Yo Truly
Saml L. Clemens
Mark Twain

Mr. Clemens
and
Mark Twain

A BIOGRAPHY

JUSTIN KAPLAN

A TOUCHSTONE BOOK
Published by Simon and Schuster
NEW YORK

A Touchstone Book

Published by Simon & Schuster, Inc.
Simon & Schuster Building
Rockefeller Center
1230 Avenue of the Americas
New York, New York 10020

TOUCHSTONE and colophon are registered trademarks of Simon & Schuster, Inc.

Designed by Eve Metz

Manufactured in the United States of America

3 5 7 9 10 8 6 4 2 Pbk.

Library of Congress Cataloging in Publication Data
Kaplan, Justin.
Mr. Clemens and Mark Twain.

(A Touchstone book)
Includes bibliographical references and index.
1. Twain, Mark, 1835-1910—Biography. 2. Authors,
American—19th century—Biography. I. Title.
II. Title: Mister Clemens and Mark Twain.
PS1331.K33 1983   818'.408 [B]   82-19597
ISBN 0-671-47071-X pbk.

*For permission to quote previously unpublished material by Samuel L. Clemens and
his family, the author is indebted to Thomas G. Chamberlain and Manufacturers
Hanover Trust Company, Trustees of the Estate of Samuel L. Clemens and of the
Trust under the Will of Clara Clemens Samossoud. The author is also indebted to
the following publishers and authors' representatives for permission to quote from:*

The Autobiography of Mark Twain,
edited by Charles Neider. Harper &
Brothers, 1959. Reprinted by permission
of Harper & Row, Publishers.
"Dear Master Wattie: The Mark
Twain–David Watt Bowser Letters."
Southwest Review, Spring, 1960. Re-
printed by permission of the *Southwest
Review* and The Mark Twain Company.
Letters from the Earth by Mark
Twain, edited by Bernard DeVoto. Har-
per & Row, 1962. Reprinted by permis-
sion of Harper & Row, Publishers.
The Love Letters of Mark Twain, ed-
ited by Dixon Wecter. Copyright 1947,
1949 by The Mark Twain Company. Re-
printed by permission of Harper & Row,
Publishers.
Mark Twain, A Biography by Albert
Bigelow Paine. Harper & Brothers, 1912.
Reprinted by permission of Harper &
Row, Publishers.
Mark Twain, Business Man, edited by
Samuel C. Webster. Atlantic Monthly
Press-Little, Brown, 1946. Copyright 1944,
1946 by The Mark Twain Company. Re-
printed by permission of Mrs. Samuel C.
Webster.
Mark Twain at Work by Bernard De
Voto. Harvard University Press, 1942.
Reprinted by permission of Harvard Uni-
versity Press.
Mark Twain–Howells Letters, edited
by Henry Nash Smith and William M.
Gibson. Harvard University Press, 1960.
Reprinted by permission of Harvard Uni-
versity Press, The Mark Twain Company,
and William White Howells.
Mark Twain in Eruption, edited by

Bernard DeVoto. Harper & Brothers,
1940. Reprinted by permission of Harper
& Row, Publishers.
Mark Twain to Mrs. Fairbanks, edited
by Dixon Wecter. Huntington Library,
1949. Reprinted by permission of Hunt-
ington Library Publications and The
Mark Twain Company.
Mark Twain's Autobiography, 2 Vols.,
edited by Albert Bigelow Paine. Harper
& Brothers, 1924. Reprinted by permission
of Harper & Row, Publishers.
Mark Twain's Letters, edited by Albert
Bigelow Paine. Copyright 1917 by The
Mark Twain Company; renewed 1945 by
Clara Clemens Samossoud. Reprinted by
permission of Harper & Row, Publishers.
Mark Twain's Letters to Will Bowen,
edited by Theodore Hornberger. Uni-
versity of Texas Press, 1941. Reprinted
by permission of Theodore Hornberger
and The Mark Twain Company.
Mark Twain's Notebook, edited by Al-
bert Bigelow Paine. Copyright 1935 by
The Mark Twain Company; renewed
1963 by Louise Paine Moore. Reprinted by
permission of Harper & Row, Publishers.
Memories of a Hostess by M. A. De-
Wolfe Howe. Atlantic Monthly Press,
1922. Reprinted by permission of Mark
DeWolfe Howe.
My Mark Twain by William Dean
Howells. Harper & Brothers, 1910. Reprinted by permission of Harper & Row,
Publishers.
The Writings of Mark Twain, edited
by Albert Bigelow Paine. Harper &
Brothers, 1922–1925. Reprinted by permis-
sion of Harper & Row, publishers.

FOR ANNE BERNAYS

CONTENTS

PREFACE

THIS BIOGRAPHY BEGINS when its subject is already thirty-one and a journalist in San Francisco. A few words to explain this abruptness may be in order. Samuel Clemens' early years—which cover his childhood along the Mississippi, his careers as printer's apprentice, itinerant typesetter, river pilot, Confederate irregular, Western prospector and newspaper reporter—were both his basic endowment in raw experience and his favorite subject. He was always his own biographer, and the books he wrote about these years are incomparably the best possible accounts, even if they may not always be the truest (and it is possible to argue that Clemens' omissions and reshapings in themselves suggest a kind of truth). But the central drama of his mature literary life was his discovery of the usable past. He began to make this discovery in his early and middle thirties—a classic watershed age for self-redefinition—as he explored the literary and psychological options of a new, created identity called Mark Twain. And this usable past, imaginatively transformed into literature, was to occupy him for the rest of his life. Moreover, the terms and directions of his discovery were dictated not only from within but also by his exuberant response to the three or four decades of American life after the Civil War. Near the beginning of this period, Mark Twain named it the Gilded Age, and to a remarkable degree his life is a function of his involvement. The way in which he first sighted the challenges and rewards of his period, grappled with them, and derived from them fulfillment as well as crushing disillusionments, is, I believe, an integral story which may also make us question some of the stereotypes of the Gilded Age.

Albert Bigelow Paine began his authorized biography of Mark Twain in 1906, while his subject was still living. The book is monumental and indispensable, and any latter-day biographer is grateful for firsthand knowledge

9

that Paine alone had. The price he paid for this knowledge was a certain sacrifice of perspective in time—a full one third of his book covers the relatively barren period between 1900 and 1910—and in materials. Since 1912, when Paine's book was published, an immense scholarly as well as critical literature about Mark Twain has sprung up. Some of this literature now makes the biographer's job in part one of synthesis. Another area of it, newly published primary materials—for example, the two volumes of Mark Twain–William Dean Howells correspondence published in 1960—comes with such a richness and scrupulosity of supporting information that part of the biographer's job is already done for him. I hope that the Notes at the back of this book will show the extent of my debt to the work of others.

Through the liberality of Paine's successors as literary editors, the vast treasurehouse of Mark Twain's papers has been opened to scrutiny. Among these papers, now at the University of California at Berkeley, are copies of material from other collections, including the Clifton Waller Barrett Library of American Literature at the University of Virginia. To Henry Nash Smith, former editor of the Mark Twain Papers, and to Frederick Anderson, their present editor, I wish to express my thanks not only for access to the collection but also for innumerable kindnesses and courtesies over the past six years. For permission to consult other manuscript materials by Mark Twain and his circle, and for help along the way, I am also indebted to Dr. John Gordan and Mrs. Lola Sladitz at the Henry W. and Albert A. Berg Collection of the New York Public Library, to Donald Gallup of the American Literature Collection of the Yale University Library, and to the curators of the manuscript collections of the Library of Congress, the Boston Public Library, The New-York Historical Society, and the Houghton Library at Harvard.

For encouragement and invigoration I shall always be grateful to James M. Cox and Howard Mumford Jones. Dr. Peter H. Knapp and Professor Roland Boyden jogged the writing of this book by kindly inviting me to try out, in a preliminary form, some of the chapters and ideas in talks at, respectively, the Division of Psychiatry of Boston University School of Medicine and Marlboro College in Vermont. It is a pleasure to thank old friends in publishing: Herbert M. Alexander, who suggested this book; M. Lincoln Schuster, who encouraged it; and Joseph Barnes, who saw it through. From the start I have benefited from my wife Anne's gifts as storyteller and judgment as editor.

—J.K.

Cambridge, Massachusetts
December 1965

Mr. Clemens
and
Mark Twain

CHAPTER ONE

"A roving commission"

I

IN 1866 PEOPLE IN A HURRY to go East from California still retraced the route of the Forty-niners. They went by ship from San Francisco down the coast of Mexico to San Juan del Sur in Nicaragua, crossed the Isthmus jungle by mule, wagon, and boat, and at Greytown, on the eastern side, they took passage in another ship for New York. If spared storm, engine breakdown, epidemic, and quarantine, they reached their destination in a little under four weeks. By 1869 the Central Pacific and the Union Pacific would be joined at Promontory Point in Utah, and on the new road the traveler would be able to ride, dine, and sleep his way in a Pullman Palace Car from San Francisco to New York in ten days. The continent would be spanned by rail, and this triumph of engineering and venture capitalism would signal a change in the face and character of the nation, the speeding of the frontier's end, and the exposure of the Crédit Mobilier, that massive scandal which, like the trial of the Reverend Henry Ward Beecher on the charge of committing adultery with a parishioner, was a symptom of what would soon be called the Gilded Age. Standing on the deck of the sidewheeler *America* of the Opposition Line as it left San Francisco at noonday in bright sunlight on December 15, 1866, Sam Clemens, just turned thirty-one, was facing eastward toward his future and leaving the frontiers which nurtured him, which he celebrated and eventually symbolized.

Diffidently and erratically, already past the age when others have chosen their vocation, he was beginning to choose his. For over four years he had been a journalist in Nevada and California, with a brief assignment in the Sandwich Islands, and the pseudonym "Mark Twain," on its way to becoming an identity in itself, was already famous in the West. In 1865, on the advice of Artemus Ward, he had sent to New York a flawless story

13

about the Calaveras mining camps. It was published in the *Saturday Press* on November 18, and soon after, by way of newspaper exchanges, it was reprinted all over the country; even so, Clemens soon found out, it was the frog that was celebrated, not its author. His most powerful ambitions, he wrote to his older brother, Orion (the Clemenses accented the first syllable of the name), three weeks before this taste of national success, had been to be a preacher or a river pilot. He had given up on the first because he lacked "the necessary stock in trade—*i.e.*, religion." He had succeeded at the second, and it was the outbreak of the Civil War, not his choice, that had cut his career short. Now he felt he had "a 'call' to literature, of a low order—*i.e.*, humorous." His vocation, though so far he lacked the education and training for it, was "to excite the *laughter* of God's creatures," and he was going to work at it. He wanted to strike a bargain with Orion, who had passed the zenith of his career after serving as secretary and sometimes acting governor of the Nevada Territory and was now embarked on thirty years of drift and vacillation: Sam would apply himself to exciting the laughter of God's creatures if Orion would apply himself to any one rational pursuit. "You had better shove this in the stove," he said at the end, in ironic reference to the seriousness of his call: "I don't want any absurd 'literary remains' and 'unpublished letters of Mark Twain' published after I am planted." In other ways, too, his vocation was becoming clear to him. During the autumn months before he sailed for New York he gave a humorous lecture about the Sandwich Islands. After a seizure of stage fright so intense that he felt he saw the face of death, he discovered a new area of triumph. He could dominate his audience, make it laugh and respond at his will. With his shuffling entrance, solemn face, and attenuated delivery he could not escape comparison with Artemus Ward, the prince of platform entertainers and his mentor, but he was developing a style and presence all his own that captivated audiences in San Francisco and Sacramento, Grass Valley, Red Dog, You Bet, and Gold Hill.

At the end of his farewell lecture in San Francisco he spoke about the California of the future as a promised land. Now, as unofficial publicist, he carried in his cabin on the *America* evidences of the Pacific Slope Golconda—specimens of quartz, fruits of miraculous size and quality, the wines which were soon to be so popular in the East that French wines were sometimes relabeled as California. He had a sheaf of letters of introduction to Eastern clergymen, Beecher among them, to politicians and editors, to solid citizens who might sponsor him if he decided to lecture. He was the shipboard celebrity, and as Mark Twain his name headed the list of cabin passengers. He was leaving behind him, he wrote to his mother in St. Louis, "more friends than any newspaperman that ever sailed out of the Golden Gate. The reason I mention this with so much pride is because our fraternity generally leave none but enemies here when they go." He craved affection and admiration, found them in the laughter and astonishment of his lecture audience, and they came to be the basic conditions he needed in order to be creative and happy. But despite his growing sense of vocation and his growing fame, at thirty-one—more than half a man's life expectancy then—he had made no real commitment to place, social goal, or identity. He belonged to a professional group that came and went and seldom rooted. He had been a wanderer on and off since 1853; his home was in his valise. His haunts were saloons and police courts, the morgue, and the stage doors of San Francisco's flourishing theaters. He moved among a subculture of reporters, entertainers, actors, theater managers, acrobats, ladies of the chorus, prospectors, and short-term promoters. As he was to tell his future mother-in-law, he was "a man of convivial ways and not averse to social drinking." This was an understatement: he had been Artemus Ward's companion on a marathon bender in Virginia City, and according to some in the West the name Mark Twain had more to do with marking up drinks on credit than it did with the Mississippi. Life on the Coast was full of queer vicissitudes, he said, and his own life there was no exception. One moment he lived high on oysters, salmon, cold fowl, and champagne at "heaven on the half shell," the Occidental Hotel; the next moment he was out of work, in debt, even in jail, having too pointedly commented on the brutalities of the San Francisco police. One night early in 1866 he put a pistol to his head. "Many times I have been sorry I did not succeed," he reflected more than forty years later, "but I was never ashamed of having tried." At one low point a local editor described him in print as a "Bohemian from the sage-brush" who was a jailbird, bailjumper, deadbeat, and alcoholic. Sam Clemens, the editor insinuated, had been rolled in a whorehouse and probably had a venereal disease; in any case, he concluded, Sam would not be missed in the city by the Golden Gate. Even for an era of scurrilous journalism this was a frightful attack, and Sam's answer was to depart, in silence, for the Hawaiian Islands. Such was the history that later caught up with him, and seriously threatened his chances, when he invaded the staidness of Elmira, New York, and asked for the hand of Olivia Langdon.

Now, scarcely two years before his first visit to Elmira, marriage and equilibrium seemed equally remote. In California he had been melancholy and restless, alternately idle and desperately industrious. His jokes and hoaxes were often strident and brassy, betraying raw nerve endings whipped by guilt about his family and by an oppressive sense of obligation to them. The youngest of the surviving Clemenses and once his mother's despair, Sam was now the hope of the family. A crippled household—his sixty-three-year-old mother, Jane, a widow since 1847, his widowed sister, Pamela Moffett, and Orion—depended on him more and more to rescue them from a long pattern of bankruptcy and foreclosure. Before, in his letters to them he had always been "Sam." Now, from time to time, he signed himself "Mark," token not only of his celebrity, which might reflect itself on them, but also of his independence. Still he missed them, and a small part of his purpose in going East was to end a separation of close to six years. With a traveling-correspondent's commission from the *Alta California* of San Francisco to supply weekly letters at twenty dollars each, he had first planned to sail for Peking on the January mail boat, to stay in China for a while, and then to go around the world to the Paris Exposition. He postponed the China trip, even though he was certain he was throwing away a fortune by not going. He wanted to see the States again. He now planned to go to New York, visit his family in St. Louis, then travel around the world by way of France, Italy, India, China, and Japan, and return to San Francisco. His plan was casual and changeable, but as the *America* carried him toward the East it carried him toward the lasting commitments of his life.

It was an inauspicious voyage. The first night out great seas broke over the steamer, sweeping away gunwales and timbers and flooding the forward staterooms with enough water to float a case of claret, and the lifeboats were readied. During the calmer days that followed, as they sailed within sight of the Mexican coast, Clemens came to know the captain who brought them through that night, a Connecticut Yankee—he was born in Westport—who by sea had followed the course of American empire westward. Ned Wakeman was already a California folk hero. He had been under piracy charges in 1850 for stealing a paddlewheel steamer from under the sheriff's nose in New York and sailing her around the Horn. In San Francisco he had served as a vigilante and hanged at least two men. For such services the citizens honored him with a silver speaking trumpet, a breast-pin cluster of nine diamonds, and a gold watch, which, along with a gold anchor and a gold ring, hung from his neck on a massy chain seven feet long. Bearded and big-bellied, he was tattooed from head to foot— with the Goddess of Liberty holding the Stars and Stripes, a clipper ship under full sail, Christ on the Cross, and an assortment of Masonic devices. Wakeman was a blasphemer of remarkable vividness, something of an eccentric theologian, and above all a teller of stories about rats as big and lean as greyhounds, about snakes as long as a ship's mainmast was high, and about the Monkey Islands, where his first mate counted ninety-seven million monkeys before the pencils wore out and his arm became paralyzed with ciphering. A week out of San Francisco Sam concluded, "I'd rather travel with that portly, hearty, boisterous, good-natured sailor, Captain Ned Wakeman, than with any other man I ever came across." More than forty years after this voyage, after a few more meetings and many more stories (including a dream of Wakeman's about sailing to heaven), Wakeman still lived in Mark Twain's imagination as an archangel. In the story

Mark Twain published in 1909 Wakeman on the deck of his storm-beaten ship became Captain Stormfield, who raced comets to heaven like a reckless river pilot, and "Stormfield" was the name of Mark Twain's villa on top of a hill in Connecticut, his last home.

When Clemens left the *America* to cross the Isthmus, he left behind, in the heroic, dominating apparition of Wakeman, the only brightness in a depressing voyage which in all other respects resembled the dark fantasy voyages he was to write about in the 1890s, when he was heartbroken and bankrupt. There had been one death already, a child, who was buried at sea. On the overland trip cholera entered the steerage class, and once they boarded the *San Francisco* at Greytown it spread through the ship and along the entire social scale, from barber to Episcopalian clergyman. Before they reached New York it claimed at least eight lives. "The passengers say we are out of luck," Clemens wrote in his notebook, plainly frightened, "and that it is a doomed voyage." He reminded himself to get a list of the dead from the first officer to telegraph to his paper, if they should ever reach port. The engine had begun to break down, there were three failures in three days, and the ship drifted by the hour. The living and the dying were filled with brandy, and for their amusement a drunken monkey, fed a brandy-soaked banana or a square drink, and dressed in black pants and a vest—gift of the ship's sewing circle—tottered and screeched in the rigging.

Throughout this voyage, even with death so near at hand, the face of gentility frowned on Clemens. A lady all in brown, backbiter, gossip—"damned old meddling moralizing fool"—said he drank too much, was often as drunk as the piper that played before Moses, played cards all night, was coarse and disgusting and clearly not a gentleman. He liked to sing, but the choir group that sang "Marching through Georgia" and "When Johnny Comes Marching Home" would have none of him. His drawl was unmistakably that of a Southerner. (He would not want to tell them that at the beginning of the war he had got himself sworn in as a Confederate irregular, but had deserted after two weeks of rain and retreat and had gone West for the duration.) On the lake steamer that took him across the Isthmus he had twice been offended by pursers who let other first-cabin passengers and even some from steerage go on deck unchallenged but said to him, "None but first cabin allowed up here. *You* first cabin?" He was ostentatiously shabby, but he was first cabin and had known celebrity, and he resented the emphatic *"you."* Among bohemians he was content to be a bohemian with a suggestion of the roughneck. The ship's manifest, drawn up by a playful officer, listed him as "Mark Twain, barkeeper, San Francisco," and he liked that.

But there was another side to his identity, a side which he had kept hidden in the West and which now bitterly minded even petty rejections by these farflung pickets of Eastern gentility. His father, John Marshall Clemens, had been a man of precise and grammatical manners, a lawyer and holder of public office. He was a chronic business failure as farmer, storekeeper, trader, and land speculator, and his wife and children were accustomed to being poor, but still he was known as Judge Clemens, was president of the Library Association and chairman of the Committee on Roads, and was accounted one of the first citizens of Hannibal. Along with pride in his Virginia ancestry he left to his family when he died in 1847 about seventy thousand acres of land in Fentress County, Tennessee, and his widow and children considered themselves prospectively rich. So far the land was good only for potatoes and wild grass, but coal, copper, and iron deposits might be discovered any day now, a new railroad would triple the value of the land, a visionary new purchaser might turn up—with such chimeras Jane, Orion, and Pamela were to occupy themselves long after Sam forswore the whole bitter business. They had been landowners and slaveholders, and among their other grandeurs they claimed a relationship to a Roundhead judge who had sent King Charles I to the block; they also claimed a wondrously exiguous connection with the earls of Durham. They were respectable gentry, poor now, but with hopes, and among these hopes, second only to the Tennessee land, was Sam.

He was, at the very least, already a double creature. He wanted to belong, but he also wanted to laugh from the outside. The Hartford literary gentleman lived inside the sagebrush bohemian. But even outwardly Sam Clemens was far different from any conventional Western journalist and rough. He had been a sickly infant, born two months prematurely, and had barely survived his first two years. He grew up sparely built, small-boned, with narrow sloping shoulders, five feet eight inches tall, a contrast with the brawny miners he knew in Nevada; all his life he liked to elaborate fantasies about small men with unsuspected gigantic strength who were always surprising people with it. His head, like a child's, seemed too large for his body. He had delicate hands, which quivered when he was stirred, and tapering fingers with pink nails. His mouth, Kipling said, was "as delicate as a woman's." He was sensitive about animals, timid about asking questions of strangers, and he was fastidious. When Clemens had been in the East for only a few years, William Dean Howells noticed something about him that was remarkable in an American of the time and especially remarkable in a Westerner: he never pawed, he was no back-slapper or arm-squeezer, he avoided touching other people. He was excitable, easily hurt, desperately hungry for affection and tenderness, often depressed, capable of great rage and greater remorse. He remained, in many ways, a child demanding attention in a nursery which was as large as the world; his wife was to call him "Youth" and "Little Man," and to Howells he had the heart of a willful boy.

"A roving commission"

On the last night at sea, off the New Jersey coast, came the last death of this voyage which had been as spectral as any of Mark Twain's voyage fantasies. The medical report, in order to circumvent quarantine, read "dropsy." On the morning of January 12, 1867, twenty-seven and a half days out of San Francisco, Clemens breathed in the biting air on the upper deck as his ship passed the snow-covered houses of Staten Island and crushed its way through the ice toward Castle Garden and the city that lay north of it, a forest of church steeples palisaded by masts.

II

To be in New York in 1867 was to be at the scrambling center of American life. Six years of war and peace had made it a city of extremes and contradictions, where the best and the worst, the highest and the lowest, existed side by side in sunshine and shadow, in splendor and squalor. The white marble palace of A. T. Stewart, the merchant prince who vied with William B. Astor for the title of richest man in the city, rose in Italianate grandeur over the shanties behind Fifth Avenue. The old aristocracy, cultivated and traveled, claimed that inflation was crushing them, and they moved into remote new streets uptown to wait for the crash that would bring back the old order. Prosperous crowds and a tremendous traffic of vehicles surged along Broadway, directed by the elite of the police force. But in the Five Points section of the lower East Side, home of ragpickers, prostitutes, new immigrants, and the desperate poor, crime reached a level of such frequency and violence that the police were afraid even to patrol. On Sundays the upright and well-dressed, acceptable in the sight of both Lorenzo Delmonico and the Deity, went to services at Bishop Southgate's or across the river at Henry Ward Beecher's in Brooklyn, to be reassured that godliness and prosperity went hand in hand, mostly to see and be seen, the ladies patting their tiny hats which looked like jockey saddles and batter cakes. On Sundays those of New York's ten thousand saloons that observed the closing laws sent their customers thronging by ferryboat to the doggeries of Hoboken.

New York's port faced east toward Europe, and the city was shipping center, temple of trade and commerce. Wartime finance had made Wall Street powerful. The city's population of nearly one and a half million, the largest in the country, supported five major newspapers, some of them with national circulation and influence. Fashion and manners were dictated from Manhattan Island. Its twelve or so theaters and palaces of entertainment—the number subject to change with each fire alarm—were supported, then as ever, by outlanders who could choose among a variety of attractions

19

that included leg shows, melodrama, and Barnum's Happy Family. The city had already become the printing, publishing, and book-manufacturing center of the nation. It was no Boston; high culture had not flourished in New York. It had a literary tradition of a sort, ranging from Washington Irving and James Fenimore Cooper to the group led by Walt Whitman and the publisher Henry Clapp that before the war had crowded into Pfaff's beer cellar under the Broadway pavement near Bleecker Street. But the tradition was miscellaneous, flavored with journalism, never deeply rooted. Both William Dean Howells and Thomas Bailey Aldrich, soon to become custodians of the Boston tradition, served briefly in the New York literary world in the 1860s. They were not sorry to leave. "Better fifty years of Boston than a cycle of New York," said Howells. The city was dedicated to popular culture, but it also originated a few literary and intellectual magazines that conferred almost as much distinction on their contributors as the august *Atlantic*, if no money at all. The *Nation*, started by E. L. Godkin three months after Appomattox, was New York in nativity even if, as some claimed, it was mainly Bostonian in spirit. Henry Clapp's urbane, venturesome, and incurably penniless *Saturday Press* had just gone broke, but not before publishing Walt Whitman as well as "Jim Smiley and His Jumping Frog." A month before Sam Clemens arrived in New York *Harper's New Monthly Magazine* published his "Forty-three Days in an Open Boat," his account of the survivors of the burned clipper ship *Hornet*. (The following May he was mortified to discover that in the magazine's annual index he was listed as "Mark Swain.")

When William Dean Howells came to Boston in 1860, at the age of twenty-three, he was a pilgrim from the Midwest worshiping at the feet of New England's literary great. It was with a sense of entering another world altogether that this postulant sat through a four-hour dinner in a private room at the Parker House with Dr. Oliver Wendell Holmes, who had given the *Atlantic* its name, James T. Fields, its publisher, and James Russell Lowell, its editor in chief. With an informality Howells would never have guessed in Columbus, Ohio, these eminences addressed each other as "James" and "Wendell," as if they were all still boys together. About the time the coffee came in, the dapper little doctor cast a smiling glance at Howells and, turning to Lowell, said, "Well, James, this is something like the apostolic succession; this is the laying on of hands." For Howells this was intoxication. Even though it was to be six years yet, and by way of a term as American consul in Venice and literary journalist in New York, before he came to the *Atlantic* as assistant editor (and eleven years before the title of editor in chief, in apostolic succession, would be bestowed upon him), Howells had a sure, unwavering vocation in Boston and in literature. Sam Clemens came to New York not as a pilgrim but as a miner staking out a claim and beginning to work it. His ambitions were not those hallowed in literary Boston. They lay in a still-unmapped area bounded by journalism, humor, entertainment, and popular literature. He was convinced, after only a few months, that he had made the right choice in coming to this city. "Make your mark in New York, and you are a made man," he reported, with a prophetic pun, to his California readers. "With a New York endorsement you may travel the country over, without fear—but without it you are speculating upon a dangerous issue."

The city offered him abundant material for his travel letters. From his rooming house on East Sixteenth Street he set out daily to cover the sights. He kept to Broadway, he said, so as not to get lost, and he went on foot. The omnibuses were overcrowded, often mired in slush and traffic, and they swayed so violently that passengers had been known to become seasick; even a veteran rider could be flung to the street by a lurch, a whipping up of the horses. It was a cruel winter; rain and slush gave way to a treacherous hard freeze during which people crossing on the East River ice from Brooklyn to New York might find themselves trapped in midpassage, the ice flashing into sudden fragments. Fourteen years earlier, as a wandering printer with a ten-dollar bill sewn into the lining of his coat, Sam had spent a brief summer in New York. He had visited the World's Fair at the Crystal Palace, where each day came six thousand visitors, double the population of Hannibal, and he had taken a liking to the city; he had found it as hard to leave as Hannibal had been easy. Since then, he felt, it had become too big a city. A business trip or a friendly visit often took up a whole day, the streets were so congested and so full of distractions. They echoed with the sounds of hammering and building, of that tremendous activity which the end of the Civil War had unleashed in America. At Fulton Street a pedestrian bridge of cast iron—along with brownstone, iron was to the Gilded Age what limestone was to the age of the Pharaohs—was going up; the Broadway traffic had become too thick to be crossed any other way. Prices for board and lodging had nearly tripled since his first visit. Waiters and bartenders, barbers and cigar vendors had become insolent with prosperity, and all things and all men conspired to keep prices up. Eggs were sixty cents a dozen, whiskey and gin fifteen cents a drink; almost everyone was feeling the pinch of inflation. All in all, he figured, a single man of moderate habits might be able to get along on forty or fifty dollars a week, but he saw no hope for the married ones. There were beggars on the streets, blind men, peddlers who sold dancing animals on India-rubber strings. But these people on the very margin of existence were not the returned soldiers, he said in a sudden celebration of the national spirit. The heroes had been absorbed into civilian life. "It is hard even for an American to understand this," he reported. "But it is a toiling, thinking, determined nation, this of ours, and little given to dreaming. Our Alexanders do not sit down and cry because there are no more worlds to conquer, but snatch off their coats and fall to shinning around and raising corn and cotton, and improving sewing machines." Sam himself, beguiled as always by mechanical improvements, reported on a primitive typesetting machine which had a bank of keys like a melodeon, and, with that fatal inclination to hope and believe the utmost of such things, he passed on the information that the patent rights had brought "fabulous sums."

Seeing the sights brought him to the fashionable churches; to the Russian Baths, where steam and ice showers, followed by a friendly drink with the manager, cured a bad cold and a feeling of oppression in the brain; to the theater, where he saw *The Black Crook*. This was a barely acceptable marriage of ballet and burlesque which nightly for years titillated huge audiences and whose appeal Sam candidly analyzed: "When they put beautiful clipper built girls on the stage in this new fashion, with only just barely clothes enough on to be tantalizing, it is a shrewd invention of the devil." "The scenery and the legs are everything," he concluded. One night he saw another facet of life in the East that would mean more to him than either church or theater. The Century Association, he told his readers, was the "most unspeakably respectable" club in the entire country. He noted the excellence of the brandy punch, the food, and the conversation and was struck by the singular fact that so few of the older members were bald. The hat sizes averaged about number eleven, he figured, and what impressed him most was that the club had a tendency to exclude those who had bank accounts but no brains. This was a long way from the land of the silver millionaires. "I have some idea of putting in my application," he joked; "I won't need to belong till I get old." Within a decade Samuel L. Clemens of Hartford, Connecticut, would be the darling of such clubs—the Players and the Lotos in New York, the Savage in London—and in his old age it was from such clubs that, surfeited with banqueting and after-dinner speeches, he would make his way late at night to Riverdale or his last New York house, on lower Fifth Avenue.

Soon after arriving in New York he went to 25 Broadway to call on an old friend from the West. Frank Fuller, whom he had known as the wartime governor of the Utah Territory, was a tireless and enthusiastic experimenter. He had studied medicine under the guidance of Dr. Holmes, practiced dentistry in Portsmouth, New Hampshire, campaigned for Lincoln, organized a regiment, been admitted to the Nevada bar. After the war he accumulated a respectable fortune selling cloth treated with India rubber, excellent for buggy tops, and he found his permanent occupation as president of his own health food company in New York. He was a speculator and a promoter—an honest one—who later, during the 1870s and 1880s, involved or tried to involve Clemens in a number of schemes, including railroad bonds as good as gold and a revolutionary new steam engine for tugboats. He was a successful Orion—gentle and charming as Orion, but with luck. This entrepreneur now proposed that Sam should lecture in New York and promised to make the arrangements and to get him the organized support of the Californians in town. To this glowing proposal Sam's response was one of cautious assent. He had not come East with any immediate plan to lecture there. His *Alta California* correspondence and miscellaneous journalism would keep him busy enough, he figured, and his Western friends had warned him he would have to be choicer in his language and more delicate in his humor lest he offend audiences in the East. A book like George Washington Harris' *Sut Lovingood's Yarns*, Western humor at the primitive base, would sell well in California, but, he predicted somewhat incorrectly, "the Eastern people will call it coarse and possibly taboo it." Before he could entrust his reputation as a lecturer to Eastern audiences he would have to be sure of his timing and approach. "I'll not do it yet," he wrote to Orion's wife. "I won't do it until I have got my cards stacked to suit me. It is too hazardous a business for a stranger. I am not going to rush headlong in and make a fiasco of the thing when I may possibly make a success of it by going a little slow"— not his customary response to a new venture, but in this case the proper one. He was taking careful aim, and he was going to use his considerable skills as a promoter, his influence as a newspaperman, and his reputation as a humorous writer to stack the cards to suit him. In February he arranged with the New York *Weekly*, which had a circulation of over 100,000, for the reprinting of the Sandwich Island letters he had written the year before for the Sacramento *Union*. Part of the return was pure publicity. The editors twice informed their readers that Mark Twain was "about to deliver in this city his great lecture on the Sandwich Islands, which for a series of nights crowded the largest lecture room in San Francisco to suffocation. He cannot help succeeding here."

His most precious letter of introduction was to Henry Ward Beecher, minister of Plymouth Church in Brooklyn, highly successful lyceum lecturer, and at fifty-four possibly the most celebrated man in the United States. By ten o'clock of any Sunday morning the pews of Beecher's church were full, the pavement crowded with people trying to get in. Sam managed only a tiny stool in the gallery, jammed into a space about big enough for a spittoon. Beecher knew how to dominate and mesmerize an audience. Not handsome, homely even, he took off his overcoat, broad-brimmed farmer's hat, and galoshes in full sight of his congregation, and then sat on a plain chair against the wall with the air of a manager who was pleased with a full house but never doubted he would have it. He exploited the contrast between these moments of repose and waiting and the time of illumination when, climbing onto a platform without rail or carpet, he read a few sentences from his manuscript and then abandoned it for an extemporaneous sermon that glittered with illustrations and worldly metaphors. His rich, resonant voice filled every corner of his elegant church, its white seats delicately beaded in brown. "He went marching up and down the stage," Clemens reported, "sawing his arms in the air, hurling sarcasms this way and that, discharging rockets of poetry, and exploding mines of eloquence, halting now and then to stamp his foot three times in succession to emphasize a point."

Beecher's style had been formed at camp meetings and forest revivals in Indiana; he dealt in broad pyrotechnic effects, and he was an apostle of enthusiasm who described himself as a "cordial Christian Darwinist." But for all this devotion to a muscular Christianity he was high-strung, a sensualist, an over-reactor. He loved flowers and would not find it grotesque that on the first day of his adultery trial his loyal parishioners decorated the courtroom with white flowers, emblems of purity ("like placing wreaths about the open manhole of a sewer," Godkin wrote in the *Nation*). He was fascinated by small rare objects, by stuffed hummingbirds and unset gems. He called the stones his "color opiates," and he carried them with him to gaze at and caress, to soothe him after his Sunday-morning performance left him limp with sweat. At the end the visiting journalist had a nearly overpowering impulse to applaud. Had it not been a church, he "could have started the audience with a single clap of the hands and brought down the house." Sam Clemens was intoxicated with oratory in an age that adored it and that turned to it for entertainment as well as persuasion, and the pastor of Plymouth Church impressed him more as a showman than as a shepherd. His introduction to Beecher proliferated in a remarkable number of ways; their relationship was crucial for Clemens, but it could never become a friendship. Beecher was more than twenty years older, but aside from this there was something in him that Clemens found antipathetic, a hint of the religious mountebank and hypocrite. At one point Beecher even symbolized for him a flyblown quality of America in the 1870s, good meat that had hung too long. But now Clemens was pleased to be a guest at Beecher's dinner table, to meet there Beecher's famous sister Harriet Beecher Stowe, to be the beneficiary of Beecher's advice on lecturing, publishing, and self-advancement in general. For a brief time he was caught in the strong toil of Beecher's personality, and for much longer he was caught in a network of Beecher connections he could never escape from and could never altogether enjoy: in Elmira, Beecher's brother Thomas was spiritual adviser to the Langdon family and married Olivia Langdon and Samuel Clemens; in Hartford there was Harriet, in her prime a phenomenon, in her dotage a nuisance; and also in Hartford there were two other sisters, one of whom, Isabella Hooker, was a snob for whom her neighbor Samuel Clemens remained coarse and a parvenu. The *Quaker City* voyage, which in a few months would take him abroad and toward fame as a writer, was at least in name sponsored by Beecher and Plymouth Church. (Twenty years later, Mark Twain the publisher figured that Beecher's death, leaving unfinished a projected auto-biography that the house was counting on, was going to cost the company at least $100,000.) "Henry Ward is a brick," Sam told his mother a year after their first meeting. Into that flat jocular statement one can read his pride at a significant conquest and also the first intimations of boredom.

His natural social element, though, was not the clergy, not yet the estab-lished middle class, certainly not the members of the Century Association. Bohemia in San Francisco had been a transplant from New York, and New York's Bohemia, in decline since the middle of the war, was in turn a trans-plant—and some, like Howells, felt it was a shallow-rooted one—from France. Postwar Bohemia in New York was an amorphous thing. It lacked the vital center that Henry Clapp, grown bitter and drinking himself to death, had once supplied at Pfaff's. It was now chiefly composed of jour-nalists living outside the conventional social order and pursuing an erratic hand-to-mouth existence. Still, "bohemian" describes Clemens' literary and social coloration during his first months in the East. "That old day when bohemianism was respectable—ah, more than respectable, heroic": so he would recall this period seventeen years later for a friend who had shared it with him, Edward H. House. House had been a music and drama critic in Boston and a Civil War correspondent for the New York *Tribune*, and he was now contributing occasional criticism to the paper. They met one morning in January at the Nassau Street office of Charles Henry Webb, poet, columnist, and editor, whom Clemens had known in San Francisco and who was credited by some as having brought New York bohemian-ism, the original, authentic article, to the West Coast. All three of them had singularly restless careers; for them to be in the same room together was a rare intersection in time. House was to have an interlude in Japan as professor of literature, return with a pension from the Emperor Mutsuhito, and become a speculator in theatrical attractions and a play adapter—a pro-fession which in 1890 pitted him against Clemens in an abusive legal con-test over stage rights to *The Prince and the Pauper*. By this time Clemens had decided that his old friend was a scoundrel, thief, "gigantic liar," and "inconceivable hound." Webb, after reading *Moby Dick* at the age of seventeen, had signed on a whaler and sailed four years in the South Seas and the Arctic; later he covered Bull Run for the New York *Times* and the passing scene for the Sacramento *Union* and the *Golden Era*. With Bret Harte he founded and edited the *Californian*, a distinguished literary journal to which Clemens contributed and which, during its short life, showed that there was real literary vitality on the Pacific Slope. The maga-zine bankrupted him, as did his mining speculations; his satires on Cali-fornia patriotism proved too uncomfortable for the natives, and if he had not left San Francisco by ship in 1866 he might have left it on a rail not long after. In New York he followed a varied course as makeshift publisher and occasional journalist, writer of light verse, banker and broker, and, something Sam would be in sympathy with, inventor and plunger in patents for a cartridge-loader and several adding and calculating machines. Like Sam, he had red hair and a mustache; he had a lisp to match Sam's distinctive drawl; he was a *bon vivant* and a lady killer; and, although he lived until 1905, his best days were already behind him. He too, like House, was to find himself on the other end of a lawsuit from Samuel L. Clemens, who, years later, remembered Webb as "a poor sort of creature, and by nature and training a fraud." These two, along with Bret Harte, were Clemens' closest links with bohemianism. He was to repudiate all of them, denounce them as crooks and parasites; their hand-to-mouth, deep-in-debt, quick-improvisation style of living he would find detestable. Bret Harte, as befitted his greater importance to Clemens, was to be repudiated with a venom and vindictiveness time could never moderate.

Several times during the previous year Clemens had planned to augment his reputation and income by publishing a book. First he considered writing about the Mississippi and his four years as cub and pilot. Now Webb, who had a firm belief in Mark Twain's rising literary star, proposed to edit a collection which would include the "Jumping Frog" and a number of miscellaneous pieces. For a share of the book's earnings Webb would do all the work and would contribute his nom de plume, John Paul, with which he already had won something of a following. Webb arranged for Sam to bring the manuscript to George Carleton, an established, aggressive, and inventive publisher who, through low prices and unorthodox advertising, sold Holmes and Victor Hugo to the burgeoning middle classes. When Sam, full of trepidation, called at Carleton's office on Broadway, meekly explained his way past a clerk, and confronted Carleton with the manuscript, it was not the first time he had given the publisher a chance at the Frog. Carleton was the man to whom the story had been sent originally, in 1865, for inclusion in a book of Artemus Ward's. Claiming that it had arrived too late, Carleton had sent it on, without enthusiasm, to the *Saturday Press.* Any number of objections would have run through his mind when he talked to the author: Mark Twain was still a relatively unknown name in the East; the Frog was two years old and could be considered to have jumped himself out, for the story had appeared not only in newspapers and magazines but even in a pirated collection called *Beadle's Dime Book of Fun;* many of the other sketches were hardly high enough above the level of humorous journalism to dizzy the beholder; and in any case the book was a miscellany of old material. Carleton rained objections. "Books—look at those shelves," he said in dismissal. "Every one of them is loaded with books that are waiting for publication. Do I want any more? Excuse me, I don't. Good morning."

The shock of this rejection was magnified two months later when Sam learned that Carleton, for all his objections, had taken on a comparable miscellany by Bret Harte. Tell Bret Harte, Clemens wrote to a friend in California—he could have written to Harte himself if he had not been so angry—that his publisher is "a Son of a Bitch who will swindle him. We of Bohemia keep away from Carleton's." He could never forget the rejection. Ten years later it was still festering: "Carleton insulted me in Feb. 1867; and so when the day arrives that sees me doing him a civility, I shall feel that I am ready for paradise." After twenty-one years, during which Carleton was near or at the head of that hate list which Clemens kept and rarely trimmed, he met the publisher in Lucerne and heard from him an apology and a confession: "I refused a book of yours and for this I stand without competitor as the prize ass of the nineteenth century." Whether the apology was really as perfect as this or whether Clemens was giving the shape of daydream to some fragments of facts, the cycle was complete, the old hurt acknowledged if not redressed. For the moment, though, in the face of what seemed a crushing rejection, Clemens fell back on Webb's belief in him. They made an oral agreement (something that led to disaster later on): Webb would produce and manufacture the book himself, arrange for the American News Company to distribute it, and pay the author a ten per cent royalty.

Clemens had approached Carleton with the trepidation of an unknown author. Now he approached another opportunity with the swagger of a toughened journalist. "Prominent Brooklynites," he reported to his paper, "are getting up a great European pleasure excursion for the coming season, which promises a vast amount of enjoyment." He was determined and confident that the proprietors of the *Alta California* would see the trip as he saw it: as a unique kind of voyage which offered him as a journalist the double challenge of observing the sightseers as well as the sights. The Brooklynites were members of Plymouth Church, and the plan had begun with Beecher himself. Having led an expedition to Charleston in 1865 to sanctify the raising of the Union flag over Fort Sumter, he wanted to lead an expedition to the Holy Land, where, in the company of his congregation, he would gather local impressions for a biography of Jesus. The man who organized the trip and was to be master of the vessel was one of Beecher's Sunday-school superintendents, Captain Charles C. Duncan. Duncan took the germ of an idea—a private group of passengers on a long voyage—cagily sized up the favoring circumstances of postwar travel hunger and the lure of the Paris Exposition, and came up with the grandfather of the modern luxury cruise. Carefully selected on the basis of character and credit, the passengers would use the steamer *Quaker City* as a traveling home while they visited Europe and the Middle East, following an itinerary which they could change by unanimous vote. Duncan did not mention it with the other attractions in his prospectus, but he shrewdly let it be known that, in addition to Beecher, among the passengers would be the popular actress Maggie Mitchell, General William T. Sherman, and Robert Henry Hendershot, an ephemeral Civil War hero known as "the Drummer Boy of the Rappahannock."

In a gay mood heightened by some drinks along the way, Clemens and House paid a visit one morning at the end of February to Duncan's office on Wall Street. The Sunday-school navigator, standing in for an awesome "Committee on Applications," greeted them with a certain skepticism. "Allow me to introduce the Reverend Mark Twain," House said, "who is a clergyman of some distinction, lately arrived from San Francisco," and he went on to describe this clergyman's exhausting labors as a missionary in the Sandwich Islands. "My congregation has concluded to start me out traveling for my health," Clemens said, but he had one or two questions about this particular voyage. Would Mr. Beecher be on board? If so, would he allow the Reverend Mr. Twain, a Baptist, to conduct services from time to time? Mr. Beecher would be on board, Duncan was certain, and would be delighted to give over his pulpit to the new preacher. The next day Clemens returned without House, identified himself correctly for Duncan, and left with him a character reference and a deposit on the price of passage, $1,250. But ten years later Duncan's rancor at the boozy hoax that had been played on him came out in a public exchange of scurrilities. Clemens, Duncan said, had stumbled in and filled the office with "the fumes of bad whiskey." "For a ceaseless, tireless, forty-year advocate of total abstinence the 'captain' is a mighty good judge of whiskey at second hand," Clemens told a reporter, and besides, "I was poor—I couldn't afford good whiskey. How could I know the 'captain' was so particular about the quality of a man's whiskey?"

III

At a "Bal d'Opéra" at the Academy of Music on March 1 Clemens masqueraded in a king's robes and reeled and roistered through a crowd in which he seemed to encounter some of the figures of his accumulating imagination. He heard a girl dressed as Joan of Arc offer to give the world for a mess of raw oysters; he heard dukes and princes call each other Jim and Joe and ask who was buying the next drink. Two nights later, in a snowstorm, he was finally on his way to St. Louis, eleven hundred miles in fifty-two hours. On the train he talked with a man who had been at Bull Run and in prison camps and who was now within a hundred miles of home for the first time in six years. It was a reminder of his own absence and of the war whose wounds were still open in St. Louis, where friendships, families, and even churches remained divided.

For him, home was Jane Clemens, his sister Pamela, her two children. Into the widowed household on Chestnut Street, to tell stories and to be scrutinized and lectured, bringing as gifts a crystal necklace and a Hawaiian Bible, came the restless hope of the family, and not in triumph. Years earlier Sam had melodramatically vowed to Orion that he would not come home again, would not look on his mother's face again or Pamela's, "until I am a rich man." He had made a certain name, no fortune. Pamela was always complaining that to run a house for Jane and support her was too great a burden, that Sam did not contribute enough and spent too much on himself. Pamela was a temperance proselytizer, and she wanted him to promise not to make jokes about sacred subjects. Reproach was in the air. Pamela's pious and melancholy domination was only partly relieved by their mother's taste for flashing colors and gaudy embroidery, for parades, circuses, funerals, and gossip. All in all Sam's six-year absence might have been six weeks for the sense of repose his return was giving him. In response to this exposure to the women of his family, a week after he arrived he started contributing to the *Missouri Democrat* some satirical articles about female suffrage. Give them the vote, he said, and the Missouri ladies would give up housekeeping and wet-nursing in order to run for "State Milliner."

Along with these appearances in the public eye came an invitation to lecture for the benefit of a Sunday school. He sized up the opportunity carefully: if you intend to publish *The Frog* before the end of March, he wrote Webb, telegraph me and I'll pass up the St. Louis invitation in favor of a New York debut. Webb would be lucky to publish before the end of April, he learned, and, having decided to make his opening move in St. Louis, he went at his publicity with the hand of a master of ballyhoo and self-promotion. Like Artemus Ward, who once publicized a lecture on the Mormons by printing up tickets which read "Admit the Bearer and ONE Wife," he wooed his audiences through crude nonsense. In San Francisco he had teased his prospects with promises of a splendid orchestra, a menagerie of ferocious animals, a fireworks display, and a grand torchlight procession—"the public are privileged to expect whatever they please"; but failing these attractions, he announced, the doors would open at seven "the trouble to begin at eight o'clock." For the citizens of St. Louis, in order to illustrate a custom of the Sandwich Islands, he promised "to devour a child in the presence of the audience, if some lady will kindly volunteer an infant for the occasion." He offered prizes as illusory as the beasts and the fireworks for the best conundrum, for the best poem on summer or summer complaint, and for a plausible essay on female suffrage.

The audience that came to Mercantile Hall on March 25, lured by the antic promotion and the exotic subject, witnessed a performance quite different from anything else on the lecture platform. He told the citizens of this thriving inland city about a precommercial and pre-Christian paradise where it was possible for the natives to be happy without being either industrious or virtuous. He gibed at the white man's gifts to the natives of "civilization and several other diseases," but still he intimated to his audience that he was on their side, the side of good works, proselytizing, progress, and democracy: the missionaries brought literacy and virtue to the natives, he assured them, especially the American missionaries. He gave them statistics and anecdotes, edification and amusement, humorous reflections with a delayed effect, and something that passed for moral philosophy, and, in order to gratify what the ladies thought of as a higher taste, he gave them stretches of word painting of a gaudy kind, "gorgeous" and "sublime." As he described it, the Kilauea volcano in eruption was "a carnival of destruction"; columns of smoke rose through the "murky pall," and "sheets of green-blue lambent flame were shot upward and pierced this vast gloom, making all sublimely grand." The volcano had erupted several years before Mark Twain ever set foot in the Sandwich Islands, but the audience sat silent before this peak of eloquence until he clapped his hands, broke the spell, and led his listeners, whose mood and pace he knew better than they did, from awe to applause and laughter. Further word painting of a more delicate sort, a flower this time; he applauded himself again, offered to repeat the passage, then declined his own offer with a comic gesture.

The lineaments of the early Mark Twain, the popular lecturer, have begun to emerge: a daring manipulator of audience psychology and values, outrageous enough to hoax, surprise, and disorient, but careful not to offend; a humorist and entertainer with moral and educational zeal to assuage a puritan conscience; a painter of word pictures who makes fun of the effect he creates, thereby both gratifying his audience's hunger for "literature" and reassuring them that he is no littérateur, that fancy talk and three-dollar words are just as alien to him as to any storekeeper or clerk. Publicly, he is not a bohemian. He is traveled and worldly, but he has an air of surprised innocence, and he manages to be a man and a boy at the same time. The vices he confesses to—laziness, petty dishonesty, lying when tempted, swearing when provoked—are, by the business-success values which most of his audience accepts, capital sins in a man. But he juggles these vices into seeming merely the bad habits of a boy playing hooky and fibbing to his mother. His audience likes him for this; in a boy such rejections of authority are taken for signs of independence and grow-ing manliness.

On his home grounds he scored a total victory. "He succeeded in doing what we have seen Emerson and other literary magnates fail in attempt-ing," the *Missouri Republican* said: "He interested and amused a large and promiscuous audience." "I think that is pretty complimentary," Clemens joked with his California readers, "considering that when I delivered that lecture I was not acquainted with a single newspaperman in St. Louis." His only chagrin came from the fact that a twenty-six-year-old reporter named Henry Morton Stanley printed the lecture nearly verbatim, thus depriving it of most of its future value—the equivalent, Clemens later said of such recurrent experiences, of asking a man for the time and then pull-ing the hands off his watch. "One never feels comfortable, afterward, re-peating a lecture that has been partly printed," he complained, "and worse than that, people don't care about what they can buy in a newspaper for less money."

A week later he lectured in Hannibal, now fallen on hard times. The railroads had taken away its river traffic, and the town was in danger of becoming once again the drowsing hamlet he had known in his boyhood. Like the cannon fire which was supposed to release the bodies of Tom and Huck from the river bottom, the brief visit sent a few connected im-ages of the past floating up to his consciousness. He recalled, and probably for the first time in print wrote about, "Jimmy Finn," the town drunkard, who for a while was won over by the temperance people, "but in an evil hour temptation came upon him, and he sold his body to a doctor for a quart of whiskey, and that ended all his earthly troubles. He drank it all at one sitting, and his soul went to its long account and his body went to Dr. Grant." He remembered that he himself, for the sake of a stunning red scarf, had once joined the Cadets of Temperance and pledged himself not to drink, smoke, or swear; after four months, during which there were no funeral processions he could march in to show off his scarf, he resigned, and within the next three weeks "pretty nearly all the distinguished citi-zens in the camp died." Except in these flashes Hannibal was still the dead and arid past from which he was escaping; it would be a while yet before the idea of a return to Hannibal would, as the roughest sort of note for *Tom Sawyer*, take some sort of imaginative shape, and even then it was not the idyl: "Return and meet grown babies and toothless old drivelers who were the grandees of his boyhood. The Adored Unknown a faded old maid and full of rasping, puritanical vinegar piety."

From Hannibal he went north to Keokuk, before the war a gate city to the headlands of the Mississippi and now, like Hannibal, in a trough between waves of expansion and speculation. Ten years before, he had left Orion's print shop there to become a pilot. Now Sam spent the week-end in the city's fashionable hotel, a visiting celebrity greeted by posters which announced a lecture to be given by "Sam. Clemens, the greatest humorist in America." The newspapers welcomed "the most extraordi-nary delineator of human character in America or upon the continent of Europe." He was at ease in his lecture to a bigger house than Emerson had drawn, and he was happy and playful. Seeing an old friend in the audience, he qualified his description of a Hawaiian ruler: "One of the greatest liars on the face of the earth, except one, and I am very sorry to locate that one right here in Keokuk, in the person of Ed Brownell." Another lecture in Quincy, Illinois, and then he started on the return trip to New York. The farther he got from home the more attractive the fields and cities of the republic seemed as he looked at them from the express. What he saw now was not the black pall that had hung over Pittsburgh on the trip west, but, all the way through Ohio and New Jersey, wonderful cities, "so cheerful and handsomely built, and so fiercely busy. It is good to come to the States occasionally, and see what a great country it is."

IV

In New York Clemens found waiting for him a check from the *Alta California* for his passage on the *Quaker City*. Frank Fuller had got the spon-sorship of two hundred Californians for the lecture Clemens was to give a few days after publication of *The Celebrated Jumping Frog of Calaveras County, and Other Sketches*. James Russell Lowell, Clemens heard, had declared the title piece to be "the finest piece of humorous writing ever produced in America." The cards finally appeared to be stacked right, and on the strength of this he moved out of his rooming house and into the elegant Westminster Hotel on Irving Place. "Full of 'bloated aristocrats,'" he described the hotel for his family, "and I'm just one of *them* kind my-self." He was pleased with his book when the first copy came from the binder near the end of April; the gorgeous gold frog stamped on the plum-colored cloth cover seemed to him worth the $1.50 all by itself. Webb had done everything—selected the contents, read proof, designed the book. In his preface he introduced Mark Twain as an author "too well known to the public to require a formal introduction." This author, Webb wrote, had already won for himself the sobriquets of "Wild Humorist of the Pacific Slope" and "Moralist of the Main," and unlike others—Webb's allusion was to Artemus Ward, Petroleum V. Nasby, and Josh Billings—Mark Twain did not have to resort to tricks of spelling or "rhetorical buffoon-ery" for his success.

"A roving commission"

"The Jumping Frog by Mark Twain will to-day jump down the popular throat": With this mouth-watering announcement in the New York *Times* on April 25 Webb offered Mark Twain's first book for sale through the American News Company. A few days later the author reported to his California paper that the book was handsome, readable, and selling well, and a shipment was on its way to the Coast. To Bret Harte, still in San Francisco working in the United States Mint, he wrote about the book in quite another vein: "It is full of damnable errors of grammar and deadly inconsistencies of spelling in the Frog sketch because I was away and did not read the proofs." And he added, "I am to lecture in Cooper Institute next Monday night. Pray for me."

Flamboyant and openhanded, Fuller aimed higher than Irving Hall or one of the smaller New York theaters and engaged the Great Hall which Peter Cooper had built a decade earlier and which had served as forum for Lincoln and Garrison. It was the largest auditorium in the city and, for a lecturer, the most august. Once the move had been made—Fuller put up five hundred dollars of his own money for hall rent and advertising—they discovered that May 6 was an inauspicious evening for a debut. Clemens was going against formidable competition: at Irving Hall Schuyler Colfax, Speaker of the House and, until the Crédit Mobilier scandal ended his political career, a contender for the Presidency, was lecturing on his trip across the United States; the Italian tragedienne Adelaide Ristori, whose repertory, although exclusively in her native tongue, still brought her full houses across the country ("It beats me entirely," Clemens confessed; "I believe the newspapers can do anything now") was giving a farewell performance; and the Academy of Music offered its stage for the debut of a troupe of Japanese acrobats, tumblers, jugglers, magicians, and contortionists.

The clusters of handbills advertising Mark Twain's lectures dangled, unplucked, in the omnibuses. The distinguished people to whom Fuller sent invitations—with Horace Greeley and Peter Cooper constituting what Clemens called the "tone-imparting committee"—all sent their regrets. Despite an elaborate eight-page prospectus and the lure of a celebrity, Senator James W. Nye of Nevada, who would introduce the lecturer, there was no box-office traffic at Chickering and Sons of 632 Broadway and at the principal hotels, where tickets for a serio-humorous lecture on "Kanakadom, or the Sandwich Islands," could be had for fifty cents. "Everything looks shady, at least, if not dark," Sam wrote home five days before the lecture, but it was too late to withdraw. "Let her slide! If nobody else cares I don't." He did care; his lecture career in the East was at stake, and the prospect of an empty house in New York was as terrifying as that of an indifferent one had been in San Francisco. A few days in advance Fuller rescued the venture from disaster by papering the house. With bushels of

33

free tickets he drew in the schoolteachers, "the choicest audience," he told Clemens, "the most intelligent audience, that ever a man stood before in this world."

Uncomfortable in the new claw-hammer coat that Fuller had insisted he buy for the occasion, Clemens arrived at the hall early, and worried. There had been no word from Nye, and the Senator never did show up; at a time when the impending release of Jefferson Davis from a Federal prison was stirring up the old hatreds Nye, who thought of Clemens as "nothing but a damned secessionist," was guided by clear self-interest. But the full house that Clemens found—over two thousand schoolteachers and Californians, representing altogether about thirty-five dollars in paid tickets —made up for the betrayal. He spoke his own introduction, looking for a tiny Nye in the cracks between the floorboards as he might look for a bug or a penny. Then he poured out the Sandwich Islands, and for an hour and a quarter he was in Paradise.

"The house was crowded, on that occasion, but it was not my popularity that crowded it," Clemens was to write to his fiancée a year and a half later. "The exertions of my friends did *that*. They got up the whole thing—suggested it, engineered it, and carried it through successfully. If any man has a right to be proud of his friends it is I, thy servant." This was after a breakfast with Fuller, who had given him a sheaf of lecture reviews which Clemens proudly enclosed with his letter. Among them was a *Tribune* review written by Ned House, described by his friend as "the most eminent dramatic critic in the Union."

> The chance offering of "The Jumping Frog," carelessly cast, eighteen months ago, upon the Atlantic waters, returned to him in the most agreeable form which a young aspirant for popular fame could desire [House wrote]. No other lecturer, of course excepting Artemus Ward, has so thoroughly succeeded in exciting the mirthful curiosity, and compelling the laughter of his hearers. Mark Twain's delivery is deliberate and measured to the last degree. He lounges comfortably around his platform, seldom referring to notes, and seeks to establish a sort of button-hole relationship with his audience. He is even willing to exchange confidences of the most literal nature. The only obvious preconcerted "effect" which he employs is a momentary hesitation or break in his narration before touching the climax of an anecdote or witticism. But his style is his own and needs to be seen to be understood.

The other reviews, too, in the *Times* and the *World*, were all he might have wished, and, sifting down through the newspaper exchanges, they were copied in Cleveland and Chicago, in Buffalo and Washington, in railheads and freshwater ports, in cities prosperous with ore and cattle, corn and wheat.

v

The aftermath of this debut was a month of depression. He was worn out and miserable, restless, full of self-accusation, worried about his neglected correspondence for the California paper. One midnight, only a few weeks away from the pieties and restraints of the European excursion, he was arrested for brawling on the street, and he spent the night in a New York jail. In the courtroom lockup the next morning he found himself in the company of the city's derelicts—drunks, a man with a battered and bleeding head, streetwalkers, an old lady who offered him a swig from her gin bottle in return for some tobacco. There he saw scribbled on the wall, in mocking parallel to the blithe advertising he had written for his San Francisco lecture, the line "The Trouble will begin at eight." He thought briefly of contesting his imprisonment. The judge assured him this would not be worth the bother: he had not been booked, and no one would know he had spent the night in the station house unless he told it himself. He told it himself, to his California readers, and he told them more about the lower depths at Harry Hill's a "concert saloon" notorious for its low entertainment, flowing liquor, and available waitresses and therefore on the basic itinerary of visiting journalists, preachers, and reformers. He had declined to see one of the young ladies home. In his account of his visit he took a stance that he constantly polished: the genteel naïf, the same bookish dupe who, having once listened to Simon Wheeler telling a story about a man named Smiley and his frog, now claimed to believe that Harry Hill's rumhole was the meeting place of philosophers and savants, that the wise man with the lady on his lap was Professor Morse and the sage treating the house to a round was Professor Agassiz.

He resumed his correspondence with the *Alta California* on May 17, and he wrote four letters in four days, fifteen thousand words or so in all, a pace which he scarcely relaxed during the three weeks before sailing. In search of copy he visited the Blind Asylum, Bible House, Henry Bergh's A.S.P.C.A., the Academy of Design, Greenwood Cemetery, and Central Park. After a trip through the Five Points and the city's worst slums, the moralist and realist, who was shortly to become a rich man himself, declared: "Honest poverty is a gem that even a King might feel proud to call his own, but I wish to sell out. I have sported that kind of jewelry long enough. I want some variety. I wish to become rich, so that I can instruct the people and glorify honest poverty a little, like those good, kind-hearted, fat, benevolent people do."

Amidst his dutiful reportage—New York for all its promise failed to spark him to any higher level—there are flickering images of a more per-

35

sonal urgency and reality, images of the passing of an older order. The onetime bushwhacker saw Jefferson Davis, three weeks short of fifty-five, standing at midnight on the sidewalk outside the New York Hotel. The man who had been, as Sam Clemens now saw him, "the head, and heart, and soul, of the mightiest rebellion of modern times" went about his business as unheralded as any country merchant visiting town. The live body of the Confederate President was on its way from a Federal prison to twenty-two years of freedom and oblivion. Early in June there arrived from England the dead body of Artemus Ward, on its way to burial in Waterford, Maine, where, as he used to say, he had been born of parents, and where the schoolchildren would soon strew flowers on his grave. At thirty-three, the watershed age, Ward was the victim of tuberculosis, alcohol, and the overwork of pleasing an insatiable public. Long ago his pseudonym had become his identity—Artemus Ward had swallowed up Charles Farrar Browne—and this problem, along with his mantle and following, now passed on to his friend and protégé.

During the week before the *Quaker City* sailed, with little left to do but buy cigars and seagoing clothing and put off packing his trunk, Clemens turned against himself. The last six months now seemed to him altogether without point or consistency. As a traveling correspondent he saw himself as a failure: corresponding was "a perfect drag," his *Alta California* letters were "the stupidest letters that were ever written from New York," and he was worried that once he was abroad he would be unable to fulfill his *Alta California* commission and a commission he had just received from Horace Greeley's *Tribune*. Despite his early reports *The Celebrated Jumping Frog* had been far from a success. Three years later, in the constant process of revising and dramatizing his own history which was to culminate in his autobiography, he told the editor of a biographical compendium that he had expected the book to sell fifty thousand copies and it sold fewer than four thousand. Now he authorized Fuller to collect whatever royalties the book might earn and to send them on to Jane Clemens, even though if she counted on them, she might be reduced to abject poverty. It would never earn anything worth a cent, he told his family, and with a rationalization born of adversity he explained, "I published it simply to advertise myself—not with the hope of making anything out of it." All winter long he had tried to find a publisher for a book about the Sandwich Islands; even late in May he still had hopes, and he planned to leave Fuller in charge of these royalties as well. But on the eve of sailing he admitted defeat, withdrew the book, and tried to salvage something out of the rejection: "It would be useless to publish it in these dull publishing times." Shaken but toughened by these two projects, he had developed a cannier and more deliberate view of his career as an author. Sizing up the potential of the *Quaker City* voyage, he told Mortimer Neal

Thomson, a minor humorist who wrote under the name "Philander Q. Doesticks," that if there was any book matter there he proposed to extract it. He had looked into the economics of subscription publishing, and he made a decision that defined the direction he was to go in and the kind of books he was to write: there was no point to writing and publishing a book, he decided, unless it earned a good deal of money.

The New York to which he had come with high expectations now seemed "a domed and steepled solitude, where a stranger is lonely in the midst of a million of his race" and "walks his tedious miles through the same interminable street every day," homeless, restless, in a state of uneasy excitement but sapped of the capacity for pleasure and curiosity. It had become a Baudelairean city of specter-thronged streets, not Walt Whitman's million-footed Manhattan, hive of democracy and temple of brotherhood. The Wild Humorist of the Pacific Slope had to apologize to his California readers for his mood. He has wandered into the wrong vein in summing up New York for them, he says, and he will try again; his repression has spilled over its private confinements. But a day later, in his final letter, he was scarcely improved. He has seen all there is to see, yet there was something missing every time. "I guess that something was the provincial quietness I am used to": he was trying to joke away an uncomfortable line of self-questioning.

He returned again and again to this something that was missing, in the letters he wrote to his family before sailing; they are almost the last truly intimate, truly inward letters he was to write to them, the letters of a private personality not yet yoked to a public one. He was maddened by the endless delays of his last torpid week in New York, he told them; he neglected every duty, and his conscience tore at him "like a wild beast." He had complained bitterly about Orion's thoughtlessness in sending him on some errand connected with his law practice. "I will have to get even with him for this somehow," he told Orion's wife. "He could have had all this attended to by writing to the man instead of to me." But he also knew he had promised his family he would go to Washington and try to lobby some sort of clerkship for Orion. He had been too busy, he had failed Orion, and he was afraid to ask how Orion's law practice in Carson City was coming along—he knew the answer. (Characteristically, Orion had been left out of the distribution of offices when Nevada became a state.)

Six years earlier, from New Orleans, where he was between piloting hitches, Sam had written for Orion an account of a visit to a local fortune-teller, Madame Caprell. The lady's analysis was so critical that it is likely Sam was simply using her as a mouthpiece for lecturing Orion. "In nearly all respects," the lady was supposed to have said to him, "you are the best sheep in the flock. Your brother has an excellent mind, but it is not as well balanced as yours. I should call yours the best mind altogether; there is more unswerving strength of will and set purpose and determination and energy in you than in all the balance of your family put together." As for Orion: "He never *does* do anything if he can get anybody else to do it for him, which is bad. He never goes steadily on till he attains an object, but nearly always drops it when the battle is half won; he is too visionary—is always flying off on a new hobby." And since that session with the deltaic sybil Orion's retreats and hesitations had filled Sam with bafflement, rage, pity, sardonic glee, but mostly guilt: the younger brother had triumphed over the older brother, in the same way that, in a certain sense, he had triumphed over his father and over his brother Henry—scalded to death in a steamboat explosion in 1858—just by outliving them. Clemens felt that he could find peace only in excitement, that only restless moving from place to place could numb his guilt. "My mind is stored full of unworthy conduct toward Orion and towards you all," he wrote home. "I have got a spirit that is angry with me and gives me freely its contempt."

The day before he sailed he wrote goodbye to an old Hannibal friend, Will Bowen; they had sat out the long mornings in Dawson's schoolroom together and later had been pilots together. Clemens' letter was blithe and overassertive to the point of being truculent, but there were some dark notes. The *Quaker City* passengers were tiptop, he said; he expected to have a jolly, sociable, homelike time of it for the next five or six months; he was going for fun only and did not expect to work hard at all—he could do his correspondence with his left hand, he said, at least until he got to Egypt. What sobered him was the thought of the return trip, and, thinking that far ahead, he decided that he might ship out again in November, "if I don't like to land when we get back." "I have a roving commission," as he had had for fifteen years as itinerant printer, river pilot, Western miner and journalist. "There is no unhappiness like the misery of sighting land (and work) again after a cheerful, careless voyage." Leaving his trunk for the last moment, he set off on what he remembered early the next morning as nine hours of farewell dinners and wine-drinking.

CHAPTER TWO

"The tide of a great popular movement"

I

EARLY SATURDAY AFTERNOON, June 8, 1867, the steamer and auxiliary sailer *Quaker City* left her Wall Street pier in a heavy rain. The weather turned rough, and she soon dropped anchor off Sandy Hook and waited there until Monday morning, riding out the storm, the Sabbath, and the first prayer meetings. It was clear that the stomachs and devotions of the seventy-five or so passengers would need considerable cosseting, and if the cruise was not quite a funeral excursion without a corpse—Clemens' epitaph for it when it was all over—neither could it be a picnic on a grand scale with young people playing cards, drinking, and dancing nightly to fiddles, flutes, and a snare drum. Creating the conditions for satire, Clemens had almost deliberately misapprehended the character of the venture from the very start. It was born under the auspices of Beecher and Plymouth Church, and it was headed for Palestine; the passengers had to be able to afford a five-month vacation and, in addition to $1,250 for passage, at least five hundred dollars in gold for expenses on land. By no strange process of natural selection most of the people on board were late-middle-aged, prosperous, pious, and abstinent.

There were exceptions. Clemens' roommate, Daniel Slote, was fifteen years older than he, fattish, balding, pampered by his mother and sisters in Brooklyn, and the owner of a commercial stationery firm. Still, he seemed "splendid, immoral, tobacco-smoking, wine-drinking, godless"; he would share two cases of champagne that an importing house had sent Clemens as a bon-voyage gift. And there were younger men, too, who offered the sort of harmonious diversity Clemens found all too little of on

39

board the *Quaker City* and on whom, in his correspondence and in *The Innocents Abroad*, he conferred a certain measure of celebrity. Among them was Charles Langdon, the eighteen-year-old scion of an Elmira coal fortune and brother of the future Mrs. Clemens, sent abroad by his father on this respectable cruise to see the world while keeping out of trouble. Occasionally, in the midst of their chatter, Clemens recalled with affection the robust voice of Captain Wakeman, who, upon hearing the hail "Stop the boat, you old pot-bellied son of a bitch," gave the order to his mate, "Stop her, John, stop her, some old friend of mine wants to come aboard." For all of them, even Slote, were boys really, callow and sheltered, tame companions for a man who had been on his own and supporting himself since the age of twelve and who was familiar with all sorts of men and degrees of life. "When I find a well-drawn character in fiction or biography," he was to write in Chapter Eighteen of *Life on the Mississippi*, "I generally take a warm personal interest in him, for the reason that I have known him before—met him on the river."

He remained as sensitive as ever to those hints of exclusion and disapproval which had vexed his voyage to New York half a year earlier; in response to what he felt to be pretension, sanctimony, snobbery, and pressures to conform, he adopted a satiric and skeptical stance which eased his tensions and angers and shaped his literary materials. Only mean people got seasick, he mused. Even when they were still within the harbor the passengers were lurching past the lashed coops of chickens, geese, and ducks on their way to the rail. He soon became acutely disgusted by the sight of these people leaving the table to vomit and then returning for more dinner. They could eat all they want, he said, mocking the ship's regulations, "but no swapping false teeth allowed." He was just as disgusted by a "Frenchy-looking woman" from Washington, D. C., who paid intimate attentions to her black-and-tan terrier, gave it bouquets of flowers, and called it "Little Boy." He was infuriated by a Dr. William Gibson of Jamestown, Pennsylvania, who, having volunteered his services as collector of facts and specimens to the Department of Agriculture and the Smithsonian, traveled under the thundering title of "Commissioner of the United States of America to Europe, Asia, and Africa." (Dr. Gibson was as grandiose in death as in life, for in the Jamestown cemetery he lies under a granite monument, ordered by him at a cost of about $100,000, which is sixty-five feet high and topped by a fifteen-foot statue of Hope.) He was infuriated also by a "simple, green, wide-mouthed, horse-laughing young fellow" who was a witless bore; by Dr. Andrews of Albany, a spouter of pretentious misinformation. And, having worked himself into a rage early in the trip, Clemens failed to find amusing even the one fullfledged and spectacular eccentric on board. This was Bloodgood H. Cutter, a Long Island farmer and a compulsive versifier who could commemorate any occasion in doggerel and who during his lifetime published at least twelve hundred broadsides of his own work. For Clemens he was nothing but a bore and an interruption, and in *The Innocents Abroad* he was written off impatiently as "Poet Lariat," an honorific which he proudly displayed in 1886 on the title page of his collected works.

There were only three ordained clergymen on board, but the prevailing atmosphere of piety and steady prayers gave Clemens the lasting impression that the *Quaker City* carried a shipload of divines. He could get along well enough with the professional clergy. He liked their conversation and their company; he had in common with them an interest in oratory; and one of the closest friends of his Hartford years was to be a clergyman, Joseph Twichell. It was the amateurs who enraged him, including one unsmiling passenger, a candidate "for a vacancy in the Trinity," who asked Captain Duncan if the expedition would come to a halt on Sundays. They could do as they wished on dry land, he was told, but Duncan couldn't anchor in the middle of the Atlantic. "There was a little difference of opinion between us—nothing more," Clemens mildly remarked about these amateurs. "They thought they could have saved Sodom and Gomorrah, and I thought it would have been unwise to risk money upon it." Consequently, with all but eight or ten of the passengers he was on terms that were at best polite and that became vexed when the touchy issues of Sabbath observance and itinerary came to the arguing point. Forty years later his rage still lay close enough to the surface to be awakened by a photograph of one of the passengers, Stephen Griswold. "Here is the real old familiar Plymouth-Church self-complacency," Clemens wrote on the frontispiece of Griswold's book about the Beecher community. "It is the way God looks when He has had a successful season."

The passengers who expected to be able to boast that they belonged to Mr. Beecher's party or General Sherman's party had been bitterly disappointed. Beecher decided to stay home and write a novel. General Sherman, possibly feeling that in such close quarters peace could be hell, went off to fight the Indians. As Clemens and some others speculated, these and a few other celebrities who defected may just have got tired of being advertised. With them gone, the "only notoriety" the group had was Mark Twain, wrote Miss Julia Newell, a maiden lady from Wisconsin, to her home-town paper. "He is a rather handsome fellow but talks to you with an abominable drawl that is exasperating. Whether he intends to be funny for the amusement of the party I have not yet ascertained." Neither she nor most of the others would, in fact, know whether he was amusing them or making fun of them. On the eve of sailing, the passengers had met at the Brooklyn house of Moses S. Beach, proprietor of the New York *Sun* and a Plymouth Church congregant. As both surviving celebrity and professional speaker, Clemens had made an announcement: "Captain Dun-

41

can wishes me to say that passengers for the *Quaker City* must be on board tomorrow before the tide goes out. What the tide has to do with us or we with the tide is more than *I* know, but that is what the *Captain* says." A mild enough joke, certainly, but when delivered with his strange, attenuated drawl and after the uncertain shuffle which, taken together with it, often laid Clemens open to the suspicion that he was drunk, it was enough to puzzle and even alarm the gentlemen in their unaccustomed swallow-tailed coats and white kid gloves and their ladies dressed *en règle* in gowns bought for the trip.

Here, facing him, was a new American middle class trying out its wealth and leisure and about to put its homegrown culture to a kind of test among the monuments of the Old World. This class, by his choice, was to be his central audience. He both entertained and mocked these people; sometimes he alienated them, but often he showed his eagerness to take on their social coloration. He was outraged by their parochialism, but he envied them their sense of rootedness, and they gave him a sense of belonging that delighted him. "I basked in the happiness of being for once in my life drifting with the tide of a great popular movement," he wrote of the middle-class discovery of Europe: basking, drifting—the terms of happy surrender. In that year of the Paris Exposition everyone seemed to him to be going abroad. During the summer, Clemens figured, four or five thousand Americans were leaving for Europe every week. The English tour party had already made such a name for itself that the novelist Charles Lever, serving a sybaritic term as Her Majesty's consul in La Spezia, was delightedly telling his Italian friends that Thomas Cook's clients were in reality convicts too depraved to be sent to the Australian colonies. Mr. Cook, he explained, had a secret contract with the Crown to release a few convicts in each Italian city quietly and then move on.

In a gentler spirit Clemens named his representative tourist "the American Vandal." Whether vandals or innocents, the Americans who were abroad in force did not represent the first or best society, Clemens acknowledged. They lacked cultivation and education, gilding and filigree and refinement; these culture-curious democrats depended on their Baedekers and Murrays to tell them not only where to go but how to deport themselves. They were capable of vulgarity, the most strident kind of chauvinism and insularity. They were skeptical and impatient; they also responded docilely and with awe if not understanding to high European culture. But this awe did not prevent them from being vandals and desecrators; people who had been accustomed to scribbling their names on the walls of water closets, Clemens said, now scribbled them on Greek ruins. Their sharp trading and acquisitive drive were, when they were abroad, just about equaled by their gullibility; European entrepreneurs, with their hastily contrived American saloons which pretended to serve

American drinks and their acres of still-wet Guido Reni canvases for sale, were plucking the American eagle. Clemens felt sympathy for the victims, and despite their unshakable belief in American superiority he found something in them to admire: their "roving, independent, free and easy character." During the five months of the *Quaker City* cruise, in close circumstances which put social identities to the test, he had his first prolonged and intimate experience of this new class which exerted its influence on him, helped shape his literary goals and social aspirations. In turn, he felt that the new class, traveling abroad and seeing new lands but unable to sing its own praises or publish its adventures, needed a spokesman. This was his formal justification of the circumstance that for the next two years, through his correspondence, his lecturing, and finally *The Innocents Abroad*, he achieved fame and considerable wealth by combining the roles of spokesman and satirist. "My audience is dumb, it has no voice in print," he wrote to Andrew Lang in 1890. "Honestly, I never cared what became of the cultured classes; they could go to the theater and the opera, they had no use for me and the melodeon."

He may have been the only spokesman on the ship, but there was no lack of chroniclers. Mrs. Mary Mason Fairbanks, under the anagram Myra, was writing meticulous and unexciting accounts of the trip which were published in her husband's newspaper, the Cleveland *Herald*. Fourteen letters by Miss Julia Newell ran in the *Gazette* of Janesville, Wisconsin. The Reverend Mr. Bullard of Wayland, Massachusetts, had an understanding with a Boston paper, as did the Reverend Mr. Hutchinson with a St. Louis paper and Dr. A. Reeves Jackson, the ship's surgeon—and, three cautious years later, the husband of Miss Newell—with one in Philadelphia. It had been rumored that Moses Beach had plans to write for his New York *Sun,* but he may have felt that an account of a luxury cruise was not altogether fitting for a paper he had taken pains to conduct as the voice of the workingman. There were these and other real or intended correspondents, perhaps a dozen in all; there were passengers who kept or intended to keep journals; and there were the letter-writers. "Everyone taking notes," observed the one professional reporter, who had to honor substantial commitments to the *Alta California* and the New York *Tribune*. "Cabin looks like a reporters' congress." Inevitably the *Quaker City* expedition developed a wide following back home.

II

To Slote and to the others who preferred poker and alcohol to dominoes and tea Clemens revealed mainly the shifting, ruffled, somewhat truculent surface of his personality. With them he was Mark Twain, satirist and mimic, profane, who joked about genuine Nubian chancres and about Bayard's motto ("*Sans peur et sans* culottes"), and who told them that contrary to all reports the ugly women of the Azores were probably virtuous—"Fornication with such cattle would come under the head of the crime without a name." (Some months earlier he had decided that the big-breasted Nicaraguan girls also were virtuous, according to their lights, but "their lights are a little dim.") He was no prude, but he did make a finical distinction between the smoking room and the drawing room, and to a few of the women on the *Quaker City*—Mary Fairbanks, her friend Emily Severance, and Emma Beach, Moses Beach's seventeen-year-old daughter—he opened himself and exposed the still plastic and uncommitted private personality of Samuel Clemens. In these friendships he gave lasting hostages to the social order.

Clemens played chess with Emma Beach and carried on a mock flirtation with her. Despite the difference in their ages, he invited her to scold and correct him, an invitation more seriously offered to and accepted by Mary Fairbanks. In comparison with most women of her day, and notably in comparison with the *Quaker City* ladies, she was highly educated and accomplished. She was an early graduate of Emma Willard's Female Seminary in Troy, New York, had taught school, could speak French well enough to get along, and was a semiprofessional writer. She was full-faced and had a rounded figure, and she was seven matronly years older than Clemens. She had two children, whom she had left behind in Cleveland in the care of her somewhat spiritless and, as Clemens saw him, exasperating unworthy, and undependable husband, Abel; she was "a Pegasus," Clemens later said, "harnessed with a dull brute of the field. Mated but not matched." For thirty-two subsequent years Clemens addressed her as "Mother" and called himself her "Cub" and her "Reformed Prodigal," and it was in the role of son to mother that he described her to his family as "the most refined, intelligent, and cultivated lady in the ship, and altogether the kindest and the best. She sewed my buttons on, kept my clothes in presentable trim, fed me on Egyptian jam (when I behaved), lectured me awfully on the quarter deck on moonlit promenading evenings, and cured me of several bad habits." It was as if Sam Clemens had never left home and was still a boy under the thumb of the thin, angular, and incomparably less cultivated Jane Clemens. Mary Fairbanks was the kind of civilizing influence that Huck Finn lit out from, but which Clemens courted for years.

She had noticed him from the start. He stood out from the others, she said, and not only because of his serious, questioning face, his look of offended innocence, his "drolleries and quaint, odd manners," and the peculiar indolence and moderateness of his movements. "There is something,

I know not what, that interests and attracts," she said. She noticed that he slouched at the table and that he was "scarcely genteel in his appearance." A challenge was offered her, and he soon made it an explicit invitation, to work her influence on him, to pass on through maternal suasion the conventions of her class and background. She was shrewd enough to see the promise in him, and at this stage he was scarcely recalcitrant. He teased her, and he continued to swear and drink when he felt like it, but he also tried to open up to her. He was not used to talking about his private self; when he did, he was a little mawkish. "I am like an old burned-out crater," he declared as they walked together on deck. "The fires of my life are all dead within me."

By the time the ship was in the Mediterranean, Mary Fairbanks had become his mentor in manners and morals, even in writing, and, willingly enough, he was surrounded by women in a scene which could have made one of the genre groups by John Rogers that went with the horsehair-upholstered parlor furniture of the time: at the right Mrs. Severance sharpens pencils for him, in the center of the group the author is bent over his writing table; while at his shoulder, a motherly figure molded in marmoreal plaster, leans Mary Fairbanks, scanning his manuscript for vulgarities and vernacularisms, for lack of charity and too much irreverence. "Now these are ready for you to make fun of us," Emily Severance once said to him, handing him his pencils. "I wish you would write something sober, to be put in the *Atlantic Monthly*, for instance." At other times the author stood at the ship's rail, gloomily tearing his manuscript into tiny pieces. "Mrs. Fairbanks thinks it oughtn't to be printed," he said, "and, like as not, she is right." (She had scolded him for writing a passage about how a lady climbing up Vesuvius in a hoopskirt would look to someone just below her on the steep path.) "Mrs. Fairbanks has just destroyed another four hours' work for me," he told Emma Beach another time. He was obedient, formative, eager to learn. Without hypocrisy but with a certain willing suspension of identity—the price of which, he would later learn, was anger and a divided heart—he wanted to experiment with her manners and standards, to imitate and possibly assimilate them. In his reliance on her taste, in his apparent submission to her literary standards, were foreshadowed some of the scenes of his life with Olivia Langdon and their children: a writer surrounded by women and seeking their approval.

In the days before the *Quaker City* called at Marseilles, Clemens played the role of the studious and reverent tourist with Mrs. Fairbanks and her friends. He was a member of a group which met for serious discussions, its high purposes only a little threatened by the fact that its presiding officer was an ex-alcoholic who had cured himself by becoming a morphine addict. Clemens studied the guidebooks. He read poetry aloud to the ladies. He even talked with confidence and reverence about the Old Masters, the holy of holies among the cultural values of Mrs. Fairbanks. In New York, at the Academy of Design, he had been entranced by academic landscapes and sentimental vistas, but he had balked: "I am glad the old masters are all dead, and I only wish they had died sooner." When he came to write *The Innocents Abroad* he would return to this jeering attitude and resign himself to the knowledge that Mrs. Fairbanks thought of him as a heretic in art. But for the moment, during this honeymoon, this period of blending in with the social foliage, he was willing to embrace her symbols of culture and status, even her religion. He dreaded the prayer meetings, but at her urging and scolding he attended them, and he went a step further. One afternoon he had a serious conversation with the Reverend Mr. Bullard, who later confided to another passenger that if Mr. Clemens proved to be not past saving they might see the rebirth of many souls on the voyage. A week later the prodigal himself, a fresh convert, led the evening devotions. This remained the ultimate outpost of his spiritual progress until a year later, when, wooing Olivia Langdon, he underwent a parallel conversion, more fervid but no more permanent than this one. Mrs. Fairbanks was gratified by his regeneration to the same degree that a friend from quite another world, Joe Goodman of the Virginia City *Territorial Enterprise*, was a few years later to be dumfounded to hear his ex-reporter saying grace at Livy's dinner table. For many of the other people on board, Mrs. Fairbanks' influence notwithstanding, he continued to be a dissolute, irreligious, uncouth Westerner, a gambler as well as a drinker. It was a role, she recognized, that he assumed partly out of perversity and in self-defense, the outsider's aggravated reaction to the already disapproving attitudes of a tightly knit social group. "You don't know what atrocious things women, and men too gray-haired and old to have their noses pulled, said about me," he explained to her after the voyage. "And but for your protecting hand I would have given them a screed or two that would have penetrated even *their* muddy intellects."

"Solemnity, decorum, dinner, dominoes, prayers, slander"—so he summed up the routine of shipboard life, which was broken at last by a stop at Horta in the Azores and by a celebration ashore for which the bill for ten people was $21.70, $15.70 of it for wine and cigars.

III

Sam Clemens, the Westerner who was to spend nearly a sixth of his life in Europe, an expatriate despite himself, came to Paris with little anticipation. Henry James's early experience of the glittering city had been so powerful that in later life he claimed to remember that as an infant, waggling his toes under long baby robes, he had seen a tall and glorious column in the Place Vendôme. For him Paris was history. For Clemens, whose first cherished memories were of drowsy dogs, ripe watermelons, and ghost stories told on his Uncle John Quarles's farm, Paris was the present, but it was progress. It was the city of the Emperor Napoleon III, who stood not six feet away from him at the Exposition grounds and who, Clemens decided, must be "the greatest man in the world today." Hadn't this ruler re-established France on a solid commercial basis? He had driven straight and broad avenues through the city and paved them with asphalt, believing that without paving stones there could be no barricades, and without barricades no revolutions.

At the city of the Universal Exposition, where the world came to enjoy the gaslit grandeurs of the Second Empire while celebrating the smiling aspects of the Industrial Revolution, America was represented by her technology as well as her tourists. Field's transatlantic telegraph, McCormick's reaping machine, and Howe's sewing machine were displayed and there were other portents of the American Century: a mill in Lawrence, Massachusetts, won a medal for its enlightened paternalism, a piano made in Boston won a commendation from the Abbé Liszt, and the painter Frederick Church was honored for his landscapes in oil. The century pointed forward, and Clemens was impatient with what Paris had to offer of the past.

He had at his command scraps of French he had taught himself on the river, and he mocked his own fumbling in the tongue as well as the affectations of others: "Quel est votre nom and how the hell do you spell it?" He wondered why so many towns in France, as evidenced by the signs on the railway stations, were called "Côte des Hommes," an indelicacy which did not survive into *The Innocents Abroad*. The paintings in the Louvre displayed a cringing spirit, he felt, "A nauseous adulation of princely patrons." At Versailles his reactions were confined within the drab limits of the observation "Nothing is small—nothing is cheap. The statues are all large." He saw Notre Dame, the Bois de Boulogne, the Morgue, the poverty of the Faubourg St. Antoine, where "the people live who start the revolutions," and he came back to his hotel on the Rue de Rivoli which had an elevator but no soap, where the candles did not give enough light to read by, and where the barbers were butchers. As he walked the boulevards and visited the cafés he was excited and pleased at first by what seemed an air of open sexuality and wickedness. He was enchanted by the cancan, by guidebook anecdotes about Louis XV and Pompadour dining naked at Versailles, and like any other tourist he thought he could tell at a glance which were the ladies of the demimonde. The city titillated him, but during the next years, as his commitments to domestic life multiplied, his curiosity and tolerance turned into anger and revulsion. Even by the time *The Innocents Abroad* was finished Peter Abelard had become something worse than just a romantic humbug—a pedant, a lecherous hypocrite, and "a dastardly seducer." He became a symbol of what Clemens later described in his notebooks as a country without morals, ruled by prostitutes, and populated by filthy-minded citizens who were the connecting links between man and monkey.

By August 2, when Clemens arrived in Naples by train from Rome, he had covered nearly twenty-five hundred miles of the Continent in a month, a heroic pace for which American tourists were already celebrated and which gave to their heightened responses to European leisureliness a comic poignancy. The *Quaker City* lay quarantined in the harbor, and from his hotel ashore Clemens wrote a letter of protest to the English-language paper in Naples: "We have not brought any cholera with us from Leghorn. They would not let us out of the country without paying duty on it." Making fun of medical fumigations, he gave play to the sort of compost-heap humor that his Western readers had enjoyed but which, he was now being told over and over again by Mary Fairbanks, would not do at all in the East: "Each and every passenger has acquired a distinct and individual odor, and made it his own, and you can recognize any one of them in the dark as far as you can smell him." During the ten days before the quarantine was lifted he made the predictable trips to Pompeii, to Capri, Ischia, and Procida; he climbed Vesuvius ("I am glad I visited it," he reported to his paper in California, "partly because it was well worth it, and chiefly because I shall never have to do it again"). He traveled by the guidebook, he was as obedient to it as any other tourist, but (as Bret Harte conceded in a review of *The Innocents Abroad*), though he was content to see only the sights everybody else saw, he saw them with his own eyes.

Aboard the *Quaker City* again, he had a breathing space. Despite the heat of the cabin, the noise of peddlers and musicians, the temptation to visit ashore—the ship was a poor writing desk, he complained—he started to catch up with his newspaper correspondence. He was worried that he had neglected it half the time and botched it the other half. To pay off his debt to the *Alta California* he spun out his impressions of Naples and Vesuvius in four long letters. He had the need and the opportunity now to consider the experience of the past month, and even while making fun of his fellow-tourists, he began to convert some of their baser attitudes—their outrage at bureaucracy and beggars, at the wealth of the Church, at superstition and the veneration of relics, their raucous irreverence and impatience with the past, their conviction that Europe was a sell, a swindle, a fraud—into a flexible, joyously inconsistent view that was wholly his own. He said the Arno might be a plausible river if it had some water pumped into it. He said that Venice looked as if in a few weeks its flooded alleys would dry up and restore the city to normal. (Some years later General Grant, no humorist and an innocent abroad as well as in peace, remarked "Venice would be a fine city if it were only drained.") "Is—is he dead?" Clemens would ask, fleeringly, in front of some ancient portrait or bust. These were his way of rejecting the past, the uncomfortable emotions of outsideness and awe, and the father image of Europe, his own way of answering Emerson's call for Americans to cease listening to the courtly Muses of Europe, to speak their own minds, make their own past.

But in certain European vistas—the fields of France and the Italian lakes —he also began to find and respond to a tranquility and gentleness that existed for him only in dreams, paintings, and his remembered boyhood and which he bitterly missed in the harsh mountainscapes and alkali deserts of the West; he said he had never seen twilight in California. From the distance of "a league"—the antique unit of measure suggests the mood —he glimpsed Venice reposing in a soft, golden setting, its towers, domes, and steeples "drowsing" in the sunset mist. "Drowsing" was his talismanic word to evoke the landscape of dream. Over Damascus he was to find, from a distance, "a drowsing air of repose" which made it seem like a city visited in sleep, and it was by the same translation of reality into dream that in *Tom Sawyer* he used "drowsing" to evoke the atmosphere of the schoolroom and in *Life on the Mississippi* he rendered the Hannibal of his boyhood as "a white town drowsing in the sunshine of a summer's morning"; even in *The Mysterious Stranger*, written late and in bitterness, the town still "drowses" in peace. The word conjured up an image of childhood purified by the years, a state of idyllic innocence which could be recaptured only in the imagination, and the image was as compelling for him as death was for Walt Whitman. These passive, whispering, dreamlike images were the token of their private alienation from the bustling present for which publicly they were often the spokesmen.

Clemens found in places such as Venice something of what Howells had reveled in during his four years as American consul there: a "vernal silence" and slowness that questioned ambition and invited surrender. The superiority of life in Europe to life in America lay in leisure and comfort, Clemens wrote, and having made this superficial and apparently static contrast, he explored it or implied it insistently. He measured American rush, gain, and early aging against a European standard; his own need to move, move, move, his restlessness and impatience expressed themselves in a heightened response to their opposites. Europe externalized what he did not have, made him question what he did have. In Milan the contrast struck him hard. The image, in *The Innocents Abroad*, is of a razor which refuses to hold an edge and which the barber puts aside for a few weeks while the edge seems to come back by itself: "What a robust people, what a nation of thinkers we might be, if we would only lay ourselves on the shelf occasionally and renew our edges." The hand is that of Samuel L. Clemens, but the voice is that of Concord, Massachusetts, not of Hannibal, Virginia City, San Francisco, or Hartford. It was a way of writing about the sources of creative energy—in his later years he was fond of simple mechanistic images ("Waiting for the tanks to fill up again," he would say during a "dry" spell)—remote in style and content from Mark Twain, the public humorist. His description of himself as "born lazy" may have the same content, phrased in socially acceptable terms, as Herman Melville's "For the greatest efficiency the harpooners of this world must start to their feet from out of idleness and not from out of toil."

Like the tenderfoot roughing it in the West, the Innocent in Europe at first finds the customs of the natives alien and obscure. His visit is a process of education, and as his sense of superiority is shaken he begins to take on some of the power and wisdom of the natives, to be able to bear their laughter at him and eventually to share it. In Europe Clemens found not only a fresh subject but also a continuing challenge to his own attitudes and to conventional American values. His correspondence from Europe was often hasty. He padded, he filled up space with easy parody and straight guidebook information. Yet it has a vividness and responsiveness, a versatile style and a flexible point of view that his New York correspondence (which he complained had been "a perfect drag") often lacked. In New York he had mentioned that he might write a book about the *Quaker City* excursion. Now his sense of the comic, inconsistent, variegated possibilities in his subject became stronger and stronger, and with a book firmly in mind he made plans for the coming winter.

From Naples he wrote to Senator William M. Stewart of Nevada accepting a private-secretaryship Stewart had offered him in June. He expected to make it one of the "best paying berths in Washington," he explained to his family, and he added that he would probably be able to find a job for Orion. To Frank Fuller, the willing impresario, who was still out about five hundred dollars on the Cooper Union debut, he reported in greater detail, but still he showed a certain secretiveness about his long-term plans:

> Don't make any arrangements about lecturing for me. I have got a better thing in Washington. Shall spend the winter there. It will be well for both of us, I think—and surely must be for me—better than lecturing at $50 a night for a literary society in Chicago and paying my own expenses. I have calculated all that and there isn't any money in it. . . . Winter after next will be early enough to dare that—and I may be better known then, after a winter spent in Washington. I must not commit myself on paper but will explain fully when I see you in October. I have had a good deal of fun on this trip, but it is costing like Sin. I will be a busted community some time before I see America again.

IV

Off Piraeus in mid-August Clemens had an adventure that supplied the material for an entire letter to the *Alta California*: wearing a red fez, he rowed ashore at night, evaded the Greek quarantine patrol, and, followed by barking dogs, climbed the Acropolis hill, where he fell into a mood of misty romantic Hellenism and had visions of the ghosts of Athenian heroes flitting past the Parthenon. After five days in Constantinople the excursion headed north through the Black Sea toward Sebastopol to visit the Crimean battlefields. Twenty hours' run away, at Odessa, where they stopped to take on coal and where Clemens amused himself watching the ladies of the city bathe naked in the harbor, there arrived an invitation for the passengers to visit the Autocrat of all the Russias, Alexander II, in his summer palace at Yalta. Committees were formed, meetings were held, white silk neckties, kid gloves, and swallow-tailed coats were furbished up, and Clemens set to work writing a formal address, a job which was not his strong suit, he complained, and which put him behind once again with his newspaper correspondence. He finished it in time for the American consul to read it aloud to the Czar and his suite. The onetime Confederate guerrilla warmed to the responsibilities of spokesmanship, hailed Alexander's emancipation of the serfs as one of the brightest passages in the history of mankind, and, reaching a certain high-water mark in Russian-American amity, concluded in a furious burst of good will: "That that friendship may still be here in times to come we confidently pray; that she is and will be grateful to Russia and to her sovereign for it, we know full well; that she will ever forfeit it by an unpremeditated, unjust act or unfair course, it were treason to believe." After the Czar, in white frock coat and pantaloons, had handed over this "rusty-looking document" to be "filed away among the archives of Russia—the stove," he and his family took the American visitors on a tour of the palace. "They made no charge," Clemens observed. Later on, in a talk with Baron Ungern-Sternberg, the chief director of the Russian railways, Clemens regained his normal stance. The Baron, "a man of progress and enterprise," told him that nearly ten thousand convicts were peaceably employed by him. Clemens responded with the blend of hoax and hyperbole that Europeans were learning to expect from American humorists: "We have eighty thousand convicts employed on the railways in California—all of them under sentence of death for murder in the first degree." He told his California readers, "That closed *him* out."

In Constantinople again, Clemens sat solemnly before the camera of Abdulah Frères. Along with the promise of a photograph, he sent to his family in St. Louis a detailed accounting of his newspaper work so far, asking them to match his catalogue against back issues of the *Alta California*. He listed forty-five letters—about ninety thousand words—representing nine hundred dollars at the rate of twenty dollars a letter, a substantial core of raw material for a book. On a visit to Scutari, on the other side of the Bosporus, the day before leaving for Palestine he stumbled on one of those apparent bonanzas that always competed with his literary plans: "Found a gold mine—good live quartz—the gold in snuff-colored suphurettes— ought to be very valuable here, where the labor is so cheap. Its presence," he concluded in his notebook, "is unsuspected." He passed this one up. On his last day in Constantinople, while Slote feverishly acquired Oriental souvenirs, Clemens frugally bought himself a Bible—not, as the Reverend Mr. Bullard might have hoped, for his devotions, but as a reference book for his Holy Land correspondence. In an offhand display of trustfulness and skepticism the new owner wrote on the flyleaf: "Sam L. Clemens— Constantinople, September 2, 1867. Please return this book to Stateroom No. 10 in case you happen to borrow it." That Sunday, Captain Duncan, who wished to sail with the evening tide, noted in his diary: "Coaling going on forward and Mr. Bullard preaching aft. It is to be hoped that our devotions will offset our wickedness in breaking the Sabbath." On its way out of the harbor that Sabbath night the ship tore the mainsail of a schooner, fouled a buoy, impaled one of its lifeboats on the bowsprit of yet another vessel, and left behind the body of a fireman who had either jumped or fallen from the ship while drunk, shocking the passengers less by his loss than by the condition in which he had been rushed into eternity.

A few days later Clemens amused himself in Smyrna and Ephesus with such anomalies as an oyster mine where, with his prospector's eye, he made out three distinct veins of oyster shells and broken crockery in a hillside five hundred feet above sea level, a new railroad that shrieked its way between the two cities, and a purely vernacular rendering of the tale of the seven sleepers. His vision, colored by the American present with its saloons and oyster restaurants, its addiction to whiskey and poker, was a foretaste of his impatient, mocking vision of Palestine and the remote, scarcely relevant past.

In Smyrna also, by a chance occurrence that compounded the deepest personal commitment with the almost comically trivial, he saw the grave and delicate face of Olivia Langdon. "I saw her first in the form of an ivory miniature in her brother Charley's stateroom in the steamer *Quaker City*, in the Bay of Smyrna, in the summer of 1867, when she was in her twenty-second year"— so, thirty-nine years later, with circumstantial understatement, he recalled this episode which he had already made part of the mythology of love in America. It was the sort of happening that he was fond of dramatizing into a "turning point": now an ivory miniature; two months later the chance invitation to write a book which became *The Innocents Abroad* and made him "at last a member of the literary guild"; another time a fifty-dollar bill he said he once found on the street in Keokuk, which heartened him to set off for the Amazon to seek a fortune in cocoa but led to his becoming a pilot instead; or the loose page he found blowing down the street in Hannibal which fired his passion for Joan of Arc; or the bout of measles caught from Will Bowen at the age of twelve which, by an exercise in selection and abridgment, he concluded was the reason he had become a writer. As he grew older he felt more and more certain that he was living in a universe which had no meaning or purpose; from these accidents, real or created, he derived for his sprawling and disorderly life the kind of order and meaning found in fiction and in dream.

At Beirut the passengers left the ship for nearly a month of traveling in Palestine, a harsh test of expectations inflamed by too much reading of Scripture and William Prime's devotional and damp-eyed guidebook, *Tent Life in the Holyland.* For their five dollars a day in gold they traveled like pashas, not roughing it in blankets on the ground, as Clemens half-seriously expected, but sleeping in stately, carpeted tents on real beds, after a huge European dinner of mutton, chicken, and goose, served on a table laid with silver and starched linen. By day the Americans rode single file on horseback, armed against the sun with white umbrellas lined with green cloth, a white cloth wrapped around their heads, thick green spectacles with blinders shielding their eyes, bouncing, short-stirruped, on their bony hard-trotting mounts, their elbows flapping like the wings of roosters about to crow. "I wouldn't let any such caravan go through a country of mine," Clemens said. He felt the absurdity of it early, and he mocked it with more vigor and bitterness after his mood had been soured by a hard ride, brutal on the horses, in order to reach Damascus before the Sabbath ("When did ever self-righteousness know the sentiment of pity?" he asked), and by an attack of cholera morbus once he got there. When Slote also came down with it, the pilgrims were all for leaving him behind while they made for Jerusalem, and the conflict became open. "Gentlemen, I understand you are going to leave Dan Slote here alone," Clemens said. "I'll be goddamned if I do." But Damascus gave him his only pleasant recollections of the Holy Land, he said in his notebook. His stay there was also the high point of his friendship with Slote, which during the next sixteen years was put to the test of a number of joint business ventures and failed it. (In February 1882, just ten days after Slote died, Clemens concluded, with the vindictiveness he reserved for his joint-venturers, that his old friend had not really been a robber, just a pickpocket.)

By this point in the journey Clemens had fallen into a gloom of the dead past. At the ruins of Baalbek, where the sun god had been worshiped, he marveled, a little hollowly, only at the size of the stones and at the ingenuity which had quarried, dressed, and raised them. The contrasts he used came too glibly, a mechanical formula for disposing of the past: the blocks were as big as omnibuses or freight cars or streetcars, with none smaller than a carpenter's chest and some larger than the hull of a steamboat. Faced with the reality of latter-day Palestine seen through dust and heat and not through the eyes of guidebook authors who said they wept when they entered Jerusalem, his drawling, anecdotal reporting became laconic, epithetic. The Arabs, he said, were "ignorant, depraved, superstitious, dirty, lousy, thieving vagabonds" who lived in caves, holes, and nasty mud cabins along with lice, fleas, horses, and jackasses amidst a shabby landscape of rocks and camel dung. What Palestine needed was a coat of paint. He renamed the cities of Canaan and Galilee Baldwinsville, Dutch Flat, Jonesborough, Jacksonville, Steubenville. By the time he reached Jerusalem his last vestiges of religious sentiment were gone—even the most pious travelers, he noted, had become a little glassy-eyed—and he became openly derisive. He shed mock tears over Adam for missing the telegraph, the locomotive, the steamboat, the Paris Exposition, and even the Flood. Moses took forty years to lead the children of Israel from Egypt to the Promised Land; the overland stage could have done it in thirty-six hours. The Jordan was just a creek, the Dead Sea a fraud, and in comparison with Lake Tahoe the Sea of Galilee looked like any ordinary city reservoir and was just about as big; still, an Arab boatman, to take a party sailing on its hallowed waters, demanded eight dollars—"Do you wonder now that Christ walked?" The man whom Bullard had hoped to save now amused himself with a fantasy about the boyhood of Christ: in front of the house was the sign "J. Christ & Son, Carpenters and Builders": "Recall Infant Christ's pranks on his school-mates—striking boys dead—withering their hands—burning the dyer's cloth, etc." By an ironical twist which delighted him, the *Quaker City* became a refuge ship for pilgrims fleeing the Holy Land, for it left Jaffa for Alexandria carrying in addition to its regular passengers forty peculiar waifs, part of a band of one hundred and sixty Maine farmers who had been led to Palestine by a man named Adams to await the Second Advent. Prophet Adams, Clemens said, had been drunk since September 1866; the crops they raised all went for taxes; and as for the rumor that they practiced free love, it was probably baseless, Clemens decided after looking at the ladies—opportunity perhaps, but no incentive. His own goodbye to the Holy Land, that howling wilderness instead of a garden, was a savage joke: "No Second Advent—Christ been here once, will never come again."

By October 9, 1867, two days after these refugees had been unloaded, the passengers were involved in a full-scale dispute over the route home.

"Coaxing won't do, abuse tried and successful," Duncan noted in his journal. "Sharp words exchanged. Prayers omitted." And on this note the excursion drew to an end, with Clemens desperate now to be off and away from this ship and all it stood for. The power of Mary Fairbanks' cool, restraining hand had begun to wane a little; he was determined to even the score with the pilgrims. He started to write a play about the trip. The hero is a correspondent named Mark Twain who comes equipped for the voyage with four reams of paper and a barrel of gin; the villains are dotards, old maids, and cripples, all of them pious, backbiting hypocrites. But it was more of a fit than a fiction, he recognized, and he gave it up, sent what he had written to Webb, just to show him that it could be done, and then succeeded in putting it out of his mind altogether. "I hate both the name and the memory of Charles Henry Webb, liar and thief," he declared categorically in 1905, "and I know of no such play. I have no memory of it."

On November 19, the day Charles Dickens arrived in Boston Harbor to begin his final American tour, the *Quaker City* returned to New York and discharged its angry humorist, his oppressors, their baggage, and their souvenirs: a Syrian eagle for the Central Park Zoo, a tree from the Mount of Olives to be dressed into pulpit furniture for Plymouth Church, Sebastopol relics, chips of monuments and mosaics, mummies for Barnum's Museum, water from the Jordan and the Pool of Bethesda, and, in addition, turbans, scimitars, fezzes, horse pistols, harem slippers, carpets, ottomans, filigree work, narghiles—all swelling the flood of exotic debris that furnished forth the cluttered period in American homemaking. Clemens fled like someone released from long captivity. That evening he planned to return to the fold briefly and have dinner with Mary Fairbanks and Charley Langdon at the St. Nicholas Hotel. But as he was on his way to meet them an editor sent by young James Gordon Bennett of the *Herald* caught up with him and persuaded him, with no great difficulty, to come to the editorial rooms and write an article about the trip. Clemens gave up the dinner. It was more than a social delinquency, for, having chosen to escape Mrs. Fairbanks' moderating influence, he now gave vent to his stored-up rage and sense of affront. "The pleasure ship was a synagogue, and the pleasure trip was a funeral excursion without a corpse," he wrote. The coffee was "unendurable," the food "not strictly first class," and the passengers patriarchs and "rusty old bachelors" who managed to accomplish quite a bit of damage. "The people stared at us everywhere and we stared at them. We generally made them feel rather small, too, before we got done with them, because we bore down on them with America's greatness until we crushed them." For all their pretensions as travelers and culture hunters, they had cared nothing for Europe or for any other place, he said. They only wanted to get back home. "Homesickness was abroad in the ship—it was epidemic. If the authorities of New York had known how badly we had it, they would have quarantined us here." It was a good night's work, this exercise in ridicule and exposure, and he was pleased. It would "make the Quakers get up and howl in the morning," he boasted to his family after midnight from his room at the Westminster Hotel. "You bet you when Charles Dickens sleeps in this room next week it will be a gratification to him to know that I have slept in it also."

The Quakers did get up and howl in the morning. "They can all go to the devil for all I care." By this time he had worked himself into a towering rage, which was aggravated further by the fact that the *Herald* had omitted his byline from the article. This score he partly settled over a dinner that night with the editors, who were busily wooing this explosive celebrity to join the staff. Before dinner, though, he went on to flay the Quakers in an even more savage letter to the *Alta California*. "I'm tired hearing about the 'mixed' character of our party on the *Quaker City*. It was not mixed enough—there were not blackguards enough on board in proportion to the saints—there was not genuine piety enough to offset the hypocrisy." One hundred and eighteen out of the one hundred and sixty-five prayer meetings had been scandalous and illegal "because four out of the five real Christians on board were too seasick to be present at them, and so there wasn't a quorum." If he had to go on such a pleasure excursion again, he said, the captain would be Ned Wakeman and the passengers would be some of the leading citizens of San Francisco, including Bret Harte, journalists and prominent eccentrics. He was not the only one who complained. A day later the *Herald* published a long anonymous letter (probably by Mrs. Severance's husband, Solon) describing the cynicism and incompetence of Duncan and his staff and the bitter feuds among the passengers. This writer attributed the trouble to the mixed character of the party, and he predicted that the *Quaker City* cruise would be the last of its kind.

In the same issue, the editors of the *Herald*, still making amends for the missing byline, ventured another prediction: "We are not aware whether Mr. Twain intends giving us a book on this pilgrimage, but we do know that a book written from his own peculiar standpoint, giving an account of the characters and events on board ship and of the scenes which the pilgrims witnessed, would command an almost unprecedented sale." It was as if Clemens had written his own prospectus. That day, while he was on his way to Washington to take up his duties with Senator Stewart and to repair his ruined finances, a publisher in Hartford, in a stiffly formal business letter, took the liberty of writing in the hope that perhaps a book could be compiled from Mark Twain's travel letters.

CHAPTER THREE

"The fortune of my life"

I

WHEN SAM CLEMENS LEFT THE WEST at the end of 1866 his fame was chrysalid, local. The editors of his California paper, counting on the sparks that new opportunities would strike against his talents, predicted that his commission for them would give him a world-wide reputation, and eventually they were right. His *Alta California* letters from abroad were enormously popular in the West, his *Herald* and *Tribune* letters in the East. His laughter and irreverence, his vernacular and skeptical accounts of Americans abroad among the holy places of Europe and Palestine, outraged some people, but they surprised and delighted most of his readers and made his venture into travel journalism an astonishing success. And it was a success that had to be measured not by the literary values of Boston but by the values of an avid, newly lettered and newly leisured mass audience, the beneficiaries of democratized culture, which had begun to come into its own just before the war and which shaped the character of the books, magazines, newspapers, and lecture programs of the Gilded Age. The parting blast at the pilgrims in the *Herald*—so sensational a valedictory that the canny publisher of *The Innocents Abroad* was to stipulate that it be included in the book—was a rocket sent up to signal not only the end of the voyage but also the arrival of Mark Twain as a national figure.

In Washington, however, despite his claim that he was lazy, Clemens threw himself into a bewildering tangle of projects and seemed to run on nervous energy flogged by ambition, restlessness, the need for money, and, above all, an indecision about who he was and what he wanted to be. As private secretary to Senator William M. Stewart of Nevada he was expected to perform a few clerkly chores in return for six dollars a day and the leisure to write. Such arrangements were common enough in the city;

not far from 224 F Street, where Clemens settled in with Stewart, lived Walt Whitman, a clerk in the Attorney General's office; and James H. Riley, who was one of Clemens' closest friends and who later figured in a bizarre and futile collaboration with him, served both as clerk to a Congressional committee on mines and mining and as political correspondent for the *Alta*. Stewart's return for taking on this unlikely secretary was the satisfaction of playing Maecenas to a literary celebrity and the use of Clemens' popularity with the Western press to advance his own reputation. The arrangement lasted barely two months. Over six feet tall, bearded like Moses, and with long flowing hair, Stewart looked like the archetypal frontier Senator, and he was also possessed by augustitude. He was no longer the lawyer and politician Clemens had known in Nevada and satirized as "Bullyragging Bill," the champion of the "honest miner"; now he was a pillar of state and nation, a rich man who had just sent his family off to Paris for the winter. Consequently he saw Clemens as "disreputable," "slouching," "seedy," "sinister"—these adjectives are from Stewart's highly colored, inevitably distorted recollections—wearing a battered hat and a frazzled cigar butt, the reverted sagebrush bohemian, now a safe three hundred and fifty miles away from Mother Fairbanks in Cleveland. According to Stewart, Clemens appeared at the apartment on F Street, helped himself freely to whiskey and cigars, took over a hall bedroom, and in the weeks that followed tormented the landlady by lurching drunkenly in the halls and smoking in bed. Clemens could not take either the Senator or the job seriously. Eventually Stewart drew himself to his full height and talked darkly about a thrashing, and Clemens resigned without regret and began to burlesque the whole business in print. In one of these burlesques, "My Late Senatorial Secretaryship," a private secretary named Mark Twain answers a request from some Nevada constituents for a post office: "Don't bother about a post-office in your camp. I have your best interests at heart, and feel that it would only be an ornamental folly. What you want is a nice jail, you know—a nice substantial jail and a free school." Such was the spirit of his brief service.

Clemens was on the move again: wretched food and shabby furniture, he complained, in five different Washington lodgings within three months. He stayed at Riley's boardinghouse: later he briefly shared with another newspaperman a room, a whiskey jug, and a scheme for working a minor swindle on provincial newspapers by sending them manifolded copies of correspondence. He had gone back to the marginal life, and in his familiar bohemian role he was enjoying one of his last flings outside the pale of respectability; the enthusiasm with which he now filled the role of tramp journalist was a measure of the enthusiasm with which he would soon fill the role of gentleman, householder, and head of a family. Years later he lamented to Howells the passing of "a life of don't-care-a-damn in a boarding-house," and in his *Autobiography*, that piece of near-fiction he thought of as the most unvarnished personal history ever written, he glorified the freedom of that life, but exaggerated the poverty and minimized the opportunities.

There were almost too many opportunities. He was Washington correspondent for Horace Greeley's New York *Tribune,* he was considering an invitation from James Gordon Bennett the younger to hold the same position for the New York *Herald,* he had other commissions from papers in the West and the Midwest. These assignments were worth about eight hundred dollars a month to him. He agreed to write occasional articles for the *Galaxy,* a literary monthly in New York. Frank Fuller pressed him to lecture during the winter, but he refused, turned down eighteen invitations at a hundred dollars each, turned down a proposition from Thomas Nast for a series of joint appearances in which Nast would draw while Clemens talked. He was determined, he told Fuller, to spend the winter building his reputation through the newspapers so it would "stand fire"; if he lectured in the spring he meant to lecture in the big cities and not in Tuttletown, Arkansas, and Baldwinsville, Michigan. But by early December, after only three weeks in Washington, he was already tired of politics and newspaper drudgery, and thinking of a Western lecture tour. "I am good for three nights in San F, one in Sac., two in Va. [Virginia City], and one in Carson—that is all *I* can swear to. It is all I would attempt on the coast. Maybe we could make it pay two of us—maybe we can't," he wrote to Fuller. "But for your overweening pride, we *could*—for you could keep door and peddle photographs—but not of *yourself,* for God Almighty's sake."

He had Orion to look out for, too, Orion who now hoped for a clerkship in the Bureau of Patents, the equivalent, if he had ever got the job, of putting a drunkard to work in a distillery. Sam's lobbying on Orion's behalf was marked by hypersubtlety, indirection, and the need to create complications in order to put off a distasteful errand. He paid a call on the Secretary of the Interior. "Said nothing about a place for Orion, of course—must get better acquainted first—must see his wife—*she* is the power behind the thone," he reported to Jane Clemens and Pamela. His heart was not in it. "I have friends in high places who offer me such things—but it is hard to get them interested in one's relatives": a cruel but accurate statement, for even in this city riddled with patronage nothing did come through for Orion. By the end of February 1868, after two and a half months of politicking, Sam claimed that, with a change in administration iminent, Washington was in such a muddle that even if Orion could get a job it would have no permanency. His determination to help evaporated into vague promise ("Sometime in the course of the present century I think they will create a Commissioner of Patents, and then I hope to get a berth for Orion") and into out-and-out rationalization: "Surely government pap must be nauseating food for a *man*—a man whom God has enabled to saw wood and be independent." It was a rationalization meant for his own benefit as well as Orion's, for he himself was tempted to become a consul or minister abroad, thought once again of going to China that spring as member of a diplomatic mission, and spent three frantic weeks lobbying for an appointment as postmaster of San Francisco. Stephen J. Field, a Forty-niner and a powerful California politician who even as an associate justice of the Supreme Court was still dispensing patronage, first proposed the post to Clemens early in December, but it had just been filled. In February it was vacant again, and Clemens went after it so energetically that after his campaign he was sick in bed, exhausted not only from overwork but also from the strain of a last-minute decision. The California delegation was pledged to him, the Senators were for him, the powers were behind him, and only then he discovered that the salary for this position (which he told Orion, San Franciscans regarded as a pinnacle of glory and public honor) was only four thousand a year. And this discovery was followed by another, surprisingly late for a man who had the subtlety to divine who was the power behind the throne in the Department of the Interior: the job was no sinecure, and the time he would have to give it would interfere with other plans. He explained to Elisha Bliss of Hartford, by this time his baffled and anxious publisher, "I have thrown away that office, when I had it in my grasp, because it was plain enough that I could not be postmaster and write the book too." Nor could he continue to be a full-time journalist either, he suddenly recognized. In order to write a book he would have to cut his newspaper correspondence to one or two letters a week, a loss of about three hundred dollars a month in income, and he asked Bliss for an advance of a thousand to help him keep writing through the spring. Until these decisions were forced on him, he was capable of continuing to drift between journalism and patronage. He still had no sure sense of identity or vocation. It was only by a wayward and dilatory process that Mark Twain, who had probably the most richly endowed natural talent in American literature, finally gave himself over to writing the book that established his fame.

II

The proposal from Elisha Bliss, Jr., secretary and managing director of the American Publishing Company of Hartford, eventually reached Clemens at the *Tribune* office in Washington on December 1. "We are desirous of obtaining from you a work of some kind, perhaps compiled from your letters from the East, etc., with such interesting additions as may be proper," Bliss wrote. "We are perhaps the oldest subscription house in the country, and have never failed to give a book an immense circulation. . . . If you have any thought of writing a book, or could be induced to do so, we should be pleased to see you, and will do so." The next day Clemens responded with equal directness. "I wrote fifty-two (three) letters for the San Francisco *Alta California* during the *Quaker City* excursion, about half of which number have been printed thus far," he wrote. "I could weed them of their chief faults of construction and inelegancies of expression and make a volume that would be more acceptable in many respects than any I could now write." He was concerned with correctness and propriety; he was less concerned with structure and direction, was willing to follow Bliss's instructions, "strike out certain letters, and write new ones," and carpenter his book to the physical exigencies of the standard subscription volume. He asked Bliss to please tell him "when the matter ought to be ready, whether it should have pictures in it or not, and what amount of money" he "might possibly make out of it. The latter clause" he wrote, "has a degree of importance for me which is almost beyond my own comprehension." (As he explained to Frank Fuller, the question boiled down to "*how much bucksheesh*.") After the disappointment of *The Jumping Frog* he had decided not to touch another book unless there was money in it; and in New York, before sailing for Europe, he had talked with Albert Deane Richardson, one of Bliss's most profitable authors, whose account of his eighteen months in Confederate prisons as a captured Northern journalist, *The Secret Service* (1865), sold nearly 100,000 copies, and whose travel book *Beyond the Mississippi* (1866) ended up selling nearly ninety thousand copies in four years. From this conversation and from others, Clemens became convinced that the only way to make a good deal of money from a book was to publish by subscription.

In stating his goal and choosing Bliss's publishing company as the way to reach it, Clemens implicitly defined his audience and the character of the books he would write for it. The subscription book, in Bliss's terms, was the people's book, and he was soon to advertise Mark Twain as "the people's author." Authors whose aspirations were of a different sort and who, while needing money no less than Clemens did, were willing for a while to accept its equivalent in reputation, went to publishers whose books were sold in bookstores. The manuscript they offered to trade publishers was as short or as long as it had to be in order to say what they wanted it to say. These authors felt that such an imprint as that of Ticknor and Fields of Boston (eventually to become Houghton Mifflin), the publishers of Emerson, Longfellow, Hawthorne, and Holmes, was critical accolade in itself. They hoped that this imprint, combined with judicious advertising, would guarantee them reviews, and they also hoped for a modest, though distant, return from their work. Their audience was educated, and it lived in communities big and prosperous enough to support a bookstore.

The subscription system, which made Mark Twain a rich author and which he later exploited as his own publisher, carried a different set of conditions. The prestige of the imprint was commercial, not literary. Eventually a stockholder and then a director of the American Publishing Company, Clemens boasted that it was the richest, most aggressive house in the country. (Incorporated in 1865, it was far from being the oldest, as Bliss claimed.) The books this and other subscription houses published had to be massive in order to justify their relatively high price ($3.50 and up, depending on the binding) and make the venture worth while for the four principals: the author, the publisher, who went to press only after he was sure of enough orders for him at least to break even; the subscription agent, who went from door to door and kept on talking; and the buyer, who was typically rural, a farmer or small tradesman with little education, for whom bulk was an index of value. But even padded out with steel engravings, decorations of all sorts, elaborate tables of contents, a six-hundred-page book could strain the integrity and imagination of an author who had only a three-hundred-page idea to begin with. It encouraged padding (Clemens once remarked that he thought about *The Innocents Abroad* pretty much as God thinks about the world: "The fact is, there is a trifle too much water in both"). It forced the author to write to fit and to fill, and it encouraged Clemens to develop his books on purely linear principles, with episode strung after episode until he reached page 600. It forced him to go on grinding out manuscript long after he lost interest in the subject, and it conditioned him to think of his writing as a measurable commodity, like eggs and corn. About the only advertising the subscription publisher bought was of a help-wanted variety, to recruit his army of selling agents. Consequently, literary editors, who kept an eye on advertising revenues, tended to ignore and resent subscription books as sub-literature and to regard the occasional review copy that came in from the publisher as an arrant attempt to get something for nothing.

The flourishing subscription system was part of the rationalizing of production and marketing that was going on all over America after the Civil War. "Anything but subscription publishing," Clemens once told Howells, "is printing for private circulation." But he was generalizing from his own special experience. "No book of literary quality was made to go by subscription except Mr. Clemens' books," Howell wrote in 1893, "and I think these went because the subscription public never knew what good literature they were." Some of the credit for this constructive deception belonged to Bliss, for he departed from his usual editorial practice by in-

viting a humorist to write a book for him that would eventually keep
company on marble-topped mahogany-legged tables with the illustrated
family Bible, with Horace Greeley's *American Conflict* and James Parton's *People's Book of Biography*, with all the other standard subscription
merchandise of moral philosophy, patriotism, and medical advice. In such
company *The Innocents Abroad* was to be, Bret Harte said, "an Indian
spring in an alkaline literary desert."

"You are one of the talented men of the age," Clemens quoted Henry
Ward Beecher as saying to him, "but in matters of business I don't suppose you know more than enough to come in when it rains." At the end
of January 1868, primed with publishing advice from Beecher and with
an invitation to be the guest of Beecher's sister Isabella Hooker, Clemens
paid his first visit to Hartford and discussed terms with Bliss face to face.
They reached a formal agreement by which Clemens was to get a five
per cent royalty on the subscription price, and this, he told his family
proudly, "is a fifth more than they have ever paid any author, except Horace Greeley. Beecher will be surprised, I guess, when he hears this" (and
so would Greeley, who was never one of Bliss's authors). He was to deliver
the manuscript of his untitled book by the middle of July; he was giving
himself six months to write or rewrite about 240,000 words, and he would
soon discover that he had to put aside nearly everything else in order to
do this. But for the moment, before the realities of work were on him, and
before his dealings with Bliss were put to the inevitable tests of impatience, suspicion and recrimination, he was, quite simply, euphoric, a man
with a new-found vocation standing in the city of plenty. Near Bliss's office on Asylum Street were the other thriving subscription houses, the
printers, the binders, and a paper mill, that made Hartford a major publishing center. All about him, as he explored this city which less than four
years later would be his home, he sensed solid security, a marriage of
prosperity and regularity which was new to him. Hartford was steady
habits and regular income, he told his California readers. The sources of
its wealth were rock-firm. The god of this celestial city was capital, invested and protected capital, and to him the people had raised altars: the
insurance companies and the banks, the revolver works and the rifle factory. The streets were broad, the houses ample, shapely, and surrounded
by "most capacious ornamental grounds." He saw hardly any smoking,
no chewing, and no saloons, although there were saloons on Asylum
Street. Poverty was not known, nor was swearing to be heard in the land.
Isabella Hooker and her husband were crushingly upright, unshakably
superior. "I don't dare to smoke after I go to bed, and in fact I don't dare
to do *anything* that's comfortable and natural," he wrote to Mary Fairbanks on January 24, after he had spent a few nights with the Hookers on

Forest Street. But he had seen the promised land, and he submitted willingly enough: "I tell you I have to walk mighty straight. I desire to have the respect of this sterling old Puritan community, for their respect is well worth having."

"I have just come down from Hartford," he wrote to Will Bowen from New York the next day, "where I have made a tip-top contract for a 600 page book, and I feel perfectly jolly. It is with the heaviest publishing house in America, and I get the best terms they have ever offered any man save one. . . . It would take a good deal of money to buy out the undersigned now, old boy." He had got a firm offer from Bennett of the *Herald* of double his usual rates for Washington correspondence, and he proposed to raise his rates to the other papers he wrote for; still, "the book is going to crowd me some—I shall have to cut off *all* outside work, and it is growing pretty lucrative." But he is not altogether occupied with rates and contracts, and in this letter to Will Bowen there begins to emerge the crucial web of motives and conditions by which Clemens would flourish as a writer: prosperity and status; Hartford, symbol of his eager acceptance, after years of drift and marginality, of a place in the social order; and marriage.

A month and a half earlier Mary Fairbanks had recommended a good wife as an incentive to steady habits, and he had countered, "I want a good wife—I want a couple of them if they are particularly good—but where is the wherewithal?" It took two newspaper letters to support him; how could he support a wife too? "I am as good an economist as anybody," he had told her, "but I can't turn an inkstand into Aladdin's lamp." Writing to Will Bowen, however, Clemens has become slightly mawkish on this subject. He envies Will for having "a most excellent wife," he says. "I wish I had been as fortunate. To labor to secure the world's praise, or its blame either, seems stale, flat, and unprofitable compared with the happiness of achieving the praise or abuse of so dear a friend as a wife." In this mood he has also begun to grope toward his materials as a writer and to begin his reconstruction of the idyl of Hannibal: "I have been thinking of schooldays at Dawson's, and trying to recall the old faces of that ancient time—but I cannot place them very well—they have faded out from my treacherous memory, for the most part, and passed away." The following July, when he returned to Hartford to deliver his manuscript to Bliss, he made a vital connection of his new life in the East to "that ancient time." "I never saw any place where morality and huckleberries flourished as they do here," he noted. He had heard of huckleberries, but he had never seen them before, and he joked that he always thought they were something like turnips. Now he saw children gathering buckets of them on the hillsides, and by the slow process of unconscious creation the huckleberry, a Hartford fact, was to become talisman for recapturing the Hannibal past.

What had happened was that, in Hartford, the sight of a promised land, and, in New York, his first meetings with Olivia Langdon caressed and quickened memory and aspiration.

Clemens met her around Christmas time 1867. He was in New York on a two-week visit with Slote, and was invited by Charley Langdon to meet his sister and his parents at the St. Nicholas Hotel, once the city's grandest palace of gold leaf and mirrors but now subsided into ultra-respectability. Clemens called on the Langdons on December 27 and was introduced to Livy. On New Year's Eve he accompanied her to Charles Dickens' reading at Steinway Hall. Among but above the other attractions of New York, Dickens had drawn the Langdons down from Elmira as he had drawn enormous crowds, five thousand at a time, who lined up in front of ticket offices before dawn on winter mornings. Speculators were riding high; Dickens' novels were selling by the tens of thousands; and the day after he arrived all but two of the nineteen hundred copies of his work in the Mercantile Library were out on loan. For all his criticism of America and his careful avoidance during the Civil War of any expression of support for the Union side, Dickens was still a Northern hero, a demigod even for abolitionists like the Langdons. The circumstances of the evening Sam Clemens spent with his future wife were appropriate. This was the valedictory reading tour of a towering literary personality, a hero of the mass audience which would soon elevate the newcomer, Mark Twain, also a great public reader as well as an actor *manqué*, to an analogous height. Despite his awe of Dickens, "this puissant god," Clemens confessed that he was disappointed: the readings from *David Copperfield* struck him as monotonous, the pathos as purely verbal, "glittering frost-work, with no heart." Dickens mumbled, and the audience, though eager and intelligent, managed to remain unexcited. So Clemens reported to his California paper. He also reported, "I am proud to observe that there was a beautiful young lady with me—a highly respectable young white woman." In an account which he dictated nearly forty years later he fitted that evening with Livy into a characteristic nexus of motives, for, at the height of his Hartford years with her, love, happiness, literary fame, and money had become convertible currency. Charles Dickens made $200,000 from his readings that season, Clemens recalled, but that one evening with Livy "made the fortune of my life—not in dollars, I am not thinking of dollars; it made the real fortune of my life in that it made the happiness of my life."

The next day Clemens paid Livy a New Year's call at the house of her friend Mrs. Berry. There, amidst the Moorish décor which marked his hostess as a lady of wealth and discrimination, he remained the entire day and part of the evening. With Livy was another friend, Alice Hooker, daughter of the disapproving Hookers of Hartford and niece of the two

Beecher clergymen. Despite the gaiety of the occasion, there was little or no alcohol and a great deal of propriety, and although Clemens spent thirteen hours at this marathon reception, he probably got to know the beautiful Miss Hooker at least as well as he could have known the "sweet and timid and lovely" twenty-two-year-old Livy. For, as he wholly idealized her, she was angelic, disembodied. The distance between them was too great for him to dare think of love; reverent worship, at best the grave affection of brother for sister, alone was possible. "You seemed to my bewildered vision a visiting *Spirit* from the upper air," he recalled a year later, "*not* a creature of common human clay, to be profaned by the *love* of such as I." After three meetings with Livy he had not progressed far enough to dare to write to her, and the one overt carry-over was an invitation from the Langdons to visit them in Elmira. He had seen her ivory miniature in September 1867; he met her at the turn of the year; he did not pay his visit to Elmira until August 1868; and before then, in February, he considered a diplomatic post in China which would keep him out of the country for a long time. Wooing her had not yet become even a possibility for him, and beyond a mention in one of his letters home—"Charlie Langdon's sister was there (beautiful girl)"—Livy vanishes from his record for over half a year.

III

On short notice and with a doorkeeper recruited at the last moment, Clemens gave a lecture in Washington on January 9 called "The Frozen Truth," a fabric of *Quaker City* impressions and anecdotes which he stitched together between ten o'clock one evening and breakfast the next morning. "I hardly knew what I was going to talk about," he told his mother, "but it went off in splendid style." Two nights later he had an unflawed success as an after-dinner speaker at a Washington Correspondents' Club banquet. Every speaker came prepared, he said: the arrangements were masterly and went as by clockwork. When midnight came, and along with it the Sabbath and the threat of adjournment, the guests voted to adopt San Francisco time, and they would have needed more than three hours of grace if the champagne had held out. Clemens was twelfth in a mammoth program of fifteen speakers, but even toward the drowsy, vinous tail of the evening his response to the toast "Women—the pride of any profession, and the jewel of ours" had the power to awaken and delight. With a sure sense of shock and transition he moved from the slightly indelicate ("She bears our children—ours as a general thing") to the colloquial ("She is a brick"), from burlesque eulogy to topical satire and back to the indelicate once again ("As a wet nurse, she has no equal among men"), and finally he put jesting aside and paid homage to what, along with the flag, was certain to bring a male banquet audience lurching to its feet: Mother. It was an extraordinarily varied performance within a span of about seven hundred and fifty words: graceful, bold, entirely original, and with a distinctive admixture of the orthodox and the outrageous. The public personality of Mark Twain, the eccentric demon born of the needs, aggressions, and reticences of Sam Clemens, was still in flux, no longer simply the bookish observer and the teller of tall stories but becoming a man of the world now, ironic, polished, and confident.

"Dear Folks," he wrote, with the triumph still fresh, "I thought you would like to read my speech, which Speaker Colfax said was the best dinner-table speech he ever heard at a banquet." Two weeks later, when he wrote to Mary Fairbanks, he had second thoughts. He was afraid she would see his speech reported in the papers and, in accordance with her standards, take him to task for using "slang," that catch-all word he and she used for indecorums, colloquialisms, indelicacies, and vulgarities of all sorts and degrees. The star performer for a toughened audience of journalists and politicians was still willing to bend his head for a scolding from a middle-aged bluestocking, proof that when he paid homage to "Mother" he had been dead serious. There *was* slang in the speech, he apologized, but the newspapers "had no business to report it so *verbatimly*. They ought to have left out the slang—*you* know that. It was all their fault. I am not going to make any more slang speeches in public."

The bolt fell nonetheless. Her letter, he said, was "a scorcher." He made his vows again—"I will rigidly eschew slang and vulgarity in future"— and he stuck by them reasonably well. In February he again spoke at a Washington banquet, and he reported to her that his speech had been "frigidly proper" and that by following her advice he had learned a lesson: "I acknowledge—I acknowledge—that I *can* be most laceratingly 'funny without being vulgar.'" A literary comedian at the start of his career, he soon discovered that many of the people whose approval he most wanted thought there was something vulgar merely about being funny; much later he discovered that there was also something confining. He assured her that he was now going to apply this hard-earned knowledge to *The Innocents Abroad* (it was to be more than a year later, after considerable agonizing over what were felt to be the blasphemous overtones of "The New Pilgrim's Progress," that he settled on the title). There was going to be no slang in the book, he told he, except "in a mild form in dialogues," as crucial a reservation as his insistence on the right of personal satire. To allay her fears that he might cause pain to his victims, he copied out for her a passage about the imposing vacuity who bore the title "Commissioner of the United States of America to Europe, Asia, and Africa." "It just touches Dr. Gibson on a raw place," he told her. (He had already touched Gibson on a raw place by arranging for him to be surrounded by a band of Arab beggars while posing for a photograph in front of the Pyramids.) Anticipating an objection from her on compassionate grounds, he added, a little disingenuously, "That complacent imbecile will take it for a compliment." For all his apparent submissiveness, he was baiting her and beginning to rebel against promises exacted by those to whom, almost mimetically, he offered himself as reconstructible sinner. For fear of exposing his "want of cultivation," he had promised Emma Beach not to joke about "those dilapidated, antedeluvian humbugs" the Old Masters; he promised Pamela there would be "no scoffing at sacred things in my book or lectures." He kept few such promises. With these women, as later with Livy, he conformed only as far as his evolving goals and standards told him to conform, and he generally had his own way.

He went through the file of his *Alta California* correspondence and discovered that there were not quite so many letters as he seemed to recall having written and that many of these letters did not measure up to Eastern taste. Even padded out with illustrations, all his letters would fill only two hundred and fifty of the six hundred pages he had to deliver. He would have to rewrite these letters and write three hundred and fifty new pages by the middle of the summer, and he needed all the help he could get. In search of ideas and raw material he borrowed Mary Fairbanks' letters to the Cleveland *Herald*, and he asked two other passenger-correspondents to collect their letters for him. Four days of illness in February, brought on by his day-and-night lobbying for the postmastership, proved to him he would have to change the way he lived. With the exception of a lecture in Georgetown later in the month, he managed to curtail other obligations, to save the nights for sleeping and the days for working, and he hoped to turn out ten pages of book manuscript a day, fifteen if things went well. But only a day after he reorganized his life in this way he found himself spending all his time in press galleries and hotel lobbies, covering the major event of his winter in Washington and observing the turmoil which for a while seemed to threaten bloodshed all over the country. On February 21 Andrew Johnson tried once again to dislodge his Secretary of War. Stanton locked himself in his office, the Radical Republicans took to the warpath, and impeachment was in the air. Johnson did not look at all like a "tyrant," Clemens wrote after watching him at a reception on the twenty-fourth, but instead like a "plain, simple, good-natured old farmer" who was uneasy, exhausted, and restless and looked in every eye for reassurance: "I never saw any man who looked as friendless and forsaken, and I never felt for any man so much."

The impeachment crisis lasted until May, by which time Clemens had been gone for over two months. His experience as a Washington reporter soured into a lifelong contempt for politicians in general and Congress-men (the only "distinctly native American criminal class") in particular, and his moment of sympathy with Johnson also passed. A year later he wrote for the New York *Tribune* a burlesque account of Johnson's last hour in office. The President lists his services to his country—he protected assassins, perjurers, and the Ku Klux Klan, and he encouraged corruption and incompetence in the government—and then he and his cabinet officers play cards for the furniture. Music is heard announcing the arrival of "the usurper Grant and his minions," and Johnson leaves wet with tears and loaded down with public property.

One other development prevented Clemens from putting his new work scheme to the test in Washington. The owners of the *Alta California* had put a high value on his services. They paid his passage in the *Quaker City*, they paid him twenty dollars for each letter from abroad, and, in a printed notice that Clemens preferred to ignore or forget, they re-served to themselves all rights in his correspondence. Now, hearing that without consulting them he had contracted with Bliss for a book based on their property, the owners decided to collect the letters as originally printed, publish them in a book to be sold on the Coast, and perhaps re-cover some of their investment. It was a double threat to his vision of pros-perity and popular success. Not only did the *Alta California*'s owners deny him the right to use his original material in his book for Bliss, but, as Clem-ens explained to Mary Fairbanks, "if the *Alta*'s book were to come out with those wretched, slangy letters unrevised, I should be utterly ruined." He tried to argue his case by telegram, but quickly gave up. On March 8, two days after the disaster was sprung on him, he decided that his only chance was to leave for California immediately, confront the proprietors and claim his rights. When he sailed from New York on March 11, with the aid of an advance from Bliss, he was in high spirits, happy to have left Washington, happy to go to sea again, and with the prospect of earning money by the Western lecture tour he had told Fuller about in Decem-ber. The ship was "magnificent," he told his mother, the passengers were pleasant and friendly, "not so stupid as on the *Quaker City*," he added. On the voyage up from the Isthmus (this time crossed by rail in three hours), in the same high mood, he once again encountered his archangel, Captain Wakeman, who told him his dream about racing comets to heaven.

Clemens arrived in San Francisco on April 2, moved into the Occidental Hotel—more than ever, after a winter in boardinghouses, his idea of "heaven on the half shell"—and presented his arguments to Frederick Mac-Crellish, the owner of the *Alta California*. MacCrellish at first compro-mised only to the extent of offering him a ten per cent royalty on the *Alta*'s book, and in the month of deadlock that followed Clemens set off on his lecture tour. On April 14 he filled Platt's Hall in San Francisco with a talk about the *Quaker City*. It drew "a little over sixteen hundred dollars in the house—gold and silver," he wrote to Mary Fairbanks, but "it was a miserably poor lecture." Despite his promise to Pamela, not to scoff at "sacred things," his lecture offended many and revived their indignation at his reports from the Holy Land. But he was pleased to hear that he had been denounced from one pulpit as "this son of the devil, Mark Twain," and he was even friendly though only politely apologetic to a young Baptist minister who scolded him as "this person who visits the Holy Land and ridicules sacred scenes and things." Some of the newspapers took up the cry and attacked the lecture as "sickening," "foul with sacrilegious allusions, impotent humor, and malignant distortion" and the lecturer himself as a "miserable scribbler," a man "lost to every sense of decency and shame." Such notoriety had its value, he recognized, and he was so little ruffled by these attacks that he explained to Mary Fairbanks that the basic fault was "the rudeness and coarseness of those Holy Land letters which you did not revise." Besides, it was only the "small-fry ministers" who attacked him. With "all those of high rank and real influence," he assured her, he was on friendlier terms than ever.

He was soon off on a two-week tour that took him to Sacramento, through the towns of the Mother Lode, and to the cities of his first celebrity, Virginia and Carson. He returned on May 5, exuberant and exhausted, having traveled two and a half hours by sleigh in a snowstorm and stayed up all night talking on the boat from Sacramento to San Francisco (he had been given the bridal suite, "a ghastly sarcasm on my lonely state"). He carried with him a gift from an assayer in Carson City, a silver bar inscribed with a Biblical citation that would dog him all his days: "And whosoever shall compel thee to go a mile, go with him twain." Friends among the *Alta California* editors had persuaded MacCrellish to give up his publication plans and settle for a face-saving acknowledgment. Having won his battle, Clemens reported to Elisha Bliss on May 5, "I am steadily at work."

IV

During May and June, working from before midnight until seven or eight the next morning, Clemens wrote over 200,000 words of *The Innocents Abroad*—thirty manuscript pages, or three thousand words, at a sitting. He bettered this staggering output only once, three years later when he was in the grip of a "red-hot interest" in *Roughing It*, and he never again equaled it for any length of time. Each book after *Roughing It*, he said, tired in the middle, its "stock of raw materials" was exhausted, but he was confident that "when the tank runs dry you've only to leave it alone and it will fill up again in time," metaphors which reflected both his mechanistic turn of mind and his frontier assumption of endless forests and numberless buffaloes. In San Francisco all the conditions seemed favorable. He was liberated from money worries and competing obligations. He had the double incentive of a short deadline and a large reward—he had turned down Bliss's offer of ten thousand dollars outright in favor of a royalty. And for once in his writing career he had no plot problems to wrestle with; the shape of the book was the shape of the voyage, and, with his *Alta California* letters, guidebooks, and other materials that he borrowed and collected, he had little fear that his tank would run dry. But he knew that his book had certain imperatives distinguishing it from a collection of newspaper pieces which needed, in the first place, to have "the wind and water squeezed out of them." It was by changing the "I" of the book —the narrator, "Mark Twain"—that Clemens not only fulfilled these imperatives but also underwent a kind of psychological integration that liberated his mature powers.

In the correspondence he wrote for the *Alta California* from New York and abroad, "Mark Twain" was accompanied by a fictitious character named Brown, a comic *Doppelgänger*. "Mark Twain" was high-minded, something of a gentleman, bookish, eager to learn, refined. "Brown" was the savage American: he was in turn gullible and outraged, he drank a lot and he washed a little, he was impatient with what he could not understand, he was raucous and derisive, his idiom was the slang that Mary Fairbanks abhorred, and he was no gentleman. "Brown" was a mouthpiece for low vulgarisms, for comments on dirt and smells, for chauvinisms and solecisms that would have been out of character for the original Mark Twain. He was in part the embarrassing dream self, the rebellious and perverse demon, that fascinated Clemens years later. In the writing of *The Innocents Abroad* "Brown" disappeared. "Mark Twain" took over some of his prerogatives, acquired a new range of mood, stance, and confidence, and became a fully created literary persona. "The irascible pilgrim, 'Mark Twain,' is a very eccentric creation of Mr. Clemens'," Bret Harte pointed out in his review of *The Innocents Abroad*; an eccentric creation of such demanding vitality that it towered over Samuel Clemens and all his books.

"Any lecture of mine," Clemens was to write to Livy a few years later, "ought to be a running narrative-plank, with square holes in it, six inches apart, all the length of it, and then in my mental shop I ought to have plugs (half marked 'serious' and the others marked 'humorous') to select from and jam into these holes according to the temper of the audiences." In *The Innocents Abroad* "Mark Twain" is comparably responsive to the demands of his readers. He can be instructive and "serious," pious, rhetorical, generous with straight guidebook information. He also wriggles in discomfort when the emotions of respect and awe, said to be especially painful for Americans, threaten him, and then he turns to burlesque and parody and he gibes at history, the Old Masters, anything new or strange or foreign. As an American democrat and announced materialist, he jeers at the European past and its foundations in superstition, cruelty, and economic exploitation; still he falls into a purple trance in front of the Sphinx, no less a loaded symbol of an alien past than the Czar's summer palace, which he also admires. His characteristic mood is indignation, but when he is not even able to simulate indignation, as Bret Harte said, "he is *really* sentimental." He can be all things to all men, a barbarian as well as a sensitive observer, for basically he is a pragmatist of audience psychology, a manipulator of the passing opportunity; and certainly the old Clemens, crying out against the aimlessness and meaninglessness of his life, must have recognized some corroborating qualities in the plasticity of the young "Mark Twain." Nevertheless, Mark Twain is not only the "I" of *The Innocents Abroad* but its single structural principle which binds together its erratic episodes and vindicates its inconsistencies, its radical shifts of attitude and allegiance, and its contrasts of the past and the present in personal as well as in historical terms. Through Mark Twain Samuel Clemens begins to rediscover his youth and translate it into literature.

In Milan, for example, the narrator of *The Innocents Abroad* is shown a stone sculpture of a flayed man. "It was a hideous thing," he says, and it calls to his mind an image of terror from his boyhood, a reminder of the frontier violence that was part of Hannibal. Hiding for the night in his father's law office, Sam had discovered on the floor, picked out by moonlight, the body of a stabbed man who had been brought in off the street to die and been left there until the next morning. "I have slept in the same room with him often, since then—in my dreams." By a train of associations that lead him further and further back in time, the Pyramid of Cheops reminds him of the Capitol in Washington, then of a high bluff on the Mississippi between St. Louis and New Orleans, and finally of "Holliday's Hill, in our town, to me the noblest work of God," where one Saturday afternoon he had sent an immense boulder crashing down the hillside and through a cooper's shack. The terror and the idyl were part of the same transformed past, just as Tom Sawyer plays on Holliday's Hill and also cowers in the graveyard hiding from Injun Joe. Even Jerusalem, a depressing experience for the *Alta California* correspondent, takes on another possibility for the narrator of *The Innocents Abroad*. Perhaps time will soften it, he reasons:

School-boy days are no happier than the days of after life, but we look back upon them regretfully because we have forgotten our punishments at school, and how we grieved when our marbles were lost

and our kites destroyed—because we have forgotten all the sorrows
and privations of that canonized epoch and remember only its orchard
robberies, its wooden sword pageants and its fishing holydays.

Intermittently through the writing of the book, insistently toward the
end of it, he measures not his distance from the past but his closeness.
"That canonized epoch"—Hannibal and the river, not purified of terror
but shaped to embrace it—is to become not only his prime subject but also
the reality that was home base, that gave him life, where he could make the
Antaean connection of sole and soil. As he described it toward the end of
The Innocents Abroad, the Sphinx itself had come to stand for this discovery: "It was the type of an attribute of man—of a faculty of heart and
brain. It was MEMORY—RETROSPECTION."

On June 17, nearing the end of his book, he broke off work to chaffer
with Mary Fairbanks in a long stock-taking letter. He was not going back
to Europe yet, he told her; he was not going to China either. His next
stops after he left San Francisco were going to be New York and Hartford (he said nothing about his invitation to go to Elmira), and then? "I
am going to settle down some day, even if I have to do it in a cemetery."
He was up to pages 2343 of his manuscript, he told her, and was homeward
bound, "voyaging drearily over accumulating reams of paper." "I wish
you could revise this mountain of MSS. for me," cut it down to size, for
he was tired of the book, bored, impatient now as throughout his career
to submit his work to someone else's judgment, follow recommendations,
be confirmed and approved. "If you wanted a thing changed, very good,
you changed it," Howells recalled years later. "His proof sheets came back
each a veritable 'mush of concession.' "

In San Francisco his Howells was Bret Harte. Supported by an unde-
manding job as private secretary to the superintendent of the Mint, Harte
was able to follow a literary career without having to do hack work for
the newspapers. In an office on Montgomery Street he was preparing the
first issue of the *Overland Monthly*, which during the two years of his
brilliant editorship became the *Atlantic* of the Pacific Coast. Clemens
watched in admiration as Harte, with a few strokes of his pencil, drew in
some rails and transformed the proposed cover emblem of the magazine
from an aimless grizzly bear into a totem of frontier California snarling
defiance at the approaching transcontinental locomotive; the raw West
was dying out, and Harte was creating the literary and picturesque West
which took its place. Early in 1866 Harte had proposed that he and Clemens publish a joint collection of their sketches. The project had fallen
through, but Clemens had been pleased and flattered at the time; he had
gladly conceded that Harte belonged "at the head of my breed of scrib-
blers in this part of the country." He had been awed by this transplanted

Easterner who was a year younger but had found his vocation so much earlier that he seemed almost of another generation. In 1868 Clemens was still dazzled, deferential, apologetic at times. He was made to feel coarse and a little clumsy by Harte's elegant manners and fashionable clothes, his graceful, even mincing movements, his neckties which flashed like butter-fly wings beneath his pock-marked but handsome face. (Five years later Harte complained that his lecture audiences were hostile to him because he looked like a gentleman and not like their idea of a miner; by then Clemens saw him as an insufferable fop.) His handwriting was tiny, pre-cise, dandiacal. He was fastidious, and as both editor and writer he had a special taste in the choice of titles and insisted on literary finish. When they first met in San Francisco in 1864 Harte had noticed Clemens' care-less outfits and apparent indifference to his surroundings, and he recog-nized in him, he said much later, an "unusual and dominant nature" sym-bolized by Clemens' "aquiline eye—an eye so eagle-like that a second lid would not have surprised me." Against this dominant nature Harte man-aged to maintain, for the protection of his own edgy ego, a condescending air, a mocking tone, and the authority of the master over the pupil. Harte "trimmed and trained and schooled me patiently," Clemens told Thomas Bailey Aldrich in 1871, "until he changed me from an awkward utterer of coarse grotesquenesses to a writer of paragraphs and chapters that have found a certain favor in the eyes of even some of the very decentest peo-ple in the land." Until their friendship finally exploded Harte had the psy-chological edge, could make him feel off balance and defensive.

The *Frog*, as Clemens said, was vulnerable; he had sent it on to Harte apologetically. Now he brought him the mountainous manuscript of his new book. "Harte read all the MS. of the 'Innocents' and told me what passages, paragraphs, and *chapters* to leave out—and I followed orders strictly," Clemens wrote in 1870. "It was a kind thing for Harte to do, and I think I appreciated it." Two of the chapters Harte told him to leave out appeared in the *Overland Monthly*: "By Rail through France" in the first issue, in July 1868, and "A Californian Abroad" in the second issue, in August, when Clemens was in Hartford delivering the book to Bliss and later in Elmira beginning his courtship of Olivia Langdon. "The Luck of Roaring Camp" ("Bret's very best sketch and most finished—is nearly blemishless," Clemens later noted) also appeared in the August number. It was bold and original, it violated all the literary taboos against prostitutes, obstetrics, and blasphemy, above all it seemed the authentic West, and it put Bret Harte's star in the Eastern sky. Three years later, having followed this success with "The Outcasts of Poker Flat" and a humorous poem, "The Heathen Chinee," he was to start for the East in a blaze of fame and excitement. When Clemens and Bret Harte said goodbye to each other in July 1868, both were about to begin their ordeals by success.

On July 2 Clemens gave a farewell lecture, "Venice, Past and Present," at the New Mercantile Library on Bush Street. Four days later he sailed for New York. "I sit here at home in San Francisco," he had written at the end of *The Innocents Abroad*; home was the Occidental Hotel, breakfast cocktails at the Cliff House, champagne dinners at the Lick House. He never in all his life came back to San Francisco or to California, and not until twenty-seven years later, when he was lecturing his way out of bankruptcy, did he even see the Pacific again.

CHAPTER FOUR

"I do not live backwards"

I

IN 1863, SHORTLY before her eighteenth birthday, Olivia Langdon of Elmira, New York, began keeping a commonplace book. "Next to possessing genius one's self is the power of appreciating it in others.—Carlyle": she copied this down, and, appropriately for the wife-to-be of a writer whose feeling for the adjective was "when in doubt, strike it out," she also copied "A man's character may be learned from the adjectives which he habitually uses in conversation.—Tuckerman." These and similar precepts from Henry Ward Beecher, Daniel Webster, Horace Greeley, and Oliver Wendell Holmes answered to her high-mindedness, her conventional Christianity, and her strong, if untested, sense of right and wrong, but (a distinction which Samuel Clemens would urge on her with some heat) she had got them from books and not from such experience as was open to a girl of her age and background.

Olivia was sheltered and adored by her parents, sister, and brother, and between her sixteenth and eighteenth years, when the juices of curiosity were flowing fast, she was an invalid and lived in a darkened room. She was tutored by Professor Darius R. Ford, the Socrates of Elmira Female College, of which her father was a founder and trustee, and she was also visited frequently by a family friend and beneficiary, Thomas K. Beecher, pastor of the First Congregational Church. Her education was at best random, but it was not a great deal worse than that of other daughters of well-to-do and respectable provincial families. Spelling remained a mystery to her, her grammar was uncertain, and her love letters, as her fiancé delighted in telling, were "darling eight-page commercial miracles," "gotten up on the square, flat-footed, cast-iron, inexorable plan of the most approved commercial correspondence, and signed, with stately and exasperating decorum, 'Lovingly, *Livy L. Langdon*'—*in full,* by the ghost of Caesar!" Her notepaper might as well have borne her father's letterhead, "J. Langdon and Co., Coal."

Jervis Langdon made some false starts as a storekeeper in Ithaca, Salina, and other upstate towns, and he ran into even worse luck in the lumber business. It was only at the beginning of the Civil War, after thirty-five years of struggle punctuated by failures and panics, that his coal and iron monopoly around Buffalo and Elmira (convenient to the Pennsylvania anthracite fields) began to pour out money enough to make him an unequivocally rich man. Jervis Langdon was born under a happier conjunction than John Marshall Clemens, also a storekeeper and a seeker after coal and iron wealth, and he lived in an age of more ruthless enterprise. Joined in a cartel with the Delaware, Lackawanna and Western Railway, his company administered prices upward and wages downward and managed to keep competition to a minimum and profits at a maximum. Like Henry H. Rogers, the Standard Oil mogul who in the 1890s helped Clemens work himself back from bankruptcy to affluence, Langdon was able to combine rectitude and benevolence in his personal affairs with a certain *laissez-faire* rapacity in business. Neither Langdon nor Rogers felt fettered by the conflict between private and business morality.

The Langdon family's wealth was new money; they used it with liberality and without ostentation. They were mainstays of church and community. Before the war Langdon was an abolitionist and aided fugitive slaves. He was now active in behalf of the freedmen, supported Negro education in the South, and was friend and host to Frederick Douglass. The Langdons had become gentry, and thirty years after he first met them, when Sam Clemens tried to rationalize in a novel what in his bereavement and bankruptcy had begun to seem an unreal past, he made a simple telescoping of his background and Livy's: she came from the first family in town and the richest, he from the second family, poorer than hers, but still gentry. (Both families in this fiction were slaveowners.)

When she was sixteen Olivia fell on the ice, suffered a mysterious injury to her spine, and became partially paralyzed. For two years she lay in her bedroom with the shades drawn. A procession of doctors gave her parents little hope for even a partial recovery. Above her bed was a pulley and tackle designed by one of these doctors to help her to raise herself to a half-reclining position. The experiment was agonizing, she became nauseated and faint, but the apparatus, though not used again, was never removed. Neurasthenia, hysteria, post-traumatic syndrome: the terms change, and there is little or nothing to go on. This was a century of sal volatile and the sick headache, of the Beautiful Invalid and the Mysterious Ailment. Elizabeth Barrett took to her bedroom with an "affection" of the spine. Even the robust Charles Sumner of Massachusetts, after his humiliating caning on the Senate floor, became an invalid although his doctors could find no organic damage. Olivia Langdon's paralysis vanished as darkly as it began. After two years of supine captivity her family tried a last resort, a mind healer named Newton who would have been as much at home in the Mississippi Valley of Clemens' boyhood as he was in the Southern Tier in the 1860s. Certainly Dr. Newton's performance in the Langdon house (he explained his power as "some subtle form of electricity" proceeding from his body) helped tickle Clemens' lifelong fascination with mind science, mental telegraphy, Christian Science, and other heterodoxies. According to the family recollection, Dr. Newton opened the shades, opened the windows, prayed, put an arm behind Livy's shoulders, and said, "Now we will sit up, my child." After a few minutes he said, "Now we will walk a few steps, my child," and she did.* During her last years asthma, hyperthyroidism, and a heart ailment made her an invalid once again, and she had periods of invalidism and nervous prostration throughout her life, but she lived to be nearly sixty and she had four children. While Clemens was courting her she was as sensitive about her health, he told Mary Fairbanks, "as I am about my drawling speech and stammerers of *their* infirmity." Perhaps his celebrated drawl served the same obscure self-protective purpose for him as her illness did for her. At the very least, his comparison suggests how direct his sympathy for her was.

Jervis Langdon could afford Dr. Newton's fee of $1,500 for his professional services. Soon after, he built the brownstone mansion at 21 Main Street in Elmira where Livy celebrated her restored health and where, in August 1868, Clemens came to woo her. Three sets of iron gates, baronially clanging when they opened or shut, gave entrance to grounds covering a city block. The Langdon greenhouse (which, like the Langdon coal monopoly in a warm winter, suffered from overproduction) supplied flowers for local funerals in such profusion that Clemens joked, to Livy's acute distress, that often the problem was, "We haven't a confounded corpse." The mansion was somber and huge, its predominant tones those of brownstone, mahogany, and rich stuffs. The parlor, where Clemens and Livy were married and where later they lay before burial, was heavily curtained, massively upholstered. Upstairs there were unexpected halls and stairways and rooms enough for the Langdon family, their servants, Jervis Langdon's eighty-six-year-old mother, a first cousin of Olivia's paying her a twelve-month visit during 1868, and such transients as Sam Clemens. Years later his daughter Clara recalled that the house had a distinctive perfume. It might have been what Clemens, who in his own house in Hartford was to

---

* "Layin' on o' hands is my best holt—for cancer, and paralysis, and sich things," says the Dauphin in *Huckleberry Finn.* When Clemens wrote this, more than twenty years had passed since Livy's own "cure"; still, she probably did not enjoy the pointed allusion. In his autobiography Clemens recalled that his mother used to go to a "faith doctor" named Mrs. Utterback. "Her specialty was toothache. She would lay her hand on the patient's jaw and say, 'Believe!' and the cure was prompt."

carry Langdon's four-square splendor to steamboat opulence, recognized as "that odor of sanctity which comes with cash." He first saw Livy—and fell in love with her, he said—in a miniature portrait encased in purple velvet; it was in a setting of equal richness that he saw her late in August 1868. He had delivered *The Innocents Abroad* to Bliss in Hartford earlier in the month, and he expected that the book would be published the following March, after a lecture tour which would publicize it and earn him some money. He wore a yellow duster and a battered straw hat when he arrived in Elmira from New York in the smoking car of a train called the Cannonball.

There were carriage rides in the city and in the hills above, walks in the Langdon garden, leisurely visiting. Evenings there were prayers and hymns in the parlor, and Clemens also sang, in his clear tenor voice, the spirituals and jubilees his uncle's slaves had taught him, strange music in the North. In this household, "the pleasantest family I ever knew," Clemens was for a while idyllically and unsuspectingly happy, and he fancied he was "quite a pleasant addition to the family circle." (A half year later Livy hurt his feelings bitterly, set him to moping about rejection and snubbing, by telling him that at one point during his first visit the family had begun to wish that he would leave.) And quite as unsuspecting were the Langdon parents, hospitable, delighted (at first) with their unusual visitor. They had not yet admitted to themselves the possibility of losing Livy to any man, least of all to Sam Clemens. He was ten years older than Livy, older still in the sights he had seen and the things he had done, Othello wooing Desdemona with tales of travels and dangers. The people Clemens had known in Hannibal, on the river, and in the West were scarcely less foreign to Livy than Othello's cannibals and men whose heads grew beneath their shoulders.

Livy was beautiful. Her black hair was drawn smooth over her forehead, framing her cameo face and dark eyes. Her smile, Howells remembered, was of "angelic tenderness," and myopia gave her a look of musing intensity. She was gentle, calm, spiritual, and refined, qualities which Clemens idealized in her and which he found all the more compelling for their contrast to his Western experience. But she also had "the heart-free laugh of a girl," he said, and he sensed in her, and later discovered, an immense capacity for giving and receiving affection. "I was born *reserved* as to endearments of speech and caresses," he wrote in his autobiography. He remembered only one kiss in his family, when John Marshall Clemens on his deathbed kissed Pamela; kissing was rare in Hannibal and generally "ended with courtship—along with the deadly piano-playing of that day." Livy "poured out her prodigal affections in kisses and caresses and in a vocabulary of endearments whose profusion was always an astonishment to me." Yet even after they were engaged the name "Sam" came from her only with the greatest difficulty, as if it represented aspects of that past of his she could never share. She was slow to grasp a joke, but he saw this as a challenge and enjoyed it, and for her benefit he patiently annotated a passage from Holmes's *Autocrat*, "That is a joke, my literal Livy." Her "gentle gravities" sometimes made him laugh. She was timid, often frightened, and when thunder and lightning came she hid in a closet. Yet, invested by him with a power she hardly suspected, when she spoke the word "disapprove" it had, he said, the force of another person's "damn." She disapproved of drinking, smoking, swearing, and, for a while, humorists.

He was in love with Livy, he wanted to marry her more than he had ever wanted anything in his life, and he found the pace of a conventional genteel courtship much too slow for him. After less than two weeks in the Langdon house he abandoned the reserve he was born with and proposed to her, and she said no. Early in September, on his last night in Elmira, he consolidated his forces behind the original line of battle. "I do not regret that I have loved you, still love you, and shall always love you," he wrote in the first of nearly two hundred love letters (a mass of manuscript as long as a subscription book) before their marriage in February 1870. He would be able to bear the bitterest "grief, disaster, and disappointment" of his life provided "you will let me freight my speeches to you with simply the sacred love a brother bears to a sister." To save him from becoming forever a "homeless vagabond," he invited Livy, as he had invited Mary Fairbanks, to supervise his regeneration. He begged her to scold and correct him, to lecture him on the sin of smoking, to send him texts from the New Testament, to tell him about Thomas K. Beecher's sermon on Sunday, to send him Henry Ward Beecher's sermon pamphlets.

He courted her by offering in all sincerity to make over his character and habits to suit her standards. Less than a year after they were married he said in half-jest, "I would deprive myself of sugar in my coffee if she wished it, or quit wearing socks if she thought them immoral." Yet he eventually withdrew many of the important concessions he made to her, and he most often had his way about things, even though he enjoyed and exploited playing the role of a man under his wife's thumb. During his courtship he took the oath, but within a few years of their marriage Livy herself was drinking beer before going to bed and he was drinking cocktails of Scotch, lemon, sugar, and Angostura bitters before breakfast as well as dinner and also hot whiskeys at night. "I believe in you, even as I believe in the Savior," he told her early in his courtship, but he went on to explain that his faith was "as simple and unquestioning as the faith of a devotee in the idol he worships." After such romantic paganism it is not surprising that he never became a Christian, and that she eventually became an unbeliever. She reigned, but she did not rule. Nevertheless, within five years of their marriage, Sam Clemens the bohemian and vagabond had undergone a thorough transformation. He embraced upper-middle-class values. He became a gentleman, and for a while an Anglophile who despised the raw democracy which bred him and the corruption and coarseness he saw all around him. He was the antithesis of Walt Whitman, also sea-changed in his thirties, for Clemens began to find himself as a writer by joining the social order instead of freeing himself from it; only later, when the mature artist came in conflict with the Victorian gentleman of property, did Clemens realize he had been scarred by his concessions. The journalist Walter Whitman became the poet Walt, but Sam became Samuel L. Clemens. He had known Whitman's open road long enough, and what he wanted was home. "The idol is the measure of the worshipper," said James Russell Lowell, and in choosing his idol Clemens chose his transformations as well. They were not forced on him by Olivia Langdon, who, although she had his love, also had what was only an instructed proxy from him. More than a year before he even saw her picture he had already, in some advice given him by Anson Burlingame, the American minister to China, glimpsed his eventual goals. "What you need now is the refinement of association," Burlingame had said somewhat pointedly after Clemens had got tight in Honolulu. "Refine yourself and your work. Never affiliate with inferiors; always *climb*."

During his courtship and first years of marriage Clemens came as close as he ever would to orthodox belief, and the echoes of this attempt could be heard long after he gave it up; the English poet and novelist George Macdonald, visiting America in 1872, was told that Jervis Langdon had expected his new son-in-law to combine his religious fervor and his broad experience of men by writing a life of Christ. He prayed, he went to church, he could even end a love letter with a "Goodbye—with a kiss of reverent honor and another of deathless affection—and—Hebrews XIII, 20, 21." He kissed by the Book, he knew that he had to reach the altar by way of the amen corner. In the exuberance of his formal engagement to Livy in February 1869 he explained his strategy to his mother: "She said she never would or could love me—but she set herself the task of making a Christian of me. I said she would succeed, but that in the meantime she would unwittingly dig a matrimonial pit and end by tumbling into it—and lo! the prophecy is fulfilled."

Visiting his family in St. Louis after Livy first refused him, he felt "savage and crazy," was angry and low-spirited, defied Pamela's temperance pledges, drank, and became even gloomier. The whole visit was a "ghastly infliction," he wrote to Mary Fairbanks on September 24; "I am afraid I do not always disguise it, either." The only good news came in a letter from Livy along with her picture: she assured him that he was in her prayers, and she said he could come for a second visit at the end of the month. He spent a night and a day in Elmira, and she seemed to give him some grounds for hope; at least she did not object to his increasing persistence within the relationship of brother and sister. Then he had a lucky accident. Early in the evening, as he was climbing into the democrat wagon which was to take him to the depot, the horse suddenly started and he fell over backward into the gutter. He was carried into the house, and there he stayed another day or two, nursed by Livy. It was one of those episodes in his life which, like his first sight of Livy's miniature on board the *Quaker City*, had the shape of daydream to begin with and which he made part of his own mythology. By the time he came to this episode in his *Autobiography*, he had turned it into an even better story, in which he played the role of wily suitor: "I got not a bruise. I was not even jolted. Nothing was the matter with me at all. . . . That was one of the happiest half dozen moments of my life." This was his version of it in 1906, but only a week after it happened he told Mary Fairbanks that he had actually been knocked unconscious, and he even wrote it up for the *Alta California:* "I fell out of a wagon backwards, and broke my neck in two places." The episode liberated the heroically masochistic Tom Sawyer within him. In a fragment which he wrote shortly after his marriage, his first explicit attempt to write fiction about the experience of boyhood filtered through the nostalgia of manhood, his boy hero stands outside the house of the girl he loves and is very nearly run over by a wagon; he is sorry that he was not hit, "because then I would have been crippled and they would have carried me into her house all bloody and busted up, and she would have cried, and I would have been per-fectly happy, because I would have had to stay there till I got well, which I wish I never would get well."

But even after this accident he found he was playing a stronger hand than he actually had. In one letter he tried to move beyond their brother-sister relationship; Livy scolded him, and from Hartford, where he was working with Bliss on his manuscript, he wrote her a repentant letter in which he begged from her "a sister's pardon" for his "hotblooded heedless-ness." He also announced that he had just met and struck up what promised to be an enduring friendship with Joseph Hopkins Twichell, the pastor of the fashionable Asylum Hill Congregational Church in Hartford. Twichell was handsome (he bore a startling resemblance to Bret Harte, in fact); he enjoyed not only Clemens' humor but also his bawdiness and profanity, and in return he preached to him a kind of muscular and nondoctrinal Christianity; and along with the physique of an athlete he retained the eagerness and enthusiasm of an undergraduate. Clemens commemorated his meeting with Twichell by writing all the details to Livy: He met Twichell at a church sociable, went home with him, had tea and spent the evening listening to Twichell talk about religion, remembered his manners and got up to go at nine-thirty, but stayed until eleven. The next morning, Sunday, he went to church and then accompanied Twichell to the Hart-ford almshouse, where the former Yale oarsman and chaplain to General

Daniel Sickles preached and sang to the inmates. Two weeks later, still in Hartford, he told her more about his new friend and more about his own earnest attempts at prayer, but, as if he already sensed victory, his tone changed. He had begun to tease her, even about such matters as her nightly prayers for his salvation, and he was no longer defensive. At Twichell's house, he told her, he had talked to a party of ministers who thanked him for having written "certain trash" which brightened their somber hours with laughter. There was something, after all, to be said for humorists. This was the last letter he addressed to her as "sister." "Some few castles in Spain going up," he told Mary Fairbanks on October 31.

On a lecture tour, he came back to Elmira and the Langdon house on Saturday morning, November 21. "The calf has returned," he said. "May the prodigal have some breakfast?" Abandoning the fiction of brotherly love, he began a six-day siege. Livy attended his lecture on Monday night. On Wednesday (he told Twichell) she "said over and over and over again that she loved me." He was in Paradise, enjoyed "supreme happiness," and, letting down the bars of his reserve, he declared, "I do love, love, *love* you, Livy." On Thanksgiving Day her parents, still in a state of shock and astonishment, consented to an engagement which they insisted should remain secret until they were able to learn a great deal more about Mr. Clemens' morality, history, character, and prospects.

II

Clemens had come to Elmira that November with a new professional confidence that supported his wooing of Livy. The lecture on Venice that he gave as his farewell to San Francisco was a success, but he told Mary Fairbanks it had been written for and delivered to a friendly Western audience and "would be pretty roughly criticized in an Eastern town." Early in October, while he was in Hartford working with Bliss, he wrote a new one specifically for an Eastern audience. He called it "The American Vandal Abroad," and it reflected his knowledge of his strong points and of the demands that would be made on him. It was almost a précis of his book, and it had the double advantage of exploiting the relatively fresh appeal of the *Quaker City* cruise and of publicizing *The Innocents Abroad*. It made fun of the American middle-class tourist, but the satire was mostly mild and good-natured. His audience hungered for faraway grandeurs, and he gave them gorgeous pictures, along with verbal fireworks, of the Acropolis and Venice, Damascus and the Pyramids. There was a moral too: travel, he said, liberalized and made a better man of the American Vandal—even though the moral was "an entirely gratuitous contribution." He spiced his lecture with nonsense, preposterous stories, and wild exaggerations, all in his increasingly individual vein of play.

Soon after he returned from California he signed on with James Red-path, the pioneer among lyceum booking agents, for a tour in the East and the Midwest. They arranged for him to open in Cleveland, where, through Mary Fairbanks, he was guaranteed the support and goodwill of her husband's *Herald*. "I would like *you* to write the first critique on this lecture," he told her. It was on the basis of such first reviews that most lyceum committees would decide whether they wanted him. His Cleveland lecture on November 17 before an audience of twelve hundred was a triumph. It had far-reaching effects not only on his own career but on the lyceum system itself, which regarded a humorist as a dubious experiment in programing. "Made a *splendid* hit last night and am the 'lion' today," he reported to his family, and to Twichell he wrote, "Congratulations to me, for lo! the child is born." The comic messiah then moved on to Pittsburgh, where on November 19 he played against Fanny Kemble, who was on her farewell reading tour, and he savored another triumph: he drew a standing-room audience of over fifteen hundred to her mere two hundred. Almost anything he wanted seemed within his grasp now, one victory could be parlayed into another, and after he gave the third lecture of his tour in Elmira on November 23 he made a suggestive linkage of courtship and career, even of love and Livy's history of invalidism. "She felt the first faint symptom Sunday," he told Mary Fairbanks, "and the lecture Monday night brought the disease to the surface. She isn't my sister any more."

Clemens was a child of the Gilded Age. At no earlier time in America would he have found conditions so favorable for his talent to flower and be richly rewarded. Just as the subscription publishing system, long committed to works of piety, patriotism, and history, welcomed a humorous writer, now the lyceum circuit, long committed to cultural and educational discourse, welcomed a humorous lecturer. In its New England origins the lyceum system had been random, local, personal, and high-minded, founded, as Edward Everett Hale recalled, on the implicit faith that "the kingdom of heaven was to be brought in by teaching people what were the relations of acids to alkalies, and what was the derivation of the word 'cord-wainer.'" In small towns without any other communal entertainment the lecture also became an important social occasion on which young men and women could mingle in a semidarkened hall. The typical lecturer—Emerson or Bronson Alcott or Thoreau—made his own precarious arrangements by letter and was resigned to accidents of time, travel, lodging, and even payment. In town after town, keeping pace with the advance of the railroad, the lyceum took its place along with the church, the schoolhouse, and the jail as part of the social order. But with the end of the war and the nation's spring westward the system was strained beyond its capabilities. With proliferation came confusion and waste, and inevitably the postwar process of rationalizing was forced on the lyceums for their survival. By joining Redpath, Clemens allied himself with a system which had the same relationship to the old lyceum circuit as, in his own terms, subscription publishing had to trade publishing. (And, to complete the cycle, when Clemens became his own publisher in the 1880s he also became an entrepreneur in the field of authors' readings.)

Redpath's Boston Lyceum Bureau, founded in 1868, had among its clients that first year Wendell Phillips, Charles Sumner, Henry Ward Beecher, and, at an average fee of a hundred dollars a lecture (of which the Bureau took ten per cent), Mark Twain. In return for its commission, the Bureau circularized its clients, made bookings, and arranged sensible itineraries. The Bureau also collected the money and thus, it was hoped, established uniform prices and eliminated the lecturer's traditional morning-after haggle with the lyceum committee. To the lyceums, in turn, the Bureau offered a complete and balanced course of speakers shaped to fit the local taste and budget and to meet the local competition.

Redpath, a reformer who had fought alongside John Brown in Kansas and was active on behalf of Negro causes, believed in the cultural and educational function of the lyceum system, and he also believed that his Bureau would help restore to the system some of the Hellenic dedication of its origins in Millbury, Massachusetts, in 1826. But he had a sure sense of the make-up and taste of the postwar audience, and in order to keep this audience he was willing to make concessions which eventually speeded a process of radical change in the old system. Before and during the Civil War the lyceums opened their platforms to political and reform subjects as well as to education, and after the war popular issues such as women's rights began to dominate the programs. The lyceum became a stump and a town hall instead of a temple of the Muses. The stars of the system continued to fill houses and earn as much as five hundred dollars an evening, but the smaller performers could compete neither with them nor with the free-lance humorists and pure entertainers who were becoming popular. Many lyceums were ending the year with a deficit; the "house emptiers" (as Mark Twain later called the small-fry performers) were losing more money than the "house fillers" could bring in. And there seemed to be a general coarsening of effects and appeals. One star, John B. Gough, a reformed alcoholic who nightly for years acted out the agonies of his alcoholic period in his temperance talk, was thought by some to be more dedicated to melodrama than to reform. A lecture system that in that one year offered hall room to Henry Ward Beecher talking about "The Ministry of Wealth" and Thomas Wentworth Higginson talking about "The Natural Aristocracy of the Dollar" had come a long way down from Emerson and Thoreau.

Redpath insisted that only enlightened variety could save the lyceums from extinction, that they would have to demonstrate their willingness to please every taste in the course of a season, and he chose his clients to cover a broad cultural range. He continued to offer the standard lyceum fare of clergymen, professors, and lay philosophers like Henry James, Sr., who expounded Carlyle for fifty dollars a night. Frederick Douglass, Julia Ward Howe, and Elizabeth Cady Stanton, among others, satisfied the appetite for topical subjects. Redpath had transitional attractions and novelties such as Paul Du Chaillu, the African explorer, and the Ottoman consul general in New York, the Honorable C. Oscanyan, who put on native costumes, chanted the cry of the muezzin, and performed the genuflexions of Moslem worship. Redpath had a stable of moderately inexpensive dramatic readers and musicians. Finally, in managing Mark Twain, Josh Billings, and Petroleum V. Nasby, the leading platform humorists of the day, he conferred on them a new if shaky status, and, having carried the system all the way from education to pure entertainment, he saw the nerve center of the lyceums move from the lectern to the box office.

"I could have cleared ten thousand dollars this lecture season if I had entered the field before the various lecture courses were filled," Clemens wrote to his mother less than a month after his Cleveland success. "As it is, I shall not clear *more* than $2,000, if so much." Having started late, he had to follow a cat's-cradle route that took him back and forth between the East and the Midwest, with occasional visits to Elmira, and Redpath's ten per cent of the gross of five thousand dollars was a modest item in comparison with Clemens' heavy traveling and living expenses. Even so, his first season opened a lucrative profession to him; invitations for the coming year poured in, and ten thousand dollars began to seem only a minimum profit. He had proved to the lyceums that he could be a draw for generally serious-minded people, and he proved to himself that he could meet and manipulate those standards of Eastern propriety and decorum which had worried him as recently as July 1868. The triumphs of his first season, during which he was recognized as Artemus Ward's successor, also inspired him with a fanatic dedication to study and polish his performances, work and rework his materials, search out dead spots, experiment with subtle changes in timing and emphasis. The once casual lecturer now learned to make his platform art a subtle and varied medium of delight.

In January 1870, during his second season as a lecturer, Clemens was to tell Livy about an experience he had with a full house in Utica. He walked on stage and said nothing, stood there patient and silent, for as long as he dared, and then, in a moment of exultant power, he realized that he could mesmerize an audience by the sheer force of his presence, could manipulate them at his will. He heard a sudden avalanche of applause and laughter, a welcome which he had earned by silence and bravado and which satisfied a fierce craving in him. "No man will dare more than I to get it," he wrote to Livy. "An audience captured in that way *belongs* to the speaker, body and soul, for the rest of the evening. Therefore, isn't it worth the taking of some perilous chances on?" He felt that he had mastered his craft and, as he later told his friend Riley, learned "*dead-sure* tricks of the platform" by which he was able, "absolutely," to "vanquish" his audience. He learned, as Dr. Holmes already had, that a popular lecture must contain nothing that five hundred impatient people could not all understand in a flash; the American, Josh Billings said, "works, eats, and haw-haws on a canter." "I used to play with the pause as other children play with a toy," Clemens recalled, and he claimed that he could measure the moment of silence with the precision of "Pratt and Whitney's ingenious machine" that was supposed to be sensitive to variations of one five-millionth of an inch. The pause preceded the "nubs," "points," and "snappers" that he fired off like Roman candles, dehiscent and gaudy, and that not only captured his audiences but subjected them to nothing less than an act of aggression. "The suspense grows bigger—bigger and bigger—your breath stops—then your heart"—he was describing the dentist's drill, but he might have been talking about his lecture art instead. "Then with lightning suddenness the 'nub' is sprung and the spindle drives into the raw nerve! The most brilliant surprises of the stage are pale and artificial compared with this."

The victories of Clemens' first seasons also left him with moments of loathing. At such moments he remembered the grime and rattling of long trips on wilderness railroads, sprints by steamboat, stage and carriage, lost sleep, lost baggage, lost engagements when rivers froze and roads were blocked by snow. He remembered shivering wayside breakfasts, gray meals of lard, fried pork, and pies with unspeakable contents. The worst lecture halls were gloomy with candlelight, were either swept by numbing drafts or were so hot and airless that audience and speaker were cyanotically groggy, and everything sounded stupid. Worst of all, for a humorist, were the churches. "People are afraid to laugh in a church," Clemens told Redpath. "They can't be made to do it in any possible way." After a day's journey and a night's work on the platform he might find himself in a cold room in a country caravansary where the stove smoked all night long and there was no light to read by and hardly any service. But even such lodgings, he discovered early, were preferable to some private houses where the host talked late into the night, served breakfast at the crack of dawn, and said smoking was not allowed. He remembered being driven around in open buggies during the day to see the customary sights of small towns, and feeling after a while that "all towns are alike—all have the same stupid trivialities to show," and that he was tired to death of being chattered at, pestered, introduced stupidly or while the audience was still coming in, and forced to talk and perform when he felt harassed, tired, and lonely. He suddenly felt revolted by the same lecture given too many times in too few weeks and by an audience which, for one reason or another, withheld sympathy and response. "These negative faces with their vacuous eyes and stony lineaments pump and suck the warm soul," Holmes wrote about his own experience. "They are what kill the lecturer." And finally there were reviews which rankled for days, the comments of small-town editors who berated Mark Twain for his mumbling and his drawl, for his "sing-song snuffling tone," for being a humorist and not a moralist, and who told him to quit lecturing altogether.

"My nerves, and my whole physical economy, are shattered with the wear and tear of traveling, lecturing, ten thousand petty annoyances and vexations and an unusual loss of sleep," he complained to Livy during his second lecture tour. "When things get to going wrong they keep it up." In January 1869, at precisely the same point in his first tour, he had the same overwhelming feeling of nemesis and of nerves strained to breaking. In Iowa City, where his lecture was reviewed as a vulgar comic humbug not worth two cents to hear again, he fell on the ice as he was stepping into an omnibus and landed with all his weight on his left hip. The manager of the hotel there made the mistake of waking him at nine in the morning and was greeted with screaming and cursing. Later, after an hour's vain attempt to go back to sleep again, Clemens tried to ring for some coffee, and when he could find no bell in his room he summoned the manager by renewed screaming and cursing and slamming the door. The manager found him half naked, abusive, out of control, and trying to kick the door off its hinges. The next day Clemens wrote to Livy about this tantrum and told her that he not only regretted it but had even written a note of apology. By this time, however, the editor of the local paper had reviewed the circumstances in print and suggested that this grotesque fracas was a truer illustration of the American Vandal than any the lecture had afforded; and as for the lecturer, "He is the only one engaged for the course whose personal character was unknown." It was a cruel jab. Clemens was still on trial with the Langdons, still, quite apart from his success on the lecture circuit, trying hard to establish his character as a Christian and a reliable citizen, and he had reason to be anxious about his progress.

III

Both Mary Fairbanks and Charley Langdon assured Livy's mother that "a great change" had "taken place in Mr. Clemens," that he was motivated by "higher and better purposes" and had "entered upon a new manner of life." But Mrs. Langdon also believed in the backward glance. A few days after Clemens' secret engagement to Livy, while, unsuspectingly, he was telling his sister Pamela that the Langdons were not much interested in his past, only in his future, Livy's mother rolled up her anxieties and perturbations into one stupendous question which she fired off at Mary Fairbanks:

> From what standard of conduct, from what habitual life, did this change, or improvement, or reformation, commence? Does this change, so desirably commenced, make of an immoral man a moral man, as the world looks at men? or—does this change make . . . one, who has been entirely a man of the world, different in this regard, that he resolutely aims to enter upon a new, because a Christian life?

Such were the terms of a character investigation which was as remarkable for its naïveté as for the amount of sheer discredit it collected.

Mrs. Fairbanks, however, came through, and on December 24—he marked the holiday by swearing off hard liquor and keeping his pledge for at least a year—Clemens acknowledged her "cordial, whole-hearted endorsement." "For that, and for your whole saving letter, I shall be always, *always* grateful to you. . . . There is no way in which I shall not prove your judgment perfect." And, as if to demonstrate his new character, he took advantage of a lecture layover in Lansing, Michigan, to write for her an unabashedly purple passage about the Nativity: "Eighteen hundred and sixty-nine years ago, the stars were shedding a purer lustre above the barren hills of Bethlehem—and possibly flowers were being charmed to life in the dismal plain where the Shepherds watched their flocks. . . ." Mark Twain, the traveler with the honest eye who remembered Bethlehem as an appalling slum full of lepers, yielded to the devotional sentimentalist and saw the little town in "the soft, unreal semblance that Poetry and Tradition give to the things they hallow." The angels sang and their music floated by: "It is more real than ever."

It was not much in the way of writing, but it moved Mrs. Fairbanks. She was relieved that her protégé was on the road up, and, without consulting him, she determined to publish his conversion to the world by publishing his letter in the *Herald*. In disregard of privacy, professional propriety, and his reputation as a writer, she would have gone ahead with this meddlesome project if he had not arrived in Cleveland a few days later, just in time to stop her. He was thoroughly jolted out of his devotional mood, barely able to disguise his horror and irritation. Yet under pressure from her he agreed to rework the Bethlehem extracts—"Their reverent spirit is more to my credit than my customary productions," he wrote to Livy—and allowed her to publish them after all. By this time he was under pressure from Livy as well: he would let the letter be published for Livy's sake, he explained to Mary Fairbanks. "Poor girl, anybody who could convince her that I was not a humorist would secure her eternal gratitude. She thinks a humorist is something pretty awful." And Livy was grateful to

Mrs. Fairbanks for raising the issue of the Christmas letter to begin with. "I want the public, who know him now only as 'the wild humorist of the Pacific Slope,' to know something of his deeper, larger nature," she wrote on January 15. "I remember being quite incensed by a lady's asking, 'Is there anything of Mr. Clemens except his humor?' "

Not many of Mrs. Langdon's searches for the real truth about Mr. Clemens ended on such an affirmative note as his Christmas letter. At her request he had given the Langdons a list of people who might be able to tell them whether he had been an immoral man or just a worldly one. This list eventually included some Nevada politicians, a variety of Western journalists, the proprietor of the Occidental Hotel, and Bret Harte's employer, Robert B. Swain, described by Clemens as "the Schuyler Colfax of the Pacific Coast"—"He don't know much about me *himself*, maybe, . . . but he ought to know a good deal through his Secretary, Frank B. Harte (editor of the *Overland Monthly* and the finest writer out there) for *we* have been very intimate for several years." It was a curiously random, even self-defeating list. Forgetting that he had included, at least indirectly, Harte and also Joe Goodman, who in 1862 had hired him for the *Territorial Enterprise*, Clemens later said that he had left out close friends because he knew they would lie for him. In most cases the Langdons were writing to people they knew not at all to ask their opinions of a man scarcely known to any of them.

While this ponderous inquiry was going on, Clemens took a number of firm, defensive stances. What counted for him, he said over and over again, was his present and his future. He was willing to admit, and he was prepared for supporting testimony from his references, that "much of my conduct on the Pacific Coast was not of a character to recommend me to the respectful regard of a high eastern civilization, but"—having established a deferential, slightly barbed polarity of standards, he now becomes surprisingly tentative—"it was not considered blameworthy there, perhaps." "I know of *nothing* in my past career that I would conceal from your parents, howsoever I might blush to speak the words," he told Livy in January, and he went on to defend himself against the charge that he was a vagabond and bohemian by nature, unable ever to settle down and support a family. "It is my *strong conviction* that, married to you, I would never desire to roam again while I lived." He complained to Mary Fairbanks that the thought of tearing Livy away from her parents and her home made him feel "like a monstrous sort of highwayman"—Mr. Langdon, it had been hinted, might wither away out of loneliness and melancholy. Was Clemens perhaps a fortune hunter with his eye on the quarter million or so that Livy would inherit? "As far as I am concerned," Clemens told her mother, "Mr. Langdon can cut her off with a shilling—or the half of it." And as a final rejoinder in the matter of reliable "references," he argued that only five people at the most had ever known him at all well and that he felt in entire sympathy with only two of them. One of the two was his dead brother Henry; the other was Livy.

During January his letters of reference began to come in. They were shockingly bad and, he told his friend Charles Warren Stoddard eight months later, they "came within an ace of breaking off my marriage." "Clemens is a humbug," a San Francisco clergyman named Stebbins reported, "a man who has talent, no doubt, but will make a trivial use of it." A San Francisco bank cashier who had once been a Sunday-school superintendent in Elmira predicted that Clemens "would fill a drunkard's grave." The alarms sounded loud in the Langdon house, and as Livy reported the returns to him he felt a kind of hopeless fury. "I do not live backwards," he pleaded. "God does not ask of the returning sinner what he *has* been." And yet the past was pursuing him. He still had visions of married happiness with Livy, intimations of the bay window and the grate in the living room, "flowers, and pictures, and books (which we will read together)," and, however perturbed her parents were, Livy's own faith in him and her love were not seriously shaken. But she had been made to suffer, he felt; she was being punished for *his* past, and the guilt was on him.

Long before the appalling reports came in he had felt restive and resentful under the Langdons' scrutiny. On November 28, in his first letter to Livy after their provisional engagement, he declared with some ferocity and exasperation, "I have been through the world's 'mill' . . . and I know it, through and through and from back to back—its follies, its frauds and its vanities—all by personal *experience* and not through dainty *theories* culled from nice moral books in luxurious parlors where temptation never comes." The parlor was, of course, the one at 21 Main Street with Livy's commonplace book and her collection of Henry Ward Beecher's *Plymouth Pulpit* pamphlets, with its abundant facts and symbols of the protected life, with its verdant hush and perfume of prosperity. Clemens' experience was something he had to justify, but it was also his endowment, as others were recognizing. A few days before his provisional engagement he had been the subject of a significant conversation in a Boston salon. Annie Adams Fields, the wife of the eminent publisher James T. Fields, wrote in her diary for November 20, 1868: "Parton thinks it would be possible to make the *Atlantic Monthly* far more popular. He suggests a writer named Mark Twain be engaged, and more articles connected with life than with literature."

In the end Clemens' refusal to deny his past was rewarded by Jervis Langdon's bluff declaration of faith. "What kind of people are these? Haven't you a friend in the world?" Langdon asked after reading the letters. "Apparently not," was the answer. As Clemens remembered the episode in his autobiography, Langdon said, "I'll be your friend myself.

Take the girl. I know you better than they do." On February 4, 1869, a half year after his first visit to Elmira, Clemens and Livy were formally engaged. He had come with a plain gold engagement ring which Mary Fairbanks helped him buy in Cleveland.

"It may be a good while before we are married," he wrote to his mother the next day, "for I am not rich enough to give her a comfortable home right away, and I don't want *anybody's* help." A week after his engagement he was back at work, lecturing in the Midwest, but dreaming, as he told Livy, of "peace, and quiet—rest, and seclusion" in his future home with her. "The long siege is over, and I may rest at last," he wrote on March 4, after his final lecture in Lockport, New York. In that industrial town on the Erie Canal he had an encounter with his boyhood. A Mr. Bennett, who once ran the Sunday school in Hannibal, called on him; in one of those episodes of recollection that were to become more and more frequent and sustained, the preacher's voice brought back for Clemens "trooping phantoms of the past," dead and forgotten faces, voices, songs.

With Livy he had begun to take on a new tone of confidence, protectiveness, affectionate mockery. "The ring continuing to be 'the largest piece of furniture in the house' is a burst of humor worthy of your affianced husband," he told her "Livy, you dear little Gravity." He began to poke a little fun at the inner workings of the Langdon coal monopoly. He admitted to her that he did not like Isabella Beecher Hooker and her husband, that he resented them for acting high and mighty with him, and that they would be at best only acquaintances of his, never friends. Nevertheless, he confessed that one evening in March he had had "a good time" at the Hookers'. Isabella, who eventually became a spiritualist, was now going through another phase of heterodox enthusiasm and believed that she was Jesus' sister. That evening she expounded her theology, in particular her ideas about Christ preaching in Purgatory, and she became so insistent and troublesome that Twichell was afraid Clemens' faith would be shaken—or so Clemens claimed, but it may have been merely his way of externalizing the discomfort of the pledges he had made both to Christianity and to the Hartford social order. Soon he was even teasing Livy about her adored pastor, Isabella's brother Thomas K. Beecher. He suggested that Beecher was miserly and selfish in his solitary pleasures and that his love for Mrs. Beecher was, even in its charged moments, merely brotherly. (Beecher himself compared his wife to "a steam engine.")

He took charge of Livy's reading, offered to mark and cut up his copy of *Gulliver's Travels* so that it would be fit for her eyes, and in the same spirit of wanting to protect her from coarseness and indelicacy he scolded himself for having let her read *Don Quixote* before he had gone at it with pencil and scissors: "I had rather you read fifty 'Jumping Frogs' than one

Don Quixote."* Their favorite book in common was *The Autocrat of the
Breakfast Table*. Livy adored it, they were both delighted by the little
doctor's wit, and for Clemens at that point Holmes stood at the pinnacle
of literary culture. Clemens marked his copy of the book for Livy and
used it as a courting book, and after they were married they kept it in a
green tin box along with their love letters. In its margins in March 1869
he tested out the final title of his book: "The Innocents Abroad—or, The
New Pilgrim's Progress"—arrived at, after more than a year's search, because (as he told Bliss) it would be "easiest understood by farmers and
everybody" and because, with "The New Pilgrim's Progress" merely as
a subtitle, hardly anyone could take offense at his reference to a "conse-
crated book." How many roots one puts down over the years, Holmes
had written. "We will plant them again, Livy," Clemens wrote in the margin. At midnight, in his room in the Langdon house, a sentence by Holmes
about women's voices made him think about his own funeral; he wished
they would sing "Even Me." The wind wailed, he was reminded of being
at sea, sadness came upon him, and he thought about what Holmes had
called the one "splendid, unfulfilled promise" every man makes to himself
when he is young and fails to keep in his age. On the last page of their
courting book Clemens wrote, "Livy, Livy, Livy, Livy, Livy, *je vous
aime. M'aimez vous?*"

---

* "It pains me to think of your reading that book just as it stands. I have thought of
it with regret time and again. If you haven't finished it, Livy, don't do it. You are
as pure as snow, and I would have you always so—untainted, untouched even by the
impure thoughts of others." "It is no reading matter for girls. I had quite forgotten
the many coarse and in themselves nauseating passages when I sent it to you. No
doubt it achieves its aim in a remarkable manner, yet even this is somewhat remote
from my princess." Both passages are about *Don Quixote*. The first is Samuel Clemens writing to Livy in March 1869; the second is another eminent Victorian, Sigmund Freud, writing to his fiancée, Martha Bernays, in August 1883.

CHAPTER FIVE

"Little Sammy in Fairy Land"

I

A FEW WEEKS AFTER his formal engagement to Livy, Clemens filled some idle time in New York by sitting in on a meeting of Jervis Langdon and some of his managers in a room at the St. Nicholas Hotel. Having been accepted into the family, he was now being given a close look at the workings of the thriving family business. For about an hour Langdon and his managers talked about coal, a "very thrilling subject," Clemens told Livy in a letter, "my blood curdled in my veins." He became interested only when they reached a relatively small item on the agenda. The landlord of one of Langdon's valuable employees in Buffalo was going to raise the man's rent; this employee, who had a large family, had put in for a salary raise to help him make up the difference. If he did not get it he would have to move out. Langdon's Buffalo manager, J. D. F. Slee, argued conclusively against the salary raise. "It is plain enough to *any* noodle that that family has got to be reconstructed," Clemens reported sardonically. "Therefore, the salary will remain just as it is, and Mr. Slee will proceed to cut down the Captain's family to fit it. Business is business, you know." (In 1905, in "King Leopold's Soliloquy," Clemens was still savoring the bitter honey of that phrase. "I have nothing against widows as a class," Leopold says in defense of slavery, "but business is business, and I've got to live, haven't I, even if it does cause inconvenience to somebody here and there?") Clemens' comment on the exploitative rigors of the family coal business—the first of several such comments, increasingly bitter—was as much a love bite as a protest. In the year of wonders that included his engagement, a successful lecture tour, and the publication of *The Innocents Abroad*, he was already troubled by the implications of his probationary membership-by-marriage in the minor plutocracy.

In the March issue of *Packard's Monthly* he published an article called

94

In Constantinople, September 1867, on the *Quaker City* cruise

Olivia Langdon: "I saw her first in the form of an ivory miniature...in the summer of 1867, when she was in her twenty-second year"

Jervis Langdon's wedding present to his son-in-law:

472 Delaware Avenue, Buffalo

Buffalo and Erie County Historical Society

In his sealskin winter outfit

Library of Congress

In Washington, July 1870,
photographed by
Mathew Brady (detail)

"One of these spasms of humorous possession": Mark Twain's Franco-Prussian
War "map," inscribed by him to the Librarian of Congress

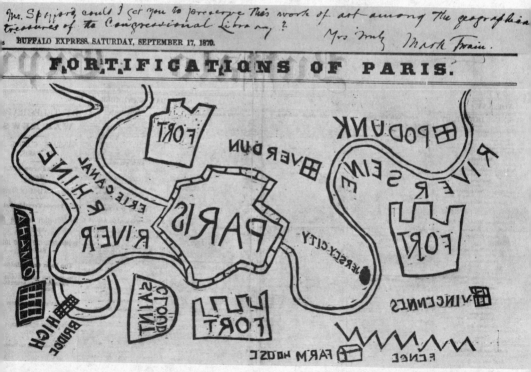

Library of Congress

Petroleum V. Nasby.   Mark Twain.   Josh Billings.

THE AMERICAN HUMORISTS.

Published by GEO M. BAKER, 149 Washington Street, Boston.

On tour, November 1869

☞ A New Book by a Well Known Author.

ROUGHING IT

BY

MARK TWAIN.

SHOWING HOW
A THREE MONTHS
PLEASURE TRIP
WAS EXTENDED TO
A TERM OF
SEVEN YEARS,
AND THE
CAUSES THEREFOR;
WITH A
RELATION OF MANY
BOTH
HUMOROUS
AND INSTRUCTIVE
INCIDENTS
CONNECTED WITH
THE EDUCATION
OF AN
INNOCENT.

A RECORD
OF VARIED
EXPERIENCES
OF THE
AUTHOR
IN
VARIOUS POSITIONS
OF LIFE,
WHILE EN-ROUTE
FROM THAT
OF A
PENNILESS
AMERICAN CITIZEN,
TO THAT OF
A MILLIONAIRE
AND
BACK TO HIS
ORIGINAL CONDITION

Hundreds of Characteristic Engravings

EXECUTED BY SOME OF THE

BEST ARTISTS IN THE LAND

ADD INTEREST TO THE TEXT.

THE VOLUME WILL CONSIST OF

Nearly 600 Octavo Pages,

AND WILL BE FOUND TO CONTAIN NOT ONLY MATTER OF AN AMUSING CHARACTER, BUT
TO BE A VALUABLE AND CORRECT HISTORY OF AN INTENSELY INTERESTING PERIOD,
WITH LUDICROUS DESCRIPTIONS OF SCENES NEVER BEFORE WRITTEN UP.

Elisha Bliss's prepublication advertising circular

Bret Harte

Orion Clemens, around 1880

William Dean Howells

Joseph H. Twichell

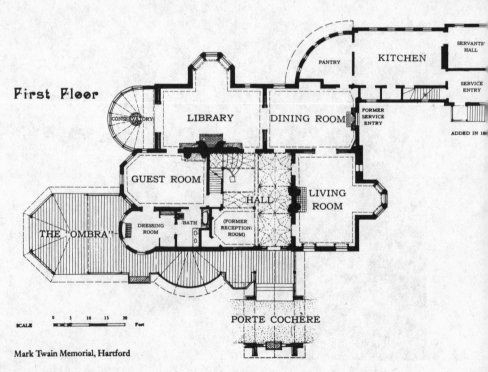

First Floor

CONSERVATORY

LIBRARY

DINING ROOM

PANTRY

KITCHEN

SERVANTS' HALL

SERVICE ENTRY

FORMER SERVICE ENTRY

ADDED IN 18

GUEST ROOM

HALL

LIVING ROOM

THE "OMBRA"

DRESSING ROOM

BATH

(FORMER RECEPTION ROOM)

SCALE 0 5 10 15 20 Feet

PORTE COCHÈRE

Mark Twain Memorial, Hartford

"Mr. Clemens seems to glory in his sense of possession," said his wife: *Opposite*, 351 Farmington Avenue, Hartford, finished in 1874. The plans show the renovations and enlargements made in 1881

Family portrait: on the "Ombra" at 351 Farmington Avenue

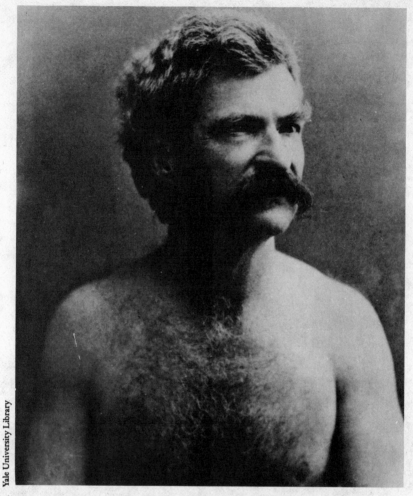

Nearing 50, probably a private joke

"Twins of Genius": with George Washington Cable, 1884

James W. Paige's typesetting machine in its present home, the basement of Mark Twain's house

"WHO DO YOU RECKON IT IS?"

The repaired illustration for page 283 of *Huckleberry Finn*

Susy Clemens at Bryn Mawr

General Ulysses S. Grant and his family at Mount McGregor, New York, 1885

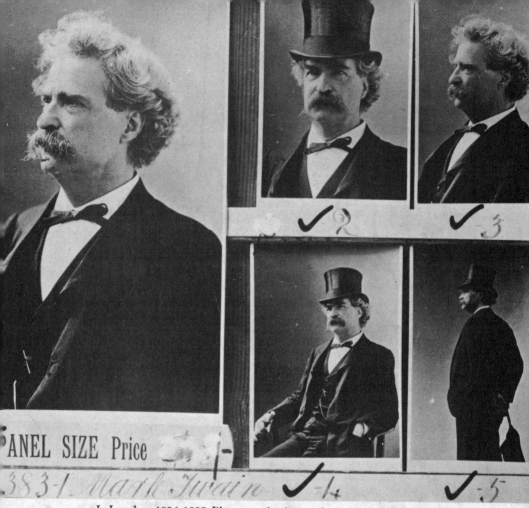

ANEL SIZE Price
3834 Mark Twain ✓-4 ✓-5

In London, 1896–1897. Photographer's proofs checked by Mark Twain

Brown Brothers

Henry Huttleston Rogers

With Livy, New York,
1900 or 1901

In Hannibal, May 1902, in front of the Clemens house on Hill Street: "It all seems so small to me. I suppose if I should come back here ten years from now it would be the size of a birdhouse."

In Hannibal, May 1902

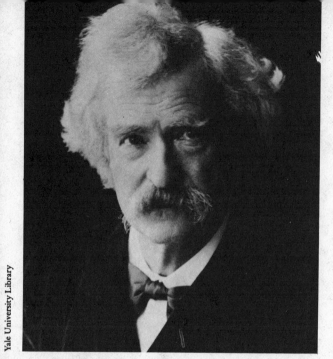

In New York, 1900: "The Hero as Man of Letters"

"The best game on earth"

Sketch by Cesare: Andrew Carnegie and Mark Twain at the Engineers' Club Banquet, New York, 1907. Carnegie's simplified spelling was "all right enough," Mark Twain said in his speech, "but, like chastity, you can carry it too far." *Right*, caricature self-portrait on copperplate: souvenir for the guests at Twain's 67th birthday dinner, 1902

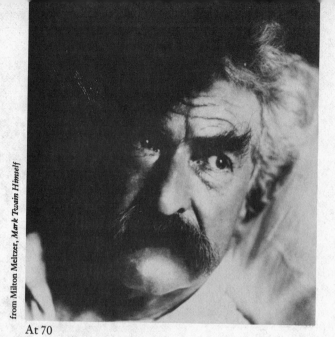

At 70

His last photograph: returning to New York from Bermuda, April 14, 1910

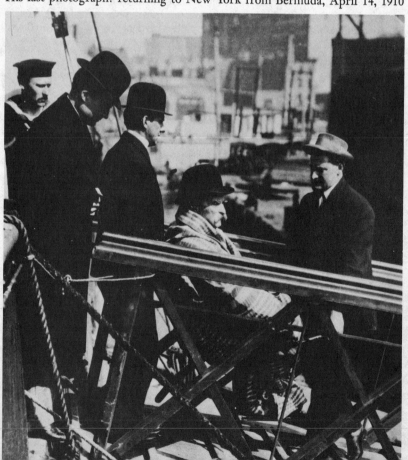

"Open Letter to Commodore Vanderbilt." It was one of the few pieces of even occasional writing he had produced since he finished his book. He was as disgusted by the fact that Vanderbilt had become something of a popular hero as he was by Vanderbilt himself, and his disgust reached its firing point at the time of his engagement to Livy. As she would have preferred, he wrote as an embattled moralist instead of a humorist, although he seems to have been too angry to write as well as he could. "Go and surprise the whole country by doing something right," he scolded the seventy-five-year-old Commodore. "I don't remember ever reading anything about you which you oughtn't be ashamed of." In Vanderbilt and his wealth Clemens saw greed, social irresponsibility, and a moral lesson: "How unfortunate and how narrowing a thing it is for a man to have wealth who makes a god of it instead of a servant." It was a lesson he himself was to study all his life; even now he was aware that there might be a price for tacitly pledging himself to the Langdon scale of living as well as to Livy. Wealth, he went on, consists in being satisfied with what one has, not in having a great deal and always wanting more:

> I am just about rich enough to buy the least valuable horse in your stable, perhaps, but I cannot sincerely and honestly take an oath that I need any more now. And so I am rich. But you! You have got seventy millions, and you need five hundred millions, and are really suffering for it. Your poverty is something appalling.

In his later years, looking back on his boyhood in Hannibal, Clemens said that the California gold rush was the watershed dividing an age of high morality and lofty impulses from an age of money lust, hardness, and cynicism.* The gold rush, he was writing even in 1869, had taken an entire generation, "the very pick and choice of the world's glorious ones," and sacrificed it "upon the altar of the golden calf—the noblest holocaust that ever wafted its sacrificial incense heavenward." In his nostalgically simplified view of history, the Golden Age of his boyhood was followed by an age which cared about gold only, and then by a Gilded Age, to whose squalid values (he attributed them to Jay Gould) money gave a specious luster. In "The Revised Catechism," published in the New York *Tribune* on September 27, 1871, he summed up the bitter credo of the age:

* The five years between 1835 and 1840 saw the birth of a remarkable number of major members of the American business elite. Andrew Carnegie, for example, was born in 1835 (five days before Mark Twain), Jay Gould in 1836, J. P. Morgan in 1837, John D. Rockefeller in 1839. These men came to financial maturity during the twenty-five years after the start of the Civil War, a period whose "most remarkable phenomenon," James Bryce wrote in 1888, was the appearance not only of "those few colossal millionaires who fill the public eye, but of many millionaires of the second order, men with fortunes ranging from $5,000,000 to $15,000,000."

What is the chief end of man?—to get rich. In what way?—dishonestly if we can; honestly if we must. Who is God, the one only and true? Money is God. Gold and Greenbacks and Stock—father, son, and the ghost of same—three persons in one; these are the true and only God, mighty and supreme: and William Tweed is his prophet.

The code he detested was also, in part, the one he lived by. He wanted to get rich, not just get along. Money was Clemens' dream, Howells said, "and he wanted more and more of it to fill out the spaces of this dream." Behind the dream lay the memory of his father's bankruptcy and the poverty of his childhood; when he himself went into bankruptcy in 1894, the dream was shattered and the family cycle had completed itself. It is hard to think of another writer so obsessed in his life and work by the lure, the rustle and chink and heft of money. Silver is the Holy Grail of *Roughing It*. All but a few of the characters in *The Gilded Age* worship the golden calf; to possess money is to be religiously possessed; and money is the main character of that book in the same way God is the main character of the Old Testament. Money corrupts Hadleyburg; the Mysterious Stranger poisons Eseldorf with it. Mark Twain wrote about a stolen white elephant, a £1,000,000 bank note, a $30,000 bequest. He sent one friend, J. H. Riley, to South Africa to gather material for a book about the diamond fields, and he encouraged another, Dan De Quille, to write the history of the Comstock Lode.

To know money was to eat of the forbidden tree. When the news of the strike at Sutter's Mill reached Hannibal and some of the villagers packed up to swell the rush, Sam Clemens was thirteen years old but already beginning to make his living as a printer. He was on the edge of adolescence and torn between the strict Calvinism of his background and the easy vice that flourished along the river. It was by no accident of memory that he was to name Laura Hawkins of *The Gilded Age* after Laura Hawkins of Hannibal, his boyhood sweetheart (and also his model for Becky Thatcher in *Tom Sawyer*). The fictional Laura is a strikingly beautiful, warmhearted, idealized girl; she is seduced and abandoned by a Confederate officer (the real-life Laura married a former Confederate Army doctor); and, a changed woman, she then uses her beauty and her intelligence, along with bribery and blackmail, in the relentless pursuit of money. The loss of sexual innocence, by Mark Twain's standards, was the equivalent of a total collapse of morality; by a process of displacement, money plays the role of sex in his work. He was notoriously reticent about depicting mature sexual and emotional relationships, but he did write a kind of pornography of the dollar.

During the year or so after his engagement Clemens was only intermittently troubled by the moral ambiguities of wealth and power. As part owner of the Buffalo *Express*, he was to enter into a touchy and vulnerable relationship with the family coal business. Only three weeks after he joined the paper he complained to Livy: "Day before yesterday there was a sneaking little communication in one of the other papers wondering why the *Express* has become so docile and quiet about the great coal monopoly question," and he was enraged when one of "those anti-monopoly thieves" wanted the *Express* to publish a letter urging coal for the people at $5.50 a ton. Grimly echoing his own "business is business" mockery, he asked: "Do they suppose we print a paper for the fun of it?" That same summer Clemens was using his influence with Whitelaw Reid of the *Tribune* on Langdon's behalf. Langdon claimed that he was owed $500,000 by the city of Memphis for a paving contract he had underwritten, and while Clemens expressed his disbelief that the money could ever be collected, he was willing to use whatever power he had. He exacted from Reid an editorial citing Langdon's difficulties in Memphis and urging the protection of Northern investments in the South. "The old gentleman is highly gratified," Clemens wrote to Reid on the day the editorial appeared (the old gentleman had apparently not been perturbed by an attack on the coal monopolies in an adjacent column). "I hope to be able to do a favor for you some time in case you will do me the honor to ask one"—this was the discourse of men of influence and power. Eleven days later he reported to Reid that Langdon was sufficiently encouraged by the editorial to plan a suit in the Federal courts.

Langdon's ligitation never passed the planning stage, however, and even the Clemens family's Tennessee land seemed for a brief period closer to cash actuality than the disputed $500,000. Commingling business interests, Clemens had got Langdon involved with the land, and, with the prospect of eventual success, he renounced his share in favor of Jane and Orion. But by November 1869, Langdon's interest began to wane, or at least grew vague. He was old and tired of business, he claimed, and even Livy could not learn whether her father intended to work the land for its supposed coal and iron deposits, act as intermediary in selling it, or just give advice. The following year Orion, once again in sole charge of the negotiations, characteristically balked at an offer of fifteen thousand dollars from a Chicago group, and the Clemenses were back in their customary state of aggravated hopes, their prospects near enough to appear glorious but still, as always, too far away to collect on. "I cannot help thinking that maybe our Heavenly Father has put obstacles in the way of our selling the land heretofore," Pamela was soon telling Orion's wife, Mollie, "that we may realize a great deal more of it hereafter, and that at no distant day." Sam himself, who abominated the Tennessee land and the wild hopes it never failed to raise, could not have written a more sardonic, if premature, epitaph.

To a certain extent the multiple distractions of courtship and the multiple prospects Clemens saw before him in 1869 foreshadowed the fever crisis as a writer, the sense of creative failure, that he was to experience during the first year of his marriage. He had worked all through the spring of 1869 on the proofs of his book, but apart from that he was writing nothing new. In June he estimated that during the past year he had written only "two little magazine squibs and one newspaper letter"; they earned him eighty dollars. He had no new project either on paper or in his mind to follow *The Innocents Abroad;* he was, in fact, not at all certain that he would ever write another book. During the year between his engagement and his marriage in February 1870, a year during which he felt he was entering an enchanted land, he was a writer only reluctantly; his materials were still lodged below the surface of his awareness. In his engagement to Livy he had pledged himself to a life of steady and respectable earning power, and though he had high hopes for Bliss's success with *The Innocents Abroad* he turned to lecturing and newspaper publishing for money and stability.

In June he found he had less than $3,600 in the bank of the eight or nine thousand dollars he had taken in during the lecture season. This was better than the two thousand he had predicted he would clear; still, he felt, it was not much of a stake with which to buy into a newspaper and marry a girl from a family whose yearly expenses were about forty thousand. "I most cordially hate the lecture field," he wrote to his mother in June; he was in a passing mood of despondency, he was afraid of being wedded to the profession, trapped in it for life like Nasby and "the other old stagers," and he hoped that a newspaper post would save him from having to go on tour again. Yet he had already promised to talk ten nights in New York State for a thousand dollars; in May he signed up with Redpath for the following season at a hundred dollars a night; and all through the first seven months of 1869 he wrestled with a plan to go West during the summer and repeat his California and Nevada circuit of the previous year. His decision to go was soon undermined by his unwillingness to be separated from Livy, but his plans and alternatives proliferated: he was going by sea, he was going the overland route with Riley, he wanted Nasby to go on a joint tour with him (and Nasby confused the issue by proposing instead that Clemens join him on the Toledo *Blade*), he dreaded the idea of having to pass through St. Louis on his way West and visit his family, he was afraid of being idle during the summer but he would not go if Livy preferred him not to. By July, when the scheme collapsed, it was too late to go anyhow, and it was clear to him that he was more interested in locating himself on a newspaper than in seeing California again.

Soon after his provisional engagement to Livy in November Clemens decided that if he could buy a share of Abel Fairbanks' *Herald* he and

Livy would live in Cleveland after their marriage, thus combining the two feminine ambiences that had most favored him. Fairbanks' hesitations, together with the hesitations, illness, and market-place subtleties of his partner, extended Clemens' negotiations through the spring. By then he had rival possibilities to consider—the New York *Tribune*, should shares come on the market, Nasby's *Blade*, and most importantly the Hartford *Courant*. Cleveland itself quickly lost its attractiveness. "Both of us," he told Livy in February, "would prefer the quiet, moral atmosphere of Hartford to the driving, ambitious ways of Cleveland." Livy's preferences, her friendships in Hartford (and, quite possibly, her reluctance to share her husband with the meddlesome Mother Fairbanks) fitted in with his own plans for reform. "I can buy into plenty of paying newspapers," he explained to Twichell, "but my future wife wants me to be surrounded by a good moral and religious atmosphere (for I shall unite with the church as soon as I am located) and so she likes the idea of living in Hartford. We could make more money elsewhere, but neither of us are much fired with a mania for money-getting."

He tried to convince General Joseph Hawley and Charles Dudley Warner to admit him to partnership on the *Courant*. He was not yet the celebrity of *The Innocents Abroad*, and these two shared Isabella Hooker's skepticism of the newcomer if not her contempt. What Clemens received from them was an aloof and tentative interest, an evasiveness and general tepidness which amounted in the end (on the advice, he later learned, of their friend Sam Bowles of the Springfield *Republican*) to a rejection. ("Nasby," he said a few months later, before he learned of the part Bowles had played in turning him down, "I have never heard anybody say a word against Sam Bowles, and he always treats me politely, but I cannot get rid of the conviction that he is a dog.") The Hartford *Post*, scarcely more interested in him than the *Courant*, was of no interest to him at all. In July, on Langdon's advice, he demanded a firm proposal from the costive Abel Fairbanks, and he got it: Fairbanks was willing to sell one quarter of the *Herald* for fifty thousand dollars. Clemens was furious, claiming that the price had been raised on him and that in any case he would not think of being political editor, the job Fairbanks had in mind for him. A few days after the negotiations collapsed Langdon proposed a new possibility: he offered to lend Clemens twenty-five thousand dollars to buy a one-third interest in the *Express* in Buffalo, a city that was well within the sphere of the family coal interests and where Langdon could be expected to be as useful to Clemens as Clemens could be to him. On August 12, 1869, Clemens made a down payment of fifteen thousand dollars, and on August 14 the former roving correspondent, police-court reporter, and puffer of mining claims took formal possession of his own newspaper.

During the first half of that year he was sending home thirty-five dollars a month as his contribution to Jane Clemens' support, and he found it was all too easy to fall behind even with this contribution. He told his family he was determined to support Livy without any help from her father. "I have paddled my own canoe so long that I could not be satisfied now to let anybody help me," he wrote in February. He was trying to save money, he explained. Citing the plain gold engagement ring he had given Livy ("when fashion imperatively demands a two-hundred-dollar diamond one"), he begged for their patience if at times he seemed stingy with them. Pamela wagged her finger at the contrast between her brother's announced thrift and the rich society and the high life he seemed to be enjoying. She, a widow with two children, was the main support of her aged mother; wasn't Sam engaged to an heiress, and wasn't he constantly talking about buying into a newspaper (and a metropolitan one, not the crudely printed provincial weekly and by-product of a job-printing shop that Orion was accustomed to)? Sam had every reason to dread a visit to St. Louis. With the exception of his work reading proof, he had spent the spring with Livy in the comforts of Elmira. "I feel ashamed of my idleness," he wrote to his mother, "and yet I have had really *no* inclination to do anything but court Livy." He had been in and out of New York, visiting friends, attending with Charley Langdon Edwin Booth's performance as Iago in Shakespeare's play about "the great Micegenationist." He spent part of May and June in Elmira. Then he accompanied the Langdons to Hartford for the marriage of Isabella Hooker's daughter, Alice, to John Calvin Day; Livy was one of Alice's bridesmaids, Henry Ward Beecher performed the ceremony. Afterward Clemens joined Livy in New York on a trousseau-shopping expedition and went back to Elmira with her for another long visit.

"You seem to think that I spend money *foolishly*—but I don't," he wrote to Pamela from New York on June 25. "My *absolute* expenses are $50 a week, just for food, lodging, and washing, and it is not possible to live for less. I have not run behind with Ma. She only asked $35 a month ($400 a year) and I have paid her as much as $500 in the last thirteen months. I ought to have done better, I know, but you must give me the little credit that is due me." And he explained that if he were not living in expensive hotels he would be able to keep up with his monthly pledges and eventually repay Pamela all the money she laid out for their mother. Pamela could not have found this a reassuring line of argument. Writing the next day from Elmira, he made the tactical error of telling her that his visit to Hartford with the Langdons to attend Alice Day's fashionable wedding had been "villainously expensive." "My expenses were ten to twelve dollars a day, and Mr. Langdon's over fifty. We were gone fifteen days."

Sam Clemens' transition from marginal journalist to newspaper proprietor, from poor man to rich man in his outlook, from bohemian to family man, was not and never would be complete; but it had been made so far with a speed that bewildered him. His reforms were still tentative. Anger warred with the Christian equanimity he was told he should strive for. He had been accepted (after much difficulty) in Elmira but rejected in Hartford, where he was still an unknown; in July the publication of *The Innocents Abroad* would begin to bring him fame and money to a degree he could never have predicted. His ironical bemusement found a certain expression in the second of the "two little magazine squibs" of that spring. Staying in Bliss's house in Hartford, he spent the night of May 13 writing a sketch called "Personal Habits of the Siamese Twins." It was a burlesque account of how the real and celebrated Chang and Eng (who had been forced by financial reverses to come out of retirement and go on exhibition once again) managed to coexist.

Twinship was one of Mark Twain's favorite subjects, often one of his fatal temptations. He could manipulate it into melodrama and farce by exploiting its possibilities for surprises and discoveries: *Pudd'nhead Wilson* became viable only after the *débridement* of a "comedy" called *Those Extraordinary Twins.* But twinship, along with the cognate subject of claimants of all sorts, also offered Clemens an enormously suggestive if misleadingly simple way of objectifying the steadily deepening sense of internal conflict and doubleness which is suggested by two sets of near-homonyms: Twain/twins and Clemens/claimants. And soon he would begin to explore the doubleness of Samuel L. Clemens and Mark Twain through concepts of "dual personality," "conscience," and, toward the end of his life, a "dream self" that seemed to lead a separate life.

Clemens elaborated certain facts about the real Siamese twins—they had been slave-owners in North Carolina, their wives were sisters, and, aggravated by Chang's alcoholism, the twins quarreled and fought violently —into a sketch which employed implicit parallels to his own life. Clemens was a Southerner turned Northerner, the son of slave-owners but now about to marry into an abolitionist family. In the same pattern of reconciliation, Chang and Eng, he wrote, fought on opposite sides in the Civil War and captured each other; a military court declared them both prisoners and exchanged them for each other. They were both in love with the same girl, but Chang won her; she abominated tobacco, and so Eng, a ceaseless smoker, had to sit by tobaccoless and listen to his twin's "fond foolishness, and to the concussion of hundreds of squandered kisses." At about the time that Livy began to pour out her "prodigal affections" in kisses, caresses, and terms of endearment, she was urging Clemens to give up smoking altogether. The twins hold different positions on most matters, for, as Clemens explained, though they are joined in body "their reasoning faculties are unfettered; their *thoughts* are free." Chang was an ardent temperance man and (like Sam and Orion on various occasions) he marched in temperance parades, but Eng would get drunk, and after a while Chang would be drunk, too. (Orion, Sam's troublesome psychological twin, once disgraced himself at a temperance parade after adopting an empiric approach to the forbidden jug; later, changeable as water, he lost the nomination for Nevada secretary of state because he suddenly announced himself unswervingly opposed to liquor, and still later he is supposed to have turned down an offer for the Tennessee land because the purchasers intended the land for a vineyard.) Finally, according to Clemens, an elaborate experiment was conducted on the twins by the suffering temperance workers. The blameless Chang was filled full of warm water and sugar, and Eng was filled full of whiskey, and within twenty-five minutes both "were as drunk as loons—and on hot whiskey punches." The moral of this, as Clemens might have been tempted to tell his fiancée's family, is that it is quite possible for a man to be physically drunk but morally sober.

II

In Hartford on May 12 Clemens looked through the manuscript and corrected galley proofs of *The Innocents Abroad* for the last time. On and off during the spring he had done his work of reading and revision in Elmira with Livy, testing out on her his sense of literary propriety and Eastern mass taste. Now the book was about to go to press, and as he handed it over to Elisha Bliss he made some emotionally charged connections between the work he had done and the life he saw before him. "Nearly every purple ink correction brought my Livy before me," he wrote to her from Bliss's house on Asylum Street the next day. "I would give much to own those rusty old bundles of paper," bundles which tokened his deepest personal and literary commitment and the shared editorial judgment which, however fictive or nominal, was one of the love rites of his thirty-four years with Livy. "I want to get located in life," he went on. "*I want to be married.*" In Elmira on June 5 he read the last pages of press proof, and he told Mary Fairbanks that he was "done with the tiresome book forever. I am ever so glad of it, and I do not want another task like it shortly.—I lost very nearly all my interest in it, long ago." He had cast his book from him as the creation of his own hand, but he was becoming jealously, anxiously, even truculently involved with its career as a publishing venture and vendable commodity. He was about to enact the legend of Mark Twain: the rocket rise, by way of the best seller and its nettling web of values, to celebrity, money, the grandest house in town, the gaudiest style of living. It was in his deliberateness, his promotional sagacity and sheer doggedness, that he departed from the dazzling pattern he set for

American writers after him. Unlike the archetypal writer who leaves his creative solitude to find himself famous, Clemens was in part the father as well as the child of the circumstances that made him.

By the terms of the formal contract he signed with Bliss in October 1868, canvassing for *The Innocents Abroad* was to begin "very early" the following spring. In anticipation Clemens zealously promoted his book from the platform all through the hard winter of his lecture tour. At the beginning of January he was urging Bliss to advertise the book and issue prospectuses while interest in his subject was still high and "while I am stirring the bowels of these communities." But Bliss, despite his initial daring in publishing a humorous book for the subscription trade, moved cautiously. He put off until March even the preliminary step of assigning territories to book agents, and the prospectus itself, without which the agent was useless, did not come from the bindery until July 12. By this time Clemens' impatience and outrage were near the limits of control. "About thirty times a day, on an average," he recalled in 1906, "I was trying to answer this conundrum: 'When is your book coming out?' I got tired of inventing new answers to that question, and by and by I got horribly tired of the question itself. Whoever asked it became my enemy at once."

Bliss had postponed the book, in favor of others on his list, from early spring to late spring, and from late spring to summer. By May 14 the delays appeared to Clemens to be at an end: twenty thousand copies were to be printed right away, he announced to Livy from Hartford, and in a second jubilant letter the same day he added that the paper for the first printing would weigh "over *thirty tons*." But eight days before the first finished copies arrived at Bliss's office from the bindery on July 20, the publisher sprang another surprise on his author. "Unfortunately we have been delayed too long to make a summer book of it"—Bliss's technique of aggressive apology kept Clemens off balance for years—"but *unavoidably* we propose to make a fall book of it with every advantage of full preparation and an early start."

By 1906 Clemens' memory had tricked him into believing that he had cut through the tangle in a decisive telegram to Bliss threatening him with a suit for damages if the book was not put on sale in twenty-four hours. What he actually sent from Elmira on July 22 was an aggrieved letter in which he voiced hurt and confusion even more than anger. "All I desire is to be informed from time to time what future season of the year the publication is postponed to and why—so that I can go on informing my friends intelligently—I mean that infatuated baker's dozen of them, who, faithful unto death, still believe that I *am* going to publish a book." But while he went on to claim that he would hold Bliss responsible in case the postponement caused the sales of the book to fall below expectations, it was on a plaintive and deferential note that this master of invective ended his protest: "I cannot think I have been treated just right." Even so Bliss had finally been forced to the wall, and with a reluctance and an air of hardship calculated to sour Clemens' victory by turning it into guilt he agreed to put the book on sale immediately. On August 1 Clemens apologized for what he now felt had been a "wicked letter" and, an easy victim of Bliss's self-justifying and hectoring tactics, admitted that "perhaps you had very good reasons for delaying the book till fall which I did not know anything about." On August 12 he was still apologetic: he attributed his "ill nature" to the collapse of his negotiations with Abel Fairbanks. "Now we will smoke the pipe of peace and bury the hatchet," he offered. Bliss had saved a final cuff in the teeth for his rebellious but curiously tractable author. "You will hereafter, if you want to say such things to me again," he scolded Clemens, "just come out plain and call me a d—d cheat and scoundrel—which will really it seems to me cover the whole ground and be a great deal more brief. Now let's let the thing drop and *sell the Book*."

Eventually, in the private hell of his autobiography, Clemens consigned Bliss to the lower circle of scoundrels, imbeciles, and publishers. "I feel only compassion for him," he reflected, after reviewing what he long before decided had been "ten years of swindlings" from Bliss, "and if I could send him a fan I would." But during 1869 and 1870, when Bliss's agents were rapping on front doors to *"sell the Book,"* Clemens was willing to back him against any publisher in the world. "It will sell. Between us we will *make* it sell," he told Bliss in August. "I like the book. I like you, and your style and your business vim, and I believe the shebang will be a success."

From his headquarters in Hartford Bliss sent out a flood of ballyhoo and promotional literature. His pamphlets blurbed the book as "the Most Unique and Spicy Volume in Existence." His memoranda for provincial newspaper editors supplied them with extravagantly favorable reviews of *The Innocents Abroad* extravagantly adapted from "leading journals." And, following the sturdy principle that success makes news and vice versa, neither Clemens nor Bliss hesitated to issue gross exaggerations of the book's sales. Early in May 1870 Clemens was proposing that when the sales reached 100,000 copies Bliss should celebrate by inviting him to an oyster supper in Hartford, the invitation, the supper, and Mr. Clemens' speech to be duly covered in the newspapers. On May 30 he was still refining the idea, and he added yet another dimension of unreality to this non-event: he did not plan to come to the dinner, he said, but if Bliss would write him an invitation he would send back a speech that the papers could have. The book would get its free publicity, Bliss would save the price of the oysters, and Clemens would be saved a trip from upstate New York. What canceled this delectable scheme was the fact that it was to be another two years before 100,000 copies were sold, progress too slow to be real news.

By the end of 1869, five months after publication, a little over thirty thousand copies had been sold. "Nothing like it since *Uncle Tom's Cabin*, I guess," Clemens said hopefully to Livy that December. (Except perhaps in dollar volume, *The Innocents Abroad* did not come anywhere near Mrs. Stowe's staggering record of 300,000 the first year.) During January, February, and March the pace decreased from December's twelve thousand to about nine thousand copies a month, and by July, a year after publication, the total was nearly seventy thousand copies. "I only expected the *Innocents* to sell 3,000 copies," Clemens wrote that December, making a good story out of it, "but it astounded me by selling 85,000 copies *within 16 months*." This time his total reflected the facts. *The Innocents Abroad* was not the besom of destruction its author and its publisher made it out to be, but it was a substantial and continuing success nonetheless. With royalties of about nineteen cents a copy coming in from Bliss, Clemens was feeling confident enough at the beginning of 1870 to pay off some debts, send a thousand dollars to his mother and Pamela, buy a ten-thousand-dollar insurance policy on his life for his mother's benefit, and still have some money in the bank—all this a few weeks before his marriage.

Bliss's army of book agents, marching out in greater numbers and generally better equipped than those of his competitors, invested every town and hamlet. The "line of battle stretches from end to end of a great continent," Clemens said in euphoric tribute to Bliss's "genuine generalship." Bliss believed in saturation, repetition, and persistency, techniques that Clemens applied when he himself published Grant's *Personal Memoirs* in 1885. The subscription agent, with a prepared talk in his head and a canvassing book in his coat, was faceless, ubiquitous, tireless, a schoolteacher, retired clergyman, or demobilized veteran, as familiar a feature of the American social order as the circuit rider and the touring lecturer. He opened his canvassing book on the parlor center table and, talking all the while, showed his prospect, who might never have seen the outside of a bookstore, the ornate title page, the voluminous table of contents, the text, the 234 illustrations, and sample bindings (which ranged from cloth at three-fifty to half morocco at five dollars). With the customer's signature on the dotted line, a down payment, and the satisfaction of having earned about a dollar for himself (more than five times the author's royalty), the agent set off on another of the fifteen or twenty calls he might be able to make on a lucky day.

Clemens missed few opportunities to promote his book in the Buffalo *Express*, where he had begun work in August, and the *Galaxy*, a magazine to which he began to contribute a regular humorous department in March 1870. He claimed in the *Express* on October 9, 1869, that there had been so far twelve hundred press notices of his book, proof (even with a generous discount for exaggeration) that Bliss's technique of saturation was as effective with editors as it was with agents and customers. Bliss concentrated on towns instead of cities, on popular papers instead of literary journals, and Clemens used his personal connections. Through their combined efforts *The Innocents Abroad*, which had started as a loosely conceived assignment from a California newspaper, was given a measure of Eastern critical attention almost unique for a book which was sold by subscription and which was consequently, and by its own novel character, outside the established literary tradition.

"Today my new book will be sent to the *Tribune*," Clemens wrote to Whitelaw Reid in August 1869, "and this is to ask you if you won't get your reviewer to praise the bad passages and feeble places in it. Those are the only ones I am worrying about, you know—the meritorious parts can get along themselves, of course." And Reid, who had already done his part for Jervis Langdon, now responded with a review that left Clemens both obliged and relieved. "I was afraid from the start that I might 'catch it' disagreeably and caustically in the *Tribune*," Clemens wrote to him in September. "Certainly and surely it isn't every adventurer's maiden experiment that fares so kindly at the hands of the press as mine has." The Cleveland *Herald* was soon to come through with a column-and-a-half front-page review which hailed Mark Twain as a "laughing philosopher" and which was followed up ten days later by an editorial blurb identifying *The Innocents Abroad* as "the literary sensation of the day—at least in this locality." His friends on *Packard's Monthly*, indebted to him for his contributions that year, could be counted on to give him the title of "first among American humorists."

But it was not from the daily press or the cheap magazine that Clemens sought and received the attention he really desired. The subscription book was the front door to prosperity, but it was, at best, the back door to literary status. Bliss was claiming in his broadsides, "Twain is entitled to the title of The People's Author." What was surprising, consequently, was that the *Nation*, on September 2, reviewed the book at all, not that it reviewed it primarily as a phenomenon of popular culture. Casting on this latest manifestation of native humor an eye more tolerant than that which saw in most aspects of the Gilded Age only evidence of a "chromo civilization," E. L. Godkin's influential weekly concluded that "if some of the book is needless, none of it is really poor, and much of it very good," acclaim somewhat better than silence.

In San Francisco, while the book was in manuscript, Bret Harte had praised it so generously that Clemens had high expectations for his review in the *Overland Monthly*. Clemens was a native son, a contributor to the magazine. He had been present at its birth, and, writing to the *Alta Cali-*

fornia from Hartford in July, he had cast, he hoped, some bread upon the waters. The magazine was well known and handsomely praised in high literary circles in the East, he reported, and as for Bret Harte (poised, like him, a few steps away from a great popular triumph), "The Luck of Roaring Camp" was the "best prose magazine article that has seen the light for many months on either side of the ocean." Clemens was sincere in his admiration, and in terms of expediency it was a good time to be so outspokenly partisan. But whatever good work had been done was undone by some ludicrous difficulty Harte experienced in getting a copy of the book for review. Clemens told Webb a year later that he found himself on the receiving end of "the *most daintily contemptuous and insulting letter you ever read*," and his friendship with Harte entered one of its cyclical periods of absolute zero. Harte's review in the *Overland* appeared in the January 1870 issue, five months after the book's publication; Clemens' hope for an early review that would trigger Western sales was already disappointed, and Harte's comments, although sympathetic and even generous in many respects, were framed in peculiarly grudging terms and narrow categories. The book was not for the "fastidious reader," Harte said, nor was it for the reader who "prefers to find books rather than let them find *him*." The humor had "very little moral or aesthetic limitation"; the indignation was closely related to sentimentalism. As a travel book, Harte said (and he had never been to Europe or the Near East), it was too conventional: the author had followed a guidebook itinerary and a treadmill round of sights. Yet in its own class, that of subscription literature, the book was a "joyous revelation," and among "Western humorists" Mark Twain was "foremost."

A Westerner writing for a Western magazine, Harte had laced his review with the literary condescension and cosmopolitan fastidiousness that Clemens feared he would find in the East. Actually, to a surprising extent and from surprising sources, he met with the opposite reaction. The copy of *The Innocents Abroad* that he sent to Oliver Wendell Holmes brought back a delighted letter paying tribute to the "sharp, twinkling Yankee (in the broader sense) eyes in his head." In that tolerant use of "Yankee" Holmes was mitigating his Hubbish pride, which sometimes made him an uncomfortable host to an outlander. (Howells had squirmed a little to hear him dismiss a stranger with the brusque statement, "If you don't know where Washington Street is, you don't know anything.") Now in praising a book which extended beyond the geography of Boston he expressed the hope that "your booksellers will sell a hundred thousand copies of your travels." But, exasperating as the weather that rattled past his study window over the Charles, Holmes beat a cautious retreat from his praise. "Don't let them get hold of this letter," he wrote, referring ostensibly to publishers in general and implicitly to what passed through Clemens' mind as he savored this superbly useful testimonial, "for the rascals always print everything to puff their books—private or not—which is odious."

"The first great man who ever wrote me a letter," Clemens said ten years later in a birthday tribute to Holmes. His pleasure at the doctor's praise and from the tacit conferral of the status of a fellow author outweighed his disappointment. From his desk at the Buffalo *Express*, where on the opposite side the political editor was scratching out the day's editorial, he wrote an effusive letter of thanks. What excuse, Holmes had asked, did Mr. Clemens have for sending so large a book? "I hadn't any real 'excuse,'" Clemens answered, "but I sent the book as a sort of unobtrusive 'thank-you' for having given me so much pleasure often and over again."

From Boston came another literary credential, and an entirely public one. The *Atlantic Monthly*, making an exception to its practice of ignoring subscription books, printed in its December issue an unsigned review of *The Innocents Abroad* by its thirty-two-year-old assistant editor, William Dean Howells. Parton's recommendation of Mark Twain as a contributor to the magazine probably had its effect in bringing the book to Howells' attention, but with the book once before him Howells was quick to recognize and declare that here was no mere comedian but a decided original who had both genius and aspiration. "There is an amount of pure human nature in the book," he said, "that rarely gets into literature." *My Mark Twain*, the biographical tribute Howells wrote in memory of his friend over forty years later, was hardly more grounded in admiration than his review of a book by a man whom he had never met and whose name he consistently misrendered as "Clements." "This book ought to secure him something better than the uncertain standing of a popular favorite," Howells concluded. "It is no business of ours to fix his rank among the humorists California has given us, but we think he is, in an entirely different way from all the others, quite worthy of the company of the best."

III

In January 1870, his marriage to Livy only a month away, Clemens celebrated his economic stability. "My book is waltzing me out of debt so fast that I shan't owe any man a cent by this time next year," he wrote to Mary Fairbanks. And he added casually, "I mean to write another book during the summer. This one has proved such a surprising success that I feel encouraged. We keep six steam presses and a paper mill going *night and day*, and still we can't catch up on the orders." The other book would be *Roughing It;* it would be two years before he finished it, and he would have experienced a time of crisis and depression that nearly destroyed him as a writer. But now, in the full pride of his year of marvels, all things seemed easy and possible, even the sequel to a popular triumph, and he was, in fact, just as occupied with other effects of *The Innocents Abroad*: lecture invitations, so many that he eventually changed his plan not to lecture at all that winter, invitations to write for magazines and newspapers, bids from book publishers. Impressed with Clemens' sweeping popularity in New England, Charles Dudley Warner was now trying to talk him into leaving the *Express* for the Hartford *Courant*. Even the haughty Isabella Hooker leaned from her buggy one day to tell Clemens that public demand made it absolutely imperative for him to join the Hartford paper and that she had asked Jervis Langdon to help persuade him to sell out in Buffalo. He was tempted by Hartford, but he felt that the money he would lose in selling out so early was more than he could afford. And besides, he recalled "the insultingly contemptuous indifference with which the very same matter was treated last June (*by every one of them*)"—to Livy he was now able to voice his anger at the Hartford establishment. "Revenge is wicked, and unchristian and in every way unbecoming," he gloated to her. "But it is powerful sweet anyway." He said no, even though his first enthusiasm for living in Buffalo and running the *Express* had cooled some months earlier.

He had his plans for the *Express;* it was that solid, remunerative newspaper post which he had made a condition of his marriage, it was something to settle down to. "I shall always confine myself to the truth, except when it is attended with inconvenience," the new associate editor declared in his "Salutatory" on August 21, 1869, and he promised, with a certain murky irony which infuriated critics of Jervis Langdon's coal monopoly, that he would not introduce "any startling reforms, nor in any way attempt to make trouble." His main program was a professional one: he was going to train his reporters, he told Livy, to "doing things my way," and he wanted adjectives, slang, and philosophic reflections curtailed and thunder-and-lightning headlines saved for real news. He was, at the start, ambitious for his paper, energetic, willing to work late hours, the veteran newspaperman settling down once again to the routine of articles and editorials, skimming through the exchanges, reading proof, receiving visitors. In a display of nonchalance meant both to impress and to shock Livy, he confided that often when he and J. L. Larned, the *Express*'s political editor and a co-owner, found themselves stuck in what they were writing and tired of biting their nails and scratching their heads, they swapped manuscripts in the middle and, sitting at opposite ends of the same table, each finished the other's piece. "Some of our patchwork editorials of this kind are all the better for the new life they get by crossing the breed."

Clemens' own singlehanded contributions to the paper reflected some of the same casualness and detachment. He was soon turning out a Saturday series of sketches, satirical commentary, burlesques, most of which reflected the strain of the regular grind, and in search of copy he turned to one of those schemes of collaboration that sum up the partialness of his commitment as a writer. Young Charley Langdon was being sent abroad by his parents once again, this time around the world, and Clemens made a loose agreement with Charley's traveling companion and tutor, the local savant Darius R. Ford, to supply travel letters which would be rewritten in Buffalo in the manner of *The Innocents Abroad.* "These letters are written jointly by Prof. D. R. Ford and Mark Twain," the *Express* announced on October 16. "The former does the actual travelling, and such facts as escape his notice are supplied by the latter who remains at home." As a collaboration the scheme was a failure. Of the twelve "travel" letters that Clemens published in the paper between October and the following March, only two were based on material from Ford. The other ten were all Clemens, accounts of his experiences in California, Nevada, and the Sandwich Islands, and, as such, in an accidental, inadvertent way they were the unacknowledged beginning of *Roughing It,* the book he was able to write only after he renounced a compromise career as newspaper publisher and decided he would be a full-time man of letters.

During his first months in Buffalo Clemens boarded at the house of an *Express* clerk named McWilliams on Oak Street. Summer evenings after work he went rowing on Lake Erie, and then he would come back to his room and write to Livy: "Little dearie, little darling, in a few minutes, after I shall have read a Testament lesson and prayed for us both, as usual, I shall be in bed." Weekends, while Larned filled in for him on the paper, he traveled the one hundred miles by train to Elmira to spend Saturday and Sunday with her. Yet by early September the old restlessness, this time aggravated by his loneliness for her during the week and by the success of his book, was on him again. "I feel a sort of itching in my feet, mother," he told Mary Fairbanks in open envy of Charley's trip around the world, "and if my life were as aimless as of old, my trunk would be packed, now." Redpath had not been able to free him from his lecture engagements for the coming winter. There was no point to learning a lecture and then giving it only a few times, he rationalized for Livy. He might as well commit himself for a full season of lecturing. Piling reason on reason, he reminded himself that he needed a cash stake to begin married life, and, besides, the tour might have some publicity value for the *Express*—Nasby, after all, was taking a leave from the Toledo *Blade* to go on the New England circuit. In a squib in his paper Clemens answered his own question, "What is your favorite season of the year?" "The lecture season." After less than two months on the *Express* he took a leave of absence and moved to Elmira to spend a few weeks with Livy while he worked up "Our Fellow Savages of the Sandwich Islands," his old Cooper Union lecture revised. Late in October he set off on a tour which began in Pittsburgh with an oyster supper and ended, after nearly sixty engagements, in Jamestown, New York, on January 21.

His Boston debut at the Music Hall on November 10 was "a handsome success—I know that whether the papers say so in the morning or not," he told Livy, and he celebrated this success, which established him on the New England circuit, by going out and spending every penny he had with him on his wedding outfit. He kept a room at Young's Hotel on Court Avenue in Boston as his base, and during November and December he lectured nearly every night and spent his days in Redpath's office on School Street smoking and talking shop with Nasby and Josh Billings. He posed with them one day in November for a group photograph which its publisher entitled "The American Humorists." These three heirs and protégés of Artemus Ward faced the camera with the undertaker solemnity that Ward had made a trademark of the platform humorist. Nasby, barrel-bodied, solidly planted, with the face of a farmer and the constitution of an ox, and Billings, corpulent, knees crossed, long hair (which concealed a birthmark on his neck), are seated. Clemens alone is standing, slight, slope-shouldered, at the age of thirty-four the youngest of the group but its visual center and dominating figure. His star alone was in the ascendant. The popularity of Nasby and Billings would soon die with them, along with their calculated but crude eccentricities of spelling and mannerism; of the three "American Humorists" only Mark Twain would survive as more than a period curiosity. In his autobiography he reflected on "the surprising fact that within the compass of these forty years wherein I have been playing professional humorist before the public, I have had for company seventy-eight other American humorists. Each and every one of the seventy-eight"—he included Nasby and Billings—"rose in my time, became conspicuous and popular, and by and by vanished." They vanished, he went on to say, "because they were merely humorists. Humorists of the 'mere' sort cannot survive." Looking back on what seemed a cemetery, he tried to isolate the reason for his survival. "Humor must not professedly teach and it must not professedly preach, but it must do both if it would live forever. By forever, I mean thirty years." And he concluded, a long way from November in Boston and the photographic studio of George M. Baker at 149 Washington Street: "I have always preached. That is the reason that I have lasted thirty years."

He was enjoying his victories and feeling his strength, and it was this aura of mastery and confidence that helped stamp his image on Howells' memory after their first meeting in Boston that autumn. Clemens had come to thank the *Atlantic* reviewer for his notice of *The Innocents Abroad*, and in the magazine's tiny office over the bookstore of Ticknor and Fields at 124 Tremont Street he was introduced to his lifelong friend, partisan, and literary conscience. Clemens was wearing a sealskin coat, whether for caprice, love of effect, or warmth Howells was not sure, but the coat was as vivid as his crest of thick auburn hair and the wide sweep of his mustache, and was, in a sense, the paraphernalia of a public personality which Howells soon recognized to be distinct from the man Clemens—"as I must call him," Howells wrote over forty years later, "instead of Mark Twain, which seemed always somehow to mask him from my personal sense." For both Howells and James Fields the crux of this first encounter was that here was an original whose vivid, utterly individual qualities fitted into no Boston category they knew.

Clemens had once called "The Jumping Frog" "a villainous backwoods sketch," and he had begged Livy not to read in the book, had told her in December 1868 that he wished every copy of "that infamous volume" were burned and gone. But in his year of triumph as author and lecturer he began to recognize his first passport to the East for what it was. "Between you and I, privately Livy dear," he wrote to her in December 1869, "it is the best humorous sketch America has produced yet, and I must read it in public some day, in order that people may know what there is in it." The following month he was suing his old friend Charles H. Webb in the New York courts in order to reclaim the copyright and the plates of the book he had published so casually when he came to New York. Late that month, he summed up the part the Frog had played in his dreamlike progress from placer miner's cabin to the Langdon mansion. Writing to Jim Gillis, who had stayed at Jackass Hill in Calaveras County, he recalled the rain and mud of Angel's Camp and the story he had heard one day around the saloon stove. "I published that story, and it became widely known in America, India, China, England," he wrote, "and the reputation it made for me has paid me thousands and thousands of dollars since." Later on, life on Jackass Hill would symbolize bankruptcy and disgrace, but now, with his passion for turning points, he traced all his good fortune from its origins in a "dismal sojourn" at Angel's Camp to its fulfillments in fame, cash, the ownership of a newspaper, and, above all else, Livy: "A week from today I shall be married."

IV

Clemens and Livy were married in the Langdon parlor on Wednesday, February 2, 1870. The next day they set off for Buffalo in a private railroad car which had been placed at Jervis Langdon's disposal, a friendly gesture from the president of the Pennsylvania Northern Central. The new couple were accompanied on their wedding journey by a crowd of family and friends: the Langdons; Pamela Moffett and her daughter, Annie (Jane Clemens obstinately stayed behind in St. Louis); Thomas K. Beecher, who had performed the service jointly with Twichell, thus more closely uniting Hartford and Elmira on a spiritual axis; and Mary Fairbanks. Mrs. Fairbanks had already noted that her protégé "filled the role of bridegroom with charming grace and dignity," and she was now mounting a further invasion of privacy in the form of a long report of wedding, wedding trip, and honeymoon house for the readers of the Cleveland *Herald*. Reacting against this spectacular lack of privacy, the plush staidness of the private car, and the boned-turkey-and-temperance-beverage propriety of the wedding supper the night before, the bridegroom entertained the company with a ballad about a woman who wanted to poison her husband for the sake of a man she loved twice as well; in *Life on The Mississippi* that ballad ("it wasn't a nice song—for a parlor") is sung by a roaring-drunk raftsman.

At the Buffalo station Clemens and Livy left the others, and there began an episode which he soon made as famous as Livy's miniature and his fall from the wagon. They boarded a sleigh which was supposed to take them to the boardinghouse he had asked Langdon's Buffalo agent to find for them; this, as well as Livy's plain gold engagement ring, which now doubled as her wedding ring, was an index of the modest scale of living he had planned at first. The driver took them on what seemed an endless trip through dark and icy streets before he delivered them at the door of 472 Delaware Avenue, a three-story mansard-roofed brick mansion on a fashionable street. "Oh, this won't do," Clemens said. "People who can afford to live in this sort of style won't take boarders." At the door Langdon presented to his son-in-law a box containing the deed to this mansion (which, with land and furnishing, had cost about $43,000) and a check to help him keep it going. Inside the house, which was ablaze with gaslight, the wedding party was waiting, and they followed Clemens as he explored the rooms, marveled at the elegance and delicateness of the blue satin drawing room and the warmth of his scarlet-upholstered study, met the coachman, the cook, and the housemaid Langdon had engaged to wait on him. In the stable behind the house were horse and carriage.

The gaudy surprise was the work both of Jervis Langdon and of Livy, who had chosen the furnishings, including a canopied and curtained bed all done in pale-blue satin. On the threshold of the house, in terms that he elaborated then and later without acknowledging their ambiguities, Clemens declared that he was the victim of "a first-class swindle," a hoax, a fraud, a practical joke. The deed in the little box was also his paper of indenture to maintain a scale of living inconceivably far above that of the boardinghouse. Ten days later he was joking about the pale-blue livery coat with monogrammed brass buttons that he had to go out and buy for Patrick McAleer, the coachman, and he said, "That coat of Patrick's cost me more than did any that ever *I* wore." But whatever feelings he may have had of anxiety, dismay, and the usurping of his prerogatives were drowned in gratitude. There were tears in his eyes, he had difficulty finding his voice, and finally, two or three words at a time, he managed to say, with something of his usual spirit, "Mr. Langdon, whenever you are in Buffalo, if it's twice a year, come right up here, and bring your bag with you. You may stay overnight if you want to. *It shan't cost you a cent.*"

Soon he was guiding visitors through his palace and saving for the last, as the final glory to take their breath away, the drawing room, its lights turned up high and the furniture covers removed. Over and over he told what he called "the story of what happened to Little Sammy in Fairy Land when he went hunting for a Boarding House," and the mansion was almost as important as Livy herself. "We are about as happy in our Aladdin's palace," he wrote, "as if we were roosting in the closing chapter of a popular novel." To his old friends on the *Alta California* he reported, "I never, never, never expected to be the hero of a romance in real life as unlooked for and unexpected as the wildest of them. The check in the bank, accompanying the gift, was not necessary, for my book and lecturing keep me equal to minor emergencies."

The Sunday afternoon after their wedding Livy lay upstairs resting before their five-o'clock dinner. Downstairs in his scarlet study Clemens began a long letter to "My First, and Oldest and Dearest Friend," Will Bowen. Out of nostalgia, inwardness, and his new happiness and release he made some crucial associations between his marriage and his materials as a writer.

> The old life has swept before me like a panorama; the old days have trooped by in their old glory again; the old faces have looked out of the mists of the past; old footsteps have sounded in my listening ears; old hands have clasped mine, and the songs I loved ages and ages ago have come wailing down the centuries.

He had "rained reminiscences for four and twenty hours," he told Will, and in a remarkable passage about seven hundred words long he catalogued their shared Hannibal past: schooldays at Dawson's, the woods on Holliday's Hill, Jimmy Finn the town drunkard, the time they tore down Dick Hardy's stable, the time Sam purposely caught the measles from Will, the time the town thought Sam drowned in the river, the time the tramp burned to death in his jail cell—the catalogue comes to an end with:

> Laura Hawkins was my sweetheart—Hold: *That* rouses me out of my dream, and brings me violently back into this day and this generation.

> For behold I have at this moment the only sweetheart I ever *loved*, and bless her old heart she is lying asleep upstairs in a bed that I sleep in every night, and for four whole days she has been *Mrs. Samuel L. Clemens!*

Livy sleeps, imagination and memory awake and seek out the past. She is a flesh-and-blood wife, but she is also a guiding principle, a symbolic figure he invests with its own power to select and purify. She has become an idealized superego which frees him from the taint of adolescent experiments and frontier lawlessness and allows him to experience a productive tension between the social order he has become a part of and the boyhood reality he can never leave behind him.

> Before the gentle majesty of her purity all evil things and evil ways and evil deeds stand abashed,—then surrender. Wherefore without effort or struggle, or spoken exorcism, all the old vices and shameful habits that have possessed me these many years, are falling away, one by one, and departing into the darkness.

In order to recapture his past he must follow a familiar pattern of rebirth and become less rather than more like his old self. Now he hears footsteps on the stairs.

> My princess has come down to dinner (bless me, isn't it cozy, nobody but just us two, and three servants to wait on us and respectfully call us "Mr." and "Mrs." Clemens" instead of "Sam" and "Livy"). It took me many a year to work up to where I can put on style, but now I'll do it.

It took the Internal Revenue Department only a few days to take note of Clemens' "style" and to greet him with a letter inquiring after his liability under the five per cent tax on gross income over one thousand dollars (a measure which was introduced during the Civil War and discontinued after universal disgruntlement in 1872). On the heels of this letter came the Internal Revenue assessor himself, who left behind a form with questions on it so ingenious, Clemens remarked, "that the oldest man in the world couldn't understand what the most of them were driving at." Clemens had considerable trouble filling out the return, used pencil and two colors of ink, and finally scribbled across the top, "Pay no attention to any figures except those in black ink—otherwise this report will drive innocent men crazy. Saml. L. Clemens, Elmira, N. Y." On March 19 he wrote and published in the *Express* a piece about the experience which he called "A Mysterious Visit."

The Mysterious Visitor, whom the narrator, Mark Twain, only later discovers to be the assessor, appears honest enough, "barring that expression of villainy which we all have." Hoping to find out what the visitor's business is, Mark Twain, with a fatal confidence in his own shrewdness, decides to draw him out by doing most of the talking himself, and soon he is giving the stranger some strange information indeed: his lecturing receipts for the past season were $14,750; his income from his newspaper, *The Daily Warwhoop*, was $8,000 in four months; and, carried away by his own extravagant visions, he tells the visitor, that his royalty income from *The Innocents Abroad* was a little over $190,000. Now the Mysterious Visitor reveals his identity. "By working on my vanity," Mark Twain laments, "the stranger had seduced me into declaring an income of $214,000." In panic he turns for advice to one of the leading citizens of the town, a man who lives like a prince. This upright man shows him how to falsify his figures, manipulate his deductions, and end up with a taxable income of $250. While the citizen is giving this advice his little boy picks his father's pocket and removes a two-dollar bill; the narrator is willing to bet that even this little boy "would make a false return of his income."

Following the example of "the very best of the solid men of the city," Mark Twain goes to the revenue office, and "under the accusing eyes of my old visitor I stood up and swore to lie after lie, fraud after fraud, villainy after villainy, till my soul was coated inches and inches thick with perjury, and my self-respect gone forever. But what of it? It is nothing more than thousands of the richest and proudest, and most respected, honored, and courted men in America do every year." It is a strangely bitter fable for a man who had owned a mansion on Delaware Avenue for only a month and a half. Clemens believed that the Midas myth had to end tragically, and his own life, culminating in bankruptcy and disasters which he felt were his punishment, was, in part, an acting out of this belief. Even in his honeymoon palace the doorbell announced a Mysterious Visitor who was not at all distantly related to some other strangers: the stranger at Angel's Camp who filled Smiley's frog full of quail shot, the Mysterious Stranger who came to Eseldorf, and the offended stranger who came to Hadleyburg and corrupted the town.

CHAPTER SIX

"A popular author's
death rattle"

I

"WE ARE BURDENED and bent with happiness," Clemens told Jervis
Langdon that May. He was at home almost all the time now and
hardly ever went to the *Express* office any more. A marble statuette of
Peace presided over the house, and Livy presided over a dining table
covered with a fringed red cloth. Evenings in his study after dinner he
read poetry to her until their bedtime at ten; breakfast was at ten the next
morning, and another quiet day began. "Am just married," he had written,
declining an invitation to lecture, "and don't take an interest in *any*thing
out of doors." He was overwhelmed by Livy's prodigal affections and
caresses, and his love for her, despite his etherealizing of her, was also
plainly and contentedly sexual. Livy, once frail and sickly, was well now;
in April she conceived.

The Innocents Abroad continued to sell. He felt prosperous enough to
plan to move his mother, Pamela, and Pamela's two children to Fredonia,
a town about forty miles from Buffalo, and give them one thousand dollars
toward building a house there. Orion's inventions—in June he was showing
a prospective backer a "modest little drilling machine"—promised a mon-
eyed success for him finally, Clemens believed, and proved that he had
"the partrician blood of intellect." Even the Tennessee land, because of an
offer of fifteen thousand dollars from a group in Chicago, seemed for once
to be not altogether chimerical. Favored by all circumstances, Clemens
made some loose and confident plans. He thought of going abroad during
the summer to write "a telling book" about England. Then he gave up
Europe and planned to spend August and half of September with the

Twichells in the Adirondacks, all his newspaper and magazine work having been done in advance. He planned to go to California during the spring of 1871. He turned down Redpath's offer of five thousand dollars a month to lecture that fall. "Have got a lovely wife," he told Redpath, "a lovely house, bewitchingly furnished; a lovely carriage, and a coachman whose style and dignity are simply awe-inspiring—nothing less—and I am making more money than necessary—by considerable, and therefore why crucify myself nightly on the platform?" In a paragraph to lyceums announcing that Mark Twain probably would not lecture during the season of 1870–71, Redpath explained that his client had made money from lecturing, from editing a newspaper, from writing a book, even from having his father-in-law perpetrate a swindle on him—"The fate of Midas has overtaken this brilliant but unfortunate lecturer." Years later, after such recitals of good fortune, Clemens would have added, *"Unberufen!"*—Let the Devil stay unsummoned.

The new life made its own demands on him. He no longer kept his hands in his pockets or lolled in his chair. He was even willing, for Livy's sake, to wear a flower in his buttonhole, indoors if not on the street. "There *is* no argument that can have even a feather's weight with me against smoking," he had once written to Livy, however. In flat rejection of all her family's reasoning on medical grounds, he cited the fact that he was in perfect health although he had smoked since he was eight, and he also passed on the information that his own mother, now a hardy sixty-seven, had been smoking for thirty years. The whole matter of giving up cigars he found ludicrous and hateful. "I am sure it has caused us both more real suffering than would accrue from smoking a million cigars," he wrote to Livy in apology for his anger. By this time he had fallen back on his last line of resistance—he would give up smoking if she desired him to, but not for any other reason. Not long after the marriage Jervis Langdon offered him ten thousand dollars and a trip to Europe if, having already given up spirits, he would now give up drinking ale and smoking. Clemens rejected the bribe—"I can't sell myself," he told Langdon—but he did cut down his smoking drastically, to Sunday afternoons only, and thus he made a sacrifice which is emblematic of the confused terms on which he lived his first year of marriage. He came almost to a full stop as a writer that year, but by the spring of 1871, when he decided to reject all the conditions of his life in Buffalo and commit himself full time to writing *Roughing It*, he had resumed his normal pace of constant smoking through the day and some drinking at night, a bottle or two of ale for a sedative. "If I had sold myself," he said to James T. Fields in 1876, after telling him about Langdon's offer, "I couldn't have written my book, or I couldn't have gone to sleep, but now everything works perfectly well."

During his thirteen months in the house on Delaware Avenue Clemens maintained the outward semblance of a religious believer. The days were punctuated at regular intervals by prayers, Bible readings, and grace before meals. "After all, what does tobacco matter?" he joked. "Let's have another chapter of Deuteronomy." But he was planning to write a book about life on Noah's Ark as seen through the diaries of Shem and Ham, was terrified that someone would steal the idea from him, and regretted ever having mentioned it to Abel Fairbanks, a compulsive publicist like his wife. "Maybe it will be several years before it is *all* written," Clemens wrote to Bliss a month before his marriage, "but it will be a perfect lightning striker when it *is* done." The "Noah's Ark Book," begun just as he was marrying into Livy's world of tranquil faith, was the seed of a book which he still working on when he was seventy and which his surviving daughter suppressed for fifty-two years after his death because of its hilarious unbelief.

"So Mark got hooked at last," Dan De Quille had written in the *Territorial Enterprise*. And in San Francisco Ambrose Bierce, who hardly knew Clemens but knew a newsworthy transformation when he saw one, had written in somewhat the same vein of frog's chorus: "Mark Twain, who, whenever he has been long enough sober to permit an estimate, has got married," and Bierce regretted that the groom's "long bright smile will no more greet the early barkeeper." Inevitably, despite Clemens' new happiness, he also suffered something like rootburn from his transplanting. From the sandy, sometimes alkaline soil of his Western independence, he moved, by his own choice, to a richer soil of money, status, and social imperatives, and although these conditions were to favor him as a writer they did not favor him right away. The past had suddenly welled up in all its old glory again, he had told Will Bowen, but the aftermath of this discovery of his literary materials was a period of restlessness and unproductivity. For the *Express* he wrote weekly sketches and only occasional squibs and editorials. Yet even with these he had difficulty, took his pen, arranged his paper, and paced back and forth, finally confessing to himself that he had no heart in what he was doing, that "my time is not come." "I am utterly empty," he said; he was determined to "*force* it" the next day. Professor Ford's meager correspondence from abroad obliged Clemens to abandon the series of travel letters, even though, in keeping the letters going singlehandedly, he had dug into his Nevada material and made a start on what would be *Roughing It*. In answer to rumors which he said had been started in Hartford, he published on the editorial page of the *Express* during five days in March 1870, a denial that he planned to leave Buffalo. "I am a permanency here," he announced. "I am prospering well enough to please my friends and distress my enemies, and consequently am in a state of tranquil satisfaction." Yet he already knew that the *Express* could never hold his interest, for he wanted more and more to write "for enjoyment as well as profit" (two years earlier he had told Orion that as soon as he married he would stop chasing "phantoms" and would "write to please myself"), and the paper seemed not only a chore and a waste of time but a hazard. He was afraid he might write himself out in the weekly grind and tire his public. He felt confined, he complained, for he had no outlet for "fine-spun stuff," and often he had to put aside an idea because it might not be "worth while" to write it for a newspaper. His notion of the literary status scale was simple: at the bottom were newspapers, at the top were books, and in the range between, with the *Atlantic* leading, were the magazines.

In March he accepted an offer from the *Galaxy*, a New York monthly founded just after the war in emulation of the *Atlantic*, to write a regular ten-page department called "Memoranda." The publishers were willing to pay him $2,400 a year—in page terms more than they had ever paid a contributor—but it was not money that was his major incentive. "I give you my word that I can start out tomorrow or any day I choose and make that money in two weeks, lecturing," he wrote Colonel William Conant Church, the *Galaxy*'s publisher, but he accepted nonetheless; remembering his difficulties with the *Alta California* proprietors, he insisted on retaining his rights in his material. In Hartford Elisha Bliss had unpleasant forebodings that his most valuable author was being seduced away from him. "I consider the magazine because it will give me an opening for higher class writing," Clemens explained to him in March, "stuff which I hate to shovel into a daily newspaper," and at the end of April, just as concerned as Bliss with maintaining the market value of his nom de plume, he assured him that if there were ever any signs of "letting down" in the *Galaxy* material he would "withdraw from literature and recuperate." He calculated that his work for the *Express* and the *Galaxy* would together take up only six days a month (often he made the same piece do double duty), leaving him time enough, he told Jervis Langdon, "to admire the house in." And, with *Roughing It* at the back of his mind as "the Calif. and Plains book," he added casually, "Need it, too, to write a book in."

Jervis Langdon once teased Livy into believing that if she ever married he would have nothing left to live for. Early in 1870 he fell ill, and that spring, as she was adjusting to her new life in Buffalo, he went South to recuperate. By the end of June it was apparent that what had started as chronic indigestion was, in fact, cancer of the stomach, and Clemens and Livy went back to the brownstone mansion in Elmira to help nurse him. For three hours in the middle of the day and from midnight to four in the morning Clemens stood his watches in the sickroom, fighting off sleep in order to wave a palm-leaf fan over Langdon's drawn, white face. Characteristically, what he remembered years later with agonizing clarity was the guilt of "my noddings, my fleeting unconsciousness, when the fan would come to a standstill in my hand and I would wake up with a start and a hideous shock."

In July Langdon seemed to be recovering, and Clemens left on a quick trip to Washington to lobby for a judicial redistricting bill for Tennessee which had a bearing on his father-in-law's Memphis involvements. He sat for his portrait at Mathew Brady's studio, talked to his friends among the politicians and reporters, and revisited the Congressional press galleries. A literary celebrity now, he was taken to the White House by Senator Stewart to be introduced to the notoriously taciturn Grant, who was considerably less at ease than Clemens and more at a loss for words once the first courtesies had been exchanged. "Mr. President," Clemens volunteered, "I seem to be a little embarrassed. Are you?" Grant's response was a grim smile. The fact was, Clemens told Livy, *the General was fearfully embarrassed himself.*" The redistricting bill did not pass, but Clemens came back from Washington with a sense of achievement all the same. He was convinced he had found "a perfect gold mine" for a book. Samuel Pomeroy, the corrupt Kansas Senator, with whom he had dined on the evening of July 8, was to be the model for Senator Abner Dilworthy in *The Gilded Age.*

Soon after he returned to Elmira, and still in high spirits, Clemens signed a contract with Bliss for a new book. He was going to "do up Nevada and Cal.," he wrote to Orion, and he was proud that his seven-and-a-half per cent royalty was the largest ever paid on a subscription book. At the end of March he had paid $9.50 to have the "coffin" containing his files of the Virginia City *Territorial Enterprise* shipped to him from his mother's house in St. Louis; now he asked for the loan of Orion's memorandum book to fill out his recollections of the route, station names, scenes and incidents of the overland trip to Carson City they had made together nine years earlier—"I remember next to *nothing* about the matter"—and he was to pay Orion a thousand dollars out of the first royalties for his help. "The book I am writing will sell," he predicted at the end of July. With equal confidence in his chances of living an orderly and productive life, he planned to deliver a manuscript to Bliss by January 1, 1871.

"Beecher, I'm going home . . . and I'm almost there": this had been Jervis Langdon's valedictory, his preacher told a memorial audience in the Elmira Opera House. The coal dealer's death on August 6 was only the first of a series of overwhelming interruptions to the six months of intensive writing Clemens had planned. Worn down by grief and by the weeks of nursing her father and sitting up nights, Livy had a nervous collapse and needed her husband's constant care; she slept only when drugged. At best Buffalo had been a city of only mild social diversions for Clemens; now, back at Delaware Avenue soon after the funeral, he was bound by the conventions of mourning to live in near-isolation with an increasingly distressed household. Jervis Langdon's widow came to stay with her daughter, and at the end of the month another visitor arrived, Miss Emma Nye, a friend of Livy's who was on her way from South Carolina to teach school in Detroit. Within a week she was sick with typhoid fever and Clemens and Livy were deathbed watchers once again. Emma Nye died on September 29 in Clemens' own bed and bedroom, a displacement that symbolizes the extent to which his life and his literary goals were to be victimized by malign and domestic harassments.

Throughout the fall he managed to work on *Roughing It*, although his pace steadily slackened. "Am up to page 180," he told Bliss ten days before Emma Nye died; "only about 1500 more to write." By the middle of October he was writing twelve to twenty pages of manuscript a day, but his usual facility had gone. It was *"very slow work,"* he complained; it went along at best "fairly tolerably" and most often "ever so slowly." He refused to admit that his difficulty was an index of his growing despair and discouragement. Instead he convinced himself that by writing so slowly he would not have to change a sentence later. But even this dogged demonstration of the stability and basic hardiness of his genius had to end. On November 11 came a cry of utter defeat. *"I am sitting still with idle hands,"* he wrote to Orion. He was too distracted, too busy with doctors and with bills, even to read Orion's Nevada notes. In October Livy had a near-miscarriage brought on, he said, by a trip over Buffalo's cobblestone streets, and she was confined to the library downstairs. On November 7 she gave birth to a son, Langdon Clemens, four and a half pounds in weight and, like his father at birth, frail, sickly, and at least a month premature. *"I am sitting still with idle hands*—for Livy is very sick and I do not believe the baby will live five days." The baby survived the winter, but Livy continued in a dangerous condition, an invalid once again, slowly recovering from childbirth complications only to get typhoid in February and come close to dying. In March 1871 she was still an invalid, and when Clemens, by this time half crazy with fatigue and despair, decided to leave Buffalo for Elmira, she had to be moved on a mattress.

At intervals Clemens' gloom lifted a little. "Mrs. Fairbanks (my best critic) likes my new book *well*, as far as I have got," he told Bliss. He kept busy during December. He finally settled the issue of the *Celebrated Jumping Frog* royalties that he claimed Webb had withheld. After suing in the New York courts Clemens agreed to waive the six hundred dollars Webb was supposed to owe him and pay an additional eight hundred for all the rights in the book and the plates besides. "Think of *purchasing* one's own property after never having received one cent from its publication!" he wrote to Mary Fairbanks. But he was relieved. He planned to melt the plates down and reissue the Frog story and some of the other pieces in the book, and he signed a contract with Bliss for a collection of sketches.

The day after Christmas 1870 Clemens wrote to the historian Francis S. Drake, who was compiling *A Dictionary of American Biography*. Clemens' entry in Drake's book, published in 1872, gave his occupation as "humorist": "Entered journalism in Virginia [City], Nevada, in 1862; continued in it three years there, three years in San Francisco, and one in Buffalo. Author of 'The Jumping Frog, & Other Sketches,' 12mo, 1867; 'The Innocents Abroad,' 8vo, 1869, of which 100,000 copies have been sold in two years." The sales of *The Innocents Abroad* had set a record, Clemens wrote to Drake, and, with the air of a man who feels that his victories are all behind him, he added: "*That* is the only thing in my life that seems to me remarkable enough to merit public attention." As the hard winter months of 1871 closed in on him and he watched the star of another California writer, Bret Harte, rise and blaze in the sky, his work on *Roughing It* came at last to a full stop, and, utterly overwhelmed, Mark Twain no longer functioned as a writer.

II

In an autobiographical dictation in 1906 Clemens said that the two or three days before Emma Nye's death were "among the blackest, the gloomiest, the most wretched of my long life." He made a significant connection between this crisis, which in one form or another continued through the spring, and the way he functioned as a humorist, and, in effect, he described the hypomania which often accompanies deep depressions: "The resulting periodical and sudden changes of mood in me, from deep melancholy to half-insane tempests and cyclones of humor, are among the curiosities of my life." With his jackknife one day he carved into a wooden printing block a map which the *Express* published on September 17 as "Fortifications of Paris"—a travesty of news from the Franco-Prussian War and also of the maps in big-city papers, which, he said, were generally more artistic than reliable. He executed this joke with the unflagging enthusiasm of near-hysteria or, as he recalled his mood, in a "spasm of humorous possession." His "map" of Paris was consistently and deliberately childish: crude block letters which would come out in reverse, impossible meanderings of misplaced rivers, the mockery of Europe and of military strategy through the designations "Fence," "Erie Canal," and "Podunk," and, finally, a series of appended testimonials from Grant, Bismarck, and Napoleon III. Republished in the November *Galaxy*, the map eventually found its way to Berlin, Clemens said, where American students roared with laughter over it. He himself was so entranced that he sent a copy to Ainsworth Spofford, the Librarian of Congress, with the suggestion that it be preserved "among the geographical treasures of the Congressional Library."

Later that fall, in another "spasm," he wrote a sketch called "Mark Twain's (Burlesque) Autobiography." He built it on the unwearying device of claiming his descent from a long line of highwaymen, forgers, thieves, pirates, and the like. It was as single-minded a performance as his map of Paris, but hostility and self-hatred are so nakedly displayed that what was meant to be a joke ends up being genuinely unpleasant. Along with a dull burlesque called "Awful, Terrible Medieval Romance"—indicative of his sense of failure at the time, the point of this story is that the author doesn't know how to end it—he allowed the "(Burlesque) Autobiography" to be brought out by the *Galaxy* publishers in February 1871. In content and aspiration this little book marks the lowest point in a bad year. Later on he regretted that he had ever written and published it, and the fact that he felt he had to destroy the plates of this book as well as those of Webb's edition of *The Celebrated Jumping Frog*—two out of his three books to date—is evidence as poignant as one could find of his fumbling grasp of his literary identity. In the fall of 1870, however, his "(Burlesque) Autobiography" seemed appropriate enough, one of those "half-insane tempests and cyclones of humor" that were his response to despair. "The secret source of humor itself is not joy but sorrow," he said many years later. "There is no humor in heaven."

As much of a measure of his changes of mood during this period was a book that was never written. He planned it in a cyclone of enthusiasm which had the same intensity as his despair. The South African diamond rush was on, and during the fall of 1870 news of spectacular finds came to America. Stories that had not been heard since 1849 were being told again. According to the New York *Sun*, three poor Capetown fishermen sold all their tackle, went out to the diamond fields, and returned with fifty thousand dollars in stones; a farmer who had gone out to the diamond fields but found nothing decided to give up, sold his walking stick for a shilling, and then stumbled over stones that brought him a fortune. Here was a dream world that also had actuality, and Clemens, placer miner and discoverer of a "gold mine" on the Bosporus, responded to it characteristically. The diamond rush, he told Bliss at the end of November, was a subject "brimful of fame and fortune for both author and publisher," and he wanted to write a book about it, immediately, but without going to South Africa. He planned to send a proxy there to spend three months gathering impressions and information. When the proxy returned, Clemens would take over his notes and write a book under the name Mark Twain, as if he had actually been to the diamond fields. He had already figured out how in his preface to the book he would justify this deception:

hadn't Daniel Defoe, after all, sent out Robinson Crusoe to find out about life on a solitary island? By February 1872, as Clemens planned it, Bliss would be able to publish a book that would "sweep the world like a besom of destruction." "Expeditious is the word and I don't want any timidity or hesitancy now," he informed Bliss. What had fired such enthusiasm and impatience was his certainty that he had found "the best man in America" to go to South Africa and do the job.

The hero, and victim, of this infallible scheme was James Henry Riley, Clemens' drinking and talking companion from newspaper days in San Francisco and Washington. Riley was a kind of flesh-and-blood *Doppelgänger* of the unregenerated Clemens, and their careers and personalities ran somewhat parallel. Riley left home in Philadelphia to dig for gold in California, Mexico, and Central America. He edited a newspaper in Alaska, and as a journalist he came to San Francisco, where for a while he was out of a job. In *Roughing It* Clemens wrote about his first impressions of the seedy and forlorn Riley in San Francisco: "He was full of hope, pluck, and philosophy; he was well read and a man of cultivated taste; he had a bright wit and was a master of satire; his kindliness and his generous spirit made him royal in my eyes and changed his curbstone seat to a throne and his damaged hat to a crown." Riley was almost always broke; when Clemens visited Washington in July he made Riley the gift of a new suit of clothes. Riley was a marathon talker, charming, ironical, deceptively solemn, "the most entertaining company I ever saw," Clemens wrote about him in the *Express* after Riley had passed through Buffalo, a bright interlude in a bleak existence. In that admiring sketch he recalled an exchange at Riley's boardinghouse in Washington. The landlady told Riley about an old Negro cook next door who had fallen asleep over her red-hot stove and was burned to death, and Riley, without a smile or a moment's hesitation, pronounced the epitaph, "Well done, good and faithful servant."

Settled for the winter in Washington as correspondent for the *Alta California* and clerk to a Congressional committee on mines and mining, Riley suddenly became the target of a barrage of solicitations from Buffalo. He was as fired up about diamonds as Clemens. The night before one of Clemens' glowing descriptions of the project reached him Riley had dreamed about digging in South Africa and finding stones of unparalleled size and brilliancy. He was eager to go over as Clemens' proxy, he said, and in the enthusiasm of the moment he put aside his habitual modesty and announced that he actually was something of an expert on precious stones, having learned all about them from a Brazilian diamond miner he once knew in California. But he had his commitments to honor; he would not be able to leave before the end of the Congressional session.

Clemens blasted Riley loose from his hesitations with a document full of manic reasoning. "This thing is the pet scheme of my life," Clemens declared, and he outlined his terms. He would pay Riley's passage to and from the diamond fields, along with expenses of a hundred dollars a month for the three months. Whatever diamonds Riley found up to five thousand dollars' worth were his; anything over five thousand dollars he would have to split with his sponsor. Clemens had thought of everything: a penalty of five thousand dollars in advance for every month Riley, presumably busy shoveling in the diamonds, overstayed the three months; a salary of fifty dollars a month and board during the time Riley would live with him "till I have pumped you dry"; manifolding notebooks to yield one copy of the field notes for each of them; and a number of security injunctions, including a blackout of private letters, designed to keep the expedition "*secret*" so that it could be "a frightfully celebrated one six months afterwards, not only here but in every language in civilized Europe."

The benefits to Riley, Clemens reasoned, would be a fortune in diamonds picked up in three months, and later on, after personal coaching, another fortune from lecturing. All in all, Riley's earnings during the next five years might come to fifty thousand dollars in diamonds and fifty thousand dollars in lecture fees, from this project alone, and in his ecstatic state Clemens envisioned other books written in the same way. Riley would go off to "some quaint country," return with his impressions, "fill me up," and another besom of destruction would be ready to sweep the world. In the winter of 1870, fifteen years before he took on in loving combat that mechanical marvel the Paige typesetting machine, he felt like a rural tinker with a box of gears, pulleys, and pendulums under his bed who thinks he has discovered perpetual motion.

"There isn't a leak in the scheme," he proclaimed. Here was a surefire way not only of scooping up a fortune in diamonds but also of rationalizing literary production, of industrializing it, in fact, in order to turn out, like so many gold bars stamped "Mark Twain," an endless stream of sequels to *The Innocents Abroad*. What this scheme lacked in respect for the working of his own talent (and in recognition of the unpredictable), it made up for in a kind of technological grandeur. Instead of the pick and shovel with which he had dug out his ores—and which he now held with faltering hands—Mark Twain was going to be foreman of a steam-driven, smoke-and-fire-belching, roaring and clanking earth delver and rock crusher.

"Will get ready to go," Riley telegraphed on December 5. The next day Bliss mailed from Hartford to Buffalo the contract which he and Clemens, confident of their man, had all the while been negotiating. After a brief visit to his mother in Philadelphia, Riley went back to Washington to pack up, and on January 7, not a day too soon for Clemens, he sailed for England, having kept his mission so secret that even his brother knew only that this was some sort of business trip to Europe. The voyage gave him time enough to study his copy of *The Innocents Abroad*, and he began to gather the kind of random impression and fact that would be suitable for a travel book by Mark Twain. "I don't drink 'spirits' but will take a small glass of brandy": he noted this "nice distinction" made in an overheard conversation. In London he equipped himself with a traveling suit, a six-dollar pair of walking shoes "that the Wandering Jew couldn't wear out," and a haversack. Along with the rumor that some Americans were planning to charter a clipper ship for the trip to South Africa, he sent Clemens an installment of travel notes and news about fresh discoveries in the Kimberley region that made the project seem more alluring than ever in Buffalo. "Your letters have been just as satisfactory as letters can be," Clemens wrote to him at the beginning of March 1871, maintaining his enthusiasm even in the face of Livy's continuing illness, his fear that the rise of Bret Harte meant his own decline, and his decision to leave Buffalo, city of cold winds and hard luck.

Riley had his first adventure sooner than he wanted. The steamship *Gambia* out of Dartmouth ran aground on a sandspit 250 miles north of Capetown and stuck fast there, pounded by the surf and taking four feet of water in her forward hold. Thirty-nine days after leaving England, Riley, still shaken by this episode, was in Capetown. "Your correspondent wouldn't repeat (with the risks) another such a voyage at sea for one hundred thousand dollars," he wrote. Clemens' blithe greeting, "Give my love to the niggers," left America just as Riley left Capetown on his way to the interior. In East London he auctioned off his excess baggage and set off on the four-hundred-mile journey by ox-cart on rough roads that crossed mountains, rocky plains, and a desert plateau before reaching the diamond fields. There he was soon absorbed into an army of prospectors, more than ten thousand of them, that had been drawn by diamond fever from all the countries of the earth. He emerged three months later, not a dollar or a diamond richer, the joint owner with Clemens of some worthless mining claims. Another Orion in a way, he also came back with an idea for a crushing and sifting machine that he never got around to patenting. Riley was back in London by August, but by then Clemens had returned to *Roughing It*, and the great diamond book no longer had the same red-hot urgency. "Let the diamond fever swell and sweat," he told Riley, and he put off work on their book. "We'll try to catch it at the right moment."

Riley was at loose ends through the winter. He worked a little on his machine, thought of lobbying for the post of United States minister to the diamond republics, but mainly he waited for Clemens. The book that Bliss published in February 1872 was not the diamond book but *Roughing It*, and Clemens, anxious about its reception and back on the lecture circuit, was still in no mood for collaboration. In January he had put off working with Riley until March, and with this cushion of two months against the reality of the project he painted a rosy if vague picture. "I shall employ a good, appreciative, genial phonographic reporter who can listen first-rate, and enjoy, and even throw in a word now and then," he promised, blind to the fact that what he and Riley, both tireless talkers, least needed was a third collaborator. "Then we'll all light our cigars every morning, and with your notes before you, we'll talk and yearn, and laugh and weep over your adventures, and the said reporter shall take it *all* down." He confidently expected to have Riley "pumped dry" in a week or so of such work.

In May 1872 the book remained just as much an intention as it had been the August before, and though the diamond fever swelled and sweated, Riley now had a more serious condition to deal with. At a distance of about forty years from the event, Clemens supplied his biographer Albert Bigelow Paine with the curious information that on the way back from Africa Riley had wounded himself with a fork while eating and had got blood poisoning. On May 16, 1872, Riley, back in his mother's house in Philadelphia and having already been treated by nine physicians, told Clemens he was engaged in "a simple contest between Cancer and Constitution." "Come see me *as soon as you can*," he pleaded, and he closed with what surely must have been intended, and received, as veiled recrimination: "Wishing myself as I was this time one year ago, and hoping you are quite well with all your cares and troubles." Clemens went to Philadelphia a few days later and encouraged Riley to spend the summer months talking his material to a stenographer, but it was clear, as Bliss was quickly informed, that there was no hope for Riley and only the meagerest hope for the book. A month later Clemens and Bliss signed a new contract which acknowledged the probability that the diamond book could never be written and applied the advance already paid against the earnings from a future book by Mark Twain.

Langdon Clemens, the sickly child born in November 1870, the month the Riley book was born, died in June 1872, the month that Howells review of *Roughing It* appeared in the *Atlantic* and helped prove to Mark Twain that he had survived his crisis as a writer. On September 17, after a summer of homeopathic medicine, electrogalvanic treatment, and clover tea, Riley, now possessed of the terminal eminence of J. Henry Riley, consul general for the Orange Free State, died in Philadelphia. He was the final fatality of this dark period, the last in a series of casualties that began with Jervis Langdon, included the infant Langdon Clemens, and very nearly included Livy, a proxy voyager who, like the victims in Clemens late fantasies, pointlessly sailed the hot ocean.

More than twenty years later, when Clemens himself was in South

Africa lecturing his way out of bankruptcy, he relived the life and death of Riley. He wanted to write a story about the mining claims Riley had bought; perhaps, he speculated, he was the true owner of the Kimberley mines. In East London he met a man who had bought at auction Riley's copy of *The Innocents Abroad*, and he held it in his hand and examined it. "Given to Riley by me—as stated in Riley's hand in pencil at top of fly-leaf," he wrote in his notebook. "It was of the earliest edition." And when, in *Following the Equator*, he wrote about his own visit to the diamond mines, which were now yielding to De Beers about ten or twelve thousand pounds' worth of stones a day, he used an image which sums up the delusions and futilities of the Riley scheme: "Nothing is so beautiful as a rose diamond with the light playing through it, except that uncostly thing which is just like it—wavy sea-water with the sunlight playing through it and striking a white-sand bottom." At the time of Riley's death Clemens was in England enjoying a triumph as lecturer, and he wrote to Livy, inadvertently echoing Riley's joke about the dead cook: "Poor old faithful Riley is dead. It seems too bad." Even the paid death notice in the Philadelphia papers was a better epitaph for this wanderer: "New York, Washington, Ohio, California, London, and South Africa papers please copy."

III

"Do you know who is the most celebrated man in America today—the man whose name is on every single tongue from one end of the continent to the other?" Clemens wrote to Riley in March 1871. "It is Bret Harte. And the poem called the 'Heathen Chinee' did it for him." The previous year Osgood and Company, publishers of the *Atlantic*, had brought out a collection of Harte's stories under the title *The Luck of Roaring Camp*. They were having only a modest success with it until a sixty-line poem called "Plain Language from Truthful James" but soon known on every street corner in the country as "The Heathen Chinee" appeared in the September 1870 issue of the *Overland Monthly*. Harte later let it be known that he wrote the poem in an idle moment for his amusement, discarded it, and fished it out of the trash basket only because the magazine was running short of copy at press time. The poem had an incredible vogue, and for reasons that are almost impossible to discover—one can describe the environment of a fad but not its cause—it created the sort of periodic short-lived national hysteria associated in the nineteenth century with streetcar and obituary poetry and in the twentieth with the hula hoop and the Beatles. Harte's dialect poem about a childlike and bland Oriental who euchres two outraged Western cardsharks "created an explosion of delight whose reverberations reached the last confines of Christendom," Clemens recalled in 1906. (By then he had convinced himself, contrary to all the facts, that until "The Heathen Chinee" was published Harte's name had been "obscure" to the point of "invisibility.") At a time when Clemens had reached what seemed like bottom, Harte's new fame made *The Luck of Roaring Camp* one of the best sellers of the decade and brought him a number of offers, including, among others that he declined, a chair in English literature at the University of California. With an air less of taking than of conferring an honor, Bret Harte was to accept from the *Atlantic*—which did not publish anything by Mark Twain until 1874—an unprecedented offer: ten thousand dollars for the exclusive rights in at least twelve poems or sketches for one year commencing March 1, 1871.

That February Bret Harte left San Francisco with his wife and two small children and traveled East—no outsider as Mark Twain had been four years earlier, but a conqueror. His journey by train was a rite in a national hero cult. The telegraph wires carried almost hourly reports of his trip. For many of his contemporaries, including Clemens and Howells, the approach of this prodigy was an event which they compared with Halley's comet, the Viceroy of India touring his domain, or the progress of a prince. His demeanor and appearance were princely. Far from being the rough-clad miner some of his readers thought he would be, he was impeccably tailored and barbered. He was aloof, ironical, deferential to no one, and he was to shock Howells, the pilgrim from Columbus, Ohio, by making fun of the way Emerson held his cigar and by suggesting to James Russell Lowell that he avoid overliterary phrasing in his poetry. The list of New England literati who feted him on his arrival in Boston and Cambridge worked in him not awe but a certain tempered amusement. "Why, you couldn't stand on your front porch and fire off your revolver without bringing down a two-volumer," he remarked to Howells. Like any princeling, he insisted on protocol and precedence. In Chicago, it quickly became known across the country, he had shunned a banquet arranged in his honor, because no carriage had been sent to call for him at the station. When Harte arrived in Boston, Howells, his host on behalf of the *Atlantic*, was careful to meet him at the station in the handsomest hack the Cambridge liveries could offer, and he was rewarded by a cordial handclasp from Harte and by his voice and laughter which Howells found "the most winning in the world." Eight years later Howells recalled that visit for President Rutherford Hayes: "He spent a week with us in Cambridge when he first came East—and we all liked him. He was late about appointments, but that is a common fault. After he went away, he began to contract debts, and was arrested for debt in Boston. (I saw this.)"

In Clemens' later years, when his feelings about Bret Harte—and Harte's chronic borrowings and debts—had turned into a barely controllable obsession, he looked back on that princely progress eastward and felt that the train might just as well have carried Harte's corpse; his best work was already behind him and "he had lived all of his life that was worth living." At the time, though, he was impressed by Harte's success and, in striking contrast to what he later said about him, both generous and circumspect. "Indeed Harte *does* soar, and I am glad of it, notwithstanding he and I are 'off' these many months," he told Webb, and to Thomas Bailey Aldrich he freely acknowledged his debt to the patient trimming and schooling Harte had given him. But at the same time it was impossible for him not to believe that Harte's rise meant his own eclipse or that the tide had already turned against him.

Even in an area of demonstrated mastery like the literary hoax Clemens now encountered frustration and failure. Hoping to stir up fresh publicity for *The Innocents Abroad*, he wrote a review of his own book, attributed it to the London *Saturday Review*, and published it in the December 1870 issue of the *Galaxy*. Even this "spasm of humorous possession" was not without self-hatred; the psychologist might not have to speculate for long about the state of mind of a man who, as Clemens did in this review, builds his joke on a statement of "the insolence, the impertinence, the presumption, the mendacity, and, above all, the majestic ignorance of this author." What Clemens intended as a spoof of the way a stolid, solemn, and literal-minded English reviewer would react to the humor and misinformation in *The Innocents Abroad* backfired entirely. The hoax was altogether too successful. The piece was accepted not only as a genuine review from an English literary journal but, despite Clemens' increasingly outraged assertions that he wrote it himself, as a joke on him. "Mark Twain has been taken in," the Cincinnati *Enquirer* said. In answer he accused the editors of "a pitiful, deliberate falsehood" and ended up offering to pay five hundred dollars to anyone who could produce a copy of the *Saturday Review* with that piece in it. The unpleasant outcome of his hoax now seemed to him only further evidence that he was living in a hostile world, for he claimed that the newspapers had turned against him. He thanked Whitelaw Reid for suppressing a snub and a slur in the *Tribune*: "I guess that emanated from some bummer who owes me borrowed money and can't forgive the offense." But when he complained about such incidents to Mary Fairbanks he recognized implications which were far more disturbing than this: "I am pegging away at my book, but it will have no success. The papers have found at last the courage to pull me down off my pedestal—and that is simply a popular author's death rattle."

Several publishers, he said bitterly, had asked him to write a volume of poetry in the style of "The Heathen Chinee"; instead of answering these letters he burned them. Even John Hay, Lincoln's private secretary and eventually Secretary of State, was feeling the pinch of Harte's rise. His own *Pike County Ballads* had brought him literary celebrity, but on January 9, 1871, from the security of his post as second in command to Whitelaw Reid, he complained to Clemens of being accused of "plagiarism B.H." And six days later the bitter charge of "plagiarism B.H." fell on Clemens himself from the *Atlantic*'s sister magazine, *Every Saturday*. Thomas Bailey Aldrich, the editor of this weekly, was, as he was fond of saying, "not genuine Boston" but only "Boston plated"; still, he represented those New England literary values which awed Clemens quite as much as they amused Bret Harte. A year or so earlier Clemens had found nothing to admire in Aldrich's *Story of a Bad Boy*; now he found a great deal to protest in a paragraph Aldrich had written in the magazine attributing to Clemens the authorship of "a feeble imitation" of Harte's poem which had appeared in the *Express*. "Will you please correct your mis-statement, inasmuch as I did not write the rhymes referred to, nor have anything whatever to do with suggesting, inspiring, or producing them. They were the work of a writer who has for years signed himself 'Hy. Slocum,'" Clemens wrote on January 15, and he concluded: "I am not in the imitation business." A week later, feeling that he had been carried away by his anger of the moment, he asked Aldrich not to print the note. But it was too late, as he learned from Aldrich; 42,000 copies of the magazine had already been printed with Clemens' angry denial and an editorial apology by Aldrich headed, "Mark Twain Says He Didn't Do It." It was Clemens' turn to apologize for "bombastic pow-wow" written in heat. "Who would find out that I am a natural fool if I always kept cool and never let nature come to the surface?" All the same there is a repeated cry of anguish: "But it *is* hard to be accused of plagiarism," and, more specifically, "But I did hate to be accused of plagiarizing Bret Harte."

On March 6, 1871, Bret Harte formally accepted the *Atlantic*'s prestigious offer of ten thousand dollars. This was only a few weeks after Sheldon and Company in New York brought out the little book which Mark Twain would eventually destroy and try to forget. The peaks of the one writer's career had a way of coinciding with the troughs of the other's; a year after *The Innocents Abroad* was published Harte's star had risen and Clemens was afraid that nothing he could write could ever reestablish him. But occasionally there seemed a trickle of hope, a sign that the hard winter was ending, a return of belief that the cycle of wave and trough would continue to his eventual benefit. He planned to stay "shady and quiet till Bret Harte simmers down a little," he wrote to Orion in March, "and then I mean to go up head again and *stay* there."

III

Clemens eventually came to believe that the supreme law was the law of one's nature—the tiger could be nothing else than a killer—and that consequently there was no such thing as freedom of choice. His own mode of decision was neither discursive nor analytical. His richest choices as man and writer came from deep imperatives of his sensibility; his determinism to the contrary, these choices take on a special dignity both because they were inescapable and because they were evolved in such adversity. During the spring of 1871 he was in the grip of circumstances profoundly disfavoring to any creation. But he managed to make a lasting commitment to his vocation as a writer, even though over the next ten years he was to have considerable difficulty in deciding just what kind of writer he was and whom he was writing for.

In the same letter in which he told Orion of his resolution to "go up head again," he explained his feeling about "seeing my hated nom de plume (for I do loathe the very sight of it) in print *again* every month." He had hoped at the start that the *Galaxy* would give him an outlet for writing which was too good for the *Express*. All too soon, though, his monthly quota of ten double-columned pages turned into a depressing chore. The bitter and angry tone of much of his writing for the magazine, the savagery and undisguised indignation in his satire, gave the lie to the myth of the genial humorist and expressed not only his personal unhappiness but his unrest in the established social order. He attacked the Reverend T. De Witt Talmage, a fashionable Brooklyn preacher who abhorred the smell of the workingman; he attacked another clergyman who refused to bury an actor from his church; and, continuing to assert a position of sympathy with the outsiders and victims of society, he wrote a series of pieces, too crammed with atrocities to be ironical, about the plight of Chinese immigrants. His *Saturday Review* hoax backfired. Jervis Langdon's death curtailed his contribution to one issue, Livy's illness forced him to miss another entirely. He quit the *Galaxy* with the April 1871 issue. "For the last eight months, with hardly any interval, I have had for my fellows and comrades, night and day, doctors and watchers of the sick! During these eight months death has taken two members of my home circle and malignantly threatened two others. All this I have experienced, yet all the time been under contract to furnish 'humorous' matter once a month for this magazine," he explained in his valedictory. "Some of the 'humor' I have written during this period could have been injected into a funeral sermon without disturbing the solemnity of the occasion." Instead of being "a monthly humorist in a cheerless time" he was going to write a book and would "write but little for periodicals hereafter."

Besides the *Express* there remained one other encumbrance to his liberty. Through a certain delicate politicking with both parties Sam had got Orion a job in Hartford with Bliss as editor of *The American Publisher*. This was ostensibly an illustrated literary monthly, but it was really a self-sustaining house organ whose function was to publicize Bliss's list and his stable of authors. Orion, who had been encouraged by Sam to show neither diffidence nor lack of confidence in his dealings with Bliss, found that his duties included what he said were girlish chores, like addressing wrappers. Bliss was not above a little exploitation; but, after all, Orion had plans for doing some writing on Bliss's time and also hoped to use Bliss to promote his inventions. Orion's main responsibility, he learned from Bliss at the start, was to make sure that his brother, a pillar of the publishing house, would not only remain one despite competing offers but would be a pillar of the magazine as well. At a cost of $1,300 a year for Orion's salary, and with the knowledge that he had got Clemens in his debt by rescuing Orion from unemployment, Bliss could feel he had bought a thrifty insurance policy on a valuable property.

In the midst of his other troubles and harassments Clemens soon found himself hounded by his own brother. Bliss would pay Sam five thousand dollars to write exclusively for the magazine and to let him publish all Sam's books, Orion would urge. At a time when he regretted his experience with the *Galaxy* and was despairing of ever writing another book, Clemens was infuriated by such propositions, and he was even more infuriated when his position was misunderstood. Early in March Orion naïvely told him how enthusiastic they all were about prospects for the magazine, now that they had an exclusive call on Mark Twain, and he added, "We *must* have something from you, or we run the risk of going to the dickens." A few days later, Orion, who was sometimes tactless as well as absent-minded, wrote in an even more exasperating role: he had finished a story for children, and he wanted his brother's professional judgment of the manuscript.

The result was a series of violent explosions from Buffalo. "There isn't enough money between Hell and Hartford to hire me to write once a month, for *any* periodical," Sam wrote, and he insisted angrily that Orion run a paragraph in the magazine to the effect that Mark Twain would doubtless appear less frequently than any other contributor. And Orion might just as well have thrown his own manuscript in the fire; Sam berated him for it, confessed that he had "no love for children's literature," and ended on a note he was to sound again and again: "I am and have been for weeks buried under beetling Alps of trouble. I am simply half-crazy—that is the truth. And I wish I was the other half." To Bliss himself on March 17, with the sounds of packing and his baby son crying in the background, Clemens wrote: "You do not know what it is to be in a state of absolute frenzy—desperation. I had rather die twice over than repeat the last six months of my life." He went on:

> Do you know that for *seven months* I have not had my natural rest but have been a night and day sicknurse to my wife?—and am still—and shall continue to be for two or three weeks longer—yet must turn in now to write a damned *humorous* article for the *Publisher, promised* it—promised it when I thought that the vials of hellfire bottled up for my benefit *must* be about emptied. By the living God I don't believe they ever *will* be emptied. . . . If I ever get out of this infernal damnable chaos I am whirling in at home, I will go to work and amply and fully and freely fulfill some of the promises I have been making to you—but I don't dare! Bliss—I don't dare! I believe that if that baby goes on crying three more hours this way I will butt my frantic brains out and try to get some peace.

But if peace had gone something else had managed to survive the dreadful winter, and at this moment of utter bottom Clemens was able to state the terms of his eventual survival: "I want to get clear away from all hamperings, all harassments. I am going to shut myself up in a farm-house alone, on top of an Elmira hill, and *write*—on my book."

He loathed Buffalo. What he remembered now was not the night he was tricked into entering the gaslit fairyland on Delaware Avenue but instead months of illness, death, drudgery, failure. On March 2 he put up for sale his two ties to the city, the house and his interest in the *Express,* both reflections not only of Jervis Langdon's beneficence but of Jervis Langdon's aspirations for him. He prepared to move Livy to Quarry Farm, her sister's summer home high above Elmira, and finish his book. Afterward he planned to move to Hartford, and already he was asking Orion to find him a storage place for his ten or twelve thousand dollars' worth of furniture. "It will not be needed by us for at least two years—I mean to take my time in building a house and build it *right*—even if it does cost 25 per cent more." Ironically, it was Livy's inheritance from her father that helped give such definiteness and amplitude to his plans to set up as a man of letters in the land of steady habits. And inseparable from his decision to leave Buffalo was a new burst of interest in *Roughing It.* Two days after he advertised his house for sale he told Orion he had decided to rewrite one of his characters from the first chapter on. "It's no fool of a job, I can tell you, but the book will be greatly bettered by it." The character he rewrote was that of the narrator himself, Mark Twain, telling in part the story of his progress from tenderfoot to toughened veteran.

At Quarry Farm that April Clemens and Livy were experiencing a parallel convalescence. After three or four bedridden months Livy was able to walk a few steps at a time supported by a chair. Clemens' support was Joe Goodman, the former *Enterprise* editor, who came to stay with him and, filling the role vacated by Bret Harte and soon to be filled by Howells, read over the manuscript. There were days of relapse in which Clemens despaired of the book and believed he was hearing "a popular author's death rattle," but, spurred on by Goodman's praise, he was writing with increasing confidence and exuberance.

On April 20 he sent Bliss a chapter for the *American Publisher.* "By all odds it is the finest piece of writing I ever did. Consequently I want the people to *know* that it is from the book." What he enclosed was Chapter Eight, the account of the pony-express rider, "a little bit of a man, brimful of spirit and endurance." "There was no idling time for a pony-rider on duty," Clemens wrote; he was ready at all times to leap into his saddle and ride through Indian country carrying his slim packets of letters "written on paper as airy and thin as gold-leaf." Like the Mississippi River pilot, he was alone in his authority. His horse was "born for a racer and fed and lodged like a gentleman," and his manner was lordly; he burst past the stagecoach and acknowledged the whoops and hurrahs of ordinary men with

> a wave of the rider's hand, but no reply. . . . So sudden is it all, and so like a flash of unreal fancy, that but for the flake of white foam left quivering and perishing on a mail-sack after the vision had flashed by and disappeared, we might have doubted whether we had seen any actual horse and man at all, maybe.

In some unconscious, unerring way Clemens was summing up his restored pride in himself as a writer and his dazzled wonderment at the workings of his imagination.

By the middle of May he was bettering his best pace on *The Innocents Abroad.* Writing "with a red-hot interest," as he told Bliss, he could turn out thirty pages a day or more, sometimes fifty or sixty. He smoked at full blast once again. "Nothing grieves me now, nothing bothers me or gets my attention—I don't think of anything but the book," and he was no longer afraid he could not equal his first success. "A bully book," "a starchy book," one that would sell: he was willing to bet that no one who started it could put it down before the end. And along with this complete swing in mood came evidence that his reputation had survived its crisis; he was flooded with offers for books and almanacs, articles and lectures. "The reaction is beginning and my stock is looking up."

More than a year and a half earlier, on October 16, 1869, Clemens published in the *Express* the first in the series of travel letters that were intended to be written with the help of Professor Ford. It was entirely Clemens' work, a description of Mono Lake in California which he later used almost unchanged in Chapter Thirty-eight of *Roughing It*. It was meant to be the setting for an episode which he had in mind but which he did not publish at the time; that episode appears as the next chapter in the book, written when his stock had begun to look up again. He described Mono Lake in the *Express* on October 16 as a "solemn, silent, sailless sea" of corrosive waters which were nearly pure lye. This Dead Sea is surrounded by a "lifeless, treeless, hideous desert." There are only two seasons, "the breaking up of one winter and the beginning of the next." The lake supports no life except a sort of worm which looks like a piece of white thread. Its shores are outlined by a belt of flies an inch deep and six feet wide. "The ducks eat the flies—the flies eat the worms—the Indians eat all three—the wildcats eat the Indians—the white folks eat the wildcats—and thus all things are lovely." These images of corrosive waters and of a brute order of nature are premonitory of the images that obsessed the despairing Mark Twain in his sixties: a drop of water turns, under the glare of the microscope lamp, into a hot, brassy sea where the monsters feed on each other and where the people on derelict ships go mad.

Something that happened to Clemens in Buffalo about a month and a half before he published the *Express* piece appears to have triggered both his recollection of Mono Lake and the episode with which he later connected it. He had gone rowing with two friends on Lake Erie; a storm broke, they were caught in a "heavy sea," and they nearly capsized. He reported this adventure to Livy on August 25. As extended in *Roughing It*, Mono Lake becomes the setting for a similar episode, which Clemens invests with powerful psychological overtones. His account has both the simplicity and the intensity of nightmare; its tone is like that of no other passage in the book, and it is difficult not to believe that the episode corresponds to a conflict within Clemens himself.

The narrator and Calvin Higbie (to whom *Roughing It* is dedicated) set out one morning to row to one of the barren lava islands in the middle of the lake:

> We had often longed to do this, but had been deterred by the fear of storms; for they were frequent, and severe enough to capsize an ordinary rowboat like ours without great difficulty—and once capsized, death would ensue in spite of the bravest swimming, for that venomous water would eat a man's eyes out like fire, and burn him out inside, too, if he shipped a sea.

They reach the island, and while they are there, having found not the fresh water they wanted but only "solitude, ashes, and a heartbreaking silence," the wind rises and a storm begins. They rush back to the shore and discover their boat has been blown away. Eventually they see it tossing about in a heavy sea fifty yards away. Their last hope now is that the wind will blow the boat close to a jutting point so that they can jump in. The moment arrives, and it is Higbie, not the narrator, who with a great spring lands in the stern of the boat and retrieves it. After a stormy and difficult passage across the lake, when they are only a few yards from shore, they capsize. But the turning point in the episode, the revelation which makes the capsizing at the end an ironical accident, is something that Higbie tells the narrator after his leap into the boat: he hadn't cared whether the boat was within jumping distance or not—he had made up his mind that if he missed he would close his eyes and mouth to the corrosive waters and swim the eight or ten yards. The narrator reacts to this with the same intensity with which Clemens, after the darkest year of his life, realized that his talent was unscathed and his vocation clear: "Imbecile that I was, I had not thought of that. It was only a long swim that could be fatal."

CHAPTER SEVEN

"I did not know I was a lion"

I

H OWELLS FOUND IT remarkable that none of the California writers who
burst on the literary scene after the Civil War wanted to go back
there; some of them even seemed to hate California, as if their frontier
image of it was the only one they could accept. Bret Harte came East, to
Boston, Newport, and New York; debt drove him to take a consular post
in Prussia; and he spent the last twenty years of his life in England, an
exile. Joaquin Miller, the bearded poet of the Sierras, headed for England
wearing his sombrero and chaps; he was taken up by William Michael Ros-
setti and his circle, and when Clemens met him in London in 1873 Miller
said he was engaged to the daughter of a baronet. During Clemens' 1873–
74 lecture season in London he hired as his private secretary and companion yet another Californian far from the scene of his first literary celebrity, Charles Warren Stoddard. And Mark Twain, having fled Buffalo
after only a year, was to revisit Hannibal a number of times but California
not even once. In none of these places could his developing needs be met.

"It takes a great deal of history to produce a little literature," Henry
James said. "It needs a complex social machinery to set a writer in motion."
In literary values James and Clemens were antipathetic: James regarded
Clemens' work as that of a buffoon and vulgarian, while Clemens, though
he included James among the "big literary fish," said of his work, at least
as it was represented by *The Bostonians*, "I would rather be damned to
John Bunyan's heaven than read that." But Clemens no less than James
needed "a complex social machinery" to set him in motion. In Nook Farm,
a tiny, coherent, and influential community nesting in the larger structure
of Hartford, he achieved a crucial balance of inner imperatives and outer
pressures that led to the most productive period of his life.

Midway in values as well as distance between New York's commerce and Boston's official culture, Hartford in 1871 was a spacious and pleasant city of about fifty thousand people. It was made prosperous by its booming insurance companies, which had proved their stability once and for all by virtually rebuilding Chicago after the great fire, by its silk and leather industries, by the skilled mechanics at its factories and machine shops, by its publishing and printing establishments, and by an appalling output of arms and munitions: peaceable Hartford supplied the Colt revolver, the Sharp rifle, and the Gatling gun to the nation and the world. The poor and the idle were not lacking in the city, though visitors had trouble finding them at first. Soon after he moved to Hartford, Mark Twain was lecturing for the benefit of Father Hawley's strenuous missions to the poor and the alcoholic, and Christmas would find the family sleigh, driven by Patrick McAleer, making the rounds of the needy to deliver baskets which Livy had loaded with turkeys, oranges, canned peas, raisins, and nuts. But despite these challenges to the social conscience the fact remained that Hartford, if its wealth were averaged among its citizens, was the most affluent of American cities.

What brought Mark Twain to Hartford was not its downtown but a small settlement on what was then the western extremity of the city. Twenty years earlier the lawyer John Hooker, husband of the formidable Isabella Beecher and descendant of Thomas Hooker, who had led a march from Cambridge Common in 1636 and founded Hartford, bought a one-hundred acre tract of wooded land known as Nook Farm. John Hooker was a sagacious real-estate developer; he was also careful in choosing his neighbors. As he sold off the land parcel by parcel and saw ample and gracious houses going up among the trees, he had the double reward of realizing a profit on his investment and of building a community of relatives and closely linked friends. Hooker's distinguished brother-in-law, Francis Gillette, United States Senator, abolitionist, and temperance reformer, built and lived at Nook Farm. Gillette's son, William, encouraged by Mark Twain, moved on to an acting career capped by the role of Sherlock Holmes; the Senator's daughter, Lilly, married George Warner and lived at Nook Farm. So did Isabella's sisters Mary, with her husband Thomas Perkins, a lawyer, and Harriet, with her husband Calvin Stowe, educator and Bible exegete and in appearance something of an eccentric: Professor Stowe's nose, ravaged by a disease, was like a cauliflower, his long white beard hung down on his chest, and, Clemens recalled, he looked like Santa Claus on the loose. Among others at Nook Farm were the co-editors of the Hartford *Courant*: Joseph Hawley, major general of volunteers during the war, and after it governor of Connecticut, Congressman, and Senator; and George Warner's brother, Charles Dudley Warner, Mark Twain's next-door neighbor and his collaborator on *The Gilded Age*. Nook Farm was as staunchly committed to liberal Congregationalism as it was to the Republican party. In 1864 the group had raised most of the $100,000 it would eventually cost to build the Asylum Hill Congregational Church, a spired edifice of Portland stone a few blocks away from the property limits of Nook Farm. Mark Twain called it "the Church of the Holy Speculators." Its minister was his friend Joseph Twichell.

In the fall of 1871, when Clemens rented the Hooker house on Forest Street, where he had once been a guest, and moved in with Livy, who was pregnant again, the white-faced and sickly infant Langdon, and their coachman, cook, and housemaid, he was at the pleasant and enveloping center of the Beecher network. A few years later, when the Beecher scandal was playing to a national audience from the center ring, the threads began to ravel. At the moment, though, for Livy, whose closest friend was Isabella's daughter, Alice Day, and even for Clemens, who had reached something of an accommodation with Isabella, the Hooker-Beecher world was home, welcoming, and so familiar that soon after they were settled on Forest Street Livy said, "You'd know this house was built by a Beecher. It's so queer."

Clemens achieved a remarkable degree of community and identification with his Nook Farm neighbors. For the first time since his boyhood in Hannibal he was part of the fabric of a stable society, and although he turned a bitter eye on practically every American phenomenon of his time he rarely questioned his life in Hartford. Nook Farm was an enclave walled off from a demoralized nation. He shared the group's faith in a dynamic aristocracy, their high responsibility, their earnest idealism, and their intellectual dedication. Harriet Beecher Stowe and Charles Dudley Warner were among the few American authors who made from their work a living comparable to that of a modest merchant prince, and they welcomed Mark Twain all the more warmly because he shared their sense of professionalism in writing and showed promise of becoming the most successful practitioner of them all.

Clemens also shared their gregariousness, their taste for entertaining each other and any eminence who happened to be passing through Hartford, whether it was Charles Kingsley, Henry Stanley, Matthew Arnold, or a Hindu Christian prelate named Protap Chunder Mazoomdar. Visitors to Nook Farm like William Dean Howells were overwhelmed by the boundless fellowship and informality. The Warners and the Clemenses, Howells wrote to a friend in Ohio, "live very near each other, in a sort of suburban grove, and their neighbors are the Stowes and the Hookers, and a great many delightful people. They go in and out of each other's houses without ringing, and nobody gets more than the first syllable of his first name—they call their minister *Joe* Twichell." The price of all this sociability, which was supplemented by teas and musicales, by billiards, discussion groups, and whist drives, was high, in energy as well as money. Mark

Twain the professional writer could work full time only during the three or four summer months he spent away from Hartford in the relative isolation of his sister-in-law's farm above Elmira. The rest of the year he thought of as enforced vacation. The Nook Farm residents tended to build as well as entertain on a scale beyond their incomes. They were always, symbolically at least, a little overdrawn at the bank. Mark Twain carried their cautious prodigality to a dimension of spectacular opulence unknown to American writers before him. When he built his own house there, that eccentric, willful, and eye-catching whatnot, $70,000 worth of turrets and balconies housing $21,000 worth of furniture and perched on a five-acre $31,000 tract of land, Nook Farm received from its newest member its gaudiest landmark, and eventually, instead of merely going into debt, Clemens went into bankruptcy.

In the fall of 1871, three years before he moved into what Howells was to call "the stately mansion in which he satisfied his love of magnificence," Clemens was in moderate financial difficulties. The price of fleeing Buffalo for the life of a man of letters in Hartford was considerable. His interest in the *Express* brought him ten thousand dollars less than he had paid for it, and the elegant brownstone house on Delaware Avenue also went at a distressed figure. Sales of *The Innocents Abroad,* which had waltzed him out of debt once before, were dwindling toward an average of only thirty-five hundred copies a year. *Roughing It,* for which Clemens had hopes that the book would never live up to, would not be published until February 1872. Early the previous summer, sizing up his situation, he had decided to return to the lecture circuit, his one sure source of quick money. "Without really intending to go into the lecture field, I wrote a lecture yesterday just for amusement to see how the subject would work up," he told Redpath with more than a trace of disingenuousness, "but now that I have read it I like it so much that I want to deliver it." Two weeks after this first announcement he told Redpath that he had already discarded this first lecture in favor of a second and then a third, with which he finally did open his season in October in Bethlehem, Pennsylvania; this last was a series of reminiscences of "some uncommonplace characters I have chanced to meet," including Artemus Ward, the Czar of Russia, and the luckless Riley, back from Africa and biding his time. After a week the reminiscences went out the window. Now Clemens was full of enthusiasm for a talk about Artemus Ward alone, but this turned out to be an uncomfortable choice. It was difficult to be funny in good taste about another humorist recently dead, especially one whose place in popular favor Clemens was claiming; above all it was awkward to have to use another man's jokes. After seven weeks the Artemus Ward lecture went the way of its predecessors and was replaced by a talk derived from *Roughing It.* "Am writing a new, tip-top lecture about California and Nevada," he wrote to Mary Fairbanks in December, "been at it all night—am still at it and pretty nearly dead with fatigue. Shall be studying it in the cars till midnight, and then sleep half the day in Toledo and study the rest. If I am in good condition there, I shall deliver it." To the usual tribulations of winter traveling had been added the strain of writing, memorizing, and perfecting three separate performances, and when he finally completed what he called "the most detestable lecture campaign that ever was," this second profession of his, for all the gratification he derived from it, was to be permanently associated in his mind with separation from Livy and with being in debt. The tour had earned him ten or twelve thousand dollars, most of which went to various creditors; he had less than fifteen hundred clear to show for a winter's work.

"I do hope that this will be the last season that it will be necessary for you to lecture," Livy wrote in mid-November. "It is not the way for a husband and wife to live if they can possibly avoid it, is it?" She minded the separation as much as he did, told him that she dreamed about his return, about stroking his hair and putting her hand in his. She hoped he was praying for her, a pathetic reversal of the roles of their courtship. She felt her own faith failing, and she wanted his support. Her feeling toward God, she confessed to him, was "almost perfectly cold," and she was afraid that if she fell away from belief this time she could never return to it. Far from being a stereotype of pallid gentility or simply a prim and parochial household figure, Olivia Clemens opened to her husband a strong, urgent, and developing nature all too easily misread by others. "His wife is a delicate little beauty, the very flower and perfume of *ladylikeness*, who simply adores him," Howells wrote after first meeting her. But it was Livy who made the hardheaded calculations of the income from coal interests and from Clemens' writing and lecturing that would enable them to settle at Nook Farm. And, she said, if after three or four years they discovered they were living beyond their means, "we will either board or live in a small cottage and keep one servant, will live near the horse cars so that I can get along without a horse and carriage—I *can not* and I *will not* think about your being away from me this way every year, it is not half living—if in order to sustain our present mode of living you are obliged to do that, then we will change our mode of living."

II

Over a long midday dinner at Ober's Restaurant Parisien in Boston early in November 1871 Clemens again encountered his friend and enemy, mentor and nemesis, Bret Harte. They were in Boston for the same purpose, for Harte too was driven by necessity to the lecture platform. The money from the glorious *Atlantic* contract had gone quickly in Newport and Cohasset, and Harte was already deep in debt, the chronic condition of his existence in the East. At Tremont Temple one night a sheriff sat behind the screen waiting for Harte to finish his talk about the California Argonauts of 1849; with arrest not more than ten feet away, Harte strung out his lecture until help arrived in the form of an advance from his publisher, and he was able to send the sheriff away satisfied. Harte's standing in New England remained as high as it had been the day Howells welcomed him and took him to dine at the Saturday Club with Agassiz, Longfellow, Lowell, Holmes, and Emerson.

Harte was the guest of honor at Ober's. Clemens was the newcomer. The others at the table were James T. Fields, recently and prosperously retired as editor of the *Atlantic*, Howells, Thomas Bailey Aldrich, and their host, Ralph Keeler, a proofreader on the magazine but also a writer, who was entertaining far beyond his means in a gesture of amity to Harte for having published an article of his in the *Overland*. Over the beefsteak and mushrooms and the omelet soufflé, which to Howells' amusement was brought to the table flat and fallen—a symbol of the punctured pretensions of the afternoon—Aldrich quipped away ("Wittiest man in seven centuries," Clemens was to say of him) and Fields told his celebrated funny stories, including one which Howells recalled years later as "a deliriously blasphemous story about a can of peaches." Harte took advantage of the easy freedom and fellowship of the dinner to describe Clemens' pleasure at being a part of this social institution of literary Boston. "Why, fellows," he said, touching Clemens' shoulder, "this is the dream of his life," a sufficiently pointed reminder that while he himself had been admitted to the sanctum by the high priests of the Saturday Club, Clemens was an outsider, and by trade a humorist, a noun which always implied the adjective "mere." ("I cannot say why Clemens seemed not to hit the favor of our community of scribes and scholars, as Bret Harte had done," Howells wrote, "but it is certain he did not, and I had better say so.") Clemens accepted the gibe in silence. Howells the peacemaker preferred to believe that the glance that flashed out from under Clemens' feathery eyebrows was one of good-natured appreciation of the fun at his expense, and he summed up in lightly mocking tones the entire occasion with its clever, inconsequential discourse, its good fellowship, and its fallen soufflé: "It was in every way what a Boston literary lunch ought not to have been in the popular ideal which Harte attributed to Clemens."

"We've been having a good many dinners together," Clemens proudly told Elisha Bliss, and he asked Bliss to send copies of *The Innocents Abroad*, with the author's compliments, to Howells, Aldrich, and Keeler. But among these dinners was one that never took place. It underscored the fact that between Mark Twain and certain aspects of literary Boston there existed, and would always exist, something less than perfect harmony. Aldrich brought him home unannounced to have dinner at 84 Pinckney Street. From the start Mrs. Aldrich, the former Lilian Woodman of New York, did not take to the arrangement. Her first impression of her husband's guest—whose name, she later claimed, had been mumbled in the introductions—was that his costume was so eccentric as to be unforgettable in all its details. He wore a sealskin coat and a sealskin hat, both with the fur out, but along with them he wore low black shoes instead of boots. His trousers and socks were yellowish-brown, his coat and waistcoat were gray, and his bow tie was violet. "May and December intermixed," she called this outfit; it gave her the disturbing impression that he had been too fuddled to dress like any other man. And as she listened to his attenuated drawl and saw him sway slightly as he spoke—mannerisms which strange surroundings exaggerated in him—she decided that he was drunk. In her fastidious allusion, "He had looked upon the cup when it was red." As Aldrich and Clemens amused each other in a waning way, she sat apart in frosty and silent disapproval, and when the dinner hour arrived and passed without any sign from her that he was to stay, Clemens read her meaning and left unfed.

"How could you have brought a man in that condition to your home," she scolded afterward, "to sit at your table and meet your wife?" Her mortification when Aldrich told her that the departed guest was Mark Twain, and cold sober, was never equal to her deep-grained disapproval. And as for Clemens, years later, in a ferociously funny account of the dedication of a memorial to Aldrich in Portsmouth in 1908, he was still chewing over the meats she failed to offer him that evening. "I conceived an aversion for her the first time I ever saw her," he said. "A strange and vanity-devoured detestable woman! I do not believe I could ever learn to like her except on a raft at sea with no other provisions in sight." She had invited sixty authors, many of them old and poor, to come to the "mortuary festival" by special train from Boston; they had to pay their own fares all the same. This incident alone, Clemens rejoiced, "restored my Mrs. Aldrich to me undamaged and just the same old thing she had always been, undeodorized and not a whiff of her missing."

The mannerisms, the eccentric costume, the sealskin coat and the unruly flow of reddish hair under the sealskin hat—these were in part the trappings of the professional humorist. What Mrs. Aldrich disapproved of was also bringing him triumph after triumph on the lecture platform. He was bound to be tormented by the distinction and the split, always invidious, between performing humorist and man of letters, and he had no way as yet of reconciling the two. S. L. Clemens of Hartford dreaded to meet the obligations of Mark Twain, the traveling lecturer—to preserve a double incognito he had registered at a Bethlehem hotel as "Samuel Langhorne,

New York." The epithet "buffoon" took on a kind of terror for him. What he liked about the *Atlantic* audience, he was to tell Howells, was that it "don't require a 'humorist' to paint himself stripèd and stand on his head every fifteen minutes." When the Duke in *Huckleberry Finn* decides that what the Arkansas lunkheads want is low comedy, the King comes prancing out on stage on all fours, naked, painted with streaks and stripes; the image corresponds to the way Clemens thought of himself during one of his sudden alternations from the buccaneering high spirits of the successful performer to depression, self-hatred, and hatred of his audience. "I am demeaning myself," he complained years later, when he and George Washington Cable were returning to their hotel after an evening on stage. "I am allowing myself to be a mere buffoon. It's ghastly. I can't endure it any longer." By then he had proved himself as a man of letters and was indulging in some self-dramatization. But in the early 1870s he was vulnerable, hypersensitive, and, with considerable justice, suspicious of some of the people around him. The private opinion of Colonel Thomas Wentworth Higginson of Boston, who visited Clemens in Hartford and then dined out in England on the strength of it, was that he was "something of a buffoon," and that grace at his table "was like asking a blessing over Ethiopian minstrels."

Soon after moving to Hartford Clemens was elected to membership in an elite twenty-man discussion group called the Monday Evening Club. Governor Hawley and the Reverend Edwin Parker, Calvin Stowe and the eminent philologist James Hammond Trumbull listened to him with respectful interest when he read papers on the license of the press, universal suffrage, conscience, organized labor. Outside Nook Farm, however, the response was quite different. When, in a letter to the New York *Tribune*, he ventured a serious criticism of the jury system, a correspondent who signed himself "H.K." sprang to the attack. No thinking man would attach any value to the view of a humorist, a class of persons who with "actors and clowns, make it a business to cater to our amusement in jest and burlesque," H.K. raged, and he concluded that in the circumstances Mark Twain's letter was a piece of "ghastly flippancy," misleading, and in the worst possible taste. But this was the merest echo of an attack on the profession of humorist during 1871 and 1872 while Mark Twain was off on his "detestable lecture campaign."

In *Scribner's Monthly*, of which he was editor and one of the founders, Dr. Josiah Gilbert Holland published his own four-part analysis of what was wrong with the lyceum system. Holland was an eminence in his day. Under the pseudonym Timothy Titcomb, he first became famous as the author of a series of moralistic letters to the young—he was an expert, as Mark Twain was to say, at arguing in support of self-evident propositions. Holland was a popular lyceum lecturer of the old stamp, dedicated to uplift and instruction, and his popularity survived the Civil War, though he was now more in demand in villages than in cities, and in the West rather than the East. The lyceums were having increasing trouble staying out of bankruptcy, Holland observed in his magazine, and he said that the prime source of their troubles was the fact that serious lecturers of his sort were being driven out of the field by "jesters and mountebanks," "triflers," and "literary buffoons." "Professional jesters and triflers are professional nuisances," Dr. Holland thundered, "who ought not to be tolerated by any man of common sense interested in the elevation and purification of the public taste." With a naïveté that was almost appealing, he demanded that the lecture bureaus purge themselves.

As a prominent "literary buffoon" and the heir of Artemus Ward, Mark Twain might just as well have been named by name. He answered Holland with a counterblast titled deceptively "An Appeal from One That Is Persecuted," and written with an irony that threatened to turn into physical violence. After some mild ad-hominem teasing, including extended references to Holland's soporific poetry and unsuccessful career as a doctor of medicine, he settled down to the main attack. The truth of it all, he said, was that the old-line moral instructors like Holland were the people who were bankrupting the lyceums; only the "literary buffoons" were bailing the lyceums out. Dr. Holland "has hung crepe on more lyceum door-knobs than any other man in America," he went on. "He moves through the lecture field a remorseless intellectual cholera," a "perambulating sack of chloroform," and "the very incarnation of the Commonplace." Finally Clemens cited two offers that he himself had just received for the coming season, one for ten thousand dollars to lecture a month and one for five thousand to lecture twelve nights. The supreme law, he might as well have said, is the law of demand; money talked louder than Holland could. Significantly, in the entire piece there are only glancing references to what was after all the heart of the argument: the function and dignity of the humorist. "Ours is a useful trade, a worthy calling," he was to say in 1888 when he accepted an honorary M.A. from Yale:

> . . . with all its lightness, and frivolity it has one serious purpose, one aim, one specialty, and it is constant to it—the deriding of shams, the exposure of pretentious falsities, the laughing of stupid superstitions out of existence; and . . . whoso is by instinct engaged in this sort of warfare is the natural enemy of royalties, nobilities, privileges and all kindred swindles, and the natural friend of human rights and human liberties.

Still later, in *The Mysterious Stranger*, he was to write that the only really effective weapon owned by the human race is laughter. "Against the assault of laughter nothing can stand," not even the most colossal humbug.

But in the early 1870s he was still unable to define and justify himself except by the sort of angry, pragmatic, and superficial arguments he used against Holland. And he never published his "Appeal from One That Is Persecuted." He realized that its basic position, determined by his misgivings and indecisions about his literary status, was no more sound or coherent than Holland's.

III

By July 1872, when Clemens wrote his answer to Holland, *Roughing It* had been out a full six months and had sold about sixty thousand copies. Publicly he tended to inflate his sales. Privately he confessed he was disappointed. He said that Bliss could have sold twice as many copies if he had not been so stingy about sending review copies to the newspapers. By May the book had earned him $10,500, less than half of what he had got from *The Innocents Abroad* over an equivalent period. "So you will see," he told his niece Annie Moffett, "we are not nearly so rich as the papers think we are."

Even so, the new book proved to him that he could support himself by writing; he had recovered from his fears that his days as a popular author were over; and he had other books in mind—an account of piloting on the Mississippi, which he would not begin for a few years, and a satirical travel book about England which would take him abroad that fall but which he would never write. He believed *Roughing It* was a distinct advance over *The Innocents Abroad*—"*much* better written," he told Livy—and his friends reported that the "general verdict" bore him out. "They like a book about America because they understand it better," he explained to Bliss. "It is pleasant to believe this because it isn't a great deal of trouble to write books about one's own country"—a claim supported by the fact that after he abandoned his book about England he wrote his share of *The Gilded Age* in less than three months.

Howells' review of *Roughing It* in the June *Atlantic* went along with the "general verdict." The grotesque exaggerations and broad ironies—which had offended some readers of *The Innocents Abroad*—struck Howells as possibly the ideal colors with which to paint life in the West, "for all existence there must have looked like an extravagant joke, the humor of which was only deepened by its nether-side of tragedy." And the unpredictable shifts from humor to pathos, from burlesque to word painting, which had seemed inconsistency in the other book now impressed Howells as creating a "complex," "a sort of 'harmony of colors' which is not less than triumphant." Although he conceded in a guarded way that the book did not always have all the literary virtues, he hardly more than hinted that the second half clearly showed haste, galloping ennui, and a tendency on the part of the author to consult his scrapbooks instead of his imagination. All in all, the review put a Boston stamp of approval on Western humor, and Clemens reacted with both gratitude and relief. "I am as uplifted and reassured by it as a mother who has given birth to a white baby when she was awfully afraid it was going to be a mulatto," he wrote, a comment which even forty years later Howells thought was too indelicate to repeat in print.

Soon after his lecture tour came to an end the Clemenses left Hartford for Elmira, where on March 19 their second child, Olivia Susan, known as Susy, was born. Among the felicitations was a characteristic message from Bret Harte. "If she behaves herself she shall marry my Franky," he wrote, "provided her father does the right thing in the way of dowry and relinquishes humor as a profession." The relationship was mended enough, though only temporarily, to support such teasing. In May, Clemens and Livy left their two children in Elmira in the care of nurses and went off to Cleveland to visit Mrs. Fairbanks. When they returned they found Langdon—the fat, alabaster-white baby who was still not able to walk—seriously ill once again. Several times before, they had given him up for dead; Clemens blamed these alarms on nurses who overfed the child by day and overdosed him with laudanum at night. This time Langdon had "a heavy cough," but he seemed to be recovering; he was well enough, in this era of guarded convalescences, for his father to take him out for an airing one morning. During the long drive in an open carriage Clemens fell into "a reverie," he said many years later, and let the fur blankets slip off Langdon, and by the time the coachman noticed this "the child was almost frozen." When they reached home he was sick again. They rushed back to Hartford, where on June 2 Langdon died, not of pneumonia but of diphtheria. Diagnostically this fails to jibe with Clemens' statement that he was responsible for the boy's death. Clemens, a lifelong guilt seeker, remembered or misremembered mainly what he wanted to; even so casual an acquaintance as Mrs. James T. Fields noted that "his whole life was one long apology." Looking back on that carriage ride with Langdon, Clemens wrote in 1906: "I have always felt shame for that treacherous morning's work and have not allowed myself to think of it when I could help it." Only once during his four-decade friendship with Howells did Clemens mention his son, and that was to say, "Yes, *I* killed him."

When the Nook Farm neighbors paid their condolence calls at the hushed house on Forest Street Clemens was in a mood of pity for the living, envy of the dead, that was to become a ground note of his celebrated despair. "Mr. Clemens was all tenderness but full of rejoicing for the baby," Lilly Warner wrote to her husband, George, "said he kept thinking it wasn't death for him but the beginning of life." Livy, who had held Langdon in her arms when he died, was "heartbroken."

Yet they quickly began to translate their grief over Langdon into a devotion to Susy that would later prove catastrophic in its excessiveness; when she died of meningitis, in 1896, they never recovered from the blow. And far from observing a period of mourning for his dead son, Clemens was soon full of hilarity and confidence, busy with all sorts of plans. "I want you to send a copy to the man that shot my dog," he wrote to Howells not two weeks after, to tease him about a published portrait. "I want to see if he is dead to every human instinct." And he boasted about the sales of *Roughing It.* He was seeing a good deal of Bret Harte. When the canvasser for the Hartford city directory called one day Clemens solemnly listed for him as a "boarder" at Forest Street "F. Bret Harte, Poet and Author." In July the heat drove them from Hartford to a hotel on Long Island Sound at New Saybrook, and Clemens kept up his high mood even when dealing with the kind of trivia that at other times put him into a towering rage. He was asking Orion's wife, left in charge of the Hartford house, to take care of his dirty laundry, to find a decent washerwoman for his shirts, to buy him a dozen pairs of cotton socks ("*Not* lisle thread, but cotton. *All* my present socks appear to have darns on them. I infinitely prefer holes"), and he was doing this with astonishing patience.

To Orion he sent tidings of a "great humanizing and civilizing invention" to be called "Mark Twain's Self-Pasting Scrapbook." "My idea is this: Make a scrap book with *leaves veneered or coated with gum stickum* of some kind; wet the page with sponge, brush, rag, or tongue, and dab on your scraps like postage stamps." He patented the scrapbook the following year and arranged with Dan Slote for its manufacture and distribution, and it actually earned him some money, making it unique among the bewildering variety of devices that Sam and Orion, each fueling the other with high hopes, were constantly thinking up. Sam already owned one patent, "Improvement in Adjustable and Detachable Straps for Garments," and he eventually acquired a number of others, including one on a board game played with pegs and pins. During this period he encouraged Orion to push on with new inventions. (Even as late as 1893, by which time Sam was thoroughly disillusioned by his own failures as well as his brother's, he was assuring Orion there was a one thousand per cent profit to be made marketing a private and infallible concoction of plain kerosene and cheap perfume under the trademark "Swift Death to Chilblains.") He proposed a railroad steam brake, only to be told by Orion that someone—named George Westinghouse—had already discarded it. He proposed a steamboat paddle wheel suitable for icy waters; he proposed some novel kind of knife. Orion, who pursued these phantoms on Bliss's time and who was already working on the grand scheme of his lifetime, a flying machine, was most

of all interested in a device that had come out of his own brain: a perfo-
rated wooden block of mountain ash to serve as a guide for gimlets and
drills. Orion was also working on a considerably more complicated project.
"My machine is creeping along," he had written to Mollie in October
1871. She was in Elmira getting hydrotherapy for an "inflamed womb,"
and she was probably glad to be that far away from the nightmare Orion
described for her:

> The clockmaker has made about 3,000 links for my chains, and has
> about 2,000 more to make. About 800 connecting parts have to be
> turned; and I suppose they have not been commenced. They were
> ordered at Bristol. I have to get them before the cogwheels intended
> for the chain can be made. While waiting on these things I am fixing
> over the pulleys, putting them on brass plates, temporarily, instead of
> wood, experimentally.

Nothing more was heard about this machine, a project of the sort that Sam
would later deride—but not before its blood brother, James W. Paige's
mechanical typesetter, had driven him into bankruptcy. During the summer of 1872, however, having more than a touch of the same fever Orion
had, Sam was full of hope and encouragement.

As for his next book, his planning was casual enough. "Shall spend the
fall and winter in England or in Florida or Cuba," he told Redpath in mid-
July. A few weeks later he decided to write the book about England, to go
there alone at the end of the summer and spend a few months taking notes.
Livy was so certain that England would inspire him that she easily resigned
herself to the separation. "I am contented to have him away," she told
Mary Fairbanks, "because I think it is just the work that he should be at
now." (It would also be for the better, she might have added, if Sam and
Orion had three thousand miles of ocean between them for a while.) On
August 21 Clemens sailed from New York for Liverpool on the *Scotia*.
Eight days later, off the coast of Ireland and nearing his destination, he
sent her an exuberant greeting: "I am standing high on the stern of the
ship, looking westward, with my hands to my mouth, trumpet fashion,
yelling across the tossing waste of waves, 'I LOVE YOU, LIVY DARLING!!!' "

IV

In all probability the most celebrated if not equally admired Americans in
England in the fall of 1872 were Henry M. Stanley and Mark Twain. Five
years earlier their paths had crossed in St. Louis. Now Stanley was back
from his journey through Zanzibar and Tanganyika, and although he was

soon to be acclaimed as the great explorer of his era he was at first the target of an extraordinary campaign of vilification. He was abused as an impostor, not an American at all but the bastard son of a poor Welsh farmer. His claim that he had found Livingstone was denounced as a lie, and the letters and journals of Livingstone that he had brought back with him were called forgeries. Eventually Livingstone's family validated the documents, Stanley's claims were accepted, and as sign and symbol of his rehabilitation Queen Victoria gave him her thanks and a gold snuffbox set with jewels. Years later, Stanley said that from the bitter bread he ate for a while in London in 1872 he could trace all his subsequent thoughts and actions.

For Mark Twain too his encounter with the English was of critical importance. Stanley's experience was of martyrdom vindicated, Mark Twain's of unalloyed triumph. Stanley was ostracized partly because he practiced what the English thought of as cheeky American journalism. Mark Twain was the hero of a vogue for American humor, a love feast which, after forty or fifty years of scorn for American culture, had begun with Lowell, Holmes, and Artemus Ward. Taste had turned to the American West; Mark Twain arrived not only as Artemus Ward's heir but as the ranking Western humorist and chronicler, and, like Whitman and Stephen Crane but to a much greater extent, he was accepted in England long before his probationary period in America had run out. Twelve volumes by or attributed to him were in print in England, and they barely satisfied the demand; half of these were cheap editions published by the enterprising pirate John Camden Hotten. Hotten's introduction to *Choice Humorous Works of Mark Twain* (1873) was one of the first biographical accounts in print, and through Hotten's piracies books by Mark Twain were made available to the English mass audience at a shilling or two a copy. Although Clemens did not get a cent from Hotten's huge circulation, he did benefit from the enormously extended reputation it gave him. Thus, while one of his secondary purposes in coming to England was to stop Hotten's piracies, he had to face up to the bitter paradox that he owed much of his standing in England to a man who not only stole from him but also took the insulting liberty of eking out little Mark Twain collections called *Eye-Openers* and *Screamers* with material by his own hand. "John Camden Hottentot," Clemens called him in a letter to the *Spectator* written soon after his arrival. "My books are bad enough just as they are written, then what must they be after Mr. John Camden Hotten has composed half a dozen chapters and added the same to them?"

Back home, he could hardly help thinking, the word "humorist" was fenced about with all sorts of restrictions. The man adored by the masses could be certain that the best he could expect from the custodians of official culture was cool tolerance. In England, despite all the class divisions he believed would make such rich material for satire, there seemed to be no class division in taste as far as humor was concerned. He was a hero of the mass audience, but he was also given almost every honor and hospitality short of the dread accolade of having to dine with the Queen. At a ceremonial dinner attended by "the brains of London" he heard the name Mark Twain greeted with an ovation so loud and enthusiastic that the introductions came to an end. The Sheriff of London, in robes of office, gave him a speech of welcome that was "the longest and most extravagantly complimentary" of the evening. "I thought I was the humblest in that great titled assemblage," he told Livy. "I did not know I was a lion."

The lion had not been in England a month before he discovered that every door was open to him, that he was welcomed everywhere, "just the same as if I were a Prodigal Son getting back home again." Charles Reade and Canon Charles Kingsley came to call on him; George Dolby, who had managed Dickens, urged him to lecture. He went to a stag hunt and dined with a direct descendant of the Plantagenet kings—"Why it had all the seeming of hob-nobbing with the Black Prince in the flesh!" At the Lord Mayor's banquet, the Chancellor of England, wigged, gowned, and followed by a lackey who bore his sword and held his train, walked arm in arm with Mr. Clemens and told him how much he admired his work, how often he read it. "He always has my books at hand," Clemens noted. "And it was pleasant in such an illustrious assemblage to overhear people talking about me at every step, and always complimentarily," he wrote to Livy at midnight from the Langham Hotel, "and also to have these grandees come up and introduce themselves and apologize for it." He did not get tired of reciting these triumphs and celebrations, so panoplied and full of medieval pageantry and yet so American in their enthusiasm and spontaneity, so different from the rejections of Dr. Josiah Gilbert Holland and from the cool and standoffish friendship, deliberately English in style, of the Boston illuminates.

He paid back his welcome in kind. "I would rather live in England than America—which is treason," he confessed to Livy. And he went about his visiting and sightseeing—to Westminster Abbey and St. Paul's, Stratford and Oxford—in a love trance, humble, as eager to learn as any of the guidebook tourists he had once made fun of, dutifully reminding himself as much as Livy that the *a* in "Avon" is pronounced like the *a* in "Kate" and that the second *w* in "Warwick" is silent. "Rural England is too absolutely beautiful to be left out of doors," he exclaimed, "ought to be under a glass case."

Even before he left for home in November, after a little over two months, he had given up his plan to write a satirical book about the English. He had been too busy going to banquets, making speeches, and having a good time to collect his material: this was the explanation he gave, but beneath it lay the simple fact that he adored the English too much to satirize them. The skepticism and indignation that had sparked the humor of *The Innocents Abroad* were gone; now he felt them only toward his own country. He joked about the English in a genial way. "The finest monument in the world erected to glorify—the *Commonplace*," he said of the Albert Memorial. "It is the most genuinely humorous idea I have met with in this grave land." In a speech at the Savage Club, which he later revised for publication, he made a further comment about it which some of the Americans present preferred to believe was a mere slip of the tongue: "I admired that magnificent monument which will stand in all its beauty when the name it bears has crumbled into dust." As for the local practice of measuring distances by cab fares: "I suppose if I were to ask a Londoner how far it is from the sublime to the ridiculous, he would try to express it in coin."

Clemens had gone to Europe and the Holy Land on the *Quaker City* a representative democrat certain of the moral and material superiority of the American present to the historical past, of the New World to the Old. In the five years since, his attitude had become more troubled, less simplistic, an index of his growing bewilderment by America in the Gilded Age. The English made a lion of him partly because he epitomized certain exotic qualities which they considered distinctly American and distinctly Western. He in turn adored the English because their way of life offered him for the first time a baseline by which he could measure his discontent with his own country, and instead of a satire on the English he wrote *The Gilded Age*, an angry and reactionary book about Americans. He was fond of remembering Hannibal as "a little democracy" which also had an "aristocratic taint" which kept class lines clearly drawn. In England his appetite for a romantic past coupled with an orderly and dignified present was roused and satisfied. He saw about him stability, government by a responsible elite, the acceptance of a gentleman's code. These were painful contrasts with the chicanery and cynicism, the demoralized civil service, the abuse of universal suffrage and legislative power, and all the excesses and failures of American society in the 1870s going through the most dynamic but least governable phase of its growth.

Eventually his Anglomania, as Howells called it, would cool, and its obverse, his disgust with American democracy, would be moderated. In 1886, when he was writing *A Connecticut Yankee*, he was to welcome Henry Stanley to Boston with a tribute to his "indestructible Americanism." "In this day and age," he said, "when it is the custom to ape and imitate English methods and fashions, it is like a breath of fresh air to stand in the presence of this untainted American citizen," and he concluded, "He is a product of institutions which exist in no other country on earth—institutions that bring out all that is best and most heroic in a man." But in Octo-

ber 1872 he saw Stanley in quite another light. The campaign of vilification was over, Stanley was a popular hero, the mood of the Establishment
was one of apology and reparation. At a dinner given by the Royal Geographical Society to make amends, Clemens was offended by Stanley's
bitterness. Instead of burying the hatchet and accepting the apologies and
the honors, Stanley, for months a pariah, was still angry and resentful, and
he flung out taunts at his hosts. Clemens' psychological stance and vocabulary sum up the extent of his commitment to the English code and the
rapidity of his transition from rough diamond to squire. The worst of it,
he told Livy, was that Stanley was not a gentleman. He was a "puppy,"
a "spaniel," a monster of ingratitude and meanness of spirit. And Clemens
was glad after all that Stanley was not really an American, having been
born in Wales, "though indeed he *must* have learned his puppyism with
us."

CHAPTER EIGHT

"Era of incredible rottenness"

I

CLEMENS' STORM-TOSSED VOYAGE home in November on the Cunarder *Batavia* only fed his Anglomania. The captain brought his ship about in a gale and sent off a volunteer lifeboat crew to pick up nine survivors of a dismasted bark. "It was worth any money to see that lifeboat climb those dizzy mountains of water, in a driving mist of spume-flakes, and fight its way inch by inch in the teeth of the gale," Clemens wrote soon after landing. "Just the mere memory of it stirs a body so, that I would swing my hat and disgorge a cheer now, if I could do so without waking the baby." And two months later, learning that the men had been rewarded by both the Royal Humane Society and the steamship line, he again paid tribute, in a letter to the New York *Tribune*, to English valor, English generosity, English benevolence, English fair-dealing, and the Cunard Steamship Company.

The English could do no wrong then, it seemed, and as the United States began a second term under the permissive leadership of its greatest military hero, a better judge of horseflesh than of human character, it appeared to Clemens that the Americans could do nothing right. Grant's Vice-President, his private secretary, his brother-in-law, his Secretary of War, and his Secretary of the Treasury all had been or were soon to be implicated in the sort of crude jobbery and cynical abuse of office and influence that William M. Tweed practiced profitably in New York. And as the century dragged on toward a mock-heroic finale on San Juan Hill, other distinctive phenomena became clear: corporations and combinations emerged to stifle competition and swallow up the individual; the bribe became a convention of political life and the vote a commodity on sale; the economy relied on gaudily launched balloons of credit ballasted with only a brick or two of assets; there was misery and alienation in the cities; the cash nexus was supreme. "The people had *desired* money before this day," Clemens said oí Jay Gould in 1906, "but *he* taught them to fall down and worship it."

To be sure, a strong case can be made for a more tolerant account of the Gilded Age. There was corruption, but there was also exposure, venality but not apathy; protest and reform were in the air. The railroad wars wasted men and money, but the railroads were built. There were panics and uncertainties, but by the end of the century the country achieved industrial maturity, and its means of production were rationalized. The age had its monuments of garish although exuberant taste such as the Philadelphia City Hall, which carried gimcrackery about as far (and as high) as it could go, but the Roeblings built the Brooklyn Bridge, a structure of purity and aspiration seeming to leap out of its times, and men of such originality as H. H. Richardson, Thomas Eakins, and Albert Pinkham Ryder were contributing to what Lewis Mumford would call a "Buried Renaissance." A surprising number of periodicals of intellectual respectability if not incandescent excitement answered the needs of a rapidly growing audience. William James, C. S. Peirce, and Josiah Royce flourished; learned societies multiplied; the universities came of age. There were parvenus and vulgarians in places of power and influence, but they were there by virtue of a new social and economic mobility; a silent revolution had made every man a potential tycoon. And from the tycoons themselves, who had all the while insisted on the coincidence of private gain and public interest, began to flow endowments for the public good.

For Clemens at the time—and involved in his time—there appeared to be overwhelming evidence that democracy was a failure. Even Nook Farm was not immune to moral decay. No one appears to have been bothered by Henry Ward Beecher's public conduct in accepting a fee of a thousand dollars to endorse a truss or, on another occasion, in accepting fifteen thousand dollars' worth of stock from Jay Cooke in return for publishing favorable editorials in the *Christian Union* about the Northern Pacific. But while Clemens was still in England walking arm in arm with titled grandees, Victoria Woodhull—protégée of Commodore Vanderbilt, feminist, clairvoyant, and shill for a bottled "Elixir of Life"—published in her paper, *Woodhull and Claflin's Weekly*, a sensational account of an adulterous relationship between Beecher and Mrs. Theodore Tilton. Victoria and her sister, Tennessee Claflin, were jailed for publishing obscene matter, but the charge remained in the air for years and was never really settled to anybody's full satisfaction. At Nook Farm Henry's intimate conduct became a shibboleth. Isabella Hooker, the queen regnant of the suburban grove and, like her friend Victoria Woodhull, a feminist and spiritualist, announced her firm belief that Henry was guilty. (Two years later Henry paid her back by announcing his firm belief that she was insane and ought to be locked up.) Harriet Beecher Stowe and Mary Beecher Perkins took up Henry's defense, and the sisterly visiting back and forth between their houses and Isabella's house came to an end; they closed their doors to her. And soon after he rejoined Livy and Susy in Hartford the newest member of the once harmonious Nook Farm community took his stand in respect to its feared and haughty leader. "Sam says Livy shall not cross Mrs. Hooker's threshold," Orion's wife reported to Jane Clemens, "and if he talked to Mrs. H he will tell her in plain words the reason."

The entire squalid and drawn-out affair—"the Beecher horror," James Russell Lowell called it—became for Clemens symptomatic of his times, a nauseating way of summing up the contrast between his own country and the England he had just left and would soon rush back to. "The present era of incredible rottenness is not Democratic, it is not Republican, it is *national*," he told Orion a few years later. "This nation is not reflected in Charles Sumner, but in Henry Ward Beecher, Benjamin Butler, Whitelaw Reid, Wm. M. Tweed. *Politics* are not going to cure moral ulcers like these, nor the decaying body they fester upon." As the republic neared the centennial celebration of its birth, images of sickness and decay were everywhere. The patrician Lowell dreaded the "festering" daily tidings of "public scandal, private fraud"; from his study at Elmwood, the great house in Cambridge where he was born and where he would die, he could watch the sun setting over a long curve of the Charles, the marshes beyond, and "the Land of Broken Promise." Lowell wondered, when he was criticized for his bitterness, whether Lincoln's government of, by, and for the people had not become instead a "Kakistocracy," a government "for the benefit of knaves at the cost of fools." In Washington, where he derived from his clerk's job a subsistence that *Leaves of Grass* never gave him, Walt Whitman took stock of his times and his country. "The depravity of the business classes of our country," he wrote in 1871, "is not less than has been supposed, but infinitely greater." In the hazy background of *Democratic Vistas* he saw the ultimate vindication of brotherhood, but for him the foreground was dominated by "appalling dangers of universal suffrage" and more "hollowness of heart" than had ever existed. For Whitman both society and politics were "canker'd, crude, superstitious, and rotten." But neither Lowell nor Whitman—one to become ambassador to the Court of St. James's, the other to become the guru of Camden, New Jersey—was involved in the same direct and painful way as Mark Twain with the failures and excesses they deplored. They looked at the American scene as through a window, not a mirror.

Mark Twain's disgust with his times was partly the index of his involvement in them, and his disgust grew more bitter through the 1870s, the decade which was the core of what he called the Gilded Age. He could observe in himself the same wild speculative mania he saw all about him.

Pamela and Orion lived all their lives in the expectation that the Tennessee land would make their fortunes, but while Sam eventually refused to have anything to do with exploiting the land (beyond writing about it), he was always, as miner, inventor, promoter, investor, and publisher, involved with some scheme that promised millions. He loved money for its own sake and for the luxury it could buy—soon after coming back from England he bought a tract of land at Nook Farm, on Farmington Avenue, and set an architect and builders to work on his stately mansion—but at the same time he feared in himself the "hardness and cynicism" which he said "the lust for money" was bound to produce. He knew the politics of the Gilded Age at first hand. "Was reporter in a legislature two sessions and the same in Congress one session," he wrote in 1890, "and thus learned to know personally three sample-bodies of the smallest minds and the selfishest souls and the cowardliest hearts that God makes." He loved the world of power and money: he was to be Grant's friend, admirer, and publisher; Andrew Carnegie was to send him barrels of whiskey from his cellars; Henry H. Rogers, a chief strategist of the Standard Oil trust, was to help him out of bankruptcy and become "the only man I would give a *damn* for." Such intimate involvements, both present and latent, with what also alarmed and disgusted him are part of the strength of the book he began to write early in 1873.

II

According to the account Clemens and his collaborator, Charles Dudley Warner, were soon circulating, *The Gilded Age* had its origin in one of those long evenings of food and talk with which the Nook Farm residents waited out the New England winter. The talk at dinner ran to contemporary novels; Clemens and Warner voiced their discontent; Livy and Susan Warner suggested that writing was better than criticizing; and so the two men accepted the challenge of writing a topical novel together.

There were certain parallels which, more than any deep personal afinity, accounted for their willingness to work together. Six years older than Clemens, Warner too had been a long time finding his vocation. He published a book when he was a little over twenty, spent two years in Missouri as a railroad surveyor, had a fling in business in Philadelphia, took a law degree and practiced in Chicago, and came to Hartford in 1860 as a newspaper editor. Like Clemens he was a civilian during the war, and, like Clemens again, he was making the transition from a career as editor to that of full-time man of letters. His reputation as an urbane and gentle if unexciting writer of essays and travel sketches was based on two books,

My Summer in a Garden (1871), which had an introduction by Henry Ward Beecher, and *Saunterings* (1872), a travel book about Europe. Like Clemens, he was also to write about his boyhood. Neither Clemens nor Warner had written a novel before, both were tentative about risking their reputations in a new form, and the most important thing they had in common, beyond their knowledge of Missouri and their skeptical outlook on American democracy, was their faith that by pooling their inexperience and anxieties they would accomplish something of greater literary value than anything either of them could do on his own. As it turned out, this faith survived the collaboration by only a few years. "This is going to be no slouch of a novel," Clemens said in April, when they were barely finished. But later he woke up to the fact that he and Warner worked together "in the superstition" that "we were writing one coherent yarn, when, I suppose, as a matter of fact, we were writing two *inco*-herent ones." In his old age he tended to grumble that it was Warner who had pressured him into the collaboration.

When the manuscript was finished they called on J. Hammond Trumbull, LL.D., L.H.D., reputedly the most learned man in Hartford, to supply them with chapter-head quotations in a vast number of tongues, including Sanskrit, Chinese, and Sioux Indian. This sort of ostentatious mystification (the appendix of translations was added in 1899 in order to prolong the copyright life of the book) corresponds to the whatnot gim-crackery and exotic junk freighting many a mantelpiece shelf; it was as if P. T. Barnum, the genius of nearby Bridgeport, had decided to exhibit a philologist in a cage. And it hardly requires a Henry James to see in more important aspects of the collaboration a certain commercial vulgarity amounting to a state of total anesthesia to the inner life of fiction.

Clemens had some elements of the story to begin with: the bitter-comic history of the Tennessee land, his knowledge of politics in Washington, the incurably hopeful and believing Orion (in the novel Washington Hawkins), and, above all, his mother's cousin, James Lampton, who became Colonel Sellers. Warner was to write a love story largely set in the twin worlds of Philadelphia Quakerism and Philadelphia commerce, and to follow the fortunes of two young men who go to Missouri and work as railroad surveyors. The story of Laura Hawkins, the *femme fatale* whose career as lobbyist in Washington is the framework for much of the political exposé, was worked out in collaboration.

With their main plots staked out, Clemens and Warner began working like tunnel crews boring from opposite sides of the mountain. Clemens wrote the first eleven chapters at white heat, coming to a temporary stop on page 399 of his manuscript with the note, "Now comes in Warner's first chapter." Through the rest of the book he contributed other blocks of chapters or single ones, paragraphs and sentences here and there, interpolated passages about corruption, the level of civic responsibility, and (from his own experience in Nevada and California) the intricacies of prospecting and mining. In general, as he liked to say, he contributed the fact and Warner the fiction.

Considering the differences in method and temperament, the collaboration was surprisingly flexible. "There is scarcely a chapter that does not bear the marks of the two writers of the book," the authors declared in their preface. Despite this united front Clemens in his copy of the first edition carefully identified his own work, even to the paragraph and sentence, and he was later to claim and receive from Warner all dramatic rights in the characters that were wholly his creation, chief among them being Colonel Sellers. Nor was he at all reluctant to supply his friends with a simplified version of the collaboration. "I think you don't like *The Gilded Age*," he wrote to Mary Fairbanks a few months after publication, "but that's because you've been reading *Warner's* chapters," and he listed the thirty-five of the book's sixty-three chapters that he claimed as his own either whole or in part. "You read *those!*"

Nearly every evening during the early months of 1873 Clemens and Warner met, read the day's work aloud to each other and their wives, and exchanged reactions. The ending of the story was settled by a kind of referendum in which Livy and Susie Warner, after some indecision, cast the determining votes. At first they were all for letting Laura Hawkins off easy, and they urged Warner to work out a chapter in which this acquitted murderer and schemer would somehow settle down to a peaceful marriage and simply disappear. Clemens' version of what he called "the 'boss' chapter" showed her trying a career as a lecturer. After a humiliating failure—she is hissed from the platform and followed down the street by an angry mob cursing and stoning her—she retreats to her hotel room and dies of a heart attack (Clemens may have been exorcising his own violently opposing feelings about lecturing).

This is the version that the authors and their wives settled upon. "My climax chapter is the one accepted by Livy and Susie," Clemens told Mary Fairbanks later that evening, "and so my heroine, Laura, remains dead." Livy and Susie were instrumental in setting their husbands to writing a novel in collaboration; they were involved with its composition throughout; they were clearly the final arbiters. All this puts into a different light the familiar claim that Livy and her circle exerted an influence on Mark Twain that was genteel to the point of emasculation. *The Gilded Age*, the first full-scale product of Mark Twain's Hartford years, is not hushed and polite literature, nor does it deal with any of the smiling aspects of American life.

The Gilded Age echoes the sounds of its times—the rustle of greenbacks and the hiss of steam, pigs grunting in the village mud, the clang of railroad iron and the boom of blasting charges, the quiet talk of men in committee rooms and bankers' offices. Its raw materials are disaster, poverty, blighted hopes, bribery, hypocrisy, seduction, betrayal, blackmail, murder, and mob violence. Written at a time when each day brought news of some revelation in the Beecher affair or the Crédit Mobilier investigation, its subject is democracy gone off the tracks.

In January 1873 a new scandal broke on an already hard-pressed Grant Administration. It supplied Clemens and Warner with their basic situation, and it set them to working six days a week to rush the book to completion. In the wisdom of his fifty-sixth year Clemens' Washington dinner companion, Senator Samuel C. Pomeroy, Radical Republican who had represented Kansas since 1861, had decided to seek a third term. Before a joint session of the state legislature in Topeka this tireless worker in the cause of temperance and the Sunday School was charged with having offered another politician eight thousand dollars for his nominating vote, and the charge was supported with evidence that was altogether damning. In two previous campaigns Pomeroy had been suspected of vote-buying. This time the convention refused to believe his story that the money was not a bribe but a loan to help a friend start a bank—Pomeroy even insisted that there was nothing unusual in making large and unreceipted loans in greenbacks from hotel rooms at midnight—and unanimously declined to support him for the nomination. To compound the scandal, Pomeroy, despite the weight of evidence against him, was later cleared by a select committee of the United States Senate who turned the hearings into an attack on his accusers. ("All being corrupt together," E. L. Godkin wrote in the *Nation* in May, "what is the use of investigating each other?") Pomeroy's Congressional biography notes merely that he was "an unsuccessful candidate for re-election." He subsided into private life, emerging briefly eleven years later as the Presidential nominee of the Prohibition party.

"Oh, I have gathered enough material for a whole book!" Clemens had written to Livy during his brief visit to Washington in 1870. "This is a perfect gold mine." With Pomeroy's downfall, he began to work the mine. Senator Abner Dilworthy of *The Gilded Age* was Pomeroy undisguised, unmistakable to contemporary readers; as Mark Twain informed them, there was "no law against making offensive remarks about U. S. Senators." The change of name was the merest bow to the conventions of fiction; Elisha Bliss's illustrators worked directly from pictures of the bearded and fatherly-looking Senator. Pomeroy-Dilworthy became a comic-corrupt archetype which Mark Twain jeered at all his life and which survives. "I think I can say, and say with pride, that we have some legislatures that bring higher prices than any in the world." (The late Earl K. Long of Louisiana once explained, "Huey used to buy the Legislature like a sack of potatoes. Hell, I never bought one in my life. I just rent 'em. It's cheaper that way.")

With equal directness the authors of *The Gilded Age* drew other characters from life and intended them to be recognizable. In Virginia City or San Francisco, Clemens may have known another Laura—Laura D. Fair, a widow-adventuress with a dazzling smile who in November 1870 boarded the ferry from Oakland to San Francisco, confronted her lover, a lawyer and politician named Crittenden, accused him of deserting her, and shot him to death in plain sight of his wife. Her trial for murder brought her national notoriety. She was acquitted and freed on the grounds that she had murdered Crittenden in a moment of "emotional insanity," a legal novelty that aroused Clemens' indignation (he very nearly dedicated *Roughing It* to Cain: "It was his misfortune to live in a dark age that knew not the beneficent insanity plea") and fed his considerable skepticism about the jury system.

Throughout the book there are other clear references, to Jim Fisk and Josie Mansfield, to Boss Tweed, to Representative Oakes Ames ("Mr. Fairoaks") and the Crédit Mobilier. Ironically, the authors ran into trouble from a totally unexpected quarter. Colonel Sellers was Clemens' distant cousin, James Lampton. "I merely put him on paper as he was," Clemens said in his autobiography. "He was not a person who could be exaggerated." Twenty years later George Washington Cable was introduced to Lampton at the Southern Hotel in St. Louis and was so fascinated by the precise correspondence of reality to fiction that he transcribed some of Lampton's conversation. It is pure Sellers: "I'll take you down to the edge of my pond surrounded by willows and—gold fish in it that long, Cousin Sam. And I've got—you know—I've got a brewery! Pipes leading to the house. Just turn on the fasset. Ah, ha, ha, ha!"

Lampton never minded his public existence as Colonel Eschol (later Beriah) Sellers. The trouble came from one George Escol Sellers of Bowlesville, Illinois, an inventor, speculator, and promoter whom Warner had heard about from a mutual friend and whose name he carelessly passed on to his collaborator. The real Sellers, warned by the mutual friend that his name appeared in the advertising prospectus for the book, made the long trip to seek redress in Hartford. He was placated by Warner's offer to have the name changed on the printing plates from Eschol to Beriah Sellers. Even so, a number of copies of the first edition carried the offending name, and several newspapers claimed that the Bowlesville Sellers was the model for the Colonel. For four or five years Clemens, Warner, and their publisher, Elisha Bliss of Hartford, lived with the threat of a lawsuit hanging over them.

The Clemens-Warner method of building a satirical story around real people and fresh social and political history showed not only a casual attitude toward the libel laws but also a casual attitude toward the power of fiction to digest an immense amount of raw topical material and still have the wholeness of fiction. The topical novel can collapse under the weight of its topics, and even the crudest inventory of *The Gilded Age* shows the high (or at least unexamined) expectations the authors had for their vehicle: frontier life before the war; the strategy and techniques of lobbying and bribery in Washington; the workings of Congress; universal suffrage; the jury system and the insanity plea; the politics of promoting a railroad; surveying; coal mining; land improvement schemes; the social structure of Washington, with particular attention to the parvenus; business, banking, and swindling in Philadelphia; the conflict of Quaker and marketplace morality; the emancipation of women; the Negro as a tool of the carpetbaggers; the credit foundation of society—"I wasn't worth a cent two years ago, and now I owe two millions of dollars" (or, as Billy Sol Estes was to explain, "If you get into anybody far enough you've got yourself a partner").

All of this was to be supported by two parallel plots—one group of characters goes East in search of wealth, the other West—embellished with romantic conventions, a trite and sentimental love story, and such melodramatic clichés as adopted foundlings, mysterious parentage, and fever crisis followed by an avowal of love. The book is awkwardly structured; there are any number of loose ends, inconsistencies, and improbabilities. Characters are mislaid. The chronology is shaky. Situations potentially rich in drama and symbol—Ruth Bolton, the Quaker medical student, uncovers on the dissecting table the corpse of a Negro—dissolve in sentimental rhetoric. Comedy and satire undermine each other. Beyond the plotting, there was the major difficulty of an incompatibility of style and scope. As a novelist Warner worked within the conventions, even if as a social critic he stood outside them and continued to write reform novels dealing with the abuse and misuse of wealth. These novels, Howells said, failed to use "experience imaginatively, structurally." Mark Twain, on the other hand, had barely tapped the springs of his endowment, but even in this first, faltering attempt at extended fiction he threatened established molds, carried realism farther than any other novel of his day, and began to discover the imaginative and structural use of what he had known, seen, and been.

"Up to the time old Hawkins dies your novel is of the greatest promise —I read it with joy," Howells wrote to Warner, "but after that it fails to assimilate the crude material with which it is fed, and becomes a confirmed dyspeptic at last." Howells' joy had ceased even before Warner's part of the story began, and he considerately offered not to comment on the book in print. Yet Howells, who was not alone in feeling that the book was a failure, was fascinated by the one character who transcends and in part redeems it, and he collaborated with Clemens on a play called *Colonel Sellers as a Scientist*. Ten years after *The Gilded Age* was published, he was encouraging Clemens in the notion that Colonel Sellers was "*the* American character," a type so representative that like the stock figures of the *commedia dell'arte* he could support any number of plots. This was not so extravagant a notion; then, as now, Sellers—"a living and distinctive type of real American and peculiarly American character," a New York *Tribune* editorial said—epitomized the aspiration, energy, optimism, and bombast of his country and his time.

Sellers is Southern gentry fallen on hard times after the war and willing to come to terms with the new men of power. He is courtly, hospitable, generous, and broke. He stands drinks in the best saloon in town, but his money is always in his other coat at home, where his family dines on turnips, cold water, and expectations. He is the mystic of the cash nexus, a visionary and spellbinder who can elevate traffic in mules, hogs, corn, and bottled eyewash to the level of Eldorado and Golconda. He is, above all, the Promoter, that distinctive profession of the Gilded Age. "I've got the biggest scheme on earth—and I'll take you in; I'll take in every friend I've got that's ever stood by me, for there's enough for all, and to spare": he spoke for his contemporaries, including Samuel L. Clemens, the promoter (and victim) of the Paige typesetter and a hundred other, less expensive chimeras. In 1897, when Clemens tried to answer the familiar European charge of American materialism, he was still so much in the grip of the Sellers passion that the best he could offer was only a half-truth: "I think that the reason we Americans seem to be so addicted to trying to get rich suddenly is merely because the *opportunity* to make promising efforts in that direction has offered itself with a frequency out of all proportion to the European experience."

In his autobiography Mark Twain looked back with love and almost in tears on James Lampton, the real Sellers, who dreamed magnificent dreams all his life and never saw any one of them come true. "A pathetic and beautiful spirit," he mourned, "a manly man, a straight and honorable man, a man with a big, foolish, unselfish heart in his bosom, a man born to be loved." And yet what gives *The Gilded Age* a degree of imaginative wholeness is the fact that this "straight and honorable man" is nonetheless completely at home with the corruptions of his time. "The Salt Lick Branch of the Pacific Railroad" that he exuberantly maps out on his tablecloth begins in St. Louis and advances by way of Slouchburg, Doodleville, and Hallelujah to its eastern terminus in Corruptionville ("after Congress itself," he explains). Soon he learns the price of pork-barrel delicacies like his railroad, the Columbus River Slack-Water Navigation Company, and the Eastern Knobs University for the Education of Negro Freedmen. In the House and the Senate it is ten thousand dollars apiece for the votes of a four-man committee majority plus another ten thousand for each of the chairmen; an ordinary Senator or representative with a high moral tone fetches three thousand dollars; and a small-fry country member goes for about five hundred dollars. Sellers goes to Washington and becomes something of an expert in the field of what is politely called lobbying.

Dilworthy is a Unionist who prospered because of the war; Sellers fought on the Confederate side and is now a poor man. But is that any reason, the authors ask, for Sellers to give Dilworthy the cold shoulder? Ultimately Dilworthy and Sellers need each other: they are two essential forces behind the horrors of Reconstruction. With varying degrees of cynicism, self-interest, and sanctimony, they are willing to work together on a grand plan which will simultaneously enrich them, tap the Federal treasury, and rehabilitate the Negro. "I'd elevate his soul, that's just it; you can't make his soul too immortal, but I wouldn't touch *him*, himself," Sellers tells Dilworthy. "Yes, sir! make his soul immortal, but don't disturb the niggro as he is." Abolitionist and slaveowner join in the common cause.

As much as Dilworthy, Sellers represents a social and political system that Mark Twain during the 1870s saw as rotten through and through, all the way from the witless citizens of Cattleville, who elect Dilworthy, to the marble halls of Congress which are adorned with the "delirium tremens" of art and where "addition, division, and silence" are daily practiced. In Mark Twain's vision of Gilded Age democracy there is no place for the romantic myth of the frontier. The villages are as corrupt and debased as the cities. In rude and tumbledown villages like Obedstown the shiftless inhabitants—"animals" and "cattle," Squire Hawkins calls them in Chapter One—live in ignorance, squalor, and somnolence; their occupations are whittling, spitting, and gossip. The citizens of New York picked to serve on the jury in Laura's trial are scarcely of a higher order: "Low foreheads and heavy faces they all had; some had a look of animal cunning, while the most were only stupid." Whatever their differences, Mark Twain and Warner shared the same acute skepticism (if not the same degree of misanthropy) over American democracy, and they derided and rejected its basic institutions—representative government, the vote, the jury system. In a much more disturbing way than Henry Adams' *Democracy*, a fastidious view of politics and society, or John Hay's *The Bread-Winners*, a conservative's fantasy about anarchism and organized labor, *The Gilded Age*, for all of Sellers' caperings and charades, is a novel of reaction and despair. Even the naïvest of its characters, Washington Hawkins, finally experiences the shock of futility: "The country is a fool."

Early in March 1873, more than a month before the manuscript was completed, Clemens assured Elisha Bliss that if Thomas Nast illustrated the book they would have free advertising "from Maine to the Marquesas." In the same blue-sky spirit he cautioned Bliss to remain absolutely silent; Clemens wanted to buy more stock in the publishing house before, as he was certain, the news would drive the shares up. No more was heard of the Nast scheme. Bliss employed a conventional stable of illustrators, and among other disappointments the book brought was Clemens' feeling that it was "rubbishy looking." As for keeping the book a secret, when the time for publicity came, the right kind of publicity was hard enough to find. At the end of March, counting on their friendships with both Whitelaw Reid and John Hay, Clemens and Warner began a strenuous campaign to get an advance review in the *Tribune*. Clemens was willing to forget his anger at the paper for having got an incompetent and humorless "old stick" to review *Roughing It* as "one of the most racy specimens of Mark Twain's savory pleasantries." At first they were jocular and bluff, strong in the faith that out of friendship Reid would ask Hay to puff the book. "I have a nice putrid anecdote that Hay will like," Clemens wrote to Reid. "Am preserving it in alcohol—in my person." Then the tone became reproachful: "You could have given us a splendid sendoff and not stepped outside the proprieties in any way." And finally Clemens wrote an epitaph over his relationship with Whitelaw Reid, after the paper had run what was at best a grudging bit of advance publicity. "He is a contemptible cur, and I want nothing more to do with him," Clemens told Warner in May. "I don't want the *Tribune* to have the book at all." By this time Clemens was in mid-Atlantic, on his way to England to arrange with the Routledges to publish the book in December 1873, simultaneously with the American edition.

Beyond a reference in his prospectus to "prominent persons and things," Bliss scarcely mentioned the topical content or the drift of the book. He emphasized instead the novelty of two prominent authors working together. As a vendor of entertaining and edifying books he was bound to fear that *The Gilded Age* carried satire too far, and many reviewers thought so, too, found the book more uncomfortable than a literary curiosity ought to be, and attacked it for presenting the country in an unfavorable light. "We should blush to see the book republished in Europe," the *Independent* said. Bliss's emphasis on the novelty of the collaboration also exposed the book to a number of damaging charges: that it was "a gigantic practical joke," that it was all Warner's work and the name Mark Twain on the title page was a cheap merchandising trick, and, worse, that all the writing had been done by a hack journalist hired by the supposed authors. Even so the book started off like a best seller: about thirty-five thousand copies were sold in the first two months. In March, however, the rate of sale fell off abruptly; during the remaining ten months of its first year in print only about fifteen thousand more were sold; and during the next five years only about six thousand. By Clemens' standards *The Gilded Age*—"the best-written and best-abused book of the age," he said to Orion —was a commercial failure.

"But for the Panic our sale would have doubled, I verily believe," he said in February 1874. He spoke out of the bitter knowledge of one of the panic's victims, for when the banking house of Jay Cooke and Company collapsed in September 1873 some of his own money, and Livy's, went down with it; the Langdon coal interests were hit hard, and Livy's income dwindled. One night in London after he heard the news of Cooke's failure, he sat up late smoking, hating himself for his stupidity in having banked with Cooke, and now facing the prospect of having to borrow from the Routledges in order to get his family home. If, as the *Nation* said, the panic was brought on partly because English investors had been frightened and disillusioned by "repeated cases of American rascality," then, in an ironically prophetic way, *The Gilded Age* was the cause of its own failure and Clemens' financial embarrassments. Eventually he recouped some of his losses. His loose dramatization of the book as a stage vehicle for the comic actor John T. Raymond as Colonel Sellers became one of the more profitable plays of the 1870s. Just this once the Tennessee land paid off. Clemens figured that in three years his combined royalties from the book and the play came to $100,000—"just about a dollar an acre."

The Gilded Age fed Clemens' anger at American democracy instead of exorcising it, and obsessively he continued his invective against universal suffrage and the jury system. He read a paper about universal suffrage to the Monday Evening Club in February 1875, and in an unsigned article, "The Curious Republic of Gondour," published in the *Atlantic* that October he proposed his solution to the problem of democracy: turn it into an aristocracy; instead of constricting the vote, which would be unconstitutional, why not expand it by rewarding men of education, property, and achievement with five or even ten votes each? Annie Fields, who with her husband paid the Clemenses a visit in April 1876, enjoyed the songs of the blackbirds in the trees surrounding his new house, but she was also exposed to a monologue that began at lunch and was resumed at dinner. Drinking beer to soothe his nerves—it seemed to her that this was about the only nourishment he took—he told her he had lost all faith in the government and wanted to see it overthrown. He inveighed against "this wicked, ungodly suffrage," she reported, "where the vote of a man who knew nothing was as good as the vote of a man of education and industry; this endeavor to equalize what God has made unequal was a wrong and a shame." At dinner he summed it up: "He is overwhelmed with shame and confusion and wishes he were not an American," Annie Fields noted.

She hoped that if he did carry out his announced plan to move to England for a while, perhaps he might "discover away from home a love of his country which is still waiting to be unfolded." And if Annie Fields was dismayed by his bitterness, what must twenty-one-year-old Mollie Fairbanks have thought when her mother's old friend, that charming, amusing, and famous man, declared to her his hatred for "all shades and forms of republican government"? He explained his reason for his tirade: "Tell your mother I am trying to do what every good citizen ought to do—trying my best to win you and the rest of the rising generation over to an honest and saving loathing for universal suffrage."

Slowly his monomania subsided. In September 1879 he was to return to America homesick after a year and a half abroad. He was also to return to the hurly-burly of politics: he became one of the favorite orators of the Republican party, campaigned for Garfield and later, as a prominent mugwump, he supported Grover Cleveland. He rejoiced that the labor movement would give the oppressed of the earth a power greater than that of any monarchy or aristocracy. In *A Connecticut Yankee*, his Anglomania now far behind him, he declared that there was "plenty good enough material for a republic in the most degraded people that ever existed," even though, at the end of the book, it has become impossible for the Yankee to impose a "new deal" on "human muck." By 1889 he was explaining to the English critic Andrew Lang that as a writer he identified himself not with "the thin top crust of humanity" but with "the mighty mass of the uncultivated," and in terms of his enduring reputation he became symbol and spokesman of the free society he once detested.

However short-lived, this fever crisis of political and social reaction still shaped the course of Mark Twain's work. "What could have sent you groping among the driftwood of the Deluge for a topic," Joe Goodman asked, astonished by the remoteness of *The Prince and the Pauper*, "when you could have been so much more at home in the wash of today?" The answer is that *The Gilded Age* had presented to him the truth that he could treat "the wash of today" only as a satirist. As his anger and disgust grew more intense satire itself became impossible. He had to find another medium flexible enough to accommodate indignation and entertainment. "A man can't write successful satire unless he be in a calm judicial good humor," he remarked to Howells in 1879 apropos of Old Masters and Wagnerian opera. "I don't ever seem to be in a good enough humor with ANYthing to *satirize* it; no, I want to stand up before it and curse it, and foam at the mouth—or take a club and pound it to rags and pulp." His recognition that he could not write sustained imaginative literature about the American—or European—present turned him to the past.

The Gilded Age was subtitled "A Tale of To-Day." Writing sustained fiction for the first time, Mark Twain found a matrix for the materials of his past: the Tennessee land, steamboating on the Mississippi, his father and Orion, village life. All of his major books were to be tales of yesterday. The next project he undertook after *The Gilded Age* was a series of articles about piloting, called "Old Times on the Mississippi," and through the rest of his career as a writer he turned further and further back into yesterdays: to the South before the war and to the South of his boyhood and adolescence, to the England of the Plantagenets and of Merlin the Wizard, to the France of Joan of Arc, to Germany in the Middle Ages, to fantasy stories in which the distinctions between past and present are blurred in nightmare. To a certain extent he became an expatriate from his own country: between August 1872, when he made his first trip to England, and July 1907, when he made his last, he spent more than eleven years abroad. To a much greater extent, however, he became an expatriate from his own times.

And in other ways *The Gilded Age* was the antecedent of *Tom Sawyer, Huckleberry Finn, The Mysterious Stranger*—a beginning, not a dead end. Obedstown and Hawkeye represent the scenes of Mark Twain's recollection that were to be the stage and setting for his imagination. These raw settlements, depicted with a precise and savage realism, are Jamestown, Tennessee, where John Marshall Clemens thrived for a while and bought the land that pressed so heavily on his heirs; Florida, Missouri, where the bankrupt Clemens moved in the hope of brighter fortune and where his famous son was born; Hannibal. In Mark Twain's fiction, and in the first part of *Life on the Mississippi*, these towns mirror the possibilities of the human condition. They are St. Petersburg, the "drowsing" setting for an idyl of boyhood; but on the streets of such towns Boggs is shot down in cold anger and the lynch mob gathers; in the surrounding forests the boys play at Robin Hood, and the Shepherdsons and the Grangerfords carry on their blood feud. As Mark Twain grew older the archetypal town enclosed his darkest vision of the race—Dawson's Landing in *Pudd'nhead Wilson*, Eseldorf in *The Mysterious Stranger*. But in the long run the upright and honest citizens of Hadleyburg are not so very different from the "animals" of Obedstown and Cattleville. Mark Twain's pessimism was a generalizing of his despair about democracy. This pessimism, as it became a powerful leveling principle which obliterated the difference between high and low, educated and ignorant, honest and corrupt, became also, by the way of paradox, a somber and cautious affirmation of democracy itself.

III

A month before Clemens went back to England in May 1873, he received from the editor of the New York *Daily Graphic* a request "for a farewell letter in the name of the American people." In his answer, which included a substantial plug for *The Gilded Age*, he explained that what was driving him abroad was merely a hunger for excitement. His morning paper brought him only news of such torpid events as riots, feuds, patricides, lynchings, massacres, and disasters. "Well, I said to myself, this is getting pretty dull; this is getting pretty dry; there don't appear to be anything going on anywhere; has this progressive nation gone to sleep?" And as for a farewell: "Bless you, the joy of the American people is just a little premature; I haven't gone yet. And what is more, I am not going to *stay*, when I *do* go."

His return to England was pure triumph. This time he could share it with Livy. In London he was sought out by Browning and Turgenev, Herbert Spencer, Anthony Trollope, Willkie Collins. Lewis Carroll—"the shyest full-grown man, except Uncle Remus, I ever met"—sat in nearly complete silence while Clemens talked; Alfred Tennyson longed to hear him lecture. "In England rank, fashion, and culture rejoiced in him. Lord mayors, lord chief justices, and magnates of many kinds were his hosts; he was desired in country houses, and his bold genius captivated the favor of periodicals which spurned the rest of our nation," Howells wrote years later, adding significantly, "But in his own country it was different." The last tatters of his plan to write a book about England were blown away in the immense ovation. He and Livy were so caught up in English social life, he told Mary Fairbanks, that they had hardly any time to see the sights of London. Eventually the pace turned out to be too intense. They went to Scotland, where Livy fell ill, and then to Ireland.

In October Clemens was lecturing in London and Liverpool to enormous and fashionable audiences; his subject was the Sandwich Islands. The English could not have enough of him, it seemed; Americans too, like P. T. Barnum, were flocking to his lectures. But Livy was homesick and tired, pregnant once again. He resolved the conflict by taking her and Susy back home late in October and then returning alone to England for a three-month lecture season. At the Langham Hotel in London, he began to feel the first pangs of separation; he had only the *Times*, a breakfast of bacon, toast, and poached eggs, and the distant sight of the Horse Guards on Portland Place to distract him. Soon enough, as a dreadful fog continued evening after evening, so thick that it trailed into the lecture hall, dimmed the gaslights, and muffled hilarity, his loneliness became intense. "If I'm not homesick to see you, no other lover ever *was* homesick," he wrote to Livy early in December, and he added a private idiom of impatience: "And when I get there, remember, Expedition's the word!" Publicly he tolerated no latitude about her. "In Salisbury," he told her, "when a gentleman remarked upon my taking the trouble to telegraph a Merry Christmas to my *wife*, saying it was the sort of thing to do with a *sweetheart*, I dosed him up very promptly, and said I did not allow any man to refer to my wife jestingly." At the beginning of January 1874, a little over a week before he sailed for home, he sketched for her a domestic scene which was a far cry from the ideals of Elmira, New York. "I want you to be sure and remember to have in the bathroom, when I arrive, a bottle of Scotch whisky, a lemon, some crushed sugar, and a bottle of Angostura bitters." In London, he told her, he had formed the habit of drinking these medicine-cabinet Old Fashioneds before breakfast, dinner, and bed, and he attributed to them the fact that his digestion was "wonderful—simply *perfect* . . . regular as a clock." "I love to picture myself ringing the bell at midnight—then a pause of a second or two—then the turning of the bolt, and 'Who is it?'—then ever so many kisses—then you and I in the bathroom, I drinking my cocktail and undressing, and you standing by—then to bed—and everything happy and jolly as it should be."

To keep him company until that midnight came he hired the poet, essayist, and rolling stone from San Francisco, Charles Warren Stoddard. They breakfasted on chops at twelve-thirty and went for long walks in the afternoon. Evenings before dinner Clemens sat at the piano and sang the Negro jubilees he had first heard as a boy, which never failed to move him. At eight o'clock he appeared on stage, moving close to the footlights to warm his toes and, in Stoddard's description, "rubbing his hands in the manner of Lady Macbeth and bowing repeatedly"—all part of the lounging informality, the mock-solemn manner, the quiet, droning monotone which captivated English critics and audiences. After the lecture the two Americans returned to their rooms to smoke, sit by the fire, drink whiskey cocktails, and talk until two or three in the morning about the trial of the Tichborne Claimant (which so fascinated Clemens that he put Stoddard to work pasting up newspaper clippings which eventually filled six large scrapbooks), about shared days in San Francisco, and about Hannibal and the river. "I could have written his biography at the end of the season," Stoddard said.

On his last night in Liverpool, despite the closeness of the long-awaited reunion with Livy, and despite his triumphs as lecturer and literary celebrity in England, Clemens was far from elated. As he talked to Stoddard his voice was lower than usual, pitched in a minor key. "He sank into a sea of forebodings," as if he felt that in returning to his own country he was leaving the best of times behind him. Looking at Stoddard from beneath his plumed eyebrows, and in a solemn voice, he recited, "Remember now thy Creator in the days of thy youth."

CHAPTER NINE

"Busiest white man in America"

I

ON a bright winter day in March 1874, Howells, Thomas Bailey Aldrich and his wife, and James R. Osgood started out on a visit to Nook Farm. They took the morning train from Boston to Springfield. In a characteristic gesture of Nook Farm hospitality, Clemens and Charles Dudley Warner, their hosts, met them there and rode with them the rest of the way to Hartford. At the Hartford station they found waiting the Clemens carriage, driven by a liveried coachman and the Clemens butler as footman. This equipage was one of many evidences of an almost magical prosperity that these visitors, accustomed to a more frugal tradition, observed with wonderment during two days and nights at Nook Farm. They drove past the site on Farmington Avenue where Clemens' new house was going up. At dinner at the Warners' the first night the heavy scent of flowers in the conservatory and the plash of a fountain surrounded by lilies seemed to transform winter into summer.

While the Aldriches were dressing for breakfast the next morning Clemens rapped on their door and, in a voice lacking in its usual gentleness, said, "Aldrich, come out. I want to speak to you." Lilian Aldrich, wrapped in her kimono, put her ear to the door and listened in horror as Clemens complained about the noises they had made in their bedroom. "Our bedroom is directly under yours, and poor Livy and her headache . . ." (Livy's delicate health was well known; she was also entering her sixth month of pregnancy.) "Do try to move more quietly, though Livy would rather suffer than have you give up your game on her account." Battered and subdued, the Aldrich couple crept timidly downstairs, where they found Livy pouring coffee from a silver urn. "I have no headache," she explained with some puzzlement after they had apologized. And as for those disgraceful noises, "We have not heard a sound. If you had shouted we should not have known it, for our rooms are in another wing of the house." "Come to your breakfast, Aldrich, and don't talk all day," Clemens broke in, and then, in an equally bewildering turnabout, he pronounced grace, having already, to his satisfaction, begun to pay back Mrs. Aldrich for that evening in Boston. Later on, in December, as part of his implicit warfare of egos with Aldrich himself, he answered Aldrich's request for a photograph by sending him one each day for two weeks; on New Year's Day Aldrich's mail included twenty photographs of Mark Twain in separate envelopes.

Their last night in Hartford, the Aldriches and the other Boston visitors saw another aspect of their extraordinary host. After dinner, with a log fire blazing in the red-curtained drawing room, he sang "Swing Low, Sweet Chariot," "Golden Slippers," "Go Down, Moses" (he sang them in Florence, thirty years later, the night Livy died). He swayed gently as he stood; his voice was low and soft, a whisper of wind in the trees; his eyes were closed, and he smiled strangely. Through the sadness and exultation of these songs which he had known since boyhood, he transported himself far from the circle of polite letters and from the New England snowscape, and he found it difficult to come back. He wanted to go for a walk. They had run out of ale, and though he could call on the servants to run errands for him, he put on his winter costume of sealskin cap and sealskin coat and low evening slippers and left for the village. (In present-day Hartford he could have bought his ale by walking a few blocks down Farmington Avenue to the Mark Twain Package Store.) He tried the whiskey at the saloon where he bought the ale. He came back excited, hilarious, distinctly overheated. His feet were wet, and somewhere along the route he had thrown away his sealskin cap. This time the butler was sent out to look for it, while Clemens changed from his evening slippers into something considerably odder for Hartford, white cowskin moccasins with the hair on the outside. And, in a crowning act of confident alienation from his guests, he twisted his body into the likeness of a crippled uncle or a Negro at a hoedown and danced strange dances for them. Howells always remembered that evening, the joy and disoriented surprise of the guests, Livy's first reaction of dismay and "her low, despairing cry of, 'Oh, Youth!' "

"The vividest impression which Clemens gave us two ravenous young Boston authors," Howells said, "was of the satisfying, the surfeiting nature of subscription publishing." He described for them the army of agents that was busy selling his books by the thousands all over the country. "It sells right along just like the Bible," he said about *The Innocents Abroad,* and he lectured them on the folly of publishing books the way Boston was accustomed to publishing books: "Anything but subscription publication is printing for private circulation." He tried to talk them into a three-man collaboration that would earn them all, he said, a fortune in the subscription market. And in the weeks after, he kept up his barrage, offered to negotiate contracts for them with Elisha Bliss, urged them to buy and settle at Nook Farm. "You can do your work just as well here as in Cambridge, can't you?" By the end of the visit Howells had been so infected by Clemens' visions of opulence that he found it difficult to follow his usual thrifty practice of walking in order to save carfare.

II

"I am the busiest white man in America—and much the happiest," Clemens had written to Mary Fairbanks two weeks before that visit; he told her that he was writing "two admirable books," had finished one five-act play (which had only a single visible character on stage) and was planning another, and was also preparing "several volumes of my sketches" and writing new material for them. That summer he dramatized *The Gilded Age* and saw it successfully produced in New York. Within the next two years he finished *Tom Sawyer* and began *Huckleberry Finn*, became a regular contributor to the *Atlantic*, and published in the magazine a seven-part series which was to be the heart of *Life on the Mississippi*. In 1875 he brought out a collection of sketches which included "The Jumping Frog" in English, French, and retranslated English, and in 1877 he made the first notes for *The Prince and the Pauper*. The exuberant variety of his energies and interests during the most productive years of his life seemed also to reflect his country and his times. He was humorist, novelist, short-story writer, social historian, dramatist, journalist, occasional lecturer and frequent dinner speaker, inventor, entrepreneur, all-night raconteur and billiard player, lavish host, devoted family man.

He was also, as his enterprises multiplied, more and more subject to fits of litigation. Within two months alone in 1874 he sued or thought of suing: a dramatist named Gilbert B. Densmore for putting on in San Francisco an unauthorized version of *The Gilded Age* (Densmore, as it turned out, did him a service by proving the stage possibilities of the book); some "swindler" in Dubuque; and the New York *Post* because they said he had paid for a complimentary dinner in his own honor, and this was libel. His feeling that newspapers in general, and Reid's *Tribune* in particular, passed up no opportunity to make him look like a fool was well on its way to becoming an obsession. "Everything goes wrong and I'm in a never-ending state of harassment," he complained to Orion in May 1874, and although he said that everybody was getting a touch of his venom these days, it was Orion who was his main target. After informing Sam that Bliss had cheated him on *Roughing It*, Orion had come to an angry parting of the ways with

his employer in March 1872. Orion and Mollie were back in Keokuk, trying to raise chickens on a farm Sam had bought for them. Instead of ideas
for new inventions Orion was now getting from Sam angry sermons that
Sam might just as well have addressed to himself. "You *are* aging and it is
high time to give over dreaming and buckle down to the simplicities *and*
the realities of life," he scolded Orion, and he told him to live and buy
cheaply, to "banish the American sham of 'Keeping up appearances.'"
"Nobody can dress as Mollie does and look like anything but a fool, on a
chicken farm." But, Sam concluded, there was no point to encouraging
Orion in anything: as a writer he was getting worse and worse (all the
same, Sam had told him to write his autobiography and to ghost-write a
book for Captain Wakeman); as a lawyer he would probably exercise the
judgment of a child of ten; and as a minister he would change his religion
too fast to make sense to anybody.

The decisive pressure on Orion, who was nearly fifty, came from his
seventy-one-year-old mother. Jane Clemens reminded him that an oath she
had once extracted from Sam not to play cards or drink whiskey on the
river had turned out to be the saving of Sam. Writing in a faltering hand
from Fredonia at the end of 1873, she now demanded a solemn oath from
Orion:

> This oath is that you will not let one single word come from your
> mouth or even one thought come in your mind about an invention of
> any kind. My dear son promise this to your aged mother this may be
> my last request my dear son don't make any excuse. . . . Sam give his
> whole attion to his book writing and managemen. But the secret with
> you is Orion is you work with your pen but your mind is not on it . . .
> your mind for years has been on nothing but the invention [his flying
> machine].

On the envelope Orion noted, "Mother wants me to swear against invention." Years later, after Orion's death, when the letter came into Sam's
hands, he too noted, "Orion's mother urges Orion to swear off inventing
and"—a final, interpolated irony—"devote his whole time to writing."
Orion complained that he was being bullied out of his flying machine.
When he did give it up and accept his mother's demands, even Sam was
sad: "I grieve over the laying aside of the flying machine as if it were my
own broken idol."

Sam's signature on the pledge would have been just as good as Orion's.
During the 1870s his entrepreneurial and other nonliterary activities took
on an increasing pace, and, at the same time that he was encouraging Orion
to buckle down to the simplicities, his own scale of living was committing
him to expenditures which after a while he found "something almost
ghastly." Through Frank Fuller he became interested in a number of prof-

itless enterprises. He passed up two opportunities, one to place $300,000 worth of railroad bonds in Hartford (Fuller sold them instead to a consortium of "bloody Britishers"), the other to buy up the patent on a modified scheme of penny postage which Fuller was certain "would take like wild fire." But two vetoes were all Clemens was capable of. By 1877 Fuller had succeeded in getting him hopelessly involved with two inventions by an alcoholic bird of passage named Bowers: a "domestic still" for desalinating water and an improved steam generator for tugboats. Soon Clemens himself was supervising the work on a prototype machine at the Colt arms factory in Hartford. But something—a coil or a nipple or a crank—always went wrong, and Bowers went off on one lost weekend after another. Finally Bowers borrowed some money from his backers and disappeared, taking his schemes with him. But by this time, his principal victim remembered years later, "I had become an enthusiast on steam and I took some stock in a Hartford company which proposed to make and sell and revolutionize everything with a new kind of steam pulley. The steam pulley pulled thirty-two thousand dollars out of my pocket in sixteen months, then went to pieces, and I was alone in the world again, without an occupation."

In Baltimore in April 1877 Clemens was to have a prevision of the world of machinery out of which would come the Paige typesetter's eighteen thousand separate parts and the mechanisms with which the Connecticut Yankee destroyed feudal England. After being shown through Alexandroffsky, the semi-automated house of the millionaire railroad engineer Thomas De Kay Winans, Clemens rushed back to his room at Guy's Hotel on Monument Square and, in order to preserve every detail of "this wondrous establishment," wrote a thirty-two-page account for Livy. He described a dining table that revolved on a pivot; a glassed-in porch, seating two hundred people, that was heated by self-regulating machinery and lighted by one hundred gas lamps; andirons, invented by Winans, which prevented logs from rolling forward; a water-driven device for regulating heat and humidity in the house; a basement wilderness of water tanks, pipes, chains, weights, pulleys, springs, knobs, cranks, and trapdoors. The main saloon, where Captain Nemo of the *Nautilus* would have felt at home, contained two pipe organs run by water power; in another room, which was sixty feet high, Winans was building a really big organ with the aid of a machine he himself had invented to compute the relationship of length, pitch, and aperture in each of the mammoth organ pipes. In the quietest corner of his workshop Winans raised brook trout from eggs in a series of glass funnels. The central marvel was Winans' bedroom, which housed workbenches, tools, a steam engine, pipes and fittings, a scale that showed weight on a dial, and all sorts of "automatic deviltries." Above the owner's bed, hanging thick about his nose when he lay on his back, was a curtain of strings by which he regulated heat, humidity, ventilation, and various signaling devices. After a long hard day, when most of the marvelous machinery in the house was stilled and even the steam engine in the bedroom had gasped to a stop, Winans pulled a string which released a board on his door and uncovered the word "ASLEEP."

III

In April 1874, after an alarm of miscarriage, Clemens took Livy to Elmira, where, on June 8, in the Langdon house on Main Street, she gave birth to their second daughter, Clara, the only one of their children who would survive him. Soon afterward they moved to Quarry Farm, high above the city, and he settled down to a summer of work. A hundred yards from the farmhouse, his sister-in-law Susan Crane had built a study for him, a single octagonal room with six large windows, a little one cut through the chimney above the mantelpiece, and a wide door facing the valley. The furniture consisted of a sofa, a round writing table, and a couple of chairs. On hot days, he said, "I spread the study wide open, anchor my papers down with brickbats, and write in the midst of hurricanes, clothed in the same thin linen we make shirts of." Each morning after a breakfast of steak and coffee he climbed up the hillside to his study, and, without stopping for lunch, he worked steadily through the day until dinnertime. Like a pilothouse, which it resembled, the octagonal room offered a commanding view; he could see city and countryside, storms sweeping down the valley, flashes of lightning over the distant blue hills. Everything lay below the study and beyond. The writer Mark Twain worked in the same solitary, untouchable splendor as Sam Clemens the pilot. He was isolated —from Livy, children, servants, the entire domestic context. He was "remote from *all* noises."

Four days after his marriage, with Livy asleep upstairs in their bedroom, he had felt "the old days" trooping by "in their old glory again," had remembered incident after incident of his schooldays in Hannibal. Now, during the summer of 1874 the fountains of his great deep were broken up again (his favored metaphor for the unlocking of memory), he rained reminiscences again, he translated nostalgia into fiction and Hannibal into "the poor little shabby village of St. Petersburg" (which is nonetheless, literally and in the glory he assigns to it, heaven), and he began *Tom Sawyer.*

He began it with no clear idea of where it would end. On the first page of his manuscript, at some point during the summer, he wrote an outline which reflected a plan to carry the story far past boyhood:

178

1, Boyhood & youth; 2 y & early manh; 3 the Battle of Life in many lands; 4 (age 37 to [40?],) return & meet grown babies & toothless old drivelers who were the grandees of his boyhood. The Adored unknown a [illegible] faded old maid & full of rasping, puritanical vinegar piety.

As he went on with the manuscript, his marginal notes—reminders to himself of episodes to be used later on in the narrative—were more in the vein of his February 1870 letter to Will Bowen: "Rolling the rock," "Candy pull," "Becky had the measles," "Cadets of Temp.," "Learning to smoke," "Burying pet cat or bird." Following the direction he had set for himself in *The Gilded Age*, he was purifying the past of the present. "The Battle of Life in many lands" and the disenchantments summed up by the "faded old maid" were to be among the subjects of his *Autobiography*. "Boyhood and youth" were the prime subjects of his fiction.

Clemens' characteristic method of improvising from chapter to chapter, of letting the story shape itself, had its pitfalls. One day's failure of invention coupled with the absence of an over-all plan could mean that his books came to a dead stop, sometimes for years. Early in September, after having written about four hundred pages of manuscript, he conceded that "that day's chapter was a failure, in conception, moral truth to nature, and execution—enough blemish to impair the excellence of almost any chapter —and so I must burn up the day's work and do it all over again. It was plain that I had worked myself out, pumped myself dry." Thirty years later he remembered this crisis as teaching him his great lesson, a basic tenet of his faith in himself as a writer: "When the tank runs dry you've only to leave it alone and it will fill up again in time." On September 4, 1874, with this lesson implicit if not completely demonstrated, he announced with no trace of concern, "So I knocked off, and went to playing billiards for a change."

As it turned out, he did not return to *Tom Sawyer* and finish it until the following summer, and even then his definitions were largely tentative ones. He had decided not to take his hero past boyhood; if he had continued with him, he told Howells, Tom "would be just like all the one-horse men in literature." He said he planned to deal in a future book (which would eventually take the form and title of *Huckleberry Finn*) with "the Battle of Life" and to "take a boy of twelve and run him on through life (in the first person) but not Tom Sawyer—he would not be a good character for it." Despite this awareness of the problem of point of view, he never did run Huck on past early adolescence. Sentence by sentence and paragraph by paragraph Mark Twain was an entirely deliberate and conscious craftsman; he insisted that the difference between the nearly right word and the right word was the difference between the lightning bug and the lightning; his ear for the rhythms of speech was unsurpassed, and he demanded in dialect and social notation nothing short of perfection. But his larger, structural methods were inspirational and intuitive. Chronically incapable of self-criticism, he relied on others to make the basic judgments of his work just as much as he relied on the tank to fill up. The Holy Ghost seemed to sit with him as he wrote. "Since there is no plot to the thing," he told Howells on June 21, 1875, "it is likely to follow its own drift, and so is as likely to drift into manhood as anywhere —I won't interpose." This was only two weeks before he finished writing *Tom Sawyer*, and he was still drifting. "I have finished the story and didn't take the chap beyond boyhood," he wrote to Howells on July 5, and he added, "It is *not* a boy's book, at all. It will only be read by adults. It is only written for adults." Late that November, after some earnest reasoning from Howells, he changed his mind altogether: "Mrs. Clemens decides with you that the book should issue as a book for boys, pure and simple—and so do I. It is surely the correct idea."

Clemens showed the same range of certainty and uncertainty about two other literary productions of the summer of 1874 at Quarry Farm. He paid the offending Densmore a total of four hundred dollars for his unauthorized script about Colonel Sellers, worked it over himself, brought it to New York in September when he was on his way back to Hartford, and spent several days rehearsing the actors. With the comedian John T. Raymond as Sellers, *The Gilded Age* opened at the Park Theatre on September 16 and was an immediate success. James T. Fields found it "simply delicious"; President Grant went backstage to compliment Raymond; and the *Atlantic*, as well as the daily papers, was full of praise. The play was a continuing success when Raymond took it on tour, earning Clemens about nine hundred dollars a week when it played in the larger cities. The daily reports of the profits arrived in Hartford around dinnertime, and Howells recalled that Clemens would spring to his feet, fling his napkin on his chair, and in "wild triumph" read aloud the "gay figures." Clemens actually had little talent as a writer for the stage, but he had approached this venture with absolute confidence, and his confidence was vindicated—unfortunately for him, as it worked out. For the success of the play, which was almost entirely due to the near-perfect match of Sellers and Raymond, led Clemens to pursue the phantom of a career as a dramatist.

The same month *The Gilded Age* opened in New York Clemens reticently and apologetically submitted to Howells a short piece called "A True Story." The narrator, an old Negress, tells how she and her favorite child were separated at a slave auction and how twenty-two years later, after her master ran away from the advancing Union armies, they were reunited. It is a moving story, one of Mark Twain's best, and in a number of ways it foreshadows *Huckleberry Finn*—in its explicit sympathy for the Negro, its level vision of the brutalities of a slaveholding society, and the enormous skill he displays in telling a first-person story in impeccably nuanced but never obscure dialect. "I've kept the True Story," Howells answered, "which I think extremely good and touching and with the best and reallest kind of black talk in it." The story was published in the November 1874 *Atlantic*. It was Mark Twain's first contribution to the magazine—six years after James Parton had suggested that "a writer named Mark Twain be engaged"—and he was paid at the highest rate the *Atlantic* had ever offered. This was only twenty dollars a page (or about two cents a word) and not really satisfactory, as he complained to Charles Warren Stoddard. "However, the awful respectability of the magazine makes up." A year later, in a review of Mark Twain's *Sketches, New and Old*, in the December 1875 *Atlantic*, Howells said that some readers had been puzzled by the seriousness of "A True Story" and had feared "a lurking joke in it." His own seasoned judgment was: "The rugged truth of the sketch leaves all other stories of slave life infinitely far behind, and reveals a gift in the author for the simple, dramatic report of reality which we have seen equalled in no other American writer."

When he submitted the piece to Howells, Clemens had written: "I enclose also a 'True Story' which has no humor in it. You can pay as lightly as you choose for that, for it is rather out of my line."

IV

Number 351 Farmington Avenue, still unfinished and swarming with workmen when the Clemens family moved into its second floor in September, impressed a reporter from the Hartford *Daily Times*, as it impressed practically everyone who ever saw it, as being "one of the oddest looking buildings in the State ever designed for a dwelling, if not in the whole country." Outside and inside it defied all categories. It presented to the dazzled eye three turrets, the tallest of which was octagonal and about fifty feet high, five balconies, innumerable embrasures, a huge shaded veranda that turned a corner, an elaborate porte-cochère, a forest of chimneys. Its dark brick walls were trimmed with brownstone and decorated with inlaid designs in scarlet-painted brick and black; the roof was patterned in colored tile. The house was permanent polychrome and gingerbread Gothic; it was part steamboat, part medieval stronghold, and part cuckoo clock.

Inside, on three stories, were nineteen large rooms, five baths (with indoor plumbing, which was still a novelty, and washbasins decorated to harmonize with the rugs), and a wealth of idiosyncratic delights which its owner worked out with Edward Tuckerman Potter, his fashionable and eclectic New York architect. The furnishings were heavy, ornate, and, like the mantelpieces, opulently inlaid and carved with cherubs, gargoyles, sphinxes, and griffins. In the dining room, where soon claret and champagne, fillet of beef and canvasback ducks, Nesselrode pudding and ice-cream angels would be dispensed with a liberal hand, a window had been cut directly above the mantelpiece and the flue diverted to the sides of it —Clemens enjoyed watching snowflakes and flames at the same time; later on he installed some tin roofing over a part of the house because he also liked to hear the rain drumming. On the west the house looked out over a small valley and the Riveret, a stream which in Nook Farm's earlier days used to be known as Meandering Swine Creek. The library opened onto a large semicircular glass conservatory, a device for moving nature indoors that Harriet Beecher Stowe developed and popularized among her neighbors; in the dark of winter a fountain played, surrounded by calla lilies and flowering vines. On the second floor, directly above the library, a luxurious study had been built for Clemens. Soon this was taken over as a schoolroom for the children, and he moved to the third-floor billiard room, which although connected to the kitchen and the servants' hall by an elaborate system of speaking tubes, had only an exiguous relationship to the furnace: the room stayed well above freezing, Howells said, when all the gas jets were on and there was a fire in the fireplace. The billiard room was the closest Clemens came to having a permanent study; even with this sprawling establishment he sometimes went to a room above the stable or in Twichell's house to find quiet enough to work in.

"We had a really charming visit, not marred by anything," Howells wrote to his father in March 1875. "The Clemenses are whole-souled hosts, with inextinguishable money, and a palace of a house." Howells later passed on his wonderment to his six-year-old son as well. "They've even got their soap painted," the boy exclaimed when he found a pink cake in the bathroom, and when he saw Clemens' Negro butler, George Griffin, in the dining room, he had a more exotic vision of life on Farmington Avenue. "Come quick!" he said to his father. "The slave is setting the table!" By 1877, in order to maintain this palace Clemens employed six servants—a German nursemaid, an Irish housemaid, an Irish laundress, a Negro cook, a Negro butler, and an Irish coachman. From time to time this slightly eccentric staff—the butler, for example, was a gambler and a moneylender to the Hartford Negro community—was supplemented by waitresses and nurses. In 1875 the Clemenses hired for Clara a wet nurse who got monumentally drunk when she was left alone. Even when she was supervised, Clemens recalled with admiration, she devoured, drank, and smoked everything in sight; then she would go upstairs and "perfectly delight the baby with a banquet which ought to have killed it at thirty yards, but which only made it happy and fat and boozy." Allowing for heroic exaggeration here, life on Farmington Avenue apparently had its robust aspects.

"Mr. Clemens seems to glory in his sense of possession," Livy said soon after they bought the land but even before the house had gone up. The stately mansion was a classic American success story, a reminder that it was possible to be born in a two-room clapboard house in Florida, Missouri, a village of one hundred inhabitants, and to become world-famous, marry a rich and beautiful woman, and live a life of domestic bliss in a house that was the marvel of Hartford. On Susy's third birthday, in March 1875, a rousing wood fire shed warmth and light in the main hall, the colored glass lamps on the newel posts were lighted, and in front of the fireplace, on a bright rug and surrounded by a circle of pink and dove-colored chairs, was a low table full of presents: a pink azalea, a Russia-leather Bible stamped in gold, a gold ring and a silver thimble, a nurseryful of dolls in Sunday dress, and—her father's gift—a Noah's Ark containing two hundred wooden animals "such as only a human being could create and only God call by name without referring to the passenger list." Here, surely, was the fulfillment of dream. For in amplitude, luxury, and freely expressed affection the house on Farmington Avenue was the opposite of Clemens' cramped birthplace and of his childhood in what he remembered as a loveless household. It was the conspicuous symbol of his success as writer, lecturer, and dramatist: the Word was made bricks and mortar, and Mark Twain dwelt among them.

"One may make the house a gaudy and unrestful Palace of Sham," Clemens explained to Mary Fairbanks' daughter, "or he can make it a Home." He was concerned with taste and correctness, but he was scarcely reticent about displaying his wealth—to give pleasure to others by displaying it was one of the social obligations of wealth—and he drew the line between Home and Palace of Sham in curious ways. For example, to celebrate the visit of Grant and his family to Hartford in October, 1880, the Clemens house, like others in the city, was decorated from top to bottom with flags of all nations, shields and coats of arms, glittering arches, mottoes and heraldic devices on gold and silver paper. Near the gate stood two figures in complete armor. But, as Clemens told Livy, he "persistently and inflexibly" forbade "the biggest and gorgeousest of the arches—it had on it, in all the fires of the rainbow, 'The Home of Mark Twain,' in letters as big as your head." Actually it would have been just as superfluous to name the owner of Iranistan or Waldemere, the unique but flammable splendors Barnum put up at nearby Bridgeport. But to own this house, Clemens soon discovered, was like being chained to a tiger. By his own choice he committed himself to an earning power more like a tycoon's than an author's, and a few years later the expense of running this establishment on the scale it demanded helped drive him to Europe. At various times Livy would be prostrated with hostess fatigue. And in this rambling palace, so antithetic to the rural simplicities and isolation of his study at Quarry Farm, he found he could get little work done. Soon after they moved in he complained he was being pestered and exasperated to death by the builder, the foreman, the architect, the upholsterer, the carpet man, the billiard-table man, the man sodding the grounds. "Just think of this going on all day long, and I a man who loathes details with all his heart." He made Livy lie down "*most* of the time." He described himself as "a headless man."

The *Atlantic* wanted more from him, Livy wanted him to get back to work. "It's no use," he wrote to Howells on October 24, "I find I can't. We are in such a state of weary and endless confusion that my head won't 'go.' So I give it up." The creature was turning on Frankenstein. It was a long walk in the woods, away from the house, that changed his mood. Later that day he wrote a second letter to Howells. He had been talking to Twichell about "old Mississippi days of steamboating glory and grandeur as I saw them (during 5 years) *from the pilot house.* He said 'What a virgin subject to hurl into a magazine!' I hadn't thought of that before." What was new was only the magazine idea. For years he had been planning a book on the subject, and in 1871 he had told Livy he intended to spend two months on the river taking notes and then "I bet you I will make a standard work." Now, with the pages of the *Atlantic* open to him, he planned to write a series that would run just as long as his material held out. As it had during the summer, the past came rushing in on him, and despite the distractions of the house he managed to put himself to work. The first of the seven installments of "Old Times on the Mississippi" was in proof by the end of November and appeared in the *Atlantic* for January 1875. "Cut it, scarify it, reject it—handle it with entire freedom," he wrote to Howells about the first installment, and Howells responded not only with specific suggestions, which Clemens gratefully accepted, but with the kind of generous praise that was reward and incentive in itself. "The piece about the Mississippi is capital," Howells wrote; "it almost made the water in our ice-pitcher muddy as I read it." And from John Hay, who had been born and raised in Warsaw, Illinois, fifty miles up the river from Hannibal, he received a tribute of the same order which he proudly passed on to Howells:

I have just read with delight your article in the Atlantic. It is perfect— no more nor less. I don't see how you do it. I knew all that, every word of it—passed as much time on the levee as you ever did, knew the same crowd and saw the same scenes,—but I could not have remembered one word of it all. You have the two greatest gifts of the writer, memory and imagination.

"Now, isn't that outspoken and hearty, and just like that splendid John Hay?" Clemens exclaimed, unaware, of course, that Hay held the private opinion that *The Innocents Abroad* was a work of "buffoonery." Spurred on by these encouragements, by January Clemens believed that he had already uncovered enough material to make a book, and, with the optimism he tended to show at the beginning and the middle of any new project, he expected the book to be published at the end of 1875. He was off by eight years.

Mark Twain's princely establishment in Hartford was visible proof that it was possible to bypass literary Boston and achieve success in America and in England as well. Now literary Boston, as represented by the *Atlantic,* welcomed him, and he responded with a troubled mingling of gratitude, residual veneration, mockery, and barely disguised hostility, all contained within a mild hoax. "Dear Redpath," he telegraphed from Hartford on November 9, 1874, "Rev. J. H. Twichell and I expect to start at 8 o'clock Thursday morning, to walk to Boston in 24 hours—or more. We shall telegraph Young's Hotel for rooms for Saturday night, in order to allow for a low average of pedestrianism." Redpath released the text to the newspapers. By Thursday morning, when Clemens and Twichell, carrying their lunch and a change of clothes, started out along the stage road from East Hartford, the Associated Press was reporting the trip to subscribers across the country. Like Barnum, whom he admired and exchanged invitations and curiosities with, Clemens believed that a man without publicity was a tinkling cymbal.

Howells thought of his own first trip to Boston as a pilgrimage; Mark Twain's subtitle for *The Innocents Abroad* was "The New Pilgrim's Progress." Now, as a whim, the celebrated humorist was setting out on foot for the Holy Sepulcher accompanied, as a princely pilgrim should be, by his confessor and almoner. They walked twenty-eight miles the first day, spent the night in a tavern at Westford, Connecticut, walked six miles more the next morning to North Ashford. There they gave up the pilgrimage and decided to go the rest of the way to Boston by train. "We have made thirty-five miles in less than five days," Clemens said in a telegram which Redpath read to a lecture audience in Boston. "This demonstrates the thing can be done. Shall now finish by rail. Did you have any bets on us?" Friday night Howells gave them a welcoming party in his new house at 37 Concord Avenue in Cambridge. "I never saw a more used-up, hungrier man than Clemens," Howells told his father. "It was something fearful to see him eat escalloped oysters." The oysters restored him, and, standing with his head thrown back, his gray-blue eyes glimmering, he told about the pilgrimage and about their encounter in the tavern at Westford with a young ostler who, as Clemens described him years later, had "oozed eloquent profanity and incredible smut from every pore." Twichell had become more and more embarrassed as the young man went on, for even on neutral subjects the ostler had been superb: "went into the crops with as fresh a zeal as ever and drove his dialectic night cart through it at as rattling a gait and with as fragrant effect as in the beginning." On Monday Clemens met Lowell, who was then in the grip of his obsession to demonstrate that everyone was in some way descended from the Jews. He seemed to be interested in Clemens' apparently Semitic nose and in little else about him; their only common ground was the Beecher affair.

One of the mementos of this well-publicized pilgrimage is a letter Clemens nominally addressed to Livy but really, as he explained a week or so later, intended for Howells. He dated it November 16, 1935, the centennial year of his birth, and he sent it, he said, from a city which used to be called Boston but which was now (a jab at the anxieties and the possibly waning vitalities of the Yankee community) called Limerick—"It is enough to make a body sick." Twentieth-century Limerick-Boston is populated by "idiots" and "fools" who communicate with each other in "dreary conversational funerals" that make Clemens want to "curse till my asthma brings me the blessed relief of suffocation." Along with Protestant hegemony, democracy and universal suffrage have withered away by the year 1935. Instead of a President the country has an emperor and a large titled nobility; Clemens is the Duke of Hartford, Howells the Duke of Cambridge, and Twichell the Archbishop of Dublin. But in this cozy reactionary fantasy, which Howells and others loved for its "deliciousness," there are hard glints not only of misanthropy but also of hostility toward the Boston peerage. Osgood, the Duke of Hartford now reports, was hanged many years ago for conspiracy. Aldrich, now Marquis of Ponkapog, was nearly hanged on the same charge; he is drunk, as usual, and spends his time telling lies. "I wish you could see old Cambridge and Ponkapog," the letter concludes. "I love them dearly as ever, but privately, my dear, they are not much improvement on idiots."

Faithful subscribers to the *Atlantic* could not have been surprised to find in the January 1875 issue two poems by Professor Longfellow and an essay by Dr. Holmes, nor would the excerpt from Henry James, Jr.'s *Roderick Hudson* have seemed much of a departure from normal editorial policies. But, beginning on page 69 of that issue, with the first pages of the first installment of "Old Times on the Mississippi," they heard a new voice and should have been electrified by it, just as, in what is surely one of the great passages in American literature, Hannibal, "the white town drowsing in the sunshine of a summer's morning," is electrified into life by the cry of "S-t-e-a-mboat a-comin'!" The gaudy packet, flying a flag from its jackstaff and tumbling clouds of black smoke from its fancy chimneys, its paddle wheel churning the water to foam, pent steam screaming through its valves, was Mark Twain announcing his arrival and declaring once and for all that his surge of power and spectacle derived not from such streams as the meandering Charles or sweet Thames but from "the great Mississippi, the majestic, the magnificent Mississippi, rolling its mile-wide tide along, shining in the sun."

Back in Boston on December 15 to attend an *Atlantic* dinner for its contributors, Clemens could see advance copies of the January issue at each of the twenty-eight places at the table. Afterward, instead of a formal speech, he remarked only that the dinner had been "nice," "really good," "admirable," and, summing up in symbolic terms his own edged, only partially revealed attitudes, he declared that the dinner had been "quite as go   as I would have had if I had stayed at home."

CHAPTER TEN

Spirits of '76

I

B<small>Y THE SORT OF COINCIDENCE</small> that delighted Mark Twain, the adultery trial of Henry Ward Beecher was at a crisis point on April 19, 1875, the one-hundredth anniversary of the first shots fired in the cause of American independence. On the sixty-seventh day of a soggy legal drama that had begun in January and was to end in the July doldrums with a hung jury, Beecher, wearing black broadcloth and holding in his left hand a small bouquet of flowers, entered the crowded Brooklyn courtroom, bowed low to the judge, and took the stand. That same morning Clemens and Howells were together in Cambridge struggling through crowds and traffic on Massachusetts Avenue to find some way of getting to the centennial ceremonies in Lexington and Concord.

A few days earlier, with Twichell, Clemens had attended the trial in Brooklyn and heard Beecher under cross-examination. Later, when Howells pressed him to talk about the trial, he became strangely reticent. "The man has suffered enough," he said wearily. His own disgust transcended the issue of guilt or innocence. As he said years later, "Mr. Beecher made the stupendous and irremediable mistake of remaining silent until all sane people"—Clemens included—"believed him guilty." Clemens' interest in the trial was not so much in its outcome as in the simple fact of its existence, evidence of what a pamphlet of the day called Wickedness in High Places. It would have been better for religion, he told Pamela, if Beecher had died in infancy. He saw the Beecher trial as a companion piece to the perjury trial of the Tichborne Claimant which he had followed with such intense interest in England in 1873. He meant to have Beecher scrapbooked, too, he told Charles Warren Stoddard, whom he had paid to paste up the six volumes of clippings about the Claimant. "At present," he told Stoddard early in 1875, "I believe I would rather go down in history as the Claimant than as Mr. Beecher." The claimant to the Tichborne title and estate had turned out to be just Arthur Orton, fat son of a ship's butcher of Wapping, and now he was convict number 10539 at Dartmoor. Beecher was a false leader who in his private behavior had betrayed the faith of his followers, as much a symptom as Boss Tweed of the ills of democracy.

All the "accidents" of Mark Twain's life had some kind of purposive meaning—so it seemed to him in his old age, when he tried to map out the turning points by which he had become a writer. His intermittent but deepening sense of alienation during the 1870s can be summed up in three "accidents": he managed to be present at the Tichborne trial in London and the Beecher trial in Brooklyn, but, despite elaborate planning and high expectations, he managed to miss the centennial celebrations. Clemens arrived in Cambridge alone on April 18—Livy was reluctant to leave her infant in the care of their alcoholic wet nurse—and spent the night with Howells. They were among the honored guests who the next day were to go by special train to Concord, where the dedication of Daniel Chester French's "Minute Man" was to be followed by an address by Emerson, an ode by Lowell, the appearance of President Grant and his cabinet, an enormous military parade led by General Burnside, and dinner in a tent for four thousand. Clemens and Howells decided to shorten the trip by skipping the train from Boston and starting out from Cambridge instead. After a leisurely breakfast they walked to the Porter Square station in North Cambridge, only to discover that there was not a place to be had on any train going to Concord; every car was full, and the roofs were covered with patriots. Every kind of vehicle from miles around was on the road and full. Not even a cat was for hire, Howells recalled. The day was cold and windy, North Cambridge was deep in mud, even Clemens' sealskin coat could not keep out the chill, and along with his anger and impatience came an attack of acute indigestion. In a final act of futility, Clemens ran after a carriage that seemed to have some empty seats; all he got for his troubles was more mud. They gave up. Through their scheme of bypassing Boston they were to miss one of the gaudiest spectacles the young republic had ever staged to celebrate itself. They also missed, as they would learn from the papers, some elements of farce: the speakers' platform collapsed twice under the combined weight of the distinguished guests; the dinner tent was blasted by wet snow and wind, and only the ice cream was warm; a town of twenty-four hundred thrifty souls was overrun by fifty thousand tourists, all cold and hungry and many of them drunk, looking for food, drink, shelter, and a way to get home. "There is no difficulty *now* in understanding the hurried retreat of the British from Concord and Lexington," the Boston *Daily News* said about the chaos.

Disappointed and humiliated and angry with each other, Mark Twain and Howells made their way as slowly as possible back to Concord Avenue and tried to convince Elinor Howells they had made a quick round trip to and from the ceremonies. She saw through the story right away, and as they stood by the library fire they began to see the morning's episode in a different light. They had, in fact, acted out the part of one of Mark Twain's favorite comic personae: the innocent, the tenderfoot, who is sure that he can outsmart the natives. The comic non-visit to Concord was, for Clemens, as loaded with psychic tensions as the comic non-walk to Boston. "I think the humor of this situation was finally a greater pleasure to Clemens than an actual visit to Concord would have been," Howells wrote in 1910. "Only a few weeks before his death he laughed our defeat over with one of my family in Bermuda, and exulted in our prompt detection."

"You left your fur cap, which I propose to keep as a hostage," Howells wrote on April 22. And in a letter the next day Clemens commemorated what was one of the many peaks in the range of their friendship of nearly forty years: "When I think over what a splendid good sociable time I had in your house I feel ever so thankful to the wise providence that thwarted our several ably planned and ingenious attempts." It was one of many such visits, to Boston or Hartford, during which they talked late into the night, Clemens in his long nightshirt, smoking constantly, telling the story of his life—"the inexhaustible, the fairy, the Arabian Nights story, which I could never tire of even when it began to be told again," Howells called it, acknowledging a mythic dimension that set his Mark Twain apart from "all the rest of our sages, poets, seers, critics, humorists." After the hot whiskeys, the beer, the champagne—whichever he happened to favor as a soporific at the time—Clemens finally went to bed, and after a while, when he had fallen asleep, Howells looked in on him and put out the last, still-lighted cigar of the night. Even after the house was aired that next morning and Clemens had gone, the smell of his tobacco remained. Worn out by smoke, drink, and late hours, completely talked out and listened out, after such a visit Howells felt like "one of those locust-shells which you find sticking to the bark of trees at the end of summer." In personal terms, Clemens' friendship with Howells had something in it of Sherlock Holmes and Watson: a nervous, impatient, unpredictable, intuitive, dominating personality finding vital satisfactions with someone who seems to present the complementary qualities of solidity, reliability, perseverance, and established values. Yet in professional terms the roles were all reversed. Clemens played pupil to Howells as master, acknowledged to him a debt as deep as the country job printer owes to the city shop foreman who teaches him the right way to do things, obediently followed Howells' editorial suggestions, valued praise from Howells above all others'. Howells, often hard pressed for money while Clemens lived in affluence, gave freely of his work and time. With the exception of Kipling much later on,

Howells was about the only writer of fiction Clemens consistently read with pleasure and admiration. "You are really my only author; I am restricted to you," he was to tell Howells in 1885. "I wouldn't give a damn for the rest." Their common ground was a basically elitist bias along with a deep loyalty to democratic roots, a refusal to sentimentalize boyhood or to cleanse it of terrors and anguish, and above all an unswerving respect and affection for each other. Through all of Clemens' vagaries and contradictions, his rages and violent rejections of old friends, his friendship with Howells was untouched by rancor or rivalry and was illuminated by a tenderness which shines through the nearly seven hundred letters they exchanged and through Howells' *My Mark Twain*, the memoir he wrote the year Clemens died. In his review of *Sketches, New and Old* Howells praised him as a dramatic reporter of reality, a friend of mankind, and a humorist of growing subtlety and seriousness. "Yours is the recognized Court of Last Resort in this country," Clemens wrote gratefully, "from its decision there is no appeal; and so, to have gained this decree of yours before I am forty years old, I regard as a thing to be right down proud of." Livy especially was grateful for the comment on his "growing seriousness of meaning," he said. "You see, the thing that gravels her is that I am persistently glorified as a mere buffoon, as if that entirely covered my case —which she denies with venom." He signed his letter with the emblem of his being as public man and professional writer, "Mark." To Livy on her thirtieth birthday, November 27, 1875—three days before he turned forty —he wrote from the depths of a different identity. She called him "Youth"; now he greeted her as daughter as well as wife. "You are dearer to me, my child, than you were upon the last anniversary of this birthday." In terms that indicate his still-bewildered response to his rapid translation from buffoon into moralist and Victorian pater familias, he concluded: "With abounding affection for you and our babies, I hail this day that brings you the matronly grace and dignity of three decades." He signed himself, magisterially, "Always Yours, S.L.C."

Clemens spent the spring and summer of 1875 in Hartford. "I work *at* work," he complained, "but I don't accomplish anything worth speaking of." He was chained to his way of living. To move his household to Quarry Farm "would be like moving a menagerie," he said, "and to leave it behind would be like leaving a menagerie behind without a keeper." There were other distractions as well. Dan De Quille, an old friend from the *Territorial Enterprise*, was in Hartford working, at his suggestion and with his help, on a history of the Comstock Lode, *The Big Bonanza*. Bliss was to publish it the following year, in conflict, as it turned out, with *Tom Sawyer*. "There *ain't* any risk," Clemens had assured De Quille, who yielded to pressure from him to take a leave of absence from the paper and come East to write the book; "I am a large stockholder and director in our publishing house, and have some influence." In part it was the Riley affair all over again, a red-hot idea which seemed as spectacular as the Big Bonanza itself, the biggest silver strike in America, and was projected in a twenty-page letter fringed with telegrams. "Here you shall stop at the best hotel, and every morning I will walk down, meet you half way, bring you to my house and we will grind literature all day long in the same room," Clemens promised. "Sundays we will smoke and lie." And, like Riley, De Quille was offered not only enthusiasm but also some dead-sure secrets. "I can show you a trick or two which I don't teach to everybody, I can tell you! . . . Bring along *lots of dry statistics*—it is the very best sauce a humorous book can have. Ingeniously used, they just make a reader smack his chops in gratitude."

In June they began their work in Clemens' study, now moved away from the domestic noises of the house to a room above the stable. Inevitably Clemens' interest in the red-hot idea cooled; the "Introductory" he wrote for *The Big Bonanza* was reserved in its enthusiasm, and the old friendship, for all the time they spent together in Hartford and during part of the summer in Newport, was never restored to its old basis. Even De Quille was troubled by the distractions Clemens seemed to look for instead of avoid. While Thomas Beecher was visiting at Farmington Avenue Clemens would do nothing but play billiards. Then Clemens went to New York on a business trip; Raymond was reviving *The Gilded Age*. Joaquin Miller was in Hartford, shorn of his shoulder-length locks and also, as De Quille saw it, of "much of his silly affectation." And Bret Harte was in town from time to time to see Bliss and talk over his novel, *Gabriel Conroy*. He was even thinking of renting a house in Hartford, a plan which must have given some uneasiness to Clemens, who seems to have made an effort to keep him and the Nook Farm group apart. On their way to a baseball game in May 1875 Clemens and Twichell encountered Harte on the street; it was the first time Twichell (who said he was "a little disappointed" in Harte's looks) had ever seen him up close.

Nonetheless, by July Clemens finished *Tom Sawyer*. He could not afford to offer it to the *Atlantic* for serial publication, he explained to Howells. "You see I take a vile, mercenary view of things—but then my household expenses are something almost ghastly." But he wanted Howells to read the manuscript anyway "and point out the most glaring defects for me." "It is altogether the best boy's story I ever read. It will be an immense success," Howells said, adding that he had made some penciled suggestions and corrections. "The adventures are enchanting. I wish *I* had been on that island." When Clemens came to "the dreary and hateful task" of revising the manuscript, he hit upon a method which sums up the extent of his almost unquestioning reliance on Howells: "Instead of *reading* the MS, I simply hunted out the pencil marks and made the emendations which they suggested." But, on occasions more exacting than all his "censors" working together, he added, "There was one expression which perhaps you overlooked," and he cited Huck's complaint about the rigors of life with Widow Douglas: "They comb me all to hell." Howells had, in fact, let it pass; so had Livy; so had Livy's mother and Livy's aunt, all "sensitive and loyal subjects of the kingdom of heaven, so to speak." Now that *Tom Sawyer* was to be "a boy's and girl's book," it was Clemens who boggled at the cornerstone vernacularism and changed "hell" to "thunder," a minor but celebrated emendation. He had an excessively fine if sometimes erratic sense of what was fitting for a juvenile audience. In general, with an adult masculine audience, he used what Howells described as "the Southwestern, the Lincolnian, the Elizabethan breadth of parlance which I suppose one ought not to call coarse without calling one's self prudish," which, unfortunately, was one word for Howells.*

II

On January 24, 1876, in the library of his house on Farmington Avenue, Mark Twain read to the members of the Monday Evening Club a paper called "The Facts Concerning the Recent Carnival of Crime in Connecticut." He had written and polished it with more than his usual care, for, as he told Howells, "I think it will bring out considerable discussion among the gentlemen of the Club." Later that night Twichell wrote in his journal that the paper was "serious in its intent though vastly funny and splendidly, brilliantly read." A clergyman present asked Clemens to read it again as a homily from the pulpit the Sunday after. And Howells, who had been among the first to recognize his friend's "growing seriousness of meaning," published it in the June *Atlantic*. "It was an impassioned study of the human conscience," Howells wrote a few years later. "Hawthorne or Bunyan might have been proud to imagine that powerful allegory,

---

* In his revision notes in the manuscript of *Tom Sawyer* Howells asked Clemens to shorten his account of Becky Thatcher looking at the "stark naked" human figures depicted in the schoolmaster's copy of "Professor Somebody's" anatomy textbook. He also marked as objectionable a phrase in Chapter Five about a vagrant poodle dog who wandered into church, absent-mindedly sat down on a fierce black beetle, let out a "wild yelp of agony," and "went sailing up the aisle, his tail shut down like a hasp." "Awfully good but a little too dirty," Howells said, and Clemens deleted the last seven words of the description. The simile of the dog's tail might have been suggested to Clemens by an entirely unobjectionable source, Oliver Wendell Holmes's novel *Elsie Venner* (1861): in Chapter Three the schoolmaster kicks a "yallah dog," who then goes "bundling out of the open schoolhouse-door with a most pitiable yelp, and his stump of a tail shut down as close as his owner ever shut the short, stubbed blade of his jack-knife."

which had a grotesque force far beyond either of them." But the public, including the *Atlantic* public, still expected Mark Twain to be a funny man only and were puzzled and dissatisfied when, as he did in this piece, he turned moralist, examined community values, and, exploring the dark side of his moon, touched on his growing sense of divisiveness.

At the beginning of "The Carnival of Crime," the author-narrator is in his study, at peace with himself, "thoroughly happy and content." Without knocking, "a shriveled, shabby dwarf" enters the room. He is about forty years old. He is a walking deformity, a "vile bit of human rubbish," covered with "a fuzzy, greenish mold." Even so, Mark Twain recognizes that he and this mysterious stranger resemble each other in appearance, and in manner as well: the dwarf talks to him with the kind of brusqueness he himself uses only with his closest friends and in the same exasperating drawl. The dwarf proceeds to cite a series of shameful episodes that Mark Twain believed no one else knew about. He allowed his best friends to be ridiculed behind their backs. Years earlier he tricked his trusting younger brother into walking blindfolded on thin ice; and the brother fell into the water and nearly froze to death. (Clemens held himself responsible for his brother Henry's presence on the steamboat *Pennsylvania* when it exploded and burned him fatally.) The dwarf goes on with these shameful secrets. "Every sentence was an accusation," the narrator says, "and every accusation a truth."

"I am your *conscience*," the dwarf says. Earlier he had accused the narrator of turning away a hungry tramp; now the narrator argues that if he had fed the tramp instead of turning him away he would still feel guilty, for he would have been condoning vagrancy and thus would have offended the conscience of the community. Then he realizes that it is the function of "conscience" to whip a man into guilt regardless of right or wrong or any absolute value; all his life he has been the slave of the tyrant "conscience." In a fit of anger he kills the dwarf, tears him to pieces, burns him. He is now liberated, having passed all the way from atonement to carnival: he is a man without a conscience, living a life of "unalloyed bliss" and free to commit every imaginable crime.

"The Carnival of Crime" lapses at the end into extravaganza: the "I" murders all his enemies, sets fire to a house obstructing his view, swindles a widow and orphans out of their last cow, and offers for sale to medical colleges dead tramps by the gross or by the ton. Still, it is a remarkably direct expression of Mark Twain's concern with multiplicity and remorse, with inner conflicts as well as conflicts with the community. He was, in certain aspects, doubly an outsider. He rejected the aberrant democracy of the Gilded Age, but while he shared certain attitudes with the intellectual reformers—their worry about unrestricted immigration and unrestricted suffrage, for example—he was also skeptical of this self-appointed elite. His sense of alienation from himself as well as from the community often forces him to hide like a hunted man. ("We are so much in the habit of wearing disguises," said La Rochefoucauld, "that we end by failing to recognize ourselves.") He has more aliases than he can remember, and he feels the need to explore the troubled twainness of Mark (or dark) Twain and his creator and Siamese twin, Samuel L. Clemens, and all the other identities clustering about a nucleus of personality called, for the sake of brevity, "S.L.C.": Sam, Mark, Youth, Samuel Langhorne, C. L. Samuel of New York, J. B. Smith, and other incognitos.

At about the same time Clemens was writing "The Carnival of Crime," his perennial interest in claimants—a sinisterly apt phonym as well as a metaphor for a riven personality—was being fed by a distant cousin named Jesse Madison Leathers of Louisville. Leathers was fixed on the belief that he was the rightful Earl of Durham, but he needed money to establish his claim. "Can we recover the estate or is it a myth?" he asked Sam in a rare moment of tentativeness. If Cousin Sam would underwrite the legal expenses, Cousin Sam would get half the estate. "You might as well tackle Gibraltar with blank cartridges," Cousin Sam advised him in October 1875. All the same, Leathers, fueled by the wild hope that ran in the family bloodstream (along with such quantities of alcohol in his own that at one time he landed in the Louisville Inebriate Asylum), believed until his death in 1887 that he was "an American Earl," the title he gave to an autobiography Clemens persuaded him to write. Clemens thought of him as an "ass," a foghorn fighting against the fog, and in *An American Claimant*, published in 1892 and one of the worst things he ever wrote, he merged Colonel Sellers with Jesse Leathers. The fantasy went deeper than that. "Suppose I should live to be ninety-two," he once said to Livy, "and just as I was dying, a messenger should enter and say—" " 'You are become Earl of Durham'!" she broke in, thus providing him with one more instance of what he called "mental telegraphy."

For Mark Twain the spirit of '76 was troubled and divided. At times he felt he had only two or three years of acceptable work left in him. We all cry when a baby dies, he told Mary Fairbanks that June, "but some are conscious of a deeper feeling of content—*I* am, at any rate." Thinking of his dead son, he was blinded by gloom and pessimism to her pride and pleasure in her own son, who had just turned twenty-one: "Never mind about that grisly future season when he shall have made a dazzling success and shall sit with folded hands in well-earned ease and look around upon his corpses and mine, and contemplate his daughters and mine in the madhouse, and his sons and mine gone to the devil." After some minor misunderstanding about the family carriage, Clemens told Annie Fields that he spent the greater part of his life, which was "one long apology," on his knees begging forgiveness. Instead of evoking the past for Will

Bowen, he now scolded him brutally for mooning over it. "Every day that is added to the past is but an old boot added to a pile of rubbish," he said. "Man, do you know that this is simply mental and moral masturbation? . . . You need a dose of salts." At times he hated everything about his past. "Ignorance, intolerance, egotism, self-assertion, opaque perception, dense and pitiful chuckleheadedness—and an almost pathetic unconsciousness of it all, that is what I was at 19 and 20," he wrote to a friend from his St. Louis days, "and that is what the average Southerner is at 60 today." Howells, who thought of him as "the most desouthernized Southerner I ever knew," recalled a conversation they had one night in Hartford. "I wonder why we hate the past so," Howells said. Clemens answered, "It's so damned humiliating."

Even the dead seemed to be returning. In 1876 the bodies of John Marshall Clemens and Henry Clemens were dug up and moved to a new cemetery. "As for a monument," Clemens wrote to John RoBards in Hannibal, "if you remember my father, you are aware he would rise up and demolish it the first night. He was a modest man and would not be able to sleep under a monument." (Nor would he have been able to sleep under the roof of 351 Farmington Avenue, the son may have felt.) As for Henry: "My darling, my pride, my glory, my *all*," he had mourned in 1858, praying to be struck dead if this would bring Henry back to life. Now Henry's death was part of the dreadful and humiliating past: "Henry Clemens. Born June 13, 1838—Died June 19, 1858—the above is sufficient for Henry's grave."

In "The Carnival of Crime" he was trying to explore the roots of his black depressions. He believed that "conscience" was the source of guilt and remorse, and of that Presbyterian sureness of damnation that he tried to joke away in his "(Burlesque) Autobiography" and in all his other public pseudo confessions that he was a liar, a thief, and a wastrel. (These pseudo confessions become an integral part of his humor: by taking the initiative in accusing and, symbolically, punishing himself, the humorist achieves a kind of immunity from the disapproval of society.) Years later, when he drew into himself after Susy's death, he no longer felt that such simple dualities as man and conscience, or Jekyll and Hyde, were adequate solutions to his own enigma, and he turned to psychology, to notions of a "dream self" and the demonic urgings of the unconscious.

During the summer of 1876, back in the solitude of his study at Quarry Farm, Clemens worked on two projects which, though they were grotesquely contrasting in quality, were related in important respects. Both were implicit rejections of the taboos and codes of polite society, and both were experiments in using the vernacular as a literary medium. The first, written for private circulation, was a harmless but soon notorious piece of bawdry called *1601; or Conversation as It Was by the Social Fireside in the Time of the Tudors*. This excursion into what Clemens imagined plain-spoken Elizabethan English to have been was, in a sense, an escape from the restraints of juvenile literature, a covert way of scribbling dirty words on Tom Sawyer's fence. The manuscript or surreptitiously printed copies passed from hand to hand among a circle of critical mediocrities (it is a wonder Mark Twain survived their adulation): Twichell; Twichell's friend Dean Sage, a Booklyn lumber dealer and authority on hunting and fishing; David Gray, Buffalo newspaper editor and pious minor poet; someone Clemens recalled as "a Jewish Rabbi in Albany, a very learned man and an able critic and lover of old-time literature." They declared *1601* to be a great and fine piece of literature; it seems now only a minor sort of curiosity.

"I am tearing along on a new book," he told Mary Fairbanks on August 4 about his second project of the summer. He could not afford any interruptions, he said, because he was afraid that his mill might get cold. Five days later he was writing to Howells in a more casual spirit. "Began another boy's book—more to be at work than anything else. I have written 400 pages on it—therefore it is very nearly half done. It is Huck Finn's Autobiography. I like it only tolerably well, as far as I have got, and may possibly pigeonhole or burn the MS when it is done." The tank ran dry, as he feared, and though he did not burn the manuscript he did pigeonhole it for two years; he worked on it again in 1879 or 1880, pigeonholed it again, and finally finished it in 1884, eight years and seven books after he first began it, a wandering process of creation that is a book-length story in itself. In the first sixteen or so chapters that Clemens wrote that first summer and liked "only tolerably well," he set Huck and Jim afloat on their raft, their fragile island of freedom between the two shores of society. When they passed Cairo, Illinois, in the night, the last free-soil outpost, Mark Twain found himself faced with an enormously difficult problem of plot and structure. He solved that problem with a persistence which reveals his deep involvement with the book both as a literary artist and as a man desperately needing to resolve his own bewilderments about conscience and the restraints and freedoms of the community.

Tom Sawyer, which Clemens once described as "simply a hymn" to boyhood, ended with the establishment of a trust fund for Tom and Huck; to have money out at six per cent meant to be part of the fabric of organized, acquisitive society. Huck's first step toward winning his freedom from the town and his father and toward beginning his education of heart and eye is to renounce his share of the trust—it has brought him nothing but trouble and confinement. He helps Jim to escape, thus symbolically destroying the institution on which the economic life of the community is built and, in actuality, committing a capital crime against the community. And at the end of the book, still rejecting civilization, Huck intends to "light out for the Territory." Throughout the book the price of these and other freedoms is remorse. Huck feels agonies of conscience not only because he is breaking the law by freeing Jim but also because he has betrayed Miss Watson by helping steal her property. In a battle with conscience, Huck finally rejects the idea of turning Jim in: "All right, then, I'll *go* to hell." He plays a practical joke on Jim, but then he realizes he has betrayed Jim's love, and he feels like "trash": "It was fifteen minutes before I could work myself up to go and humble myself to a nigger—but I done it." Like Huck, Jim has memories which shrivel his soul. Once, he says, he struck his little daughter because she ignored what he said to her; then he learned she was deaf and dumb. "Oh, Huck, I bust out a-cryin' en grab her up in my arms, en say, 'Oh, de po' little thing! de Lord God Almighty forgive po' ole Jim, kaze he never gwyne to forgive hisself as long's he live!' " In the manuscript Mark Twain emphatically underlined "de Lord God Almighty fogive po' ole Jim." "This expression shall not be changed," he wrote in the margin. He too would cry to heaven for forgiveness.

Nearly twenty years after he began *Huckleberry Finn* Clemens described it in his notebook as "a book of mine where a sound heart and a deformed conscience come into collision and conscience suffers defeat." Ignoring for the moment the fact that he himself, despite his Hannibal background, had grown up to become the most desouthernized of Southerners, he went on to describe how unquestioned the institution of slavery had been in his boyhood: "The conscience—that unerring monitor—can be trained to approve any wild thing you *want* it to approve if you begin its education early and stick to it."

The dwarf conscience was not necessarily the voice of God, he had discovered; it might be only the voice of the people. If he, like Huck, could reject the community, or at least maintain a critical distance from it, he could win his freedom from the tyranny of conscience. When Clemens broke off his story at the end of the summer of 1876, Huck and Jim are only halfway to freedom. They have passed Cairo, crossed the invisible frontier, and entered enemy territory. A steamboat, the image of avenging society, pounds down on the raft, her wide-open furnaces blazing in the night. Huck dives deep, deep down to escape the thirty-foot paddle wheel, holds his breath until he thinks his lungs are bursting. Mark Twain was also diving deep down into sensibility and memory and preparing himself for a searing examination of the society—part of "the damned human race"—which nurtured him. As man and artist he was to find his first, only, brief liberation.

III

That Mark Twain wrote even as much of *Huckleberry Finn* as he did during the summer of 1876 is proof, if any were needed, that the book sprang from a deep inner necessity. Chronically subject to rages and depressions which at other times might have stopped him altogether, he managed to work on it at the same time that he looked on helplessly while *Tom Sawyer*, the augur of a decline in his fortunes, headed for disaster. Bliss had had the manuscript since the end of November 1875 and had put his best illustrator, the alcoholic and eccentric True Williams, to work. In England Chatto and Windus were rushing toward a June publication. With his expectations high, Clemens sent Howells a set of untitled proofs; Howells finished his review at the end of March and scheduled it for the May number of the *Atlantic*. "It is a splendid notice, and will embolden weak-kneed journalistic admirers to speak out, and will modify or shut up the unfriendly," Clemens wrote on April 3, and he unfolded his plan: "About two days after the *Atlantic* issues I mean to begin to send books to principal journals and magazines."

All of this was, of course, based on the assumption that Bliss was doing his part, but a visit downtown to 284 Asylum Street in mid-April shocked Clemens out of his confident strategy. Bliss mumbled some excuse about the engravers falling behind schedule; not a single advertisement had been issued, not a single canvasser had gone out to take an order. "A subscription harvest is *before* publication (not *after*, when people have discovered how bad one's book is)," Clemens explained to Howells—in considerable embarrassment, for the book could not possibly issue before the autumn. "Howells, you must forgive me if I seem to have made the *Atlantic* any wrong. I—but I'll talk to you about it and show you that it was one of those cases where 'the best laid schemes of mice and men, etc.' "

He wanted Howells to believe that it was his own idea to postpone *Tom Sawyer* to autumn, when it would sell as a holiday gift book, but the truth of the matter was quite different, humiliating and infuriating. Made prosperous by Clemens' past successes, Bliss had expanded his list and taken on too many other books to be able to handle *Tom Sawyer* on schedule. Many of these books were by authors brought into the house by Clemens himself, by now a director as well as a stockholder; among them were Dan De Quille, Charles Dudley Warner, and Bret Harte. He had pleaded with Bret Harte to give his novel, *Gabriel Conroy*, to Bliss, in the expectation that it would make money for the publishing house. The author was acting as businessman, a double role that was to become more and more tempting for Clemens, and he was caught between conflicting interests. The previous December Harte, who was broke, had begged Clemens "in the common interests of our trade" to get him another thousand dollars from Bliss. But in September 1876 Harte complained to him about Bliss's delays with *Gabriel Conroy*. Use your influence, Harte demanded. "You are a stockholder in the Concern." The following spring he was at Clemens again. *Gabriel Conroy* had been a failure. "Either Bliss must confess that he runs his concern solely in *your* interest, and that he uses the names of other authors to keep that fact from the public, or else he is a fool." For Clemens, who was all the while watching the failure of his own book and whose feelings for Harte were by now permanently poisoned, this was too much. "I have read two pages of this ineffable idiotcy," he scrawled on the back of Harte's letter. "It is all I can stand. S. L. C."

During the summer Clemens was in a rage against Bliss. Ignoring his conflict of interest as stockholder and as author, he went about in Hartford and New York denouncing Bliss's incompetence and double-dealing. Even the mild Williams, whose sole interests were illustrations and the rum bottle—Orion had once seen him climbing up a lamppost in front of Tim Dooley's saloon—was so fired up by one of these diatribes that he started taunting Bliss, his employer. Bliss made a frantic appeal to Clemens to stop the campaign. "For myself I care nothing," he said, with a touch of sanctimonious injury, "but it seems poor policy to injure the stock this way, and our stock is too valuable to be made to suffer." Put in these frank profit terms, his appeal was irresistible, and Clemens the investor apologized at the same time that Clemens the author remained absolutely certain that Bliss had botched *Tom Sawyer*.

Howells' enthusiastic review came out too long before publication to do the American edition much good and, as Clemens hoped, to set the pattern for other reviews; Howells' was, in fact, about the only review of any critical importance that the book received at the time. But his review did serve a certain purpose: it was picked up by Canadian pirates, who used it to advertise their edition, reprinted from the Chatto and Windus edition, and they skimmed off a large part of the American market, without paying a penny to the author, before Bliss finally had books to sell in December. *The Gilded Age* sold 50,000 copies during its first full year of publication, *Sketches, New and Old* about 27,000. *Tom Sawyer,* far from being an early best seller, sold only about 24,000 copies. Its relative failure, which hastened Clemens' eventual break with Bliss and his fatal involvements as publisher of his own books, made unmistakable a pattern of declining popularity for Mark Twain. During 1877 his most popular and profitable book was the blank adhesive scrapbook. "It seems funny that an invention which cost me five-minutes' thought in a railway car one day," he said to Mary Fairbanks, "should in this little while be paying me an income as large as any salary I ever received on a newspaper."

IV

As the year drew to an end, the calm surface of life at Nook Farm, already broken by feuding among the Beechers, was further disturbed by a series of curious schemes and squabbles. Bret Harte, in deep with his creditors in New York, was a more or less constant guest at Farmington Avenue. His borrowings from Clemens were approaching the three-thousand-dollar mark, and in other respects he showed himself equally capable of exploiting his literary seniority over Clemens, his confident wit, and his dazzling facility. One Friday night in December he came to dinner with a double deadline to meet: he was scheduled the following morning to read a story to the Saturday Morning Club, a select circle of Hartford young ladies, and Dana of the New York *Sun* was counting on this story and had promised a bonus of one hundred dollars if Harte delivered it on time. Harte had until morning to write it. Instead of rushing to his room after dinner, he sat up in the library talking and drinking whiskey. By one o'clock Clemens was ready for bed. Harte was ready for work and for more whiskey. He went up to his room and worked and drank steadily through the night, although Clemens' estimate that Harte consumed two quarts of whiskey between one and nine in the morning is clearly a heroic embellishment of the facts. Harte came down to breakfast alert, sober, and with a finished story called "Thankful Blossom." The young ladies were delighted, Dana got his story, Harte got his bonus, and thirty years later Clemens was still awed by Harte's ability to work under pressure and by the story itself: "It is my conviction that it belongs at the very top of Harte's literature."

Clemens was still deferential, defensive, a little off balance with Harte, still, in many ways, the obedient disciple as well as anxious collaborator, and there were those at Nook Farm who saw in Harte's hold over him something altogether undesirable. Recently, at a lunch of chicken and oysters with Susan Warner, Livy, and a number of other ladies, Isabella Hooker had been readmitted to probationary standing in the community. Now, prowling through the house on Farmington Avenue—Nook Farm was noted for its open-door policy—she looked into the billiard room and saw the two men together; in plain sight were some bottles of whiskey. "I felt a new distrust of such companionship," she wrote in her diary, "and ever since the thought has haunted me that perhaps I have something to do there by way of warning—yet I dread to lose the friendship of that house which is but a slender thread already." Despite her circumspection, however, that slender thread had very nearly been severed a few minutes earlier by Clemens himself. The tireless gossip of the neighborhood had supplied Isabella with a trivial anecdote, with which she taunted him: Clemens, it seemed, had outspokenly admired a lampshade in his house, but had stopped admiring it when he learned how little Livy had paid for it. Now, hounded by Isabella, he admitted with considerable exasperation that in all probability he had no knowledge or taste, and she set him down in her diary as "Mark Twain, the parvenu." He resented her nosiness and her condescension, and he checked his anger only because Livy interceded. Isabella departed with a sense of moral and intellectual superiority, leaving Bret Harte to work his influence on "the parvenu."

The fruit of "such companionship," it developed, was a quick-money scheme. Mark Twain, who only a month or so earlier was writing *Huckleberry Finn*, had since the beginning of October been collaborating with Bret Harte on a comedy set in the Mother Lode country. It was called *Ah Sin* after its main character, the shrewd Chinese laundryman who was the original "Heathen Chinee" of Harte's celebrated poem. They were to work together on the main character; Clemens was to bring in Scotty Briggs, the virtuoso of Western vernacular who made the arrangements for Buck Fanshaw's funeral in *Roughing It;* and each of them, independently, was to construct a plot and then synthesize the best parts of each plot into a third. Whatever lesson Clemens may have learned from collaborating with Warner on *The Gilded Age* was forgotten in the excitement of the scheme and the prospect of dividing huge profits. Both of them were in the grip of that theater mania which possessed so many of their contemporaries; singlehandedly, Harte was later to try at least two more plays, one of them a dramatization of "The Luck of Roaring Camp." For *Ah Sin* they expected eager producers and actors, and large audiences who would flock to the theater to see the novelty of a comedy written by two leading Western humorists and built around a world-famous character. As the play progressed, Clemens' admiration for Harte continued to rise. "He worked rapidly and seemed to be troubled by no hesitations," he dictated in his autobiography in 1907. "What he accomplished in an hour or so would have cost me several weeks of painful and difficult labor and would have been valueless when I got through. But Harte's work was good and usable; to me it was a wonderful performance."

Ah Sin was finished by the middle of December, and Harte went back to New York to make arrangements with the actor Charles T. Parsloe. He left behind him, however, some injury—a remark about Livy's faith or furniture or style of living—which was localized enough at the time but which eventually poisoned the entire relationship. "My dear Mark," he apologized from New York on December 16, "tell Mrs. Clemens that she must forgive me for my heterodoxy—that until she does I shall wear sackcloth (fashionably cut), and that I would put ashes on my forehead but that Nature has anticipated me. . . . I feel her gentle protests to my awful opinions all the more remorsefully that I am away." And along with the friendly hope that "Nature has let up generally on your bowels," he added some news, suggestive of trouble to come, about the revisions he was making: "Writing myself *up* and you down, that is, trying to make myself more easily intelligible, and you not quite so *prononcé*."

"Yes, one of the brightest gems in the New England weather is the dazzling uncertainty of it," Mark Twain was saying prophetically on December 22, in one of the best speeches he ever gave. "There is only one thing certain about it: you are certain there is going to be plenty of it." The permanent revival of the feud between him and Bret Harte was more certain, though, than some of the other episodes of the winter. Isabella Hooker's interest in the spirit world had grown to the extent that she now believed that on New Year's Eve, in her house on Forest Street, a sign would come from beyond the veil that she had been elected president of a universal matriarchy which, like a giant corporation, would later effect a merger on a share-for-share basis with the kingdom of heaven. A celebration was in order, especially in this community where there was a generalized interest in spiritism (Clemens, for example, would make an attempt in 1879 to talk to his brother Henry through a medium named Mansfield, would visit other mediums after Susy died, and was throughout his later life fascinated by mind science and faith healers). Isabella invited two sets of guests: the secular neighbors—including the Clemenses, the Charles Dudley Warners, and General Hawley—who were there primarily to celebrate the arrival of 1877, and a covey of local mediums, spiritualists, and clairvoyants who were there to witness her elevation and whom she hid upstairs in a bedroom. At midnight the bells rang, but nothing else happened. The raisins and the walnuts were all eaten. Awkwardly and indignantly the believers came out of hiding—"There is the queerest-looking lot up there," Isabella's daughter Alice said a little too loudly—and one medium, Dr. Williams, was mistaken by Clemens for somebody's coachman. The long-suffering John Hooker, destined by his wife to be secretary of foreign affairs under the new order, was attacked by a muscular lady medium, and they scuffled in the hallway. In the early hours of the new year Hooker confronted Isabella in the study and said she was suffering from monomania.

The entire Beecher hegemony was collapsing, in fact. Henry had said that Isabella was crazy and ought to be locked up. John Hooker was afraid that he himself was about to become the victim of hereditary insanity from one of his grandfathers. Harriet Beecher Stowe was only about ten years away from a state of schizoid anility in which (Clemens recalled) she "would slip up behind a person who was deep in dreams and musings and fetch a war whoop that would jump that person out of his clothes." Harriet's husband, Calvin, was constantly visited by apparitions, and their son Fred was an alcoholic.

During February 1877 Clemens, who had maintained a discreet public silence about Henry Ward Beecher, launched an attack on an old Beecher protégé which was so venomous and out of scale to its target that it is probable that at the back of his mind was lurking the black-clad figure of Beecher himself. Charles C. Duncan, captain (or, as Clemens chose to call him, "head-waiter") of the *Quaker City*, was now back in the public eye lecturing about the cruise and also being investigated for alleged embezzlement and nepotism while serving as shipping commissioner of the port of New York. There were obvious parallels between Duncan and Beecher —neither lived up to his moral pretensions—and Clemens may have been hiding his true intentions from himself when he said, privately, that the vilest thing Duncan ever did was to turn against Beecher when Beecher was in trouble. The pretext for his public statements, which were printed in the New York *World*, was the charge made by Duncan in his lecture that Clemens had been drunk when he first applied for passage. "I have known and observed Mr. Duncan for ten years," Clemens wrote, working himself into a blind rage, "and I think I have good reason for believing him to be wholly without principle, without moral sense, without honor of any kind. . . . I know him to be a canting hypocrite, filled to the chin with sham godliness, and forever oozing and dripping false piety and pharisaical prayers." A week later he resumed the attack: "A man whose stock in trade is sham temperance, sham benevolence, religious hypocrisy, and a ceaseless, unctuous drip of buttery prayers."

If Livy's powers of restraint were actually as considerable as her husband pretended they were, Duncan should have been spared. When Bret Harte's turn came, her counsels of moderation were no more effective. "Don't say harsh things about Mr. Harte, don't talk about Mr. Harte to people," she pleaded. "We are so desperately happy, our paths lie in such places, and he is so miserable, we can easily afford to be magnanimous to him." Harte's original insult had been aggravated by a battle over revisions, but, contrary to Clemens' recollection of the feud in his autobiography, it was Harte who rejected Clemens. Clemens, in fact, even offered him a salary of twenty-five dollars a week plus room and board to come back to Hartford and collaborate on another play. Harte flung the offer back at him, charging that Clemens was merely speculating on his poverty and making him, in effect, an indentured playwright, and he added a welter of recriminations: Clemens and Bliss were responsible for the failure of *Gabriel Conroy;* Clemens' idea of sending Parsloe to San Francisco to study his Chinese part was outrageous; Clemens' revisions were only marring the play and demonstrated a total misunderstanding of Harte's characters. All in all, Harte concluded, it would not be "advisable" for them to write another play together. This was in March 1877; by the beginning of April, a month before *Ah Sin* opened in Washington, Harte was writing to him only about business matters—"My dear Mr. Clemens."

"Is the name of your play 'Arse in'?—sounds like a sitz bath," Frank Fuller teased him a week or so before it opened at Augustin Daly's Fifth Avenue Theatre on July 31. Clemens was in New York supervising the rehearsals, seething with anger at Harte for not putting in an appearance, planning, he told Livy, to extract from his collaborator "$50 a day for my work here, or I will know the reason why—that is, if the play succeeds." The Washington tryout had been a backward affair; the New York run was a failure, and after five weeks of dwindling attendance it closed, leaving Daly with a considerable loss.

On opening night Clemens saw Parsloe act the part and speak the lines miscreated by two celebrated humorists and artists of the vernacular: "Walkee bottom side hillee—stage bloke down—plenty smashee uppee. Plunkee plenty helpee, plenty makee allee rightee—Plunkee vellee good man." At the end of the third act that evening, Clemens stood before the curtain in a summer white suit and spoke what might just as well have been the play's epitaph. The more Daly had cut, he explained, "the better the play got. I never saw a play that was so much improved by being cut down; and I believe it would have been one of the very best plays in the world if his strength had held out so that he could cut out the whole of it."

v

The first months of the Hayes administration raised Clemens' spirits. "It's been a long time since we've had anybody to feel proud of and have confidence in," he told Howells. "I mean to take my fill now while the meat's hot and the appetite ravenous." But in July and August the anthracite miners and the railroad workers went out on strike; the walkouts were followed by pitched battles between militia and labor; there was rioting, pillage, and arson in Baltimore, Pittsburgh, and Buffalo. All this fanned once again his hatred for republican government, and he returned to his habitual tirades against democracy, the vote, the jury system, and the modern world in general. When he visited Bermuda with Twichell in May —"First actual pleasure trip I ever took"—he was dazzled by the whiteness of the houses (he always remembered the Hannibal of his lost childhood as a "white town"), but he was certain that in only a year or so this Eden too would be ruined by civilization's "triple curse" of railroad, telegraph, and newspapers.

Livy was often on the edge of nervous collapse from the fatigue of entertaining and of tutoring her children; the Hartford house was getting more and more expensive and complicated to run, and the Clemenses were feeling the need to cut back on little things here and there. Livy's income had dwindled—the coal business, after making only a slow recovery from the panic, was hard hit by the strikes. As usual, when the storm signals went up, Clemens could turn to lecturing. But he declined the usual invitations, because he dreaded traveling alone and carrying the entire show by himself. Instead, still in a collaborative mood even after combat with Bret Harte, he tried to talk Thomas Nast into making the same joint tour —one of them to draw pictures while the other talked—that Nast had proposed to him in 1867. But Nast was no longer interested, and the scheme died. As a humorist, Clemens felt himself more than ever at a disadvantage. "When a humorist ventures upon the grave concerns of life," he explained when Howells asked him to take public part in the Hayes campaign, "he must do his job better than another man or he works harm to his cause." *Ah Sin* had been his second failure within a year. At the end of November 1877 he began *The Prince and the Pauper*, a tale set in Tudor England; as a further defensive withdrawal from his life and times and profession, he intended to publish it anonymously, "such grave and stately work being considered by the world to be above my proper level."

He voiced his sense of both independence and alienation in several public gestures whose hostile content, as it seems now, was too painful for him to acknowledge consciously. On one occasion, the Whittier birthday dinner in December 1877, he implicitly rejected and mocked the official culture of New England as represented by its septuagenary eminences, some of them entering their dotage and all of them products of another taste and another time, when that culture reigned without rival. On another occasion, two months earlier in Hartford, he attacked the sacred values of patriotism, the martial spirit, and New England solidarity.

On October 1, 1877, two hundred and thirty-five members of the Ancient and Honorable Artillery Company of Massachusetts, the oldest military organization in the country—Governor John Winthrop signed their charter in 1638—arrived in Hartford after a four-hour train trip fom Boston. They had come to celebrate their annual fall field day as guests of the city. They were greeted at the depot with a thirteen-gun salute. Led by the Putnam Phalanx, Hartford's elite marching group, and by a drum corps and two bands, the Ancient and Honorable paraded through the city and passed in review before the old State House. Like the rest of America, Hartford was in the grip of a passion for pageantry and display, for marching groups and drilling societies and fraternal orders; this was the beginning of the golden age of Masons, Elks, and Knights of Pythias. Hartford was also a parade-loving city—Mark Twain later moved the kitchen of his house closer to Farmington Avenue "so the servants can see the circus go by without running into the street"—and its citizens turned out by the thousand. Flags and banners and bunting, evergreens and inscriptions and patriotic devices were everywhere—on private houses, on the buildings of the great insurance companies, on the Wadsworth Athenaeum and on the statue of Israel Putnam in the west park. Near the main entrance of the City Hall was a huge pillow of red, white, and blue flowers enclosing the word "Welcome," and over Asylum Street an arch of banners, shields, flags, and coats of arms stretched from sidewalk to sidewalk. That night there was a reception, a ball, and a supper. The next morning the Ancients were taken by carriage on a tour of the city, including Colt's armory, where Dr. Gatling demonstrated his remarkable repeating gun; and shortly before noon there was a band concert attended by four or five thousand people in the park.

The climax of this patriotic celebration was a midday banquet at Allyn Hall. Mark Twain sat at the main table with the eminences of Connecticut and Massachusetts and the commanders of the Ancients and the Putnam Phalanx. The martial strains of Mr. D. W. Reeves's American Band of Providence were followed by the clash of cutlery. Then came the speeches. Commander Stevenson tended the thanks of the Ancients. And then Major Brown of the Phalanx said he was unaccustomed to speaking in public. And then Judge-Advocate Barber delivered a rousing patriotic and historical oration in the course of which he re-created the battle of Bunker Hill, the thundering cannon, the crack of musketry, the charges and repulses, the desperate hand-to-hand struggle, and the voice of Israel Putnam crying out above the noises of battle, "Make a stand here; in God's name form, and give them one shot more!" (Applause.) And then Governor Hubbard recalled how the men of Massachusetts and the men of Connecticut had always been brothers in arms: "The grim earth has drank richly of their common blood—in the Indian Wars, in the French War, in the Revolutionary War, in the Mexican War, and finally in the greater war which shook for four years, as with a rending earthquake, the foundations of the republic." And then General Banks said that in the War of the Rebellion he found no more courageous and vigilant supporters of the Union flag than the sons of Connecticut. And then, and then, and then.

Toward the end of this Pentecostal rite of self-congratulation, Northern brotherhood, and inflamed patriotism, Mark Twain spoke. "If you fight as well as you feed, God protect the enemy," he remarked as he began his account of what he called a forgotten chapter in the military history of the United States and of the Southern Confederacy: his own career as a rebel soldier ("I find myself in a minority here") who signed up because war seemed a lark and who deserted after two weeks because he discovered it was a bore. In a sense, it had taken him sixteen years to prepare this speech. What he had learned in the sixteen years was how to turn the "damned humiliating" past into a comic weapon.

"Mark Twain's speech at the 'Ancients' is rather flat reading," the Boston *Evening Transcript* reported the next day, "but they say it was full of sparkle as it was delivered," and without a doubt the frequent "bursts of laughter" which interrupted the speaker had a nervous quality. Mark Twain told these warriors of Connecticut and Massachusetts that for him it had all been like a camping trip at first. But then the rats and the mosquitoes and even the horses started biting; the rain fell, his feet were wet all the time; there were not enough umbrellas to go around, and the Worcestershire sauce gave out; insubordination was the only order of the day ("Who was your nigger last year?" the orderly sergeant answered a command) and military discipline was unknown; boredom set in. "Then Ben Tupper lost patience. Said he, 'War ain't what it's cracked up to be; I'm going home if I can't ever get a chance to sit down. Why do these people keep us a-humping around so? Blame their skins, do they think this is an excursion?' " Worst of all, there were reports the enemy was in the vicinity and meant business:

There was mutiny and dissatisfaction all around, and of course here came the enemy pestering us again—as much as two hours before breakfast, too, when nobody wanted to turn out, of course. This was a little too much. The whole command felt insulted. I sent an aid to the brigadier, and asked him to assign us a district where there wasn't so much bother going on. The history of our campaign was laid before him, but instead of being touched by it, what did he do? He sent back an indignant message.

Brigadier Tom Harris ("Why, I knew him when he wasn't nothing but a darn telegraph operator") threatened them, in fact, with court martial. But contrary to the code which Judge-Advocate Barber and Governor Hubbard and General Banks and all the others were glorifying, Mark Twain's band of volunteers, instead of saying, This is war, said, To hell with it. The brigade disbanded and tramped off home, deserters, but safe. "We were the first men that went into the service in Missouri; we were the first that went out of it anywhere." Like Huck Finn, Mark Twain said to himself, "I reckon I got to light out for the Territory ahead of the rest," and as the readers of *Roughing It* knew, he spent the war years far from cannon and battlefields: as Orion's secretary in Nevada, he was at least the symbolic beneficiary of Federal patronage, and then he went on to mine for silver, work as a journalist, and in general have a pretty good time.

Rebel, deserter, slacker—he had been all these, but by his confession in such bold, ironic terms he is free from punishment and also free to channel his accumulated anger and contempt. He has become the humorist as rational coward, Falstaff declaring that "Honor is a mere scutcheon." He rejects war because war is boring, uncomfortable, and dangerous. He makes an offensive weapon out of the sort of experience the veterans of the Ancients and the Phalanx would normally find shameful. Against the background of the flatulent and bloodthirsty oratory that preceded it, his speech was implicit insult and explicit deflation of the hallowed martial values—What was the war all about, anyway? he seems to be asking—but he contained his satire within a convention his audience was powerless to reject: "I ask you to fill your glasses and drink with me to the reverend memory of the Orderly Sergeant and those other neglected and forgotten heroes, my foot-sore and travel-stained paladins, who were first in war, first in peace, and were not idle in the interval that lay between."

For years afterward Clemens continued to work over this speech, the germ of his darker and more extended account of his military service in the December 1885 *Century*, "The Private History of a Campaign That Failed." But the speech he gave in Boston on December 17, 1877, at the dinner in honor of Whittier's seventieth birthday was one that he added, for a while, to the long list of *mea maxima culpas* that ran back to his boyhood. "That disastrous cataclysm," he noted thirty years later on a copy of the seating plan for the Hotel Brunswick's dining room. After the chablis and the claret, the Mumm's Dry and the Roederer Imperial, Clemens faced toward the honored guests at the head of the U-shaped table and told a long—to some, interminable—story within a story. In 1864, he said, when the name Mark Twain was beginning to be known in Nevada and California, he stopped off at a miner's cabin in the Sierra foothills and introduced himself. The miner said Twain was "the fourth literary man that has been here in twenty-four hours," and told him a story about three boozy and rough-looking tramps—"Consound the lot!"—who had stopped off the evening before and said they were Emerson ("a seedy little bit of a chap"), Holmes ("fat as a balloon"), and Longfellow ("built like a prize-fighter"). They took over the cabin, gorged themselves on the miner's bacon, beans, and whiskey, played cards with a greasy deck and cheated, and at seven the next morning left with the miner's only pair of boots. "I'm going to move," the miner says to Mr. Twain. "I ain't suited to a littery atmosphere."

> I said to the miner, "Why, my dear sir, *these* were not the gracious singers to whom we and the world pay loving reverence and homage; these were impostors."
> The miner investigated me with a calm eye for a while; then said he, "Ah! impostors, were they? Are *you?*"

During the performance the three "gracious singers," according to Howells, were to be seen in various attitudes of removal from reality: Mr. Longfellow looked puzzled, Dr. Holmes was busy writing on his menu, and Mr. Emerson was in one of his chronic senile trances. The expression of interest on the other faces, Clemens remembered, "turned to a sort of black frost." Howells stared down at his plate; once he looked up out of his embarrassment to see Clemens "standing solitary amid his appalled and appalling listeners, with his joke dead on his hands." Afterward Howells could manage only a gasp. There was a heavy silence, "weighing many tons to the square inch," and it was "broken only by the hysterical and bloodcurdling laughter of a single guest whose name shall not be handed down to infamy." "Well, Mark," Warner said, "*you're* a funny fellow." That night, having been convinced by himself and by Howells that this speech, so gaily conceived, was fundamentally an insult and a "hideous mistake," Clemens tossed sleeplessly in his bed, and his agony of shame and remorse, aggravated by some newspaper references to his "offense against good taste," lasted for months. Tacitly acknowledging the satiric drift and content of his speech, he, like Howells, persisted in exaggerating the dimensions of the scandal. In actuality, the speech had been greeted with a fair amount of laughter; Emerson, it is true, had been in a trance, but Whittier, Longfellow, and Holmes had shown some polite amusement; and the evening had not broken up in paralyzed horror, but had gone on as planned, speeches and all, for at least an hour more.

Ten days after his speech, with Howells' consent, Clemens wrote a formal letter of apology to Emerson, Longfellow, and Holmes. Two points run through it: his own continuing mortification as well as Livy's ("As to my wife's distress, it is not to be measured. . . . We do not talk about this misfortune—it *scorches*") and his certainty that his original or at least his conscious impulse had been innocent: "I do not ask you to forgive what I did that night, for it is not forgivable; I simply had it at heart to ask you to believe that I am only heedlessly a savage, not premeditatedly." The dwarf conscience, he seemed to be saying, had no right to tear at him for being "only heedlessly a savage." He made the point again in a speech of amends two years later at an *Atlantic* breakfast celebrating Holmes's seventieth birthday. This time Howells read over the speech beforehand, approved it, and then emphasized the penitent nature of the occasion by his introduction: "We will now listen to a few words of truthfulness and soberness from Mark Twain." And quite simply and directly Clemens told how he had inadvertently plagiarized the dedication of *The Innocents Abroad* from Holmes and, when he discovered this a few years after the book was published, had written a letter of apology; pleasantly and forgivingly Holmes wrote back to say "he believed we all unconsciously worked over ideas gathered in reading and hearing, imagining they were original with ourselves." "I am rather glad I committed the crime," Clemens said at the end, "for the sake of the letter." The parallel with the Whittier disaster was clear enough. One of the tramps borrowed Holmes's poetry and identity, Mark Twain stole his dedication from Holmes. If plagiarism deserved forgiveness because it had been committed "unconsciously," then an insult offered "heedlessly" deserved equally to be forgiven.

But along with such explicit and implicit admissions of insult and wrongdoing Clemens could present an entirely different stance. "I am sincerely sorry if it in any wise hurt those great poets' feelings—I never wanted to do that," he told Mary Fairbanks in February 1878, not much more than a month after his letter of apology. "But nobody has ever convinced me that that speech was not a good one—for me; far above my average, considerably. I could as easily have substituted the names of Shakespeare, Beaumont, and Ben Jonson." (Shakespeare and Beaumont, it is worth noting, participate in the taboo fireside conversation in *1601*.) "But my purpose was clean, my conscience clear, and I saw no need of it. Why anybody should think three poets insulted because three fantastic tramps choose to personate them and use their language, passes my comprehension. Nast says it is very much the best speech and the most humorous situation I have contrived." And in 1906, having again blinded himself to the content of the evening, he wondered what had been the matter with that audience at the Hotel Brunswick—"It is amazing, it is incredible, that they didn't shout with laughter, and those deities the loudest of them all." By then, after wrestling long with the enigma of dual personality, he might have recognized that his speech about three tramps was the kind of speech his "dream self" (another "impostor") would give. Clemens' performance that evening in Boston, Howells wrote to Charles Eliot Norton, "was like an effect of demoniacal possession." The demons were to be increasingly with him and to lead him even farther away from benign entertainment and toward highly complex and conflictive comic molds. His "hideous mistake," though he did not know it, was really a portal of discovery.

CHAPTER ELEVEN

"The free air of Europe"

I

ON APRIL 11, 1878, Mr. and Mrs. Samuel L. Clemens of Hartford and their two children—Susy, six, and Clara, going on four—sailed from New York, Europe-bound, on the steamship *Holsatia*. With them were Clara Spaulding, an Elmira friend who had accompanied Livy to England five years earlier; a nursemaid, Rosina Hay, who was to give the children instruction in German; and the Clemenses' butler, George Griffin, who came along as valet and baggage agent. From time to time this sizable party was supplemented by cicerones and couriers.

Neither in itinerary nor in scale of living did Clemens and his family depart much from the conventional pattern of well-to-do Americans. They landed at Hamburg, visited Hanover and Frankfurt, and spent most of the summer in Heidelberg. At the beginning of August Twichell arrived from America, his passage and expenses paid by Clemens, who counted on him to help in gathering material and adventures for a European travel book. The two went off on the "tramp abroad" of the book's title, a walking tour—by rail, carriage, and boat, as it turned out—through the Black Forest and the Swiss Alps to Lausanne and Geneva. After a month and a half of sightseeing, shopping, and visiting the American colonies in Venice, Florence, and Rome, the Clemenses settled for the winter in Munich, where, in a rented workroom at 45 Nymphenstrasse, Clemens struggled with the book. In February they moved to Paris; they stayed there until July, then went to London by way of Belgium and Holland. On August 23, 1879, they left Liverpool on the *Gallia*, and they reached New York on September 3. They were gone a little over sixteen months.

The tourist looks ahead of him, anticipating a different landscape and a change of heart; the expatriate looks also behind him, fearfully or in anger, and measures where he has gone against where he has been. Although he observed most of the conventions of the family grand tour, Clemens himself, disillusioned, pressured, and, he believed, made soft and self-complacent by ten years of celebrity in the East, became for part of his stay abroad a self-exile from his homeland. A voyage was a dreamless sleep, a stupor, he said when he went to Bermuda. As he prepared to leave for Europe he felt that to go abroad was to die, to escape from the living. "I know you will refrain from saying harsh things *because* they can't hurt me, since I am out of reach and cannot hear them," he wrote in his notebook, addressing his own country. "That is why we say no harsh things of the dead." To go abroad was to leave behind the sting of the Whittier dinner, the failures of *Tom Sawyer* and *Ah Sin*, and certain portents of declining creativity: between September 1877 and March 1880 Mark Twain published only one book, called *Punch, Brothers, Punch!*, and this little collection of reprinted sketches was designed primarily to promote his scrapbook, a book with no writing in it at all.

"Life has come to be a very serious matter with me," Sam wrote to his mother two months before sailing. "It comes mainly of business responsibilities and annoyances, and the persecution of kindly letters from well-meaning strangers." He was the victim of his own success and fame; he felt hounded by autograph hunters, and life in the house in Hartford, with its ever-mounting expenses and stream of visitors, was swallowing him up. "I want to find a German village where nobody knows my name or speaks any English, and shut myself up in a closet two miles from the hotel and work every day without interruption," he told Mary Fairbanks in March 1878. A little over a year later, however, he was writing to her not from a German village, but from Paris. Now he said, "We are in Europe mainly to cut down our expenses." He did not explain that in none of the places where he had tried to settle down had he been able to work at all satisfactorily on his new book and thereby escape what seemed a web of futility.

Disgusted by the mishandling of *Tom Sawyer* and convinced that his publisher was out to fleece him, Clemens signed a contract with Elisha Bliss's son, Frank, a month before sailing. The younger Bliss, working secretly at first, planned his own publishing house and as a start was raiding his father's. But the ghost of Riley walked again (as it does in Chapter Twenty-six of *A Tramp Abroad*). Alerted to Frank's raid, Elisha Bliss reminded Clemens that the old Riley contract of 1870 was still unfulfilled: under its terms Clemens owed Bliss a book-length manuscript and the two thousand dollars that Riley had got as an advance. Frank Bliss stepped in between his father and Clemens to point out that conditions of the Riley contract had been satisfied by *Tom Sawyer*, and for a while Clemens seemed to be winning his freedom. Eventually, however, Frank failed to raise enough money to start the new house and Elisha Bliss reclaimed his valuable but discontented author, who found himself trying to finish a book which he did not want to write and which was to be published by a house he no longer liked nor trusted. His only victory was in getting Elisha Bliss to agree "not to publish any other new book within nine months from the time of publication of my new book." Remembering the lesson of *Tom Sawyer*, he was determined that *A Tramp Abroad* should not be an orphan. He was equally determined that it should not be an outlaw, and, to make sure that he would offend no one at home, he wrote a pointed reminder to himself to put all criticisms of America in the mouth of a foreigner.

He was discreet publicly, but in private he continued to rage at the familiar corruptions and abuses. "Noble system, truly," he grumbled, where a man who should be in jail or practicing shyster law in the Tombs goes to the Senate instead. He wanted to write a biography of Whitelaw (or "Outlaw") Reid and also a biography, *The Genial Thief,* of Mayor Oakley Hall, puppet and patron of the Tweed Ring. But there were new forces, too, which troubled Clemens and which, though he barely understood them, were changing the nation he thought he knew so well: the rise of organized labor, the wave of immigration which in the years 1880–89 added five and a quarter million newcomers to a population of fifty million. Sixty thousand "communists," someone told him, were drilling in the streets of Cincinnati, Chicago, and St. Louis; anxious cities were putting up armories to put down rebellion. The radicals, foreigners many of them, the hearsay went on, were inflamed by socialist revolutionary theory, and Clemens believed they might very well overthrow "the asinine government" of this "leatherheaded Republic," which he would not mind, except that his money and property and Livy's were hostages to the status quo. As the *Holsatia* headed for the open sea, where it would pass ships carrying some of those five million immigrants waiting for the first sight of the New World, Mark Twain sniffed the Old World in the breeze. It was good, he reflected, "to go and breathe the free air of Europe."

II

"Oh, I have such a deep, grateful, unutterable sense of being 'out of it,'" Clemens wrote to Howells from Frankfurt. "I think I foretaste some of the advantages of being dead. Some of the joy of it." After the Beecher scandal he was all the more eager to drink in the *bürgerlich* virtues he saw all about him. "What a paradise this land is," he exclaimed. "What clean clothes, what good faces, what tranquil contentment, what prosperity, what genuine freedom, what superb government!" The German trains ran on time, the brass was polished every morning and the sidewalks swept and washed down, the Empress dressed like anybody else and went to Church of England services. For Clemens, as for many Americans of his generation and a few after it, Germany stood for Protestant rectitude and industriousness, orderliness and thrift. The contrast was with the disordered America of the Gilded Age, its urban squalor and meager municipal services. The contrast was also with England, still condescending to most of American culture, and above all with France and Italy, Catholic countries and, as Clemens saw them, sensual, torn by radicalism or reaction. The German revolutionaries of 1848–49 had emigrated to America, seeking an ideal of popular government; now, thirty years later, the German-American cultural entente was never stronger. American universities looked to Germany for models of academic freedom and scholarship; Germany took the lead in music, in philosophy and science, medicine and jurisprudence. Carl Schurz, a German revolutionary in 1849 and, during the Civil War, American minister to Spain and a divisional commander, was now President Hayes's Secretary of the Interior; and, in a sense reciprocally, Mark Twain's fellow passenger on the *Holsatia* was Bayard Taylor, translator of Goethe's *Faust* and professor of German literature at Cornell, on his way to Berlin to take up his new post as American minister.

The Prince and the Pauper, which Clemens began in November 1877, was the sign of his growing disenchantment with England, now replaced in his enthusiasms by Germany. Before leaving America he began to study German, and he kept on with it even though its intricacies of sentence structure exasperated him as much as they amused him. "Yes, sir," he wrote in his notebook, "once the German language gets hold of a cat, it's goodbye cat," and he decided he would rather decline two drinks than one verb. He admitted to Bayard Taylor that he was fighting a losing battle, and this was obvious to others. "Speak in German, Mark," Twichell whispered to him as Clemens was discussing some private matter within earshot of some Germans, "some of these people may understand English."

His enthusiasm for the Germans was matched by their enthusiasm for him. *Roughing It* had come out in a German translation in 1874, a year after Bret Harte's *Die Argonauten-Geschichten;* four other Mark Twain books were translated between 1875 and 1877 (between 1890 and 1913 a hundred German translations of his work were published); and Baron von Tauchnitz's paperback Continental reprints in English brought him additional popularity among the Germans (as well as modest but entirely voluntary royalties). "They all quote him before they have spoken with you fifteen minutes, and always give him a place so much higher than we do," the Bostonian Thomas Wentworth Higginson, visiting Coblenz in August 1878, said in amazement. "I don't think any English prose writer is so universally read." It was in the flush of this requited love affair with Germany and the Germans that Mark Twain, discovering that he needed a passport, sent an application to Bayard Taylor in Berlin with an exuberant self-description:

> Geborn 1835; 5 Fuss 8½ inches hoch; weight doch aber about 145 pfund, sometimes ein wenig unter, sometimes ein wenig oben; dunkel braun Haar und rhotes Moustache, full Gesicht, mit sehr hohe Oren und leicht grau practvolles strahlenden Augen und ein Verdammtes gut moral character. Handlungkeit, Author von Bücher.

Yet into Clemens' paradise at the Hotel Schloss in Heidelberg came an unescapable demon in the form of news that Bret Harte, another hero to the Germans, had been given a consular appointment in Germany—in the textile center of Krefeld, it developed, only about two hundred miles north of Heidelberg. "Tell me what German town he is to filthify with his presence." Clemens wrote to Howells in June 1878; "then I will write the authorities there that he is a persistent borrower who never pays." Fully in the grip of a monomania that only grew more violent with age, he intended to protect the Germans from the new American consul. "Harte is a liar, a thief, a swindler, a snob, a sot, a sponge, a coward, a Jeremy Diddler, he is brim full of treachery, and he conceals his Jewish birth as if he considered it a disgrace." For Bret Harte, a diplomatic appointment was one way of solving his money problems, and he had had an anxious time in Washington politicking for a position, aware all the time that he had enemies working against him, among them his former collaborator. Clemens had taken the trouble to write to President Hayes and denounce Harte as unfit for any public office. Now, as he admitted to Howells, he felt "personally snubbed," because the President "silently ignored my testimony." Certainly Clemens did not know—and neither did Harte, probably—that in an attempt to cut through all the wheedling and backbiting Hayes had written directly to Howells, who was his cousin by marriage and author of his campaign biography, asking for an opinion, and that Howells, after admitting that Harte had "the worst reputation as regards punctuality, solvency, and sobriety," concluded cautiously that he was making an effort to reform and therefore deserved help. "*Personally*, I should be glad of his appointment, and I should have great hopes of him—and fears."

"Billiardly-speaking," Clemens wrote, when Hayes appointed Harte "he simply pocketed his own ball," and he asked Howells: "Have you heard any literary men express an opinion about the appointment? Who were they—and what said they?" Howells maintained an embarrassed silence which after three months had Clemens wondering, "Have I offended you in some way? The Lord knows it is my disposition, my infirmity to do such things . . ." Among those offended was Frank Harris, former bartender and cowboy, now, at the age of twenty-two, a student at Heidelberg, who called on Clemens to ask him to address the local Anglo-American literary society. Like Kipling, Harris idolized Bret Harte, and he was treated to a venomous account of how his idol was a cheat and fraud who had bilked the American Publishing Company. "I told the publishers that they ought to have put him in prison," Clemens went on, ignoring the effect he was having on Harris. "A man should be honest above everything." At that moment Harris lost his last bit of respect for Clemens. "I never want to see that man again; never again do I want to talk to him," he said to a friend. "Fancy his running down Bret Harte on such paltry grounds." And more than forty years later, after Clemens' death, Harris wrote him off as a small man who wanted success and popularity in his day and was willing to pay any price for it.

Behind the litany of Clemens' grievances against Bret Harte during the summer of 1878 was an infuriating parallel. Harte was coming to Germany as consul at Krefeld (at a salary of two thousand dollars a year) because he could no longer make a go of it as a literary man in America. *Gabriel Conroy* was a failure, *Ah Sin* was a failure, he was in debt, and his achievement and fame were already behind him. Mark Twain was in Germany partly to save money, partly because of the declining American sales of his books, partly because he was unable to work at home and finish any one of the six or so books (among them *Huckleberry Finn*) he had begun, partly because he wanted to return to proven ground and write another travel book. In Heidelberg he spent weeks waiting for "a 'call' to go to work"; when the call came it was not a strong one, and he ended by tearing up most of what he wrote there. Europe, for all his first enthusiasm, did not excite him in any deep sense; soon, in fact, he realized that he hated travel, hated the food, hated hotels and opera and Old Masters, hated them so much (as he told Howells) that he was afraid he was too angry to write "successful satire." As Clemens struggled with his book in Heidelberg, and then in Munich, Paris, Elmira, and Hartford, he had reason to be afraid that he was going the way of Bret Harte.

Clemens paid for Twichell's trip to Europe because he needed the stimulus of Twichell's company for *A Tramp Abroad*, and he freely acknowledged Twichell's importance. When he heard that a Hartford paper said it was improper for a clergyman to accept patronage from a humorist, he commented that it was Twichell who was doing the favor; in eventual terms if the book turned out to be a success, that money was "a trivial share of the money which he has lavished upon me." When Clemens finished the book in 1879 he made a significant calculation: he had spent fourteen months in Europe collecting material; Twichell had been with him only one and a half months of the fourteen; yet Twichell, thinly disguised as "Mr. Harris," a hired "agent," figures in about two thirds of the book. One way of describing the inadequacies of *A Tramp Abroad* is to

say that it reflects the personality and viewpoint of the boyish and fundamentally conventional Twichell altogether too much.

Yet even along the barren ground of *A Tramp Abroad* Mark Twain
stumbled on outcroppings of his native vein. Two brilliant chapters near
the very beginning of the book deal not with dueling, the Alps, or the
pleasures of bourgeois tourism but with the California hermit Jim Baker,
who understands the language of animals and birds and tells a yarn about
a gullible bluejay. There is a story about Riley and a Washington office
seeker. Toward the end of a digressive chapter there is a story about Nico-
demus Dodge, a printer's apprentice in Hannibal, who had a skeleton put
in his bed as a practical joke; the skeleton was that of Jimmy Finn, the
town drunkard, who auctioned off first claim on it for fifty dollars, spent
the fifty dollars on a long binge, and after two weeks was dead. And in
other ways, even in the unlikely context of a European travel book, Mark
Twain was rehearsing *Huckleberry Finn*, put aside in 1876 when the tank
ran dry. Weaving together Chapters Fourteen through Nineteen of *A
Tramp Abroad* is a curious raft episode, almost wholly invented, which
Mark Twain wrote in Munich during January and February 1879. The
raft episode suggests both the waywardness and the persistence of his creative process: he came back to his block and stopping point in *Huckleberry
Finn*, the destruction of the raft, in the same way that the tongue comes
back to the site of the missing tooth.

Adjoining his rooms at the Hotel Schloss in Heidelberg, Mark Twain
writes at the beginning of this fictional episode, was a glassed-in balcony
looking out over a swift stretch of the winding Neckar, the arched stone
bridge, and the thick traffic of rafts. "I used to sit for hours in my glass
cage, watching the long, narrow rafts slip through the central channel,"
he recalls. "I watched them in this way, and lost all this time hoping to
see one of them hit the bridge-pier and wreck itself sometime or other,
but was always disappointed." To begin with, this is a curious preoccupation for the man Twichell was describing in his journals as timid, shy,
delicate, absorbed in flowers, petting a lamb—"can't bear to see the whip
used, or to see a horse pull too hard."

Visiting Heilbronn, thirty-five or so miles up the river from Heidelberg,
the narrator is suddenly possessed by "the daredevil spirit of adventure."
He tells his companions, "*I* am going to Heidelberg on a raft. Will you
venture with me?" He charters a raft, and they push out into the current
and into the repose and freedom Huck and Jim knew. "The motion of a
raft is the needful motion," the narrator says, "it is gentle and gliding, and
smooth, and noiseless; it calms down all feverish activities . . ." The idyl
has begun again, but as a parody of the raft episode in *Huckleberry Finn*.
The hazards of the journey—a storm, dynamite blasts, the river steamers—
are burlesques of travel adventure. The narrative is padded out with

German "legends" about knights, lords, and Crusaders and with the words, variant translations, and even the music of "Die Lorelei." In place of Huck and Jim, fugitives from justice, we have Mark Twain and his thinly disguised pastor, Mr. Twichell. Huck is certain he will go to hell, Mark Twain is certain he will get to Heidelberg.* He gets there at sunset . . .

> . . . perceiving, presently, that I really was going to shoot the bridge itself instead of the archway under it, I judiciously stepped ashore. The next moment I had my long-coveted desire: I saw a raft wrecked. It hit the pier in the center and went all to smash and scatteration like a box of matches struck by lightning.

Clemens' anxiety about *Huckleberry Finn* is in a subtle way exorcized by substituting for it an old anxiety about the river. ("My nightmares, to this day," he noted in 1882, "take the form of running into an overshadowing bluff, with a steamboat—showing that my earliest dread made the strongest impress on me.") The narrator of this story is now back where he started, back in Heidelberg—one derivation of which is from a telescoping of *Heidelbeereberg*, meaning Huckleberry Mountain. The writer Mark Twain, whose creative unconscious lies closer to the surface than it does with most men, and whose life, consequently, is full of psychologically loaded accidents and coincidences, is now back at the end of Chapter Sixteen of his greatest book.

III

In 1909, reading over a letter he had written Howells from Munich in November 1878, Clemens thought back over his life as a traveler. Up to the time of the *Quaker City* trip, he said, he had a normal appetite for travel. Every voyage since then—he counted over forty of them, including a trip around the world—he made only out of necessity, "with rebellion in my heart, and bitterness." For all his initial relief at being out of America, for all his delight in Bavarian *Gemütlichkeit* and *Lebkuchen* and Christmas trees hung heavy with sugared dates and candy sticks, the winter of 1878–79, in Munich and Paris, was long and troubled. The cold weather lasted late into the spring; it snowed in May, and even in July and August he shivered by the fire. Someone was always sick: the baby, Clara, came near

* "Hell or Heidelberg, whichever you come to, first," Clemens wrote in his notebook in 1891, when he was again in Europe. "Hadleyburg" is an anagram of "Heidelberg." The passing stranger's note, in the short novel Clemens wrote in Vienna in 1898, reads: ". . . *some day, for your sins, you will die and go to hell or Hadleyburg* —TRY AND MAKE IT THE FORMER."

dying in January, Clemens thought; he himself was laid up with rheumatism and dysentery. "I broke the back of life yesterday and started downhill toward old age," he wrote to his mother on his forty-third birthday, jokingly enough. "This fact has not produced any effect upon me that I can detect." Yet the sudden death only a few weeks later of Bayard Taylor in Berlin, worn out at fifty-three, came as a somber reminder. "It is too sad to talk about." Throughout the winter Clemens had such trouble with *A Tramp Abroad* that he hoped he could find a pretext for abandoning it altogether.

Somewhere in Florence or Rome, or on the way to Munich, Clemens lost, or so he thought, one of the two notebooks of his tour with Twichell. Considering the disproportionately important role that Twichell plays in *A Tramp Abroad*, the loss of one of these notebooks would have been staggering; the book would have become "simply impossible." For Clemens, a man who in his professional and personal life hardly ever lost anything and generally preserved everything, this "accident" had a meaning which he grasped. "If it remains lost," he wrote to Twichell from Munich in November, "I can't write any volume of travels, and shan't attempt it, but shall tackle some other subject." He was, he admitted, relieved, glad— "I was getting an idea that I had lost my faculty of writing sketches of travel." And a month or so later, when the "lost" notebook was finally found, "down went my heart into my boots," and he set to work grimly on the "dismal" task of writing this "confounded book." He finished *A Tramp Abroad* more than a year after he "found" the notebook, a year during which he seemed to be groping for some way to escape the sterile obligation of writing "sketches of travel" and to regain the freedom he was to find in fiction and in imaginative uses of the past. "My Long Crawl in the Dark" was the title he eventually gave to one of the chapters in the book, an account, extravagantly adapted from an incident with Livy in Munich, of how he crawled forty-seven miles on his hands and knees in a dark bedroom looking for one of his socks. In the same vein was a remark he made in Paris to Moncure Conway, the clergyman, reformer, and literary man to whom he had entrusted arrangements for the English publication of *Tom Sawyer*. On a cold March morning in 1879 Clemens was on his way to call on General Noyes, the American ambassador, when Conway overtook him on the Champs Élysées and asked him what he was writing these days. "Well," Clemens answered, "it's about this: A man sets out from home on a long journey to do some particular thing. But he does everything except what he set out to do."

"Those mountains had a soul: they thought, they spoke—one couldn't hear it with the ears of the body, but what a voice it was! and how real." This was Clemens writing to Twichell in January 1879 in an effusion of sentimental rhetoric. "Deep down in my memory it is sounding yet. Alp calleth unto Alp!" If, as André Gide once said, the worship of mountains is a Protestant invention, a confusion of the beautiful with the merely lofty, then Clemens' other European reactions were also running true to form: he worshiped the Alps, a Protestant invention, and he reacted with discomfort to the sensual, Catholic arts of Italy. He objected to the fig leaf not only because it was prudish but because it made nakedness "most offensive and conspicuous," and his prurient but still amused eye noticed fig leaves in all kinds of places, even under the tails of animals, noticed also that these fig leaves and, when exposed, the genitals on statues were "handled so much that they are black and polished. Which sex does this handling?" But in Italy, too, visiting a life class in Rome, he was merely amused when the professional model who had been naked only minutes before adjusted her skirt because too much of her ankle was showing.

It was not until he came to France at the end of February 1879 that he began to voice the full and anguished extent of his conflicts over sexuality and sexual morality, censorship and controls, double standards in taste and conduct. As usual, he was feted and sought after. He drank tea from Turgenev's samovar, exchanged visits with him, gave him a copy of *Tom Sawyer*. "My dear Mr. Chatto," he was writing to his English publisher in May, "Please send a copy of *Roughing It* to Monsieur Ivan Turgenev, 50 rue Douay, Paris." With Conway and General Noyes he went to a reception at President Grévy's; with Clara Spaulding and General Lucius Fairchild, the American consul in Paris, he went to see the Grand Prix run at Chantilly. At a session in Paris of a convivial masculine group called the Stomach Club he heard with delight the illustrator Edwin Abbey give an unprintable speech; in his own talk, not tested out on Livy and Clara Spaulding, he paid tribute to the high antiquity of masturbation and joked that modern progress and improvement now assigned to it somewhat the same social dignity as flatulence. (His talk, "Some Thoughts on the Science of Onanism," could be traced back to a favorite joke of Artemus Ward's about "playing the lone hand.")

Despite all this pleasant and apparently untrammeled activity, the notebooks he kept during five months in Paris are those of a man obsessed. "Stomach Club has good times," he noted. But the very next entry is, typically, a diatribe against a "grossly obscene," "wholly sensual," and "bestial" Venus by Titian that he saw at the Louvre. He was afraid a young lady could be "defiled" simply by looking at it. The conjunction of Clemens' note about "good times" at the Stomach Club and this diatribe is, of course, a little like Baudelaire's experience with the five-franc prostitute who said the indecencies on exhibit at the Louvre made her cover her face and blush. Clemens' split attitude reflected in part a built-in American puritanism; fifty years earlier, for example, Samuel F. B. Morse, who began his career as a painter, said that it was the duty of American art to support truth and virtue and not to imitate the sensualism and "stench of decay" of European art. Clemens was also a Victorian gentleman who tacitly accepted a double standard even if he did not take advantage of it and who, at one and the same time, believed that prostitution was a necessary evil and occasional convenience but also denied the existence of any kind of urgent sexuality in the women of his own circle and social rank. He also made a rigid distinction between smoking-room sexuality and drawing-room purity. At the back of this same Paris notebook, as in other notebooks kept over about thirty years, he listed the "nubs" and "snappers" of dirty jokes that he never seemed to tire of: jokes about dogs copulating; about the bride who had stenciled across her stomach "Try Helmbold's Balsam Coperia," a patent gonorrhea medicine; about the old maid on her wedding night on a steamboat explaining, "I never *could* worth a damn on a steamboat"; about the man so short his doctor could not tell whether his trouble was a sore throat or hemorrhoids. And in examining such splits between the taboo and the permissible he was, as a writer, concerned with what seemed to him clear injustices. Watching a group of Salon pictures being carried into the Palais d'Industrie, he reflected sourly on the fact that an artist could exhibit a nude in public and even get a prize for it, while any writer who described nakedness would have his book banished from the parlor table. There were further inequities within printed literature. "It depends on who writes a thing whether it is coarse or not," he said, thinking back on *1601*. Along with a number of other schemes—including a plan to exhibit the tomb of the Virgin Mary in New York City —he made a note to collect his "profane works," including the Stomach Club speech, and have them privately printed.

Yet in Clemens' reactions to the French and what he thought of as French morality there is a quality of fury and unrelenting invective—of obsession—which suggests that his troublement went far beyond the conventional split in the Victorian psyche, and far beyond France itself; *Tom Jones*, just as much as Titian's Venus, he found simply "disgusting." His comments on France and the French were veiled expressions of his own intensely troubled, incurably divided concern with sexuality. He was, in all senses, bothered: the Titian, he said, "inflames and disgusts at the same moment." The "two great branches of French thought," he said, were science and adultery. France was a nation governed by prostitutes, a nation without winter, summer or morals, a nation whose "filthy-minded" citizens were "the connecting link between man and monkey" and practiced unspeakable "bestialities." "A Frenchman's home is where another man's wife is," he went on, and on: scratch a Frenchman "and you find a harlot"; " 'Tis a wise Frenchman that knows his own father" ("When all other interests fail," he was to say in 1895, his anger unabated, a Frenchman "can turn in and see if he can't find out who his father was"). And explicit in this invective is the contrast with America, the once rejected, now beckoning homeland. The contrast was quite as much an act of shaping history to the daydream as his claim that the gold rush was the watershed dividing an era of purity and innocence (sexual as well as commercial) from an era of cynicism and money lust. America, he now began to say, was the most civilized of nations: American "*native-born*" (the italics are his) women and men were pure-minded; American girls did not read smutty novels, and, he was absolutely certain, they were unacquainted with "unclean thoughts."

He was homesick, eager to rejoin the mainstreams of American life. He would never again be an expatriate out of choice. He wanted "hot biscuits, *real* coffee with *real* cream—and *real* potatoes. Fried chicken, corn bread, *real* butter, *real* beefsteak, *good* roast beef with *taste* to it." Even England, where he spent July and August, had lost most of its glory and glitter for him; his Anglomania had waned. He now predicted a widening cultural gap between England and America. In resources and technology his own country had pulled ahead, and he felt that the American century was at hand. A visit to Darwin failed to excite him much more than did dining out in London society with two eminent Americans, Whistler and Henry James, the occasion for a possibly apocryphal but perfectly credible exchange between James and Clemens: "Do you know Bret Harte?" "Yes, I know the son of a bitch."

Mark Twain returned to New York with his family on September 3. The *Sun* reporter noted that his hair had turned quite gray.

IV

Also returning from a stay abroad in the autumn of 1879 was another American anomaly. The life of Ulysses Grant, like Mark Twain's, had been a saga of the unpredictable and the unlikely, of a man without promise who, after years of drift, failure, alcoholism, and disgrace, was touched by history and the Holy Ghost and achieved greatness. "Useless" Grant, an unprepossessing man who turned out to have the powers of a giant, was an archetype that never ceased to fascinate Mark Twain, also a twice-born man, who could never explain his own gifts and powers and who wrote a book about Joan of Arc, an ignorant country girl who had the unaccountable military genius of a great general like Grant. This strange, brooding man took Vicksburg, but he could not stand the sight of rare meat. He was imperturbable and almost expressionless, but as a commander he had unequaled charisma. Even Sherman, a nonbeliever, said that he fought under Grant with "the faith a Christian has in his Savior." To the North, during the war years, Grant seemed God's tool, but, like Mark Twain, he was God's fool as well: his cabinet officers betrayed him, he demeaned himself with Jay Cooke, and he was later to be the cat's paw and victim of his Wall Street partner, the swindler Ferdinand Ward.

Since May 1877 Grant and his family had traveled through Europe and the Orient sightseeing, collecting souvenirs and addresses of welcome, and, as they came into conflict with the protocol of courts and royalty, spreading a peculiarly democratic brand of consternation. At Windsor, young Jesse Grant had insisted on his right to dine with his parents at Victoria's table, given her an ultimatum through her master of the household, bent her to his will, and then celebrated his victory over a bottle of her brandy. Ulysses Grant at the age of fifty-seven came back to America rehabilitated by time, absence, and foreign celebrity, and he shone with some of the old heroic fire. He seemed once again, as Sherman was to say, "the typical hero of the great Civil War." The scandals and the plain ineptitudes of his two disastrous terms in office were now forgotten sufficiently for there to be open talk of a third term for him in 1880. Their fervor fanned by the waving of the bloody shirt, Republican stalwarts (including the desouthernized Mark Twain) who had once been mortified by President Grant now offered up three cheers. The cheers were not for the "Let Us Have Peace" Grant of the White House but for the pre-political Grant of Fort Donelson, Vicksburg, Spottsylvania, and "Unconditional Surrender" (a phrase with his own initials as well as his country's, it was pointed out). In November Grant made his way to Chicago, where, in the course of a week-long patriotic and military celebration, he was to be welcomed home by Sheridan and Sherman and by eighty thousand men marching under ten thousand banners. The city belonged to its "Man of Destiny," as a broadside called him, "our own General Grant," "the admitted and undisputed Military Genius of the whole world, the man especially created by Providence to triumphantly trample out the most wicked rebellion of the Christian era, and crush to the earth those uncompromising TRAFFICKERS in human flesh, in their heinous, unholy and unpardonable crime of attempting to destroy the most indulgent government the sun ever shone upon."

In Elmira, struggling to finish *A Tramp Abroad* and sinking deeper into a creative torpor, Clemens felt the mighty appeal of the occasion and he expressed it in terms which suggest the almost religious nature of his hero worship. "My sluggish soul needs a fierce upstirring," he wrote to Howells, "and if it would not get it when Grant enters the meeting-place I must doubtless 'lay' for the final resurrection." He compared Grant's journey from San Francisco to Napoleon's progress from Grenoble to Paris; to see the great reunion in Chicago, he said, would be like seeing Napoleon meeting his Old Guard. He eagerly accepted an invitation, offered him as a popular spokesman for the Republican party, to come to Chicago as honored guest of the Army of the Tennessee and to speak at the banquet to Grant at the Palmer House on November 13.

In Chicago, by his account, Mark Twain reached the high point of his career as speechmaker; still, a mingled strain runs through the various roles he played there. He worshiped Grant, he identified himself with Grant. Their lives, it now seems, became interlocked: when Grant died in 1885 Mark Twain started on the long road downhill toward ruin. But as a former Confederate who comes to terms—of intimate friendship, it developed—with the Union commander, he combats, in subtle and symbolic ways, Grant's tremendous authority, competes with him, even seems to want to destroy him.

At times Mark Twain was the comic alter ego of authority, Grant's court jester. On November 11 Clemens found himself on a flag-canopied reviewing stand with Grant and others. They watched the endless processions march past, led by Sheridan, in martial cloak and plumed hat, mounted on his giant black horse. In plain sight of the crowd—"It was dreadfully conspicuous," Clemens told Livy—the mayor of Chicago presented him to Grant, and Clemens, in some embarrassment, made a move to withdraw to the back of the platform. "I'll step back, General," he said, "I don't want to interrupt your speech." "But I'm not going to make any," Grant said. "Stay where you are—I'll get you to make it for me." Clemens delightedly reported the conversation to Livy that afternoon. (Less than a year later, again in this relationship of comic hero to military hero, Clemens put on Sherman's coat and military hat, stepped out on a train platform, and made a speech impersonating him. "Say, that ain't Sherman," came a voice from the crowd, "that's Mark Twain.")

On the stage of Haverley's Theatre that night, sitting elbow to elbow with the Union generals, Clemens again took the measure of his hero. Through all the patriotic rant, the bombardments of praise and adoration, the unfurling of a shredded battle flag and the roar of a thousand men singing "Marching through Georgia," Grant sat slouching in his chair, his right leg crossed over his left, not moving a muscle, an iron man. Twice, at Sherman's urging, he rose to acknowledge the storms of applause. And: "He broke up his attitude once more—the extent of something more than a hair's breadth," Clemens carefully noted for Livy the next morning, "to indicate me to Sherman when the house was keeping up a determined and persistent call for me." The anti-hero vied with the hero, and the hero deferred to him. Clemens, a Grant-intoxicated man in an age that loved heroes, oratory, and patriotic ceremony, "went to sleep without whiskey," he wrote. "Ich liebe dich."

The climax of the Chicago celebration was the Palmer House banquet. Surfeited with claret, champagne, and rum punch, with oysters, fillet of beef, and buffalo steaks, five hundred Union veterans settled down with their brandies and whiskeys for six consecutive hours of oratory, applause, and military music, an orgy of the spoken word which increased in passion and intensity as the night wore into morning. "I doubt if America has ever seen anything quite equal to it," Clemens told Howells. "I am well satisfied I shall not live to see its equal again. How pale those speeches are in print—but how radiant, how full of color, how blinding they were in the delivery!" In the accent of the angel of mercy, as it impressed Clemens, Colonel Robert Ingersoll declaimed, "Blood was water, money was leaves, and life was only common air until one flag floated over a Republic without a master and without a slave." He seemed, Clemens said, "the most beautiful human creature that ever lived," and his speech, which brought his audience to their feet clapping and stamping and waving their napkins, was "the supremest combination of English words that was ever put together since the world began." As he waited his turn to speak, Clemens was transfigured by oratory, too excited to eat or to drink anything but ice water, his "sluggish soul" certainly now upstirred to a pitch he would hardly reach again.

Somewhat after two in the morning, Clemens, the fifteenth and final speaker—"I was to 'hold the crowd,'" he told Livy—mounted the banquet table and responded to the toast he himself had devised for the occasion: "The babies—as they comfort us in our sorrows, let us not forget them in our festivities." By the end of his third sentence—"When the toast works down to the babies, we stand on common ground"—he knew he had mastered his audience, and, all the while watching Grant, who was no longer impassive now but laughing like the others, he marched through an elaborately double-edged tribute to the man of war, majestic on the battlefield but ridiculous in the nursery with an infant. "You could face the death storm at Donelson and Vicksburg and give back blow for blow," he told these veterans, "but when he clawed your whiskers, and pulled your hair, and twisted your nose, you had to take it." He even worked in a reference to Sheridan's recent twins: "As long as you are in your right mind don't you ever pray for twins. Twins amount to a permanent riot." And, having appeared to deflate the military, he now went on to glorify the babies. He summoned up visions of the America of fifty years thence, a vast country to be governed by the future leaders who were now lying in three or four million cradles. It was worth risking everything in order to win an audience over, body and soul, he once told Livy; now he led up to a climax which for a brief moment seemed more like a disaster. Relentlessly, with an apparent unawareness of the reverence in which these veterans held Grant, he described the future commander in chief of the American armies lying in his cradle and occupied with "trying to find some way of getting his big toe in his mouth." (Grant had, in fact, spent eight years in the

White House trying to get it out.) This goal, Clemens went on, "the illustrious guest of this evening turned his entire attention to some fifty-six years ago." Here he remembered that the laughter ceased, there was only "a sort of shuddering silence," which he associated with the Whittier dinner, and then he sprang his masterful and breathtaking surprise: "And if the child is but a prophecy of the man, there are mighty few who will doubt that he *succeeded*."

Two days later the Philadelphia *Press* described Clemens' speech as "a humorous and highly-appreciated satirical eulogy"; the Chicago papers did not make even this much of it; and George Warner reported from Des Moines that the Western papers ranked the speech as number three of the evening. Yet three or four hours after his performance, in long letters he was writing to Livy in Hartford and Orion in Keokuk, Clemens saw himself as the hero of the banquet, as if he had been borne aloft in triumph after a symbolic tournament in which he had vanquished Grant himself. By making this iron man laugh and cheer with all the others he had, in a sense, destroyed him. And in keeping with a speech which, until its very last sentence, had seemed headed toward catastrophic insult, the images that Clemens used to describe his triumph suggest that on this occasion, as well as on so many others, he thought of his humor as something violent and painful that he did to someone else. "I fetched him! I broke him up utterly!" he wrote to Livy. "The audience *saw* that for once in his life he had been knocked out of his iron serenity." "I knew I could lick him," he told Howells. "I shook him up like dynamite . . . my truths had wracked all the bones of his body apart." And to Orion: "He laughed until his bones ached."

Tornadoes of applause and laughter continued to ring in his ears. "I say it who oughtn't to say it," he wrote to Livy a little after five that morning, "the house came down with a crash. For two and a half hours, now, I've been shaking hands and listening to congratulations." The Army of the Tennessee was his, an officer told him—"You can *command* its services." "Mark, if I live to be a hundred years, I'll always be grateful for your speech," Ingersoll said. "Lord, what a supreme thing it was!" The following noon, in his own eyes a new hero, he attended a breakfast given in his honor by a group of Chicago journalists, and after his fast of the night before he feasted on mushrooms, sweetbreads, quail, coffee, and cognac. "Grand times, my boy," he wrote to Howells, "grand times."

CHAPTER TWELVE

"Everything a man could have"

I

On JANUARY 7, 1880, in a fit of impatience followed by wild elation, Clemens thrust the final manuscript pages of his despised travel book into the hands of Elisha Bliss. The next day, leaving their children behind in Hartford, he took Livy to Elmira for a rest. Pregnant again, she had been brought to the edge of one of her periodic collapses by the strain of reopening the house on Farmington Avenue, redecorating it, and installing five or six thousand dollars' worth of European bric-a-brac and furniture, including a four-hundred-dollar music box and a massive Venetian bed adorned with carved cherubs. That Clemens and Livy had bought this much abroad at a time when they were "feeling poor" and economizing on hotel rooms and cab fares was one more proof of their self-sacrificial devotion to their eccentric mansion. Clemens thought of the house in sacramental terms. "Our house was not unsentient matter—it had a heart, and a soul," he was to write in 1897, having derived from Susy's death the single consolation that she had died at home; "it was of us, and we were in its confidence, and lived in its grace and in the peace of its benediction." But he and Livy also feared the house and fled from it—it committed them to a frenzied pace of management, entertainment, and expenditure which devoured their energies and their money. Within a year and a half after this winter flight from Hartford, Clemens was to spend over thirty thousand dollars to buy up a strip of adjoining land, lower some of the grounds in order to "bring the house into view," reroute the driveway, tear down the kitchen and build one twice as big, remove the reception room and enlarge the front hall, install temperamental new plumbing, heating, and burglar-alarm systems, and decorate the walls and ceilings of the first floor with hand-stenciled designs by Louis Tiffany of New York. When all this work was done, Clemens joked, he "had three hundred dollars in the bank which the plumber didn't know anything about," and he felt that what the house needed most of all was an incendiary to put them out of their misery. Later on he compared Susy's death to the fire which destroys a house and everything in it.

Clemens had finished *A Tramp Abroad* with even less interest than he had had when he began it. Still, by several standards, it was a success. "You are a blessing," Howells told him. "You ought to believe in God's goodness, since he has bestowed upon the world such a delightful genius as yours to lighten its troubles." Howells' review in the May *Atlantic* paid tribute to what Livy agreed were her husband's strong points—his underlying seriousness, common sense, and moralistic fervor. Published in March 1880, the book sold sixty-two thousand copies during its first year in print. This was far better than any of his previous three books and only about seven thousand copies fewer than *The Innocents Abroad*. In returning to the proven mode if not the true vitality of his first success Mark Twain reversed a six-year declining trend of sales and popularity, and he was well on his way to achieving the eminence of a national institution. "You Americans," an English guide was to say to some tourists in the summer of 1882, "have Mark Twain and *Harper's Magazine*." The obligations of such celebrity, which at times he accepted with delight, were self-imitation, constant exposure and performance. He walked along the streets of Hartford as if they were a stage and he were doing a cakewalk. He had a rolling gait like a sailor or one of Tim Dooley's patrons, and, whenever he could, he wore the sealskin coat and fur hat which set off his cascade of gray curls. The people stopped and turned around to stare, and if they did not know who he was they asked and always found out. Everywhere he went they hung on every word he spoke. In June 1881 he visited West Point and stayed with Lieutenant Charles Erskine Scott Wood, the post adjutant (who, the following year, supervised the printing of *1601* on the Academy's press), and for an entire evening he held a group of cadets spellbound with his monologue. He was at his best, he knew, with a stag audience; even "male corpses," he once said, could give him more satisfactions than the young ladies of the Saturday Morning Club. The next morning over coffee he gleefully tormented Wood's spinster sister, who had brought in her infant nephew. "Don't you adore babies, Mr. Clemens?" she asked unsuspectingly. "No, I hate them," he answered, and he told her how once, when he was convalescing from typhoid, his own sister's infant son had climbed on his bed and kissed him. "I made up my mind, if I lived I would put up a monument to Herod," he said, and an expression of horror crossed his face. "Miss Wood, since then I have hated babies." Miss Wood refused to believe he was joking; she was glad when her brother's "coarse" visitor left.

Often, however, the price of celebrity seemed to him too much to pay.

More and more he traveled under incognitos and signed hotel registers as "Samuel Langhorne," "C. L. Samuel," "J. P. Smith," "J. P. Jones." From time to time, as when he finished *The Prince and the Pauper*, he thought of publishing anonymously, because his celebrity as a humorist would do harm to a "serious" book. Samuel Clemens had created Mark Twain, and now he had to run away from him. Interviewers and autograph hunters pursued him; in Australia there was even an impostor who passed under the name Mark Twain. Standing near the pinnacle of a world-wide fame, Clemens faced it with a double-edged attitude, wallowing in attention one moment, and in the next becoming snappish and resentful and feeling sorry for himself. The day's mail brought him letters begging money and advice, letters from strangers and cranks, letters asking for an answer and an autograph. He scribbled his comments on them—"From an ass," "No, Sir," "Persecution," "And a curse on *him*"—but he saved the letters all the same. In a moment of mild vindictiveness he asked the Howells children to sign a batch of postcards for him "S. L. Clemens—per J. L. McWilliams." "It is wonderful," he explained to their father, "how that little 'per' does take the stuffing out of an autograph." Even the distinguished Moncure Conway, visiting Hartford, found himself pressed into service as an amanuensis. This time it was "S. L. Clemens, per M. D. C.," and Clemens smiled triumphantly. Yet only a few hours later, in the middle of a billiard game with Conway, Clemens was perfectly delighted to put down his cue and write a sentiment and a signature in the autograph book of a ten-year-old boy who had stopped by and rung the doorbell. It was all a matter of accident and approach, it seemed. George Washington Cable, playing an April Fool's joke on him in 1884, had a moment's fear that he might provoke Clemens' celebrated temper, which could be hair-triggered to tantrum even by such annoyances as a missing button (he once shattered the peace of a Sabbath morning in Hartford by screaming and throwing his shirts out of his bathroom window). Cable arranged for 150 or so of Clemens' literary acquaintances to write in for autographs. Some of them, like Aldrich, pushed the hoax a step further and pretended to confuse Mark Twain and Bret Harte. The letters poured in on April 1. After a flash of annoyance Clemens saw the joke and enjoyed it so much that he gave out the story to the papers. New interviewers appeared, and soon there was a fresh flood of genuine requests from strangers for his autograph. So celebrity fed upon and reproduced itself, and the cycle quickened.

In mid-March 1880 one stranger, a twelve-year-old Dallas boy named David Watt Bowser, wrote a letter to "Mr. Twain." Out of a list of favorites which included Edison, Tennyson, Holmes, and Longfellow, Wattie had chosen him as the living great man with whom he would most like to change places. As the boy explained in a school composition which he enclosed, along with his report card, Mark Twain was "jolly," "happy," and rich ("worth millions") and had "a beautiful wife and children." In short, Wattie concluded, his hero had "everything a man could have." Would Mr. Twain be willing to change places with him and be a boy again? he asked. "I hope you will send me at least your autograph for my album. I do not think Mr. Longfellow, Mr. Whittier &c. can stand a joke like you, so I feel surer than the other boys, that I will have a line in return." Acting in Wattie's favor, beyond the flattery and charm of his letter, was something he mentioned in his postscript: "Our principal used to know you, when you were a little boy and she was a little girl, but I expect you have forgotten her, it was so long ago." For a long time Clemens had nursed romantic recollections of this principal, Laura Dake, whom he had met when he was a twenty-two-year-old pilot.

Wattie received in return an extraordinarily intimate and revealing letter, which was followed by four others over the next two years. As always, recollections of the river awakened Clemens. He *would* be willing to be a boy again, he told Wattie, but only under certain conditions. "The main condition should be, that I should emerge from boyhood as a 'cub pilot' on a Mississippi boat, and that I should by and by become a pilot, and remain one." Among the other conditions he listed eternal summer, with the oleanders in bloom and the sugar cane green, the middle watch in the pilothouse on moonlit nights, friends to talk to and sing with, long trips and short stays in port, a big freight boat that would ignore passenger hails and lay up whenever the fog got thick, and a crew that would never change and never die. "One such crew I have in mind, and can call their names and see their faces: but two decades have done their work upon them, and half are dead, the rest scattered, and the boat's bones are rotting five fathom deep in Madrid bend." But even though, in this daydream, he is isolated from society on shore and outside the pilothouse, he still insists on fame and recognition:

> And when strangers were introduced I should have them repeat "Mr. Clemens?" doubtfully, and with the rising inflection--and when they were informed that I was the celebrated "Master Pilot of the Mississippi," and immediately took me by the hand and wrung it with effusion, and exclaimed, "O, I know *that* name very well!" I should feel a pleasurable emotion trickling down my spine and know I had not lived in vain.

He was remembering the grandeur that surrounded the lightning pilot, the gold-leaf, kid-glove, diamond-breastpin sort of pilot who lived on a princely salary and answered to no man. But steamboating was dying on the Mississippi now, the railroads were killing it off, the pilot was prince no longer. Within five years after this letter to Wattie, Clemens published two books celebrating the river of bygone days, and in these books he demonstrated as a writer the freedom and command he had once had as a pilot. "Master Pilot of the Mississippi" is a metaphor for the literary achievement of Mark Twain, a name born of the river and by then so linked with it that in 1886 young Clara Clemens, hearing the leadsman on a steamboat sing out soundings, said, "Papa, I have hunted all over the boat for you. Don't you know they are calling for you?"

For a brief period between 1880 and 1885 Mark Twain achieved a maturity and a balance which permitted him as a man to live fully in the glorious, opulent present and as an artist to live imaginatively in the transfigured past. During these years of exuberance and creation his imagination embraced two transcendent figures who suggested to him what remained inexplicable in his own genius. The first was Grant, who even over a sent-in lunch of beans, bacon, and coffee at his Wall Street office still seemed to have the stature of Julius Caesar or Alexander. Visiting Grant frequently there and at his house uptown, Clemens smoked in silence, listened to Grant spin his "sensational history" in a soft Ohio River accent, and urged him to write his memoirs. But Grant was still feeling too rich and lazy to get to work. The second figure was another "Master Pilot," Captain Edgar Wakeman. Year after year Clemens struggled with his story about Wakeman, as Captain Stormfield, entering heaven. He was afraid it was too blasphemous for print, often thought of giving it up, and at least once thought of burning it, before he published part of the story in 1906. The grandeur of "Captain Stormfield's Visit to Heaven" is not in its theological extravaganza or in its relatively mild burlesque of the Protestant heaven as a place where the better sort of people mingle. The drive and the vitality of the story spring from its images of total freedom—of Stormfield, the Master Pilot, racing with comets and hurtling through outermost space at about a million miles an hour and pointed straight as a dart for the hereafter.

Grant and Wakeman represented limitless possibility. But limit, failure, futility were made visible for Sam Clemens in Orion, his mirror image, his burden, his baseline for judging the distance he himself had traveled from Hannibal. True, Orion had, in his brother's eyes, one recent achievement that stood to his credit and was a conspicuous blot on a nearly unblemished record of ineffectuality. During his brief service with Bliss Orion had studied the company's account books and warned Sam that Bliss was misrepresenting his expenses and profits. Sam insisted on revising the terms of his contract for *A Tramp Abroad*, and in October 1880 told Orion that because of his advice the new book had earned about twenty thousand dollars more than it would have under the old contract; from now on, he said, Orion was going to receive the income from this extra twenty thousand, about seventy-five dollars a month. "This ends the loan business," Sam wrote to Orion (who for five or six years had lived on the quixotic plan of "borrowing" from Sam and sending him a check for the interest by return mail). "Hereafter you can reflect that you are living not on borrowed money but on money which you have squarely earned and which has no taint or savor of charity about it." At other times Sam looked on his brother with amusement and affection, remembering, for example, three occasions on which Orion demonstrated an absent-mindedness more extreme than his own: In Hannibal late one night Orion climbed into the upstairs bedroom of the wrong house and found himself sharing a bed not with his brothers but with two terrified spinsters. ("You really *mustn't* let Orion have got into the bed," Howells said in 1906 after reading Clemens' account of the episode in his autobiography. "I know he did, but . . .") Once he forgot what time it was, paid a courting call on a girl at three in the morning, and stayed to breakfast. During the period he was working for Bliss and living in a Hartford boardinghouse, Orion forgot to lock the bathroom door and was discovered by a maid lying in the tub with his head under water and his bottom in the air (this was Orion's way of getting relief from the hot weather). The maid ran out screaming that Orion was drowned. "How do you know it is Mr. Clemens?" Orion's wife asked. According to Sam's delighted retelling of the story, the maid answered, "I don't."

For years Sam tried to exploit Orion's possibilities as literary material, first starting a novel about him called *Autobiography of a Damned Fool* but giving it up after 114 pages of bad farce: its vacillating hero, named Bolivar, is a convert to Mohammedanism and becomes the disgrace of his Mississippi River village when he tries to round up a harem there. In 1878 and again in 1879 he urged Howells to write a book or a play about Orion. He also proposed that they collaborate on the play. "Orion is a field which grows richer and richer the more he manures it with each new top-dressing of religion or other guano," he wrote. "I imagine I see Orion on the stage, always gentle, always melancholy, always changing his politics and religion, and trying to reform the world, always inventing something, and losing a limb by a new kind of explosion at the end of each of the four acts." Probably afraid of the backlash of satirizing this exasperating but beloved brother, Howells declined all these invitations, which were renewed from time to time over the next three years, and Clemens tried another approach to what he believed was a comic gold mine.

In February 1880 he wrote Orion a letter which suggests his own scattered interests. "I believe I told you I bought four-fifths of a patent some ten days ago for several thousand dollars." This was "Kaolotype," a chalk-plate process for making printing plates and, as later refined and applied, for casting brass stamping dies; soon the letterhead of the Kaolotype Engraving Company, of 104 Fulton Street, New York, listed S. L. Clemens as president. This characteristic venture, the direct antecedent of Clemens' disastrous investment in the Paige typesetter, was to end in financial loss, litigation, and, worst of all, an inescapable involvement with business affairs. In the same letter he told Orion that he was working away "with an interest which amounts to intemperance" on *The Prince and the Pauper* and in all likelihood would never in this life get around to writing two other books he had had in mind for a long time, *The Autobiography of a Coward* and *Confessions of a Life That Was a Failure*. With what now seems open cruelty he suggested that Orion tackle one of these books—they were hardly distinguishable—and write an autobiography which for unswerving candor would rival Cellini, Casanova, and Rousseau.

Not the least bit discouraged by Sam's charges that he lacked literary training, Orion got to work at once. The first installments struck Sam as so "killingly entertaining" that he sent them on to Howells hoping that the *Atlantic* would pay Orion at the customary rate for anonymous contributions. Howells backed away. Orion's autobiography had wrung his heart, but he found it "shocking." It was altogether too candid, and he was horrified by a passage which described young Sam at the keyhole watching the post-mortem being performed on his father. "Don't let anyone else even see those passages about the autopsy," Howells wrote. By 1883, after three years of weekly and even daily installments from Orion, Clemens had lost all interest in the book, and what he originally envisioned as a classic of autobiography had become just "the autobiography of an ass" and "more damned lunacy." As a writer, he now told Orion in brutal dismissal, "you cannot achieve even a respectable mediocrity," and he demanded that Orion sign an oath which pledged him for two years not to submit any writing or any literary or business proposition to Sam, to give up lecturing, to stop interpreting Sam's silences as assent (there had been a misunderstanding about an "electric project"), and to turn all his attention to the law. Some of the manuscript ended up as fire-starter to warm the boardinghouse that Orion and Mollie kept in Keokuk.

Recognizing that Orion was bound by the laws of his nature to a lifelong fickleness of purpose and a butterfly vagrancy, Sam once meant to reassure him that there was no reason why a kaleidoscope should not have as good a time as a telescope. But the melancholy Orion, continually hounded by every member of his family to focus on a single star, did not have a good time. Both brothers followed the same pattern of red-hot enthusiasm followed by almost catatonic indifference, but Sam's peaks lasted longer—his genius as a writer gave a small but sufficient number of them validity and staying power. Orion, the victim of a hundred fresh enthusiasms each day, lived in the troughs of the waves, not on the crests. Despite this difference, and despite the staggering contrast of his own fame and success with Orion's total failure, Sam could still read Orion's career as a cautionary tale.

The one constant in Orion's life in the ten years after he and Bliss parted company was change. For a while he worked as a proofreader on the New York *Post* and lived on milk and graham crackers. With money advanced by Sam he bought a chicken farm outside Keokuk, but he soon gave it up. "He casually observed," Clemens reported to Howells, "that his books had shown there was no money in fattening a chicken on 65 cents' worth of corn and then selling it for 50." The next step was to move into Keokuk, where he lived frugally enough on Sam's money and in Sam's castoff clothing (Mollie wore Livy's), but still rented a pew in the First Presbyterian Church. This extravagance outraged Sam, and it did Orion little good when, in 1879, after he gave a lecture entitled "Man, the Architect of Our Religion," he was excommunicated by the church elders. He kept up an office as a lawyer, but he was about the only person who ever saw the inside of it. He earned five dollars the first year, nothing the second, and six dollars the third; he occupied himself with various schemes concerning the Tennessee land, and he planned to raise goats. Besides the autobiography he had other literary projects: an article, "Immigration and Wages," which the *Atlantic* refused, newspaper paragraphs, a burlesque of *Paradise Lost,* and a burlesque of Jules Verne in which (as suggested by Sam) the main character was a gorilla who turns out to be Jules Verne himself, "that French idiot." Only a scream of rage from Hartford stopped Orion from going on the lecture circuit billed as "Mark Twain's Brother." He was short of everything except advice from Sam.

By 1881 Mark Twain's scale of living was so high that just running the house and providing champagne, canvasbacks, fillets of beef, and ice-cream cherubs for his procession of visitors cost about as much as he earned from royalties and investments. He was already pledging his capital toward a number of major expenditures. During 1881 he spent about $100,000 in all. Over $30,000 went toward expanding and renovating the house. About $5,000 went into conventional investments such as securities of the New York Central, the American Bank Note Company, Adams Express. The largest single amount, about $41,000, went into the sort of irresistible speculation that would later bankrupt him—Kaolotype (he was putting up a building in New York to house this shaky venture), the Paige typesetter (whose acquaintance he made in 1880 with a down payment of $2,000 on the eventual cost to him of close to $200,000). He supervised and financed, to the extent of $4,500, the Paris art education of Karl Gerhardt, a young sculptor, formerly a mechanic at the Pratt and Whitney works. He was on the way to becoming his own publisher. Later that year he brought out *The Prince and the Pauper* at his own expense, and he made a trip to Canada to protect his copyright there. (Certain recent improvements in copyright relations, he said at a dinner in Montreal, made him hope and believe that a day will come when, in the eyes of the law, "literary property will be as sacred as whiskey, or any of the other necessaries of life.") He made plans to coedit with Howells an elaborate *Library of Humor;* by March 1882, when he left Hartford to go on a six-week trip on the Mississippi, he had made selections for the anthology running to more than 93,000 words. He believed he had a "perfectly stunning literary bonanza" in the autobiography of that "tramp" and "bummer," Cousin Jesse Leathers, the American Earl. He began a burlesque book of etiquette, and he worked with such zeal on a burlesque *Hamlet,* an old idea come to life again after a talk with Howells, that after three days he was flat on his back, "burned out, devastated, and merely smouldering."* He worked up a scheme for the citizens of Elmira to petition Congress for the exclusive right to erect a monument to Adam in their city. According to his Barnumlike calculations, the Adam Monument would have been as powerful a tourist draw as the Tomb of the Virgin or, something he began to plan about 1884, the bones of Columbus exhibited in the base of the Statue of Liberty or in the Capitol rotunda in Washington. He abandoned the Adam Monument after Senator Joseph Hawley of Connecticut, who had agreed to sponsor the petition, fled to Europe in embarrassment.

All in all, Mark Twain was living beyond his means financially, and it was in the belief that he was also living beyond his energies that at the end of April 1881 he appointed as his business manager his twenty-eight-year-old nephew by marriage, Charles L. Webster of Fredonia, sometime civil engineer, real-estate agent, and stock promoter for a Fredonia watch company and now about to become a Jack of all trades. His function at first was to supervise Kaolotype, which was already a disaster, but by the beginning of August he was in charge of everything, publishing contracts and the scrapbook included, and with considerable bewilderment he told his wife, Pamela's daughter Annie, that he had enough assignments from Uncle Sam to keep a dozen men busy: he had to get after the plumber and the builder, talk to John T. Raymond about the contract for the old *Colonel Sellers* play and make arrangements with a French actor to produce the play abroad, track down some delinquent royalties, renegotiate the *Tramp Abroad* contract with Elisha Bliss, discover the extent of Dan Slote's peculations with the scrapbook royalties. In the years following,

---

* Since 1873, when he first mentioned the idea to Edwin Booth, Clemens had been unable to solve a problem of propriety: how to write a burlesque of *Hamlet* without altering the text. His solution was to invent an extra character who made humorous comments on the other characters but was totally ignored by them. The character he hit upon after talking with Howells was a subscription book salesman named Basil Stockmar (the last name borrowed from Victoria and Albert's *éminence gris*) whose mother was supposed to have been Hamlet's wet nurse. "They're on the high horse all the time," Basil mutters about court life at Elsinore. "They swell around, and talk the grandest kind of book-talk, and look just as if they were on exhibition." Howells, customarily cautious and decorous, predicted "a great triumph" for Basil the book agent, but the project soon died. Clemens eventually believed that the author of *Hamlet* was not William Shakespeare of Stratford, who was just another claimant.

until neuralgia, blinding headaches, fatigue, and galloping anxiety compelled him in 1887 to retire from business, Charley Webster was to be publisher, sales manager, auditor, researcher, private detective, watchdog, and errand boy, as the whim or the fury of his tireless uncle dictated.

Two years earlier Clemens had scolded Orion for wasting money on pew rent "and other idiotic vanities." "I am not proposing what I would not propose to myself," he explained, "that is, live clear within my income, whether it was a thousand dollars a week or fifteen." And in May 1880, riding the crest of his fame and energies, he addressed Orion as if Orion were the man he saw each morning in his shaving mirror: "The bane of Americans is overwork—and the ruin of *any* work is a divided interest. Concentrate—*concentrate*. One thing at a time. Yrs in haste, Sam."

II

By May 1880 it was clear that Elisha Bliss was dying of heart disease—he had only four and a half months to live. His most important author, having been alerted by Orion to Bliss's liberal interpretation of "half profits," now looked back on their relationship, including even the triumphant experiment of *The Innocents Abroad*, as merely "ten years of swindlings," and he looked forward to going off in a new direction and earning a great deal more money than ever before. Bliss's son Frank, who had failed in his attempt to set up business on his own, now seemed to Clemens far too ineffectual to take over from the father; besides, Frank was in poor health. Despite Clemens' own education in subscription publishing he made a strangely self-defeating choice to replace Bliss and the American Publishing Company. James R. Osgood of Boston had been heading unerringly toward bankruptcy since 1871, when he had bought out James T. Fields, publisher to the American pantheon. Bret Harte, Harriet Beecher Stowe, and even Fields complained loudly about Osgood's carelessness and flickering application. In 1880 Osgood sold out to Henry O. Houghton, but he was soon ready to make a fresh start as a publisher with two important authors—Howells, who resigned from the *Atlantic* early in 1881, and Clemens, who yielded after years of being importuned by Osgood over billiards and dinner. By choosing to do business with Osgood despite so many clear warnings, Clemens made it inevitable that after three books he would become as disgusted as he had ever been with Bliss—Osgood made a "mighty botch" of subscription publishing, he later said—and would take the fateful step of setting up his own publishing house. His arrangement with Osgood was a step in that direction, for instead of receiving royalties while the publisher bore the capital risks, Clemens decided to finance his own books and to pay Osgood—nominally the publisher, actually only an agent—a seven-and-a-half-per-cent royalty for selling them. The traditional roles of publisher and author were reversed, just as in the first book by Mark Twain that Osgood brought out under this arrangement a pauper changes places with a prince.

Since November 1877 Clemens had worked intermittently, at times (as he told Orion) "with an interest that almost amounted to intemperance," on his tale about sixteenth-century England. By mid-September 1880 he believed he had finished it. As usual he was premature; it was not until January or February that it was really completed and revised. But despite this vagrant process of composition, Clemens was guided by an absolute singleness of purpose. Unlike *A Tramp Abroad*, which he undertook as an act of commerce, *The Prince and the Pauper* was to be an act of culture. He had no hesitation, as he had had with *Tom Sawyer*, over whether this was a book for children or for grownups. From the very start he knew that he was writing for children and the family circle, and he was determined that the book would exhibit him not as a humorist (he thought for a while of concealing his authorship), but as a serious practitioner of polite, colorful literature meant to entertain and inform children instead of arousing them to mischief (as might be charged of *Tom Sawyer*) or to violence (as was charged of "blood and thunder stories" and Beadle's Dime Novels). He was going to write a costume drama full of ceremonials and historical information which would, at one and the same time, cater to the fashionable taste for monarchical England and also assert the superiority of democratic ideals without offending anyone. He was determined to give genteel culture exactly what it wanted.

The "Master Pilot of the Mississippi" had stepped ashore, and there to welcome him were the women and children and clergy of Hartford. "Your rank as a writer of humorous things is high enough," the Reverend Edwin Pond Parker, pastor of the Second Church of Christ Congregational, wrote on December 22, 1880, "but do you know, Clemens, that it is in you to do some first-class serious or sober work. . . . It might not pay in 'shekels,' but it would do you vast honor, and give your friends vast pleasure. Am I too bold?" "I thank you most sincerely for those pleasant words," Clemens answered on Christmas Eve. "They come most opportunely, too, at a time when I was wavering between launching a book of the sort you mention, with my name to it, and smuggling it into publicity with my name suppressed. Well, I'll put my name to it, and let it help me or hurt me as the fates shall direct." And in search of further blessings from Parker he went on to ask of him a service which he had already been promised by Twichell: "Will you, too, take the manuscript and read it, either to yourself, or, still better, aloud to your family."

Even Howells, champion of naturalism, was willing to abet the transformation of his "sole and incomparable" Mark Twain into a practitioner of the art of Frances Hodgson Burnett, who in due time received an inscribed copy of *The Prince and the Pauper* from its author. There were a couple of things in the book Howells found "rather strong milk for babes," but on the whole he liked it "immensely," even though, as he delicately ventured, the book could have used a little more satire and a little more humor. "This would not have hurt the story for the children, and would have helped it for the grownies." (Howells too was a captive of the children's hour.)

During the winter months of 1881 the women and children had their say. Sitting by a blazing fire, with Susy and Clara on the arms of his chair, with Livy and their visitor, Mary Fairbanks, listening intently, Clemens read his manuscript aloud, and they pronounced it good. "A lovely book," Mary Fairbanks said, pleased that her protégé had finally come all the way around, "your masterpiece in fineness." In recognition of his ideal audience he was to dedicate *The Prince and the Pauper* to Susy and Clara, "those good-mannered and agreeable children," adjectives which scarcely suggest his remembered boy life in Hannibal. "Unquestionably the best book he has ever written," Susy said some years later, after she had learned to dislike *Huckleberry Finn* and dread her father's ghost story about the Golden Arm. "The book is full of lovely, charming ideas, and oh the language! It is *perfect!*" Even the Reverend Dr. Parker would have felt this was going too far, for he acknowledged Mark Twain to be a master of "forcible, racy English." It is the language of *The Prince and the Pauper* —nerveless, bookish, conventional, totally denatured—that is the measure of Mark Twain's chameleon identity as a writer, his crablike progress toward his true idiom, and most of all his luck, in the sense that over all the exclamations of the women and the children he heard inner voices and eventually paid attention to them. *The Prince and the Pauper* received an official critical acclaim that was new to him, but he soon went back to work on his masterpiece of the American vernacular, *Huckleberry Finn,* "a language experiment" (as Whitman said of *Leaves of Grass*) in which Mark Twain employed three main dialects and four Pike County varieties, all carefully shaded.

When Joe Goodman first heard about *The Prince and the Pauper,* he was distressed by the remoteness of the subject. After he had read it, he was frankly disappointed and told Clemens so. He also said that he hoped Clemens would come to his senses and get back to what he ought to be writing about. But Goodman's unawed Western judgment was the exception. "I find myself a fine success as a publisher," Clemens wrote in 1882 to the critic and scholar Hjalmar Boyesen, another discovery of Howells', "and literarily the new departure is a great deal better received than I had any right to hope for." With hosannas and rejoicing the custodians of official culture celebrated the taming of the maverick. The Hartford *Courant* greeted its publication at Christmas time 1881 with an editorial that echoed the sentiments of Susy Clemens: "Mark Twain has finally fulfilled the earnest hope of many of his best friends, in writing a book which has other and higher merits than can possibly belong to the most artistic expression of mere humor." And in the New York *Herald* and the Boston *Transcript*, the *Atlantic* (under Aldrich, Howells' successor), and the *Century*, the words "pure," "lovely," "subdued," "delicate." "refined," and "ennobling" recurred as part of a grateful appreciation of just those qualities which any conventional romancer might be expected to possess: professional polish, descriptive power, neatness of plot construction, and an over-all correctness. Even the English reviews, as Clemens told his London publisher, Andrew Chatto, were "surprisingly complimentary." "I am reading your *Prince and Pauper* for the fourth time," Harriet Beecher Stowe was to tell Clemens in 1887, pressing his hands in hers and speaking with such fervor it brought the tears to his eyes, "and I *know* it is the best book for young folks that was ever written."

Howells, given his usual freedom to "slash away" at the proofs—he suggested deleting such objectionable words as "devil," "hick," and "basting" —gave the book a final reading in October 1881, a month or so after he had solicited from John Hay, who was managing the New York *Tribune* during Whitelaw Reid's wedding trip in Europe, a commission to review the book. Howells' unsigned review, twice as long as most in the paper, ran on October 25, two full months before publication, and as far as Clemens was concerned it served its purpose: it helped prepare the press and the public for his new incarnation as a writer of serious, morally sound romance. "That is the kind of review to have," Clemens said happily, remembering the bitter episode with Hay and Reid over their grudging treatment of *The Gilded Age*. "The doubtful man, even the prejudiced man, is persuaded, and succumbs."

For Clemens there was nothing improper in having his adviser and editor act as his reviewer; Howells, whom he respected as a man of high literary ethics, had made a practice of it in the *Atlantic* and was never bothered by the conflict of roles. The *Tribune* review, moreover, was unsigned, and Howells had taken pains to explain to Hay that he wanted the commission so that he could have an opportunity to publicize the "unappreciated serious side of Clemens' curious genius." He believed he was performing a service to both the public and the *Tribune*, for which Reid had cultural aspirations. Yet John Hay, a more worldly and diplomatic man than either Clemens or Howells, realized that they were headed for trouble with Reid. He explained to Reid that Howells had asked for the commission and had argued that it would be a good thing for the *Tribune* if it set a pattern of recognizing new literary departures. "I took into account your disapproval of Mark in general and your friendship for Howells—and decided for the benefit of the *Tribune*," Hay wrote on September 4. "If it does not please you—wait for his next book and get Bret Harte to review it. That will be a masterpiece of the skinner's art." ("Now, isn't that outspoken and hearty, and just like that splendid John Hay?" Clemens, all unsuspecting, had written to Howells in December 1874.)

The decision did not please Reid. "It isn't good journalism," he wrote from Vienna on September 25, "to let a warm personal friend and in some matters literary partner, write a critical review of him in a paper which has good reason to think little of his delicacy and highly of his greed." And with the recollection of the *Gilded Age* episode still fresh in his mind, he concluded: "As you remember, we agreed, years ago, a new book by Twain is *not* (as he modestly suggested) a literary event of such importance that it makes much difference whether we have our dear friend Howells write the review, or whether indeed we have any review." But it was too late. Howells, whose good will Hay and Reid valued, had already been commissioned.

Confidential though this correspondence was, some notion of its drift reached Charles Dudley Warner by the editorial grapevine. In a rash moment Warner cautiously "intimated," as Clemens told Howells, "that the N. Y. *Tribune* was engaged in a kind of crusade against me." Following up this intimation, Clemens questioned other friends, who told him that as soon as Reid returned from abroad in November the *Tribune* had begun to fling a series of sneers, insults, and brutalities his way—some said frequently, others said "almost *daily*." Someone told him Osgood was worried that these "constant and pitiless" attacks would destroy his reputation. But Osgood had real cause to worry when Clemens told him that the sequel to *The Prince and the Pauper* was going to be the "dynamitic" biography of Whitelaw Reid that he had been contemplating for a couple of years. In the spirit of vendetta he was working day and night collecting material and taking notes; he had researchers at work in England; for three hours in New York he spewed out his rage to a stenographer. He was going to write a book, he said, "which the very devils and angels would delight to read, and which would draw disapproval from nobody but the hero of it, (*and* Mrs. Clemens, who is bitter against the whole thing)."

While the reviewers were praising his new delicacy and refinement, Clemens was filling page after page of his notebooks with the rubrics of his great revenge: "skunk," "idiot," "eunuch," "missing link," "receiver of stolen goods," "property of Jay Gould," "Guiteau with the courage left out," "chased after all the rich girls in California" (Reid's new bride was the daughter of Darius Ogden Mills, the California mogul), "Grant calls him Outlaw Reid." The preface was going to be simply a compilation—which he would get around to making by and by—of Reid's slurs and sneers at Clemens from 1873 on. Howells, hearing the news of the impending holocaust from Osgood, who begged him to intervene, decided to remain strictly neutral. "I did not know how you would take unprovoked good intentions from me," he explained to Clemens on January 20, and he used precisely the same reasoning which Clemens habitually used with Orion: "I believe you will be sick of the thing long before you reach the printing point."

After three weeks of frenzied involvement with this biography which Clemens was sure would wipe Reid off the face of the earth, a touch of cold reality was introduced in the form of a suggestion, apparently from Livy, that before he went any further it might be well for him to look up these "almost daily insults." So far the revenge machine had been running on hearsay only. As a start, he subscribed to the *Tribune* and read it daily. On January 21 he instructed Webster, who was already supervising more business affairs than he was able to handle (including several litigations and all the bills for remodeling the house), to "put in an hour or two" and "quietly copy off and send to me every remark which the Tribune has made about me *since the end of October* up to the present date." An air of autocratic unreality, like Lear commanding the hurricane, now enveloped the project. Four days later, disappointed by what Webster had culled from three months of the paper, Clemens asked John Russell Young of the *Herald* to investigate. Young's findings were the same as Webster's: four minor items, critical but not malicious, no crusade, just a "prodigious bugaboo." "What the devil can those friends of mine have been thinking about?" Clemens asked ruefully as he abandoned the biography to which he had devoted three weeks of intense work and total attention. This spurt of creativity, misguided and fruitless like many of Orion's enthusiasms, was followed by the inevitable fallow period of visiting and entertaining, getting deeper and deeper into business, working on the *Library of Humor*. Clemens calculated, in a characteristic way, that he could have earned ten thousand dollars in those three weeks and with infinitely less trouble, if only he had had the motivation. "I am too lazy, now, in my sere and yellow leaf," he said to Howells, resigning himself to the less than mouse his mountain had produced, "to be willing to work for anything but love."

III

In search of love he left Hartford in mid-April 1882. "After twenty-one years' absence," he was to write later that year in *Life on the Mississippi*, "I felt a very strong desire to see the river again, and the steamboats, and such of the boys as might be left; so I resolved to go out there." Ever since his piloting articles in the *Atlantic* seven years before, he had intended, given suitable company (he wanted Hay or Howells), to go back to the river and collect enough new material to make a book. The subscription book, by which he lived, was making its usual demands on him. What he had to do was take a three-hundred-page series, already seven years old, and make a six-hundred-page book of it. And, as he soon discovered, the trouble was that the original three hundred pages, for all their apparent factuality, had been a work of the imagination, an attempt to recapture the past; the new material was by and large a chore, a work of travel journalism, an attempt to document the present. Eventually, after believing that "the powers of earth and hell are leagued against it," he managed to finish *Life on the Mississippi*. Then he dismissed it as "this wretched God-damned book." This was to be expected. What was unexpected and showed once again the vagrant but also purposive workings of his creative process was that his river trip and his struggles to finish his river book were directly related to the finishing of *Huckleberry Finn*, itself the child of six years of sporadic inspiration.

The *Atlantic* piloting articles as well as *Tom Sawyer* were Mark Twain's celebrations of life and adventure in the South before the Civil War. The second part of *Life on the Mississippi*, with its constant reminders of the decline of piloting and steamboating from their former glory, and the last two thirds of *Huckleberry Finn* are the work of a matured and more reflective Mark Twain who has not yet taken the final turn in his road toward cynicism and despair. Even before leaving on his 1882 river trip he had begun to attack the South and to tell himself what he expected to find. The South was poverty-stricken, barren of any progress, he wrote in his notebook. Except in the arts of war, murder, and massacre, the South had contributed nothing. It had no architecture, it was sophomoric, its speech was "flowery and gushy." (By the time he finished the book he had worked up such a rage against the South that Osgood asked him to omit certain chapters and passages as offensive and damaging to Southern sales.) And along with this growing disenchantment with his homeland came recollections of loss, violence, and dread: Henry Clemens, scalded to death; the tramp who burned to death in the village jail; men shot down or stabbed on the streets of Hannibal; a slave man struck down with a chunk of slag for some small offense. In his age as well as his youth, these recollections filled his nights with remorse.

Getting ready for his Southern trip, Clemens put away the *Library of Humor* books that littered his billiard room on the third floor, reminded himself to buy some whiskey flasks and to bring enough cigars and pipe tobacco for the trip (he attributed his good health to the fact that he took no exercise, drank in the morning and again in the evening, and smoked continuously, with all his might when he was working). In New York on April 17 he made a careful inventory, including certificate numbers, of the $110,000 in securities he kept in a box at the Mount Morris Bank. The next morning he left for St. Louis on the Pennsylvania's eight-o'clock train. With him were Osgood and a Hartford stenographer, Roswell Phelps, hired at a hundred dollars a month and expenses to take down not only Clemens' travel impressions but also, inevitably, reminders of the business turmoil he left behind: a letter to Charley Webster suggesting litigation to recover some of the scrapbook royalties, a letter advising a certain R. E. Elliott, Esq., that the American Publishing Company was not a reliable concern, inasmuch as on one book alone the late Elisha Bliss had swindled the undersigned out of twenty-five thousand dollars.

From the start Clemens was oppressed by a sense of change and loss. The levee at St. Louis, once packed solid with steamboats, was empty now except for half a dozen, their fires banked or dead. The pilot and the steamboat man were heroes no longer—in the old days, he said, the pilot was "the only unfettered and entirely independent human being that lived in the earth." The young men in river towns who used to delight in re-peating the names of the gaudy, smoke-plumed boats that passed each day now rolled on their tongues the names of railroads. Even the sight of a steamboat named *Mark Twain*, tied up inside the wooded mouth of the Obion River, did not relieve the general air of desolation—it was the only steamboat he saw that day. The second day out of St. Louis, on board the packet *Gold Dust* bound for New Orleans, Clemens tried to pass himself off in the pilothouse as a credulous visitor. He was recognized right away. The pilot remembered his voice, remembered his habit of passing his fin-gers through his hair, and, as a punishment, put him at the wheel. The pilothouse was as familiar to him as if he had never left it. It was the river that had changed, Clemens said. It was "as brand new as if it had been built yesterday," and there were new islands, landings, towns. The chang-ing river had cut away the banks at Parker's Bend where Sam Bowen, Will's brother, was buried and had washed his grave away. All that now remained of the wondrous pilot knowledge and pilot memory that Sam Clemens had acquired under Horace Bixby, who taught him the river, was a landsman's skill in remembering names and addresses.

In Concord on April 27, 1882, four weeks and six days after Longfellow, died Ralph Waldo Emerson, long remote from the world of the living. Two of the three "gracious singers" were dead, and along with the old order were passing the centers of literary vitality. In New Orleans in late April and early May, while New England mourned, Mark Twain and two other masters of Southern vernacular, George Washington Cable and Joel Chandler Harris, were meeting in friendship and festivity. At thirty-seven, Cable, a tiny mandarin-looking man, was "the South's finest literary genius," said Clemens, who liked and admired him so much that he went along on Cable's usual Sunday round of sermons and church services. "I got nearer to heaven than I hope I ever shall again," Clemens said about the Sunday he spent with Cable in New Orleans. During the day, Harris arrived from Atlanta, where he was an editor on the *Constitution*, and Clemens called on him at his hotel. They had never met, although a year earlier they had corresponded and exchanged versions of the Negro ghost story Clemens told as "The Golden Arm." According to Clemens, Harris, whose first collection of Uncle Remus stories had been published in 1880 and became one of the best sellers of the decade, was "the only master" of Negro dialect. Monday afternoon they all spent together at Cable's red-and-olive cottage, surrounded by orange trees and a garden, on Eighth Street, on the lip of the Garden District. A crowd of children had come to see their beloved old Uncle Remus, who disappointed them, because he turned out to be white, young, rather Irish-looking, and, even with a three-year-old in his lap, still too shy to read his stories. To console the children, Clemens and Cable talked about Brer Rabbit, told "The Tar Baby," and read some of their own work. In the evening the festivities continued at the house of James Guthrie, a friend of Cable's. There was piano music by some young ladies, Cable sang a Creole song, Clemens read from *The Innocents Abroad* and some unpublished travel sketches, Guthrie recited Shakespeare, and two of Guthrie's children, a six-year-old boy and a four-year-old girl, played Romeo and Juliet in the balcony scene. "I have never seen anything that moved me more," Clemens wrote to Livy. The children had performed with "perfect simplicity and unconsciousness" and they "required prompting only once."*

This day of love-feasting climaxed a stay in New Orleans which Clemens, exhilarated and tireless, described for Livy as "a whirlpool of hospitality." Despite his hostility to the South and to much of its culture, which he said was a feudalistic sham borrowed out of Walter Scott, it was still *his* South he had come back to, a region but also a background and experience he could never wholly share with Livy. His days began early with social breakfasts and ended late at night after rounds of banqueting on pompano and crayfish and soft-shell crabs. He explored the French Quarter with Cable as his guide, attended mule races and cockfights, went on a visit to an ice factory and an excursion on Lake Ponchartrain. He left New Orleans on May 6, having waited until then so that he could make the trip upriver with Horace Bixby, now captain of the resplendent *City of Baton Rouge*. From the crowd of friends and admirers standing near

* This children's performance, combined with a passage (from Chapter 51 of *Life on the Mississippi*) about "a couple of young Englishmen" who "got themselves up in cheap royal finery" and "did" the swordfight from *Richard III*, ends up in the program given by the Duke and the King in their "Shakespearean Revival" in Chapters 20 and 21 of *Huckleberry Finn*.

the gangplank stepped a young man who said, "I have not read all of your writings, Mr. Twain, but I think I like 'The Heathen Chinee' best of all." According to Cable, the young man's wits had been rattled by the excitement of meeting Mr. Twain. But the compliment was not wasted. "A thousand thanks," Clemens said heartily, taking his hand. The young man replied, "You are perfectly welcome. I am sure you deserve it."

He saved for the end of his Southern trip a three-day visit to Hannibal. He arrived on a still Sunday morning. The town seemed deserted. "Everything was changed," he noted, "but when I reached Third or Fourth street the tears burst forth, for I recognized the mud." He was to say in *Life on the Mississippi* that he felt that morning like a prisoner seeing Paris again after years of captivity in the Bastille. The scenes of his Hannibal boyhood liberated him as a writer from the captivity of prosperous middle age in his house in Hartford, itself a kind of Bastille which he sometimes wished could be razed to the ground. He climbed Holliday's Hill again and looked out over the drowsing white town. Inevitably Master Wattie's question about being a boy again came back to him, and with it came his own nagging sense of unreality in the face of change. Years later, after he had tasted failure and loss, he would ask, Which was the dream—the hideous present or the remembered past? But now, in the confidence of his forty-sixth year and on the eve of his greatest fulfillment as a writer, it was still possible to move from present to past and back again, to move in and out of the dream. The Pauper, after all, is a bad dream from which the Prince awakens, but the Connecticut Yankee, only six or seven years later, will not have this freedom—his dream of ruined chivalry and self-destroyed technology has become the addled reality from which he cannot escape. In Hannibal, Mark Twain could believe he was a boy again, a boy who had never left the town in 1853 to set out on his travels but instead had a dream twenty-nine years long about growing up. He woke up each morning a boy, but at night, after visiting with old friends who were rich or fat or grizzled and had children long since grown up and gone away, he went to bed feeling a hundred years old. "That world which I knew in its blossoming youth is old and bowed and melancholy now," he wrote to Livy. "It will be dust and ashes when I come again. I have been clasping hands with the moribund—and usually they say, 'It is for the last time.'"

He reached St. Paul after a "hideous trip." May 21: it snowed, he lay in his bed at the Metropolitan Hotel homesick, hiding from the cold, waiting for the eastbound train. For once the reporters did not clamor for interviews with S. L. Clemens of Hartford, who had given up registering under some other name. They were much more interested in talking to a party of English peers led by the seventh Duke of Manchester—grand parallels to the titled rapscallions of *Huckleberry Finn*—who were passing through St. Paul on their way to Manitoba to look into some land speculations.

IV

In mid-June 1882, just as Clemens was about to leave Hartford for his summer's work at Quarry Farm, the infant, Jean, came down with scarlet fever. The house was quarantined, and they unpacked the trunks and undid the elaborate preparations for the trip. A few days later, Susy became delirious with some undiagnosed fever, and Clemens himself was laid up in bed with a fever and lumbago. All in all, the departure for Elmira was postponed about a month. During the following winter, when there was an epidemic of pneumonia in Hartford and the city's death rate rose about thirty-five per cent over the season's norm, Clemens had colds and rheumatism, Susy had scarlet fever, and they were quarantined again. After a fright that Clara had diphtheria, Livy not only came down with it but also had quinsy and high fever. By the end of the spring she was so emaciated. Clemens joked bitterly, "it's been like sleeping with a bed full of baskets." Eventually, dogged by chronic ill health in his family—he once remarked that two such highstrung people as he and Livy should probably never have had children—Clemens became something of a faddist, and he looked for miraculous cures through hydrotherapy, osteopathic manipulation, electric treatments, mind cure and mind science, health foods, and such homemade nostra as a daily shampoo with strong soap to keep his hair from falling out and a mixture of turpentine and scent to cure chilblains. He believed that he could cure myopia and astigmatism by abolishing eyeglasses, and in consequence he and Livy, Howells recalled, came "near losing their eyesight." He kept grim inventories of his physical ailments, including hernia and chronic constipation. Susy was to die of meningitis; Jean's pattern of physical and emotional disturbance was diagnosed finally as epilepsy; Clara had nervous breakdowns; and Livy had hyperthyroid heart disease. By the time all of this had become clear to him, during the last twenty years of his life, he had developed, with considerable justification, a sense of horrible nemesis.

But in the early 1880s, even though he often felt he was running a hospital in his home, he was still able to find a kind of humor in it all. In his notebook he made a list of names for the characters in some fictional pathology he never got around to writing; among them were Gonorrhea Jackson, Pneumonia Bascom, Cancer Collins, Lockjaw Harris, and Rectum Jones. "Yes, sir," he exclaimed to Cable after the terrible winter of 1882–83, "my poor wife must get sick, and have a pulse that ran up to 150 in the shade." He had just been sick in bed, was finicky and anxious, and impatient with Cable, who wanted to go out without an overcoat in April and had said, "The air is full of a soft warm glow." "Soft warm glow!" Clemens said. "It's full of the devil!—the devil of pneumonia," and he made

Cable borrow an overcoat to wear for the few yards that lay between his house and Charles Dudley Warner's, where Cable was staying. Two days later Clemens was able to bounce back completely. On April 4 he introduced Cable to a full house at Unity Hall and gave a party for him after the reading. The next morning, after Cable read for the Saturday Morning Club at Mary Perkins' house, Clemens bubbled with delight and enthusiasm and praised him as a reader over Howells, Henry James, and Bret Harte. Then they went to a three-hour lunch.

In all ways other than health the external conditions and the accidents of Clemens' life were now as favorable as they would ever be. He was rich (although not so rich as Wattie Bowser imagined him to be); his business ventures, and failures, were constantly mounting in number and in cost, but they were still not the catastrophic drain on his resources and energies that they would soon become. He was still expanding in a carefree way. "Dear Charley," he wrote on September 9, 1882, taking the next-to-last step toward starting his own publishing house, "I want you to be the General Agent for my New Book for the large district of which New York is the centre. I can make it pay us both." The praise which *The Prince and the Pauper* brought him was given canonical form by Howells' full-length critical essay in the *Century* magazine that September, an appraisal of Mark Twain's total literary achievement in terms of his moral fervor, the "ethical intelligence" underlying his humor, and his strength and artistry as a storyteller. "I hope the public will be willing to see me with your eyes," Clemens said in gratitude. The public, and others as well, were willing indeed. Thomas Hardy, his own reputation already firmly based on *The Return of the Native*, remarked at a London dinner party in 1883, "Why don't people understand that Mark Twain is not merely a great humorist? He is a remarkable fellow in a very different way," and Hardy went on to praise *Life on the Mississippi*.

Clemens' six-week trip of hail and farewell to Hannibal and the river gave him material and impetus for more than a year and a half of productive work on two books. In *Life on the Mississippi* he described *Huckleberry Finn* as "a book which I have been working at, by fits and starts, during the past five or six years, and may possibly finish in the course of five or six more." The two books were by now symbiotic, and he used one to jog the other. (In 1885, by which time he had finished both of them, he planned a book in which Huck was to ship as a cabin boy on a steamboat; the book would enable Mark Twain to "put the great river and its bygone ways into history in the form of a story.") His working notes for the two books overlapped, and while he was wrestling with *Life on the Mississippi* during the summer and fall of 1882—"I never had such a fight over a book in my life before," he told Howells—he managed to make some progress on *Huckleberry Finn*. And, in turn, to pad out his river book to its inexorable subscription bulk he not only followed his usual practice of quoting extensively (in one long day's work, from nine one morning until one the next, he added 9,500 words, most of them quotations from earlier travel writers), but also borrowed from the novel. Almost the whole of Chapter Three of *Life on the Mississippi* is the raftsmen's chapter from *Huckleberry Finn*, seven thousand words or so, and he also adapted or rehearsed other material from the novel, including the feud and his period-piece description of the Grangerford parlor as the "house beautiful."

By January 1883, when the book was finally ready to be set in type, Clemens had cut about fifteen thousand words, most of the deletions reflecting Osgood's fear that sentimental Northerners as well as loyal Southerners might find grounds for offense. Even so, there remained one more editorial hurdle. Howells was away in Europe, and Clemens now turned to Livy. She "has not edited the book yet," he told Osgood in January, "and will of course not let a line of the proof go from her till she has read it and possibly damned it. But she says she will put aside *everything else* and give her entire time to the proofs." Osgood's role was getting smaller. He was accountable to his author, who was the sole financier of the publishing project. He was also, as he learned, accountable to Charley Webster, no mere general agent now but his uncle's vicar in all publishing as well as business matters. "I will not interest myself in *any-thing* connected with this wretched God-damned book," Clemens told Charley, and he ordered him to take charge. "We must give Webster all the thunder-and-lightning circulars and advertising enginery that is needful," Clemens had instructed Osgood that January. "We must sell 100,000 copies of the book in 12 months, and shan't want him complaining that we are the parties in fault if the sale falls short of it." Now, with all these pressures on him, Osgood was ordered both to rush the book through and to wait for word from his author's wife, whose changes in galley and page proof were likely to cost time as well as money. As it turned out, some of the changes Livy insisted on, though reasonable enough in terms of taste, were more troublesome than Osgood's worst expectations. That May, with fifty thousand copies already printed and forty thousand of them bound, Osgood had to delete two illustrations which Livy objected to. One showed the author being cremated, with an urn initialed "M.T." standing in the foreground to receive the ashes. The other showed a corpse in graveclothes, chopfallen and with staring eyes—"She says the chapter is plenty dreadful enough without," Clemens told Osgood.

It was to be more than sixty years before *Life on the Mississippi* approximated the 100,000-copy success that Clemens and Webster demanded for it. The scapegoat, inevitably and also with some justice, was Osgood, whose brief career as Mark Twain's publisher was clearly coming to a close. Years later Clemens was to remember him as "one of the dearest and sweetest and loveliest human beings to be found on the planet anywhere." But in December 1883, after the book had been out for half a year, Clemens put all the blame for what he considered its failure on Osgood. "The publisher who sells less than 50,000 copies of a book for me has merely injured me, he has not benefitted me," and he charged that Osgood's "apprenticeship" in the subtleties of subscription publishing had cost fifty thousand dollars on this book alone, not to mention *The Prince and the Pauper*. Nevertheless, despite the agonies he had writing it and despite its disappointing sales, the publication of *Life on the Mississippi*, eight years after he first began it as an *Atlantic* serial, was part of a constellation of circumstances which favored Mark Twain as he worked and flourished during the summer of 1883.

That summer he achieved a state of creative euphoria in which all things seemed possible and, to a sufficient extent, actually were. The genius works in a dazzling darkness of his own which normal modes of explanation hardly penetrate, and to describe Mark Twain as he neared the age of forty-eight, one has to invoke the same rich symbols that occupied his imagination. This master of quotidian reality, whose life was a sort of love affair with the transient, gaudy satisfactions the Gilded Age offered him, was in the grip of the same benign and transcendent force that raised Grant and Joan of Arc from obscurity to greatness, gave a small man unsuspected strength, enabled Jack to kill the giant. Like the best of his literature, Mark Twain himself had his roots in myth and folklore, thought of himself as a prodigy of nature or an "unaccountable freak" like Halley's comet, which had blazed over his birth in 1835 and which he expected to go out with when it returned. "Ah, well, I am a great and sublime fool," he had written to Howells after the Whittier disaster, "—but then I am God's fool, and all His works must be contemplated with respect."

Clemens took Livy, still "thin as a rail" after a hard winter, and his children and servants to Elmira in the middle of June by a private sleeping car on the Delaware, Lackawanna and Hudson. They stayed at Quarry Farm until mid-September. Six days a week, and sometimes Sundays, during these three months he hurried through breakfast and spent the entire day working in his study. His normal summer pace, he calculated, was four or five hours a day five days a week. Now he was working just about twice as long and as hard as he was accustomed to and doing "two seasons' work in one," and though he had brief spells of exhaustion, during which he would spend a day or two in bed reading and smoking, he was more robust than ever. In the euphoria of an immense release of creative energies his miseries and symptoms of the previous year vanished. To describe his own state he repeatedly used the same word, "booming," that he used for entrepreneurial ventures, steamboats and rivers in full course, and anything splendid or grand ("We can just have booming times—they don't have no school now," Buck Grangerford tells Huck). "I'm booming these days," Clemens wrote to Howells in July, "got health and spirits to *waste*—got an over-plus." "The children are booming and my health is ridiculous." "I haven't had such booming working-days for many years," he told his mother. "This summer it is no more trouble to me to write than it is to lie." In a surge of creation which, he recognized, was unique in his experience, he finished *Huckleberry Finn* and began revising it, a job on which he continued to work enthusiastically, although intermittently, during the following winter and spring. And instead of being dubious about his novel, as he was in 1876, when he thought he might "pigeon-hole or burn the MS when it is done," he proclaimed his enthusiasm for it. "*I* shall *like* it, whether anybody else does or not," he told Howells even before he finished, and in September, with a finished manuscript on his table, he wrote to Andrew Chatto, "I've just finished writing a book, and modesty compels me to say it's a rattling good one, too."

That summer was the high point of his creative life—at the end of the next summer he complained that he did not have a paragraph to show for three months of work—but, like microtomized tissue, it both recapitulated and predicted his entire career. *Huckleberry Finn*, which had fought him to a standstill several times during the previous seven years, fitted into a characteristic mosaic of other projects and preoccupations, literary and unclassifiable, to which, incongruously, he seemed to give equal enthusiasm and energy. In the ecstasy of booming along at the rate of three or four thousand words at a sitting he became self-intoxicated to the point of having the blind staggers about his own work. More or less concurrently, he finished two books that summer. One was his masterpiece. The other was something quite different, a burlesque continuation of the *Arabian Nights* on the thousand-and-second night of which Scheherazade, lying in bed with King Shahriyar, is talking him to sleep; in literary terms, she is really talking him to death. But Clemens was so taken with this new book that, as he told Charley Webster, he wanted it published "right after Huck." Confronted with the manuscript of this numbing extravaganza, Howells felt himself just as much a victim of Scheherazade's "prolixity" as the King and was nothing if not frank. "It was not your best or your second-best," he told Clemens, who eventually put the manuscript away in his archive of false starts and exhausted inspirations. Other, equally misbegotten schemes occupied him that summer. Through Charley Webster he planned to manufacture and put on sale sixty dozen pairs of grape scissors of a type invented and patented by Howells' father. Joe Goodman interested him in investing in California vineyards. He was in danger for a while of being involved in Captain Duncan's libel suit against the New York *Times*. He was storing up ideas for a play, which he wrote that fall with Howells, in which Colonel Sellers, now become a scientist and an American Claimant, capered around the stage equipped with wings and, as a firm believer in homeopathic principles, with a fire extinguisher full of Greek fire strapped to his back. Among other projected literary works was a burlesque account of the Second Advent in which Paddy Ryan and some other disciples talked in a music-hall brogue.

On July 18, after three and a half weeks of "booming along" on his two mismatched books, Clemens had a premonition of overwork, quit for the day, and, characteristically, gave himself entirely over to something altogether different but also, as he found it in his high mood, equally absorbing. On this idyllic summer day, with Susy, Clara, and Jean by his side, he measured off with a yardstick 817 feet on the winding driveway that ran up the hillside. Then, using as markers pegs which he whittled and drove himself, he measured out on the scale of one foot per year all the reigns of the English rulers from William the Conqueror on. His idea was to amuse and instruct his children by teaching them history (as he regarded such collections of dates and facts) by the running foot. Standing in the door of the farmhouse and surveying history, they could see 1066 near the foot of the hill and, with opera glasses, the forty-sixth year of Victoria's reign uphill, past his study. The game at first consisted of running past the markers, calling out the names and dates of the rulers, and trying to reach 1883 first and with fewest mistakes. The following night, however, Mark Twain's demon sprang on this innocent pastime. Lying in bed, churning with the idea, Clemens devised a way of playing this game indoors, on a cribbage board with pins and cards. He began to see it as a commercial venture which, patented and manufactured, would sweep the world with his own mania for facts ("I never care for fiction or story books," he told Kipling in 1889. "What I like to read about are facts and statistics of any kind").

The next day he fired off the news of his invention in several directions. "The reason it took me eight hours," he wrote to Twichell, "was because with little J's interrupting assistance, I had to measure from the Conquest to the end of Henry VI. three times over," and he outlined his plans for the indoor version. Soon Orion, never hard to inflame, was at work collecting all kinds of facts and dates and working on the typographical problems of designing a board for the game. Webster too got the news and was ordered to drop his other responsibilities and rush up to Elmira "for a couple of hours"—the round trip might have taken up the better part of two days—to discuss patents and manufacturing. Twichell quickly got himself in deep trouble with his friend, for in a moment of boyish indiscretion he had given Clemens' description of the game to the *Courant*, which published it. Other papers, in Boston and New York, picked up the story, and Howells felt that he had to counsel Clemens to "patent it or copyright it before someone else gets hold of it." Twichell "not only made me feel ridiculous," Clemens said to him, "but he broke up and ruined a fine large plan of mine," part of which was to publish a small illustrated book about the game. Even so Clemens was not discouraged. He was back pacing and repacing his driveway, whittling and hammering new pegs and stakes, working on the board and the pins and the cards, filling his notebooks with lists of other categories of fact and date that the game could be played with, including authors, geography, Irish history, religion, and the rulers of France.* He even considered imposing a three-point penalty on the player who stumbled over Judas Iscariot or—his animosities faded very slowly—Whitelaw Reid: "It is called being smirched."

Even in the booming summer of 1883 this exuberant plunge displayed his fatal addiction, which he observed with an amused and angry eye in Orion, to drowning his important goals and also his judgment in some 180-proof, hypomanic tipple of speculation. He was in the grip of a compulsion to think and act always in terms of exploitation and profits; even a game intended to teach chronology to little girls had to become a commercial venture right away. This is not to say that Mark Twain could have written another *Huckleberry Finn* or two in the time and with the energy he gave to such ventures. But these ventures eroded and colored his literary interests, and by trapping him into such irreversible involvements as his publishing house and the Paige typesetter they ofen made any writing, of any quality, next to impossible. In 1883, however, Mark Twain was still able to put *Huckleberry Finn* aside in favor of his history game and, in the plenitude of his creative powers, come back to his book later and finish it. The door was still open, the future ahead of him. History was still only a "game."

---

* Clemens eventually got a patent for his game apparatus in 1885, and in 1891 his own publishing house, which was already shaky on its feet, went one step further toward bankruptcy and brought out "Mark Twain's Memory-Builder: A Game for Acquiring and Retaining All Sorts of Facts and Dates." It consisted of a board, a small pamphlet of "facts," and a box of straight pins.

CHAPTER THIRTEEN

"Our great Century"

I

O N A WEEKDAY MORNING in mid-February 1884, tired out after a
winter's work, Clemens declared a half holiday for himself and lin-
gered over his breakfast steak and coffee with his house guest, George
Washington Cable. Cable was close to overstaying his welcome. While
passing through Hartford on a reading tour two and a half weeks earlier,
he had developed a fever and racking pains in his lower jaw, and he had
been an invalid at Farmington Avenue since. Even though the three Clemens children and the private nurse hired to take care of him all came down
with the mumps not long after, Cable maintained that whatever he had was
noncommunicable, probably just neuralgia. The seeds of Clemens' profound disgruntlement with him were already planted. Privately Clemens
blamed him for the mumps epidemic and told Ned House that Cable complained altogether too much about his pains—"Lord, if I dared laugh as I
want to laugh—but Mrs. Clemens would kill me." And later Clemens refused to deny published rumors that Cable had demanded a steady flow of
champagne and tried to duck out of his medical bills. "Don't give yourself
any discomfort about the slander of a professional newspaper liar," he
wrote to Cable in May 1885, after having been asked for the second time
to discredit a particularly demeaning account of their personal differences.
"Why, my dear friend, flirt it out of your mind," he concluded, disingenuously—for while soothing Cable he was also writing reminders to himself to "tell the *truth*" about Cable and about one other house guest, Bret
Harte. But whatever his resentments of Cable were to be, Clemens admired
him as a writer and social thinker, and Cable repaid his admiration in kind.
They had in common a passionate interest in the shadings of spoken vernacular, a histrionic talent, a deep-grained but liberalized Southernness,
and an outspoken humanitarianism. That morning in February they talked

with an intensity and a shared concern that overshadowed all their differences, present and future.

In the library after breakfast Clemens sat smoking his yellow corncob pipe, one slippered foot flung over the arm of his chair, his chin cradled in his right hand. As they talked, Cable could see coming out on Clemens' face the vivid pink spots that meant his mind was racing along with excitement, and soon they were both on their feet, pacing up and down and across the library floor, Cable a tiny man weighing a hundred pounds or so, Clemens, by a contrast that was to jog and delight their audiences when they appeared together on lecture platforms, seeming to be six feet tall. They stopped a moment to watch a strange bird hopping in the wan sunlight outside the window, tried to identify it in Clemens' Audubon, went back to their pacing. They talked, Cable wrote to his wife later that day, "about our great Century and the vast advantages of living in it—the glory and beauty of it." Clemens' brave world was still new, he had not yet been betrayed by the machine, nor had he composed his sad and sardonic farewells to what he called "the drive and push and rush and struggle of the raging, tearing, booming nineteenth century." In his lifetime alone, he believed, the human race had made more progress toward achieving its full stature than in any five centuries in history, and he celebrated the advance of technology and medicine, the toppling of the monarchies and the triumph of democracy, the emancipation of serf and slave.

They talked for hours that morning. Only once did Clemens become "ferocious and funny," Cable recalled, and that was when he came to his favorite subject of publishers who swindled him. "Oh," Clemens groaned, contemplating some ideal revenge, "if it could be, I could lie in my grave with my martial cloak around me and kick my monument over and laugh and laugh." Then he was at the piano singing "Tannenbaum" in German, banging the bass notes hard with one finger, while Cable followed the tune in his high tenor. The January 1885 issue of the *Century* magazine was a commemoration of such fellowship as this between two writers at the peak of their powers, for that bastion of intellectual respectability carried both an installment of *Huckleberry Finn* and Cable's "The Freedman's Case in Equity," a demand, stated in terms of legal and moral imperatives, for full civil equality for the Negro. Cable's position, which he stated in other reform articles, inevitably made him a pariah in the South. Clemens acknowledged Cable's courage and correctness; he himself had already, as his part of "the reparation due from every white to every black man," put a Negro student through Yale, and was determined to make this reparation in other ways, including small courtesies, reading at Negro churches, and interceding with Garfield on behalf of Frederick Douglass. There were certain residual attitudes, however, which he could never shake. He had a Negro butler, he explained to Howells, because he did not like to give orders to a white man, and with some anxiety he said that in a hundred years there would be Negro supremacy in America, the "whites under foot."

Out of Clemens' mind that morning also sprang one of his innumerable collaborative schemes. He, Cable, Howells, Frances Hodgson Burnett, and one or two others were each to write a long story based on the same characters and roughly the same situations. As Cable recognized, this "little literary scheme" bore a family resemblance not only to *The Ring and the Book,* which Clemens would soon be explicating for the ladies of his Browning circle, but also to another kind of scheme which they talked about that morning. Clemens had been thinking about his "travelling menagerie" for several years; the plans called for Howells, Aldrich, Joel Chandler Harris, and Cable, with Clemens as both impresario and star, to live in a private railroad car served by a private cook and to go around the country reading from their works on a tour which was bound to make them all rich, fat, and happy. By one o'clock, when Livy made her first appearance of the day and called them in to lunch, Cable's head was spinning with possibilities. Three days later Mark Twain, the great projector, was still working his spell on him. They were in New York, riding uptown in a carriage from their hotel near Union Square and on their way to 3 East Sixtieth Street to call on General Grant—"whom Mark knows well," Cable noted admiringly—to ask him if he would preside at "a big show for the relief of the Ohio River overflow sufferers," the entertainment to be provided by Mark Twain, Cable, and Henry Ward Beecher.

"If the book business interferes with the dramatic business, drop the *former*—for it doesn't pay salt," Clemens instructed Charley Webster at the beginning of January 1884. Only a few months later, after a disagreement with Osgood over costs, Clemens set Charley up in the book business, as Charles L. Webster and Company, to publish *Huckleberry Finn* and the rest of Mark Twain's works. But all that winter, even though he was making elaborate preparations to bring out his book, he was in the throes of a hopeless passion for a seductive but totally incompatible Muse. The stage obsessed him, as it did Henry James, Howells, and Bret Harte, and it exhausted him. Despite mounting evidence that he had little talent for either dramatic plotting or stage management, Clemens persisted in believing that the theater, like a bonanza mining strike, would yield him a maximum of income from a ludicrous minimum of effort. He dramatized *Tom Sawyer,* only to have it turned down by Augustin Daly, the leading producer of the day who had already staged *Roughing It* as well as *Ah Sin.* "Tom might be played by a clever comedian as a boy," Daly wrote to him that February, "but the other parts would seem ridiculous in grown people's hands." (Three years later Clemens himself decided that *no one* could put that celebration of youth on the stage—"One might as well dramatize any other hymn.") That February also he applied for a dramatic copyright on his adaptation of *The Prince and the Pauper*, but the only stage this version saw was the makeshift one in the carriage house at Farmington Avenue. Even Howells had not bothered to soften his disapproval. The play was "altogether too thin and slight," he said; it lacked life and incident, it was only half as long as it should have been, "and the parlance is not sufficiently 'early English.'" Clemens began a novel set in the Sandwich Islands, piled his billiard table high with source books, and tacked his notes all over the walls, but even before he had an outline of the book he was talking dramatization to Howells, who, for all his realistic appraisal of a script, was generally just as beguiled by the theater and by his own fancied talent for it. Together he and Clemens also planned an abolitionist melodrama and a play set in the time of Oliver Cromwell, and all through the winter, spring, and summer they followed with dismay, befuddlement, and exasperation Charley Webster's desperate campaign to negotiate with the original Mulberry Sellers, the actor John T. Raymond, a production of their joint play, *Colonel Sellers as a Scientist*. "If the play is altered and *made* longer I should be pleased to read it again," Raymond finally said in September; he was certain that "in its present form it would not prove successful." "Never mind about the play," Howells said wearily to Clemens. "We had fun writing it anyway."

Such discouragements prefigured worse to come. After having had gout during the spring ("I suppose this comes from high living when I was a boy," he told Osgood, "—corn-dodgers and catfish"), Clemens was spending a couple of hours every other morning that July writhing in the dentist's chair in Elmira, having his teeth scaled, "gouged out and stuffed." He sent away for personal narratives of Indian fighters and plainsmen—he was planning a novel about Tom and Huck out West among the Indians "40 or 50 years ago"; but nothing came of the idea except a few chapters. It had been a lost summer, he told Charley in September; "I haven't a paragraph to show for my 3-months' working season." That summer he had often seemed to be considerably more interested in a "perpetual calendar" he had developed. He optioned a half interest in a patented "bed clamp" meant to keep children from kicking off their sheets and blankets at night, presumably when they had bad dreams. Then he discovered that the bed clamp was too cheap to yield a decent profit margin, and he "invented" one that was "more expensive and more convenient." Hardly any of his investments had been anything but a disaster. Paige and his typesetting machine clamored for more attention, more time, always more money. Clemens already had a considerable amount tied up in manufacturing *Huckleberry Finn* and in supporting a publishing house which had nothing else to publish as yet; the drain was to go on through the beginning of 1885. He was feeling the old money pinch again. He could not afford to go to Europe, as he had vaguely planned in the spring—he had to stay home and earn some money. He even had to put off paying two thousand he owed to Howells for work on the *Library of Humor*. "I am like everybody else—everything tied up in properties that cannot be sold except at fearful loss," he apologized to Howells at the end of June. "It has been the roughest twelve-month I can remember, for losses, ill luck, and botched business." A week later he decided that to recoup his losses he would have to go back on tour again, but this time not alone. "I want good company on the road and at the hotels," he later told a reporter. "A man can start out alone and rob the public, but it's dreary work and a cold-blooded thing to do." His companion and fellow performer was to be Cable, and their joint tour—an abridged, austerity version of the grandly conceived "travelling menagerie"—was to begin in November.

Clemens had been rocked out of prosperity by one of the systolic events that set the life rhythm of the Gilded Age. For him and many of his contemporaries, no fewer than fourteen of the years between 1873 and 1897—the period of his own economic rise and fall—seemed to have been either "recession" or "depression" years. The little panic of 1884 distempered the nation's business and doubled the rate of bank failures. Even the canny and conservative financier Russell Sage, caught short for once in his career, lost seven million dollars in a few days' time. General Grant's stockbroking firm failed early in May, and the Marine Bank collapsed under the weight of Grant and Ward's overdrafts. The General, who a few days earlier had reckoned his assets at over two million dollars, discovered, at the age of sixty-two, that his partner had picked him so clean that the Grant family could put together only $180 in cash on the parlor table at Sixtieth Street. The Union commander and eighteenth President of the United States, a dupe in business as well as in politics, was paying the butcher and the baker with rubber checks. Soon after this humiliation, when he was beginning to fail in health, he was to write a book which would link his life pattern to Mark Twain's once and for all. For the General's *Personal Memoirs*, which he wrote to get his family out of bankruptcy, earned so much money that Mark Twain, his publisher as well as his friend, was encouraged—in terms of his bonanza psychology, compelled —to extend himself in bigger and bigger ventures until, ten years after the panic of 1884, he found himself a bankrupt, too, the victim of his own success. And again because of this, ten years after the money pinch forced him to take to the road with Cable, he had to plan another tour, this time around the world, a voyaging which became for him the sign and symbol of despair.

"I think we are only the microscopic trichina concealed in the blood of some vast creature's veins," Clemens wrote in his notebook that August,

"and it is that vast creature that God concerns himself about and not us."
Like the tragic figures in some of the stories he was later to begin but
never finish, he spent hours at the eyepiece of his English brass microscope. Its objective was focused on a drop of rainwater or of blood; its
mirror cast upward the harsh glare of his gas lamp. His fantasies of plurali-
ties of worlds, of intolerable disparities in time and size and distance, of a
dark area where dream and reality meet and shatter each other, embraced
a growing despair and confusion and prefigured the decline of his powers
as a writer. The miscroscope, the dream, the voyage became dominant
symbols of a great hopelessness that existed side by side with his faith in
the great century. The summer before, he had made notes for a story
about life in the interior of an iceberg which drifts in a vast circle year
after year for 130 years, by which time generations of people inside are
dead and frozen; he would return to this theme after Susy died. In January 1885, as if anticipating just such a loss, he translated into English the
last part of a German prose version of "The Pied Piper." He called this
episode "The Great Loneliness"; the mothers wake out of sleep, push open
the doors of their children's rooms, see that the beds are still empty and
always will be, call out in a last hope, and then turn away—"Ah, dear God,
if it could have been but a dream."

II

During those barren summer months at Quarry Farm Clemens was also
occupied with the unfamiliar challenge of his imminent reading tour. In a
laggard response to Charles Dickens' last visit to America, the vogue had
shifted from the humorous lecture, which Clemens had mastered after a
long apprenticeship, to the "author's reading," a semidramatic form with
its own set of demands and conventions which he had to learn almost from
scratch. He aimed to make writing sound like talk, but in order to do this
and create the illusion of a man telling a story instead of just reading it, he
had to modify as well as memorize the printed word; it was the audience
that had to be watched, not the page. And by now Clemens was entrepreneur as well as platform artist, and through the summer and fall he sent
out a flood of impresario instructions to Charley, who negotiated the contracts for the tour, and to Redpath's successor, Major James B. Pond, veteran of long tours with Henry Ward Beecher and with Ann Eliza, nineteenth wife of Brigham Young. Out of the proceeds Pond was to pay
Cable $450 a week plus expenses and to get ten per cent of the profits him-
self; the rest was to go to Clemens. For although Pond billed them as
"Twins of Genius," and Clemens said that Pond was the "boss and head

ring-master," there was no doubt about who the real boss was. The programs had to be planned, Clemens insisted, not to exceed two hours, including laughter and applause; the time was to be divided so that he had the edge over Cable. As the tour progressed, in fact, every minute Cable was on stage became something of an agony for his partner, and their constant fiddling with the program began to reflect not just accumulated knowledge of their audience but also a naked contest between two hungry egos. "He keeps his programs strung out to one hour, in spite of all I can do," Clemens was soon complaining. "I am thinking of cutting another of his pieces." His own readings included "advance sheets" of *Huckleberry Finn*, but even this sort of promotion was in general tempered by a shrewd public-relations strategy. "I may possibly get up one or two original things for the series," he told Pond at the end of July, "but I shan't want the fact mentioned that they *are* new. I think it dangerous policy to let the people suppose we need any attraction but just our *names* alone." No detail escaped him, from the printed programs, which had to be small enough to be useless as fans and stiff enough not to rattle, to "vast red posters" bearing the single line, "MARK TWAIN—CABLE." His promotional as well as his artistic judgment turned out to be correct, for despite lean times that followed the panic, the fifteen-week tour was to earn him seventeen thousand dollars and Cable six thousand.

With Livy in the audience, Clemens and Cable opened in New Haven on November 5. A week later, after polishing their performance in Melrose, Lowell, and Waltham, they were in Boston, their first major city, reading at the Music Hall. "You were as much yourself before those thousands as if you stood by my chimney corner," Howells said in admiration. "You *are* a great artist, and you do this public thing so wonderfully well that I don't see how you could ever bear to give it up." Livy wrote to him, not yet recognizing how such comparisons fed his resentment of Cable: "Mr. Charles Warner said the other evening that he enjoyed your reading so much more than Mr. Cable's, because it was so much more natural." And many others, including Hamlin Garland, then a young student of elocution in Boston, were also struck by this chimney-corner naturalness, which was actually a triumph of actor's artifice and a deliberately heightened contrast to Cable's stylized, dramatic, somewhat stagy manner. Mark Twain lounged about the platform solemnly (Cable said that only once during their 104 performances had he seen him smile), coughed dryly from time to time, wrung his hands, passed them through his hair, stroked his chin, pulled at his mustache, and, lulled by his own long drawl and buzz-saw voice, seemed to be half asleep only an instant before he sprang those nubs and snappers which made his audience "jump out of their skins," he told Livy, after which his ears rang with "a long roll of artillery laughter" punctuated by "Congreve rockets and bomb-shell explosions." It was after tasting such invincibility that at the end of a reading on Tuesday evening, November 18, in New York, he embarked on a venture which, in its meanings and consequences for him, dwarfed the successes and the problems of his tour with Cable.

Dictating his autobiography in 1906, Clemens provided the event with the atmosphere of a Poe story:

> I had been lecturing in Chickering Hall and was walking homeward. It was a rainy night and but few people were about. In the midst of a black gulf between lamps, two dim figures stepped out of a doorway and moved along in front of me. I heard one of them say, "Do you know General Grant has actually determined to write his memoirs and publish them? He has said so today, in so many words." That was all I heard—just those words—and I thought it great good luck that I was permitted to overhear them.

As a matter of fact, however, Grant, who was desperate for money, had been talking about his book since early September with Roswell Smith and Richard Watson Gilder (one of the "two dim figures"), both of the *Century*. He agreed in principle to give them the book for trade publication when he finished it, and he even declared himself to be "very disgusted" with most subscription publishers and their army of "scalawag canvassers." He also eagerly accepted the offer of five hundred dollars for the first of eventually four articles in the *Century*'s notable series "Battles and Leaders of the Civil War." And Clemens learned about these negotiations, which were about to be consummated by contract, in the considerably less dramatic and more refined circumstances of a late supper at Gilder's studio on East Fifteenth Street, which he attended with Livy after the Chickering Hall reading. The overheard conversation between two mysterious strangers on a dark street was Clemens' way of acknowledging that the hard facts of his dealings with Grant also had a dimension of myth and mystery. To become Grant's publisher, as he shortly did, was to combine piety with commerce, to administer as sacrament to the dying General and his family what Clemens described as the largest single royalty check in history.

"I wanted the General's book," Clemens later said, "and I wanted it very much." In all likelihood, until that evening at Gilder's he never meant to publish anyone's books but his own. The next morning—while Cable was worrying that his portion of the performance might have been "a wee bit too long"—Clemens, with the reading tour entirely out of his mind for the moment, was in the library of the house on Sixtieth Street, hot on the track of a publishing bonanza and turning the full power of his dazzling personality on Grant and his son Fred. He recalled for them his attempt three years earlier to persuade Grant to write his memoirs and his prediction then that the book was worth a fortune. Having established his moral claims, he described his own experience as author, director of one publishing house, and owner of another, and he argued the merits of subscription publishing in general and the particular superiority of Charles L. Webster and Company. As Grant listened, that army of "scalawag canvassers" began to seem noble joint-venturers in a great and profitable cause. Within the limits of tact Clemens scored the *Century*'s timid offer of a ten per cent royalty (an offer, he confided to his notebook, which was "the most cold-blooded attempt to rob a trusting and inexperienced man since Ward's performance"). He made a princely offer: ten thousand dollars against a twenty per cent royalty or, as he preferred for Grant's sake seventy per cent of the publisher's profits. Grant yielded to these persuasions to the extent of putting off any agreement with the *Century* until they had had a chance to match these terms. It was to be over three months before the book was Clemens' by contract. Still, that morning he could celebrate a possibility, a change in his fortunes and, as he sincerely intended, a change in the Grants'.

After the session in the library, the General showed Clemens his swords and medals and Oriental souvenirs and took him into the parlor to talk to Mrs. Grant and their guest, Lew Wallace, back from his post as American minister to Turkey and enjoying the snowballing success of *Ben Hur*. Even Grant, who had no appetite for novels, had stayed up thirty hours straight to read *Ben Hur*—he wanted to see, he explained, what kind of book another Union general could write. "There's many a woman in this land that would like to be in my place," Julia Grant said, "and be able to tell her children that she once stood elbow to elbow between two such great authors as Mark Twain and General Wallace." In the festivity of the moment Clemens, as he told Susy, turned to Grant and said, "Don't look so cowed, General. You have written a book, too, and when it is published you can hold up your head and let on to be a person of consequence yourself."

The next day he was back on the road with Cable, swinging south to Philadelphia, Baltimore, and Washington and then northwest to Toronto and Cleveland before coming back to Hartford for a holiday at Christmas. The continuing negotiations with the Grants he left to Charley Webster as item number one in a roll call of responsibilities which now included the history game, the perpetual calendar, the bed clamp, various litigations either in progress or being planned, an investment in a fire extinguisher that worked like a hand grenade, the purchase of a $250 or $300 diamond solitaire ring at Tiffany's for Livy's birthday ("You must guess at the size"), and the publication, apparently jinxed from the start, of *Huckleberry Finn*.

III

"The book is to be issued when a big edition has been sold—and not before," Clemens repeatedly told Charley. His goal was an advance sale of forty thousand copies, and he said he was willing to wait seven years for it if he had to, but he was sure they would reach it early in December 1884, in time for the holidays. In Elmira that summer Clemens sat long hours for a portrait bust by his protégé, Karl Gerhardt, had it photographed in profile, and ordered reproductions printed and bound in the book, facing the frontispiece and protected by a basic furnishing of the fancy book, the tissue guard. By his own as well as by critical fiat he was now a standard author, and along with this status came a heightened sense of accountability to his public. Consequently, even though Howells combed the manuscript and some of the proofs, Clemens subjected the book to Livy's final scrutiny and gave her the page proofs to "expergate" (this was Susy's word for the editorial act). Livy's standards of decorum were scarcely more rigorous than his own. They were, in fact, considerably more liberal than those of Gilder, who, in editing selections from *Huckleberry Finn* for the *Century*, deleted references to nakedness, blasphemy, smells, and dead cats, and made such genteel emendations as changing "in a sweat" to "worrying." When Clemens came to judging the illustrations by E. W. Kemble, a then unknown artist whom he had chosen himself, he displayed the extremest Victorian severity. Kemble's Huck, at first, was a trifle too "Irishy" or "ugly" for Clemens' taste. Some of the pictures were too violent, "forbidding," or "repulsive," and one of them had to go altogether, he told Charley—"the lecherous old rascal kissing the girl at the campmeeting. It is powerful good, but it mustn't go in—don't forget it. Let's not make *any* pictures of the campmeeting. The subject won't *bear* illustrating. It is a disgusting thing, and pictures are sure to tell the truth about it too plainly." Caught in a conflict between realism and decorum, he had worked himself into the uncomfortable position of relying on the printed word to muffle "the truth" about "a disgusting thing."

Despite all these precautions, it seemed for a while that a kind of wicked justice would prevail. An engraver, whose identity was never discovered even though Webster posted a five-hundred-dollar reward, made a last-minute addition to the printing plate of Kemble's picture of old Silas Phelps. In the mischievous tradition of graffitti he drew in a male sex organ, and what was originally a pleasant scene shared by an appreciative Aunt Sally asking, "Who do you reckon it is?" suddenly became a flagrant case of indecent exposure. The alteration was discovered by one of Webster's agents only after thousands of the pictures, including those for the

agents' canvassing books, had been printed and bound. "Had the first edition been run off our loss would have been $250,000," Webster told a re-
porter from the New York *Tribune* on November 28. "Had the mistake
not been discovered, Mr. Clemens' credit for decency and morality would
have been destroyed." At J. J. Little's plant in New York the offending
illustration was cut out by hand and replaced by a new printing of the
plate, but though decency and morality were rescued, damage of another
sort had already been done. Webster had to postpone publication until
February 1885, thus missing the holiday trade, and the inevitable publicity
that the affair of Uncle Silas' organ won for the book only confirmed the
opinion of some custodians of public morals that the book was coarse and
degrading.

Back in Hartford for a Christmas vacation, Clemens found another
emergency. His eye fell on the catalogue of Estes and Lauriat, booksellers,
of 111 Nassau Street, New York, and the pink spots came to his cheeks,
for there, in cold print, was the announcement that *Huckleberry Finn* was
"now ready" and available at a reduced price of $2.25. (The lowest price
at which the book could be bought from Webster's agents was $2.75.)
Tearing out the page, he penciled a note across it: "Charley, if this is a
lie, let Alexander & Green sue them for damages instantly. And if we have
no chance at them in law, tell me at once and I will publish them as thieves
and swindlers." And he wanted each of Webster's agents to get a facsimile
of a handwritten note signed "Mark Twain": "These people deliberately
lied when they made that statement. . . . They will have an immediate
opportunity to explain, in court." Five days later, on the train going to
Pittsburgh, he met one of the Estes and Lauriat men, who offered the feeble explanation that his company had supposed the book would be out in
time for the holidays. "I said we couldn't help what they 'supposed,' "
Clemens reported to Charley, "and we should have to require them to pay
for supposing such injurious things." It took him hardly any time to become implacable. Now Livy entered the fray, but her control over him
extended, as usual, only to what he volunteered to her control. "Youth
dear," she began mildly enough. Then she told him bluntly that his conduct in the Estes and Lauriat affair, in particular a menacing letter he was
about to send them, was making her "sick." "How I wish you were less
ready to fight, and more ready to see other people's side of things . . . If
you write, write civilly." But he was already past writing civilly or un-
civilly to Estes and Lauriat; his attorney had applied for an injunction
against cut-rating the book. In Boston on February 10 Judge Le Baron
Colt of the United States Circuit Court denied the injunction, a ruling
which, according to Clemens' disgusted and sardonic interpretation, gave
his opponent the right to "sell property which does not belong to him but
to me—property which he has not bought and which I have not sold.

Under this ruling I am now advertising that judge's homestead for sale; and if I make as good a sum out of it as I expect I shall go on and sell the rest of his property."

Even the simplest transactions were going wrong. A request from Allen Thorndike Rice, the thirty-three-year-old owner and editor of the *North American Review*, for an excerpt from the book quickly became in Clemens' eyes a kind of Byzantine intrigue. Seduced by Rice's celebrated glitter, an assistant of Charley's named Bromfield was handing over literary property without authorization, and Rice apparently planned to pay less for it than he told Clemens he would. "Bromfield is an idiot," Clemens decided after getting, as he believed, to the bottom of it all, "and Rice—well, Rice seems to have acted very much like a rascal."

Inevitably Clemens' impatience and mounting discontent with his book spilled over into his reading tour with Cable and magnified the normal tensions between two high-strung men compelled to share ten thousand miles of travel, four months of homeless nights in the hotels of seventy different cities. On peaceful days they sang together, shadow-boxed, joked for reporters, allowed their manager to register at a Cincinnati hotel as "J. B. Pond and two servants." In Albany they were entertained by Grover Cleveland, the President-elect, properly grateful to Hartford's most prominent mugwump, who now sat on the governor's desk and by accidentally sitting on the electric bells as well summoned a squad of pages. In St. Louis they talked to Cousin James Lampton, whom Cable immediately recognized as the model for Colonel Sellers—Lampton invited them to visit his imaginary house and drink beer out of the water taps. They read together at the Opera House in Hannibal, where Clemens once again felt, as he told Livy, "infinite deeps of pathos" and where he carried his heart in his mouth the whole day. Jane Clemens, eighty-one and full of dance and gossip, was in the audience at Keokuk. "What books she could have written!" Clemens said after an evening of her talk. In a Rochester bookstore one Saturday night in December Cable had introduced him to Malory's *Morte d'Arthur*—"You'll never lay it down until you have read it from cover to cover," he promised—and thereby became, as Clemens acknowledged a year later, the "godfather" of *A Connecticut Yankee*. Despite the frictions, his admiration for Cable grew. "Cable is a great man," he was writing to Livy in February, and if he continued his fight on behalf of the Negro "his greatness will be recognized." "Cable's gifts of mind are greater and higher than I had suspected," he told Howells a day before the tour ended. "But . . ."

The "but," he went on to explain, had to do with Cable's religion, his piety and abstemiousness, and, above all, his inflexible Sabbath observances. Sunday in any town found Cable at church services and Bible classes. Clemens either stayed in bed resting and spinning tales of the mutiny on the *Bounty* and the Pitcairn Islanders to Major Pond's brother, Ozias, or applied a lesson from Cable. "He has taught me to abhor and detest the Sabbath-day," he told Howells, "and hunt up new and troublesome ways to dishonor it." And although Cable was hardened after a while to being teased about his religion, he was tormented by some of the masculine company Clemens deliberately exposed him to, company which, Cable was afraid, showed all too well one side of his partner's personality that had remained hidden during that morning talk in Hartford a year before.

On January 6 Clemens' distant cousin "Marse" Henry Watterson of the Louisville *Courier-Journal* took them to lunch at the Pendennis Club. Cable was horrified by Watterson's rough language, his talk about getting drunk, and his appearance, which, according to Cable, mirrored a "moral distortion": Watterson had one blind eye, the other was nearsighted, and his face was hard, razor-scraped, and suffused with blood. A few weeks earlier they had spent an evening with Petroleum V. Nasby, publisher of the Toledo *Blade*, who took them out for a supper of birds. "I'll tell you, Clemens," Nasby said as Cable flinched in distaste, "I've settled down upon the belief that there is but one thing in this world better than a dollar, and that's a dollar and a half." Nasby was a big, coarse-looking man with a knotted forehead and thick, disheveled hair; Cable was relieved to see that in contrast "the fine lines" in Clemens' face seemed to shine out. Nasby was drinking only ginger ale and lemonade now; he had sworn off drinking, he told them, after twenty years of going to bed drunk every night. He had often lectured, he said, so drunk that his audience was "invisible" —"I knew it was going right only by the laughter and applause." After dinner he insisted on going back with them to their hotel and talking late into the night, the kind of talk he and Clemens had had in Hartford and Boston in the old lecturing days, all part of a distressing past, and not the kind Cable was accustomed to. "I'm glad he's gone," Cable wrote to his wife at the end of the ordeal. "He's a bad dream."

These encounters were one way in which Clemens could pay back Cable for a series of petty grievances which seemed more and more infuriating as the tour went on. In November Livy had cautioned him not to get angry at Cable, to guard everything he said about him, even in fun. The only concession he made was to send her indignant accounts in which Cable, in fulfillment of some idea of discretion, was referred to as "K." K., he complained, saved up a whole trunkload of dirty laundry from his vacation and intended to have it washed at Clemens' expense when they were on the road again. Ozias passed on the veto to Cable, and although a crisis was averted Clemens continued to fume about Cable's parsimony—"His closeness *is* a queer streak," he told Livy—and about countless other objections and episodes, most of them just as ludicrous. "He has never bought one sheet of paper or an envelop in all these 3½ months," he wrote after he found that Cable had been using his paper. "He is the pitifulest human louse I have ever known." Cable had interrupted him in the middle of a story; Cable had marched out of a hotel dining room rather than sit with some children; Cable was arrogant with servants; Cable starved himself when he had to pay for his own meals and gorged himself when he was on expenses. The complaints went on and on, always coming back to the favorite target of Cable's religion. "This pious ass" (or, "this Christ-besprinkled, psalm-singing Presbyterian"), Clemens recounted to Livy, had never gone to hear Beecher give a sermon, because he refused to cross over to Brooklyn on a Sunday. Tiny differences were blown up to monster size by too much proximity, and also by plain jealousy. In 1899 Clemens was still brooding—"With *his* platform talent he was able to fatigue a corpse." The fact was that Cable was being well received, and that on occasions Mark Twain was dismissed by some small-town citizens and reviews as a humbug and a buffoon. But even by mid-January Clemens was fed up with more than Cable: he was fed up with performing every night, fed up with early rising and daily railroad trips. One morning, to his annoyance, they had to leave Springfield, Illinois, at 6:35 A.M. Four hours later, crossing the Eads Bridge into St. Louis, the engine jumped the tracks, and as the cars clanked and swayed Clemens rushed for the door. (He explained later, his irascibility temporarily drawn by emergency, that he would rather fall on top of the train than have it the other way, and besides, the river was perfectly familiar to him.) Three days later, however, the prospect of taking another morning train so vexed him that as Ozias Pond (who had earlier noted that Clemens had "a heart as tender as a child, as loving as a woman") and Cable watched in silent amazement, he worked himself into a tantrum, went after a window shutter with his fists, and clubbed it off its hinges.

In time *Huckleberry Finn* would be read in ten million copies printed in nearly every tongue, and nobody would question its rank as literature. But during the winter and spring of 1885 it seemed to promise its author-publisher a scarifying lesson in bad luck, bad planning, bad timing, entrenched orthodoxy, and public humiliation. On February 10, two days after Judge Colt ruled against him in Boston, Clemens was in Columbus, worrying. "I am not able to see anything that can save Huck Finn from being another defeat," he told Charley. Charley, it was clear from his answer, still hoped for the best, but he was prepared for the worst and he already had an explanation for it. "Huck is a *good* book," he wrote soothingly on February 14, only four days before publication, "and I am working intelligently and *hard* and if it don't sell it won't be your fault or mine but the extreme hard times. It *shall* sell however." But "extreme hard times" had nothing to do with the fact that they still did not have a single

American review of any influence or importance to overcome both genteel hostility to a novel of vernacular naturalism and the traditional hostility that editors had toward subscription books in general. This once, Howells, who had set the critical tone for nearly every one of Mark Twain's books, was without a regular reviewing forum. (His admiration for the book and his editorial involvement with it would have been sufficiently good reasons, in Whitelaw Reid's view, for him to remain silent.) The *Century* waited three months after publication to run a review. "A vivid picture of Western life of forty or fifty years ago," the Bostonian scholar and critic Thomas Sergeant Perry wrote in the May issue, and he went on to praise the book's "immortal hero" and Mark Twain's grasp of truth and reality which enabled him—a key issue in the stormy career of *Huckleberry Finn* —to teach "by implication, not by didactic preaching." But Perry's was a nearly solitary voice, and even that November Joel Chandler Harris concluded a public letter of praise for the book with the pointed acknowledgment that "some of the professional critics will not agree with me." What most of the professional critics may have been saying, when they said anything at all, was indicated by a savage attack, in two issues of the comic magazine *Life*, on the book's "blood-curdling humor," gutter realism, "coarse and dreary fun," and total unsuitability for young people. The genteel tradition, far from dead, had simply been lying in wait.

For nearly a month *Huckleberry Finn* existed in a kind of critical outer darkness until, one day in March, the Library Committee of Concord, Massachusetts, made a public announcement. After deliberation, these custodians of the town's flickering transcendental flame pronounced the book rough, coarse, and inelegant, expelled it from the library shelves, and began to earn for Mark Twain the now traditional rewards of being banned near as well as in Boston. "If Mr. Clemens cannot think of something better to tell our pure-minded lads and lasses," said Louisa May Alcott, with the moral weight of a lifetime of well-loved books behind every word, "he had best stop writing for them." Soon enough, the newspapers, silent until then, came to life. "It is time that this influential pseudonym should cease to carry into homes and libraries unworthy productions," the Springfield *Republican* said, and, in the course of anathematizing both *Tom Sawyer* and *Huckleberry Finn* as degrading, immoral, and no better than dime novels, it whipped up the old horse of the Whittier dinner; now, as in 1877, "the trouble with Mr. Clemens is that he has no reliable sense of propriety." The Boston *Advertiser* connected the failure of the book with his "irreverence." According to the *Transcript* the Concord banning was unnecessary—"The book is so flat, as well as coarse, that nobody wants to read it after a taste in the *Century*."

"Dear Charley," Clemens wrote on March 18, "The Committee of the Public Library of Concord, Mass., have given us a rattling tip-top puff which will go into every paper in the country. They have expelled Huck from their library as 'trash and suitable only for the slums.' That will sell 25,000 copies for us sure." This letter, released to the papers, stirred up a second wave of reaction. For some editors Clemens' confident prediction was only further evidence of his venality and cynicism. But many agreed with him that the Concord committee had assured the success of the book. At the end of March a Concord group called the Free Trade Club proffered an amende honorable by electing him to membership, and he immediately seized on this opportunity for publicity as well as public vindication by writing a graceful and ironic letter of acceptance, which was published in the New York *World* and other papers. His new membership, he said, "endorses me as worthy to associate with certain gentlemen whom even the moral icebergs of the Concord library committee are bound to respect." The excommunication of *Huckleberry Finn* was going to benefit him in several ways beyond doubling the sale:

> For instance, it will deter other libraries from buying the book and you are doubtless aware that one book in a public library prevents the sale of a sure ten and a possible hundred of its mates. And secondly it will cause the purchasers of the book to read it, out of curiosity, instead of merely intending to do so after the usual way of the world and library committees; and then they will discover, to my great advantage and their own indignant disappointment, that there is nothing objectionable in the book, after all.

Instead of "another defeat" he soon found that *Huckleberry Finn* was "a handsome success" which sold better in its first two months than even *The Innocents Abroad*—forty-two thousand copies by March 18, fifty-one thousand by May 6—and there was every indication that it would never stop.

Through all of this Clemens managed to present to his public the image of a confident, masterful, and good-humored author. "Those idiots in Concord are not a court of last resort," he told Pamela, "and I am not disturbed by their moral gymnastics." But he *was* disturbed. Why banish Huck from the family circle, he fumed, but let in not only the Bible but also a paper like the New York *World* which carried tidings of adultery, abortion, and prostitution into a million homes every week? ("The truth is," he said more than twenty years later, "that when a library expels a book of mine and leaves an unexpurgated Bible around where unprotected youth and age can get hold of it, the deep unconscious irony of it delights me and doesn't anger me.") Until Howells talked him out of it, he planned to give the Concord library a blast at a public dinner in New York. "You can't stir it up," Howells reasoned, "without seeming to care more than you ought for it." Until Livy forbade it, Clemens intended to hand out to the papers and insert in all future printings of the book a "Prefatory Remark" in which he would pay back some of his enemies: "Huckleberry Finn is not an imaginary person. He still lives; or rather, *they* still live; for Huckleberry Finn is two persons in one—namely, the author's two uncles, the present editors of the Boston *Advertiser* and the Springfield *Republican*." He added that "in deference to the taste of a more modern and fastidious day" he had taken the liberty of departing from his models in one respect: "This boy's language has been toned down and softened here and there."

The spokesmen for the genteel tradition, who had taken Mark Twain to their bosoms for *The Prince and the Pauper*, a piece of literary playacting which they praised for its finish and refinement and delicacy, turned their backs on the book which sprang from his deepest personal and creative imperatives. Betrayed, rejected, and seriously confused in goal and standard, Mark Twain henceforth looked back on *Huckleberry Finn* with mingled pain, pride, and puzzlement, as on a favorite child who had brought disgrace on his father and whom the father would at times reluctantly acknowledge as his favorite and at other times reject in favor of the chaste and unexceptionable Maid of Orleans. His own conflict was mirrored within his family. Livy was fond of "dear old Huck," but was never at all comfortable with the book. Susy, whose disapproval he dreaded, disapproved of Huck, because she wanted her father not to be a humorist, a naturalist, or a teller of dreadful ghost stories but a writer of high seriousness, moral uplift, and thrice-purified English. Prophetess of the cultural values he seemed all too often to be flouting, she was, fittingly, his model for Joan of Arc.

The popular success of *Huckleberry Finn* in the face of official disapproval and indifference made it finally clear to him that there was no such thing as a unitary society in America and that he would have to decide whether to write "for the Head" or for "the Belly and the Members," for the "uncultivated class" or "the mighty mass of the uncultivated." Huck Finn lit out for the Territory, but Mark Twain had to stay at home to nurse his wounds, and he submerged some of his goals in enterprises that appeared more rewarding than writing books: the publishing house, the typesetting machine, and, in general, making money. Before he published another book, four and a half years were to pass—his longest silence since he came East—and in this book, *A Connecticut Yankee*, he translated into a fantasy of warfare some of the tensions he felt between vernacular and genteel values, between laity and clerisy. *A Connecticut Yankee* was to be his "swan-song," he said more than once, his "retirement from literature permanently." He planned to make certain that "those parties who miscall themselves critics" did not have the chance to "paw the book at all"—"I wish to pass to the cemetery unclodded."

"One of the highest satisfactions of Clemens' often supremely satisfactory life was his relation to Grant," Howells wrote in 1910, but in suggesting the range and intimacy of the relationship Howells also suggested its ominousness. The Grant bonanza led Clemens to "excesses of enterprise" and to a preoccupation with business which debilitated him as a writer and nearly destroyed him as a man. From the start, Clemens himself recognized the importance of the Grant chapter in his life. He went to unusual lengths to set down accounts of it which he could recite as history and in self-vindication and possibly use as material for fiction. He kept a detailed record in his notebook. During the summer of 1885, to combat ugly rumors about his dealings with Grant and the *Century*, he dictated about seventeen thousand words for his autobiography. In a long letter to Henry Ward Beecher two months after Grant died of throat cancer, he reviewed the story once again. And in 1906 he dictated another long account, this one colored by his venomous recollections of Charley Webster.

In February 1885, Charley, still in favor with his uncle, sounded one of the ground notes of the enterprise: "There's big money for us both in that book and on the terms indicated in my note to the General we can make it pay *big*." Throughout the winter Clemens and Charley argued their case before Grant and his advisers, presented testimonials and various evidences of their business fitness, and also fell back on small diplomatic maneuvers such as the gift of a leather-bound *Huckleberry Finn*, suitably inscribed by the author, to Colonel Fred Grant's eldest little girl. A week after Charley's letter, on his way to read in Brooklyn with Cable, Clemens called on Grant, and he was shocked to see how weak and thin the General was despite a newspaper report that his throat symptoms were gone. "Yes," Grant said uncomplainingly, "if it had only been true." But Clemens came away reassured on one point at least. "I mean you shall have the book," Grant said, "I have about made up my mind to that." On February 27 he signed a contract with Charles L. Webster and Company, publishers—as Clemens proposed their new letterhead should read—of "Mark Twain's Books and the forthcoming *Personal Memoirs of General Grant*," the five last words "in just a *shade* larger type, and in RED INK." The day after the contract was signed Clemens' reading tour ended in Washington, and, utterly absorbed in his new career as publisher, he stopped being a writer as well as a public performer. By February 1886, while Livy and Susy worried that he had forgotten his own work altogether, Clemens was making some round-sum calculations. His $15,000 investment in the publishing house was now worth $500,000, and he was about to pay Mrs.

Grant $200,000 against her eventual earnings of nearly half a million.

But, as part of the price he paid for this success, he was at the mercy of every detail of the enterprise. He simply could not hand over authority, and Charley's days as publisher were numbered. "I wish to be close at hand all the time General Grant's book is going through the press and being canvassed," Sam wrote to Orion in March to explain why he had canceled plans for a reading tour in England and Australia. "I want no mistakes to happen, nothing overlooked, nothing neglected." He worked up an incentive plan for canvassers, and he undoubtedly had a hand in writing an aggressive sales manual which exhorted the canvasser to avoid "the Bull Run voice" and to "keep pouring *hot shot*" until the cowed prospect signed his name on the line. He was occupied with circulars, handouts for the press, photographs, medallions, the index, security measures to keep books out of the hands of pirates and cut-raters, a de luxe edition to be sold at auction. He praised Charley for the serene and capable way he was guiding "the vastest book enterprise the world has ever seen," and he warned him to slow down: "overwork killed Mr. Langdon, and it can kill you." But he was constantly at Charley with instructions and errands to run, and he grumbled about the clerks Charley took on to absorb some of the overwork, about new offices on Union Square, and about expenses like postage, telegrams, and thick letter paper. He arranged for a portrait bust of Grant to be made by Karl Gerhardt, who was now systematically exploiting his patron's influence for all it was worth.* At the beginning of April, when the country sat a premature death watch over Grant and expected momentarily to hear the muffled fire bells toll out sixty-three strokes, he delicately interceded to get Gerhardt the death-mask commission. By December Gerhardt and the Grant family were involved in an acrimonious and ghoulish squabble over property rights in the death mask, and Clemens, now thoroughly disillusioned with the sculptor, offered to buy him off in order to avoid the "degrading scandal" of a lawsuit which would drag Grant "out of the rest and peace of the grave."

At the end of April Clemens took Susy with him to visit Grant. The General, Clemens noted, had made a remarkable recovery. He looked and felt better than he had in months, his throat had stopped hurting him, and, in his terse fashion, he was talkative again. "Neither of us originated the idea of Sherman's march to the sea," he said, answering one of the crucial questions about his campaign. "The enemy did it." Clemens came

* "I wish you were here, to let me tell you about Gerhardt and the Nathan Hale Statue," Clemens told Howells on December 7, 1885. "A 14-months' history and the funniest in the whole history of art." Gerhardt had spent months sulking in his studio while the committee in charge of awarding the commission for an equestrian statue in the State Capitol at Hartford demanded formal assurance from him that the $5,000 price included the horse.

away encouraged, for Grant was back at work again on his unfinished book. That morning he had spent two hours dictating an account of Appomattox, and his manuscript needed no revision at all.

As always, however, there were enemies out there to be dealt with after the manner of the Comanches. First, there were the *Century* people, who, Clemens heard, were spreading the story that he stole the book from them and was out to fleece the helpless Grants. There were rumors that he was writing the book himself. At the end of April he decided to go after the New York *World*—"that daily issue of unmedicated closet paper"—for publishing the manifest lie that Grant's aide General Adam Badeau was the author of the *Memoirs*. No compromise or apology would do, he told Fred Grant, and he urged him to press for punitive damages "that will cripple—yes, *disable*—that paper financially." On second thought he decided to let it drop; since no other paper had bothered to repeat the *World*'s "libel," obviously the *World* was not worth suing. The next year the target was to be "that unco-pious butter-mouthed Sunday school-slobbering sneak-thief" John Wanamaker, "now of Philadelphia, presently of hell," who was cut-rating the book. When a court decision failed to support his claim against Wanamaker, Clemens called for a new tactic. In the hope of provoking a libel suit, he planned to have William Laffan of the New York *Sun* publish a fictitious interview in which, after accusing Wanamaker of "picking Mrs. Grant's pocket," Clemens asked, "Is there really *any* kind of property he wouldn't take, in case he wasn't being watched?" The interview, however, apparently went no farther than Webster's office.

But the major problem had been, of course, whether Grant would live long enough to finish the book. After his brief remission, the suffering came back again redoubled; he depended on larger and larger amounts of cocaine. Under the drug his mind reeled back to the cannon, and he clutched at his throat. Water, he said, went down like molten lead. In a hoarse whisper he talked his book to a stenographer for hours at a time. Then he fell back, exhausted, for two or three days, and slept half reclining in his easy chair, a heavy scarf wrapped round his throat. It seemed to Clemens, sitting quietly near him in the bedroom at Sixtieth Street, that Grant in his last days had fully regained the stature of a hero and also that no one had ever sufficiently noted Grant's "exceeding gentleness, goodness, sweetness." "He had dictated 10,000 words at a single sitting," Clemens noted in awe and envy. "It kills me, these days, to write the half of it." He had almost forgotten that he was a famous author and was startled, he said, when Grant, diffidently and through another person, asked what he thought of the *Memoirs*. He later said he felt the way Columbus' cook would have felt if Columbus had asked his views on navigation. But he recovered from his embarrassment, compared the

Memoirs to Caesar's *Commentaries,* and told Grant that his book belonged with "the best purely narrative literature in the language." (His opinion was shared over the years by Gertrude Stein as well as by Howells; today the book seems as remarkable as ever for its muscular directness and its avoidance of chest-thumping and martial rhetoric.) In 1886, after Matthew Arnold had criticized Grant for writing "an English without charm and high breeding," Clemens rushed to the defense of his dead author with a show of indignation and injured pride that suggests that what shrank the distance between Columbus and his cook was the threat of a common enemy: Arnold's high culture—"*superficial polish*," Clemens once called it —which looked down on Grant because he made mistakes in grammar and looked down on America because it lacked "the discipline of awe and respect." Clemens' thundering answer described his own as well as Grant's lack of formal literary training and orthodox antecedents, his own conscious and defiant nativism: "This is the simple soldier, who, all untaught of the silken phrase-makers, linked words together with an art surpassing the art of the schools and put into them a something which will still bring to American ears, as long as America shall last, the roll of his vanished drums and the tread of his marching hosts."

Clemens examined his relation to Grant not only in his notes and his autobiographical accounts but also, implicitly, in the only extended writing he did during his year as Grant's publisher. "The Private History of a Campaign That Failed," his characteristically anti-heroic contribution to the *Century*'s "Battles and Leaders" series, was, in a way, an answer to the question of why a former Confederate irregular should be publishing, and ostensibly making a good deal of money doing so, the *Personal Memoirs* of the commander of all the Union armies. The speech Clemens gave in Hartford in 1877, his first public account of his military service, ended with the footsore paladins disbanding in disgust, having realized that rain, corncribs, and retreat were not what they had had in mind when they signed up to be soldiers. Early in 1885, at the urging of Robert Underwood Johnson of the *Century*, Clemens started to rework his speech into a long article, ran into trouble, and found that he was too busy and would have to put it off until August at Quarry Farm. He finished the article in November, and it was published in the December issue. In the intervening eight or nine months its character changed radically: a comic adventure became a dark and troubled reading of his experience of war. "Such a bloody bit of heartache in it," Howells was to remark. The change is clearly connected with Clemens' careful reading of Grant's manuscript and proofs, with conversations between the two in April and May, and with Grant's death on July 23, an event loaded with real and symbolic meaning for Clemens.

During the spring, Grant—and his family—read an early draft of "A

Campaign That Failed." In conversation afterward Grant elaborated on his already-written account of his service as colonel of the Twenty-first Illinois Volunteers in July 1861 in the vicinity of Florida, Missouri, Mark Twain's birthplace and the scene of his military service. Grant said this had been his first independent command of the Civil War; the responsibility had terrified him at first; then his fright had left him for good. Grant and Clemens, it turned out as they compared notes, had come within a few weeks and a few miles of facing each other as enemies in the field. Clemens immediately began to play with this discrepancy in time and distance. In a notebook entry which he made soon after one of these talks it became a difference of "a day or two." "How near he came to playing the devil with his future publisher," Clemens wrote, and in conversation with Grant he said that if he had known the identity of the Union colonel who was pursuing the Marion Rangers he would have turned and attacked instead of retreating. Finally in the published version of "A Campaign That Failed" he wrote, "I came within a few hours of seeing him when he was as unknown as I was myself."

Intrigued by this fantasy of facing Grant in battle, Clemens tentatively titled the article "My Campaign against Grant." For a while he planned to put aside the article and in its place to give the *Century* a chapter from a novel he hoped to write that summer; the novel was to take Tom, Huck, and Jim through his Missouri campaign, at the end of which Tom would be accosted by a Union officer named U. S. Grant. Clemens soon put the novel aside and went back to the article. All this went on at a time when he was busy with his publishing venture and when, as he said, "It kills me" to write. It is not too much to say that this persistence reflects the intensity and complexity of his feelings toward Grant. Several levels of relationship can be suggested: the Rebel son and the punishing figure of power and authority (who, as President, later assumed a more explicitly paternal office); the parallel and ironic relationships of anti-hero ("I knew more about retreating than the man who invented retreating") to hero, and humorist to victim (in his 1879 speech at Chicago Clemens set an ambush for Grant; "I knew I could lick him," he said, "I shook him up like dynamite"). And, reversing these relationships, the former Rebel son, now reconstructed, had become, as publisher, the strong and benevolent figure who rescues the Grant family from poverty.

By the time Clemens finished writing "A Campaign That Failed," his decision to desert was no longer based on boredom and discontent. It was directly related to a new episode, almost surely invented, which compressed a number of symbolic situations into an apparently simple narrative and which was also consistent with some of the recurrent motifs in his experience and memory: bitter remorse and guilt; the direct witnessing of violence ("I saw him die," he wrote, in his *Autobiography*, of a killing in Hannibal, "I saw the red life gush from his breast"); discovery and horror (the post-mortem, the corpse on the floor of his father's office). "It is curious and dreadful to sit up this way and talk cheerful nonsense to General Grant," Clemens said after one of many talks about their common war experience, and he added, with a meaning his article was to underscore, "and he under sentence of death with that cancer."

Toward the end of "A Campaign That Failed" Clemens says that he and the fifteen other Marion Rangers received a warning one night that the enemy was in the vicinity. Excited and terrified, they hide in the corncrib where they usually sleep and look out through the cracks at where the forest path emerges into veiled moonlight. They hear muffled hoofbeats, and a dreamlike figure comes out of the forest darkness. "It could have been made of smoke, its mass had so little sharpness of outline." It is a man on horseback, and as he rides toward the corncrib he too is "under sentence of death." The narrator is almost paralyzed with fright, but he manages to fire off his gun (the only time during the campaign that he fires it in combat). The man falls to the ground on his back, his arms stretched to the side, mouth open, chest heaving. His white shirtfront is splattered with blood. He is dressed in civilian clothes, and he is unarmed.

The narrator's first feeling is one of "surprised gratification." But then: "The thought shot through me that I was a murderer, that I had killed a man, a man who had never done me any harm. That was the coldest sensation that ever went through my marrow." In sudden remorse he would give up his own life to undo what he has done. The stranger, he imagines, gives him "a reproachful look out of his shadowy eyes" and, dying, mutters "like a dreamer in his sleep" about his wife and child. And all the narrator will ever know about his victim is that "he was a stranger in the country," a description which fits into the dreamlike ambience of the episode and which also suggests that the victim is related to all the other "strangers" who populate Mark Twain's fiction. And having read with special interest Grant's own account of service around Florida, Missouri, Clemens borrowed enough details to suggest that in a number of covert ways the "stranger" is also Grant himself.

One of Grant's worries when he received his orders to go to Missouri had to do with his wife and child; he arranged to ship his eleven-year-old son back to Mrs. Grant in Galena. When Grant appeared in Cairo to take command of the district of southeast Missouri the officer in charge "looked a little as if he would like to have someone identify me," Grant says. Not only was Grant a stranger in the country at that point, but he was also wearing civilian clothes; as he explains, his brigadier's uniform had not yet arrived from the tailor in New York. Later on, at the battle of Belmont, Grant was wearing "a soldier's overcoat" when he galloped past a detachment of Confederate troops hidden in "a dense forest." As he learned later, a Confederate officer recognized him despite the private's overcoat and said to his men, "There is a Yankee; you may try your marksmanship on him as you wish." (The question of "marksmanship," quite aside from the accidental pun, becomes a crucial one at the end of "A Campaign That Failed.") No one fired at Grant then. However, soon after galloping his horse over a single plank onto the Union steamer that was waiting in the river, he had "a narrow escape." He lay down to rest in the cabin adjoining the pilothouse—a familiar enough setting for Mark Twain—but he heard the sound of gunfire and got up to go on deck. "I had scarcely left when a musket ball entered the room, struck the head of the sofa, passed through it and lodged in the foot." If he had not fought the futile battle of Belmont, Grant says at the end of his account, he might have lost three thousand men. "Then I should have been culpable indeed."

Second Lieutenant Clemens is overwhelmed by culpability, and he looks for absolution. Other Marion Rangers had fired at the same moment—"There were six shots fired at once but I was not in my right mind at the time, and my heated imagination had magnified my one shot into a volley"; any one of the others could be the real murderer. But even though he has now made the killing completely ambiguous,

> morbid thoughts clung to me against reason, for at bottom I did not believe I had touched that man. The law of probabilities decreed me guiltless of his blood for in all my small experience with guns I had never hit anything I had tried to hit and I knew I had done my best to hit him. Yet there was no solace in the thought. Against a diseased imagination demonstration goes for nothing.

The killing of strangers, the taking of unoffending lives, now seems to him not only "a wanton thing," but also "an epitome of war," and he turns from nightmare to self-ridicule in order to shift his burden of guilt: "It seemed to me that I was not rightly equipped for this awful business, that war was intended for men and I for a child's nurse" (an entertainer of children and also precisely the role in which he claimed responsibility for the death of his infant son Langdon). "I resolved to retire from this avocation of sham soldiership while I could save some remnant of self-respect." "My campaign was spoiled," he says. "My Campaign against Grant" has become, by an ironic questioning and reversal of the terms of success, "A Campaign That Failed."

v

Mark Twain delighted in figuring the precise dimensions of the gigantic success he was to have with Grant's book. In May 1885 he predicted—conservatively, as it turned out—a sale of 300,000 sets (600,000 books), a profit of $200,000 for his publishing house, and royalties to the Grant family of over $400,000 (or, as he translated it, seventeen tons of silver coin at twelve dollars a pound). Howells imagined him smoking and swearing in "wild excitement" as he kept count of the twenty presses and the seven binderies that worked day and night to meet the demand. The firm was in debt to the banks, his personal money was so tied up in the venture that he was feeling squeezed again, yet he was far from being worried. "I am merely a starving beggar standing outside the door of plenty," he was to tell Howells in October, "—obstructed by a Yale time-lock which is set for Jan. 1st." As the months ticked away and Grant, at Mount McGregor, New York, slipped slowly from life, Clemens' mood climbed higher and higher. He was giddy with the anticipation of a hundred other successes, all of which, without a pang to him, overshadowed his own writing. Among the grandiose schemes was one which he discussed that summer with Grant and Jesse Grant, and by letter with Leland Stanford; it involved getting from the Sultan of Turkey the charter to build a railroad between Constantinople and the Persian Gulf.

Clemens' domestic idyl, which he celebrated publicly but kept closed to all but the intimates of the Nook Farm circle, was still undisturbed. Livy, nearing forty, was in good health, still beautiful. She was adored, it seemed, by everyone who knew her. Visitors were struck by her luminous dark eyes, broad white forehead, and gleaming smile, by the grace with which she wore gowns of blue and red silk, by the unruffled and commanding way she was able to run a gracious and opulent household and also be mother and companion to three children, whom she tutored at home and trained to simple pleasures and few pretenses. They were always to be carefully chaperoned, they were to be kept ignorant as long as possible of ball gowns and coquetry, and despite their wealth Livy intended all three to go to the public high school in Hartford. On a June evening the Clemens family had an early dinner together out on the veranda. Then they went for a twilight drive around the city. Their carriage was still the one Jervis Langdon had given as a wedding gift; it was driven by the same coachman whose brass buttons and livery overcoat Clemens had admired during his first married days in Buffalo. After the children had been put to bed, visitors drifted along the worn path that led from the Warner house to the conservatory door. Charles and George Warner arrived with their wives, then President Smith of Trinity College and others—enough for two tables of whist. Afterward there was ice cream and a long evening of talk and funny stories, "of which latter Mr. Clemens was full," Livy wrote in her diary. (To Twichell and to many others he had become "the Prince of Raconteurs"; after such an evening at Farmington Avenue, Howells remarked in pleasure and wonderment, "There is certainly no one else alive who can equal it.") Later that week, there was another informal evening of whist, ice cream, and talk. Friday nights Livy played cards with the two Warner wives while Clemens had his weekly stag billiard session on the third floor and the lager flowed. But even such quiet happiness as Clemens enjoyed at Farmington Avenue he insisted on measuring in terms of the material riches that were about to pour in on him. "What a profitable return," he wrote to Livy on the sixteenth anniversary of their engagement, "from the invested capital of a single word." "I am frightened at the proportions of my prosperity," he said one evening. "It seems that whatever I touch turns to gold."

On August 8 Clemens stood for five hours at the windows of his publishing house on Union Square in New York and watched the Grant funeral procession passing along Fourteenth Street toward Fifth Avenue, on its way to the temporary tomb of brick trimmed with bluestone and granite that stood open at Riverside Park. Swathings of black drapery covered marble and brownstone fronts; the streets were lined with mourning-hung portraits of the dead hero. Forty thousand men in uniform marched behind the catafalque drawn by twenty-four black horses. In sign of union, old opponents Sherman and Johnston, Sheridan and Buckner, walked side by side as pallbearers. A President and two ex-Presidents rode in the cortege. Two days earlier Clemens had sat with Sherman at the Lotos Club and talked with him about Grant. "He was a *man*—all over —rounded and complete," Sherman said; but, for him as well as for Clemens, neither of them possessing a shred of religion, Grant was also more than a man. Now, as the sounds of muffled drums and muted brass came to him from the street below, Clemens might have been hearing the strange music which in Plutarch signified that the god Hercules was forsaking Antony. For with Grant's death the period of Mark Twain's brief flowering—five years—began to end. "Our faces are toward the sunset," he told Livy later that year. He was fifty years old.

CHAPTER FOURTEEN

The Yankee and the Machine

I

A T THE AGE OF THIRTEEN, SUSY CLEMENS, a fascinated observer of her
father's moods and fluctuations, began to write his "biography."
"Mama and I have been troubled of late," she wrote in February 1886,
"because Papa since he has been publishing Gen. Grant's book has seemed
to forget his own books and work entirely." Susy was also troubled,
briefly, by a remark he made to her. His arm around her waist, slowly
pacing in the library during the time of intimate talk that he saved at the
end of the day for her, his oldest and clearly his favorite, he said he expected to write only one more book. "Then he was ready to give up
work altogether, die or do anything. He said that he had written more
than he had ever expected." Thinking about this, and about "the proofs
of past years," Susy decided after a while that there was really nothing
to worry about. He had said things like this before and then gone back
to writing.

Twenty-one years later, the old and lonely Mark Twain, dictating his
autobiography, remembered the occasion. "It was quite natural that I
should think I had written myself out when I was only fifty years old,
for everybody who has ever written has been smitten with that superstition at about that age." Yet behind this casual explanation, and behind
the hyperbole and calculated shock of his remark to Susy—he often, as he
said later, posed for his biography—were two strands of circumstance
which became tangled with each other and had the effect of making
what he said to her come very nearly true.

That January and February, while riding the crest of his new prosperity from the Grant book, Clemens had started serious work on *A
Connecticut Yankee in King Arthur's Court*, his story about a Hartford
master mechanic, superintendent at the Colt arms factory, who is hit on

280

the head with a crowbar during an argument and begins to imagine himself bringing nineteenth-century technology, enlightenment, and venture capitalism to sixth-century England. "I have begun a book whose scene is laid far back in the twilight of tradition," Clemens told Charley on February 13, and he explained that he was too engrossed to tend to the publishing business in New York. Yet only a week before this apparent return to full-time writing he organized a company to perfect, manufacture, and market all over the world James W. Paige's typesetting machine, that "mechanical marvel," Clemens declared, which made "all the other wonderful inventions of the human brain"—he cited the telephone, telegraph, locomotive, cotton gin, sewing machine, Babbage calculator, Jacquard loom, perfecting press, and Arkwright frame—"sink pretty nearly into commonplace" and seem "mere toys, simplicities." For five years he had been a quiet backer; now, along with boundless expectations of wealth, he took on the entire financial and managerial burden of the machine, and it crushed him.

The Yankee and the Machine were twinned in his mind. Both were tests of a perfectible world in which, contrary to all his insights and experience, friction and mechanical difficulties were equivalents of ignorance and superstition. Both expressed a secular religion which had as an unexamined article of faith a belief not in eternal life but in perpetual motion. "Wait thirty years and then look out over the earth," he was to write in 1889, on the occasion of Walt Whitman's seventieth birthday. "You shall see marvel upon marvels, added to those whose nativity you have witnessed; and conspicuous above them you shall see their formidable Result—Man at almost his full stature at last!—and still growing, visibly growing, while you look." He was capable of sustaining two moods of belief at the same time: the opposite of this paean to progress is *A Connecticut Yankee*. The ambivalences, disillusions, destructive fury, and, finally, homicidal tantrums of the novel were fire drills in his imagination for the actual failure of the machine, machine values, and his dream of capitalist democracy in which he expected to be a tycoon among tycoons.

The writer Mark Twain saw omens of disaster long before the promoter Mark Twain, who all his life believed that he was lucky and also, like inventors and prophets in general, maintained a mulish faith that despite constant delays and breakdowns his machine would turn up trumps eventually. "I want to finish the day the machine finishes," he kept saying of his new book, acknowledging a magical kinship between a writer writing words and a machine setting them in type. Yet he fatalistically accepted the fact that the life history of the machine would have to be written in terms of those delays and breakdowns. "Experience teaches me that their calculations will miss fire, as usual," he said of Paige and his workmen. Four years before he formally conceded that he was beaten, he wrote of himself as a victim of his own and the machine's powerful spell, and he made it clear that what was at stake for him was not just a business venture bigger and more promising than most but an entire framework of aspiration, for himself and for his century:

> And I watched over one dear project of mine five years, spent a fortune on it, and failed to make it go—and the history of that would make a large book in which a million men would see themselves as in a mirror; and they would testify and say, Verily this is not imagination, this fellow has been there—and after would they cast dust upon their heads, cursing and blaspheming.

II

In 1880 Dwight Buell, a Hartford jeweler, cornered Clemens in the billiard room, described a typesetting machine that was being built at the Colt arms factory, and persuaded him to buy two thousand dollars' worth of stock. Clemens invested three thousand more after he visited the factory and saw the machine at work. With an operator seated at its keyboard, the machine set entire words at a time; it fed itself from a galley of dead matter and distributed its own case. An assistant removed the sticks of type from the machine and did the hand work of inserting space to align it at the right; later on this assistant was replaced by a built-in mechanical justifier. Even at this early stage of its development the machine was doing the work of four men. It set six-point type at the rate of about three thousand ems an hour (four times the best speed the seventeen-year-old Sam Clemens had achieved as an itinerant practical printer), and it would eventually be capable of setting five thousand ems and then eight thousand and more an hour.

Until he saw it in action Clemens had not believed such a machine could exist. Soon after he saw it and fell under the spell of its inventor, James W. Paige of Rochester, New York, he began to believe that it was about the only machine of its kind that did exist. Actually, the Pianotype, a similar machine designed by Henry Bessemer, the inventor of the iron converter, was used to set type commercially as early as 1842; a number of other machines since then had seen limited practical service; and the basement of the London *Times* was said to be filled with typesetting machines that had been tried and discarded. For all of them, including the one Mark Twain backed, represented successively intricate elaborations, unworkably delicate and temperamental, of the same outmoded principle. These machines were designed to imitate the work of a man setting, justifying, and distributing single foundry types by hand. Actually, type distribution, which was one half the function of Paige's early machine, was no longer necessary or practical, as Clemens might have discovered if he had not been so beguiled by Paige's eloquence and ingenuity. The London *Times* was using a rotary type caster, patented in 1881, which worked so fast—it turned out sixty thousand characters an hour from one hundred molds—that instead of distributing type at the end of the run the printers simply melted it down and started all over again with fresh type. This bypass of the human analogy was the basic principle of Ottmar Mergenthaler's Linotype machine, which cast its own type from its own matrices in single slugs of a line's length which were afterwards thrown back into the melting pot. Mergenthaler was to sweep the field.

A mechanical typesetter would have to *think* in order to work, Clemens persisted in believing, and the machine he saw at Colt's appeared to be able to think. The inventor of such a machine must be a divine magician, he also believed, and the machine itself a living, intelligent organism which, as it was improved and articulated, paralleled human ontogeny. It became "an inspired bugger," "a cunning devil," and, after passing through a "sick child" stage, a "magnificent creature" ranking second only to man.*
What Clemens was expressing in personifications such as these was not only his hope for the machine but also his basic layman's ignorance, his credulity in the face of what seemed to him a divine mystery only because he knew hardly anything about mechanics.

Clemens later remarked of his second investment and total commitment to the machine, "It is here that the music begins." Urged by William Hamersley, a lawyer and fellow investor (later to earn from Clemens the accolade of having the pride of a tramp, the courage of a rabbit, the moral sense of a wax figure, and the sex of a tapeworm), he took on the job of raising money to bring the machine to an unattainable perfection. For perfection, not just working order, had been the goal of its inventor, James W. Paige, ever since 1872, when he filed his first patent application for "an Improvement in Type-setting Machines." Paige got his patent in December 1874 (ten years before Mergenthaler finished his first Linotype machine). The following August he was married in Rochester and soon after, listing his occupation as "patentee," and equipped with a smart wardrobe, remarkable gifts of persuasion, and the confidence that he had the lead in his field, he moved to Hartford, attracted there by its com-

* In July 1889 Clemens was telling Livy about another wonder, a "charming machine" that could make 9,000 envelopes an hour, gum them, print them, count them, package them. "It oils itself, it attends to its own glue and ink." And years after Paige's typesetter had bankrupted him Clemens still had the same tendency to humanize machines (and mechanize people). Watching one of McClure's giant presses stop and signal for a foreman to shift its roll of paper, he exclaimed, "My God! Can that thing vote, too?"

bination of abundant investment capital, machine shops, and skilled mechanics.

"He is a poet," Clemens wrote of Paige even in 1890 (when he entertained the fantasy of locking Paige in a steel trap and watching him die), "a most great and genuine poet, whose sublime creations are written in steel. He is the Shakespeare of mechanical invention." (The first proper name set on Paige's improved keyboard in 1889 was Shakespeare's, misspelled.) Years earlier Sam had written about Orion, for whom he tried to lobby a clerkship in the Patent Office, in the same devout terms: "An inventor is a poet—a true poet—and nothing in any degree less than a high order of poet." Mark Twain, a passionately believing child of the Great Century, defined his writer's role as that of teacher, entertainer, and moralist for the masses. He deferred to another order of "poet" altogether, for the inventor, as the Yankee says, was "after God" the creator of this world. And Paige bestrode the two temples of nineteenth-century meliorism, the patent office and the printing office.

The Yankee's first official act in Arthur's England is to start a patent office. "I knew that a country without a patent office was just a crab," he says, "and couldn't travel any way but sideways or backways." Then the Yankee goes on to hammer away at sixth-century mind shackles by teaching people how to read and by starting a newspaper. At eighteen Sam Clemens stood before Benjamin Franklin's wood-bed printing press in the Patent Office Museum in Washington and marked the changes that one hundred and twenty years had brought. Franklin's press printed 125 sheets an hour, while the whirling cylinders of the Hoe press shed twenty thousand, fast and steady. For Mark Twain and for Walt Whitman, both of them journeyman printers in their youth, the Hoe press—as, later, the perfecting press, which printed both sides of a continuous sheet at the same time—symbolized dynamic democracy. It whetted and fed the word-hunger of the mass audience which Whitman aspired to and which nurtured Mark Twain. Clemens remembered all his life the drowsing summer afternoons he and another apprentice, Wales McCormick, had spent in Joseph Ament's printing office in Hannibal. Wales once had to reset three solid pages of sermon because Alexander Campbell, a founder of the Disciples of Christ, refused to allow one abbreviation, made for convenience's sake, of "Jesus Christ" to "J. C." The angry preacher got more than he bargained for: Wales restored the name in full and also added a middle initial, "H." For Sam Clemens this prank redeemed the afternoon's lost fishing and the tedium of setting type by hand. At seventeen Sam was still a laggard typesetter, slower than the slowest in the composing room of the Philadelphia *Inquirer*—he could set only ten thousand ems on a Sunday while the others were doing fifteen thousand. "For some cause," he wrote to Orion, "I cannot set type so fast as when I was at home." All his life he was interested in improvements that would take some of the work out of writing and communicating: he was probably the first author to turn in a typed manuscript, he was a connoisseur of fountain pens, he owned the first private telephone in Hartford, he dictated part of one of his books into a phonograph.

In its most advanced state Paige's machine had eighteen thousand separate parts, including eight hundred shaft bearings. The patent application he filed in 1887 contained 275 sheets of drawings and 123 pages of specifications, and it was pending for eight years. The typesetter was a remarkable piece of machinery, the most ambitious and complex device of its kind, and when it worked it worked like a miracle. Eventually, in the hands of an operator of average skill, it could set twelve thousand ems an hour, compared with the 1890 average of eight thousand ems an hour for a practiced Linotype operator. But the typesetter was also impossibly delicate and high-strung, broke down frequently, needed specially trained workmen in attendance at all times, and was something like a mechanical human being, dazzling for a demonstration but not so sturdy and reliable as the real thing.

The inventor's "noblest pleasure dies with the stroke that completes the creature of his genius," Sam had written in 1870. It was scarcely likely that the typesetter would ever be pronounced finished. "It did seem to me the last word in its way," said Howells (another former practical printer) after seeing a demonstration of "the beautiful miracle," but he felt that that last word "had been spoken too exquisitely, too fastidiously." He recognized that Clemens and Paige were trying to bring the machine "to a perfection so expensive that it was practically impracticable." Clemens' psyche as well as his fortune came to be disastrously overinvested in the typesetter's gears and levers. For him the machine was poetry and power, the brass and steel fulfillment of his century. When the machine died, more than money died with it.

"Very much the best investment I have ever made," Clemens said to Charley in October 1881 about his five-thousand-dollar stake in the typesetter. "I want an opportunity to add to it—that is how I feel about it." He predicted an initial world sale of 100,000 machines. For the next four years he made a series of progress statements which had a Phrygian music of their own (the music was the merest overture, it turned out): "finally got it right" (April 1881), "now flawless" (February 1883), "could be perfected" (March 1883), "in lucrative shape at last ... in perfect working order" (April 1885). But the "perfect working order" of April 1885 was only the start of another cycle; during the five years that followed, Paige discarded the old machine and built a new one with a coupled mechanical justifier and Clemens was drained of hope and money.

By the summer of 1885, when he was pushing the Grant book along, the original Hartford typesetter company had become a tangled corporate possibility which needed large administrations of cash. Clemens and Hamersley projected a parent company with a capitalization of $1,100,000 and subsidiaries in America and England to manufacture machines and then rent them at $2,500 a year. The schemes proliferated: they would need money to build two hundred machines before the dollars would start flowing back in; perhaps they ought to hold the justifier back for fifteen years so as to extend the patent life of the machine for an additional seventeen; in return for the net profits from foreign sales and rentals, Clemens undertook to secure and maintain the foreign patents. "Ask the President"—a notebook reminder—"if he will not give me a note to the government printer." Hartford's most prominent literary man was now to be seen in New York at the Union League Club and on Wall Street singing the virtues of the machine to skeptical investors who agreed with him that the purse was big but were not so sure he had picked just the right horse to win it. (Some of them, as he discovered when it was too late, had been betting all along on Mergenthaler's Linotype.) In return for the promise of a half interest, he was also acting as agent for an improved printing telegraph, another Paige invention. On May 27 he visited President Norvin Green of Western Union. The next day, back at the Western Union tower on Broadway and Dey Street, he met Jay Gould and his son George—the Goulds owned the controlling interest in the company—and talked about the printing telegraph over lunch, without success. "Damned insignificant looking people," he noted. (Still, the unmistakable face and beard of the senior Gould appear in Dan Beard's picture of "the Slave Driver" in *A Connecticut Yankee*.) He met with little more encouragement from his old friend John Mackay, the Comstock millionaire who was now trying to break Gould's telegraph monopoly. Paige's invention soon merged into the somber background of the typesetter.

On January 20, 1886, Clemens held an evening business meeting in his billiard room. Paige, heading for perfection, had decided to start all over again on a combined typesetter and justifier. He estimated that all the expenses connected with building a prototype machine, including wages, drawings, and patent applications, could not possibly go over thirty thousand dollars. He offered Clemens a half ownership of the new machine if he would underwrite this expense and then go on to capitalize, manufacture, and promote it. Clemens, who had already surrendered over thirteen thousand dollars to keep Paige going, jumped at the offer even though his business adviser, Franklin G. Whitmore, warned him that his obligation to support the venture from beginning to end could easily bankrupt him. "Never mind that. I can get a thousand men worth a million apiece to go in with me if I can get a perfect machine," he answered, the captive of his own dream. Two weeks later, he formally took over the new venture and hoisted all the gaudy banners of his expectations. If money was needed, he reminded himself, Andrew Carnegie was the man; he planned to see Thomas Edison. Bigger schemes of capitalization filled his head: by autumn he was thinking of a $5,000,000 stock issue; the next year, as his hopes and needs grew, it became $10,000,000. He wanted to measure his market, and he ordered surveys of the amount of new matter set each day by all the newspapers in the United States and Canada. He tried to find out the membership and organization of printers' and compositors' unions; when a union official objected to these inquiries Clemens answered cagily—and through an intermediary to keep his name out of it—that he was interested in some sort of printing invention and "wanted to get an idea of how small the market for such a thing might be." He was tangled in a paradox. As Howells once characterized him, he was a theoretical socialist and a practical aristocrat; but he was also a practical capitalist and, by Howells' definition, a plutocrat, a man who dreams of and pursues enormous wealth regardless of whether he gets it or not. That March, speaking as a theoretical socialist to the Monday Evening Club in Hartford, Clemens hailed the rise of organized labor. Labor was "the new dynasty," he said, which would rule and own the coming age; the Haymarket Square riots in Chicago in May showed that the transfer of power was near at hand and might not occur without bloodshed. Yet as a plutocrat and a practical capitalist Clemens figured that Paige's machine did the work of four or five men, did not get drunk, did not join the printers' union.

For years Whitelaw Reid had been a majority stockholder in the Mergenthaler syndicate and had encouraged the inventor to experiment with his machine in the *Tribune*'s composing room. When the machine vindicated his patience and backing, it was Reid who had the satisfaction of coining the name "Linotype." On July 3, 1886, the first of the *Tribune*'s battery of twelve Linotype machines set a part of the day's issue. Soon after came *The Tribune Book of Open Air Sports*, the first book printed from machine-composed type. And it was clear that even though it was still in an early stage, the Linotype, unlike Paige's machine, could function continuously and reliably. A printing invention as important as the rotary press had finally been proved workable after half a century of trial and failure. But even this development did not shake Clemens' confidence. Hearing that the Linotype machine had worn out a $1,500 set of typecasting matrices within a month, he concluded that it was little better than "a costly luxury" which was also, he was pleased to hear, occasionally plagued by faulty alignment. Even two years later, when an observer at the *Tribune* told him that an improved Mergenthaler machine was now giving reliable service without expensive wear on its matrices, he was still positive that it was "just a racehorse" and consequently "can't run no competition with a railroad." His own machine was rarely together in one place for more than a week at a time, but he planned a series of public contests, handicapped at one Paige machine versus two Mergenthaler machines, to be witnessed by assorted financiers, newspaper owners, and the government printer.

Years later Clemens told Albert Bigelow Paine that the Mergenthaler promoters had offered to exchange a half interest in their venture for a half interest in his and that, full of scorn and confidence at the time, he did not even bother to say no but "only smiled." Paine would have done well to smile, too. Among all the hundreds of Mark Twain's business memoranda concerning the machine there is not a glimmer of evidence that the offer was ever made. This ironic, rueful tall story told on himself has a family resemblance to his claim that he once turned down a chance to buy a whole hatful of stock in Alexander Graham Bell's new invention, the telephone, for only five hundred dollars. He may simply have been telescoping a hope and an actuality. In October 1894, just two months before Paige's machine failed its final test, he said he hoped that "some day the Mergenthaler people will come and want to hitch teams with us." The actuality was that in 1897 the Mergenthaler Company bought out Paige's prototype machines and all his rights and patents for twenty thousand dollars, just to clear the decks.

For all his hubris at the time Clemens had the growing feeling that the mire was sucking at his boots. Even when he wanted to write, he told Whitmore, he found that all his energies had been eaten up by the machine. During most of 1886 and 1887 the combined expense of Paige's salary and the bills at Pratt and Whitney averaged about two thousand dollars a month; then the Pratt and Whitney bills went up enough to bring the monthly drain to three thousand dollars. By December 1887, the typesetter had already cost Clemens about fifty thousand dollars, which was twenty thousand dollars more than Paige's top estimate, and it was feeding strong and fast. "We go on and on, but the typesetter goes on forever—at $3,000 a month," Sam complained to Pamela. He apologized for being able to afford only five dollars each as a Christmas present for Orion, Mollie, and Jane Clemens in Keokuk. The predictions went on and on, too—finished by April, finished by May, finished by August, finished in eighty-five days. The old familiar money pinch was on again, and with it came the feeling that he was once again a beggar standing outside the house of plenty. His fortune and Livy's, he began to say, was "interred" in the "eternal machine." There are two times a man should not speculate, he soon noted privately: "When he can afford it, and when he can't."

III

Passing through St. Paul, Minnesota, at the end of June 1886, on his way to visit his mother and Orion, Clemens impressed a local reporter as the sort of grandee who customarily traveled by private Pullman with his family and servants. Dressed in alligator slippers, a light-gray suit, and a pearl-colored high hat, Mr. Clemens said that his friend Mark Twain had little time for writing these days because he was really in the publishing business. His firm, he went on to say, had so many books under contract—enough for four years—that even if Mark Twain did get around to writing a book, some other house would have to publish it.

Charles L. Webster and Company did, in fact, have an ambitious program, and, despite all his grumblings, it was Clemens who had the commanding voice in the partnership, who was responsible for most of the books the firm took on (over Webster's blunt veto he insisted on making the neighborly gesture of publishing the Reverend N. J. Burton's Yale lectures on preaching), and who, unwilling to share top billing in his own house with any of the vast number of literary men he knew, remained the firm's only major literary author.* The list was by and large a mishmash of undistinguished books by or about famous people, frank attempts at celebrity publishing on the pattern of the Grant book: King Kalakaua's collection of Hawaiian legends; memoirs by Sherman, Sheridan, and Mc-Clellan; *The Genesis of the Civil War*, by Major General Samuel Wylie Crawford, who was at Sumter when the shooting began; Elizabeth Custer's book about General George Armstrong Custer and Almira Hancock's book about General Winfield Scott Hancock, the hero of Gettysburg; "Sunset" Cox's *Diversions of a Diplomat in Turkey*; and two books which epitomize the firm's style and fortunes—Father Bernard O'Reilly's *Life of Pope Leo XIII* ("the greatest book of the age," Webster and Company trumpeted, written with the Pope's "Encouragement, Approbation, and Blessing") and Henry Ward Beecher's *Autobiography*.

When Clemens talked with the St. Paul reporter he was still savoring the triumph of having signed up what he would always call "the Pope's book." He believed every Catholic in Christendom would have to buy a copy as a religious duty. Even Twichell, who should have known better but didn't—he too had an awesomely exaggerated idea of the power of the Pope—was taken in by this categorical logic. "The issue of this book will be the greatest event in the way of book publishing that ever oc-

* In 1892 the firm published two books by Walt Whitman, *Selected Poems* and *Autobiographia*. By this time, however, Clemens was an absentee partner, and the company was run by Webster's successor, Fred Hall.

curred," he wrote in his diary, "and it seems certain M.T. will make a vast amount of money by it." (Some years afterward he added the comment, "Proved quite otherwise in the event.") Clemens had told Livy, who had been hesitant about buying some new furniture, that they could now afford a thousand new sofas out of their future bank account, and he planned a presentation copy for the Pope with a solid-gold binding by Tiffany. In July a hired carriage with a plumed footman delivered Charley Webster at the Vatican for a private audience with his Holiness, who infallibly knew how many copies Grant's book had sold and professed amazement when Charley assured him that his biography was guaranteed a minimum sale of 100,000 copies. Charley returned with a rosary blessed by the Pope that caused so much excitement at Farmington Avenue that Clemens said he would not take a thousand dollars for it. (In fact he wanted to buy three more through Father O'Reilly.) But although Clemens was sure the promotional literature was good enough to sell a Chocktaw Bible, *The Life of Pope Leo XIII*, published in 1887, did not bring in a golden harvest of the faithful and in fact fell considerably short of Charley's promised minimum of 100,000 copies. "The failure was incredible to Clemens," Howells recalled. "His sanguine soul was utterly confounded, and soon a silence fell upon it where it had been so exuberantly jubilant."

Other books, too, plotted a declining course for Mark Twain's publishing house. In January 1887 Henry Ward Beecher, who twenty years earlier had advised Sam Clemens to hold out for a royalty contract with Bliss on *The Innocents Abroad*, took a five-thousand-dollar advance to write his autobiography. Clemens' enthusiasm went up the more he thought about the book, and he predicted a profit of $350,000 if only Beecher "heaves in just enough piousness." Three weeks after this chicken-counting Beecher was dead at seventy-three of a cerebral hemorrhage and Clemens was left with an unfinished manuscript and a paper loss which he estimated at $100,000 and maybe more. Along with Beecher's death came the discovery that the firm's bookkeeper and cashier, F. M. Scott, had made off with about twenty-five thousand dollars. Clemens assured Orion that this was a trifling "momentary annoyance"—"a thing which slips out of one's mind of its own accord"—compared with the Beecher loss; still even though the bookkeeper turned himself in and paid back a third of the money, Clemens became the avenging fury, impatient at Charley for urging leniency. Hire a detective to find out where Scott hid the greenbacks, he instructed Charley; sell Scott's house in New Jersey for eleven thousand dollars and keep the money; and, finally, make sure that Scott gets five years in Sing Sing—which he did. Soon enough Charley himself was to feel the force of his uncle's implacability.

The Paige typesetter, for all the fiscal monkeyshines and anxieties that surrounded it, was still a creature of poetry, a marvel in steel. The publishing house, Clemens increasingly felt, was merely an act of commerce and a corporate trap which compelled him to assume the liabilities but share the profits. He made a choice between the two. He began to use the publishing house as a private bank to finance the machine; he drew off the profits, demanded more, and left the firm undercapitalized, overexpanded, and fatally committed to publishing a ten-volume *Library of American Literature* without the money to manufacture it. When he felt hopelessly whipsawed by publishing reverses and Paige's delays, he cast a baleful eye on Charley Webster and chose him as the first human sacrifice to placate the machine god. In his rage against Webster he summed up his doubts that the machine could ever be finished or the firm rescued from a course "straight down hill, towards sure destruction."

Webster was vulnerable and accessible. He had his share of vanity and self-importance: at thirty-four he was head of a publishing house that bore his name, he associated with the powerful and famous, and he was proud of it. He was also cruelly overworked. Years of running fool's errands for Uncle Sam and Aunt Livy, when he should have been tending strictly to business, began to tell on his command of details and on his health. By the summer of 1887, after the double fiasco of the Beecher manuscript and the embezzlement—both of which Clemens blamed him for—he was suffering from acute neuralgia and blinding headaches; he was as irascible as his uncle. The year before, he and Clemens had taken in a new partner, Fred Hall; at the end of 1888 Webster sold his interest to Hall for a mere twelve thousand dollars, retired permanently from business, and, bearing a photograph inscribed "with the affectionate regards of S. L. Clemens," went back to Fredonia. There he spent his days building ships' models, assembling a museum on the top floor of his house, and scanning the landscape with a telescope from a cupola with a revolving roof. On occasion he appeared in the streets wearing the uniform—complete with sword, tricorn hat, blue tunic, gold epaulets, and white cashmere pants—of a Knight of the Order of Pius, an honor bestowed upon him by Leo XIII (which provoked from his uncle the comment that if Charley Webster deserved to be a Papal Knight, Mark Twain deserved to be an archangel). The village newspaper referred to him as "Sir Charles."

When Webster died, in April 1891, only forty years old, Clemens absented himself from the funeral and sent Orion in his place, but his wrath, which had followed Charley to the mild eccentricity of his Fredonia retirement, followed him to the grave, and then beyond that, a persistence reflecting Clemens' own struggle and failure. The charges hardly varied in their shrillness: incompetence, wastefulness, glory-grabbing, stupidity, ignorance, greed, arrogance, dishonesty. "Not a man but a hog," Clemens told Pamela (who was Charley's mother-in-law) in July 1889. "I have never hated any creature," he told Orion at the same time, "with a one hundred thousandth fraction of the hatred which I bear that human louse." That hatred never abated; until his own dying day Clemens with stern Presbyterian logic held Webster responsible for every terrible thing that happened, including bankruptcy and the deaths of Susy and Livy. Charley, it seems clear, was in actuality less than a villain but considerably more than a scapegoat. He became the chief actor in one of those demented fantasies which Clemens increasingly relied on to preserve his own sanity, a fictional character supporting a fabric of bearable reality.*

At the end of 1888, however, with Charley out of the business, it seemed that the machine was finally about to be perfected, as though all along he had been the real and symbolic obstruction. In July Clemens said the machine (and the book) would be finished in August. On October 3 he said there were twenty-one full working days to go. He was about to pay ten thousand dollars to Pratt and Whitney, the last such bill, he was sure, and the last lean Christmas. Even Jean, eight years old, had learned to measure her simplest needs against the machine's. She told a maid to put off buying a box of shoe polish—"The machine isn't done," she explained. Livy's brother-in-law Theodore Crane was an invalid at Farmington Avenue, paralyzed on one side after a stroke that September, slowly dying, and needing care night and day. Hoping to escape from the gloom and confusions of his overburdened household, Clemens moved his workroom to Twichell's house, only to discover that the usual noise of the Twichell children was nearly drowned out by an army of carpenters hammering away at a new ceiling directly beneath his feet. Still, in this boiler-factory setting he managed to turn out eighty pages of *A Connecticut Yankee* in a week. He was as determined as ever to finish the book the day Paige finished the machine. But the strain was beginning to tell. "Don't imagine that I am on my way to the poorhouse, for I am not," he raged at Orion, who had provoked him with a letter about petty economies, "or that I am uncomfortable or unhappy—for *I never am.*" Even on December 29, when he hopefully drafted a New Year's greeting for Livy which he planned to set on the machine, he was prepared for delays and more delays: he spoke of the possibility that it would be finished in a few days, but he added, "We never prophesy any more."

"Machine O.K.," Paige telegraphed to him in New York on January 2. "Come and see it work." Three days later, a date that Clemens noted for history—"Saturday, January 5, 1889, 12:20 P.M."—he scrawled in block letters, "EUREKA!" and jubilantly underlined the word. "I have seen a line

---

* "Webster kept back a book of mine, *A Connecticut Yankee in King Arthur's Court*, as long as he could," Clemens said in 1906, with a malevolent disregard of fact that the mere thought of Charley brought out in him, "and finally published it so surreptitiously that it took two or three years to find out that there was any such book." Actually, Webster was out of the business before the manuscript was even finished.

of movable type, *spaced and justified by machinery!* This is the first time in the history of the world that this amazing thing has ever been done," he wrote, and he signed the statement. A few hours later, writing to Orion, he went on to describe "the immense historical birth" at which every one of the six men present seemed "dizzy, stupefied," "stunned," drunk although they had had nothing to drink. The machine even made a perverse demonstration of its powers, for just when it seemed that the marvel was misbehaving and might have to be taken apart all over again, Paige discovered the trouble. "We are fools," he said, "the machine isn't." Its superfine intelligence—which went along with its unviably fastidious nature—had simply been making allowance for an invisible speck of dirt on one of the types. But even in this demonstration the future of the delicate machine was foretold. While Clemens was writing his account and Livy was celebrating downstairs—and two weeks later, when a newspaper as far away as London announced that Mark Twain's "patient toil" had at last been "crowned with success"—Paige was taking it apart once more. His purpose, as his backer believed, was to work the stiffness out of its joints and make it as smooth and supple as a human muscle. The same story, already nine years old, was beginning all over again. No more experiments, Clemens was soon protesting in his notebook; they must get it finished by July. He told Orion he was sorry they had ever taken the machine apart; it had been good enough as it was, and besides, now that the work and the bills at Pratt and Whitney had resumed, he was cramped for money, and expected to be for some time. Never mind, he added wearily. "All good things arrive unto them that wait—and don't die in the meantime."

IV

For all practical purposes the machine was never finished. Still, supported by a faith in homeopathic magic and also spurred on by the need for money, Clemens managed to finish *A Connecticut Yankee* in May 1889, four and a half years after reading *Morte d'Arthur* and making his first note:

> Dream of being a knight errant in armor in the middle ages. Have the notions and habits of thought of the present day mixed with the necessities of that No pockets in the armor. No way to manage certain requirements of nature. Can't scratch. Cold in the head—can't blow— can't get at handkerchief, can't use iron sleeve. Iron gets red hot in the sun—leaks in the rain, gets white with frost and freezes me solid in winter. Suffer from lice and fleas. Make disagreeable clatter when I enter church. Can't dress or undress myself. Always getting struck by lightning. Fall down, can't get up.

But over the years this comic idea changed its course and headed away from burlesque and toward an apocalyptic conclusion in which chivalric England and Hank Morgan's American technology—failures both, as the author had come to see them—destroy each other. Writing this book, Mark Twain was in effect acting out his own disintegration, measuring the failure of a precarious equilibrium. In response not to a traumatic reversal but to a steady erosion of belief, his center ceased to hold, and for the rest of his life his imaginative energies would be scattered and baffled.

By the early part of 1886, when he was writing the first three chapters, the comic idea had already taken on grim overtones. At the same time that he planned for Hank Morgan to do battle armed with a hay fork instead of a lance, Mark Twain also planned a conflict with the supreme medieval authority. "Country placed under an interdict," he noted, anticipating his account (not written until 1888 or 1889) of a desolate and muted England, punished by the Church for accepting Morgan's ideas. From the very start, the dream about knight-errantry was joined in Mark Twain's mind by the idea of a great battle, at first between crusaders and a modern expeditionary force fitted out with ironclad warships, observation balloons, torpedoes, hundred-ton cannon, and Gatling guns ("labor-saving machinery" which, like the Yankee himself, was the product of Colt's Patent Fire Arms Manufacturing Company of Hartford). In other early notes for the book the Yankee, like Mark Twain yearning for Hannibal as it was around 1846, yearns for an Arcadian past which "exists" only in his dream, a pre-Boss Camelot (poverty, slavery, and ignorance forgotten for the moment) as drowsing and idyllic—"sleeping in a valley by a winding river"—as that other fictive town, St. Petersburg. Caught between dream and reality, between past and present, the Yankee has arrived at the impossible position of needing to return to a place which never existed—or no longer exists, because he destroyed it himself.

Visiting Hannibal in January 1885, just when he was under the spell of Malory, Clemens had felt himself swept under by "infinite great deeps of pathos," by waves of helpless longing for a lost Eden and his boyhood there. His distance from the receding past was symbolized for him by the pathetic figure of his "cradle-mate, baby-mate, little boy-mate," Tom Nash, deaf and dumb now as he had been for almost forty years, since the night he went skating with Sam and fell into the river. Sam's mother too, with whom he spent "a beautiful evening" of reminiscence, was increasingly dislocated from the present; she was eighty-two now and would live to eighty-seven. "Poor old Ma," he noted, "asking in haste for news about people who have been dead forty, fifty, and sixty years." Like Jane Clemens, sinking so far and fast into anility that soon she would have to ask Orion what relation Sam was to her, the Yankee, even as first conceived, has lost the power and desire to shake off his dream. "He mourns his lost land—has come to England and revisited it, but it is all so changed and become old, so old—and it was so fresh and new, so virgin before." Thus Clemens outlined the frame story surrounding Hank Morgan's yellowed palimpsest, and he supplied the only possible ending: "He has lost all interest in life—is found dead next morning—suicide."

The implications were too unpleasant to face up to directly, and neither Clemens (at first) nor those on whom he tried out the idea acknowledged that it might lead to something other than a splendidly funny book. "That notion of yours about the Hartford man waking up in King Arthur's time is capital," Howells said in January 1886, after the story had been talked to him; and even in 1908, when he was reading the book for at least the second time, Howells still called it "the most delightful, truest, most humane, sweetest fancy that ever was." The book also seemed pure fun to a group to whom Clemens read the first three chapters and outlined the rest on November 11, 1886, at Governor's Island in New York; this group was the members and guests of the Military Services Institution, fittingly enough for the subject matter a society dedicated to the promotion of the military interests of the United States. The final battle had reached the tadpole stage: under contract from King Arthur, the Yankee (then known as "Sir Robert Smith of Camelot") undertakes to kill off at a tournament fifteen kings and acres of hostile knights. Squadron after squadron they charge, while from behind an electrified barbed-wire fence he mows them down with the inevitable Gatling gun. Having done this, knocked the ogres out of commission and abolished both courtly love and armor, Sir Bob is able to put the kingdom on a strictly business basis: Arthur's knights set themselves up as a stock exchange, and the going rate for a seat at the Round Table reaches thirty thousand dollars.

In the audience were two men with experience to judge this mingling of fantasy and *laissez-faire* capitalism: General Sherman, destroyer of the cotton kingdom, and his millionaire brother John, Hayes's Secretary of the Treasury and, later, sponsor of the Anti-Trust Act. Neither Sherman appears to have left any recorded comment even though the Yankee had just re-enacted one of the General's favorite lessons. "In all history," Sherman had warned a Southern friend in 1860, "no nation of mere agriculturalists ever made successful war against a nation of mechanics." But from Cleveland, where a newspaper synopsis of the entertainment reached her, came words of alarm from Mary Fairbanks, asserting her role of censor and mentor to her fifty-one-year-old protégé, who still addressed her as "mother" and signed himself "Saml." Predictably, she was afraid he was about to commit a crime of cultural lese majesty against King Arthur and that body of Arthurian legend and association hallowed by time, Thomas Malory, and, lately, the Poet Laureate's *Idylls of the King*. Clemens' attempt to set her mind at rest reflects some of his own tangled, mutually exclusive aims, still so obscure to him that he seems to be playing the fool. Now, as at the Whittier fiasco, it was possible for him to entertain a demon and not suspect it.

"The story isn't a satire peculiarly," he wrote to her five days after his Governor's Island performance, "it is more especially a *contrast*" of "daily life" in Arthur's time and now. He had no intention of smirching or be-littling any of Malory's "great and beautiful *characters*," and he went on to explain—in a literary-lofty-sentimental vocabulary that he favored when dealing with women in general and Mrs. Fairbanks in particular—that Galahad ("the divinest spectre") will still gallop through "the mists and twilights of Dreamland," Arthur still keep his "sweetness and purity," and Launcelot (his unmentionable passion for Guinevere unmentioned) still be the sternest of enemies and the kindest of friends. He was deter-mined, he said, that the disruption of the Round Table and the final battle —"the Battle of the Broken Hearts, it might be called"—should lose none of their "pathos and tears" through his handling.

Writing a book which, as far as it preaches anything, preaches ir-reverence, the guillotine, a reign of terror, and a kind of generalized de-spair, he still believes that he is writing a blameless, instructive tale for women and children. Nowhere in this long letter does he make a single mention of the Yankee. Also to demonstrate his high seriousness Clemens told Mrs. Fairbanks that he was writing "for posterity only; my posterity: my great grandchildren. It is to be my holiday amusement for six days every summer the rest of my life. Of course I do not expect to publish it; nor indeed any other book . . ." Along with this image of a writer who, presumably rolling in money from the typesetter, could afford to retire from the market place, he left her with a final, reassuring glimpse of cul-tural orthodoxy: he was now reader to a dozen or so ladies who met every Wednesday in his billiard room—the favored theater for his reper-tory of identities—to hear him explicate the poetry of Robert Browning. ("I can read Browning," he liked to say, "so Browning himself can under-stand it.")

The following April Clemens appeared before another military group, the Union Veterans' Association of Maryland, and gave an abbreviated version of "The Private History of a Campaign That Failed." In the re-telling he made an important change which relates his Civil War experi-ence directly to his book in progress and suggests that the unresolved ten-sions of his uncomfortable role as a Confederate irregular and deserter were now being translated into the major conflicts of the book itself. The turning point of "A Campaign That Failed" had been the moonlight shoot-ing of the unarmed, unidentified soldier thought to be the vanguard of a pursuing Union force. In Mark Twain's Baltimore speech the killing of this solitary stranger becomes just another hyperbolic joke: "So began and ended the only battle in the history of the world where the opposing force was *utterly exterminated*, swept from the face of the earth—to the last man." Having demonstrated that he (like the Yankee) is invincible in battle, Second Lieutenant Clemens, in awe of his own powers, decides to withdraw to civilian life, let the Confederacy collapse, and allow the Union to survive—a wise decision, he told the Baltimore veterans, because the United States in 1887 was the "one sole country nameable in history or tradition where a man *is* a man and manhood the only royalty."

To a great extent Hank Morgan *is* Mark Twain. Both are showmen who love gaudy effects. But this, as Clemens said in criticism of a stage version of the Yankee, is only "his rude animal side, his circus side." For the Yankee, like Mark Twain, is also "a natural gentleman," with a "good heart" and "high intent." Both combine idealism and nostalgia with shrewd practicality and devotion to profit. Their revolutionary, humanitarian zeal is tempered and at times defeated by their despairing view of human nature. By an ironic reversal, the Rebel soldier's historic battle with the Yankee scout has the symbolic content of the Connecticut Yankee's battle with the enemies of his "republic." Having made the connection in terms of his own experience, Mark Twain went on to explore in his book a number of implicit parallels between Arthur's England and the American South: slavery; an agrarian economy which came into armed conflict with an industrial economy; a chivalric code which, Clemens said, was second-hand Walter Scott and kept the South mawkish, adolescent, verbose, and addicted to leatherheaded anachronisms like duels and tournaments. In both frameworks a civil war destroys the old order, and the Yankee has as acute a sense of loss as Mark Twain did. In the course of writing *A Connecticut Yankee*, Mark Twain compelled his original matrix (not a stable one to begin with) of a "contrast" rather than a "satire" to accept and contain a remarkable range of conflict and anger. Finally the matrix burst. He pronounced a curse on both parts of the "contrast" and ended his battle of ancients and moderns with a double defeat.

"It is a perfect day indeed," he wrote to Orion's wife on a Sunday in July 1887. From his study at Quarry Farm he looked out, in enormous contentment, over the purple shaded valley. Livy was resting, the children had gone for a walk in the woods, his cats were sleeping nearby. Later, at the piano, he sang—"Go Down, Moses," "Gospel Train," "Old Folks at Home," "Die Wacht am Rhein," "Die Lorelei"—and then he read late into the night. Yet the sixteen chapters he wrote during what began as a "perfect" summer trace a pattern of mounting anxiety, bitterness, and invective; all his experience, his business involvements as well as his reading of history, pointed to a single conclusion and a single mood. Early in July he had been too occupied with the typesetter to get started. Later that month, just as he hit his stride again, he had to stop for a week to wrestle with the machine in Hartford and the publishing house in New York. Webster, now nearly incapacitated by neuralgia, was less and less able to deal with the mounting anarchy of too many titles and too little capital to publish them with, and the outlook was gloomy.

Working seven hours a day on his book, Clemens was tense and anxious, unable to sleep at night. He sat up late, smoking and thinking—"not pleasantly." "I want relief of mind," he complained to Charley after one of these bad nights; in the deepest depressions of his Buffalo year he had felt the same urgency. "The fun, which was abounding in the *Yankee at Arthur's Court* up to three days ago, has slumped into funereal sadness, and this will not do—it will not answer at all. The very title of the book requires fun, and it must be furnished. But it can't be done, I see, while this cloud hangs over the workshop." Two weeks later his mood, characteristically, had turned around completely: now he was proudly writing "an uncommonly bully book" which would sell twice as many copies as *Huckleberry Finn*, and for a while he even deluded himself into believing he could finish it by November. By this time, though, the machine and the publishing house were in the saddle again and riding him hard. "This kind of rush is why parties write no books," he said with a minimum of regret, as if relieved not to have to follow the Yankee in the direction he had taken. Mired deeper and deeper in business, he took up the manuscript again the following summer too late, as he told Andrew Chatto, to finish even in 1888; and it was partly his urgent need for money that compelled him to keep on against extraordinary distractions during the winter and spring of 1889 in Hartford—the social season and therefore the equivalent for him of working a night shift—and write the final chapters in May, five months too late, for all his determination to celebrate the apparent perfection of the machine.

During all this time the abounding "fun" never wholly returned. *A Connecticut Yankee* contains episodes as richly comic and satirical as anything he ever wrote, but they are more and more frequently, finally compulsively, presented in terms of havoc. It was apparent to Clemens himself that he was passing through some crisis of ebbing faith in the Great Century, a "negative conversion" that he could hardly help but dramatize in the final chapter of his book. "The change," he declared to Howells (in a flash of self-illumination totally absent from his letter to Mary Fairbanks), "is in *me*—in my vision of the evidences."

When he said this in August 1887, he had just been rereading Carlyle's *French Revolution*, and he recognized that "life and environment" had made him "a Sansculotte!—And not a pale, characterless Sansculotte, but a Marat"—calling for death to all ancient forms of authority: monarchy, aristocracy, the Catholic Church. None of these posed much of a threat to him or to America in the 1880s. Like Arthur's England, their remoteness made them permissible scapegoats for an anger whose real objects were much closer to home. True, modern Europe offered him few "evidences" that it was any better than it ever had been; European morals, as he read over and over again in Lecky, had scarcely been improved by social or material progress. Clemens hated the French more than ever; their sexual code, and their incapacity for independent thought and action seemed what they had been in the days of Saint-Simon, whose *Memoirs*, along with Lecky's *History*, he often read at night. Matthew Arnold's celebrated strictures on American civilization enraged him when they were published in 1888,* because they seemed merely to demonstrate that the English were as servile, conformist, and brutalized as they had been in the darkest ages, their national character combining the primary traits of the dog and the lion (so far behind him had he now left that Anglomania which had distressed his friends fifteen years earlier). Almost monthly, from 1887 on, in lectures and in articles in the *Century*, the traveler George Kennan described the savagery of life under the Czar. His accounts of Siberian slave labor, which Clemens borrowed from in *A Connecticut Yankee,* shed in the contrast a wanly charitable light on slavery even as it had been in England and the United States. "If such a government cannot be overthrown otherwise than by dynamite," Clemens exclaimed in a voice thick with emotion after hearing Kennan lecture in Boston, "then thank God for dynamite!"

Yet what the Yankee dynamites is not only the old chivalric and autocratic order—Europe, symbolically—but also all the apparatus of the "new deal"† that he tried to impose on what he bitterly acknowledges is "human

* In "Civilization in the United States" Arnold argued that despite America's material prosperity the basic "human problem" had not been solved. He cited the lack of "what is elevated and beautiful, of what is interesting," and, choosing Lincoln as an example, he also cited the lack of "distinction." "In truth, everything is against distinction in America, and against the sense of elevation to be gained through admiring and respecting it. The glorification of 'the average man,' who is quite a religion with statesmen and publicists there, is against it. The addiction to 'the funny man,' who is a national misfortune there, is against it. Above all, the newspapers are against it." In a speech which he never delivered but set in type on the Paige machine, Clemens replied to Arnold's attack on the newspapers; "a discriminating irreverence is the creator and protector of human liberty," was his general point.

Arnold's attack on the status of "the funny man" in America had home-grown counterparts, and Clemens was all too familiar with them. For example, the author of a literary history published in New York in 1886 made the following assessment: "The creators of *Uncle Remus and his Folklore Stories* and of *Innocents Abroad* must make hay while the sun shines. Twenty years hence, unless they chance to enshrine their wit in some higher literary achievement, their unknown successors will be the privileged comedians of the republic. Humor alone never gives its master a place in literature."

† On Oct. 12, 1876, years before he used this famous phrase in Chapter 13 (which was apparently Franklin D. Roosevelt's source) Clemens had written to Howells, apropos of an abortive literary scheme, "We must have a new deal." But in that same sense the phrase had been American usage as early as 1834.

muck." "All our noble civilization factories went up in the air and disappeared," he says. "We could not afford to let the enemy turn our own weapons against us." And it becomes clear that the apparatus of enlightenment and progress introduced by the Yankee is in some way a "weapon" which destroys its beneficiaries as well as its enemies. The busy factories hidden all over England, he says, are like a "serene volcano, standing innocent with its motionless summit in the blue sky, and giving no hint of the rising hell in its bowels." Throughout the book there are similar metaphors which suggest that Clemens, for all his expressed enthusiasm for what he called "machine culture,"* nursed the covert belief that the machine was a destructive force. For him and for many of his contemporaries the most familiar epitome of the two-facedness of the machine was the steam locomotive tearing and shrieking its way through the heart of the American Eden (and destroying two of his most cherished idyls, river steamboating and the self-sufficing agricultural life he remembered at his Uncle John Quarles's farm). Clemens' concurrent experience with Paige's typesetter confirmed his worst fears. The very names the Yankee gives to his institutions—"civilization factories" and, a dehumanizing pun, "man factories" —suggest not the fervent brotherhood of Whitman's utopian democracy but instead a bleak, industrial collectivism, the nightmare society of a monolithic state ruled by the Boss.

Working through a crisis of belief in fictional terms, Clemens found himself unable, either ideologically or emotionally, to cope with the historical extremes that lay on either side of his pastoral, drowsing Hannibal. Out of desperation and bafflement he chose the way of the anarch. The final combat, more a massacre along the lines of Little Bighorn than a "Battle of the Broken Hearts," is a gruesome practical joke. Virtuoso of dynamite, electricity, pent-up water, and the Gatling gun, the Yankee surveys twenty-five thousand dead lying on the field (for reasons of taste Clemens suppressed a reference to four million pounds of human meat). In a moment of tragic overconfidence he declares, "We fifty-four"— Clemens' age in 1889—"were masters of England!" But he is actually trapped within three walls of dead men, he is the victim of his own victory. Wounded and apparently dying, he has only one place to go: backward into the cave. He is carried there by his band of boys—Sam Clemens has

* In February 1887, before he had finished the first half of the book, Clemens read a paper with this title to the Monday Evening Club in Hartford. A fragment of the paper survives as an interpolated passage in Chapter 10 of *An American Claimant* (published in 1892). The speaker is identified as a middle-aging man who has got his education in a printing office. He argues that "the imagination-stunning material development of this century" has so drastically "reconstructed" America that 17,000 persons can now accomplish the same work that 50 years ago would have kept 13 million busy. Restating, he figures that the 1887 population of 60 million has the productive potential of 40 billion. He does not speculate about possible concentrations of wealth and power or surpluses of goods, labor, and leisure.

come back to Hannibal for good. Having already rejected all the values and both the "contrasts" of the book, the Yankee makes a further withdrawal, as Clemens himself was shortly to do, into the dream.

By an ironic accident, Livy, her husband's vigilant editor, had a severe case of pinkeye during the spring, and even in August, when the proofs of *A Connecticut Yankee* were nearly ready, she was still forbidden by her doctor to use her eyes for reading or writing. She insisted that Clemens ask Howells to read the proofs. "She is afraid I have left coarsenesses which ought to be rooted out, and blasts of opinion which are so strongly worded as to repel instead of persuade," Clemens explained to Howells. For once, despite their remarkable rapport, the two might have been talking to each other across the Grand Canyon. "Last night I started on your book, and it sank naturally into my dreams," Howells wrote from Cambridge on September 19, 1889. "It's charming, original, wonderful—good in fancy, and sound to the core in morals." And from Hartford three days later answered a man who knew that in the course of writing the *Yankee* his demons had been loosed and could never be kenneled again: "Well, my book is written—let it go. But if it were only to write over again there wouldn't be so many things left out. They burn in me; and they keep multiplying; but now they can't ever be said. And besides, they would require a library—and a pen warmed up in hell."

v

Under the terms of a new agreement signed in December 1889, Clemens undertook to manufacture the typesetting machine and to pay Paige about $160,000 plus $25,000 a year for seventeen years. In return Paige assigned all rights in the machine. Clemens' stake in the venture, which included not only the enormous profits he reckoned on but also the $150,000 or so which he had been paying out with increasing hardship since 1885, thus became, in what proved to be a catastrophic gamble, altogether contingent on his success as a promoter. The smooth-talking Paige, whom he always believed at the moment of talking, no matter what evidence there was to the contrary, once assured him they could dispose of the English patent rights for ten million, and Clemens assumed a universal supply of eager money. Far from worrying about his obligations under the new contract with Paige, he was confident that from now on negotiations ought to be quite simple. "It will not be necessary for the capitalist to arrive at terms with anyone but me," he said. And, the entrepreneurial logic went on, once he had one major capitalist in tow, the smaller ones would not be hard to find.

That summer Charley Langdon no longer the playful cub of the *Quaker City* but a toughened money manager who looked with anguish on the uses to which Livy's shrinking patrimony were being put, flatly turned down his brother-in-law's offer to sell a one per cent interest in the company for $25,000. "The stock is either worth ten times that or it is worth nothing," Clemens reassured himself after this was followed by comparable rejections; "maybe the latter, although I think otherwise." Nor would Charley even give the company a loan secured by guaranteed royalties, which took precedence over dividends. John Marshall Clemens' "heavy curse of prospective wealth" was once again laid upon his son, the Tennessee land this time compacted into the shape of a brass-and-steel machine. By all his calculations Clemens was about to be gargantuanly rich, utopianly rich. The owner of a historic American fortune, he would never again have to write, much less lecture, for money. He was absolutely certain that he could sell 350 machines in New York City alone right away, and that this sale would breed a minimum sale of two thousand a year for the life of the patent and earn for the company an annual profit of at least twenty million dollars, with other millions pouring in each year from Europe. What he needed was the money to build the first 350 machines (he assumed that Paige's prototype was about to be perfected momentarily). Yet for months he could scarcely raise a dollar; even an old friend and fellow promoter like Frank Fuller backed away although Clemens assured him a return of fifteen hundred per cent on his investment. His own resources nearly exhausted, he frankly acknowledged that he was in a desperately tight corner. That December he again apologized for being able to send only five dollars each for Christmas trifles for his mother, Orion, and Mollie, "The machine still has its grip on our purse." But as always he kept his eye fixed on the glorious future. Surely, he reasoned, Andrew Carnegie or the Standard Oil Trust would want to come in with him.

In fact, however, there was never much for an investor to see. For all their money calculations, Clemens and Paige were also reluctant to expose their gleaming model of perfection to the scrutiny and the probably corruptive touch of the market place. The machine was so obsessively tinkered with and "improved" that it was rarely in working order. It had been taken down in January 1889, right after its triumphant demonstration, and it stayed in pieces until the summer. Clemens insisted that there be no new experiments, but, beguiled as much by his own dreams of perfection as by Paige's, he easily relented: the machine was taken down again so that Paige could install a device to keep the keys from jamming. By the time it was put together again in September, Charley Langdon, who might have been convinced by a demonstration, had left for a year abroad. Sometime during the year the machine was kept in commission long enough to set all that Clemens had written since 1884, or ever would write, of his adventure novel about Tom and Huck out West among the Indians; the twenty-three galleys are a double monument to an unfinishable book and an unfinishable machine. Throughout its life span the typesetter again and again showed the same character defects—grimly traceable to its two parents—of a foolish virgin and an overprotected child, precocious but accident-prone. In November, even though it was already "as perfect as a watch," it was taken down again, this time with Clemens' approval. This was to be the last polishing, he and Paige believed, which would eliminate "even the triflingest defect" and make the prodigy "perfecter than a watch," "letter perfect." Such rapt phrases were about to become epitaphs for the enterprise.

Clemens finally pinned all his hopes on John Percival Jones, the millionaire Senator from Gold Hill, Nevada. He had recently re-established contact with Jones through Joe Goodman. Fifteen years earlier, the solicitations had flowed in the opposite direction: using Goodman as middleman, Jones had persuaded Clemens to become a stockholder and director in the Hartford Accident Insurance Company, incorporated in June 1874; Clemens' publicity value to the new company was so great that Jones offered to indemnify him against loss on his investment and Clemens assumed his responsibilities gleefully. "There is nothing more beneficent than accident insurance," he said in a speech which the company later issued as an advertising pamphlet.

> I have seen an entire family lifted out of poverty and into affluence by the simple boon of a broken leg. I have had people come to me on crutches, with tears in their eyes, to bless this beneficent institution. In all my experience of life, I have seen nothing so seraphic as the look that comes into a freshly mutilated man's face when he feels in his vest pocket with his remaining hand and finds his accident ticket all right.

The company foundered after about a year and a half; $23,000 of Clemens' money appeared to be going down with it despite Jones's promises, and during a period of confusion and alarm Clemens listed him as "that lying thief U.S. Senator Jno P. Jones." But Jones finally made good on his pledge —the villain, it turned out, was Jones's brother-in-law, G. B. Lester, secretary and director of the company—and the anger was forgotten. Now Clemens was ready and eager for new dealings. Jones had sailed around the Horn to California in 1849 in search of wealth. He had found it in Virginia City during eight months in 1872 when he watched his shares in the Crown Point Mine rocket from two dollars to $1,800. He could be expected to have the appetite for another big bonanza and also the cash and influence to find ways to feed it.

At the end of February 1890, when the machine was in a brief and rare state of readiness for a demonstration, Jones ("my capitalist," Sam wrote to Orion) was delayed on business somewhere. Paige took advantage of the delay to work on a new improvement in the machine, an air blast to blow motes off the types. "News today that some vast capitalists want to come and talk business with us," Clemens wrote to Goodman on April 18. "We have appointed next Thursday—the final touch, the air-blast, will be in then." Clemens began to count on Thursday for his liberation from worry and want; he had extracted a fifty-thousand-dollar pledge from a banker in Elmira which was contingent on Jones's decision. Jones and his group arrived from New York around noon. Clemens met them at the station and drove them to Farmington Avenue. There he fed them a dinner calculated to make them grateful and happy, plied them with Roman punch, champagne, brandy, and his best stories, and then loaded them into the family carriage. At the Pratt and Whitney machine shop they found that Paige had miscalculated his time. The air blast was ready, but the machine was not. What was on display instead of the mechanical marvel Clemens had promised over dinner was a crazy tangle of gears, keys, cams, wheels, springs, cogs, levers, and other hardware. The Senator and his consortium marched out in disgust and headed for the first train back to New York. After this disaster, a psychologically predetermined "accident" in which his own motives figured quite as much as Paige's, Clemens began to sink into what Livy recognized as a serious depression. "I don't believe you ought to feel quite as desperate as you do," she wrote to him at the beginning of May, when he was in New York trying to raise money. "Things are not quite as desperate as they appear to you."

During the summer Clemens and Goodman pursued Jones in Washington and by some miracle of persistence and persuasion got him to come back to Hartford. This time the machine worked, and Jones was impressed. He bought a five-thousand-dollar share of Clemens' anticipated royalties and, more important, on August 13 he acquired a six-month option to organize a parent company to make and market the machine. Soon it was Jones who seemed to have Paige's old job of issuing constant assurances. Jones said he intended to start raising money in December and January (his option was to run out in February), when the machine would be ready to be moved to New York for a demonstration, and, he went on, he anticipated no difficulty whatsoever, provided Paige and the machine, both still financed by Clemens, did their part. And not only Jones was behind the machine, but John Mackay as well. "Do everything you can for Sam and his machine," Mackay told John Russell Young of the New York *Herald*. The Comstock millionaires had come around; now Clemens could bring in the smaller fish, all the way down from the Elmira banker, who resumed paying his fifty-thousand-dollar pledge, to assorted relatives and friends, including the Shakespearean actor Sir Henry Irving and his manager, Bram Stoker, the author of *Dracula*. Even the news of competing machines—Mergenthaler's Linotype at the New York *Tribune* and John Rogers' compositor at the New York *World*—still failed to temper Clemens' restored enthusiasm, but struck him, by some surreal logic, as further proof that Paige's wonder ("a perfect machine at last," Clemens was saying in October) had nothing to fear. The only problem for him was to keep Paige and his mechanics at Pratt and Whitney going through the winter; he had begun to borrow—$10,000 from Livy's mother, $2,500 from Hamersley. Still, he told Orion, he was "feeling reasonably comfortable."

All the conditions were now ripe for that entrepreneurial tragedy of aspiration and credulity in which, as he said, "a million men would see themselves as in a mirror." In the Yankee's image, the volcano was about to pour out its hellfire.

At the end of December Paige and his assistant Davis were still tinkering, still promising that within an hour or a day or a week the machine would be permanently blemishless—"the hoary old song," Clemens wrote in his notebook on December 20, "that has been sung to weariness in my ears by these frauds and liars!"

"Dear Mr. Clemens," Paige wrote on January 2, 1891, "The cast iron lever which owing to the poor quality of the iron broke the other day, and the cast iron part accidentally broken by Mr. Parker, have both been replaced by new, substantial, and durable *steel parts*, and the machine has run since that time without bruising, breaking, or damaging a type of any sort and gives promise of working continuously without delays of any kind. This is the best New Year's greeting that I can send you." And it was now time, he was soon saying almost daily, for Jones and his consortium to exercise their option before it was too late.

In Washington Clemens waited impatiently for two days, mainly reading *Cymbeline* and Anatole France's recent novel *The Crime of Sylvestre Bonnard* in his hotel room, before Jones consented to talk to him. On a Thursday morning less than a month before the deadline, Jones gave him a grudging few minutes, told him he was too busy with Senate affairs, and rushed him out. Suddenly sick with worry, Clemens went back to Hartford and began bombarding Jones with letters that grew more and more shrill and desperate in their claims. The machine would pay about $55,-000,000 a year to begin with and therefore, Clemens argued, "we are offering hundred-dollar bills at a penny apiece"; the machine filled a more urgent need than the telephone or the telegraph; "We occupy the field utterly and permanently," without competition from Mergenthaler or anyone. Jones would not answer. From Paige came harsher reminders that the option would run out, "absolutely," February 13. Livy was away visiting

Susy at Bryn Mawr, and Clemens, alone in the house which he could no longer afford, paced and figured and waited. Late one evening, expecting the worst, he told Paige not to expect another dollar from him. On February 11 Jones finally telegraphed; it was impossible for him to do anything, he said, a letter would explain. But when it arrived on the thirteenth his letter added to this flat refusal only a transparent contradiction: he and other prudent men of substance felt that conditions in the money market were not at the moment favorable for such a venture; moreover, he said, a number of these same men of substance already had large investments in Mergenthaler's Linotype.

"For a whole year you have breathed the word of promise to my ear to break it to my hope at last," Clemens started to write. "It is stupefying, it is unbelievable."

VI

A week or so later Clemens was able to return to a more nearly normal idiom. Jones, he wrote to Goodman, was nothing but a fraud, a "penny-worshipping humbug and shuffler," "really a very good sage-brush imitation of the Deity." On February 20 he noted that it had been two weeks since he had seen Paige or the machine and that during that time—while Livy, a victim of the disaster as much as of the fatigues of her trip to Bryn Mawr, was once again confined to her bed—he had been hard at work on the history game he invented at Quarry Farm and on the first chapters of a novel about Colonel Sellers. Implicitly, in both of these projects he recognized a therapeutic as well as a commercial value. Five days later he gave Orion further news (horribly premature) of his apparent withdrawal from a deep addiction. "I've shook the machine and never wish to see it or hear it mentioned again. It is superb, it is perfect, it can do ten men's work. It is worth billions; and when the pig-headed lunatic, its inventor, dies, it will instantly be capitalized and make the Clemens children rich." Soon after, he surrendered his contract with Paige. "I am out in the cold," he told Goodman, but back at work again. For the first time in twenty years, he was compelled to be a full-time writer, and a platform performer too, if necessary; to rebuild his wasted fortunes he planned to do enough work in the next three months alone to earn $75,000.

The vital signs seemed to be reappearing. Still, it soon became clear that he and the machine had not really let go of each other, that he had not even begun to grasp the extent of his involvement, and that meanwhile some corrosive process of change, prefigured and rehearsed in the Yankee, had taken place in his vision and morale as a writer. He finished a new novel, *The American Claimant*, and he found it so hilarious as he wrote it that he would wake up in the middle of the night laughing. (In Buffalo during the dark autumn of 1870 he had had the same near-hysterical response to his "map" of the fortifications of Paris.) But this farce about Colonel Sellers, now not only an inventor but the claimant to the earldom of Rossmore, is a negligible book. At the same time he was making a note for another novel, which he never wrote but which is another index of his real mood in the spring of 1891: Huck and Tom, both sixty, come back from wandering the world, talk about old times and mourn all the good things that are now gone, and agree that life for each of them has been a failure. "They die together."

Mark Twain's body too, as well as his imagination, was rebelling against the present in a significantly selective way. Forced back to writing for a livelihood, he found that his right hand was almost crippled by rheumatism. During the spring it spread from his fingers all the way up to his shoulder—"Every pen-stroke gives me the lockjaw." His usual handwriting, remarkably clear and even, became angular, cramped, and irregular. He tried for a while to dictate to the wax cylinders of a phonograph that Howells rented for him from a company in Boston. Later in the year, when he was in Europe trying to grind out travel journalism and also taking the cure for his rheumatism at Aix-les-Bains, he painfully taught himself to write with his left hand; all the symbolic meaning the act usually carries is relevant. But the same spring, when every time he picked up a pen the pain shot through his arm, this lifelong exponent of non-exercise —he said his biceps had the tone of an oyster wrapped in an old rag—was learning how to ride a bicycle. Evenings, with Jean running alongside, he wrenched and wobbled down his driveway onto Farmington Avenue, his ailing right hand clamped to the handlebar, and he discovered new ways to fall off. He was pretty well battered up with bicycling, he told Livy, but he was making progress and was satisfied. Somehow his rheumatism stopped hurting when he didn't have to write.

Over the past five years he had become fretful and unpredictable with his children, more and more difficult to understand. "Yesterday a thunderstroke fell on me," he had written to Howells in 1886. "I found that all their lives my children have been afraid of me! have stood all their days in uneasy dread of my sharp tongue and uncertain temper." Even after discounting this for his customary self-accusation, enough truth remains. "How he would be affected by this or that no one could ever foresee," Clara wrote after his death. She still remembered that as children she and her sisters were often terrified of being left alone with him. He was charming and entertaining with them, told endless stories and invented games and romps, but his mood might shift without warning from light to dark, his brow suddenly cloud over, and he would speak to them in anger or with autocratic severity. As they grew up they saw in him a Victorian sternness. He seemed determined to keep them away from men. Clara also remembered disturbing inadvertencies, seeming moments of demonic possession. She was in a rest home recovering from a nervous breakdown brought on by Livy's death when Jean was hurt in a riding accident and, according to the newspapers, crushed. Clemens telephoned to Clara's doctors to keep the papers away from her—he himself would come and gently tell her about the accident. When he arrived he showed her the headlines nonetheless, and then he gave her his own highly colored and needlessly suspenseful account (Jean's injuries, it turned out, were minor). "The dear man certainly intended to spare me a shock," Clara said years later about this display of mingled concern and cruelty, "and some strange spirit led him into contrary behavior."

On Susy fell the burden of a relationship compounded of hectoring and worship. He idealized all her gifts and was disappointed when she decided she wanted to study to be an opera singer, for he always hoped that she would be a writer. "She was a poet," he said. "Every now and then in her vivacious talk she threw out phrases of such admirable grace and force, such precision of form, that they thrilled through one's consciousness like the passage of the electric spark." In everything she did he subjected her to demands for perfection, but he himself was vulnerable to her slightest criticism and was easily angered, pursued by a guilty sense that he had failed her. Volatile, tense, and moody, she responded to him in an equally conflicted way. When she was nearly eleven she drew up a list of famous men which delighted him: "Longfellow, Papa (Mark Twain), Columbus, Teneson, Ferdinad." As she grew older she knew he was a great man, but she was not at all sure a humorist was any better than a clown, and more and more she wanted him to be a great man in some other way. "In a great many directions he has greater ability than in the gifts which have made him famous," she wrote in her biography. She wanted him to be a moral philosopher, for example, and the author not of *Huckleberry Finn* but of *The Prince and the Pauper* and especially *Joan of Arc;* much more than her mother she demanded purity, gentility, high sentiment—the criteria of the female reading audience described by one of Clemens' contemporaries as "the iron Madonna who strangles in her fond embrace the American novelist". Susy sometimes expressed her aspirations for him, with a cruelty she could hardly have acknowledged, in open resentment of the fame and identity of that deliberate creation, Mark Twain. "How I hate that name! I should never like to hear it again!" she told the New Orleans writer Grace King, and she said that she had suffered during every moment of a court ball in Berlin because she received no attention "save as the daughter of Mark Twain."

For his part he minded so much her leaving home in the fall of 1890—

"Susy is a freshman at Bryn Mawr, poor child"—that he was half glad to hear she was almost too homesick to stay at college. "The last time I saw her was a week ago on the platform at Bryn Mawr," he wrote to Pamela, and his sentence has the cadence of his own grief and loneliness without Susy. "Our train was moving away, and she was drifting collegeward afoot, her figure blurred and dim in the rain and fog, and she was crying." To his "private regret," he confided to Howells a few months later, she was beginning to love Bryn Mawr. She had managed to put aside her homesickness and was busy practicing the part of Phyllis in *Iolanthe*. But Clemens was reluctant to leave well enough alone, and he cast about for pretexts for visiting Susy. He would even have delivered her laundry from home if he had been allowed to, Livy told one of Susy's classmates. It was clear that Livy, who had wanted her to go away to college to begin with (and had arranged for the tutoring to prepare her for the entrance examinations), thought it was a good thing for father and daughter to be separated.

Clemens eagerly accepted an invitation from President James E. Rhoads to read to the students at Bryn Mawr on Monday, March 23, 1891, and he took unusual care in planning his program, even though this was the sort of reading he had done time and time again, with Cable or alone. Even the special audience was nothing new to him—he had read at Vassar in 1885 and had taken Susy along with him. In the three successive programs Clemens wrote out in his notebook, the crucial number came to be (as it was at his Vassar reading) the Negro ghost story he had learned as a boy on his uncle's farm near Florida, Missouri, and had been telling ever since, on the stage, at dinner tables, in living rooms: A man digs up his wife's body to take her golden arm, solid gold from the shoulder down; he hears her accusing voice—"Who got my golden arm?"—growing nearer and louder; he himself is half dead of terror; the voice, now at his head, cries out, "*You've* got it!" He made it a hair-raising story, even for those who heard him tell it over and over again.

For Clemens "The Golden Arm" had an extraordinary range of associations and covert meanings. (At the time, his own golden arm was worthless from the shoulder down.) It was one of his most effective performances (the actor Hal Holbrook recently showed just how effective the story still is). As Clemens theorized about it, and he theorized very rarely about his craft, it became the supreme illustration of the art of the oral story—the basic model for his best work. It depended for its effect "upon the *manner* of the telling" and the timing of the pause before the "snapper" at the end. "If I got the right length precisely," he said in 1897 in *How to Tell a Story*, "I could spring the finishing ejaculation with effect enough to make some impressible girl deliver a startled little yelp and jump out of her seat—and that was what I was after." But, as he described "The Golden Arm" to

Joel Chandler Harris years earlier, it was more than "a lovely story to tell." It was also a kind of cautionary economic fable about a man who was willing "to risk his soul and his nightly peace forever" for the sake of wealth. Here again in Mark Twain's pattern of associations the relationship with a woman has got turned into money.

Susy had been hearing her father tell "The Golden Arm" as long as she could remember; by the time she heard it at Vassar she had made up her mind not to be frightened, but she was frightened all the same. She hated the story not only because it terrified her but also because there were implicit parallels that were bound to set up some disturbing subliminal vibrations. An anxious and sensitive child like Susy could easily believe that her adored and invalid mother was dying every time she fell ill; there was something unpleasant in this story of her father's about a dead wife. The children knew also that their father, in order to support his household and his ventures (and to send Susy to Bryn Mawr) was increasingly dependent on his wife's wealth (and it might as well be mentioned that Livy's money, derived from coal, was dug up out of the ground, just like the golden arm).

Susy begged him not to read his ghost story at Bryn Mawr; her reason, as she explained to a classmate, was that it was not right for a "sophisticated group." "*Promise* me that you will not tell the ghost story," she said when she met him at the station. He laughed, patted her on the head, and promised, even though at no time had he considered leaving it out of the program. She trembled through the reading. Toward the end she whispered to a friend, "He's going to tell the ghost story—I *know* he's going to tell the ghost story. And he's going to say 'Boo' at the end and make them all jump." When he started the story, she ran up the aisle and out of the room, weeping.

"All I could hear was your voice saying, 'Please don't tell the ghost story, Father—promise not to tell the ghost story,'" he said later, taking her in his arms, "and I could think of *nothing* else. Oh, my dear, my dear, how could I!" For this and for so much else, willed and unwilled, that had happened over the past five years he was back where he seemed determined to be, on his knees begging forgiveness.

VII

"Stop street sprinkling—and electric lights—and publications—and clubs, three years—and pensions," Clemens reminded himself that spring; stop the telephone, sell the piano, the pew, the horses, find places for the butler and the coachman. Hamersley, the first of a long line of creditors he would eventually have to face, demanded his money back; the best Clemens could offer was a seventy-five-day note. He told Howells that for Livy's health they had decided to go to Europe for an indefinite stay, take the baths during the summer and spend winters in Berlin. It was a matter of necessity, he said. "Travel has no longer any charm for me. I have seen all the foreign countries I want to see except heaven and hell." Howells could have guessed another reason for going: the house had finally become too much for Clemens to keep up. After seventeen years the mansion on Farmington Avenue was stripped bare, furniture, carpets, and books had gone to the warehouse. Clemens' footsteps echoed in the empty rooms. Outside the conservatory door waited another symbol of Nook Farm's twilight: Harriet Beecher Stowe, holding flowers in her hands, smiled vaguely, and made strange noises. "This maniac," as he now called her, escaped daily from her hired Irish companion and wandered about frightening people with "her hideous gobblings."

"We are going to a world where there are no watermelons, and not much other food or cookery." On June 6, 1891, the Clemenses sailed for France on the *Gascoigne*, to be gone for more than eight of the next nine years and as a family never to live in Hartford again. On shipboard he wrote down some topics for the travel letters he had just contracted to write for the McClure Syndicate, and he added a familiar note of quite a different sort: "Tom and Huck die."

CHAPTER FIFTEEN

"Get me out of business!"

I

DURING THE SUMMER of 1891 Clemens and Livy placed their two oldest daughters at boarding school in Geneva and, looking for relief for the rheumatism that now crippled both of them, visited the fashionable watering places, Aix-les-Bains and then Marienbad. In between, with tickets bought months in advance, they attended the equally fashionable Wagner festival at Bayreuth. Clemens' feelings about this rite of cultural piety, performed in the cavernous Festspielhaus (he called it "the Shrine of St. Wagner") were those of an unreconstructed admirer of spirituals and minstrel shows who would always apologize to his children for his taste in music. He preferred Wagner in pantomime, he said; the singing in *Lohengrin* reminded him of "the time the orphan asylum burned down."

Clemens' travels and appearances were in part dictated by his standing as the most celebrated American in Germany. He dined at the right hand of the Kaiser, who, having dropped one pilot recently, was happy to entertain another and told Clemens that *Life on the Mississippi* was his best book. Helmholtz called on him. He was twice mistaken for the students' idol, the seventy-five-year-old Mommsen, a little man with long hair and an Emersonian face. A new six-volume edition of his works was being published in Stuttgart. He had a reputation to live up to, whatever the price in money and privacy might be. In Berlin that winter the family lasted only two humiliating months in a cheap apartment across Körnerstrasse from a warehouse before they moved into an eight-room suite in an Unter den Linden hotel from which they could watch imperial Wilhelm ride past. They saved money by taking their meals in the public dining room, where Clemens' entrance created a sensation. Sometimes, as he ate with his family, strangers stood only a few yards away to watch him and perhaps overhear a scrap of table talk. He was not at all embarrassed; to

Clara he even seemed "utterly unconscious" of such attentions. Howells, walking on Fifth Avenue with him years later, recognized how much Clemens actually delighted in the turned head and the undisguised stare.

Years of wealth and social pre-eminence had made Clemens and Livy unable to economize for long in any significant way. The enormous villa in Florence that they were soon to rent needed a brigade of servants to make it habitable. Their style of living in Berlin and elsewhere, boarding schools and all, made only small, nominal concessions to the pressures that weighed heavier and heavier upon him. "I have never felt so desperate in my life," he had written to his publishing partner, Fred Hall, soon after the collapse of yet another scheme to rehabilitate the typesetter, "for I haven't got a penny to my name." They were altogether dependent on what he could earn with his disabled writing hand and on the small sum—barely enough to keep them two months even in Europe, he figured in July 1891—that Livy's brother was holding for her.

Late that summer Clemens made a symbolic return to the river, to the one source of vitality that had never yet failed him. He left his family in Lausanne, bought a flat-bottomed boat, hired a man to steer it and a courier to take care of the travel arrangements, and set out on a ten-day trip down the Rhone from Châtillon on Lake Bourget to Lyons, Vienne, Avignon, and finally Arles. He drifted downriver by day, smoking, reading, and writing under a canopy that reminded him of a covered wagon, and spent the nights ashore. Nothing compares with a raft voyage, he wrote to Twichell, recalling the delight he always took in such trips, for "extinction from the world and newspapers, and a conscience in a state of coma, and lazy comfort, and solid happiness. In fact there's *nothing* that's so lovely." But for all its associations with his boyhood idyl, Samuel's Rhone journey, his attempt in late middle age to recapture some of the simplicity and freedom of Huck and Jim on their raft, had somber Nibelung overtones. This passive surrender to the river's larger rhythm—"to glide down the river in an open boat, moved by the current only" and to experience a "strange absence of sense of sin, and the stranger absence of the desire to commit it"—might, he hoped, refresh and replenish him as a writer. But it also prefigured the next five or six years, whose tragic symbols were to be so many futile voyages across the oceans; his will, talents, and powers increasingly frustrated, the luck he always counted on clearly running out, Clemens became a victim of circumstance, a man on the run.

And in fact this once the river did fail him. His ten days became all too deliberately a search for travel copy for William Laffan's New York *Sun*. His posthumously published account, "Down the Rhone," is Albert Bigelow Paine's devitalized abridgment of a projected book-length manuscript which Clemens began, returned to over the next ten or so years, and could never finish. Its title, *The Innocents Adrift*, describes his own state.

During his years in Europe the volume and range of quality of his work was considerable, but even that part of it written in haste but with dead aim for ready money reflects his compulsion not only to go back over familiar ground but also to let the current of the river take him further and further back in time. In *Pudd'nhead Wilson*, a sustained, powerful satire in which as a novelist he took his last long look at America, he returned to Hannibal, now become Dawson's Landing, like Hadleyburg an archetypal town enclosing a somber but not totally despairing vision of the race. The confused course of the composition of the book reveals all too well Mark Twain's faltering sense of direction during the 1890s. He began this novel about slavery, moral decay, and deceptive realities as a mistaken-identity farce about Siamese twins, a subject which had long fascinated him. "It changed itself from a farce to a tragedy," he said, explaining the painful process—the rewritings nearly killed him—by which *The Tragedy of Pudd'nhead Wilson* came to be equipped with a pendant piece called *The Comedy of Those Extraordinary Twins*. "I pulled one of the stories out by the roots, and left the other one—a kind of literary Caesarian operation."

He also returned once again to the matter of Hannibal in *Tom Sawyer Abroad*, an adventure story with antecedents in Jules Verne. Tom and Huck are "still fifteen years old" when they set out on their voyage in a self-propelled balloon. The "genius" who invented this mechanical marvel —which, for purposes of the story, is basically just an airborne raft—is a combination of Pap Finn and James W. Paige. He is a mad professor who falls into a drunken, paranoidal rage and is, in effect, murdered by Tom, who pushes him overboard into the Atlantic. After this start the story was more or less conventional going for the young readers of Mrs. Mary Dodge's *St. Nicholas Magazine*. After writing *Tom Sawyer Abroad* Mark Twain continued to go back in time. During 1893 and 1894 he seriously made plans for a monthly magazine of which he was to be editor and publisher, figured costs for a first issue of twenty thousand copies, and wrote a draft of a prospectus. The contents were to be gathered from old autobiographies and reminiscences, from "moldy old newspapers and moldy old books." The purpose of the magazine was to call up "the great yesterdays, the sublime yesterdays, the immemorial yesterdays of all time." Clemens tried to explain his own sense that the past was becoming more immediate to him than the present: "The word 'yesterday' seems to whisk us back and set us face to face with the occurrence and make it a personal affair to us." And the title of this venture, suggesting his awareness of time passing and powers failing, was to be *The Back Number*. But he was never able to persuade any publisher to make the experiment; years later, in 1906, he was still sorry that the idea remained only an idea.

In 1893 he had turned instead to the distant yesterday of Joan of Arc's Domrémy. Having been betrayed by the dynamo, he threw himself at the feet of the virgin and wrote an idealization of nonsexual (and, as he understood it, constitutionally non-nubile)* young womanhood which was so single-mindedly devout and so unabashedly sentimental that for once even Susy (from whom he secretly drew Joan's physical portrait) was thoroughly proud and pleased. It promised to be "his loveliest book," she told Clara, "perhaps even more sweet and beautiful than *The Prince and the Pauper;*" to hear him read aloud from his manuscript was "uplifting and revealing." *Joan of Arc* was an act of piety for him, and he explained over and over again that he wrote it out of love, "not for lucre." If it was to be published at all he wanted it published anonymously, as if Mark Twain and his laughter had never existed.

Joan was to be his refuge from hard work, quick business trips to America, and poor health. In Berlin during October 1891 he worked himself into exhaustion by spending three days and nights translating into English Dr. Heinrich Hoffman's children's classic, *Struwwelpeter*. He wanted his translation either published as a book right away, in time to catch the Christmas trade, or sold to McClure as a serial "for several hundred dollars." Fred Hall, by now accustomed to Clemens' hand-to-mouth planning and impatience with the normal pace of book publishing, said he could manage it neither way, and along with other abandoned manuscripts Mark Twain's *Slovenly Peter* went into the trunk, not to be published until 1935. During the winter of 1891–92 Clemens was in bed for over a month with what started out as a racking cough and turned into influenza and congestion of the lungs. He came out of his sickroom at the end of February with one lung permanently damaged, an unshakable head cold, and rheumatic threatenings so severe he could hardly pick up a pen. Months later, his own health apparently restored, he reported to Orion that he was "in the clouds": the doctors at Bad Nauheim were now positive that Livy did not have heart disease but only a "weakness of the heart muscles" which they said would improve with rest. But by the time Clemens was ready to leave Bad Nauheim for Italy in September Livy was suffering from severe headaches, and her neck and face were grossly swollen. The same doctors said it might be erysipelas. More likely it was the onset of acute hyperthyroid heart disease. Throughout the rest of her life she was subject to attacks of shortness of breath, complained of the heat and of overexcitement, and was terrified, when her attacks were severe, that she was choking to death. That summer Clemens

---

* In his copy of Jules Michelet's *Jeanne d'Arc* (1853), opposite a passage citing the testimony of some Domrémy women that Joan had never menstruated, Clemens noted: "The higher life absorbed her and suppressed her physical (sexual) development."

and Livy observed an alarming change in Jean's personality: she had become contrary, rude, and sullen. He harshly concluded that her "*real nature*" had finally emerged and that her former gentle and lovable personality had been only "an artificial production due to parental restraint and watchfulness." Four years later he gave up this sort of moralizing, for she had had a convulsion at school and all her earlier symptoms were now explained: she was an epileptic.

"A fine soft-fibered little fellow with the perversest twang and drawl, but very human and good," William James wrote to Josiah Royce from Florence in 1892. "I should think one might grow very fond of him." Clemens had come to Florence in search of a house for the year. He settled on Villa Viviani at Settignano, a hill village about five miles outside the city. Livy's health seemed to improve when they moved there late in September, "and the best is yet to come," he believed. Soon, however, she had dysentery and was weak and wasted away. Clemens was afflicted with some scalp ailment and had to have all his hair cut off. "I seem able to forget everything except that I have had my head shaved," he noted. He was bothered by drafts and itching, by flies walking on his head. He was bothered most of all by a real and symbolic divestment of identity and power, and he went into seclusion, which he welcomed. Yet he made the most of it, in his way, for he sprang the bald surprise on his daughters one morning. He stood silently in the doorway of Susy's bedroom. She saw him, gave a little cry, and blushed. He had paid her back, no doubt, in this cruel but self-abasing way, for some friction between them, some infraction of the cast-iron Victorian code by which he sternly forbade his daughters to go unchaperoned in Europe or to be exposed to public view. Clara too suffered. Still shuddering at the image of her father's naked head, she escaped for the winter to Berlin, where she was studying music, but letters of strictest advice from him followed her. "We want you to be a lady—a lady above reproach," he scolded; he heard that she had allowed herself to be the only female in a room full of admiring German officers. He had recently locked her in her hotel room after he caught her exchanging glances with a young man. Years later, after he saw some Italian officers in a tearoom staring at her, he took a scissors to her hat and cut off the artificial fruit because he thought it was coquettish and provocative. Nor was Susy to be happy in Florence. She went to the theater and the opera "to ease the dullness of eternal study," he recognized sympathetically, but still there were tensions between them—she dreaded going down to breakfast with him, "altho' Papa hasn't stormed yet."

The square stone house was so vast that he thought of setting a time and a room for the family to find each other once a day. There was a constant confounding of tongues among the servants and their employers:

the cook and the butler were Italian, the housekeeper was French, one maid was German and one Irish. Still, both Clemens and Livy managed to find quiet and rest. "There is going to be absolute seclusion here—a hermit life, in fact," he said. He needed a "serene and noiseless life," and he was able to turn out an enormous volume of work: eighteen hundred pages in five months, he told Hall. There was a chance, he now began to feel, that he might be able to keep his family out of the poorhouse. He stopped work only when the sun set over the hills west of Florence, and then he had tea on the terrace under the olive trees, smoked his pipe, took his ease. He was enchanted with the view—"drunk with pleasure all the time"—but still he remembered other views. "It cannot be compared with the sun on the Mississippi," he told Grace King, and he talked about pilots and steamboating and, one evening, half jokingly about hell. "I don't believe in it," he said, "but I'm afraid of it. When I wake up at night, I think of hell, and I am sure about going there." "Why, Youth," Livy said, "who, then, can be saved?"

II

Between June 1892, when he returned to the United States alone for a month, and May 1894, when he came back to Europe a bankrupt, Clemens made eight Atlantic crossings and was away from Livy for about a year altogether; one period of seven months during 1893 and 1894 was the longest separation of their married life. He was called from his European seclusion by the worsening condition of his publishing house, which was now collapsing under the weight of the ten-volume *Library of American Literature*, and also, at first, by a revival of hope in the typesetter. Clemens estimated the potential value of that one publishing project at well over half a million dollars; his share of the machine he carried on his psychological books at about a quarter of a million plus the value of his one sixth of Paige's patent. What both ventures needed, of course, was a large administration of cash. Directly and through Hall he was plotting a $100,000 loan from Carnegie, who resisted all invitations to diversify his investments and even, in an epigram which Clemens soon made famous, defended a contrary policy. "Put all your eggs into one basket," Carnegie is supposed to have said, "and watch that basket."

One problem with the machine, as always, was that it was worthless until a company could start manufacturing it, and here, Clemens recognized, was the deadlock. "Nothing *but* a Co. can manufacture—and P is determined there never shall be one, except on his terms—and they will never be granted." After less than a month in New York and Hartford he concluded it was futile even to visit Paige, and, distraught and lonely, he sailed for Europe once again and played the fool. "I am a Yale man now, you know," he said, citing the honorary M.A. he had received in 1888, and he injected himself into the company of a group of sixteen members of the class of 1892, on their way to taste the wicked pleasures of the Continent. On the last night out he submitted to a mock trial on the charge of "outrageous and habitual lying" and was sentenced to solitary confinement in his cabin with only his own books to read. He talked too much, monopolized attention in the first-class smoking room, and told mildly smutty stories which shocked the boys, who remembered him long after as a not so entertaining humorist, a garrulous older man who had drunk more champagne than was good for him and was up past his bedtime.

Eight months later, in April 1893, he was back again in New York, hoping to break the Paige deadlock but also full of remorse for having left his family behind in what he still considered near-penurious exile. "My dear darling child," Livy tried to console him, "you *must not* blame yourself as you do." But soon he was as deeply involved with the machine as he had been before he swore off. It actually seemed to be in production at a factory on Eighteenth Street and Broadway. Fifty machines were well along, Paige assured him, but this would never do; the factory could turn out only one a day, and how could the immediate market for ten thousand machines be satisfied? The answer, Paige went on hypnotically, ignoring the rumblings of the panic that was soon to sweep the country (the Philadelphia and Reading Railroad had already gone into receivership; in May the rope trust was to fail), was to shift the manufacturing operation to Chicago, where some huge company seemed to be willing to put up all the money for a factory with an eventual capacity of five machines a day. Paige's improved machine could now set thirteen thousand ems an hour: "Competition is impossible." Once again under Paige's spell, with the future suddenly seeming quite bright, Clemens sent off jubilant letters to Livy which made her "just about wild with pleasurable excitement. It does not seem credible that we are really again to have money to *spend*," she answered from Florence. "It is astonishing to think that perhaps there is not yet a very long time for us to keep up this economy." He celebrated by going off on a round of lunches and dinners, with Rudyard Kipling and his wife, Howells, Mary Mapes Dodge, Charles Warren Stoddard, and Andrew Carnegie, who tried to interest him in a scheme for absorbing Great Britain, Ireland, and Canada into an American commonwealth.

In mid-April he went to Chicago with Hall, only to spend eleven days sick in bed with a bad cold at the Great Northern Hotel, smoking against his doctor's orders, reading Mrs. Gaskell's *Cranford*, and receiving a stream of visitors, including Eugene Field. Orion came up from Keokuk to see Sam and the machine, and to look for work. Paige, overflowing with confidence and good will, came to apologize for all past bitterness and misunderstanding and promised Clemens half the money forthcoming from the Chicago backers. Clemens still wanted proof that all along he had not been dealt with "in an absolutely shameless and conscienceless way," but, as usual, he was impressed by Paige, "the smoothest talker I ever saw," who gave him "an abundance of gilt-edge promises." Hall, who had listened to praises of the machine all the way from New York to Chicago, rushed to see it in action. As usual, it was dismantled. Whatever premonitions Clemens had he took out on Orion, and Hall was shocked not only by Clemens' sarcasms but by the unprotesting silence with which Orion received them. Sam's sixty-eight-year-old brother sitting by his bedside now seemed more than ever failure and futility in the flesh, a warning. Unaware as always of his effect on Sam, Orion a week or so later gave him a pretty comprehensive report of unsuccess. He had tried to get the job of Columbian Exposition correspondent for the Keokuk *Gate City* and then the St. Louis *Republican;* he had tried to get a job with a Keokuk law firm; he had tried to sell an article to a magazine; and he failed in every one of these attempts. He and Mollie would have to scrimp along on their monthly remittance from Sam, keeping careful account of ten cents' worth of coffee beans and fifteen cents' worth of crackers, and dodging the collector from the water works.

With a sense of having accomplished absolutely nothing, Clemens left Chicago without even a preliminary glimpse of the White City at the World's Fair; he returned to New York too late to see the great international naval parade on the Hudson. The Columbian year had also come and gone without seeing the realization of his cherished scheme to buy up the Discoverer's bones and put them on exhibit. "It was wonderful to find America," he was soon to write at the end of *Pudd'nhead Wilson,* "but it would have been more wonderful to miss it."

Back in Europe that summer he was racked with worry. The stock market crashed in June. One after another—the Erie in July, the Northern Pacific in August—the great railroads, more than seventy of them, were failing. Before the year was out five hundred banks and nearly sixteen thousand businesses had collapsed, and the American people, a London financial journal remarked, were "in the throes of a fiasco unprecedented even in their broad experience." Clemens' publishing house, an unsound enterprise even in the most favoring business circumstances, had borrowed heavily and was clearly headed for ruin. "Get me out of business!" he wrote to Hall, "and I will be yours forever gratefully." "I think Mr. Clemens is right in feeling that he should get out of business, that he is not fitted for it," Livy agreed. "It worries him too much." Yet in "these hideous times" of a panic year it was going to be hard to find anybody to buy anything, especially a company in trouble. Although Clemens knew that the machine offered only "a doubtful outlook," that it was tough on prophets, and that even now (thirteen years and about $190,000 since his first investment) it might not be ready for a long time to perform reliably in a printing office, he kept hoping. And then the hope began to fade. "I watch for your letters hungrily," he wrote to Hall from London on August 9, "as I used to watch for the cablegram saying the machine's finished—but when 'next week *certainly*' suddenly swelled into 'three weeks *sure*' I recognized the old familiar tune I used to hear so much." A week later, with not a glimmer of daylight visible and now terrified that he might have to assign even his copyrights and thus become "a beggar," he made the reluctant decision: "I am coming over, just as soon as I can get the family moved and settled."

When he returned to New York early in September, leaving the others in Paris for the winter, the business cyclone was gusting harder than ever. At first he saw some hope for his personal finances: he sold a story to *Cosmopolitan* for eight hundred dollars, which he kept for his expenses in New York, and he sold the serial rights in *Pudd'nhead Wilson* to the *Century* for an eventual $6,500. A week later, though, he was plunged once again into the entrepreneurial nightmare. "The billows of hell have been rolling over me," he wrote Livy from Frank Fuller's New Jersey farm, where he had gone to recuperate after a terrible week. With eight thousand dollars in notes about to fall due, the publishing house seemed to be going under. Clemens could not raise the money in New York. Nor could he raise the money in Hartford, where the friends of the old affluent days, hard hit like everyone else, seemed to him hardly interested, hardly moved by his distress, and he came back to New York ashamed of himself for having tried. He was resigned to another round of futile appeals up and down Wall Street. Even the Langdon family could come up with only five thousand dollars in negotiable bonds, not enough to save the firm, Hall told him. At the Murray Hill Hotel on Friday evening, September 15—the notes fell due the following Monday—his friend and physician, Clarence Rice, with whom he was staying, arranged for him to talk to someone Rice described as a rich businessman who admired Mark Twain's books and read them aloud to his wife and children. This man had learned of Clemens' troubles, and wanted to help, if he could. They talked, and at the end of the evening the businessman told Clemens to send Hall in the morning to 26 Broadway, where a check for eight thousand dollars, with the firm's assets as security, would be forthcoming. Utterly worn out in mind and body, and suffering from a cough so violent that, as he was told a week or so later, it had caused a hernia, Clemens came back to Rice's apartment on East Nineteenth Street and before falling asleep managed to write a few lines to Clara on a prescription blank: "The best new acquaintance I've ever seen has helped us over Monday's bridge. I got acquainted with him on a yacht two years ago." A few months later, after this benefactor had taken over all the problems of the typesetter and had also arranged another transfusion for the publishing house in the form of a purchase offer from a publisher (the benefactor's son-in-law, it turned out) for the firm's millstone, the *Library of American Literature*, Clemens described him as "the only man *I* care for in the world; the only man I would give a *damn* for." In 1902 he wrote, "He is not only the best friend I ever had, but is the best man I have ever known."

This benefactor, it soon became public knowledge, was Henry Huttleston Rogers, fifty-three years old, one of the chief architects of the Standard Oil trust and, according to the common stereotype of that trust as all horns and tail, one of its arch villains.* Together with John D. Archbold and William Rockefeller he was in operating control of the trust's daily affairs. Of the twenty companies that in 1895 made up the "interests" of the vast amalgamation, Rogers was a director of thirteen and of these was president of six, and he might just as well have been president of the other seven, for he let it be known that "all meetings where I sit as director vote first and talk after I am gone." From his offices on the eleventh floor of the Standard Oil Building at 26 Broadway his interests eventually extended beyond oil and pipelines into gas, copper, steel, coal, municipal traction, nails, rails, insurance, and the stock market, and he often left behind him a wake of ruined competitors and thwarted investigations. "We are not in business for our health," he said in a moment of candor to a governmental commission, "but are out for the dollars," and to defend that principle he became as skillful a master of the evasive answer—and of the finely controlled inexactitude just this side of outright perjury—as John D. Rockefeller was of plain silence. In an era of freeboot-

* Howells, whose critical judgments about American plutocracy were more consistent if less passionately stated than Clemens', had played a role in creating this stereotype. Just before resigning his *Atlantic* editorship at the beginning of 1881, he arranged to publish in the March issue, some pages ahead of an installment of Henry James's *Portrait of a Lady*, a pioneering exposé, "The Story of a Great Monopoly," by Henry Demarest Lloyd, then one of the editors of the Chicago *Tribune*. Lloyd's article, previously rejected by the *North American Review* on the grounds that it was explosive and possibly actionable, was the first all-out attack on Standard Oil for general circulation and the source of the basic image of that trust as the implacable enemy of competition and the public interest. The March *Atlantic* went through seven printings in order to meet the demand for Lloyd's article, which was subsequently reprinted in England and circulated in Australia. "The Story of a Great Monopoly" was also the germ of Lloyd's dissection of monopoly and Spencerian economics in general, *Wealth against Commonwealth* (1894). Again Howells was responsible for placing it—with Harper and Brothers, who, as fearful of the consequences as the several other publishers to whom Lloyd submitted the manuscript, had originally declined it. We shall come to Mark Twain's tangential but highly charged connection with Lloyd's book.

ing Rogers distinguished himself for daring, rapacity, intrigue, and a total lack of business scruples. In his *Who's Who* listing he called himself simply a "Capitalist." His enemies, among whom were victims with life-long scars and grudges, called him "Hell Hound" Rogers, invoked comparisons with rattlesnakes, sharks, and tigers, and in compassionate moments saw him as the victim of a "cannibalistic money-hunger" which turned him into "a fiend."

But the same enemies recognized a paradox. Any man who had Rogers as a friend, it seemed, was thrice blessed as the beneficiary of his company, protection, and fiscal advice. He was handsome and vigorous, he had hypnotic charm and social brilliance, he was a superb host and storyteller, and he was capable of enormous kindness, generosity, and delicacy. His services to Mark Twain, which rescued a great writer from probable destruction and the entire Clemens family from shame and poverty, were founded on affection and admiration, and Rogers had to render these services with especial tact as well as shrewdness. From the start Livy's pride as well as Clemens' eliminated the possibility of a disguised gift or personal loan, although by Rogers' standards the amounts involved were relatively small. Later on he took considerable pains to deny the imputation that he had been speculating for Clemens' account. He was helping a writer, but, unlike an Otto Kahn, he had to do it in ways that were acceptable to a fellow man of affairs and standing who was also his friend. His association and frequent appearances with Mark Twain could only help rehabilitate his own (and Standard Oil's) public image. Still, he put no overt demands on Clemens. Rogers also paid for Helen Keller's education, was a patron of the arts, and with Carnegie gave money to Cooper Union in New York. To the town of Fairhaven, Massachusetts, where he had delivered groceries and newspapers as a boy and was still known to some as "Hen," he gave paved streets, school buildings, a Masonic lodge, a town hall, a library and a Unitarian church and parsonage. He was not, therefore, lacking in social utility. The trouble was that, like any *condottiere*, he believed that justice consisted in being kind to his friends and ruthless to his enemies, and since he, like his compeers, understood economic life to be a raw state of nature, anyone who stood between him and his next acquisition was likely to be treated as an enemy.

For Mark Twain, who all his life had plutocratic ambitions but at the same time believed that money was evil and created evil, there had to be a price for any alliance he would make with archetypal plutocracy. The representative of a broad spectrum of paradox, as a writer he stood outside American society of the Gilded Age, but as a businessman he embraced its business values. When he went bankrupt and then not only paid off his creditors to the last cent but even became a rich man all over again, he re-enacted the capitalist passion and resurrection. "Our friend entered the fiery furnace a man," Andrew Carnegie said of him, "and emerged a hero." He was the idol of the common man and also the pet and protégé of the very rich, but though he was naïve at times about the very rich he rarely became their apologist. He once said about Rogers, "He's a pirate all right, but he owns up to it and enjoys being a pirate. That's the reason I like him." The satirist and moralist was always breaking in. "The political and commercial morals of the United States are not merely food for laughter," he said in an autobiographical dictation in 1907, "they are an entire banquet." He took a savage pleasure in the egotistic gambols of Andrew Carnegie. "He has bought fame," he said of Carnegie's public libraries, "and paid cash for it." He took the same savage pleasure in examining the marriage of plutocracy and Christianity. John D. Rockefeller, Jr., applied "the fox fire of his mind" to arguing that "Sell all thou hast and give to the poor" didn't apply to money at all, but to anything that stood between a man and salvation; by this interpretation, Clemens reasoned, the Rockefellers' millions were "a mere incident in their lives," of no importance to them at all. (The Rockefellers' notion that they were merely the custodians of wealth, Mr. Dooley said at about this time, made them "a kind iv a society f'r th' previntion iv croolty to money.") When in 1907 Judge Kenesaw Mountain Landis fined Standard Oil of Indiana a total of $29,240,000 for violating the Elkins Act against rebates, Clemens was reminded of what the bride said the next morning: "I expected it but didn't suppose it would be so big." But this sort of hilarity he generally kept as private as the diatribes against money, money men, and money morality which he spoke as from the grave, intending them for his posthumous autobiography.

The price of his becoming a provisional member of the plutocracy was a certain blunting and demoralizing of purpose, a sense of powerlessness and drift. He began to see himself, and everyone else, as driven by self-interest and the compulsion to conform. "You tell me whar a man gits his corn pone," he liked to quote, "and I'll tell you what his 'pinions is." The price was also the stilling of a magnificent public voice presented with a magnificent public subject. He had not been bought out. It was largely a matter of loyalty to Rogers, to whom he felt he owed his life and whom he worshiped, and this loyalty excluded all other considerations. Clemens accepted this personal code despite all the contradictions it carried with it. And it was clear from the start that the price he volunteered to pay was public silence. By some horrendous misjudgment George Warner, Charles Dudley Warner's brother and a friend of Henry Demarest Lloyd, approached Clemens during the autumn of 1893 and suggested that there might be a "splendid chance" open to him as a publisher if he were to take on Lloyd's *Wealth against Commonwealth*, which was then making the rounds at Harper, Houghton Mifflin, and Appleton. "I know a man—

a prominent man—who has written a book that will go like wildfire," Warner said, "a book that arraigns the Standard Oil fiends, and gives them unmitigated hell, individual by individual. It is the very book for you to publish."* Clemens swallowed his rage and the temptation to tell Warner that it was one of those fiends who (in contrast to the genial folks at Nook Farm) was keeping him and his family out of the poorhouse. He was proud enough of the self-control he had shown with Warner to tell Livy about it. He had answered that he "wanted to get out of the publishing business and out of *all* business" and therefore was not interested in taking on any sort of book. Orion too, having learned of the role that Rogers was playing, accepted his brother's simple code, and with characteristic ease he disembarrassed himself in one instant of a conviction he and a good part of the American population had held for years. "I have been abusing the Standard Oil Company," he apologized to Sam. "I did not know it was run by angels."

III

During the bleak autumn and winter of 1893–94 over two and a half million men were out of work. The tramp, wandering from city to city, was as familiar on the American landscape as the silent factory and the deserted mine pit. "If we have built many railroads, we have wrecked many," Howells wrote in the February *North American Review*, "and those vast continental lines which, with such a tremendous expenditure of competitive force, we placed in control of the monopolies, have passed into the hands of the receivers, the agents of an unconscious state socialism. . . . In our paradise of toil, myriads of workingmen want work." Writing to Livy from his economy room at the Players Club on Gramercy Park, Clemens also expressed the national despair, in terms of his own situation. He was full of shame and remorse at having brought his family to the edge of ruin. He foresaw the terrible necessity of mounting the lecture platform again, first in India and Australia while presumably his own

* Clemens' account of this conversation does not mention the author or the title of the book Warner proposed to him. But it seems clear that the book was Lloyd's *Wealth against Commonwealth*. Warner's description fits no other book by "a prominent man" at that precise time, when Lloyd was having trouble finding a publisher. Warner was a close enough friend of Lloyd's to act as his informal intermediary in placing the book. When Warner visited him at Winnetka Lloyd confided to him that "he expected to be *crushed* by the Standard people" for what he had said in the book. It is ironic, in view of Clemens' categorical refusal to have anything to do with the book, that in it Lloyd, discussing Rockefeller's elusive South Improvement Company, quoted Mark Twain on sin in the Sandwich Islands: "no longer exists in name —only in reality."

country was recovering from the depression. He was desperately lonely, minding their separation more and more, absent-minded at times, distracted enough with anxiety to forget to mail his letters to Livy. "A body forgets pretty much everything, these days, except his visions of the poorhouse," he wrote.

Rogers, who had taken over the supervision of all of Clemens' business interests, including the typesetter, had said to him, "You stop walking the floor," and while one rescue scheme or another was being tried out, Clemens, hungry for public activity to keep his mind off his troubles, hungry for public adulation, submerged himself in an intense social life. He was busy from the beginning of one day until far into the beginning of the next. Then, wanting sleep and oblivion, he went back to his room and fell asleep immediately, or he drugged himself with whiskey and slept as soundly as a dead person. He led the sort of public existence which, years later, would prompt Howells to regret that his friend was eating too many dinners and writing too few books.

He was busy turning down invitations, inventing ways to cut short some of those that he did accept. During one day alone he might have a breakfast engagement, dinner engagements at three and again at seven, a couple of business conferences, and then an evening party of magic-lantern slides and stories at Mary Mapes Dodge's apartment off Central Park, or billiards at the Racquet Club with William Laffan, or supper and dancing to a Hungarian band until four-thirty in the morning. The Lotos Club gave a banquet in his honor at which, in response to superabundant praise and welcome, he gave no fewer than three speeches. He dined at Charles Dana's house, where he had a "shouting good time" telling "Captain Stormfield's Visit to Heaven" and learning from a retired diplomat that copies of *Tom Sawyer* and *Huckleberry Finn* had been seen on Bismarck's writing desk, in the Czarina's boudoir, and in the private parlor of the President of Chile. He dined at Delmonico's with Sir Henry Irving, a five-hundred-dollar investor in the typesetter. He dined without fear of indigestion on oysters and corned beef and cabbage with John Mackay, traded Comstock anecdotes, inscribed to Mackay a copy of *Roughing It* in token of a thirty-one-year friendship. Mackay told him that any message, any time, that he wanted to send to Livy would go free via Postal Telegraph cables, with Mackay's personal frank. He went to Fairhaven to speak at the dedication of Rogers' town hall. In Boston, at Annie Fields's house on Charles Street, he dined with Sarah Orne Jewett and with Dr. Holmes, now eighty-four and failing in sight. Holmes tired easily and he rarely went out, but this evening he was as sparkling as ever, refused to go home until late, was full of compliments, and was delighted to be told once again that his *Autocrat* had been Clemens' courting book and was kept along with the love letters in Livy's green tin box. Holmes said he had the *Century*'s monthly installments of *Pudd'nhead Wilson* read aloud to him as they came out. These installments were causing a stir everywhere, even on the floor of the New York Stock Exchange—one of its governors, Theodore Wilson, was suspected of being the original Pudd'nhead and someone circulated a petition for his removal.

The chorus of praise was unremitting, and Clemens generally fed on it. "I can stand considerable petting," he said. He was delighted to be told that his fame was both "substantial and permanent," to be accosted on the El by a prosperous-looking master mechanic who said, "You look enough like Mark Twain to sit for his portrait." Dr. Rice told him that his welcome to New York had been "phenomenal," that the people loved him. John D. Archbold, who each morning whistled "Onward, Christian Soldiers" as he entered his office at 26 Broadway, took him and Rogers to the prize fights at the New York Athletic Club to see a boxer named the Coffee Cooler flatten a white man in five rounds. As Clemens reported it to Livy, Rogers remarked to Archbold, rather pointedly, it seems, "that other people's successes in this world were made over broken hearts or at the cost of other people's feelings or food, but my fame had cost no one a pang or a penny."

He never felt tired any more, he said. Supporting this manic stamina was a renewed faith in "mind-cure," which he had dabbled in for years as a remedy for colds, headaches, and even astigmatism. Now he and thousands of others were taking it up seriously; the far from gay Nineties saw the founding of Mrs. Eddy's Mother Church in Boston, an event which dramatized the remarkably brief evolution of Christian Science from a sect to a religion. "Do find that Christian Scientist for Susy," he told Livy. Susy now had what a Paris doctor diagnosed as a chest condition stemming from anemia and proposed to treat by gymnastics and massage. Susy and later Clara were to become converts to what their father called "that rational and noble philosophy." Clemens himself, suffering from bronchitis and a chronic cough, was going to a Dr. Whipple at 328 Madison Avenue in New York, recommended to him by George Warner and credited with having so successfully cured a Hartford boy of "heart disease" that the boy was playing football for Yale. During these treatments Whipple sat silent in a corner with his face to the wall while Clemens walked around the room and smoked. Mind cure seemed to work on him (although he conceded the possibility that some homeopathic powders given him by Rogers might have helped, too); it also seemed to work on Elinor Howells, who was going to a lady named Mrs. E. R. de Wolf at 1418 Broadway and whose improvement in health won over even her husband from his view of the whole business as a hoax. Sadly, Clemens told Livy that there were no mind-curists in Europe;

"Get me out of business!"

Whipple said anyone who tried to practice his healing art in France would be put in jail right away. Soon, however, convinced by Elinor Howells that mind cure and hypnotism were really all the same thing, Clemens had a new and urgent proposal for Susy's therapy. "The very source, the very *centre* of hypnotism is *Paris*. Dr. Charcot's pupils and disciples"—among whom, seven years earlier, had been Sigmund Freud— "are right there and ready to your hand," he wrote to Livy, and he asked her to get from John Mackay's wife the name of one of them. "*Do*, do it, honey. Don't lose a minute." Mind cure, beyond the real or imagined physical relief it was giving him, offered Clemens a cure for the blues and an antidote to "the religion of chronic anxiety" (the phrase is William James's) in which he had been raised.* Above all, by making "what in our protestant countries is an unprecedentedly great use of the subconscious life" (again William James), it helped liberate that vast body of dream and fantasy material which, in the late 1890s, he relied on to preserve his sanity.

In addition to his genius as a corporate organizer and manager, Rogers had a strong technological bent. In his late twenties he developed and subsequently patented the first workable process for separating naphtha from crude oil. Consequently, through the tremendous power of his endorsement there occurred a sort of electroconvulsive movement in the late career of the typesetter, which suggested to Clemens that the old dream of being a millionaire might come true after all, if he could only hold on for a while. "I have got the best and wisest man in the whole Standard Oil group of multi-millionaires a good deal interested in looking into the typesetter," he wrote to Livy on October 18, 1893, and he warned her that a rumor of Rogers' even perfunctory interest would send the shares way up. After a preliminary study of several weeks Rogers went to Chicago with a son-in-law, Urban Broughton, for a demonstration. "Let all tests be applied," Clemens ordered. They were, and along with all its sophistications and improvements the machine performed brilliantly. At the same moment that the operator was setting a line on the 109-character keyboard, the machine was testing the previous line for broken and turned types, measuring it, and justifying it, using eleven sizes of space. Since the entire cycle of machine composition was now accomplished almost simultaneously, a skilled operator could turn out unheard-of amounts of work every hour. Rogers was convinced. Cutting through the dense tangle of royalties and options that had been suffocating the venture

* Writing in 1885 to Charles Warren Stoddard, a convert to Catholicism, Clemens said: "I look back with the same shuddering horror upon the days when I believed I believed, as you do upon the days when you were afraid you did not believe."

almost from the start—there were at least three companies involved, including one represented by Hamersley, now described by Clemens as "that cask of rancid guts"—Rogers devised a contract which, it seemed certain, Paige would have to sign. Paige, in Chicago, was down to his last seven dollars; as Orion told Sam, Paige had acted like a snake, but "now you've got the fork on his neck."

"A singularly clear-headed man is Mr. Rogers—this appears at every meeting," Clemens told Livy. "And no grass grows under his feet." From time to time Clemens was treated to displays of Rogers' genius at hard and soft bargaining. He moved easily from hauteur and ultimatum to sudden displays of affability and compromise, even to pleas for sympathy and haste on the grounds that he simply had to get Mr. Clemens off his back. It was better than a circus, Clemens told Livy. "It was beautiful to see Mr. Rogers apply his probe and his bung-starter and remorselessly let out the wind and the water from the so-called 'assets' of these companies."

Three days before Christmas Clemens and Rogers traveled to Chicago in a private car put at their disposal by a vice-president of the Pennsylvania Railroad. In this rolling symbol of the Gilded Age Clemens breakfasted on steaks, chops, and baked potatoes, dined on canvasback duck, claret, and champagne, and after a couple of hot Scotches slept in opulent comfort. They spent a day bargaining with Paige, then returned in the same car and style and got off at Jersey City, where Rogers' coachman was waiting to drive them to New York. Clemens was back at the Players in time to cable a greeting to Livy: "Merry Xmas! Promising progress made in Chicago." And although it would be more than a month before Paige signed the final contract, Clemens could barely control his elation as he moved toward what now seemed certain victory. On January 15, 1894, he learned that Paige had reached an agreement to manufacture; the machine was finally going into production under a sensible contract and that autumn would be put into experimental service at the Chicago *Herald*. Undressing in his room after an evening of billiards, he suddenly felt the weight of three and a half months of desperate worry slip away, suddenly began to believe that he was no longer a pauper deep in debt, and he was overwhelmed. He walked the floor in excitement; at the same time he wanted to sit down and cry. He vowed never to touch business again, but to finish *Joan* and for the rest of his life wallow in writing and swim in ink. "Nearing success," he cabled on January 19, cautious after years of disappointment. Then it became "a ship visible on the horizon, coming down under a cloud of canvas." Finally, on February 2, 1894, he cabled, "Our ship is safe in port."

But the publishing house, as he told Pamela at the end of February, was an altogether different story. Even the Grant *Memoirs*, the towering success of Clemens' career as a publisher, now seemed to him "that terrible book!"; all it had done for him was to get him in deeper. He now had about $110,000 in the firm, which owed Livy $60,000 and various banks and suppliers $83,000. Against this indebtedness there were assets of perhaps $60,000. Determined to get out at any cost, Clemens had considered going into receivership as early as January 1894. After a brief visit to Livy that March and early April he came back to New York to find a repetition of the September crisis and its "billows of hell"; the Mount Morris Bank demanded immediate payment of $10,000 on the firm's notes. There was no point to looking for another transfusion, Rogers told him; he had to decide whether to raise a great deal of money to put the company on a new and solid footing or to give up altogether. On April 16, in the middle of this latest crisis, *Tom Sawyer Abroad* was published in New York and London. That same day, figuring that according to all the signs (including a movement for beatification) Joan of Arc was going to be "the commanding figure" in literature, Clemens decided that he wanted to be at the head of the procession and that he should finish his book as quickly as possible and rush serial publication. To do this he would have to put aside his business distractions. Rogers had told him that bankruptcy was the only rational solution, and also the only compassionate one. How else, Rogers asked, could Clemens ever be relieved of his "fearful load of dread" and go back to writing? Two days later, on Wednesday afternoon, April 18, Clemens entered into voluntary bankruptcy proceedings.

"Cheer up," he wrote to Livy early the next morning, and, in his state of initial shock, before he knew what he was doing he had written, "the worst is yet to come." Yet during the weeks that followed he felt relieved, blithe at times, convinced that this was only a temporary setback and without dishonor. At meeting after meeting with the creditors Rogers was engineering the financial salvation of the Clemens family. He insisted that Livy's $60,000, the largest single claim on the firm, entitled her to be a preferred creditor and that in payment of her claim all of Clemens' copyrights, which later proved to be worth $25,000 and more a year, and his typesetter stock be assigned to her. He insisted that the Hartford house was her personal property and could not be attached. Coached by Rogers before these meetings, Clemens learned to keep silent or at least to resist attempts to anger him into damaging admissions. He even became adept at the legal convention of always referring to "Mrs. Clemens'" copyrights, "her" books, "her" typesetter stock, "her" house and "her" plans for *Pudd'nhead Wilson*.

All his friends told him there was no tinge of disgrace in going into bankruptcy. "Don't let it disturb you, Sam," John Mackay said, "we all have to do it at one time or another, it's nothing to be ashamed of," and historically Mackay was right.* But in Paris after "the hideous news" reached her, Livy was feeling old and wrinkled, convinced that her life was now a failure, full of "*horror* and heartsickness." The ethical implications of bankruptcy practice, always more lenient in America than anywhere else, confused and depressed her. "I cannot get away from the feeling that business failure means disgrace," she wrote. She could not understand how Rogers, as Clemens had reported to her, could be "caustic" with the creditors; "I should think it was the creditors' place to say caustic things to us." She did not want to be a preferred creditor, and she was afraid that in order to protect the family Clemens and Rogers would turn to brutal bargaining and sharp business practices. "My first duty is to you and the children—my second is to these others," Clemens answered, and he tried to explain Rogers' long-term strategy: unless the property, and especially the literary copyrights, remained in her hands, the creditors in all likelihood would never get any money back.

From then on, settlement in full, down to the last penny, became Livy's ironclad law, and in this she was backed up by Rogers; between the two of them, as Clemens recalled in 1906, he was effectively prevented from taking any short cuts. He had no legal obligation to pay one hundred cents on the dollar, but he began to say publicly that "honor is a harder master than the law" and he intended to serve it. Rogers had told him that an author's only stock in trade was character, and Clemens, remembering the example of Bret Harte, readily believed him. Soon Pamela's grown-up son, Samuel Moffett, editorial writer on the San Francisco *Examiner*, was trumpeting to the world at large that in his uncle's case "honor knows no statute of limitations." Certified by this gassy refrain, which after all had nothing to do with his craft or his purpose as a writer or with commercial realities as he understood them, Clemens was to become the sacrificial hero of a dollar code and of an artistic standard somehow confused with dollar honor. He was compared with Sir Walter Scott, whom he loathed but who had spent six years paying off his creditors and thereby worked himself into an early grave. The paradoxes of Clemens' double commitment as writer and entrepreneur added up to a clear case of double jeopardy: he had assumed the risks but was denied the recourse of the businessman.

It was about eight months before the real consequences of what had happened came home to him. Living in Normandy and later Paris, having cut the family's expenses to what he considered the bone—$1,700 a month,

---

* In 1835 Tocqueville had written: "The Americans, who make a virtue of commercial temerity, have no right in any case to brand with disgrace those who practice it. Hence arises the strange indulgence that is shown to bankrupts in the United States; their honor does not suffer by such an accident." The Scotsman David Macrae, describing the economic climate right after the Civil War, wrote: "Men are up today, down tomorrow, and up again the day after. . . . No man loses caste because he has failed, unless he has allowed himself to fail for a trifle."

he told Orion, "scrimp and economize as we may"—Clemens had returned to *Joan of Arc* and he was writing away with such freedom that the book seemed to write itself. "I merely have to hold the pen," he told Rogers in September—fifteen hundred or two thousand words a day, sometimes three thousand. Despite the ease with which he wrote he began to feel that his head was worn out, full of cobwebs. What sustained him was not only the subject itself, as etherealized and remote as ever, but his absolute certainty that at any hour now the machine would rescue him. It was the same old tune all over again, except that he was hearing it for the last time.

In October, when the machine started its test at the Chicago *Herald* and Clemens saw actual samples of its work, he began to feel again like Columbus sighting land. At the end of a long exuberant letter to Rogers about his nightshirt adventures in the black corridors of a Rouen hotel while looking for the toilet, he returned to his old daydream: the Mergenthaler people were about to be brought to their knees, their $10,000,000 capital of no use to them at all in competition with the indisputable boss machine of the world. Then, following its usual form, the machine broke down, the stoppages became longer. The newspaper proprietors had seen all they needed to. Rushing to Chicago in December, Rogers watched the machine in action and inaction as it declined into invalidism. He decided that the test had proved once and for all that the dazzling machine could never be made practical and that the typesetter company, with its shrewd contract and glorious expectations, had better be dissolved right away. The news hit Clemens like a "thunder clap," he told Rogers, and, "with just barely enough head left on my shoulders to protect me from being used as a convenience for the dogs," he stumbled through the Paris streets, driven by the idea that either his "dream" must be rescued or he would have to go back to America to see it die. At the end of the afternoon, before he had collected his senses, he found himself at a steamship office on the Rue Scribe, about to buy a ticket on the 6:52 boat train to Le Havre. Still, when he returned to his Left Bank apartment, he had not given up. He sent Rogers six closely written pages of notes for improving the machine at least to a point at which Mergenthaler would have to buy them out: talk to Thomas Edison about using die-cut brass type; run the circular typedriver slower but the machine faster; lighten and simplify the machine, reduce the number of type channels and keys to sixty. These and other improvements, he told Rogers in desperate seriousness, still believing what he wanted to believe, could all be made "in a few months."

By the beginning of January 1895, the machine had taken on "the aspect of a dissolved dream," and with it had gone Clemens' certainty that his luck would never run out. He was born lucky, he told Rogers, he had escaped drowning in the Mississippi nine times before he even learned how to swim, had been somewhere else when the steamboat *Pennsylvania* blew up and Henry Clemens was scalded to death; he even avoided business dealings with certain relatives and friends because he considered them "unlucky people." "All my life I have stumbled upon lucky chances of large size, and whenever they were wasted it was because of my own stupidity and carelessness." And he summed up his bitter experience with the machine, his faith that had never until now allowed itself to yield to certain knowledge: "It disappointed me lots of times, but I couldn't shake off the confidence of a lifetime in my luck."

At Clemens' age, friends of Rogers had remarked, ninety-eight per cent of men who failed in business "never got up again." With the death of the machine Clemens began to comprehend his bankruptcy as more than a financial reverse. With it came a loss of faith and a sense of betrayal, a kind of symbolic failure of manhood, failure as husband and father. That February, on the twenty-fifth anniversary of his marriage to Livy (and roughly the fifteenth anniversary of his marriage to the machine), he took out of his pocket a silver five-franc piece—"It is our silver wedding-day, and so I give you a present." They would never be able to live in the Hartford house again, he now realized, "though it would break the family's hearts if they could believe it." Back in America, alone, in March to wind up his shattered business affairs, he visited Farmington Avenue. They had decided to rent the house, furnished, to Alice Hooker Day and her husband, whose wedding Clemens and Livy had attended in the summer of their own engagement, and all of the family's possessions had come back out of the warehouse and were in place again. He wanted never to leave, never even to go outside the grounds again, never certainly to go again to Europe. It was all so bright and homelike and splendid, and for a moment he imagined that Livy in a rustling silk gown was coming down the stairs and that the family idyl would begin all over again, just as it had been. "It seemed," he wrote to her, using the image which was now indispensable to the way he read his experience, "as if I had burst awake out of a hellish dream, and had never been away."

IV

Clemens tried to go back to writing. In January 1895 he finished *Tom Sawyer, Detective*, a frank attempt to cash in on the current rage for Sherlock Holmes and detective fiction in general. At the end of the month, after what he figured had been twelve years of preparation and two years of intense but intermittent work, he finished *Joan of Arc*, and with the long strain gone, he told Rogers, "I am in a sort of physical collapse." Rogers had negotiated for him a contract with Harper and Brothers, who would publish the two new books in the trade. Afterwards the books were to go into an edition of his collected works, to be sold by subscription under the familiar imprint of the American Publishing Company of Hartford, now run by Frank Bliss. All the same, despite income Clemens anticipated from these projects, it was clear that he would have to lecture that year and the next. His dread of "the impending horror of the lecture platform" made him depressed and tired, unable to write—"The mill refuses to go." He began to feel that he had been condemned to walk in a large circle. Approaching sixty and about $100,000 in debt, he was to start on a year-long tour which even a young man might find too strenuous. Thirty years earlier he had planned to travel around the world, visit China and the Paris Exposition, come home, and maybe start out all over again. Now in order to pay off his creditors he had to lecture his way to the Pacific Northwest and from there to Australia, New Zealand, Ceylon, India, and South Africa; even after that he would not go home but would go instead to England, where, in some quiet village with his reunited family, he hoped to spend six months or so writing a travel book, again for the benefit of his creditors, about his round-the-world lecture tour.

In May the Clemenses landed in New York from Southampton, which Clemens considered his starting point for circling the globe, and spent a few days at the Everett House on Union Square. (Livy had felt that "it wouldn't look modest for bankrupts" to accept her brother's invitation to be his guests at the Waldorf, William Astor's brand-new German Renaissance hotel at Fifth Avenue and Thirty-third Street.) At Quarry Farm, confined to his bed for three weeks with carbuncles and gout and half expecting to start his travels on a stretcher, Clemens prepared his programs and worked over his itinerary. Pond, grown more prosperous in the decade since the Cable tour, shrewdly talked Clemens out of a plan to make a nostalgic return to California by lecturing six consecutive evenings in San Francisco; in August, Pond argued, the city would be empty. At ten-thirty on the evening of July 14, Clemens, with Livy, Clara, Pond, and Mrs. Pond, left for Cleveland, the first of a hundred cities he would call at. As the train drew out of the Elmira station, Clemens watched Susy standing on the platform in the glare of the electric lights, waving goodbye. "She was brimming with life and the joy of it," he recalled more than a year later. It was the last time he ever saw her.

As Mark Twain began once again to be a public performer and celebrity and tasted the first of a nearly unbroken succession of welcomes and ovations, the colds, the carbuncles, and even the sense of futility were, for a while, pushed into a corner of his awareness. Wherever he went he read to capacity audiences; the halls were hardly ever big enough and the cash account Rogers kept for him against the time he would be able to pay one hundred cents on the dollar grew. He netted five thousand dollars from his one month in North America; he was to net twenty-two hundred just from his first two weeks in Australia.

He was in need of ego-building and was getting it, and it was in expectation of more that, as he left Vancouver in mid-August for the long voyage across the Pacific, he succeeded in inducing a state of self-exhilaration approaching euphoria. He now knew that he had friends all over the United States, he told Samuel Moffett. For Moffett's *Examiner* he supplied a self-interview in the form of a letter to the editor.

> Perhaps [he wrote] it is a little immodest in me to talk about paying my debts, when by my own confession I am blandly getting ready to unload them on the whole English-speaking world. . . . Lecturing is gymnastics, chest-expander, medicine, mind healer, blues destroyer, all in one. I am twice as well as I was when I started out. I have gained nine pounds in twenty-eight days, and expect to weigh six hundred before January. I haven't had a blue day in all the twenty-eight.

He wrote to Rudyard Kipling the next day, about his visit to India:

> I shall arrive next January, and you must be ready. I shall come riding my ayah with his tusks adorned with silver bells and ribbons and escorted by a troop of native howdahs richly clad and mounted upon a herd of wild bungalows; and you must be on hand with a few bottles of ghee, for I shall be thirsty.

He told Henry Harper there was no longer any point to publishing *Joan* anonymously. He wanted to keep his name before the public, for, as if he expected never to be tired again and even to live forever, he intended to start on another American lecture tour just as soon as he got back.

He had heard, he noted, that people in India knew only three things about America: "George Washington, Mark Twain, and the Chicago Fair." Everywhere he went every word he said was hung upon and repeated. Sometimes this backfired. In Australia he praised unadulterated whiskey, but when he went on to dispraise Bret Harte as "sham and shoddy" he had to answer a storm of protest. (He told a reporter, only half apologetically, "If one criticizes a man one should do it thoroughly.") Later on, entertaining the Jameson Raid prisoners in Pretoria, he spoke across the prison dead line and praised the comforts of life in jail. He told the prisoners they were better off there than anywhere else, luxurious indolence being preferable to the struggle for bread and shelter, and promised to ask President Kruger to double their sentences—which Kruger nearly did: Clemens had to call on him to explain that it was all a joke.

Yet he had "a steady, unceasing feeling," as Livy had written to Susan Crane in September 1895, "that he is never going to be able to pay his debts. I do not feel so." By the following June, as he was nearing the end of a triumphant tour, his despair had deepened; the voyage seemed endless, without purpose or achievement. "I don't think it is of any use for me to struggle against my ill luck any longer," he wrote to Rogers from Queenstown, South Africa. "If I had the family in a comfortable poorhouse I would kill myself." Two weeks later he seriously considered applying for the vacant post of American consul in Johannesburg and staying there; Livy said no. In actuality he was retracing the steps of the ill-fated Riley, whom he had sent on that futile trip twenty-five years earlier. In East London he saw the inscribed copy of *The Innocents Abroad* which Riley had sold at auction before starting his trek overland to the diamond fields. He visited Kimberley, where, he was told, over fifty thousand dollars a day in diamonds was being taken out of the ground, and he played with the fantasy, which he intended to spin into a story for his travel book, that it was here that Riley had bought a claim for him and that during all those years someone had been searching for the true owner, now finally identified as Samuel L. Clemens.

On July 15, a year and a day after he left Susy on the station platform in Elmira, Clemens ended his tour in Capetown and sailed for England. There, in a rented house in Guildford, he waited for her and Jean to come over. Instead he received first a letter saying that she was ill, then a cable saying that her recovery would be slow. Livy and Clara rushed back to America. They were still on the high seas on August 18 when, as Clemens stood in the dining room at Guildford thinking about nothing in particular, he was handed a cable that told him Susy, twenty-four years old, had died of meningitis. "It is one of the mysteries of our nature," he reflected when nearly ten years had gone by, "that a man, all unprepared can receive a thunder-stroke like that and live."

CHAPTER SIXTEEN

"Never quite sane in the night"

I

I N GUILDFORD CLEMENS PLAYED BILLIARDS UNTIL he dropped with exhaustion. He gathered together the circumstances of Susy's death, tasted the pain and the shame of each, and used them in daily and nightly rituals of self-accusation. She had been staying with the Warners in Hartford, but each day she had visited the house next door. "She seems quite happy where she is," Pond wrote at the beginning of July. He was in Hartford to attend the funeral of Harriet Beecher Stowe. "She says it seems very much like home to her, and she wished you would come back. The place is beautiful, but there is a terrible atmosphere of lonesomeness there." She spent her last two weeks back in her own house, walked the floor in pain and delirium, became blind, and died after being in a coma for two days. What Clemens desperately searched for was some sign that before she died she had him in her thoughts, spoke of him in pride or love. "I wonder if she left any little message for me," he wrote to Livy imploringly. "I was not deserving of it." He wanted everything of her last days kept, even the agonizing pages she wrote in her delirium and with the light failing. "Mr. Clemens, Mr. Zola, Mr. Harte," she had written in a large scrawl across the length of the page, "I see that even darkness can be great. To me darkness must remain from everlasting to everlasting." In her delirium, he learned, she found a dress of Livy's in a closet, believed that Livy was dead, and kissed the dress and cried. In her delirium also she heard the rumble of the trolley cars outside and believed that they were running because she was "Mark Twain's daughter." ("How I hate that name," she had said only a few years before.) He was grateful, Clemens said, casting about for other straws, that she had died in the home of her childhood and surrounded by friends, that she had not lived on insane or enfeebled but that the light of her mind, whose quickness

336

and subtlety he always marveled at, "passed swiftly out in a disordered splendor." "When out of her head," he wrote in his notebook, "she said many things that showed she was proud of being my daughter."

When his brother Henry died, he told Livy, he had not allowed himself to think of it, in case the grief should become too heavy. But now he had no desire to put Susy out of his thoughts—he wanted to think about her death all the time. "I have *hated* life before—from the time I was 18—but I was not indifferent to it," and his indifference and catatonic grief were only punctuated by a sudden, self-preserving need to vomit up rage and blasphemy. After a lifetime of hunting for a crime which he could say he had committed, his guilt had finally crystallized so massively around this real event that his grief at Livy's death eight years later hardly compared in intensity. Their loss, he now said, "would bankrupt the vocabularies of all the languages to put it into words," and, in another image as central to his experience, he said that Susy's death was like a man's house burning down—it would take him years and years to discover all that he had lost in the fire. At times he allowed himself to turn his rage on the memory of Charley Webster—"He was all dog," he wrote to Pamela months later, "the primal cause of Susy's death and my ruin"— but even then he held himself responsible, for he remembered that he had not backed up Pamela when she opposed her daughter's marriage to Charley, and so he turned his rage on himself all over again. "My crimes made her a pauper and an exile," he said to Livy. He had been selfish and neglectful with Susy, an indolent father; he was sure, he said, that if she were brought back from the dead he would still be selfish and neglectful, condemned to obey the inexorable and brutish laws of his own nature. "It is an odious world, a horrible world," he began to be fond of saying. "It is Hell; the true one." His grief and anger, unchecked and turned against himself, were driving him toward destruction, and the only thing that saved him was work.

That fall, settled with Livy, Clara, and Jean at 23 Tedworth Square in Chelsea, he began writing his new travel book. He had already decided that as soon as he finished it he would begin on some other book, with no more than an hour between. "I have many unwritten books to fly to for my preservation," he told Twichell. By December he was working from directly after breakfast each day until seven in the evening, without a break. "It puzzles me to know what is in me that writes," he told Howells, "and that has comedy fancies and finds pleasure in phrasing them." He was writing a travel book "whose outside aspect had to be cheerful," he explained later, "but whose secret substance was all made of bitterness and rebellion," and, needing to prove that his gift was still intact, he was deliberately invoking and following old precedents. He thought of naming his travel book *Another Innocent Abroad;* he held it up to the standards not only of that first success but also of *Roughing It;* and he had also returned to his original audience. For in signing up with Frank Bliss's American Publishing Company, which guaranteed him a minimum of ten thousand dollars, and not with Harper, he was back with "the factory hands and the farmers," readers who had to be hunted down by the publisher's agents. "When a subscription book of mine sells 60,000 I always think I know whither 50,000 of them went," he explained to Rogers. "They went to people who don't visit bookstores." And it was out of compulsion both to keep busy and to prove himself that he devoted an extraordinary amount of work and rework to this book, whose final character as *Following the Equator,* for all this care, still reflects the conflicting and demoralizing circumstances of its writing. He revised it at least three times and, as much to help her as to help him, submitted it to Livy's careful editing.

But Livy, before this task was given her and especially after she finished it, had nothing to turn to and felt utterly purposeless. She was in a "submergence," Clemens said, and was clearly declining into full invalidism. She had lost her interest in books, refused to see anyone, and sat solitary day after day wondering how it had all happened. She was interested in palmistry and spiritualism; they became friendly with the editor of a journal of psychical research, and they even went to séances together, but neither of them ever acknowledged a convincing contact. One of the mediums, Clemens remembered five years later, was a fraud, the other a vacancy. He had long ago undermined Livy's religious faith, another thing he could claim guilt for. Now, when she looked for comfort in orthodox notions of a just or purposeful deity, he told her that the universe was governed by some sort of malign thug. He raged on and on, but when his storm subsided he stroked her hair and said softly, "Don't mind anything I say, Livy. Whatever happens, you know I love you." And then he took his daughters for a walk by the Thames and told them how vile the human race was.

In their house of mourning, which Clemens and Livy intended to keep so until they themselves were dead, the holidays and anniversaries passed and were marked only in sorrow. Susy's two sisters became priestesses at her shrine. Thanksgiving Day 1896 reminded Clemens that seven years ago in Hartford Susy had put on a play for them, that both his mother and Livy's mother had died around Thanksgiving in 1890. Christmas morning in London the family breakfasted together and talked quietly. No one mentioned that it was Christmas; there were no presents. The following August in Switzerland, on the first anniversary of Susy's death, Clemens and Livy spent the day apart from each other. She took the steamer up Lake Lucerne and spent the day alone at an inn. He sat under some trees and wrote an in-memoriam poem. For years afterward wedding anniversaries and birthdays and holidays were observed only as they had some tenuous but harrowing connection with Susy. The milestones had become gravestones, Clemens said. "The cloud is permanent now."

II

For both Mark Twain and his America the frontier was closed. That "great historic movement" which Frederick Jackson Turner, reading his celebrated paper to his fellow historians in 1893, said had come to an end in America had also come to an end in Mark Twain. Like his country, which he eventually symbolized for many, he was at an age at which he could no longer afford to be prodigal. In 1861, roughing it on the shores of Lake Tahoe, he had carelessly started a forest fire. He had been intoxicated by the spectacle, described it as "superb! magnificent! beautiful!" "Blazing banners" of flame, a hundred feet in the air, roared through the forest, were reflected in the lake, climbed up and over the mountain and left a charred wasteland behind. As a writer he judged his craft by the same standard of gaudy, profligate spectacle: he liked effects that worked like Fourth of July rockets or a torchlight procession. His writing table and manuscript trunk could never hold the projects he began in a forest fire of enthusiasm and then put aside, when the flames stopped leaping, in favor of some other conflagration. Like America's untouched forests and inexhaustible herds of buffalo, there was always more where the first or fiftieth or hundredth came from.

Now, in the early twilight of his life, having suffered frightful affronts to his sense of plenitude and possibility, he felt frugality and defensiveness forced upon him, conservation, limits, self-inquiry, inwardness. He was no longer working a bonanza claim. He had already struck barren rock, had seen the failure of his frontier talent for improvising a way out of trouble and of his frontier faith that things always come out right in the long run. In 1897 an American paper ran a headline five columns wide, "Close of a Great Career," and under it the baseless story that Mark Twain, abandoned by his wife and daughters, was living in abject poverty. He raged in disgust after he read it. Only a man, he said, could be capable of such lying and vileness, not a dog or a cow. But he knew that his luck, which he trusted all his life, had finally run out, even though he was far from poverty, and one day that winter he wrote out a list to prove it: the cook's sweetheart was dying, one of the maids might go blind, the porter had pleurisy, a friend's baby had died, another friend had fractured his skull, and on the way back from a visit to him in the hospital Clemens' cab had nearly run over a little boy. "Since bad luck struck us," he concluded from all this, "it is risky for people to have to do with us."

In order to reach a kind of accommodation with the guilt and casualty that seemed to be his daily bread, he began to write what he thought of as his "Bible," a one-sided Socratic dialogue called *What Is Man?* He believed that it was theological dynamite, that all the creeds which gave dignity to man and God would crumble under the force of its angry logic. Livy loathed it, shuddered over it, would not even listen to the last half, much less permit him to publish any part of it. He published the book only after her death, and even then privately and, he believed, anonymously. But its despairing ideas dominated his conversation from 1897 on. His children and friends dreaded the inevitable monologue of gloom and vituperation, and one of Livy's consolations, maybe even one of her motives, as she spent more and more time isolated in a sickroom, was that she was spared these performances.

Writing in 1897 to the British psychologist John Adams—his longest letter in years, Clemens explained, unable to stop once he had started on his favorite subject—he outlined the few and pathetic basic ideas of *What Is Man?* He described it as a book on psychology. Life had no dignity or meaning, he said, for each and every member of "the damned human race" was driven wholly by self-interest, the need to conform, the need, powerful above all others, for "peace of mind, spiritual comfort, *for himself.*" The Paige typesetter which once seemed to him capable of thinking and therefore second only to man, had now become, by a turnabout which sums up the whole bitter experience, the model for human personality: "Man's proudest possession—his mind—is a mere machine: an automatic machine." Adams recognized one fallacy right away: If man is truly a machine, why should he need "spiritual comfort?" But there is another, and a poignant, contradiction. Without choice there can be no responsibility, and—as if Clemens dimly perceived the logical goal of his illogic—without responsibility guilt has no meaning. "No one," Bernard DeVoto wrote, "can read this wearisomely repeated argument without feeling the terrible force of an inner cry: Do not blame me, for it was not my fault."

At the same time that he was writing his "Bible" Clemens was following another line of inquiry, one which turned out to be too complex and baffling to give him what he wanted, simple self-exoneration, but which was far more productive and relevant to his needs as a writer. Living in mourning and seclusion, he also went underground and turned inward to the enigmas of his own life. "S.L.C. interviews M.T."—the idea is repeated throughout the notebooks he kept during the late 1890s, when he was also planning his autobiography, the one major work of the last decade of his life. He explored his dream life, and in brief notes or in long, unfinished manuscripts he tried to articulate his fantasies into fiction. In the nocturnal and irrational he found material which seemed richer, more suggestive, and more disturbing than anything he could find on the level of consciousness. "In my age as in my youth," he was to say in his autobiography, "night brings me many a deep remorse. I realize that from the cradle up I have been like the rest of the race—never quite sane in the night."

Was it dream or reality, he had asked in 1893, that he had been a pilot on the Mississippi and a miner and journalist in Nevada, that he had come East and then sailed to Europe and written a book that made him famous, that he had a wife and children and lived in a villa above Florence? "This dream goes on and on and *on*, and sometimes seems so real that I almost believe it is real," he wrote. "I wish I knew whether it is a dream or real." Years earlier he had found the confusion of dream and reality to be a subject for comedy. The Pauper was a bad dream that the Prince had, but with the Yankee, who is unable to wake from his dream, the comic possibilities vanished, and now, in the dark mood of Mark Twain's old age, the confusion has another aspect. It has become, by itself, a nightmare.

"Every man is a moon and has a dark side which he never shows to anybody," he wrote, tacitly suggesting that this dark side might be hidden from himself as well. By the second half of his century the speculative notion of an unconscious mind had become almost an intellectual commonplace, and like many of his contemporaries Clemens was fascinated by ungovernable forces in the workings of the mind. In "The Facts Concerning the Recent Carnival of Crime in Connecticut," the paper he read to his Monday Evening Club in 1876, he had tried to explain his feeling of duality and conflict, of having a demon inside him. He called this demon conscience, and in his fantasy he vented on it and on society in general the stored-up self-doubt and anger which are the price of possessing a conscience. Later, in Robert Louis Stevenson's *Dr. Jekyll and Mr. Hyde* (1886), he found a further explanation, "nearer, yes, but not near enough," for he recognized a falsity: unlike Jekyll and Hyde, "the two persons in a man are wholly unknown to each other." But in his sixty-first year, during the winter of 1896-97 in London, he found, he believed, the solution to what had become for him "a haunting mystery." He found the solution in a dream:

I was suddenly in the presence of a negro wench who was sitting in grassy open country, with her left arm resting on the arm of one of those long park-sofas that are made of broad slats with cracks between, and a curve-over back. She was very vivid to me—round black face, shiny black eyes, thick lips, very white regular teeth showing through her smile. She was about 22, and plump—not fleshy, not fat, merely rounded and plump; and good-natured and not at all bad-looking. She had but one garment on—a coarse tow-linen shirt that reached from her neck to her ankles without break. She sold me a pie; a mushy apple pie—hot. She was eating one herself with a tin tea-spoon. She made a disgusting proposition to me. Although it was disgusting it did not surprise me—for I was young (I was never old in a

341

dream yet) and it seemed quite natural that it should come from her. It was disgusting, but I did not say so; I merely made a chaffing remark, brushing aside the matter—a little jeeringly—and this embarrassed her and she made an awkward pretence that I had misunderstood her. I made a sarcastic remark about this pretence, and asked for a spoon to eat my pie with. She had but the one, and she took it out of her mouth, in a quite matter-of-course way, and offered it to me. My stomach rose—there everything vanished. . . . My, how vivid it all was! Even to the texture of her shirt, its dull white color, and the pale brown tint of a stain on the shoulder of it.

The sixty-one-year-old man who dreamed this dream had grown up in a slaveholding society which had among its commonest institutions Negro wet nurses and Negro concubinage. As a young printer's apprentice in Hannibal Sam Clemens ate in the kitchen with the "very handsome and bright" young daughter of the slave cook. Wales McCormick, the other apprentice, was always flirting with the girl. Her mother, Clemens remembered, "well understood that by the customs of slaveholding communities it was Wales's right to make love to that girl if he wanted to." And only a few years before having this dream, Clemens, in *Pudd'nhead Wilson*, had put aside his usual reticence about sex, portrayed the one mature and explicitly sexual woman in all his fiction, Roxy the slave, and dealt squarely with the intertwined themes of micegenation and the corruptive effect of slavery. But Clemens did not acknowledge to any great extent the sexuality of his dreams. And it is, in fact, precisely his casualness about symbolic content that permitted him to write down his dreams without being afraid of violating any taboos. His solution to the "haunting mystery" was to accept the existence of a "dream self" who comes alive during sleep, is liberated, and does things which the waking self would never dare. "I go to unnameable places," Clemens wrote, in the excitement of his discovery, "I do unprincipled things; and every vision is vivid, every sensation—physical as well as moral—is *real*." Clemens' dream self lost his way in caves and in "the corridors of monstrous hotels." He appeared at social gatherings dressed only in nightshirt and told the people, "I am Mark Twain," and no one believed him. He stood on the lecture platform without a subject to talk about (Martin Luther had comparable nightmares), his audience started to leave, and after a while he found himself alone in the semidarkness talking to an empty house. Sometimes he was standing at the wheel as his steamboat approached a black shadow, and he could not tell whether it was Selma Bluff, Hat Island, or a wall of night. Clemens' dream self stumbled off the edge of cliffs, went into battles and hid from bullets, even made jokes which seemed funny in the morning (Queen Victoria, adrift at sea, was cross all the time—"This was the origin of the V.C.").

"Never quite sane in the night"

For about two years after Susy died Clemens lived in a sort of deliberate, self-induced dream state in which the reality was what he dreamed and the fantasy was what he lived by day, and he wrote story after story about men whose dreams turned into reality. By releasing himself from daytime rationality and consciously wooing the creatures of the night he found new ways to look at himself. He also found new literary material. He exposed himself to madness, and for a while was close enough to it to realize that the dream, as Freud said, was simply "a psychosis, with all the absurdities, delusions, and illusions of a psychosis." But by turning his dream life into a literary problem—into *work*—he saved himself from madness. He thought and felt as a writer, and he was interested primarily in the overt shape and content of his dreams and fantasies, in their literary and anecdotal value, and not in interpreting their latent content. Like other writers of his period, he was satisfied to seize the literature and let the psychological mysteries go by.* But under the stress of his disasters he became more than ever a traveler in the spectral world of Poe and Haw-

* The period is framed by the work of two doctor-novelists. Holmes wrote several psychiatric (or, as he called them, "medicated") novels, and around the turn of the century the Philadelphia neurologist Silas Weir Mitchell wrote fictional studies of dual personality. But a number of nonmedical writers were turning to dreams or psychotic states for sources as well as subjects for fiction. Robert Louis Stevenson arrived at the idea for *Dr. Jekyll and Mr. Hyde* in a dream. One stalwart of New England intellectual society (whose chivalry in helping a fat lady onto a trolley car in Harvard Square is commemorated by the lines, "The noble man by whom this deed was done/ Was Colonel Thomas Wentworth Higginson") wrote a novel, *The Monarch of Dreams* (1886), about a man who is unable to come out of his dreams; at the end he lies in bed helplessly as the train carrying his Union regiment starts south. Higginson became so engrossed in the novel that his sister thought he was sick or seriously depressed. "Ten Years Dead" (1885), Hamlin Garland's first published story, is about a man (in almost all respects the author himself) who returns to familiar scenes after a deathlike dream absence of ten years; Garland said that the subject came to him "in a dream." Two years later Howells (who said he had been having dreams "worth dreaming") told Garland he was planning to write a story about the effect of one dream on a man's life. Garland, he reconstructed the conversation years later, tried to discourage him: "There are plenty of men, Mr. Howells, who can do 'the weird kind of thing,' but there is only one man who can imagine *A Modern Instance* and *The Rise of Silas Lapham*." Howells wrote the novel anyhow, *The Shadow of a Dream* (1890), and he continued to investigate the relationship of dreams to fiction. By 1895, however, in an article in the May *Harper's*, he had decided that "the plots of dreams are not much more varied than the plots of romantic novels, which are notoriously stale and hackneyed." In Rudyard Kipling's *The Brushwood Boy* (1895) the dream becomes merely the central plot device for a charming romantic story. Mark Twain's "My Platonic Sweetheart" (written in 1898 but not published until 1912), about a girl he consistently encountered in his dreams, is similar to Kipling's and may have been suggested by it. Soon after Clemens sent the story off to Gilder at the *Century*, he had a change of heart, and just as he began to hope that Gilder would reject it he heard that Gilder already had done so. Typical of his interest in all sorts of psychic phenomena, he concluded that this was one more example of "mental telegraphy." "I have had 21 years of experience of it," he wrote to Gilder, "and have written a novel with that as *motif* (don't be alarmed—I burned it) and I know considerable about it."

thorne and among "the invisible spheres" that Melville said "were formed in fright."

Mark Twain's dream stories have a number of symbols and situations in common. A rich and happy man at the peak of his powers falls asleep, and in the brief moments his eyes are closed—whether he sleeps for an instant or for a billion years, Clemens said, "the time to you is the same"—he dreams a life of disgrace and horror. His house has burned down and he is bankrupt. Or he has gone on a chartless, mutiny-torn voyage that lasts for years, and at the end of the voyage the passengers and the crew are all either dead or crazy. His consuming need is to beg forgiveness of his wife and daughters. When he wakes from his dream his hair has turned white and he cannot tell which of his two existences is the "real" one. Along with these instantaneous dislocations of psychological time and reality, which had fascinated Clemens for years, there are radical dislocations of place, scale, and perception of the sort usually associated with hallucinated and psychotic states. In some of these stories a man goes on a voyage inside a drop of water, or—an idea which Clemens first had in the early 1880s and was still working on in 1905—he has become a trichina in the intestine of God or a micro-organism in the bloodstream of a tramp named Blitzowski. Among the dominant symbols are Mark Twain's own finely tooled brass microscope and, at the other end of the scale, the house on Farmington Avenue and all the ocean voyages that for thirty years and more he had gone on and written about. Two years after Susy's death Clemens was writing an article for the *Century*, "My Debut as a Literary Person," in which he recapitulated some of the recurrent symbols as well as his 1866 newspaper story, written for the Sacramento *Union* and reprinted in *Harper's*, about the clipper ship *Hornet*. The ship had been set on fire by the disobedient first mate; fifteen of the thirty-one men on board survived hunger, delirium, exposure, and the threat of cannibalism and mutiny and arrived in Honolulu after "a voyage of forty-three days in an open boat, through the blazing tropics, on *ten days' rations* of food." In general, the dream stories deal with the question of guilt and responsibility, with the experience of the destruction of identity and of the sudden recognition of the possibility of never having existed at all. The chronological and thematic relationships between these stories are almost impossible to disentangle; Clemens probably began writing the first of them in May 1897, a few days after he finished *Following the Equator*. Most of the stories are autobiographical epitomes in which, framed by the relentless questions, What have I done wrong? How can I make amends?, he introduced the people around whom his life was built: Livy and their daughters, especially Susy; Orion; villains—Paige, Charley Webster, various publishers, businessmen, bankers; friends and heroes—Grant, the silver-tongued agnostic Robert Ingersoll, Joe Goodman, Ned Wakeman. Mark Twain had always believed that his best work came out of his own direct experience. Now the accumulated, bitter experience of a lifetime came flooding in over him with such a rush and volume that he was barely able to give it a voice and a shape. Fearing madness if he became the creature and not the master of his past, he worked like a man pursued by furies and turned out manuscript after manuscript, most of them unsatisfactory to him. It hardly seems possible, said Bernard DeVoto, the first to recognize their role in this ordeal of Mark Twain, that any man could write so much.

One long manuscript, "Which Was the Dream?," concerns a brilliant and famous general, happily married to a rich wife and at the age of thirty-four certain of being the next President of the United States. His name, Tom X (X was the "mark" with which Huck signed his oath as a member of Tom Sawyer's gang) is but one of any number of autobiographical references—for example, it was at the age of thirty-four that Clemens became famous as the author of *The Innocents Abroad* and married Livy. One evening, while Alice, his wife, and their three daughters entertain Washington society in their great mansion, Tom goes up to his study to write and falls asleep. When he "wakes," the house is on fire, and it burns to the ground. An undistinguished and unpromising lieutenant known to his friends as "Useless" Grant leads the guests to safety. Tom plans to build an even grander house. Suddenly and irreversibly—and all proceeding from the fire (Clemens' metaphor for Susy's death)—his fortunes turn. His accounts are all overdrawn, his insurance policies are all fraudulent; the California mine—called the Golden Fleece—in which he invested all of Alice's money is also a fraud. The villain, who has made off with all their money, is Tom's business agent and confidential secretary, Jeff, whom he had trusted against Alice's advice. Jeff's handwriting and even his set of mind are so similar to Tom's that he writes and signs Tom's letters.* He is Tom's alter ego, the *Doppelgänger* of Poe's William Wilson, and the "dream self" Clemens had recently discovered—"my double, my partner in duality, the other and wholly independent personage who resides in me." Tom is now a ruined man, not only a bankrupt but an accused swindler.

---

* In Stevenson's novel, Mr. Hyde's handwriting was Dr. Jekyll's sloped backward. Clemens may have borrowed the detail of the counterfeit hand from newspaper accounts of a breach-of-promise action brought against the American journalist William Henry Hurlbert in England in 1891. Hurlbert presented the amazing defense that the letters in question, some of them obscene, had been written by his secretary, who had learned to imitate his handwriting so successfully that it was impossible even for Hurlbert to detect a forged letter. The secretary, Hurlbert further testified, had somehow disappeared and could not be found. Tom X's career was undoubtedly suggested by that of General John C. Frémont, who, after a career as explorer and soldier and his marriage to Senator Thomas Hart Benton's daughter, was nominated for the Presidency in 1856, at the age of 43; after he was defeated by Buchanan he went back to mining in California, and his last 34 years, before his death in 1890, were spent in relative obscurity.

On March 19 (Susy's birthday) he meets with his creditors, who provoke him into a paroxysm of rage, and he falls unconscious. Over a year later, on August 18 (the day of Susy's death) he "wakes." He is lying on a straw mattress in a humble cabin, one with an earthen floor, tin plates, a sack of navy beans, and a cracked mirror, in a California mining camp called Hell's Delight. (Outside Angel's Camp, in just this sort of cabin on Jackass Hill, Clemens, a fugitive from the San Francisco police, had spent a depressed winter in 1864-65.) In order to leave his disgrace behind, Tom now has a new name, Jacob Edwards. The manuscript is unfinished: Clemens had brought Tom's life up to the point his own had reached.

Another one of these stories, entitled by DeVoto "The Great Dark," also concerns a man named Edwards who moved from a domestic idyl into nightmare. While looking through his microscope at a drop of rainwater, to which he has added a little whiskey to stir up the microbes, he falls asleep. An ominous figure, really a Satanic stage manager, identified as "the Superintendent of Dreams" arranges for a ship and a crew to take Edwards and his family on a long voyage inside the drop of rainwater. (In a related and also unfinished story Edwards is supposed to have committed some unspecified crime; everyone on board is certain that he is guilty, but he is never allowed, and never tries, to deny his guilt.) His favorite daughter is kidnapped, and for years, as the ocean grows hotter and hotter and begins to dry up under a merciless white light (from the microscope lamp), they follow a phantom ship. They are surrounded by sea monsters, including an enormous blind cuttlefish, who battle each other to the death. The compasses spin crazily. The crew mutinies. In Mark Twain's notes for the completion of this story, the narrator, his hair turned white, is awakened by his wife and children, but by now he has been crazed by his voyage. He thinks *they* are the dream.

Few of the recognizable people in these stories come from Mark Twain's boyhood, his years as a pilot, or his years as miner and journalist in the West. Even Orion here is not the hope of the Clemens family as newspaper editor in Hannibal and august secretary of the Nevada Territory who took his younger brother with him to Carson City as his unpaid assistant; instead he is the chronic failure that he later became. The experience of the years before he came East was Mark Twain's basic endowment in raw materials and sensibility, his working capital, the bank note sewn inside the coat of the country boy coming to the big city. He came East and plunged into the life of the Gilded Age wholeheartedly, hungry for reward and recognition, willing to submit his only half-formed identity to a bewildering number of adaptations—literary, intellectual, social, economic. But though his Eastern years often appeared to him to be meaningless, in these dream stories, whose shape and symbols they supply, they have a tight and urgent coherence: a man makes a spectacular rise to eminence, lives on a plateau of triumph and fulfillment, is betrayed by something within him which he can never discover, and falls. At the end of *Roughing It* Clemens described what he did in the autumn of 1866, soon after writing his *Hornet* story:

> When I returned to San Francisco I projected a pleasure journey to Japan and thence westward around the world; but a desire to see home again changed my mind, and I took a berth in the steamship, bade goodbye to the friendliest land and the livest, heartiest community on our continent, and came by way of the Isthmus to New York—a trip that was not much of a picnic excursion, for the cholera broke out among us on the passage, and we buried two or three bodies at sea every day.

The difference between that account, casual despite its horrors, and the story of Edwards' nightmare voyage inside a drop of water is the difference between the young Clemens and the broken one.

Reciting the past over and over again, he still never found out why he was accusing himself or how he could earn forgiveness. His insights into the workings of his dream self had carried him as far as he could go. He eventually came back to the gospel of *What Is Man?* and to a shrill, philosophically shallow nihilism which enabled him to dismiss responsibility and to obliterate all distinctions between the real world and the dream world, or, using other favorite co-ordinates, between truth and lies. "*Nothing* exists," Satan declares at the end of *The Mysterious Stranger*. "Strange, indeed, that you should not have suspected that your universe and its contents were only dreams, visions, fiction! Strange, because they are so frankly and hysterically insane—like all dreams." He rationalized his guilt away, but this left him with an insatiable appetite for approval and adulation, and he spent a good part of the last ten years of his life trying to feed it. He had begun his career as a teller of tall stories. Then, as his craft matured, fiction became a delicately controlled illusion in which the "truth," in order to be believed, had to be disguised as a lie. "I disseminate my true views," he told an interviewer in 1900, "by means of a series of apparently humorous and mendacious stories," and at other times he was willing to argue with some passion that all spoken lies put together existed in a proportion of "1 to 22,894" to "the silent colossal National Lie" that supported such "tyrannies and shams" as Negro slavery and the imprisonment of Captain Dreyfus. But at some point in this development fiction, dreams, and lies had become confused, and he could not tell them apart. They were all "frankly and hysterically insane." The fiction he wrote after his ordeal no longer has the rich sprawl of accident and anecdote of his mature work. Instead it is marked by spareness in structure and invention and by moral and logical clarity; the best of this fiction has a sardonic power, the worst of it is merely sentimental. In addition to these quasi-philosophical tales the forms he was to be most at home with were reminiscence and polemic, and to bring himself to write or dictate he relied for stimulus on larger and larger doses of indignation directed against larger and larger objects: Mary Baker Eddy, King Leopold II, William Shakespeare, and God. I do not agree with DeVoto that Mark Twain came out of this ordeal with his gift "whole," and that *The Mysterious Stranger* vindicated and solved the problems of all those despairing manuscripts he could never complete. But he survived, and that, considering what he went through, is in itself something of a triumph. It illuminates with a grim, retrospective irony the celebrated public statement he made in June 1897 to the London correspondent of the New York *Journal:* "The report of my death was an exaggeration."

III

His travel book finished, his literary energies committed to his cycle of dream stories, Clemens was also occupied during the summer of 1897 with what sometimes seemed the hopeless task of paying off his debts. He continued to be obsessed with gravestones instead of milestones, but still there were certain triumphs of the distant past that he looked back on with satisfaction. In July the first twenty-eight-year copyright term of *The Innocents Abroad* expired; he had already, during the darkest part of the winter, applied to Ainsworth Spofford, the Librarian of Congress, for a renewal. In June, hearing that friends in New York and San Francisco wanted him to come back for a gala benefit lecture, he devised a characteristically nostalgic and gaudy scheme. His vanity, he admitted, was tickled by the possibility that he might make the largest single money scoop in lecturing history. A group of millionaires, including Adolph Sutro, would put up twelve thousand dollars and invite him to lecture at the Waldorf. The choice seats were to be auctioned off "at Jenny Lind prices," and the others were to go at whatever the market could bear. The man he wanted to entrust with "the engineering of so delicate and so large an undertaking" was Frank Fuller. As a further re-enactment of his Cooper Union debut of May 1867, he proposed to tell the story of that lecture, of how he and Fuller had taken in only thirty-five dollars in paid admissions and papered the rest of the vast hall, and to show lantern slides of all the famous people—Grant, Emerson, Whittier, Greeley—whom they had invited but who had sent regrets. A week after broaching the idea to Fuller he tacitly acknowledged that though it might get him out of debt it was also contrary to the spirit of the code stubbornly imposed by Livy and Rogers, which committed him to earn dollar for dollar. "If that project is doubtful," he wrote to Fuller, "don't consider it for a moment. And in writing to me or in talking to people don't indicate that *I* know anything about it." Fuller took to the plan with enthusiasm, but his work went to waste. Livy learned about the benefit, said no, and insisted that if Clemens returned to the lecture platform it would have to be "in the old way and at the ordinary prices." And even this grim solution was closed to him. A few days later, having decided that a hard winter of traveling would destroy Livy's health and unwilling to leave her behind in her depression, he turned down an offer from Pond of fifty thousand dollars and all expenses for 125 nights in America.

At the same time Clemens had been flirting with yet another way out. The New York *Herald*, for which in November 1867 he had written his sardonic valedictory to the *Quaker City* and its pilgrims, organized a Mark Twain subscription fund. It represented, James Gordon Bennett's writers editorialized, a debt of gratitude for "the sunshine spread among the American people by the writings of the author." The *Herald* itself put up a thousand dollars, Andrew Carnegie another thousand; on June 24 the *Herald* said the fund amounted to $2,601.65, and that day one of its readers sent in a dollar and proposed that everyone who had read *Huckleberry Finn* do likewise. "All friends think *Herald* movement mistake," Rogers had cabled on June 16. "Withdraw graciously." Three days later Frank Bliss, certain that the fund would hurt Clemens, asked him to cable his disapproval immediately. Up to this point Clemens had maintained an attitude of silent—and therefore, to one way of thinking, blameless—acquiescence. But the pressure mounted, especially from his family. "I have grown so tired of being in debt," he wrote to Bennett in Paris on June 19, "that I often think I would part with my skin and teeth to get out." Still, he went on, his family had convinced him that he had no right to take other men's money to discharge his debts. (As he later wrote to Carnegie, declining his contribution, "My wife won't allow me to accept any money so long as I am not disabled.") But, indicative of his own sorely tempted and wavering feelings about the fund, his first letter to Bennett somehow miscarried; five days later he had to repeat his request for the *Herald* to close its subscription list and return the money. Apparently determined to help him in other ways, that October, a month before *Following the Equator* was to be published, the *Herald* ran a full-page advance review which included, without permission, about six thousand words of quotation as well as six pictures. This time, his pride stiffened, and apparently forgetting his own bitter maxim about the difference between feeding a starving dog and feeding a starving man, he told Bliss to go ahead and sue and "put the damage at a good figure."

On November 30 Orion wrote to congratulate him on his sixty-second birthday and on the success of *Following the Equator*. Orion, who had spent the money from their mother's estate to enlarge his boardinghouse in Keokuk, was busy with a new literary scheme, a biography of Judas of Galilee which would penetrate the mystery of the Essene sect known as the Society of the Dead Sea. "I imagine those Essenes to have been Buddhists established there about 150 B.C.," he wrote, "and that their secret was the Buddhist worship, as now seen in Roman Catholic Churches." And, turning to another project, he proposed himself as model for "a fool character" in a comic novel he wanted Sam to write. Eleven days after this letter Orion was dead. "He was good—all good and sound: there was nothing bad in him, nothing base, nor any unkindness," Sam wrote to Mollie from Vienna. Then, falling back into his customary bitterness, he went on with a condolence letter remarkably lacking in comfort: "It was unjust that such a man, against whom no offense could be charged, should have been sentenced to live for 72 years."

Soon after Orion's death the tide of Clemens' affairs began to turn. "I hear that your latest work is succeeding splendidly," Howells wrote from New York in January 1898, "and I have lately heard people talking proudly and gladly of your rehabilitation in the business line." *Following the Equator* had sold thirty thousand copies right away; the royalties and the other earnings Rogers had invested for Clemens added up, by the end of that January, to enough to pay off the creditors in full and still leave thirteen thousand to spare. "The debts ... took the *spirit out of my work*," Clemens had told Rogers in December. "For the first time in my life I am getting more pleasure out of paying money than pulling it in." He began to feel "abundant peace of mind" once again, and even Livy showed signs of coming out of her depression. Rogers had sent on the letters of thanks and acknowledgment from the satisfied creditors, and Livy, reading them over and over again, told Clemens that this was the first happy day she had had since Susy died. Within the next two years a substantial measure of the old prosperity returned to him. Reflecting his life in two divided and distinguished worlds, his notebook entries are a sort of antiphony of dream stories and records of his rising cash balances. Between October 1898 and April 1899 his account with Rogers increased from $18,068.89 to $51,995.29. In January 1899 "a quite unexpected $10,000 tumbled in here," he joyously told Howells. "Come—respect the capitalist!" Cables between Rogers and Clemens now told a new story. "Profit $16,000," Rogers reported after closing out a stock investment. "Splendid bird," Clemens replied. "Set her again," and he watched the swelling of his "hen-fruit": Federal Steel up in two weeks from 32 to 38½, Brooklyn Gas up from 75 to 155. He was feeling young and comfortable again, free of the long nightmare of leaving his family in want. Livy, keeper of the accounts and the bankbook, figured up with pencil and paper for her own satisfaction that they owned a house and furniture in Hartford, that his royalties in America and England were equivalent to the income from an invested capital of $200,000, and that they had $107,000 cash in the bank. "I have been out and bought a box of 6 cent cigars; I was smoking 4½ before," he told Howells after this accounting in January 1899, and he said that they were thinking of coming back to New York to live next year. Meanwhile, in Vienna, they were living in de luxe hotels, in enormous suites of four bedrooms, a dining room, drawing room, three bathrooms, and three antechambers.

Every once in a while he was presented with reminders of the old disaster. Since April 1890 Pratt and Whitney had been trying to collect $1,744.20 from him for estimating the cost of a typesetter factory; Whitmore, his Hartford business agent, assured him that by and by the company would give up. And in April 1903, after mistakenly calculating that his expenses had grown 125 per cent greater than his income, he was to spend a night of dread thinking himself back "in the black days when I was buried under a mountain of debt." He came down in the morning "a gray and aged wreck" and then discovered his arithmetic had been off. "It is quite within the possibilities," he said, "that two or three nights like that night of mine could drive a man to suicide." As it was, he came down with a chill and was sick in bed for a month after.

He had still kept his fatal hunger for a sure thing that would make him millions. In March 1898, only two months after paying off the last of his debts, Clemens encountered another "Shakespeare of mechanical invention," Jan Szczepanik, a Pole whom he promptly named "the Austrian Edison." A few years earlier, at the age of only twenty-five, Szczepanik had made a name for himself as the inventor of the *Fernseher*, or "telectroscope," a rudimentary television system. When Clemens met him in Vienna he was occupied with textile machinery. He had invented a weaving machine that reproduced photographic images, and as Clemens watched in amazement the machine wove his unmistakable portrait into silk. Szczepanik had also invented a computerlike machine that stamped out the basic instruction matrices for the Jacquard loom, and Clemens, after a conversation with the inventor's backer, a man named Kleinberg, became fired with the idea of becoming the Carnegie of carpet weaving, and began to think of forming a syndicate to buy the option on the American rights for a half-million dollars or so. From Rogers, fortunately, came the report that there were not enough Jacquard looms in America to make the invention worth while, and the bonanza was abandoned, without regrets. Progress, Clemens reflected, is generally achieved through the cooperation of an Inventor and a Fool, the Fool being the man who finances the venture until the Wise Man takes over and sends the other two to the poorhouse. But now there was a difference: "Sz is not a Paige, but a gentleman; his backer, Mr. Kleinberg, is a gentleman, too, yet is *not* a Clemens—that is to say, he is not an Ass."

Even so, the self-styled Ass turned without hesitating from carpet weaving to the profit-breeding and medicinal properties of Plasmon, a granulated high-protein food concentrate certified by the German pathologist Rudolf Virchow. It appeared, Howells recalled, that " 'the damned human race' was to be saved by Plasmon" stirred into its milk, soup, coffee, chocolate, or oatmeal, or taken dry. Soon after investing twenty-five thousand dollars—"all the cash I could spare," he explained to Carnegie—in a London-based international Plasmon syndicate, Clemens was urging this tasteless, odorless, but supposedly sovereign powder on anyone who had ever suffered from constipation, indigestion, seasickness, or just plain hunger. Plasmon, he said, "digests as easily as water," and it was almost as cheap. One pound of it, costing half a crown, would feed a family of four for four days and yield the nutritional equivalent of "sixteen pounds of the best beef." He himself was able once again to eat raisin cake, plum pudding, lobster salad, candy and ice cream, all of which had been "deadly to me, and taboo" before he started taking Plasmon. But soon the old story of the Inventor, the Fool, and the Wise Man began over again. Early in 1900 Clemens was elected a director of the Plasmon syndicate and promoted stock in the United States. By April 1901 things looked rosy: Plasmon sales were up to seven or eight tons a month. But by January 1906 two Wise Men, "by nature and training rascals," had taken over and, Clemens charged, had stacked the cards on him: they planned to start a new Plasmon company, throw the American one into bankruptcy, and freeze him out altogether. Under the circumstances, he told a fellow organizer, he would not put another penny into Plasmon, "not on your life."

At the time of his love affair with Plasmon, Clemens had also become a convert to osteopathy (then also known as "the Swedish movements"), and in Mr. Heinrick Kellgren's office in London or at his sanatorium at Sanna, Sweden, he and his family submitted to daily manipulations. The osteopath plowed him up and down, Clemens said, "leaving no muscle and no nerve unvisited . . . waking and shaking up all my machinery," and he felt refreshed and renewed, as if he walked on air, and considerably lightened of the chronic discomforts of his rheumatism, piles, constipation, dysuria, hernia, headache, and heartburn; even an unpleasant tingling in his left arm had stopped, now that the "gas" which had caused it was given a free passage by manipulation. Clemens had found another cure for the blues, a passive pleasure corresponding to his lifelong taste for self-punishment and perhaps as effective as drifting down the river on a raft. He also believed that Kellgren's miracle-workers cured Livy of bronchitis and influenza. Jean, for whom there had seemed to be no hope at all, stopped taking large doses of bromides to suppress her convulsions, and her attacks of *petit mal* had become less frequent. In accepting rather than fighting Kellgren's treatment she had lowered the flag of her hostility and contrariness, and this, Clemens noted, was "the first flag she has voluntarily lowered in two years."

"Damn all the other cures, including the baths and Christian Science and the doctors of the several schools," he wrote to Gilder in August from Sanna, "*this* is the satisfactory one!" He became a publicist for the new cause, and even, in 1901, went to Albany to testify in support of a bill to recognize and regulate osteopathy. "The objection is, people are curing people without a license," he told a public-health committee there, "and you are afraid it will bust up business." To anyone who would listen to him he declared that Kellgren (in conjunction with Plasmon, as he told William James) could cure any disease that a regular doctor could and some that a regular doctor couldn't. Sir Henry Stanley, he said, had been dying of gastralgia and jaundice; Kellgren had raised him from the dead, along with five or six Rothschilds of Vienna and a Frau von Kopf of Bremen, who had chronic heart disease but was enabled by her annual two months of Kellgren treatment to go mountain climbing. Osteopathy and its attendant mood of benevolence became associated in Clemens' mind with other worthy causes. In Vienna at the end of 1897 he planned a book about the Dreyfus Affair. As he told Chatto and Windus, the book would show "the French backside" as well as justice triumphant (he expected Dreyfus to be vindicated momentarily). As an offshoot of his interest in the Dreyfus Affair he wrote an admiring article on the Jews—"a marvelous race," he told Twichell, "by long odds the most marvelous that the world has produced, I suppose." When Zola published *J'accuse* in January 1898, Clemens was quoted in the American press as declaring, "Such cowards, hypocrites, and flatterers as the members of military and ecclesiastic courts the world could produce by the million every year. But it takes five centuries to produce a Joan of Arc or a Zola." On September 19, 1899, Dreyfus was released from prison, pardoned but still not vindicated. Five days later, at the suggestion of Frau von Kopf, Clemens asked Chatto, who was to use Zola as an intermediary, if necessary, to pass along a constructive suggestion: to "get Madame Dreyfus to consider the idea of entrusting to Mr. Kellgren the restoration of Captain Dreyfus' health," and Clemens enclosed an elaborate letter of testimonial to go to her in the south of France.

IV

In Vienna during 1898 and 1899 Mark Twain was treated like a Hapsburg. He enjoyed his special privileges. "For God's sake, let him pass," said a mounted officer ordering a police barrier opened. "Don't you see it's Herr Mark Twain?" "My," Clemens said to Clara after they had passed through, "but that makes me feel damned good." He and Livy had begun to come out of seclusion. Afternoons, from five o'clock on, a stream of visitors poured into their drawing room, which was becoming a sort of second American Embassy. He felt that during his nearly ten years of self-exile he had been serving as "self-appointed Ambassador at Large of the U. S. of America—without salary." And from America itself were coming unmistakable evidences that during this time of his low creativity and morale his reputation had passed through a remarkable change. Popularity had turned into fame. He had become a part of his nation's history as well as its literature.

In 1884 the *Critic* had asked its readers to nominate forty American "immortals." Holmes, Lowell, and Whittier led the list, Howells was fifth, Bret Harte eighth, and Mark Twain fourteenth, one place ahead of Charles Dudley Warner and two places ahead of Henry Ward Beecher. In 1899 John Kendrick Bangs, editor of the American edition of the transatlantic journal *Literature*, asked his readers to nominate ten living writers for a hypothetical American Academy. Howells was first with eighty-four votes, the popular philosopher and historian John Fiske was second with eighty-two, and Mark Twain was third with eighty. "Your 84 votes place you where you belong—at the head of the gang," Clemens wrote from Vienna. The readers of *Literature* had already been told by Howells in June 1898 that the greatest American literary center was at present neither in New York nor in Boston but in Vienna, and from Howells directly Clemens had received a string of heartfelt tributes compounded of love, admiration, and Howells' unswerving conviction that, polls and academies and other literary men aside, his friend was "sole, incomparable, the Lincoln of our literature." "I wish you could understand how unshaken you are, you old tower, in every way," Howells wrote in January 1898. "Your foundations are struck so deep that you will catch the sunshine of immortal years and bask in the same light as Cervantes and Shakespeare." And that October, after rereading "The Recent Carnival of Crime," he concluded, "You are the greatest man of your sort that ever lived, and there is no use saying anything else."

In 1899 Hamlin Garland, carrying letters of introduction from Howells, called on Clemens and Bret Harte, who were then both in London. Garland was shocked by the changes which had come on Clemens since the Cable tour fifteen years earlier. His shaggy hair had turned white, his shoulders were stooped, he seemed smaller than he had been, and at first he was curiously aloof, as if he had forgotten he had a visitor. But when Garland, who had written a biography of Grant, asked him about the publishing history of the *Memoirs,* his interest was finally engaged, and his eyes became as keen and piercing as ever. It seemed to Garland that this old man—"the largest and most significant figure in American literature" —had lost little of his vigor or his indignation. Actually, as Garland may have realized years later, Clemens was also in the grip of one of his monomanias. For he said—contrary to all the facts, as Garland was to find out—that Charley Webster had "chouselled" him out of fifty thousand dollars and had brought about the ruin of the publishing house. He cursed Charley with fervor and Oriental magnificence, going on and on with "cold malignity" and "deadly hatred in face and voice," and he told Garland that what he had written about Charley in his autobiography "would make the son-of-a-bitch turn in his grave." Suddenly changing from this vein to an ironic prank, he gave Garland permission to publish the interview in *McClure's*, provided, of course, that Livy also gave her permission, and Garland went off on his fool's errand, to ask and be refused.

Garland's visit to Harte, who was living in a dainty apartment in Lancaster Gate, shocked him more deeply, for this man who had almost single-handedly created the literary image of the American West, and who had been idolized by an entire nation, now "looked and spoke like a burned out London sport." He was dressed like an American actor's idea of an English clubman, in striped trousers, a cutaway coat over a fancy vest, and lavender spats, he wore a monocle, and he carried a pair of yellow gloves. "*My* California is gone," he told Garland. "Sometimes I wish I had never come away." He had not lived in America since 1878. At thirty-five his best work had been behind him, and for twenty years and more Bret Harte had lived on what he knew to be hackwork—"I grind out the old tunes and gather up the coppers," he had written to his wife long ago, when he was consul at Krefeld. Now, jaded with London society, whose pet he was, he was tired and sick, his hair was white and his figure stooped, his eyes were yellowish, and his skin was puffy. Three years later he was dead of throat cancer, having acted out to the letter F. Scott Fitzgerald's observation that there are no second acts in American lives.

"*My* California is gone," Bret Harte had said. Mark Twain, aware of the passing of the frontier and touched by a *fin-de-siècle* wistfulness, also felt that time and history were passing him by. The century to come was not his century. As if to mark the close of a literary era, Frank Bliss during 1899 and 1900 published a signed and numbered twenty-two volume edition, *The Writings of Mark Twain*. Bliss appeared to be having an easy time selling it, Clemens told Chatto—"President McKinley and other big guns have subscribed." For this "Autograph Edition" Clemens, while in Vienna in March 1899, wrote fourteen manuscript pages of an autobiographical sketch. He submitted it to Livy, who made a few small but characteristic changes (for example, she suppressed his reference to "one James W. Paige, a fraud"). Then, with the reminder that what he hated above all was "gush and vulgarity," he sent the manuscript to his nephew, Sam Moffett, who was to put it in his own words, add to it or elaborate according to his judgment, and sign it for publication. Clemens was to have final approval of this piece, which contained much that he said himself—in the freedom of anonymity—and nothing that he disapproved of. "Mark Twain, A Biographical Sketch, by Samuel E. Moffett," which appeared at the end of Volume Twenty-two (just after "In Memoriam," Clemens' poem about Susy), is therefore more than an authorized biography. It can be read as a statement about himself by a man who had already in his lifetime become a legend, who continued to manipulate and redefine the symbols on which his legend was based, and who was driven by the need to impose order on a sprawling life which he often felt was without meaning.

Viewing his life as history from the very start, the sketch places Mark Twain's birth in the context of America's new "Western empire" and of the frontier, defined, in terms similar to Turner's, as "the extreme fringe of settlement" between cultivated land and wilderness. The "sleepy river towns" of the frontier, which Mark Twain grew up in and later knew as a pilot, are now a "vanished estate" whose charm and "warm, indolent existence" are preserved in his books, from *Tom Sawyer* to *Pudd'nhead Wilson*. Later on the sketch introduces another symbol as powerful for Americans at the turn of the century as the frontier: Mark Twain's "humor is as irrepressible as Lincoln's," and, again like Lincoln's, it has a profound aptness "in spite of the surface incongruity."

Instead of being swept on to wealth by the great westward tide of American expansion, Mark Twain's parents, we are told, had an almost "miraculous" faculty for the "eddies and back-currents," and they remained poor. But they still owned land and slaves, and the ancient Anglo-Saxon antecedents which the sketch cites complete a stereotype, familiar in success literature, of poor but blood-pure and proud gentry: Mark Twain's father was descended from Gregory Clemens, identified as one of the judges who condemned King Charles I to death, and through his mother the boy was descended from the titled "Lamptons of Durham." His formal education ended at the age of twelve (as late as 1890 the average American did not go beyond the fifth grade); "his high school was a village printing-office," and "his education in real life" had begun. The traditional anti-intellectualism—or, at the very least, mistrust of higher education—of the self-made man is heavily underscored: "It is a fortunate thing for literature that Mark Twain was never ground into smooth uniformity under the scholastic emery wheel." He "made the world his university." His preparation to be a pilot was "a labor compared with which the efforts needed to acquire the degree of Doctor of Philosophy at a university are as light as a summer course of modern novels."

At one point the sketch turns, without warning, into tall story. Mark

Twain while a journalist in Nevada had in fact been challenged to a duel by a rival editor; the duel had ended in apologies, but to escape imprisonment under the territory's anti-dueling statute Mark Twain had left for California. In the sketch he and his second go out to a gorge to practice with Colt revolvers. "A small bird lit on a sagebrush thirty yards away, and Mark Twain's second fired and knocked off its head." The opponent thinks this was Mark Twain's work, and, suddenly terrified by this deadly display, he offers a formal apology, thus "leaving Mark Twain with the honors of war." These details are borrowings from a comic story long familiar in the West in countless versions.

After this brief interlude the sketch goes on with a number of historically oriented or overtly self-vindicating statements. *The Innocents Abroad* established him as "a literary force of the first order." His acquaintance with Livy led "to one of the most ideal marriages in literary history." The house in Hartford was neither a practical joke nor a public demonstration of "the financial success possible in literature," but instead "one of the earliest fruits of the artistic revolt against the mid-century Philistinism of domestic architecture in America." The sketch tells in considerable detail about his career as a businessman, emphasizing "the series of unfortunate investments" that followed the "brilliant *coup*" of the Grant *Memoirs*. Bankrupt, he "could easily have avoided any legal liability for the debts," but he "felt bound in honor to pay them," and he paid them in full. His work as a writer has been "irresistibly laughter-provoking," but its more important purpose has been to make people "think and feel," and in *Joan of Arc* he emerged most distinctly as "a prophet of humanity." The sketch concludes with a discussion of Mark Twain as "characteristically American in every fiber," yet possessing a "universal quality" which has made him "a classic, not only at home, but in all lands whose people read and think about the common joys and sorrows of humanity."

His life had become history and biography, legend and stereotype, expressing the values and achievements of his country and his century. He had become a hero of the American experience, and when he came home in 1900 he was given a hero's welcome and led a hero's public life. Meanwhile, impatiently living out in London his last year of "this everlasting exile," Clemens looked back on history, and against the perspective of time his bitterness faded momentarily and he remembered only the fulfillments. "The 20th Century is a stranger to me," he wrote in his notebook. "I wish it well, but my heart is all for my own century. I took 65 years of it, just on a risk, but if I had known as much about it as I know now I would have taken the whole of it."

CHAPTER SEVENTEEN

"Whited sepulchre"

ON OCTOBER 15, 1900, after an exile of nearly ten years and an unbroken absence of over five, Mark Twain returned to America and to an ovation that went on for the rest of his life. "He looks like a fighting cock," Livy said, her own health apparently restored. Howells also recognized that this homecoming corresponded to a sense of triumph that pervaded Clemens, body and soul. "Younger and jollier than I have seen him in ten years," he told Thomas Bailey Aldrich. "He says it's all Plasmon, a new German food-drug he's been taking, but I think it's partly prosperity. He has distinctly the air of a man who has unloaded." The same remarkable change, along with its suggestion of renewed youth, was evident to the reporters who met Clemens in New York that October evening as he walked down the gangplank of his ship, appropriately the *Minnehaha* of the Atlantic Transport Line. They found him smiling and ruddy, generous and playful while being interviewed. As funny as ever, one reporter noted, and a little better-natured. Soon newspapers all over the country hailed the return of "the bravest author in all literature" and followed the lead of the New York *Times* in paying tribute, with unvarying comparison with the career of Sir Walter Scott, to "the Hero as Man of Letters." "It is a great thing to possess genius," the Boston Weekly *Transcript* said; "it is a greater thing to be a man of unsullied honor." Mark Twain's "splendid fight" against the dread enemy, debt, had made him the hero of a morality supported by a sound currency. "In this age of selfishness and commercialism," said a Southern church paper with an inadvertent gift for paradox, "he has taught the world a lesson that will bear fruit." It was clear to the custodians of public values that this lesson gave them an opportunity to congratulate themselves. "It makes us proud of our race and age," the

New York *Evangelist* said, "all the more as he comes off a winner." He had just been elected to a life membership in heaven, and while one of his favorite characters, the Recording Angel, was exploding in laughter, Clemens lightheartedly discussed with the press his belief that "the trouble with us in America is that we haven't learned to speak the truth," and he outlined his short-range plans to spend the winter in New York, to work and travel as little as possible, and to run for President on the broad platform of being in favor of everything.

Hartford had already become "the city of heartbreak." After attending Charles Dudley Warner's funeral there at the end of October Clemens realized that there was no longer any possibility of coming back to live in the house on Farmington Avenue. He was willing to sell it at a substantial loss and managed to talk Livy out of her refusal to allow it to be advertised. In 1903, following complicated negotiations, he finally sold it, to the president of the Hartford Fire Insurance Company. Clemens settled his family for the winter of 1900–1901 in a furnished house at 14 West Tenth Street which had been scouted for him by F. N. Doubleday. There, while Livy entertained quietly, while Clara prepared for her debut as a mezzo-soprano in Washington that January, and while Jean took treatments from Dr. George Helmer, an osteopath at Thirty-first Street and Madison Avenue, Clemens received a stream of visitors and interviewers who solicited his opinions on just about everything, including heaven, hell, the Boer War and the Boxer Rebellion, and his favorite method of escaping from the Indians. "It always puzzled me," Clara later recalled, "how Mark Twain could manage to have an opinion on every incident, accident, invention, or disease in the world." Less than thirty years before, he had been dismissed by the H. K.s and the J. G. Hollands of the time as a trifler and a clown whose opinions on subjects of any gravity were at best presumptuous. Now, Howells felt, Clemens was in danger of being taken so seriously as a sage that people might forget that he was, after all, a humorist. Almost daily and nightly he set out on a round of lunches, banquets, speeches, and appearances that nearly devoured him and that left him after two or three months worn out, pale, and coughing. "I hate to have him eating so many dinners," Howells told Aldrich, "and writing so few books." The Lotos Club and the Aldine, the Nineteenth Century Club and the City Club, the Society of American Authors and the New England Society gave banquets in his honor, in honor of the American Century, and in honor of the eliteness and achievement that the club way of life was supposed to foster. And for the sake of the redeeming moment when he rose to speak and gave public play to his spellbinding personality Clemens was willing to endure the "dreadful ordeal" of hearing dinner music, clashing cutlery, and shrieking human voices compete with each other and finally rise to a level of sheer pandemonium. After a while, "in order to save my life," he learned to skip the banquet, arrive after the speeches had begun, enjoy his moment, and leave early.

Late in 1901, after a summer at Lake Saranac and a visit to Elmira, Clemens rented a baronial mansion in Riverdale which was only twenty-five minutes from Grand Central and the banqueting world. It had a dining room sixty feet long and a commanding view of the Palisades, the Hudson, and the steamboats passing. Soon after, he bought for nearly fifty thousand dollars a house in Tarrytown overlooking the Tappan Zee; they never moved into it, for Livy's health had begun to crumble for the last time. In all this, Clemens' style of living matched his status as a steady guest, on cruises to Nova Scotia and Bermuda, of Henry Rogers on his steam yacht *Kanawha;* he was seated at the poker table one night off the coast of Florida when Tom Reed, former "czar" of the House of Representatives, took twenty-three pots in a row. Clemens was now a man of property, a major celebrity, and a semi-retired man of letters who no longer kept notebooks but instead pocket diaries in which he recorded a few literary ideas and a lot of social and business engagements. He could afford to pick and choose among a variety of lucrative offers and reject most of them. During 1900 he turned down Pond's offer of ten thousand dollars for ten lectures. (In 1902, he said, he would give benefit performances only, and only in private houses.) He turned down S. S. McClure's visionary offer of five thousand a year (and later an estimated twenty-thousand-dollar share of the expected annual profits) to edit a magazine of "rising young American literature" to be called *The Universal.* He turned down an offer from the humor magazine *Puck* of ten thousand a year (or more, Clemens believed, if he insisted) for one hour a week of his editorship. During 1902 his cash income from all sources was over $100,000, of which book royalties accounted for sixty thousand. In October 1903 he signed a contract, negotiated by Rogers, by which Harper acquired the inventory and rights in his work from the American Publishing Company, became his exclusive publisher, and guaranteed him a minimum of twenty-five thousand dollars a year for five years. As he noted at the time, he expected his books to "yield twice as much as that for many a year, if intelligently handled"; fifty years after his death, with many of his books having passed into the public domain, the royalties received by his estate were averaging about twenty thousand dollars a year.* His new and assured affluence was proof even against his investments in Plasmon, which inevitably turned into another "chouselling," and in smaller ventures such as a new kind of cash register, a patented spiral hatpin, and a stock promotion called the Book-

* Including cash and securities, house and land in Connecticut, two horses, a cow, and several vehicles, his estate was worth about $200,000 in 1910, according to Mr. Thomas G. Chamberlain, a trustee. At the final accounting in 1963, after the death of Clara Clemens Samossoud, the estate totaled $867,565.

lover's Library. Livy herself became interested for a while in a revival of the Tennessee land, having been told by Sam Moffett that because of a possible defect in the title some of the land, long since sold, might now revert to them. Soon, however, she was advising Moffett to proceed with caution. "Be *very* guarded in what you do," she wrote to him in January 1902, and she warned him that it was unlikely that his Uncle Sam would take any interest in recovering the land—"He is afraid it will bring you trouble as it has brought it to those who went before you." (As late as 1906 Clemens was still hoping to be rid of such vicarious claims on the land, claims which only swelled its sixty-year-old burden of "accumulated misapprehensions.")

On the streets and in theaters and restaurants Clemens was so often recognized and applauded that, as Clara said, "it was difficult to realize he was only a man of letters." He had, in fact, become something else. His career had followed a mythic pattern of journey from poverty and obscurity, of mortal struggle, and of victory and return. His hero's fame was transformed by a revolution in the printing of news and the appetite for news, and he became a celebrity—in Daniel Boorstin's definition, "a person who is known for his well-knownness." The reporters who dogged his steps were attracted not so much by his literature, which they rarely read or understood, as by his personality, his mane of white hair, his drawl, his astonishing opinions and mannerisms—all of which, having already been the subjects of bales of news clippings, now, by the dynamics of celebrity and his own skillful management, made him even better copy. Two old friends of his, survivors of the Boston group which years earlier had received if not exactly welcomed him, pondered his new dimension. "Mark's spectacular personality is just now very busy all over the world," Aldrich wrote to Howells in December 1901. "I doubt if there is another man on earth whose name is more familiar." "What a fame and force he is!" Howells remarked, and he described for Aldrich the experience of accompanying Clemens to the train for Riverdale. Clemens did not have to carry a timetable. When he arrived at the station the gatemen and the starters, who were proud to know him, arranged for him to board something that stopped at Riverdale, and even then he made them hold the train while he went to the station toilet. "But they would not let it go without him," Howells said, "if it was the Chicago limited!" Impressed and amused, Howells was also aware that Clemens' celebrity was becoming a barrier in itself. Howells called him "Clemens"; the pseudonym Mark Twain "seemed always somehow to mask him from my personal sense." He preferred, he said in a critical essay in the February 1901 *North American Review*, his friend's "personal books"—the books of travel and reminiscence—for there "we come directly into the presence of the author, which is what the reader is always longing and seeking to do." In a humorous letter to Clemens two years later Howells stated, in an oblique way, his sense of bafflement and isolation. He had had a dream about visiting Clemens in Riverdale, and in the dream he had encountered a servant named "Sam" who was planting potatoes in a plowed field. "Sam" had insolently refused to allow Howells to go up to the house, refused even to bring his card in, and Howells had gone back home humiliated. "I must really complain to you of the behavior of your man Sam," he said in his letter. "Bet Howells is drunk yet," Clemens noted on the envelope. He wrote back immediately to apologize and to tell Howells that Sam had been fired.

At the same time that he luxuriated in celebrity, Clemens broodingly recognized that it had its costs and imperatives and also that it was only the delicate child of public opinion. "We all do no end of feeling and we mistake it for thinking," he wrote in 1900 at the end of "Corn-Pone Opinions." "And out of it we get an aggregation which we consider a boon. Its name is Public Opinion. It is held in reverence. It settles everything. Some think it is the Voice of God." He then put this bitter little essay away in his box of "posthumous stuff," but, remembering its lesson well, he displayed in his public behavior over the next five or six years an irregular pattern of magnificent courage and fervor punctuated by retreats and compromises which he managed to rationalize in one way or another. The Spanish-American War (which Howells, more of a political realist, predicted would inaugurate "an era of blood-bought prosperity") impressed Clemens at first as a noble cause, the only occasion in history when one man was willing to fight for another man's freedom. But soon the application of this principle to the "liberation" of the Philippines fused in his mind with the Boer War and the Boxer reparations. By the time he returned to America he was, like most intellectuals and writers, a professed and outspoken anti-imperialist. In December 1900, when he introduced the twenty-six-year-old Winston Churchill to his first American lecture audience at the Waldorf-Astoria, he could not pass up the opportunity to elaborate on the circumstance that it was not alone through Churchill's mother that America and England were kin. "I think that England sinned when she got herself into a war in South Africa, just as we have sinned in getting into a similar war in the Philippines," he said. "And now that we are also kin in sin, there is nothing more to be desired." A few weeks later, disgusted by what he saw as an unholy alliance of Christianity, cash, and colonialism going under the collective name of civilization, he published in the New York *Herald* a salutation to the twentieth century: "I bring you the stately matron named Christendom, returning bedraggled, besmirched, and dishonored from pirate raids in Kiao-Chou, Manchuria, South Africa and the Philippines, with her soul full of meanness, her pocket full of boodle, and her mouth full of pious hypocrisies. Give her soap and a towel, but hide the looking-glass." Finally, in the February 1901 *North American Review*, Clemens published "To the Person Sitting in Darkness," an impassioned attack on "the Blessings-of-Civilization Trust," its managers—Mr. McKinley, Mr. Joseph Chamberlain, the Kaiser, and the Czar—and its chosen representatives, the Christian missionaries who marched to distant lands to conquer in the double sign of the cross and the black flag. "We can even make jokes," Clemens said, after noting that these missionaries were now busy collecting reparations, sometimes hundreds of taels of silver and the life of a Chinese for each believer killed by the Boxers: "Taels, I win, Heads you lose."

"I am not expecting anything but kicks for scoffing, and am expecting a diminution of my bread and butter by it," he wrote to Twichell, "but if Livy will let me I will have my say." Livy was sometimes angry with him for pursuing some personal vendetta until, she said, "you seem almost like a monomaniac." But on large issues of conscience she respected his indignation, and it was not Livy but Twichell who urged him to be silent. "*I* can't understand it!" Clemens raged. "You are a public guide and teacher, Joe, and are under a heavy responsibility to men, young and old; if you teach your people—as you teach me—to hide their opinions when they believe the flag is being abused and dishonored, lest the utterance do them and a publisher a damage, how do you answer for it to your conscience?" A few years later, during Theodore Roosevelt's campaign, Clemens was scolding the solidly Republican Twichell for writing a campaign speech built "on the oldest and best models. There isn't a paragraph in it whose facts or morals will wash." For not the least among all the changes Clemens had seen in his lifetime was the decline of the Protestant clergy in influence and function. The social and moral leaders of his youth were now, he believed, merely apologists for dollar civilization and the status quo. The pulpit, he said, had become about as indispensable as "the sun—the moon, anyway."

One afternoon in December 1907 Clemens and Carnegie had a talk about the news that Theodore Roosevelt—"the Tom Sawyer of the political world of the twentieth century," Clemens called him—had impetuously decided to abolish the motto "In God We Trust," because coins "carried the name of God into improper places." The fact was, Carnegie said, that "the name of God is used to being carried into improper places everywhere and all the time." It *was* a beautiful motto, Clemens said. "It is simple, direct, gracefully phrased; it always sounds well—In God We Trust. I don't believe it would sound any better if it were true." But the fact was, he went on, it hadn't been true since the Civil War; what the country trusted in was not God but "the Republican party and the dollar—mainly the dollar." And as for the United States being a Christian country (as twenty-two clergymen, protesting Roosevelt's order, had just declared in a formal resolution), "Why, Carnegie," Clemens said, and one can hear the triumphant drawl, the soft and deadly pounce, "so is hell."

Twichell had predicted a storm of abuse over "To the Person Sitting in Darkness," and the storm broke. One New York Congregationalist minister publicly denounced Clemens as "a man of low birth and poor breeding." But Clemens was also applauded and supported by people he respected, and, far from backing down, he pressed the attack in a second article, "To My Missionary Critics." That October he and Howells came to Yale to receive honorary degrees. Theodore Roosevelt stood apart at the ceremony; since the assassination of McKinley he had been forbidden to mix in crowds or shake hands. As a long ovation went up for Clemens, Roosevelt declared privately, "When I hear what Mark Twain and others have said in criticism of the missionaries, I feel like skinning them alive." But Mark Twain was the students' hero. After the exercises, when he was touring the campus, a crowd of them gave the college cheer and roared out his name. He took off his hat and bowed.

"Praise to the Eternal!" said a leading anti-imperialist. "A voice has been found." Serving as a public conscience, Mark Twain was applauded for his courage, anger, and truth. Yet at the same time, privately, he was capable of the kind of *volte-face* which, by his own standards, made him scarcely less culpable than Twichell. Over 1,500 Negroes and whites were lynched during the 1890s; in 1900 there were 115 lynchings, in 1901 there were 130. "In ten years this will be *habit*, on these terms," Clemens noted in September 1901. The citizens of Pierce City, Missouri, a village in the southwest corner of his native state, had just gone on a rampage, lynched three Negroes, burned out five households, driven thirty families into the woods. Stirred by the outrage, Clemens occupied himself that summer at Saranac with two related projects. One was an article, "The United States of Lyncherdom," which he intended for the *North American Review*. "O compassionate missionary," he pleaded, "leave China! come home and convert these Christians!" The disease of moral cowardice was epidemic, and it could be fought only by brave men taking a stand, for "no mob has any sand in the presence of a man known to be splendidly brave" (the same point Colonel Sherburn made to the Arkansas lynch mob in *Huckleberry Finn*). The second project, which he proposed to Frank Bliss, was a subscription-book history of lynching in America— maybe three thousand cases in all, he figured. His article was to be the introduction. "Nothing but such a book can rouse up the sheriffs to put down the mobs and the lynchings," he told Bliss. Moreover, "No book is so marketable as this one—the field is fresh, untrodden, and of the strongest interest." The idea continued to excite him—at one time he thought of asking George Kennan to take it over—but in the end he abandoned the

book and turned instead to writing "A Double-Barrelled Detective Story,"
a heavy-handed burlesque of Sherlock Holmes and "his cheap and ineffectual ingenuities." For he had felt compelled to agree with Bliss that
in one crucial respect the lynching book was a poor idea: it would kill
sales in the South. "I shouldn't have even half a friend left down there,
after it issued from the press." "There is plenty of vitriol in it and that
will keep it from spoiling," he rationalized as he consigned the article to
his pile of posthumous manuscript. (Paine had an even more desperate
rationalization: "The moment of timeliness had passed.")

His need to be loved dictated the answer to the question of whether
to speak out about lynching or remain silent. "Desouthernized" as he was,
his imagination and his youth still lived down there in Hannibal. During
1902 he was intermittently occupied with further Tom and Huck stories,
elegiac in tone and with a new element frankly acknowledged: now there
are girls in Tom Sawyer's gang, kissing parties, and even a suggestion
that one girl, as Huck says, was a "horlat." Clemens' notes call for the
boys and girls to promise to meet after fifty years at midnight on Holliday's Hill. Tom and Huck call the roll: they are old and withered like
the others; "Old Jim" answers for all the absent ones. There are railroad
tracks now where once there had been open land; the levee is dead; the
steamboats are all gone.

It was in this valedictory mood that at the end of May 1902 Clemens
returned to Hannibal—for the last time, he was certain. He was on his
way to receive an honorary doctorate of laws from the University of
Missouri at Columbia on June 4. The five days he spent in Hannibal represented the accumulated and reciprocated loyalties of a lifetime. On the
first morning he visited the tiny frame house on Hill Street where he
had spent most of his boyhood. "It all seems so small to me," he said.
"I suppose if I should come back here ten years from now it would be
the size of a bird-house." Wearing a white shirt and a pale-gray suit, he
stood hatless in the sunlight, his hands in his coat pockets, and leaned
against the open screen door. The photographers took his picture while
crowds of townsfolk, boys in galluses and girls in smocks, watched from
the sidewalk. Then he drove off in a carriage to visit the family graves
in Mount Olivet Cemetery. In the afternoon he went to the Decoration
Day exercises at the Presbyterian church. He rose to speak, and the entire audience rose with him and applauded and applauded. When they
stopped he had to stand silent for a long minute before he was able to
speak without his voice breaking in emotion. That evening he dined
in formal dress with two old schoolmates, Helen Garth and Laura Hawkins
Frazer, both widows now; Laura, who had been his "very first sweetheart,"
was a plump old lady, gum-fallen and purse-mouthed. Later, at the Opera
House, he gave out the diplomas to the high-school graduating class and

shook hands for an hour. When he left from the depot in Hannibal at the end of his stay, he posed once again for the photographers, this time holding a bunch of flowers. Over the din of the huge crowd that had come to say goodbye, his boyhood playmate Tom Nash shouted to him in a deaf man's whisper, "Same damned fools, Sam." At way stations on the trip to Columbia and then back to St. Louis, where he stood at the pilot's wheel of the harbor boat *Mark Twain*, other crowds waited for him, with applause and flowers, and his eyes filled with tears. For such love who can blame him for putting aside, out of a lifetime's work, one book and one article?

Clemens was as certain that American democracy was headed toward "monarchy" (or dictatorship) as he was that Christian Science was the coming religion—"I regard it as the Standard Oil of the future." "When we contemplate her and what she has achieved," he said about Mary Baker Eddy, "it is blasphemy to longer deny to the Supreme Being the possession of a sense of humor," and in articles published in 1902 and 1903 he went at Eddyism with the same savage glee he took in cataloguing Fenimore Cooper's literary offenses. A few years later his target became the Belgian depredations in the Congo, and he wrote "King Leopold's Soliloquy," the most effective and most widely circulated piece of American propaganda in the cause of Congo reform. But he declined to commit himself to being a systematic reformer. He was a lightning bug, not a bee, he said, explaining why he could not go on to write a second piece about the Congo. "My instincts and interests are merely literary, they rise no higher; and I scatter from one interest to another, lingering nowhere." There were other explanations. The Harper firm, he said, had been doubtful all along of his commercial wisdom in dipping into Leopold's "stinkpot" as well as Mrs. Eddy's, and he accepted their proposal to publish *Christian Science* "silently" and to allow "King Leopold's Soliloquy" to be published as a pamphlet, illustrated with atrocity photographs, by the Boston Congo Reform Association, a gratis contribution from the author. Underlying even his most courageous and outspoken public positions was the demoralizing gospel of "Corn-Pone Opinions." His response to years of bankruptcy and disaster, during which he felt his powers and his popularity waning, was a kind of post-traumatic syndrome, part of which was a refusal to take serious risks with what he had regained. By 1905 his celebrity had become addictive and had begun to blunt his purpose as a public conscience. Sometimes he was not at all sure that it had been worth while to give up the freedom of the humorist in order to become a sage. In a satire called "The War Prayer," not published until 1923 in *Europe and Elsewhere*, he wrote a Swiftian indictment of the martial spirit, of patriotism which was basically blood lust. But Jean told him it was sacrilegious: it did, after all, suggest the paradox of God being on both sides in any war between two Christian countries. Clemens accepted her veto, and, pacing the floor in his slippers and dressing gown, he admitted to Dan Beard that he was not going to publish it in his lifetime. "I have told the whole truth in that, and only dead men can tell the truth in this world," he said, perhaps recalling that Montaigne admitted to speaking the truth not as much as he wanted but only as much as he dared. "He did not care to invite the public verdict that he was a lunatic," Albert Bigelow Paine wrote in his biography, "or even a fanatic with a mission to destroy the illusions and traditions and conclusions of mankind."

He was a pragmatist, and it was in a spirit of bowing to the inevitable that he survived, not without dishonor and embarrassment, the agonizing farce staged by Maxim Gorky's American hosts in April 1906. The speed with which this celebrated episode moved only strengthened Clemens' conviction that public opinion was as delicate a fabric as "the webs of morning" and shriveled at the lightest touch. On April 10 Gorky arrived on a mission to solicit money and support for the Russian revolutionary movement. He was accompanied, according to the newspapers, by his "young charming wife." Despite the rain he was greeted at the pier in Hoboken by thousands who hailed him as another Kossuth or Garibaldi. Wearing boots and a blue peasant blouse, he was feted the day after at a dinner at which plans were announced for a great gala fund-raising banquet; its sponsors were, among others, Clemens, Howells, Finley Peter Dunne, and Jane Addams. "If we can build a Russian republic to give its persecuted peoples the same freedom which we enjoy," Clemens said that evening, with the guest of honor seated at his right, "let us by all means go on and do it." "Let there be light!" said a cartoon in the New York *World* on April 12; it showed the Statue of Liberty bending down to light Gorky's torch. The *World*'s cartoon the next day showed Mark Twain, a "Yankee in Czar Nicholas' Court," toppling the Romanov throne with a mighty push of his pen. ("The Czar's Soliloquy," Clemens' most extended statement on the subject, had appeared in March 1905 in the *North American Review*.) But by Saturday, April 14, just four days after Gorky's arrival, the honeymoon was over. In reprisal against Gorky, who, after all these nice gestures, had just signed an exclusive contract with a rival paper, Hearst's *American*, the *World* broke a story apparently based on information supplied by the Russian Embassy. "Gorky Brings Actress Here as 'Mme. Gorky.'" the headline ran. Gorky's "young charming wife," as his inner circle of supporters had known and worried about from the start, was his mistress, Maria Andreyeva, an actress (he had been separated from his legal wife for years). The scandal reverberated. Gorky and Madame Andreyeva, turned out of one hotel after another by irate managers, finally found a place to stay with friends on Staten Island (the

Sun warned that "the purity of our inns is threatened"). That Saturday afternoon Paine ran into Howells coming out of Clemens' house at 21 Fifth Avenue. Howells was wearing "an unhappy, hunted look"; upstairs was Clemens, agitated and brusque. Paine wondered if the two had quarreled; they had only been trying to solve the problem of what to do with the reporters downstairs. "I am a revolutionist—by birth, breeding, principle, and everything else," Clemens finally told them, but he explained that Gorky's "efficiency as a persuader" was now seriously "impaired"— "I was about to say destroyed"—by his violation of certain "laws of conduct." Soon after this he and Howells resigned as sponsors, and the fundraising banquet was abandoned.

It had been a remarkable week, the sociologist Franklin Giddings wrote in an article which Clemens found uncomfortably, remorselessly severe: In Missouri three innocent Negroes had just been physically lynched, in New York two visiting Russians had just been socially and morally lynched, and no one protested. There was no doubt that as advance man for the revolution Gorky had botched his job. He should have had a guardian to keep him out of trouble, Clemens said—"The man might just as well have appeared in public in his shirt-tail." Soon, in an attempt to justify his own uncomfortable retreat, he was saying that Gorky had violated custom and that this was worse than violating the law, because law is only sand, while "custom is custom; it is built of brass, boiler iron, granite; facts, reasonings, arguments have no more effect upon it than the idle winds have upon Gibraltar." Still, it was humiliating to have to postpone the liberation of 150,000,000 Russians just because one of them had left his pants at home; it was humiliating to say hurrah for Gorky's program of bloodshed and dynamite and then balk at what was only a domestic irregularity (the Russian divorce laws prevented Gorky from marrying Madame Andreyeva). And Clemens had cause to worry that his own "efficiency as a persuader" had been seriously impaired by the episode. It took nothing less than an act of God, the San Francisco earthquake on April 18, to spare him and the other amateur revolutionists further mortification in the newspapers.

II

At York Harbor, Maine, in the summer of 1902, Clemens watched hopelessly as Livy lapsed into her last illness. They had traveled from Riverdale in Rogers' yacht shortly after Clemens returned from Hannibal, and, in a rented house overlooking the York River and only a few miles away from Howells at Kittery Point, they expected a quiet time with a few visitors. Nonetheless, by the beginning of August it was apparent that a breakdown was coming on; in order to breathe, Livy now sat upright in her bed most of the night. Clemens blamed it on the accumulated strain of five years of anxiety about Jean. On August 12, a day after she entertained at tea for what proved to be the last time—among the guests were Howells and a singing teacher named Madame Hartwig who came with a letter of introduction from Queen Elizabeth of Rumania—she had a choking fit, brought on by a combination of asthma and heart strain. She and Clemens believed she was dying. For weeks afterward, while the *Kanawha* waited for orders to take them back to Riverdale, she hardly improved, seemed once or twice again to be dying. The doctors said her collapse was due to organic heart disease and nervous prostration. In between their visits, while they did what they could, appeared the inevitable Dr. Helmer, the osteopath, who came over from his vacation in Vermont to give her a treatment that left her aching all over. By the middle of October she had recovered sufficiently to be taken to Riverdale in a special through train, with a locomotive on either end, that Clemens had gone to Boston to arrange for. Howells spent a "ghostly afternoon" with him there lunching at Young's Hotel, where Redpath's lecturers used to meet at the start of the season, and fighting off the specters of the old days.

From that day in August until she died in Florence twenty-two months later, Livy declined steadily. She often thought she was suffocating, and after she was revived by oxygen or injections of brandy she lay back haggard and quivering with fright. "I don't want to die," she said to Clemens. The time had come for a heroic ruse. He told her, "I more believe in the immortality of the soul than misbelieve in it," and at first she was reassured and grateful. But by this time her orthodoxy had been too deeply eroded by him to give her much comfort; she knew he said this only for her sake. "Almost the only crime of my life which causes me bitterness now," he told Clara after Livy's death, was to violate the sanctities of her "spiritual shelter and refuge." And it was certainly one of the bitter ironies of their marriage that after all these years he should be singled out, by Livy's doctors and implicitly by Livy herself, as the chief external cause of the nervous states that went along with hyperthyroid heart disease. In Riverdale during the fall and winter of 1902 she was isolated in her room, and Clemens was prevented from paying her even a brief visit. On December 30 he saw her for five minutes, the first time in three months, and on their thirty-third wedding anniversary in February he again had only five minutes with her. He communicated with her by notes, playful, affectionate, some of them written in a private code: "Sozodont and sozodont and sal ammoniac synchronously pax vobiscum, S.L.C."—by which he meant to say that he was ever passionately hers.

"Poor Livy drags along drearily," Clemens had written to Twichell in October, just as her long isolation from him was beginning. "It must be hard times for that turbulent spirit. It will be a long time before she is on her feet again." Without her he felt "helpless" in literary matters. He now had "no editor—no censor," he told Frederick Duneka of Harper; even Howells failed him, for after reading a story ("Was It Heaven? Or Hell?") in manuscript, Howells said it was "all right—whereas it wasn't." It was Clara who told him there was too much sermon in it, and he took the manuscript back from the magazine and revised it. In Clara and Jean and a little later in his private secretary, Clemens looked for a symbolic replacement for Livy, just as Livy had replaced Mary Fairbanks. During the sixty-seventh-birthday dinner given in his honor at the Metropolitan Club, Clemens spoke about old friends who were present, about the "great and beautiful country . . . a delectable land" where he had spent his boyhood, and finally about his debt to Livy, "the larger part, the better part" of him. Three days later, writing to Livy from Elmira, where he attended a niece's wedding in the Langdon parlor, he recalled for her the joy and excitement and hilarity of their own wedding, and then he told her about the "grand and flattersome" birthday banquet. "It was the last name and the last praise (yours) uttered that night that brought the *mighty* burst" of applause, he wrote, and he added Howells' comment that it was the best speech he ever made. "It was splendid to close, like that, with Mrs. Clemens." But in Livy's state such jubilance had to be handled with care. "Clara dear," he wrote at the head of the page, aware that a strange spirit sometimes possessed him even when he was vigilant, "this is to your mother but you must not risk showing it to her without reading it first yourself."

Livy's doctors told him to take her to Florence to stay the following winter. His friends guessed they would stay indefinitely. That summer, in between business trips to New York, he worked in his study at Quarry Farm for the last time. At the beginning of October he visited Susy's grave in Woodlawn Cemetery and placed some flowers there. Later that month he and Livy sailed from New York. With them were Clara and Jean; a trained nurse; their maid, Kate Leary; and Miss Isabel V. Lyon of Hartford, thirty-five years old, Clemens' personal secretary. At Genoa, on the orders of the Italian ambassador, they were passed through customs without examination, and they moved into Villa di Quarto on the outskirts of Florence, an enormous, gloomy, and unsatisfactory house with the comforts of a fortress. Soon Clemens was hunting for a better place and all the while carrying on a vendetta against their American-born landlady, Countess Massiglia, who seemed as determined to get him out as he was to leave. They quarreled at first because she had removed some furnishings that were supposed to go with the villa. He suspected her of cutting the telephone wires, locking the gates, turning off the water, even smearing her large dogs with kerosene and then loosing them to rub up against his visitors. By April he had begun a suit against her for breach of contract and failure to maintain her cesspools properly; in the same litigious mood, after Livy's death he planned a campaign against the Hamburg-America Line and accused the doctor who attended her in Florence of overcharging and of maliciously withholding the death certificate.

Throughout the cold and rainy winter, no improvement over the climate of Riverdale, Clemens was allowed to see her once a day; she continued to grow weaker. She was worried about their medical expenses, which were prodigious. To set her mind at rest he turned out about thirty-seven thousand words of magazine material for *Harper's* in less than a month, and then, beginning in January, he dictated his autobiography to Isabel Lyon for two hours each morning. After a winter of hard work, bronchitis, and rheumatism, he was beginning to look older than his sixty-eight years. "I am passing off the stage," he joked with William Lyon Phelps when they met at a concert of Clara's in April, "and now my daughter is the famous member of the family." When Phelps called at Villa di Quarto a few days later he noted a constant twitching in Clemens' right cheek; Clemens seemed nervous and restless, smoked three cigars during an hour's talk. The old triumphant slow-paced drawl came back only when Phelps asked him how he felt about his legendary rise from obscurity. "Well," he answered, "I do look back upon my career with considerable satisfaction."

By May, although Livy talked about moving to another villa for the summer, it was clear that she had given up. She talked to Kate Leary about being buried in the lavender satin dress she had bought in New York. After a brief remission, when she suddenly looked bright and young again, Clemens saw in her gaze "that pathetic something," he wrote to Gilder, "which betrays the secret of a waning hope." It was what he had learned to expect, and when she died on the evening of June 5, sitting upright in bed with the oxygen tube in her mouth, it came to him not like the thunderclap of Susy's death but as inevitable, and a portent of his own. Looking at her for the last time, he remembered the face he had first seen in Charley Langdon's ivory miniature, and he was "full of remorse for things done and said in the 34 years of married life that hurt Livy's heart." A few weeks later he made note of "a calamity": "I cannot reproduce Livy's face in my mind's eye." He described himself, characteristically, as feeling penniless and fifty million dollars in debt. After an accident in which he nearly fell out of one of the Countess's second-story windows he felt certain that "in my bereaved circumstances the world would have been sure it was suicide." But it was his daughters who were in a state of shock. Jean had had her first epileptic seizure in over a year; during most of the five years after Livy's death and before her own in 1909 she would be in and out of various sanatoriums. Clara had a nervous breakdown, and she kept to her bed for the trip home from Naples to New York at the end of June. That fall she entered a rest home on Sixty-ninth Street and saw no one but a trained nurse and a specialist. The pattern of Livy's last years was ironically, perhaps vindictively, repeated: for a year Clemens was not allowed to visit Clara, telephone her, or even write to her.

III

The furniture from the Hartford house was unpacked and installed at 21 Fifth Avenue, on the corner of Ninth Street, and in the fall of 1904 Clemens moved into what was to be his home for the next four years. The loneliness of his life here was only deepened by the melancholy music of an Aeolian Orchestrelle, a sort of player organ for which, as Clemens later told Clara apologetically, he had paid $2,600. He always had a passion for the hurdy-gurdy, for ballads and jubilee hymns; now, at least, his taste was being elevated, he told her, for among the composers of the sixty pieces of music that the machine rendered were Beethoven, Wagner, and Schubert. Lying back on a sofa, smoking and musing, he listened for two or three hours every night while Isabel Lyon worked it for him. With Clara away and Jean unpredictable, he had come to depend on her. She had his entire confidence. He had, after all, dictated to her portions of that autobiography which he believed was the most truthful book ever written, which would show him nakeder than Adam and Eve and would tell what Howells said could never be told about any man—"the black heart's-truth." In his dressing room or at the dinner table he spoke to her with a freedom he would not have dared with Livy or his daughters. (At dinner early in 1906 he remarked to her about the estrangement between Taft and Theodore Roosevelt, "I thought Taft was Roosevelt's miscarriage preserved in alcohol.") She supervised his social and business affairs and ran the house at 21 Fifth Avenue; the living expenses were over fifty dollars a day by 1906, Paine was shocked to realize, and Clemens never questioned anything.

Isabel Lyon had also taken over some of Livy's role as editor. During the summer of 1905 Clemens went back to his old habit of working on a number of projects almost simultaneously, abandoning one in the middle when his interest flagged and jumping to another; he had always worked this way, he told Colonel Higginson, and he liked it. That summer, with his customary suspension of self-criticism, he was working sporadically on *The Mysterious Stranger,* on *Three Thousand Years among the Microbes,* on a revision of "Adam's Diary," and, at the farthest end of the scale, on a sentimental story about cruelty to animals, "A Horse's Tale," whose human heroine was Susy. One of the constants running through this gamut of quality was the editorial voice of Isabel Lyon. "Miss Lyon voted against the revision," Clemens noted after he had worked over "Adam's Diary," "but she wouldn't vote against it now." "Miss Lyon likes it nearly as much as I do," he told Duneka about "A Horse's Tale." She had a voice in family affairs, too. It was because of her, Clemens later said, that he believed Jean was crazy and should live in an institution instead of at home, where, he mourned, she had belonged all the while. Miss Lyon followed the family pattern of "nervous collapses," needed isolation and rest, had hysterics and tantrums; later he claimed that all her disturbances came out of the whiskey bottle. He also claimed later that she had sexual designs on him. Whether this was true or not, it was certainly true that she became possessive of her influence over him and jealous of others, and that she was largely responsible for creating a court atmosphere in which "the king" was surrounded by plots and counterplots straight out of Saint-Simon's Versailles if not Graustark itself. It took a palace revolution to depose Isabel Lyon in 1909, when she went into permanent banishment.

To celebrate Mark Twain's seventieth birthday, men and women of letters and of eminence in general were invited to attend a great banquet at Delmonico's, the society sanctum, on December 5, 1905. After meeting the guest of honor at a reception, they filed into Delmonico's red room to the music of a forty-piece orchestra from the Metropolitan Opera House. Surrounded by potted palms and huge gilt mirrors, they dined on fillet of kingfish, saddle of lamb, Baltimore terrapin, quail, and redhead duck washed down with sauterne, champagne, and brandy. Then they settled back to absorb five hours of toasts, poems, and speeches, every word of which, together with photographs of the guests by Byron, was preserved in a special thirty-two-page supplement to the Christmas issue of *Harper's Weekly.* In the small hours the guests started for home carrying as souvenirs of the occasion foot-high plaster busts of Mark Twain.

When he first heard of the plans for this banquet Clemens was enchanted. Bang away, he told Colonel George Harvey, editor of both *Harper's Weekly* and the *North American Review;* Harvey's genius as organizer, publicist, and kingmaker was soon to be applied to the political career of Woodrow Wilson. "The dinner scheme is unique and just and a jewel," Clemens said, and when it was all over he thanked "Harvey the Magnificent" for "the most satisfying and spirit-exalting honor done me in all my seventy years, oh, by seventy times seventy! By George, nobody but you could have imagined and carried out that wonderful thing." During the weeks before the banquet, however, he grumbled to Miss Lyon that the whole thing was a publicity stunt for the Harper list. With his chronic mistrust of publishers (and of practically everyone with whom he had business dealings), he had already, on various occasions, damned Harvey, Duneka, and all the Harpers to the same hell he reserved for Elisha Bliss and Charles Henry Webb, "liar and thief." (In the category of "Permanent," Bliss, Charley Webster, and Paige were on a list of "Hated Persons" Clemens drew up around 1904 or 1905; Countess Massiglia and Fred Hall, on the other hand, occupied only a kind of purgatory under the heading "Temporary—fleeting. Good for one year and Train only. To be taken up in idle moments and hated for pastime.")

As he approached his seventieth year—"the time of life when you arrive at a new and awful dignity," he was to say at the banquet—he alternated between such angers and pastimes and a mood of warm sunset. Sometimes he saw himself as saying goodbye to a long procession in which he himself marched not far from the end. Livy, Mollie Clemens, and Pamela all died in 1904. He made a new will. "Who is it I *haven't* known?" he asked that May when he heard that Sir Henry Stanley was dead; he had known him since 1867, when Stanley had covered his St. Louis lecture. Any man whose death was worth cabling he was sure he had met somewhere or other, and when he thought back to Nevada and California he felt that just by naming the names he could almost start a resurrection. "Those were the days!—those old ones," he wrote in 1905 as he declined an invitation to go West again. But his time for wandering was over: he planned "to sit by the fire for the rest of my remnant of life and indulge myself with the pleasure and repose of work." It was in one of these evanescent mellow moods that he composed his birthday speech, said he was greatly satisfied with it, and rehearsed it twice in front of Miss Lyon.

"I will not say, 'Oh King, live forever,'" Howells addressed him as the great evening neared its climax, "but 'Oh King, live as long as you like!'" The hundreds who waved their napkins, cheered, and paid tribute to Mark Twain summed up his years in the East and the rewards he had sought from the Gilded Age: Howells, the only man of letters he deferred to, whose praise certified Clemens to a literary status higher than any he had first aimed for as humorist, entertainer, and lecturer; Twichell, who had conducted Livy's wedding service and then her funeral service, bridging the heartbreak and the enormous bliss and triumph of the years at Nook Farm; his barnstorming partner, Cable, who had come from his sickbed this evening to declare a lifetime of affection for a humorist who was never the king's jester—"He is always the King"; his friends the plutocrats Henry Rogers and Andrew Carnegie, who had seen him through financial ruin and in whose favor and admiration he now luxuriated—"He stands forever with Scott," Carnegie said later that evening, "he has done everything that Scott did." There was even a representative from the Four Hundred, Perry Belmont, the future doyen of Newport, where Clemens felt quite as much at home as he did at Tuxedo Park, Pierre Lorillard's enclave for sifted millionaires. The molders and the servants of official opinion, the editors and the critics, were here; so were the stars of a new generation of humorists, George Ade and Finley Peter Dunne, who would never match Mark Twain's enduring popularity; sitting among them were women as varied in the directions their talents would take as Willa Cather and Emily Post. But mostly facing Mark Twain were the respectable, workaday practitioners who would soon be forgotten but were the night sky for the brilliance of his departing comet.

Seated at their flower-decked tables, participating in what they felt was a memorial service for a living writer, they expected a valedictory, and that is what he gave them. In his funny and sad speech, a feat of illusionism which was the first in a long series of swan songs, he looked back over the seventy years since his birth in "a little hamlet, in the backwoods of Missouri, where nothing ever happened," and, joking about his cigars and his morals and his habits in general, he said that each person listening to him now would have to find his own way of living to seventy —"We can't reach old age by another man's road." Old age had its desolations, he said. After the banquet he would come out into the night, the winter, and the deserted streets—alone again, as he had been nearly forty years before when his cholera-torn ship came into New York Harbor. Even so, having reached "Pier Number Seventy," he was prepared, he told them—and he believed it himself for the moment—to sail again with "a reconciled spirit" and "a contented heart."

One of the many Harper authors at the Delmonico banquet was Albert Bigelow Paine, editor, writer of fiction for children and adults, and author of a distinguished biography of Thomas Nast, published the year before. Paine had been raised in the Midwest; at the age of eight he listened night after night to his parents reading aloud from a new book called *The Innocents Abroad*. For a while he was an itinerant photographer and a dealer in photographic supplies at Fort Scott, Kansas. He came to New York in the 1890s and joined the group of writers and editors who made their social headquarters at the Players Club on Gramercy Park. It was there that he first met Clemens, in 1901. Later, after one or two other meetings, Clemens gave him permission to quote from some letters to Nast. At the beginning of January 1906 they met again; at a Players dinner in Clemens' honor. They talked about *Joan of Arc;* nearly twenty years later Paine was to publish his own painstaking and scholarly book about her. On Saturday, January 7, after having been encouraged by a friend to propose himself as Clemens' biographer, Paine called at 21 Fifth Avenue. In the dark red room upstairs which doubled as workroom and bedroom, Paine found Clemens propped up in his carved mahogany bed smoking a cigar and answering some letters. Paine told about his lifelong admiration for Clemens' work and then, with considerable trepidation, explained the purpose of his visit. There was a long silence, and Clemens said, "When would you like to begin?" The next Tuesday morning Paine moved into the adjoining room. So began a relationship which lasted until 1910: Paine was his biographer, constant companion, steward, and finally editor and literary executor.

At first, as notes for the biography, Clemens dictated long answers to Paine's questions. These answers quickly turned into the daily monologues which now make up the greater part of Clemens' published and still unpublished autobiography: in two and a half years he dictated something like half a million words. To supplement this outpouring he gave Paine access to his letters and papers—limited access only, as Paine, Howells, and others soon found out—and also a credential, dated March 1, 1906, introducing "my biographer and particular friend, who is seeking information concerning me for use in his book."

The summer before Paine appeared on the scene, Clemens had made vague plans for Clara and Jean, assisted by Miss Lyon, to arrange and publish his letters someday. "I don't want it done by any outsider," he told Clara. "Miss Lyon can do the *work*, and do it well." He had in mind an orthodox and dutiful life-and-letters treatment which, customarily in two imposing volumes, was as inevitable a reward for a man of letters as his gravestone and sometimes pressed a little more heavily. Later on, in order to avoid conflict between Paine's biography and what had to become simply an edition of the letters, he made the stipulation that Paine limit his quotations from them to ten thousand words. For years, with curses and threats of litigation, he had fought off unauthorized biographers and people who made unauthorized use of his letters; he regarded them all as invaders of his privacy, and, beyond this, he wanted his story told in his own way. He once thought that he might have to go to law in order to stop his old friend Pond from quoting from letters. Even Twichell, who injudiciously released a private letter to the papers, was denounced as a "damned fool." "I shall never thoroughly like him again," Clemens told Sam Moffett in 1907. Years earlier he had explained to Moffett, "All private letters of mine make my flesh creep when I see them again after a lapse of years." It was in the hope of avoiding this kind of distress that in 1904 he told the administrator of Mollie Clemens' estate to destroy any letters of his to Mollie, Orion, or Jane Clemens (he wanted saved only his father's old *Britannica* and his mother's illustrated family Bible). He hated the past, as he once told Howells—"It's so damned humiliating." Now, with an accredited biographer in full pursuit of the past, Clemens had his worries, and so did Paine. Isabel Lyon, watching with some satisfaction the inevitable cross currents and tensions, noted in January 1908: "Mr. Clemens has lost confidence in Paine." The maid Kate Leary, always loyal to the family, had seen Paine going through Clemens' letters to Livy and reported this to Clemens, who was angry. Paine asked Isabel Lyon to use her influence. She not only refused but also seems to have reported to Clemens that Paine, without permission, had obtained directly from Howells and Sam Moffett "a lot of the King's letters." Now Howells as well as Paine was in trouble. The impossible situation was finally resolved: Clemens was to go over all letters before Paine was allowed to consult them. "I don't like to have those privacies exposed in such a way even to my biographer," he told Howells: "If Paine should apply to you for letters, please don't comply."

Clemens had been writing or dictating his autobiography off and on since the 1870s, when he wrote some fragments about the Tennessee land and his early years in Florida, Missouri. In 1877 he planned to write "and *publish*" an account of his life up to the time of his marriage. In 1885 he dictated detailed accounts of his dealings with General Grant. He took up his autobiography again around 1896 and planned to write it in full, with "remorseless" accuracy. In Florence the year Livy died he dictated a substantial amount of material to Isabel Lyon. The impulse behind most of these starts was, of course, that of a professional writer whose favorite modes were autobiographical and oral. Behind his Florence dictations of 1904 was a special purpose, somewhat in violation of the spirit of the copyright laws, it now seems: he intended to tack pieces of these dictations as "new matter" onto each of his old books and thereby extend their life in copyright. By the summer of 1906, when George Harvey, who at first had been dubious about the autobiography pronounced it the "greatest book of the age" and started selecting installments for the *North American Review,* Clemens felt that a gold mine had been opened up. He was sure he could turn out fifty thousand words a month for the rest of his life. With the money that began to come in from the *Review* he bought 248 acres near Redding, Connecticut, and on his hilltop there over the Saugatuck valley he commissioned John Howells, his friend's son, to build him an Italianate villa. Isabel Lyon wanted to call it "Autobiography House." Clemens held out for "Innocence at Home," but finally let Clara have her way with "Stormfield."

All his life Clemens juggled with shifting notions of lies and truth. In his autobiography—which, with only an occasional caution, he was giving to his authorized biographer as primary material—he planned to write the truest book ever written. It is a "true" book, in the sense that he poured into it his deflected angers and heterodoxies. He had said that only the dead have free speech. Speaking "as from the grave," he could tell "the truth" about some of the people he had known; he could dictate passages about God and religion which he was sure would get his heirs and assigns burned at the stake if they dared take them out of his box of "posthumous stuff" and publish them before 2006 A.D. But this was only one kind of truth. "You are dramatic and unconscious," Howells wrote to him, "you count the thing more than yourself." Clemens too acknowledged tacitly that introspection and self-analysis were not his strong suit. The truth about *himself* might have to be deduced from his own inevitable lies, evasions, and (as with the letters that Paine was not allowed to read without supervision) reticences. "The remorseless truth *is* there, between the lines," he assured Howells, "where the author-cat is raking dust upon it which hides from the disinterested spectator neither it nor its smell." But by this time Mark Twain was too scarred an author-cat, and also too habituated a storyteller and performer, to give the spectator much of a chance at the truth. Even the vein of self-accusation which runs through the autobiography, and which he regarded as sure proof that he was baring his soul, is in part dramatic rationalizing. Self-accusation was one of his bulwarks against chaos, an act of obedience to the laws of an official and historical identity, Mark Twain, whose authorized biography Clemens himself, long before Paine, had been writing for years.

Only a few weeks after they began working together, Paine realized that Clemens' spellbinding reminiscences "bore only an atmospheric relation to history." He could recall something that had happened only the day before with absolute conviction but with all the essential circumstances turned around, and when Paine reminded him what the facts really were his face took on a blank look, as if he had just waked up. "When I was younger I could remember anything, whether it happened or not," he said to Paine, "but I am getting old, and soon I shall remember only the latter." The question of "whether it happened" is not much more relevant to certain parts of the autobiography than it is to *Huckleberry Finn*. But throughout this chronicle is the talk, the like of which, Howells said, we shall never know again—and we never have. As a record of magnificent talk, magical, hilarious, savage, and tender, the autobiography is a major work, Mark Twain's last, a sprawling and shapeless masterpiece whose unity is in the accent and rhythm and attack of his voice.

In the fifty-four years since his first sketch was published, Mark Twain had written novels, travel books, short stories, essays, plays, plain and fancy journalism. Formal construction baffled him; he wrestled constantly with the problem of point of view, solved it often by writing in the first person, sometimes had to give up altogether. For a while after Susy's death he could finish nothing and was afraid that he could no longer write at all. But in the autobiographical dictations he discovered an anti-form which allowed him a perfect and joyous freedom. "What a dewy and breezy and woodsy freshness it has," he exclaimed to Howells. He might have been speaking from Eden the day talk was invented. Each morning he took up whatever subject interested him and developed it whatever its logical or chronological direction might be; his method was associative, naturalistic, random; in a week's work humor, diatribe, and nostalgia would be all mixed together. In the afternoon he went over the typescript of the morning's dictation and polished it, but he was careful not to eliminate the slips and halts and stumbles which added up, he said, to "the subtle something which makes good talk so much better than the best imitation of it that can be done with a pen." There were drawbacks, of course, when others than Paine and the stenographer were exposed to the method. "Poor man," William James wrote to his brother Henry after dinner with Clemens in February 1907, "only good for monologue, in his old age, or for dialogue at best, but he's a dear little genius all the same." James could have saved his pity, because for two and a half years Clemens, spinning out his wild and wonderful history, lived in a creative ecstasy of talking, talking, talking.

He lay in bed and talked, smoking, clenching his fist, pointing with his index finger. When he paused and waited for the word to come he folded the sleeve of his robe or cocked his head at an angle and looked about him. At Dublin, New Hampshire, where he rented a summer house, he paced the long veranda or, when it stormed, the living room, talking all the while. "When I think of that time," Paine wrote, "I shall always hear the ceaseless, slippered, shuffling walk, and see the white figure with its rocking, rolling movement passing up and down the long gallery." And Clemens continued his dictations until the summer of 1908, when he moved into his new house at Redding, discharged his stenographer, and entered, he said, "upon a holiday whose other end is in the cemetery." That year he stopped keeping even the little engagement books that had been serving him for his notes. The last entry he made was the single word, "*Talk*."

IV

On December 7, 1906, Clemens was in Washington to testify before a Congressional joint committee on copyright. When his turn came, he stripped off his long overcoat; he was dressed from shoulder to foot in white serge, and, with his great mane of white hair, he stood out in the dimly lighted committee room at the Library of Congress like a blaze of sunlight. "Nothing could have been more dramatic," Howells remembered. "It was a magnificent *coup*"—which Clemens followed with a talk, equally magnificent, in defense of intellectual property rights. Dining at Willard's Hotel that evening he wore full dress and insisted on entering the dining room by the most conspicuous way—not by a secluded elevator, as Paine had supposed he would prefer, but by the stately steps at the F Street entrance and by Peacock Alley, the corridor that ran the length of the hotel. It was only after this that Paine realized "the fullness of his love for theatrical effect." That winter Clemens began to wear white suits more and more frequently. He had ordered six from his tailor to begin with, and by spring he was wearing them all the time, on every sort of occasion. He had a dress suit of white broadcloth, swallow-tail coat and all, which made him white as a ghost. It was "just stunning," he told Clara and Jean, "my don'tcareadamn suit," "a very beautiful costume—and conspicuous."

His favorite recreation in New York, when he was not playing billiards, was to stroll up and down Fifth Avenue in his white suit, chat with the police, and be stared at. Sometimes he walked as far as Carnegie's house at Ninety-second Street and rode back on the open deck of a Fifth Avenue coach, smoking and looking down. On Sunday mornings he walked to Fifty-ninth Street, and before starting downtown again he waited in the Plaza lobby until the churches were out and the sidewalks crowded with fashionable strangers who lifted their hats to him. "It was his final harvest," Paine said of this public homage, "and he had the courage to claim it." But it was as much a matter of need as of courage. His white suits, which focused on him such attention—love, really—were the fetish of what had become an obsession with guilt, with forbidden and therefore unclean thoughts. (His "box of posthumous stuff" and all the letters he wrote in anger but never sent provided him with one outlet for this sort of uncleanness.) In a rambling but curiously insistent dictation in July 1908 he went on about the subject of cleanliness. He had kept his hair, he said, by scouring it every morning with soap and water; after ten hours the "microscopic dust floating in the air," even in the country, made it dirty again, and after twenty-four "raspy" and "uncomfortable." People washed their hands several times a day, but what about the dirt on their heads? In addition, the dark clothes that most men wore carried so much dirt that "you could plant seeds in them and raise a crop." "I wear white clothes both winter and summer," he said, "because I prefer to be clean in the matter of raiment—clean in a dirty world; absolutely the only cleanly-clothed human being in all Christendom north of the Tropics. And that is what I am." To be clean was to be deserving of love, and, as the scribes and Pharisees were supposed to have believed, to be clean outside was as good as being clean inside. When Clemens was just beginning to wear white suits morning and evening he reported to Clara, not only with delight but also with a full and scriptural knowledge of the implications, that Howells had given him a new title: "Whited sepulchre."

In other ways he seemed to be realizing an ambition to be the "most conspicuous person on the planet." At the Oxford convocation in June 1907, Lord Curzon, the new chancellor of the university, was to confer honorary degrees on two Americans, Mark Twain and Ambassador Whitelaw Reid. (A third American, Thomas Edison, declined on the grounds that he was too busy in his laboratory to make the trip.) Howells had been honored by Oxford in 1904; now Clemens saw it as his turn to have "a secret old sore of mine" healed. For over a generation, he said two weeks before leaving for England, he had been "as widely celebrated a literary person" as America had ever produced. Now the Oxford degree, "a loftier distinction than is conferrable by any other university," he said, was to be his final credential for immortality. He had planned never to cross the ocean again, but, he told Paine, he "would be willing to journey to Mars for that Oxford degree." On June 8, forty years to the day since the start of his first voyage to the Old World, on the *Quaker City*, he sailed on his last. He took with him as secretary Ralph Ashcroft, a young Englishman originally hired to manage the Plasmon affairs.

During the voyage's quiet interval between his American sendoff and his English welcome, Clemens stripped off some of the lineaments of his incomparable celebrity and showed himself in all his private loneliness. He had never recovered from the death of Susy. Clara was thirty-three now, busy with her singing career, away much of the time. He and Jean quarreled when they were together. She said he was rude, impatient, and angry with her; she felt her life was useless. Off in some rest home or other, tormented by daydreams about men and by the fear that she would never marry and have children, she complained about the food and accused him of wanting simply to get her out of the way. He barely had daughters any more, he felt, and here he was old enough to have grandchildren almost as old as Susy had been when she went off to Bryn Mawr. So he had taken to adopting grandchildren. To the end of his life he liked to be surrounded with bright and pretty young girls, his "Angel Fish," the members of his "Aquarium." He wrote them overflowing, sentimental, curiously feminine letters. He gave them tiny pieces of jewelry and the adoration of a bereaved old man. What he expected in return was gaiety and innocence, love, and flattery. "Butter wanted," he once joked. "Any Kind: New; Old. *Real* preferred, but Oleomargarine not turned away." On his way to England now he met one of these girls, Carlotta Welles, whom he called Charley. She was eighteen and, as someone in Paris told her later, she looked like Susy. He asked her to sit at his table, wanted her to spend every waking moment with him, and although he was delightful she became restless after a while and avoided him. He was disappointed when she did not come to hear him read from the manuscript of *The Mysterious Stranger*. "Well," he said sadly, "she's very young." He waited outside her stateroom one morning and sent in a little note on his calling card: "Charley, dear, you don't know what you are missing. There's more than two thousand porpoises in sight, and eleven whales, and sixty icebergs, and both Dippers, and seven rainbows, and all the battleships of all the navies, and me. SLC." The steward told her it was a shame to keep the old gentleman waiting like that, just walking back and forth and waiting. There was something tender, sad, and heart-broken about him, she remembered. The night of the ship's concert he read aloud from Susy's biography, and he was close to tears.

But with the first cheer from the stevedores at Tilbury dock—the most precious kind of love, he wrote to Jean, because it was from the *people*, "my own class"—the public Mark Twain, wearing a derby and spectacles and carrying a cotton umbrella ("the only kind the English won't steal"), reappeared in all his brilliant gaiety and told the reporters that he had come to show Oxford "what a real American college boy looks like." Crowds lined the street when he drove to the royal garden party at Windsor. There he had a private talk with Edward VII; the Queen com-manded him to keep his hat on—she was afraid he might catch cold. He was honored at the Lord Mayor's banquet, by the Savage Club and by the proprietors of *Punch*. The parties and celebrations never stopped; there were so many invitations coming in that Ashcroft had to hire an assistant. During Mark Twain's stay in England, *Harper's Weekly* said, "he was the most advertised man in the world."

On the platform at St. Pancras Station he had been introduced to George Bernard Shaw, who described him to a reporter as "by far the greatest American writer." Shaw talked about one of the several parallels between them: "He is in very much the same position as myself. He has to put things in such a way as to make people who would otherwise hang him believe he is joking." A few weeks later, after Clemens had lunched with the Shaws, Max Beerbohm, and Sir James Barrie at 10 Adelphi Ter-race, Shaw (fifty-one then and therefore, according to Clemens, "merely a lad") touched on something else they had conspicuously in common: a public personality. "My dear Mark Twain," Shaw began a letter on July 3, "—not to say Dr. Clemens (although I have always regarded Clemens as mere raw material—might have been your brother or your uncle)." He said that like William Morris ("an incurable Huckfinno-maniac") he believed that Mark Twain was one of the great masters of the English language, and besides: "I am persuaded that the future his-torian of America will find your works as indispensable to him as a French historian finds the political tracts of Voltaire. I tell you so because

I am the author of a play in which a priest says 'Telling the truth's the funniest joke in the world,' a piece of wisdom which you helped to teach me."

In the same vein of homage, at Oxford on June 26 Curzon had read out the citation, *"Vir jucundissime, lepidissime, facetissime . . .* Most amiable, charming and playful sir, you shake the sides of the whole world with your merriment." Even the dons stood up in the Sheldonian Theatre and cheered, Kipling remembered in 1936. Afterward, wearing the scarlet robe that he cherished and flaunted until the end of his life, Mark Twain marched into the sunlight in procession with the King's brother and the Prime Minister, with Rodin, Saint-Saëns, and Kipling. When he returned to America toward the end of July he seemed lonely, Paine said, not for companionship but for what seemed the high point of his life, which he had just passed. "Get your cue," he said to Paine. "I have been inventing a new game."

In 1909 a writer in the *North American Review*, Eugene Angert, asked the question "Is Mark Twain dead?" and made out an amusing case for the probability that he had died in 1906 in an obscure village in Switzerland. Reviewing *Is Shakespeare Dead?*, Angert applied Clemens' analytic methods and reached the conclusion that the writer currently known as Mark Twain was as much an impostor as "Mark Twain" said Shakespeare was. This new book, for example, was subtitled "From My Autobiography" and dealt with Shakespeare as a false claimant who could take his place in history with Mark Twain's other anti-heroes, Satan, Louis XVII, Arthur Orton, and Mary Baker Eddy. But this new book had been copyrighted by, and possibly written by an employee of, a legal entity called "The Mark Twain Company," chartered by the state of New York in 1908. A careful study of Baconian cyphers might even prove that the "Mark Twain" of *Christian Science* and *Is Shakespeare Dead?* was none other than the sage of East Aurora and author of *A Message to Garcia*, Elbert Hubbard.

Underneath the lighthearted ingenuity of all this ran the serious suggestion that by 1906, four years before his death, Mark Twain had outlived not his fame but the identity that had made him famous. The stagecoach and the river boat, symbols of the Western Mark Twain, had become the motorcar and the steam yacht, symbols of the plutocracy. He had shed his negligence about what he wore and was now, in his highly individual way, even something of a fashion plate. Sometimes he wore what Howells called "that society emblem," a silk hat. He lived on Fifth Avenue, rented a summer house at Tuxedo Park. He was to be seen in the company of Henry Rogers and other moguls at Palm Beach and Bermuda. His friendship with Rogers had continued to deepen—"I am his principal intimate and that is my idea of him." Stretched out on the sofa in Rogers' private office in the Standard Oil Building, smoking or reading while Rogers conducted his daily affairs, Clemens was completely at home and completely trusted. He was now a family friend as well: he had dedicated *Following the Equator* to Rogers' son Harry; to Rogers' daughter-in-law, Mary, he was "affectionately, your uncle"; and almost day and night for the rest of his life he played billiards, "the best game on earth," on a luxurious table given him as a Christmas present by Rogers' wife. He was Andrew Carnegie's crony and dinner companion, the recipient and consumer of bottles, cases, and finally barrels of Carnegie's private-stock Scotch—"the best and smoothest whisky now on the planet" —which always seemed to come at the right time. "Whisky never comes at the wrong time," Clemens said in one of a cycle of such thank-you notes. To each other they were "Saint Mark" and "Saint Andrew."

"Money-lust has always existed," Clemens could say to Twichell, "but not in the history of the world was it ever a craze, a madness, until your time and mine." But the moralist and the people's author had also become the pet and the peer of the moguls, and on a personal plane he was loyal to them in return. In 1905 he contributed anecdotal material to Isaac Marcosson's profile of Rogers for *World's Work;* that profile was meant to counteract Thomas Lawson's slashing attack in *Frenzied Finance.* Earlier Clemens had arranged for Ida Tarbell, just starting on her epochal history for McClure, to interview Rogers. This was Rogers' opportunity to present the Standard Oil side of the story (and possibly also his opportunity, as John D. Rockefeller, Sr., believed, to divert as much censure as he could from himself to his associates). On occasions Clemens could even be convinced that the Standard Oil captains were simply the victims of an unremitting public hostility whipped up by magazine publishers like McClure and a demagogic trust-busting President. The simple fact that in forty-five years the employees of Standard Oil had never gone out on strike, he said, proved that their "chiefs cannot be altogether bad," and in this benevolent mood he was willing to be an agent in the public rehabilitation of John D. Rockefeller, Sr. Frank Doubleday, one of Rockefeller's golfing companions, made a strategic approach: he told Clemens about the work of the Rockefeller Institute for Medical Research, especially about its research into meningitis, the disease that had killed Susy. On the strength of these good works Clemens agreed that the Standard Oil leaders deserved a fair hearing; he also agreed to appear on their behalf. At the Aldine Club on May 20, 1908, about fifty magazine publishers had the dramatic surprise of seeing the Rockefellers, father and son, file into their lion's den. With them were Henry Rogers and Mark Twain, who made a conciliatory speech, after which the elder Rockefeller, "speaking sweetly, sanely, simply, humanly," told them about the work of his Institute. As Clemens described the speech and its reception in an autobiographical dictation the next morning, Rockefeller "achieved one of the completest victories I have ever had any knowledge of." Doubleday's published impressions of Rockefeller as a "modest and friendly man" were soon followed by other revisionist accounts in the newspapers and magazines. A year later, after Rogers died suddenly of an apoplectic stroke, Andrew Carnegie wrote a condolence letter to the shocked and grieving Clemens which also contained a plea for his loyalty. "Mr. Rogers had to bear the odium of a system, one blamed for unavoidable consequences. Rebates were part of transportation in the early days and railways fought each other as private manufacturers did," Carnegie wrote from Stresa. "Well, his memory will be kept green in your heart and I doubt not history will do him justice because you will take care to record him as your friend in need, showing the real man. Goodnight, Saint Mark."

v

"The country home I need is a cemetery," Clemens had grumbled when the house at Redding was built. But when the house was ready for him he was in a mood for holiday. At the end of his first day there, in June 1908, he played billiards with Paine until midnight, and during the weeks and months that followed he played endless billiards and games of hearts, walked, went for rides around the countryside in the carriage that had been part of Jervis Langdon's wedding gift; its springs were stiff with age. There were almost always visitors at Stormfield: Howells, Colonel Harvey—bringing with him Lord Northcliffe—Helen Keller, Laura Hawkins, always the Angel Fish with or without their mothers. Occasionally Clemens came out of his retirement. In November he gave a performance—"the same old string of yarns"—for the benefit of the free library he presented to the town. "Poor fellow," Howells said, declining his invitation, "I thought you went to Redding to get rid of Mark Twain." And even though Clemens had begun the vacation that he felt sixty years of work had earned him, he still spent his mornings writing in bed. He was busy with letters, his Shakespeare book, and *Letters from the Earth*. In 1909, for *Harper's Bazaar*, he wrote "The Turning-Point of My Life": reviewing his life and legend once again, he saw everything he had done and become as predetermined from the beginning of time, each event only another link in a chain forged by "circumstance, working in harness with my temperament"—he was still pushing away the heavy burden of his freedom. He had discharged his stenographer, but he had not finished his autobiography. He even hit on a new scheme: to write it in the form of letters to friends, letters he would never mail. More than ever he seemed to live in the past and among great expanses of space and time which he figured in light-years. "My father died this day 63 years ago," he wrote to Clara on March 24, 1910, less than a month before his own death. "I remember all about it quite clearly." He remembered standing in the pilothouse in 1858 and reading a newspaper by the white spray of light of Donati's comet. He had come in with Halley's comet in 1835. In the fall of 1909 the returning voyager was visible again, at first as a faint nebulous star not far from Orion. "Here are those unaccountable freaks," he imagined God to be saying about Halley's comet and Mark Twain. "They came in together, they must go out together." And he added, "Oh! I am looking forward to that." Like his Connecticut Yankee, he was "getting up his last effect": he was to die at sunset on April 21, one day after the comet reached its perihelion.

During Jean's last six months, when she came to live with him and worked as his secretary, Clemens and this willful, troubled, and pathetic daughter of his finally achieved a brief and loving peace together. "Oh, the irony of it," he told Clara in July 1909. "That reptile Lyon mistress of our house these several years and Jean barred out of it." The long power struggle behind the King's back between Clara, "Painchen," "the Lioness," and Ashcroft had reached a horrible dénouement which Paine was sure undermined Clemens' health. Urged on by Clara and Paine, he looked into the way Miss Lyon and Ashcroft had been administering his affairs, including the payrolls for his staff and his children's allowances, and discovered that he had grounds enough to charge them with mismanagement and possibly larceny. He threatened legal action, including a suit to recover a small house on the property that he had given her as a Christmas present (he accused her of diverting money to improve this house). Ashcroft and Miss Lyon married in haste and left for England— in order to avoid testifying against each other, according to Clemens and Paine. "I caught Miss Lyon stealing (she had been at it for more than two years), and I bounced her," Clemens told Melville Stone of the Associated Press in September. "That is the whole of the dispute." By this time he had had the pleasure of seeing her "stretched on the rack" by his lawyers and every last detail of his connection with her legally erased. Having been suspicious of so many all his life, now, at the end of it, he seethed with hurt and anger at this new betrayal, not the least agonizing part of which was his separation from Jean. "A liar, a forger, a thief, a hypocrite," he described Isabel Lyon for Clara, "a drunkard, a sneak, a humbug, a traitor, a conspirator, a filthy-minded and salacious slut pining for seduction and always getting disappointed, poor child."

At Stormfield in October 1909 he gathered his scattered and pitifully shrunken family together for the last time. On a clear autumn day Clara and the pianist Ossip Gabrilowitsch were married by Twichell, and after the wedding service Clemens posed with his daughters, his Oxford gown over a white suit, a last flash of brilliant plumage in sunlight. When the couple had driven off, Clemens was alone with Jean, trusted and adored, "a surprise and a wonder" to him now that she had finally come into her own. Some of his youth was restored to him briefly. Each morning during Howells' last visit to Stormfield that autumn, before Howells was even dressed he heard Clemens calling his name through the house, "for the fun of it and I know for the fondness; and if I looked out of my door, there he was in his long nightgown swaying up and down the corridor, and wagging his great white head like a boy that leaves his bed and comes out in the hope of frolic with someone." On December 23 Jean telephoned to the New York manager of the Associated Press Clemens' denial of a familiar rumor: "I hear the newspapers say I am dying. The charge is not true. I would not do such a thing at my time of life. I am behaving as good as I can. Merry Christmas to everybody!" The next morning it was Jean who was dead; she had had an epileptic seizure in her bath. On Christmas Day, too ill to travel, Clemens stood at the window and watched the hearse moving downhill through a heavy snowstorm. "I have never greatly envied any one but the dead," he said to Paine. "I always envy the dead." It was only then, after writing his account of her life and sudden death, that he considered his autobiography, and his career, finished: "I shall never write any more."

In August 1908 Sam Moffett drowned in the surf off New Jersey. Clemens came back from the funeral in New York broken by the heat, depressed and tired. He was sick in bed for a few days; as soon as he was on his feet again and back at the billiard table with Paine he had a sudden dizzy spell and lost his memory. He forgot which was his ball, even which game they were playing. The following June he went to Baltimore to talk at the graduation exercises of one of his Angel Fish at St. Timothy's and to tell the girls not to smoke, drink or marry to excess. In his room at the Belvedere he had an undisguised attack of angina pectoris, and he came back to Stormfield sick. He said it was "tobacco heart" and he tried to cut down his cigars from forty to four a day. He was resigned to a drawn-out invalidism and decline. With this form of heart disease, he said, "you get run over by a freight train before you can get rid of yourself." His attacks became more frequent and severe, some of them brought on by "mental agitation." He read a passage from "The Turning-Point of My Life" to Paine and Jean, sensed they were disappointed, clutched at his chest. He began to lose enough sleep, he said, "to supply a worn-out army." At first he could relieve his chest pains by drinking hot water.

Later on only hypodermic injections helped. "I can't hurry this dying business," he said to Paine. "Can't you give me enough of the hypnotic injunction to put an end to me?"

In New York on January 5, 1910, a day before he sailed to Bermuda, he had his last meeting with Howells. They talked about labor unions as the "sole present help of the weak against the strong"; they also talked about dreams. "You never wrote anything greater, finer than that turning point paper of yours," Howells wrote two weeks later, and Clemens, cherishing this praise as much as he had cherished Howells' review of *The Innocents Abroad* forty years earlier, wrote across the top of the page: "I reckon this spontaneous outburst by the first critic of the day is good to keep, ain't it, Paine?"

He began to fail rapidly in Bermuda, was afraid that he would die there and lie in an undertaker's cellar. Paine came for him, and they sailed for home on April 12. On the trip back Clemens drowsed under the morphine, and when he half woke he talked about his dreams: He was at some college, on the platform, but by now he had had his fill of honors—"Isn't there something I can resign and be out of all this? They keep trying to confer that degree upon me and I don't want it." Or there was a play, but he could never find anyone to be the general manager—the Superintendent of Dreams had gone for good. At Stormfield before he slipped into coma his last continuous talking was about "the laws of mentality," about Jekyll and Hyde and dual personality. To the end he remained as much an enigma and prodigy to himself as he was to the thousands at the Brick Presbyterian Church in New York who filed past the casket, topped with a single wreath of laurel, where he lay in a white suit.

NOTES

The notes that follow are keyed to the text by page number and catch phrase. In general I have cited primary sources only. The following abbreviations and short titles have been used:

PERSONS

EB	Elisha Bliss
OLC	Olivia Langdon Clemens
MMF	Mary Mason Fairbanks
FBH	Francis Bret(t) Harte
WDH	William Dean Howells
HHR	Henry Huttleston Rogers
JHR	James H. Riley
WR	Whitelaw Reid
JHT	Joseph Hopkins Twichell

BOOKS, PERIODICALS, AND MANUSCRIPT SOURCES

AL	*American Literature: A Journal of Literary History, Criticism, and Bibliography*, Durham, N.C., 1929——.
AU-1924	Albert Bigelow Paine, ed., *Mark Twain's Autobiography*, 2 vols. New York: Harper and Brothers, 1924.
AU-1959	Charles Neider, ed., *The Autobiography of Mark Twain*. New York: Harper and Brothers, 1959.
Barrett	Clifton Waller Barrett Library of American Literature, University of Virginia, Norfolk, Va.
Berg—NYPL	Henry W. and Albert A. Berg Collection, New York Public Library.
BM	Samuel C. Webster, *Mark Twain, Business Man*. Boston: Little, Brown, 1946.
Bowen	Theodore Hornberger, ed., *Mark Twain's Letters to Will Bowen*. Austin, Tex.: University of Texas, 1941.
Brown	Franklin Walker and G. Ezra Dane, eds., *Mark Twain's Travels with Mr. Brown*. New York: Alfred A. Knopf, 1940.
Eruption	Bernard DeVoto, ed., *Mark Twain in Eruption*. New York: Harper and Brothers, 1940.
F	Dixon Wecter, ed., *Mark Twain to Mrs. Fairbanks*. San

	Marino, Calif.: Huntington Library, 1949.
L	Albert Bigelow Paine, ed., *Mark Twain's Letters*, 2 vols. New York: Harper and Brothers, 1917.
Life as I Find It	Mark Twain, *Life as I Find It*, ed. Charles Neider. Garden City, N.Y.: Hanover House, 1961.
LinL	Mildred Howells, ed., *Life in Letters of William Dean Howells*, 2 vols. Garden City, N.Y.: Doubleday, Doran, 1928.
LL	Dixon Wecter, ed., *The Love Letters of Mark Twain*. New York: Harper and Brothers, 1949.
MF	Clara Clemens, *My Father, Mark Twain*. New York: Harper and Brothers, 1931.
MMT	William Dean Howells, *My Mark Twain*. New York: Harper and Brothers, 1910.
MTH	Henry N. Smith and William M. Gibson, eds., *Mark Twain–Howells Letters*, 2 vols. Cambridge, Mass.: Harvard University Press, 1960.
MTN	Albert Bigelow Paine, ed., *Mark Twain's Notebook*. New York: Harper and Brothers, 1935.
MTP	Mark Twain Papers, University of California Library, Berkeley.
NF	Kenneth R. Andrews, *Nook Farm: Mark Twain's Hartford Circle*. Cambridge, Mass.: Harvard University Press, 1950.
Paine	Albert Bigelow Paine, *Mark Twain, A Biography*, 3 vols. New York: Harper and Brothers, 1912.
Record	Arlin Turner, *Mark Twain and G. W. Cable: The Record of a Literary Friendship*. East Lansing, Mich.: Michigan State University Press, 1960.
Speeches	*Mark Twain's Speeches*. New York: Harper and Brothers, 1923.
TIA	D. M. McKeithan, ed., *Traveling with the Innocents Abroad*. Norman, Okla.: University of Oklahoma Press, 1958.
W	Albert Bigelow Paine, ed., *The Writings of Mark Twain*, "Definitive Edition," 37 vols. New York: Harper and Brothers, 1922–25.
Yale	Yale University Library.

Chapter One (pages 13-38)

14. "Necessary stock in trade": SLC to Orion and Mollie Clemens, Oct. 19, 1865, from San Francisco (MTP).
14. "More friends": BM, 89.
15. Pistol to his head: The most explicit of SLC's several references to the episode is a marginal comment, Apr. 21, 1909, in his copy of J. R. Lowell's Letters, quoted in Los Angeles Times, Apr. 15, 1951.
15. "Bohemian from the sage-brush": Albert S. Evans ("Amigo") in Gold Hill News, Feb. 12 and 19, 1866, quoted in Mark Twain, San Francisco Correspondent, ed. Henry Nash Smith and Frederick Anderson (San Francisco, 1957), 39-40.
15. Venereal disease: Also Artemus Ward to SLC, January 1864, Austin, Tex. (MTP): "Why would you make a good artillery man? Because you are familiar with Gonorrhea (gunnery)." Paine omits this passage, which may be just a pointless joke, from his text in L, 93-94.
16. "I'd rather": MTN, 35. Wakeman is described in his daughter's introduction to his autobiography, The Log of an Ancient Mariner (San Francisco, 1878), 10.
17. "Out of luck": MTN, 47.
20. "Well, James": WDH, Literary Friends and Acquaintance (New York, 1910), 35-39.
21. "Make your mark": Brown, 176.
21. "Hard even for an American": Brown, 163.
22. "Clipper built girls": Brown, 88-89.
23. "I'll not do it yet": BM, 90-91.
24. "He went marching": Brown, 92-94. Beecher's pulpit style and mannerisms: David Macrae, The Americans at Home (New York, 1952), 65-71; Constance Rourke, Trumpets of Jubilee (New York, 1927), 149 ff.
25. "That old day": SLC to Edward House, Jan. 14, 1884, Hartford (Barrett—photostat in MTP). SLC recalled the meeting in a letter to Charles H. Webb, Feb. 16, 1896, Darjeeling (Yale).
26. George Carleton: Eruption, 143-46.
27. "Son of a Bitch": MTH, 133.
27. "Carleton insulted me": MTH, 132.

27. "Prominent Brooklynites": Brown, 111.
28. "Allow me to introduce": Brown, 113-15.
28. "Fumes of bad whiskey": N.Y. World, Feb. 18, 1877.
29. He wrote Webb: Mar. 19, 1867, St. Louis (Barrett—photostat in MTP).
30. Mercantile Hall: For SLC's promotion compaign and the text of his talk see Fred W. Lorch, "Mark Twain's Sandwich Island Lecture at St. Louis," AL, XVIII, No. 4 (January 1947), 299-307.
31. "Pretty complimentary": Brown, 136.
31. "One never feels comfortable": Alta California, Feb. 5, 1868. SLC used the watch metaphor in LL, 116-17. On Feb. 1, 1894, SLC told Frank Fuller: "That old lecture is not in existence— I tore it up. Stanley made a pretty full report of it . . ." (Yale).
31. Lectured in Hannibal: Brown, 143-46.
31. "Return and meet grown babies": Hamlin Hill, "The Composition and Structure of Tom Sawyer," AL, XXXII, No. 4 (January 1961), 386.
32. "One of the greatest liars": Paine, 107.
32. "So cheerful": Brown, 156-57.
33. "Damnable errors": L, 124.
33. "Everything looks shady": L, 124.
34. "Damned secessionist": BM, 93.
34. "The chance offering": N.Y. Daily Tribune, May, 11, 1867. SLC paid tribute to Fuller in 1868 (LL, 26-27) and 1906 (AU-1959, 170-73).
35. Night in a New York jail: Brown, 187-91. Years later, in a dinner-table conversation with Clara and WDH, SLC said, "I passed a night in jail once. . . . Drunk, I guess" (MTN, 400).
35. "Honest poverty": Brown, 236.
36. "I published it": L, 127.
37. Mortimer Neal Thomson: Fred W. Lorch, "Doesticks and Innocents Abroad," AL, XX, No. 4 (January 1949), 446-49.
37. "Domed and steepled solitude": Brown, 259-61.
37. "I guess that something": Brown, 277-79.
37. "I will have to get even": BM, 90.
37. Madame Caprell: BM, 52-57.
38. "Full of unworthy conduct": L, 128.
38. Wrote goodbye: Bowen, 15-16. SLC's

last night in New York before sailing is described in his letter to John Mc-Comb early the next morning (published in the Boston *Sunday Globe*, Nov. 29, 1964).

Chapter Two (pages 39–56)

40. "Stop the boat": *F*, xxiv.
40. "Swapping false teeth": SLC's comments on the other passengers are in *MTN*, 56-60, and Notebook No. 7, MTP.
40. Gibson: Henry F. Pommer, "Mark Twain's 'Commissioner of the United States,' " *AL*, XXIV, No. 3 (November 1962), 385-92.
40. Cutter: John T. Winterich, "The Life and Works of Bloodgood Haviland Cutter," *Colophon*, I, Part 2, May 1930.
41. "Vacancy in the Trinity": *Brown*, 275-76.
41. "Sodom and Gomorrah": *TIA*, 309.
41. Griswold's book: SLC's copy of *Sixty Years with Plymouth Church* is in MTP.
41. "The only notoriety": *Rock County Chronicle*, II, No. 2 (June 1956).
42. "Captain Duncan wishes": MMF, "Cruise of the Quaker City," *Chautauquan*, January 1892.
42. "I basked": *W*, I, 11.
43. "My audience is dumb": *L*, 528.
44. "Most refined": *BM*, 97.
45. "Burned-out crater": MMF, *Chautauquan*, January 1892.
45. "Something sober": *Journal Letters of Emily A. Severance* (Cleveland, 1938), 217.
46. "You don't know": *F*, 3.
48. "I am glad": *TIA*, 97.
50. "Don't make any arrangements": SLC to Frank Fuller, Aug. 7, 1867, Naples (Yale).
51. The visit to the summer palace at Yalta: *TIA*, 142-62.
52. "Coaling going on": C. E. Shain, "The Journal of the *Quaker City* Captain," *New England Quarterly*, XXVIII, September 1955, 388-94.
52. "I saw her first": *AU*-1959, 183.
53. "I'll be goddamned": *MTN*, 89. For SLC's later opinion of Slote, see *F*, 247-49.

54. "Ignorant, depraved": *MTN*, 93.
54. "J. Christ & Son": Notebook No. 9, MTP.
55. He started to write: SLC told Webb about the play in a letter from Washington, Nov. 25, 1867 (facsimile in *The Quaker City Holy Land Excursion, An Unfinished Play*, privately printed, 1927). But he denied its existence in a letter to "Mr. Buell," Dec. 29, 1905, New York (Barrett—photostat in MTP).
55. "The pleasure ship": *TIA*, 313-19.
56. "Make the Quakers get up": *BM*, 94-95.
56. "I'm tired hearing": *TIA*, 309-13.

Chapter Three (pages 57–75)

57. Senator William M. Stewart's account of SLC in Washington is in his *Reminiscences* (New York, 1908), 219-24.
59. "Good for three nights": SLC to Frank Fuller, Dec. 5, 1867, Washington (Yale).
59. Lobbying on Orion's behalf: *BM*, 96; *L*, 149, 150.
60. "I have thrown away": *LL*, 61-62.
61. "We are perhaps": *L*, 140.
61. "I wrote fifty-two": *L*, 141-42.
62. "No book of literary quality": WDH, "The Man of Letters as a Man of Business," *Scribner's*, October 1893.
63. "Talented men of the age": *L*, 145-46.
63. "Don't dare to smoke": *F*, 15-16. SLC's first newspaper impressions of Hartford were published in the *Alta California* Mar. 3, 1868.
64. "I want a good wife": *F*, 7-8.
64. "I wish I had been": *Bowen*, 16-17.
64. "Morality and huckleberries": *Alta California*, Sept. 6, 1868.
65. "Proud to observe": *Alta California*, Feb. 5, 1868.
65. "The fortune of my life": *AU*-1959, 174. I follow the chronology of H. G. Baetzhold, "Mark Twain's 'First Date' with Olivia Clemens," *Missouri Historical Society Bulletin*, XI, January 1955, 155-57.
66. "A visiting *Spirit*": *LL*, 43.
66. "I hardly knew": *L*, 144.
67. "Dear Folks": *F*, 12. The text of the speech is in *Speeches*, 31-33.

67. There *was* slang: *F*, 13.
67. "I acknowledge": *F*, 18-21.
69. New York *Tribune:* "The White House Funeral," dateline Washington, Mar. 4, 1869 (clipping in MTP).
69. "If the *Alta*'s book": *F*, 24.
70. "Son of the devil": *F*, 29.
70. Some of the newspapers: The reviews are quoted in Paul Fatout, *Mark Twain on the Lecture Circuit* (Bloomington, Ind., 1960), 89-90.
71. "Any lecture": *LL*, 165-66.
72. "School-boy days": *W*, II, 330-31.
73. "Settle down": *F*, 29-30.
73. "If you wanted": *MMT*, 19.
73. "Head of my breed": *L*, 102.
74. "Unusual and dominant nature": T. Edgar Pemberton, *The Life of Bret Harte* (New York, 1903), 74-75.
74. "Trimmed and trained": *L*, 182-84; this is also the source for the story about the *Overland*'s cover emblem. Among others testifying to FBH's brilliance as editor and mentor was Charles Warren Stoddard, in his *Exits and Entrances* (Boston, 1903), 248.
74. "Harte read all the MS.": SLC to C. H. Webb, Nov. 26, 1870, Buffalo (Barrett—photostat in MTP).
74. "Bret's very best sketch": SLC's marginalia in his copy (MTP) of *The Luck of Roaring Camp* (Boston, 1870).

Chapter Four (pages 76-93)

76. Commonplace book: MTP.
76. "Square, flat-footed" *LL*, 33.
77n. "Her specialty": *AU*-1959, 11.
79. "Born *reserved*": *AU*-1959, 185-86.
80. "I do not regret": *LL*, 18-20. The salutation is: "My Honored 'Sister.'"
80. "I believe in you": *LL*, 25.
81. "What you need now": Paine, 287; *Bowen*, 14.
81. George Macdonald: Greville Macdonald, *George Macdonald and His Wife* (London, 1924), 457-58.
81. "Goodbye": *LL*, 9.
81. "Said she never": *LL*, 64.
82. "Not a bruise": *AU*-1959, 187-88.
82. "I would have been crippled": Bernard DeVoto, *Mark Twain at Work* (Cambridge, Mass., 1942), 26 ("Boy's Manuscript").

83. "The American Vandal Abroad": A 52-page manuscript is in MTP; *Speeches*, 21-30, is a fragmentary version.
84. "I would like *you*": *F*, 46.
84. "*Splendid* hit": *BM*, 102.
84. "Congratulations": SLC to JHT, Nov. 18, 1868, Cleveland (Yale).
84. "First faint symptom": *F*, 48-49.
84. "The kingdom of heaven": Edward Everett Hale, *A New England Boyhood* (Boston, 1927), 19. Other sources for the development and makeup of the lyceum system are: Paul Fatout, *Mark Twain on the Lecture Circuit* (Bloomington, Ind., 1960); Thomas Wentworth Higginson, "The American Lecture System," *Macmillan's Magazine*, XVIII, May 1868, 48-56; Charles F. Horner, *The Life of James B. Redpath* (New York, 1926); R. B. Martin, ed., *Charles Kingsley's American Notes* (Princeton, N. J., 1958); David Mead, *Yankee Eloquence in the Middle West* (East Lansing, Mich., 1951); "The Lyceum Lecture," *Nation*, VIII, April 8, 1869; J. B. Pond, *Eccentricities of Genius* (New York, 1900). Redpath's promotional bulletin, *The Lyceum* (Boston, 1869-75), gives a direct index to the taste of the audiences. For example, among the 125 lecturers Redpath offered for the season 1869-70 there were 38 clergymen, 35 authorities on history and foreign travel, 18 women, and only 3 humorists. There were at least 6 humorists the following season.
86. "I could have cleared": SLC to Jane Clemens, Dec. 10, 1868, New York (MTP).
86. "No man will dare more": SLC to OLC, Jan. 15, 1870, Utica, N.Y. (MTP).
87. "The suspense grows": *W*, XXIX, 162-63.
88. "My nerves": *LL*, 137.
88. In Iowa City: *LL*, 52-53. The Iowa City *Republican*'s account and review ("We would not give two cents to hear him again") are quoted in Fred W. Lorch, "Mark Twain in Iowa," *Iowa Journal of History and Politics*, XXVII (1929), 507-47.
89. "From what standard": *F*, 53.
89. Nativity passage: *F*, 59-60.

89. "Their reverent spirit": *F*, 63n.
89. "Poor girl": *F*, 63.
90. "I want the public": *F*, 67n.
90. "Much of my conduct": *LL*, 37.
90. "I know of *nothing*": *LL*, 60.
90. "As far as I am concerned": *LL*, 66.
91. "The world's 'mill' ": *LL*, 26.
91. "Parton thinks": *Memories of a Hostess*, ed. M. A. DeWolfe Howe (Boston, 1922), 111.
92. "It may be a good while": *LL*, 64.
92. "The long siege": SLC to OLC, Mar. 4, 1869, Lockport, N. Y. (MTP).
93n. "It pains me": *LL*, 76. "No reading matter for girls": *Letters of Sigmund Freud* (New York, 1960), 44.
93. In its margins: Bradford Booth, "Mark Twain's Comments on Holmes's *Autocrat*," *AL*, XXI, No. 4 (January 1950), 456–63.

Chapter Five (pages 94–116)

94. "My blood curdled": *LL*, 68–69. A later (*ca.* 1887), extended comment by SLC on the Langdon coal business is published as "Letter to the Earth" in *Letters from the Earth* (New York, 1962), 117–22.
95. "Pick and choice": Buffalo *Express*, Nov. 13, 1869.
95n. American business elite: See Irvin G. Wyllie, *The Self-Made Man in America: The Myth of Rags to Riches* (New Brunswick, N. J., 1954), 24. "Most remarkable phenomenon": James Bryce, *The American Commonwealth* (London, 1888), II, 616.
97. "Day before yesterday": *LL*, 108–9.
97. "The old gentleman": SLC to WR, June 15, 1869 (MTP).
97. "I cannot help thinking": Pamela Moffett to Mollie Clemens, June 23, 1870, Fredonia, N. Y. (MTP).
99. "Both of us": SLC to OLC, Feb. 15, 1869, Ravenna, O. (MTP).
99. "I can buy": SLC to JHT, "St. Valentine's, 1869," Ravenna, O. (MTP).
99. "Never heard anybody": *LL*, 123–24; Nasby answered that "a very great many people had very convincing proofs" that Bowles was a dog.
100. "I feel ashamed": *L*, 158.
100. "You seem to think": SLC to Pamela Moffett, June 25, 1869, New York (MTP).

100. "My expenses": SLC to Jane Clemens and Pamela Moffett, June 26, 1869, Elmira (Moffett–MTP).
102. "Nearly every purple": SLC to OLC, May 13, 1869, Hartford (MTP).
102. "Tiresome book": *F*, 98.
103. "Thirty times a day": *AU*-1959, 158–59.
103. "Been delayed": EB to SLC, July 12, 1869, Hartford (MTP).
103. "All I desire": SLC to EB, July 22, 1869, Elmira (Yale).
104. "Ill nature": SLC to EB, Aug. 12, 1869, Buffalo (MTP).
104. "You will hereafter": EB to SLC, Aug. 4, 1869, Hartford (MTP).
104. "It will sell": SLC to EB, Aug. 12, 1869, Buffalo (MTP). Bliss's promotional techniques and the publishing history of *The Innocents Abroad* are discussed in: Leon T. Dickinson, "Marketing a Best Seller," *Papers of the Bibliographical Society of America*, XLI (1947); Hamlin Hill, "Mark Twain's Book Sales, 1869–1879," *Bulletin of the New York Public Library*, LXV, No. 6 (June 1961), 371–89; Hamlin Hill, "Mark Twain's Quarrels with Elisha Bliss," *AL*, XXXIII, No. 4 (January 1962), 442–56.
105. "I only expected": SLC to F. S. Drake, Dec. 26, 1870, Buffalo (Berg–NYPL).
106. "My new book": SLC to WR, Aug. 15, 1869, Buffalo (MTP).
106. "I was afraid": SLC to WR, Sept. 7, 1869, Buffalo (MTP).
107. "Sharp, twinkling Yankee": O. W. Holmes to SLC, Sept. 26, 1869, Boston (MTP); in part in *L*, 166–67.
108. "I hadn't any": SLC to O. W. Holmes, Sept. 30, 1869, Buffalo (Library of Congress).
108. "My book is waltzing me": *F*, 114.
109. "Insultingly contemptuous": *LL*, 131–32.
109. "Patchwork editorials": *LL*, 105.
110. "Little dearie": *LL*, 105.
110. "A sort of itching": *F*, 108.
111. "The surprising fact": *AU*-1959, 272–73.
111. Howells' memory: *MMT*, 3–4.
112. "Between you and I": *LL*, 41.
112. "I published": *L*, 170–71.
114. "Mr. Langdon": JHT, "Mark Twain," *Harper's*, May 1896.

114. "My first, and Oldest": *Bowen*, 18-21.
115. "Pay no attention": SLC's copy of the return is in MTP; OLC told her mother that this return was "a matter of most intense anxiety to him, he could not *possibly* comprehend it" (*LL*, 146).
115. "A Mysterious Visit": *Mark Twain's Sketches* (Hartford, 1875), 316-20.

Chapter Six (pages 117–138)

118. "A lovely wife": *L*, 172-73.
118. "No argument": *LL*, 135.
118. "I can't sell myself": *Memories of a Hostess*, ed. M. A. DeWolfe Howe (Boston, 1922), 245-46. See also SLC, "Smoking as Inspiration," in *Life as I Find It*, 202-3.
119. "Maybe it will be several years": SLC to EB, Jan. 22, 1870, Elmira (typescript in Berg–NYPL).
120. "I give you my word": F. L. Mott, *A History of American Magazines* (Cambridge, Mass., 1938), III, 364.
120. "Higher class writing": SLC to EB, Mar. 11, 1870, Buffalo (Berg–NYPL).
121. "My noddings": *AU*-1924, II, 114.
121. Trip to Washington: *LL*, 154.
121. Orion's memorandum book: *L*, 175.
122. "*I am sitting still*": SLC to Orion, Nov. 11, 1870, Buffalo (Moffett–MTP). SLC told Orion the expenses at Delaware Ave., including doctors, nurses, and insurance, were about $1,000 a month.
123. "*That* is the only thing": SLC to F. S. Drake, Dec. 26, 1870, Buffalo (Berg–NYPL).
123. "Among the blackest": *Eruption*, 250-52.
124. "Brimful of fame": SLC to EB, Nov. 28, 1870, Buffalo (MTP).
125. "He was full of hope": *W*, IV, 148.
126. "Pet scheme": *Colophon*, XIII, March 1933.
127. "Your letters": SLC to JHR, Mar. 3, 1871, Buffalo (Berg–NYPL). JHR had written to SLC from London on Jan. 22 (MTP) and had enclosed the first installment of his travel journal (MTP). The next installment of the journal, sent from Capetown around Mar. 23, told the story of the *Gambia* running aground (MTP).

127. "Diamond fever": SLC to JHR, Oct. 9, 1871, Hartford (Berg–NYPL).
128. "I shall employ": SLC to JHR, Jan. 4, 1872, Dayton, O. (Berg–NYPL).
128. "Simple contest": JHR to SLC, May 16, 1872, Philadelphia (MTP).
129. "Given to Riley": Notebook No. 30, MTP.
129. "Rose diamond": *W*, XXI, 375.
129. "Do you know": SLC to JHR, Mar. 3, 1871, Buffalo (Berg–NYPL).
130. Halley's comet: These comparisons occur in SLC's accounts, in Charles Warren Stoddard's *Exits and Entrances* (Boston, 1903), 252-53, and in WDH's extended account in "Editor's Easy Chair," *Harper's*, CVIII, December 1903.
130. "He spent a week": *LinL*, I, 251.
131. "Some bummer": SLC to WR, Feb. 22, 1871, Buffalo (MTP).
131. "I am pegging away": *F*, 153.
132. "Plagiarism B.H.": John Hay to SLC, Jan. 9, 1871, New York (MTP).
132. "Will you please correct": The exchange of letters is in *L*, 181-84, and Ferris Greenslet, *Life of Thomas Bailey Aldrich* (Boston, 1908), 95-99.
132. "Shady and quiet": SLC to Orion, Mar. 11, 1871, Buffalo (MTP).
134. "Beetling Alps of trouble": SLC to Orion, Mar. 15, 1871, Buffalo (MTP).
135. "Absolute frenzy–desperation": SLC to EB, Mar. 17, 1871, Buffalo (Berg–NYPL).
135. "It will not be needed": SLC to Orion, Mar. 10, 1871, Buffalo (Berg–NYPL).
135. "No fool of a job": *L*, 186.
136. "By all odds": SLC to EB, April 20, 1871, Elmira (MTP).
136. "Wave of the rider's hand": *W*, III, 54.
136. "Red-hot interest": *L*, 187-88.
137. "We had often longed": *W*, III, 241.

Chapter Seven (pages 139–155)

139. "John Bunyan's heaven": *MTH*, 534. The quotation by Henry James is from his *Hawthorne* (1879). Kenneth Andrews' *Nook Farm* (Cambridge, Mass., 1950) is an invaluable study of the complex social and intellectual "machinery" of SLC's Hartford circle.

141. "A sort of suburban grove": *LinL*, I, 187.
142. "Without really intending": SLC to James Redpath, June 10, 1871, Elmira (New-York Historical Soc.).
142. "Tip-top lecture": *F*, 157.
143. "I do hope": *LL*, 164.
143. "We will either board": *LL*, 168-69.
144. "A Boston literary lunch": *MMT*, 6-7. I have also drawn on WDH's account in *LinL*, I, 157.
145. Less than perfect harmony: Mrs. Thomas Bailey Aldrich, *Crowding Memories* (Boston, 1920), 127-32. In *AU*-1959, 357-67, SLC talks about her and the Portsmouth memorial to Aldrich.
146. "Demeaning myself": Paine, 786.
146. "Ethiopian minstrels": Mary Thacher Higginson, *Thomas Wentworth Higginson* (Boston, 1914), 259-60.
146. Letter to the N. Y. *Tribune*: Mar. 10, 1873. "H.K.'s" answer appeared the next day.
146. Holland: His attacks ran in the March 1871, April 1871, February 1872, and July 1872 issues of the magazine. SLC's "An Appeal from One That Is Persecuted" is in Berg—NYPL.
147. "A useful trade": Hartford *Courant*, June 29, 1888.
148. "So you will see": SLC to Annie Moffett, May 17, 1872, Elmira (MTP). SLC said he and OLC each had about $30,000 in the bank.
148. "They like a book about America": SLC to EB, Mar. 20, 1872, Elmira (MTP).
149. "I am as uplifted": *MTH*, 10-11. In *MMT*, 3, WDH mistakenly recalled this as SLC's thank-you for the *Atlantic*'s review of *The Innocents Abroad* and explained that "the mock modesty of print" forbade his quoting from the letter.
149. "If she behaves herself": FBH to SLC, Apr. 1, 1872, New York (MTP).
149. "Always felt shame": *AU*-1959, 190.
149. "*I killed him*": *MMT*, 11-12.
149. "All tenderness": Lilly Warner to George Warner, June 3, 1872, Hartford (Warner cycle, MTP).
150. "*Not* lisle thread": SLC to Mollie Clemens, Aug. 2, 1872, Saybrook, Conn. (MTP).
150. "My idea is this": *L*, 196-97. "Swift

Death to Chilblains": SLC to Orion and Mollie, Feb. 2, 1893, Florence (MTP). Steam brake: SLC to Orion, Sept. 16, 1871, Elmira (MTP). Drilling block: Orion to SLC, Sept. 22, 1871, Hartford (MTP). On Mar. 3, 1873, SLC signed an enthusiastic letter of testimonial for another "humanizing" invention, "White's Portable Folding Fly and Musketo Net Frame." "We shall see the summer day come," he wrote, "when we shall all sit under our nets in church and slumber peacefully, while the discomfited flies club together and take it out of the minister" (manufacturer's circular, Yale).
151. "The clockmaker": Orion to Mollie Clemens, Oct. 23, 1871, Hartford (MTP).
151. "I am contented": *F*, 164.
151. "I am standing": *LL*, 176.
152. Vogue for American humor: Discussed in Clarence Gohdes, *American Literature in Nineteenth Century England* (New York, 1944), 83-94. SLC's reciprocal Anglomania (as WDH called it) is traced in H. G. Baetzhold, "Mark Twain: England's Advocate," *AL*, XXVIII, No. 3 (November 1956), 328-46.
153. "I was a lion": *LL*, 178-79.
153. "Always has my books": *LL*, 181-82.
154. Mere slip of the tongue: Moncure D. Conway, *Autobiography* (Boston, 1904), II, 143. The revised text is in *Speeches*, 37-41.
154. "In this day": *Speeches*, 131-32.
155. A "puppy": SLC to OLC, Oct. 25, 1872, London (MTP).

Chapter Eight (pages 156–172)

156. "Worth any money": Boston *Transcript*, Nov. 26, 1872.
157. Jay Gould: *Eruption*, 77.
158. "Sam says Livy": *NF*, 39.
158. "The present era": SLC to Orion, Mar. 27, 1875, Hartford (MTP).
159. "Was reporter": *L*, 542.
160. "In the superstition": Paine, 477.
161. "I think you don't like": *F*, 184.
161. "My climax chapter": *F*, 171.
162. "I think I can say": *Speeches*, 35.
163. "I'll take you down": Cable's notes of the conversation (Cable Coll., Tulane

Univ.) are published in Arlin Turner, "James Lampton . . . ," *Modern Language Notes*, LXX, December 1955, 592-94.

164. "Up to the time": *MTH*, 13.
165. "*The* American character": *MTH*, 479.
165. "I think that the reason": "What Paul Bourget Thinks of Us" (*W*, XXII, 162).
165. "A pathetic and beautiful spirit": *AU*-1959, 19.
167. "Putrid anecdote": SLC to WR, Mar. 28, 1873, Hartford (MTP).
167. "Splendid sendoff": SLC to WR, early April 1873 (MTP).
167. "Contemptible cur": SLC to C. D. Warner, May 1873, "Under way" (MTP).
168. "But for the Panic": *L*, 215.
168. One night in London: OLC describes SLC's state of mind in a letter to her mother from London, September 1873 (MTP).
168. "Wicked, ungodly suffrage": *Memories of a Hostess*, ed. M. A. DeWolfe Howe (Boston, 1922), 251-53.
169. "Tell your mother": *F*, 208-9.
169. "Driftwood of the Deluge": J. T. Goodman to SLC, Oct. 24, 1881 (MTP).
169. "A man can't write": *MTH*, 248-49.
171. "A farewell letter": *L*, 204-5.
171. "In England": *MMT*, 46.
171. "If I'm not homesick": *LL*, 186.
171. "In Salisbury": *LL*, 189.
172. "Scotch whisky": *LL*, 190.
172. Stoddard: *Exits and Entrances* (Boston, 1903), 61-74.

Chapter Nine (pages 173-187)

173. Visit to Nook Farm: Mrs. T. B. Aldrich, *Crowding Memories* (Boston, 1920), 143-60; *MMT*, 5, 7-8.
175. "Busiest white man": *F*, 183-84.
176. "You *are* aging": SLC to Orion, May 10 or 11, 1874, Elmira (MTP).
176. "Keeping up appearances": SLC to Jane Clemens, May 10, 1874, Elmira (MTP). SLC voiced his general exasperation with Orion in *L*, 245-46.
176. "This oath": Jane Clemens to Orion, *ca.* November 1873, Fredonia, N.Y. (MTP).

176. "I grieve": SLC to Orion, Feb. 4, 1874 Hartford (MTP).
177. Bowers: *AU*-1959, 229-30. Frank Fuller's letters to SLC between May 1877 and February 1878 (MTP) corroborate SLC's account.
177. "This wondrous establishment": SLC to OLC, Apr. 26, 1877, Baltimore (MTP); SLC appears to have confused the owner of the house, Thomas De Kay Winans, with his father, Ross Winans.
178. "I spread the study": *L*, 295.
179. "Boyhood & youth": quoted in Hamlin Hill, "The Composition and Structure of *Tom Sawyer*," *AL*, XXXII, No. 4 (January 1961), 386. The manuscript is in the Riggs Memorial Library, Georgetown Univ.
179. "So I knocked off": *L*, 224.
179. "One-horse men": *MTH*, 91-92.
180. "No plot": *MTH*, 87.
180. "*Not* a boy's book": *MTH*, 91.
180. "A book for boys": *MTH*, 112.
181. "Kept the True Story": *MTH*, 24.
181. "No humor in it": *MTH*, 22.
182. "Charming visit": *MTH*, 70. Young John Howells is quoted in Paine, 572-73.
182. "Fat and boozy": *MTH*, 72.
183. "Palace of Sham": *F*, 195.
183. "Home of Mark Twain": Paine, 691-92.
184. "No use": *MTH*, 33-34.
184. "Cut it": *MTH*, 42.
184. "The piece": *MTH*, 42-43.
184. "Memory and imagination": SLC quoted Hay in *MTH*, 55. Hay's opinion of *The Innocents Abroad* is quoted in John Bigelow, *Recollections* (New York, 1913), IV, 478-79.
185. Setting out on foot: *MMT*, 45; *Eruption*, 366-72: the telegrams are quoted in *MTH*, 36n.
186. "Make a body sick": SLC to "Dear Livy," *MTH*, 37-40.
187. Back in Boston: Arthur Gilman, "*Atlantic* Dinners and Diners," *Atlantic*, C, November 1907, 650-51.

Chapter Ten (pages 188-211)

188. "Mr. Beecher": Marginal comment (92-93) in SLC's copy of Griswold,

Sixty Years with Plymouth Church (MTP).

188. "At present": SLC to Charles Warren Stoddard, Feb. 1, 1875, Hartford (Boston Public Library).

189. Centennial celebrations: *MMT*, 39–41. A general account of the festivities is D. B. Little, *America's First Centennial Celebration* (Boston, 1961).

190. "Fur cap": *MTH*, 73.

190. "When I think over": *MTH*, 74.

190. "Arabian Nights": *MMT*, 9–10.

191. "My only author": *MTH*, 533.

191. "Court of Last Resort": *MTH*, 107.

191. "Dearer to me": *L*, 268–69.

191. *"Ain't* any risk": SLC's correspondence with Dan De Quille is printed in Oscar Lewis' introduction to *The Big Bonanza* (New York, 1959).

192. "Vile, mercenary": *MTH*, 92.

192. "Best boy's story": *MTH*, 110–11.

192. "Dreary and hateful task": *MTH*, 121–22.

193. "Breadth of parlance": MMT, 3–4.

193. "An impassioned study": *MMT*, 141.

195. "Can we recover": Jesse Madison Leathers to SLC, Sept. 27, 1875, Louisville, (MTP).

195. "Tackle Gibraltar": SLC to Leathers, Oct. 5, 1875, Hartford (MTP).

195. "Mental telegraphy": *W*, XXII, 125–28.

195. "Never mind": *F*, 200.

196. "Every day": *Bowen*, 23–24.

196. "Ignorance, intolerance": *L*, 289.

196. Recalled a conversation: *MMT*, 30.

196. "As for a monument": SLC to John RoBards, Apr. 17 and June 10, 1876, Hartford (MTP).

197. "Another boy's book": *MTH*, 144. The fullest account of how the book came to be written is Walter Blair's *Mark Twain and Huck Finn* (Berkeley, Calif., 1960). The range of critical discussion is indicated in the text and bibliography in Richard Lettis *et al.*, eds., *Huck Finn and His Critics* (New York, 1962).

198. "A book of mine": Notebook No. 28A, MTP.

199. "About two days": *MTH*, 129.

199. "A subscription harvest": *MTH*, 132.

200. "You are a stockholder": FBH to SLC, Sept. 5, 1876 (MTP).

200. "Either Bliss": FBH to SLC, Mar. 1, 1877 (MTP).

200. "For myself": EB to SLC, July 18, 1876, Hartford (MTP).

200. "It seems funny": *F*, 220.

201. "A new distrust": Isabella Hooker Diary, Dec. 1, 1876 (Conn. Historical Soc.—typescript in MTP).

202. "Worked rapidly": SLC's highly colored account of the collaboration and falling-out with FBH is in *AU-1959*, 297–99.

203. "Tell Mrs. Clemens": FBH to SLC, Dec. 16, 1876, New York (MTP).

203. "One of the brightest gems": *Speeches*, 55. The sources for Isabella Hooker's New Year's Eve party are her diary and *NF*, 59–62.

204. "Fetch a war whoop": *AU-1924*, II, 242–43.

204. "Mr. Duncan": N. Y. *World*, Feb. 18 and 25, 1877.

204. "Don't say harsh things": *LL*, 203.

205. "Arse in": Frank Fuller to SLC, July 20, 1877, Glen Cove, N.Y. (MTP).

205. "$50 a day": SLC to OLC, July 30, 1877, New York (MTP).

205. "Walkee bottom side": *Ah Sin*, ed. Frederick Anderson (San Francisco, 1961), 10.

205. The more Daly cut: Joseph Daly, *The Life of Augustin Daly* (New York, 1917), 235–36.

205. "Been a long time": *MTH*, 187.

206. "When a humorist": *MTH*, 146.

206. October 1, 1877: *The 240th Annual Record of the Ancient and Honorable Artillery Company of Massachusetts* (Boston, 1878), 3–30 (this includes the text of SLC's speech); Boston *Evening Transcript*, Oct. 2 and 3, 1877.

209. Whittier birthday dinner: SLC, "The Story of a Speech" (*Speeches*, 63–76). Henry Nash Smith, whose *Mark Twain: The Development of a Writer* (Cambridge, Mass., 1962), 92–112, contains the most searching account of the occasion, concludes that the notion of a great public scandal was largely invented by SLC and WDH.

210. "My wife's distress": Dec. 27, 1877, Hartford (MTP).

211. "I am sincerely sorry": *F*, 217.

Chapter Eleven (pages 212–227)

213. "I know you will refrain": *MTN*, 131.
213. "Life has come to be": *L*, 319.
213. "I want to find": *F*, 222.
213. "We are in Europe": *F*, 230.
213. The contract with Francis (Frank) Bliss, dated March 8, 1878, is at Yale. Hamlin Hill summarizes the negotiations over *A Tramp Abroad* in *AL*, XXXIII, No. 4 (January 1962), 451-53.
214. "Noble system": *MTN*, 130. In Notebook No. 12, MTP, SLC listed the "biography" of WR and related projects.
214. Sixty thousand "communists" . . . "free air of Europe": Notebook No. 12, MTP.
214. "Oh, I have such": *MTH*, 227.
215. "It's goodbye cat": *MTN*, 139. SLC quoted JHT's whispered comment in his letter to Bayard Taylor, Munich, Dec. 14, 1878 (*AL*, VIII, No. 1 [March 1936], 50).
215. German translations: E. H. Hemminghaus, *Mark Twain in Germany* (New York, 1939), 9-11. Higginson's comment is in his *Letters and Journals* (Boston, 1921), 300.
216. "Geborn 1835": Heidelberg, May 7, 1878 (*AL*, VIII, No. 1 [March 1936], 48).
216. "Harte is a liar": *MTH*, 235-36. FBH cited the plots against him in an 1877 letter to his wife (*The Letters of Bret Harte* [Boston, 1926], 67-68).
216. "The worst reputation": *LinL*, I, 251-52.
216. "Have I offended you": *MTH*, 239.
217. Frank Harris' account of the Heidelberg encounter is in his *Contemporary Portraits*, 4th series (New York, 1923), 162-64, 173.
217. SLC's comments on the importance of JHT in the writing of *A Tramp Abroad* are quoted by A. E. Stone, Jr., "The Twichell Papers . . . ," *Yale Univ. Library Gazette*, XXXIX, No. 4 (April 1955), 155-64. "If you had staid at home," SLC wrote on the flyleaf of JHT's copy of *A Tramp Abroad*, "it would have taken me 14 *years* to get the material."

219n. "Hell or Heidelberg": *MTN*, 216.
219. "Perceiving, presently": *W*, IX, 164.
219. "My nightmares": Notebook No. 16, MTP.
219. "Rebellion in my heart": *MTH*, 242.
220. "I broke the back of life": *L*, 343.
220. "If it remains lost": Nov. 20, 1878, Munich (Yale).
220. "Down went my heart": *L*, 349.
220. "It's about this": Moncure D. Conway, *Autobiography* (Boston, 1904), II, 146.
220. "Those mountains had a soul": *L*, 351.
221. Fig leaves: Notebook No. 13, MTP.
221. SLC and Turgenev exchanged visits on May 8 and 12, 1879 (Notebook No. 14, MTP). SLC's letter to Andrew Chatto (May 29, 1879, Paris), is in Berg–NYPL.
221. "Bestial" Venus: Notebook No. 14, MTP.
222. "It depends on who writes": *MTN*, 151.
222. SLC's attacks on French character and morality are in Notebook No. 14, MTP; a few excerpts are published in *MTN*, 153.
222. "When all other interests fail": "What Paul Bourget Thinks of Us" (*W*, XXII, 169).
223. "*Real* coffee with *real* cream": Notebook No. 13, MTP; published with some minor changes in *MTN*, 149.
223. "Do you know Bret Harte?": Philip Dunne, ed., *Mr. Dooley Remembers* (Boston, 1963), 244.
223. Grant's charisma: Sylvanus Cadwallader, *Three Years with Grant* (New York, 1955), 181-82; Jesse Grant, *In the Days of My Father, General Grant* (New York, 1925), 320; W. T. Sherman, quoted in Edmund Wilson, *Patriotic Gore* (New York, 1962), 142.
224. "The typical hero": "Grant more nearly impersonated the American character of 1861-5 than any other living man. Therefore he will stand as the typical hero of the great Civil War in America."—Sherman's 1885 speech to the Army of the Tennessee, quoted in Lloyd Lewis, *Sherman* (New York, 1958), 639.
224. "Man of Destiny": The broadside is in MTP.

224. "My sluggish soul": *MTH*, 274. SLC made the comparisons of Grant with Napoleon in a letter (unsent) to the chairman of the Chicago reunion committee (*L*, 364-65).
225. "Dreadfully conspicuous": *L*, 367. Paine, 710-11, is the source for the anecdote about SLC's impersonation of Sherman.
225. "He broke up his attitude": *L*, 368-69.
226. "I doubt if America": *MTH*, 279-80.
226. "The babies": *Speeches*, 58-62.
227. "A sort of shuddering silence": In 1885 SLC dictated an account of the banquet and the speech (*AU*-1924, 13-19).
227. "I fetched him": SLC's letter to OLC is in *L*, 370-73; his letter to WDH is in *MTH*, 278-80; his letter to Orion (Nov. 14, 1879, Chicago) is in MTP.

Chapter Twelve (pages 228–253)

228. Bric-a-brac: The purchases were itemized in a blue leather wallet-notebook (MTP).
228. "Our house": *L*. 641.
228. Over $30,000: *BM*, 150; *F*, 245-46.
229. "You are a blessing": *MTH*, 293.
229. "You Americans": JHT, "Mark Twain," *Harper's*, May 1896.
229. Rolling gait: W. L. Phelps, *Autobiography* (New York, 1939), 63-64, describes SLC's walks in downtown Hartford.
229. "Adore babies": Wood's account of the West Point visit and the encounter with Miss Wood was published by Dixon Wecter in *Mark Twain in Three Moods* (San Marino, Calif., 1948), 28-32.
230. "It is wonderful": *MTH*, 277. Conway wrote about his services as amanuensis and the boy's visit in his *Autobiography* (Boston, 1904), II, 143-45).
231. "I hope you will send me": Wattie Bowser's letter to SLC and SLC's answer are from Pascal Covici, Jr., "Dear Master Wattie: The Mark Twain–David Watt Bowser Letters," *Southwest Review*, XLV, No. 2 (spring 1960), 105-21.
232. "Papa, I have hunted": Paine, 845.

233. "The loan business": *L*, 389-90.
233. Orion's absent-mindedness: SLC listed "Orion's 3 famous adventures" in Notebook No. 13, MTP. In 1906 he dictated an account of Orion's later career (*AU*-1959, 218-24). WDH's objection: *MTH*, 803.
233. "Orion is a field": *MTH*, 269.
233. "I believe I told you": *BM*, 142-44.
234. "Don't let anyone else": *MTH*, 315. The post-mortem is discussed in Dixon Wecter, *Sam Clemens of Hannibal* (Boston, 1952), 115-17.
234. "You cannot achieve": SLC to Orion, Feb. 22, 1883, Hartford (MTP). SLC demanded Orion's pledge in a letter from Hartford Feb. 27 (MTP).
235. "He casually observed": *MTH*, 255.
235. Spent about $100,000: The figures on SLC's income and expenditures during 1881 are from Paine, 729.
235. "Sacred as whiskey": quoted in *BM*, 176.
237. "Not proposing": SLC to Orion, Feb. 9, 1879, Munich (MTP).
237. "Bane of Americans": SLC to Orion, May 12 [1880], n.p. (MTP).
238. "Rank as a writer": Dec. 22, 1880 (MTP).
238. "I thank you": SLC to E. P. Parker, Christmas Eve 1880, Hartford (Berg–NYPL).
239. "Rather strong milk for babes": *MTH*, 338.
239. "A lovely book": *F*, 245n.
239. "Unquestionably the best book": Susy Clemens' biography of SLC, quoted in *AU*-1924, II, 88.
239. "I find myself a fine success": SLC to H. H. Boyesen, Jan. 11, 1882, Hartford (Barrett Coll.–photostat in MTP).
240. The reviews have been analyzed in Arthur L. Vogelback, "*The Prince and the Pauper*: A Study in Critical Standards," *AL*, XIV, No. 1 (March 1942), 48-54.
240. English reviews: SLC to Chatto & Windus, Mar. 3, 1882, Hartford (MTP).
240. "I am reading": Mrs. Stowe is quoted in SLC to Charles L. Webster, Apr. 26, 1887, Hartford (Berg–NYPL).
240. "That is the kind of review": *MTH*, 377.

241. "I took into account": John Hay to WR, New York, Sept. 4, 1881 (Whitelaw Reid Papers, Vol. 106, Library of Congress).
241. "Outspoken and hearty": *MTH*, 56.
241. "It isn't good journalism": WR's letter (John Hay Library, Brown Univ.) is published in George Monteiro, "A Note on the Mark Twain–Whitelaw Reid Relationship," *Emerson Society Quarterly*, XIX, 2nd quarter 1960, 20-21.
241. "A kind of crusade": SLC gives a rueful version of the vendetta in *MTH*, 386-89.
241. "Skunk," "idiot," "eunuch": SLC's notes for the biography of WR run through Notebooks Nos. 15 and 16, MTP.
242. "I did not know how you would take": *MTH*, 386.
242. "An hour or two": *BM*, 183.
243. "Flowery and gushy": Notebook No. 16, MTP. By contrast with the South, SLC felt, Boston was "about the prettiest city in the world."
244. R. E. Elliott, Esq.: draft of the letter in River Notebook, 1882, dictated to Roswell Phelps (MTP).
244. In New Orleans: details of the meeting are in *Record*, 5-8, 132, and Arlin Turner, *George W. Cable* (Durham, N. C., 1956), 121.
245. "Never seen anything": *LL*, 212.
246. "I like the Heathen Chinee": New Orleans *Times-Democrat*, May 6, 1882, quoted in Arlin Turner, "Notes on Mark Twain in New Orleans," *McNeese Review*, VI, spring 1954, 10-22. Cable repeated this story at the memorial service for SLC on Nov. 30, 1910.
246. "Everything was changed": *MTN*, 163.
246. "That world which I knew": *L*, 419.
246. Reached St. Paul: J. T. Flanagan, "Mark Twain on the Upper Mississippi," *Minnesota History*, XVII, December 1936, 369-84.
247. "Bed full of baskets": *MTH*, 435. WDH comments on SLC's reliance on "superstition, usually of a hygienic sort" in *MMT*, 81.
247. Fictional pathology: The list is in Notebook No. 17, MTP.
247. Cable's visit: *Record*, 12-13, 16-18.
248. "Dear Charley": *BM*, 195.

248. "I hope the public": *MTH*, 405.
248. Thomas Hardy: WDH quoted Hardy in *MTH*, 434.
248. "By fits and starts": *W*, XII, 19.
248. "Put the great river": Notebook No. 18, MTP.
249. "Not edited the book yet": SLC to Osgood & Co., Jan. 6, 1883, Hartford (Newberry Library, Chicago); first published in Benjamin Lease, "Mark Twain and the Publication of *Life on the Mississippi*, *AL*, XXVI, No. 2 (May 1954), 248-50.
249. "Wretched God-damned book": *BM*, 207.
249. "She says the chapter": quoted in Caroline Ticknor, "Mark Twain's Missing Chapter," *Bookman*, XXXIX (May 1914), 298-309.
250. "Dearest and sweetest": *Eruption*, 157.
250. "The publisher who": SLC to J. R. Osgood, Dec. 21, 1883, Hartford (MTP).
250. "Great and sublime fool": *MTH*, 215.
251. "Booming these days": *MTH*, 435.
251. "Booming working-days": *L*, 434.
251. "*I* shall *like* it": *MTH*, 435.
251. "Just finished writing a book": SLC to Andrew Chatto, Sept. 1, 1883, Hartford (British Museum); first published *AL*, XI, No. 1 (March 1939), 78-81.
251. "Right after Huck": *BM*, 249.
251. "Not your best": *MTH*, 443-44.
252. "Never care for fiction": Rudyard Kipling, *From Sea to Sea* (New York, 1912), II, 180.
252. "It took me eight hours": Paine, 752.
253. "Made me feel ridiculous": *MTH*, 439.
253. "Being smirched": Notebook No. 17, MTP.

Chapter Thirteen (pages 254-279)

254. "If I dared laugh": SLC to E. H. House, Feb. 27, 1884, Hartford (Barrett—photostat in MTP).
254. "Don't give yourself any discomfort": The letter is in MTP. The episode is discussed in Arlin Turner, "Mark Twain, Cable, and 'a Professional Newspaper Liar,'" *New Eng-*

land Quarterly, XXVIII, March 1955, 18-33.

254. "Tell the *truth*": Notebook No. 19, MTP.

255. In the library: Cable left a detailed account of the morning, and of the later visit to Grant, in letters to his wife, published in *Record*, 31 ff. SLC told WDH (*MTH*, 471) that the talk went on for four hours after breakfast.

255. "Drive and push and rush": *Speeches*, 145.

255. The human race had made more progress: This was the gist of the letter SLC wrote on the occasion of Walt Whitman's seventieth birthday (*Camden's Compliment to Walt Whitman*, ed. Horace Traubel [Philadelphia, 1889], 64-65).

255. "The reparation due": *MMT*, 35, and Paine, 701.

256. Negro supremacy: Notebook No. 18, MTP.

256. "Whom Mark knows well": *Record*, 33-34.

256. "If the book business": *BM*, 230.

256. "Tom might be played": *BM*, 236.

257. "Altogether too thin": *MTH*, 485.

257. "If the play is altered": *BM*, 236.

257. "Never mind": *MTH*, 507.

257. "Corn-dodgers": SLC to J. R. Osgood, March 20, 1884, Hartford (MTP).

257. "I haven't a paragraph": *BM*, 274.

258. "I am like everybody else": *MTH*, 493.

258. "I want good company": Minneapolis *Tribune*, Jan. 25, 1885, quoted in *Minnesota History*, XVIII, No. 1 (March 1937).

258. "Recession" or "depression": E. C. Kirkland, *Dream and Thought in the American Business Community* (Ithaca, N. Y., 1956), 6-7.

258. "Microscopic trichina": *MTN*, 170.

259. "The Great Loneliness": SLC to OLC, Jan. 11, 1885, St. Louis (MTP).

260. "Thinking of cutting": *LL*, 236.

260. "I may possibly": SLC to J. B. Pond, July 28, 1884, Elmira (Berg–NYPL).

260. $17,000: My figures come from the entries in Pond's cash book (Berg–NYPL). The fullest accounts of the Twain-Cable tour and relationship are: Guy A. Cardwell, *Twins of Genius* (East Lansing, Mich., 1953); Arlin Turner, *George W. Cable* (Durham, N. C., 1956); and *Record*.

260. "As much yourself": *MTH*, 513.

260. "Mr. Charles Warner": OLC to SLC, Nov. 10, 1884, Hartford (MTP).

260. "Jump out of their skins": SLC to OLC, Nov. 24, 1884, Washington (MTP). SLC's other reports of success are quoted from *LL*, 230-31.

261. "Been lecturing": *Eruption*, 170. In the account he wrote in 1885 (*AU*-1924, I, 32) SLC said that it was at a "late supper" at Gilder's house that he heard about the *Century's* plans.

261. "Very disgusted": *Letters of Richard Watson Gilder* (Boston, 1916), 123-24.

261. "I wanted": *AU*-1924, I. 36.

262. "Cold-blooded attempt": Notebook No. 19, MTP.

262. "There's many a woman": *LL*, 219-20.

263. "*The book is to be issued*": *BM*, 248.

263. "Lecherous old rascal": *BM*, 260.

264. "Had the first edition": The Webster interview is quoted in Walter Blair, *Mark Twain and Huck Finn* (Berkeley, Calif., 1960), 365-66.

264. "Charley, if this is a lie": *BM*, 284.

264. "I said we couldn't help": *BM*, 289.

264. "Youth dear": OLC to SLC, Jan. 2, 1885, Hartford (MTP).

264. "Sell property which does not belong to him": From the text of SLC's letter to the Concord Free Trade Club, March 1885, as edited by WDH (*MTH*, 876-79).

265. "Bromfield is an idiot": *BM*, 295.

265. "You'll never lay it down": Cable cited the prophecy in his speech at the Mark Twain memorial services Nov. 30, 1910.

265. "A great man": SLC to OLC, Feb. 3, 1885, Chicago (MTP).

265. "Cable's gifts of mind": *MTH*, 520.

266. Henry Watterson: Cable supplies the details of the encounters with Watterson and Nasby in letters to his wife published in *Record*, 72-75, 83.

266. "His closeness": SLC to OLC, Jan. 2, 1885, Paris, Ky. (MTP). The litany of SLC's complaints runs through *LL*, 234-37.

267. "With *his* platform talent": Notebook No. 32, MTP.
267. "A heart as tender as a child": Ozias Pond's diary (Berg–NYPL). Ozias describes the derailment and SLC's bout with the window shutter.
267. "I am not able to see anything": *BM*, 300.
267. "Huck is a *good* book": *BM*, 303.
268. "A vivid picture": The *Century* and other reviews are quoted and analyzed in A. L. Vogelback, "The Publication and Reception of *Huckleberry Finn in America*," *AL*, XI, No. 3 (November 1939), 260-72. The two reviews in *Life* were reprinted in *AL*, XXI, No. 1 (March 1959), 78-81.
268. "Dear Charley": *L*, 452-53.
269. "Endorses me as worthy to associate": *MTH*, 876-79 (text of the letter as edited by WDH).
269. "Those idiots in Concord": *BM*, 317.
269. "The truth is": *L*, 805. SLC's comments on the N.Y. *World* are in Notebook No. 19, MTP.
269. "You can't stir it up": *MTH*, 526.
270. "Prefatory Remark": The text is quoted in *MTH*, 535n. SLC cites OLC's proscription in *BM*, 309.
270. "Swan-song": *MTH*, 610-11.
271. "One of the highest satisfactions": *MMT*, 72.
271. "There's big money": *BM*, 302.
271. "If it had only been true": *MTN*, 174.
271. New letterhead: *BM*, 323.
272. "I wish to be close at hand": *BM*, 305.
272. "The Bull Run voice": The sales techniques are discussed in Gerald Carson, "Get the Prospect Seated . . . ," *American Heritage*, IX, No. 5 (August 1958), 38-41, 77-80.
272. "Vastest book enterprise": SLC to Orion, May 16, 1885 (MTP).
272. "Overwork killed": *BM*, 307.
272. "Neither of us": *AU-1924*, II, 144.
273. Would "cripple": *BM*, 319.
273. "Butter-mouthed Sunday school-slobbering": *MTH*, 572. The fictitious interview is published in *MTH*, 573n. SLC's designs on Laffan were stated in his letter to Fred Hall, Aug. 6, 1886 (Berg–NYPL).
273. "He has dictated 10,000 words": *MTN*, 182.

274. "This is the simple soldier": *Speeches*, 137. In his notebook for 1866 (Nos. 4-5, MTP) SLC singled out Grant's "I propose to move at once upon your works" as an example of circumstances forcing eloquence on the noneloquent. SLC's comment on Matthew Arnold is in Notebook No. 22, MTP.
274. "Bloody bit of heartache": *MTH*, 541.
275. "How near he came": *MTN*, 183.
275. "I came within a few hours": "The Private History of a Campaign That Failed," *Century*, December 1885 (*W*, XV, 281).
276. "It is curious and dreadful": *MTN*, 182.
276. Grant's worries: Grant's account of his service in Missouri is in Chapters 18-20 of his *Personal Memoirs*.
277. 300,000 sets: *MTN*, 180.
278. "A starving beggar": *MTH*, 539.
278. On a June evening: OLC's diary, June 13, quoted in *NF*, 92-93.
279. "Profitable return": SLC to OLC, Feb. 4, 1885, Chicago (MTP).
279. "I am frightened": Paine, 831.
279. Grant funeral procession: SLC's accounts in *MTN*, 185-86, and *LL*, 244; Boston *Evening Transcript*, Aug. 10, 1885; *The Riverside Souvenir: A Memorial Volume* (New York, 1886); Grace M. Mayer, *Once upon a City* (New York, 1958), 462-63.
279. "He was a *man*": *L*, 460.
279. "Toward the sunset": *LL*, 246.

Chapter Fourteen (pages 280-311)

280 "Mama and I": *North American Review*, Aug. 2, 1907, 689-90.
281. "I have begun a book": *BM*, 355.
281. "Mechanical marvel": *L*, 508.
281. "Wait thirty years": *Camden's Compliment to Walt Whitman*, ed. Horace Traubel (Philadelphia, 1889), 64-65.
282. "And I watched": *The Portable Mark Twain*, ed. Bernard DeVoto (New York, 1946), 775.
282. A typesetting machine: SLC wrote extended accounts of Paige and his typesetter in notebooks, correspondence, and autobiographical material.

Among other sources are: Paige's various patents; the files of *The Inland Printer*, Chicago, which from the 1880s on trace the evolution of machine composition from mere novelty to a mainstay of the printing trades; John S. Thompson, "Composing Machines—Past and Present," *Inland Printer*, XXX, No. 5 (February 1903), 697-99; W. Turner Berry, "Printing and Related Trades," a chapter in Charles Singer et al., *A History of Technology* (Oxford, 1958), V, 685-87; Royal Cortissoz, *The Life of Whitelaw Reid* (New York, 1921), II, 105-6; Waldemar Kaempffert, *A Popular History of American Invention* (New York, 1924), I, 228-33; Willi Mengel, *Ottmar Mergenthaler and the Printing Revolution* (New York, 1954). A suggestive discussion of SLC's involvement is Tom Burnham, "Mark Twain and the Paige Typesetter: A Background for Despair," *Western Humanities Review*, VI, winter 1951-52, 29-36.

283*n*. "My God!": Peter Lyon, *Success Story: The Life and Times of S. S. McClure* (New York, 1963), 139.

284. "He is a poet": *MTN*, 72-73.

284. "An inventor is a poet": *BM*, 114.

284. "I knew that country": *W*, XIV, 68.

284. "For some cause": *L*, 29.

285. "It did seem to me": *MMT*, 80.

285. "Very much the best": *BM*, 173.

286. "Ask the President": Notebook No. 20, MTP.

286. On May 27: SLC's memoranda concerning Western Union are in Notebook No. 19, MTP.

286. "Never mind that": Paine, 906.

287. "Wanted to get an idea": SLC to Fred Hall, Sept. 11, 1886, Elmira (Berg—NYPL). Writing from Elmira on August 28, SLC had told Hall, the junior partner in Charles L. Webster & Co., "I want to know where each of these unions is—and what its strength is" (Berg—NYPL).

288. "Only smiled": Paine, 906.

288. "The Mergenthaler people": SLC to HHR, Oct. 7, 1894, Rouen (Berg—NYPL); DeVoto omits this passage from the text of the letter he printed in *The Portable Mark Twain* (New York, 1946), 778-80.

288. "We go on and on": *BM*, 339.

288. "When he can afford it": Notebook No. 23, MTP.

289. Impressed a local reporter: The interview (Minneapolis *Tribune*, June 30, 1886) is reprinted in J. T. Flanagan, "Mark Twain on the Upper Mississippi," *Minnesota History*, XVII [December 1936], 369-84.

289. "The issue of this book": JHT's unpublished journals (Yale) are quoted in *LL*, 247.

290. "The failure was incredible": *MMT*, 74.

290. "Enough piousness": *BM*, 376.

290. "Momentary annoyance": *BM*, 377-78.

291. Back to Fredonia: Samuel C. Webster supplies the details of his father's last years in *BM*, 388-90.

291. "Not a man": SLC to Pamela Moffett, July 1, 1889, Elmira (Moffett—MTP).

291. "I have never hated": SLC to Orion, July 1, 1889, Elmira (Moffett—MTP).

292*n*. "Webster kept back": *Eruption*, 189.

292. "Don't imagine": *L*, 503.

292. "Machine O.K.": Telegram in MTP.

292. "I have seen a line": *MTN*, 205.

293. "Immense historical birth": SLC's fullest account of the event is *L*, 506-8.

293. "All good things": SLC to Jane Clemens and Orion, Apr. 3, 1889, Hartford (Moffett—MTP).

293. "Dream of being": *MTN*, 171. In general I have followed the chronology in H. G. Baetzhold, "The Course of Composition of *A Connecticut Yankee*: A Reinterpretation," *AL*, XXXIII, No. 2 (May 1961), 195-214.

294. The idea of a great battle: Notebook No. 18, MTP.

294. Tom Nash: SLC wrote to Livy about the visits to Hannibal and Keokuk in *LL*, 228-29.

294. "Poor old Ma": SLC's note on envelope of letter from Jane Clemens (MTP).

295. "He mourns his lost land": Notebook No. 20, MTP.

295. "That notion of yours": *MTH*, 550. WDH's later comment is in *MTH*, 833-34.

295. The final battle: H. G. Baetzhold, "The Autobiography of Sir Robert Smith of Camelot," *AL*, XXXII, No. 4 (January 1961), 456-61.

295. "In all history": Lloyd Lewis, *Sherman* (New York, 1958), 158.

296. "The story isn't a satire": *F*, 257-59.

296. Union Veterans' Association: SLC's speech, "An Author's Soldiering," is in *Life as I Find It*, 216-18.

297. "Rude animal side": *LL*, 257-58.

297. "A perfect day": *L*, 488-89.

298. "Relief of mind": SLC to Charles L. Webster, Aug. 3, 1887, Elmira (Berg–NYPL).

298. "This kind of rush": *F*, 262.

298. "My vision of the evidences": *MTH*, 595.

299n. Arnold argued: Matthew Arnold, "Civilization in the United States," *The Nineteenth Century*, XXIII, April 1888. "The creators of *Uncle Remus*": Charles F. Richardson, *American Literature, 1607-1885* (New York, 1886), I, 521.

300. Most familiar epitome: Bernard Bowron, Leo Marx, Arnold Rose, "Literature and Covert Culture," *American Quarterly*, IX, winter 1957, 377-87.

301. "She is afraid": *MTH*, 608-9.

301. "Last night I started": *MTH*, 612.

301. "Well, my book is written": *MTH*, 613.

301. "It will not be necessary": *L*, 521.

302. "The stock is either": Notebook No. 24, MTP.

302. "The machine": SLC to Orion, Dec. 10, 1889, Hartford (MTP).

303. "An entire family": *Speeches*, 81. The advertising pamphlet was issued in Hartford, 1874, as *Mark Twain's Speech on Accident Insurance*.

303. "That lying thief": Notebook No. 12, MTP. SLC tells the story of his accident-insurance career in *AU-1959*, 230-32.

304. "News today": SLC to J. T. Goodman, April 18, 1890, Hartford (Yale). There is an account of Thursday's disaster in Mary Lawton, *A Lifetime with Mark Twain* (New York, 1925), 107-8.

304. "I don't believe you ought to feel": OLC to SLC, Hartford, May 2 (?), 1890 (MTP).

304. "Do everything you can": SLC quoted Mackay in Notebook No. 24, MTP.

305. "The hoary old song": *MTN*, 211.

305. "Dear Mr. Clemens": James W. Paige to SLC, Jan. 2, 1891, Hartford (MTP).

305. In Washington: SLC described the visit in two letters to OLC from Washington, Jan. 13 and Jan. 14, 1891 (MTP). Three increasingly frantic letters from SLC to Jones Jan. 17, Jan. 20, and Feb. 7 are in MTP, as are Jones's telegram and letter of Feb. 11.

306. "For a whole year": SLC to Sen. J. P. Jones, Feb. 13(?), 1891, Hartford, incomplete, not sent (MTP).

306. "Penny-worshipping humbug": SLC to J. T. Goodman, Feb. 22 or 24, 1891, Hartford (MTP).

306. "I've shook the machine": SLC to Orion, Feb. 25, 1891, Hartford (Moffet–MTP).

307. "Yesterday a thunder-stroke": *MTH*, 575.

308. "Some strange spirit": *MF*, 256-57.

308. "She was a poet": *MTN*, 315.

308. List of famous men: *MTH*, 424.

308. "In a great many directions": *North American Review*, May 17, 1907, 120.

308. "How I hate that name": Grace King, *Memories of a Southern Woman of Letters* (New York, 1932), 173-74.

309. "The last time I saw her": SLC to Pamela Moffett, Oct. 12, 1890, Hartford (MTP).

309. One of Susy's classmates: Mrs. Charles M. Andrews. Mrs. Andrews' letter of Feb. 26, 1949, to the late Dixon Wecter is in MTP and is the basis for my account of Susy at Bryn Mawr and of the "Golden Arm" episode there.

309. "The right length precisely": *How to Tell a Story* (New York, 1897), 9-10.

310. "A lovely story to tell": SLC's letters of Aug. 10 and Dec. 12, 1881, are published in *Mark Twain to Uncle Remus, 1881-1885*, ed. Thomas H. English, Emory Sources and Reprints, Series VII, No. 3. (Atlanta, Ga., 1953), 1-23. Harris' version of the story had a silver sevenpence, and this, SLC told him,

seemed "rather nearer the true field-hand standard than that achieved by my Florida, Mo., Negroes with their sumptuous arm of solid gold." SLC's version, dealing with a return from the dead to punish the theft of a golden arm, has folklore analogs in France, Germany, and the British Isles.

310. "Stop street sprinkling": Notebook No. 25, MTP.

311. "Travel has no longer": *MTH*, 645.

311. "This maniac": Notebook No. 25, MTP.

311. "We are going": Notebook No. 25, MTP.

Chapter Fifteen (pages 312–335)

313. "So desperate": SLC to Fred Hall, July 18, 1891, Paris (Berg–NYPL).

313. "Extinction from the world": *L*, 558.

313. "To glide down": "Down the Rhone" (*W*, XXIX, 129).

313. "Down the Rhone": Arthur L. Scott, "The Innocents Adrift . . . ," *Publications of the Modern Language Association of America*, LXXVII, No. 3 (June 1963), 230-37.

314. "Changed itself": *W*, XVI, 208.

314. "Great yesterdays": SLC's prospectus, or "explanatory note," is DV 233, MTP. He later described the project in a dictation in January 1906 (*AU*-1924, I, 335-37).

315n. "The higher life": A. E. Stone, Jr., *The Innocent Eye* (New Haven, Conn., 1961), 209.

315. "Loveliest book": Susy is quoted in *MF*, 126-27.

316. "*Real* nature": "Jean's Illness" (MTP).

316. "Fine soft-fibered little fellow": quoted in R. B. Perry, *The Thought and Character of William James* (Boston, 1935), I, 806.

316. "I seem able": *AU*-1924, I, 227. Clara describes the episode in *MF*, 120.

317. "Cannot be compared": quoted in Grace King, *Memories of a Southern Woman of Letters* (New York, 1932), 172-73.

317. "Nothing *but* a Co.": Notebook No. 26, MTP.

318. "I am a Yale man": H. A. Bayne, "Mark Twain Crosses the Ocean" (unpublished account—Yale). There is a brief account of the same episode in M. B. Leavitt, *Fifty Years in Theatrical Management* (New York, 1912), 595.

318. "My dear darling child": *LL*, 264.

318. "Just about wild": *LL*, 512.

319. He had tried to get the job: Orion to SLC, April 20, 1893, Keokuk (MTP). Orion described his economies in a letter to Mollie from Keokuk, July 7-9, 893 (MTP).

319. "A fiasco": *Banker's Magazine*, quoted in H. U. Faulkner, *Politics, Reform and Expansion* (New York, 1959), 142.

319. "Get me out": *L*, 584.

319. "I think Mr. Clemens": *L*, 586.

320. "I watch for your letters": *L*, 594.

320. "I am coming over": *L*, 595.

321. "The best new acquaintance": *LL*, 269.

321. "The only man": *L*, 612.

321. "He is not only": "A Tribute to Henry H. Rogers," in Paine, 1659.

321. Rogers: One account by SLC is *AU*-1924, I, 250-65. For material about HHR here and in later chapters I have drawn on: *Dictionary of American Biography*, XVI, 95-96; R. W. and M. E. Hidy, *History of Standard Oil Company (New Jersey): Pioneering in Big Business* (New York, 1955); Thomas W. Lawson, "Frenzied Finance: The Story of Amalgamated," *Everybody's Magazine*, August 1904; Allan Nevins, *John D. Rockefeller: The Heroic Age of American Enterprise* (New York, 1940); Ida M. Tarbell, *History of the Standard Oil Company* (New York, 1904).

322. "Our friend": Andrew Carnegie, *Autobiography* (Boston, 1920), 296. Carnegie said this in his speech at SLC's seventieth-birthday celebration in 1905.

323. "He's a pirate": Dan Beard, *Hardly a Man Is Now Alive* (New York, 1939), 348.

323. "Political and commercial morals": *Eruption*, 81.

323. "Bought fame": *Eruption*, 39.

323. 'Sell all thou hast": *Eruption,* 85-86.
323. "I expected it": Notebook No. 38, MTP.
323. "You tell me": "Corn-Pone Opinions" (*W,* XXIX, 399).
324*n.* Clemens' account: *L,* 612-13. The publishing history of *Wealth against Commonwealth* is summarized in Daniel Aaron, *Men of Good Hope* (New York, 1951), 153. Warner's account of his Winnetka visit is quoted in Caro Lloyd, *Henry Demarest Lloyd* (New York, 1912), I, 206. "No longer exists": *Wealth against Commonwealth* (New York 1894), 58.
324. "I have been abusing": Orion to SLC, Feb. 2, 1894, Keokuk (MTP).
325. "A body forgets": *LL,* 275.
326. "Other people's successes": *LL,* 287.
327. "The very source": SLC to OLC, Jan. 27-30, 1894 (MTP).
327*n.* Writing in 1885: SLC to Charles Warren Stoddard, June 1, Hartford (Univ. of Notre Dame Library).
327. "I have got the best": *L,* 596.
328. "The fork on his neck": Orion to SLC, Feb. 2, 1894 (MTP).
328. "A singularly clear-headed man": *LL,* 280.
328. "It was beautiful to see": *LL,* 282.
328. "Nearing success": SLC kept a record of his progress bulletins to OLC (*MTN,* 235-36).
329. "That terrible book!": SLC to Pamela Moffett, Feb. 25, 1894 (MTP). In this letter SLC supplies the figures on the firm's indebtednesses.
329. "Cheer up": *LL,* 299.
329. "Don't let it disturb you": In an attempt to console OLC, SLC quoted Mackay to her (*L,* 614).
330*n.* In 1835: Alexis de Tocqueville, *Democracy in America,* tr. Phillips Bradley (New York, 1945), II, 236. "Men are up today": David Macrae, *The Americans at Home* (New York, 1952), 34.
330. "I cannot get away": Paine, 986-87.
330. "I should think": *LL,* 309.
330. "My first duty": *LL,* 306.
331. "Thunder clap": *L,* 617-18; Paine omits the sentence about "convenience for the dogs"; the manuscript letter is in Berg–NYPL.

331. He sent Rogers: SLC to HHR, Dec. 22, 1894, Paris (Berg–NYPL).
332. "All my life": *L,* 621-22.
332. Five-franc piece: OLC tells this in a letter to Susan Crane (Paris, Feb. 2, 1895) in Paine, 996.
332. "It seemed": *LL,* 312.
333. "She was brimming with life": *MTH,* 663.
334. Friends all over the United States: SLC to S. E. Moffett, Aug. 15, 1895, Vancouver (MTP); published in J. B. Pond, *Eccentricities of Genius* (New York, 1900), 225.
334. "Arrive next January": *L,* 629.
334. Told Henry Harper: SLC's letter is printed in J. Henry Harper, *The House of Harper* (New York, 1912), 575-76.
334. "George Washington": Notebook No. 28A, MTP.
334. "Sham and shoddy": SLC's comments on FBH are quoted in C. O. Parsons, "Mark Twain in Australia," *Antioch Review,* XXI, winter 1961-62, 458.
334. Jameson Raid prisoners: *L,* 632-33; *MTN,* 293-94; John Hays Hammond, *Autobiography* (New York, 1935), II, 398-400.
335. "Steady, unceasing feeling": OLC to Susan Crane, Sept. 5, 1895, at sea (MTP).
335. "I don't think": SLC to HHR, June 6, 1896, Queenstown, Cape Colony (MTP).
335. Riley: Notebooks Nos. 28A, 29, and 30, MTP.
335. "One of the mysteries": *AU*-1924, II, 34.

Chapter Sixteen (pages 336-357)

336. "She seems quite happy": *NF,* 219.
336. "I wonder": *LL,* 326.
336. "Mr. Clemens": Susy's deathbed writings are in MTP.
337. "When out of her head": Notebook No. 31, MTP.
337. "I have *hated*": *LL,* 324.
337. "All dog": SLC to Pamela Moffett. Jan. 7, 1897, London (MTP).
337. "An odious world": *LL,* 328.
337. 'I have many": *L,* 641.
337. "It puzzles me": *MTH,* 664.

337. "Whose outside aspect": SLC to Laurence Hutton, Feb. 20, 1898, Vienna (MTP).

338. "Subscription book": SLC to HHR, November 1896, London (MTP).

338. "Don't mind anything": Quoted in *MF*, 180.

339. "The cloud": *MTN*, 354.

339. Forest fire: *L*, 56; SLC describes the fire in Chapter 23 of *Roughing It* (*W*, III, 164-67)

339. "Close of a Great Career": *MTN*, 327.

339. "Since bad luck": Notebook No. 32A, MTP.

340. Writing in 1897: Sir John Adams, *Everyman's Psychology* (New York, 1929), 202-3.

340. Bernard DeVoto: *Mark Twain at Work* (Cambridge, Mass., 1942), 116.

341. "In my age": *AU*-1959, 43.

341. Was it dream: Paine, 964.

341. Speculative notion: L. L. White, *The Unconscious Before Freud* (New York, 1960), 169-70.

341. "Nearer, yes": *MTN*, 348.

341. "I was suddenly": *MTN*, 351-52.

342. Wales McCormick: *AU*-1959, 88.

343. "A psychosis": Sigmund Freud, *An Outline of Psychoanalysis* (New York, 1940), 61.

343*n*. Higginson: Anna Mary Wells, *Dear Preceptor* (Boston, 1963), 272-73, 307. Garland: Hamlin Garland, *Roadside Meetings* (New York, 1930), 37, 60-61; Jean Holloway, *Hamlin Garland* (Austin, Tex., 1960), 15, 21. SLC to R. W. Gilder: Nov. 6 and Nov. 13, 1898, Vienna (Yale).

345. "Which Was the Dream?": Manuscript in MTP.

345*n*. Hurlbert: Frank Maloy Anderson, *The Mystery of a Public Man* (Minneapolis, 1948), 133.

345. "My double": *MTN*, 349.

346. *The Great Dark:* Published in *Letters from the Earth* (New York, 1962), 233-86.

347. "When I returned": *W*, IV, 303.

347. "*Nothing* exists": *W*, XXVII, 140.

347. "I disseminate": N.Y. *Herald*, Oct. 16, 1900.

347. "Silent colossal National Lie: "My First Lie and How I Got Out of It" (*W*, XXIII, 169).

348. Gala benefit lecture: SLC to Frank Fuller, May 27, June 3, and July 2, 1897, London (3 letters—MTP).

349. "All friends think": The cables from HHR and Frank Bliss are in MTP.

349. "Grown so tired": SLC to J. G. Bennett, June 19, 1897, London (MTP).

349. "My wife won't allow me": SLC to Andrew Carnegie, July 7, 1897, London (Carnegie Papers—Library of Congress).

349. "Put the damage": SLC to Frank Bliss, Nov. 4, 1897, Vienna (MTP). The N.Y. *Herald* review appeared Sunday, Oct. 10.

350. "I imagine those Essenes": Orion to SLC, Nov. 30, 1897, Keokuk (MTP). On the envelope SLC wrote: ". . . his last letter. Preserve it. SLC."

350. "He was good": Published in *Palimpsest*, publication of the State Historical Soc. of Iowa, X, No. 10 (October 1929), 396.

350. "Your latest work": *MTH*, 668.

350. "The debts": *L*, 653.

350. "A quite unexpected $10,000": *MTH*, 685.

351. "I have been out": *MTH*, 684.

351. "The black days": *L*, 734-36.

351. "Sz is not a Paige": Paine, 1057.

352. "Not on your life": SLC to J. Y. MacAlister, Jan. 16, 1906, New York (Barrett Coll.—photostat in MTP).

353. "The first flag": "Jean's Illness" (MTP). SLC also kept a "Diary of the Kellgren Cure" (MTP), in which he catalogued his own ailments.

353. "Damn all the other cures": SLC to R. W. Gilder, July 23, 1899, Sanna, Sweden (photostat at Yale).

353. "The objection is": Newspaper clipping in MTP.

353. "A marvelous race": *L*, 647.

353. "Such cowards, hypocrites": Nicholas Halasz, *Captain Dreyfus* (New York, 1955), 135.

353. "Get Madame Dreyfus to consider": SLC to Andrew Chatto, Sept. 24, 1899, Sanna, Sweden (Berg—NYPL).

354. "Damned good": *MF*, 202.

354. "Self-appointed Ambassador": Notebook No. 32, MTP.

354. "Your 84 votes": *MTH*, 696. See Allen W. Read, "The Membership in

Proposed American Academies," *AL*, VII, No. 2 (May 1935), 155-60.

354. "I wish you could understand": *MTH*, 668.

354. "The greatest man": *MTH*, 679.

354. Hamlin Garland: Garland's account of his meeting with SLC and FBH is in his *Roadside Meetings* (New York, 1930), 447-53.

355. "President McKinley": SLC to Chatto & Windus, Apr. 25, 1899, Vienna (Berg–NYPL).

355. Autobiographical sketch: A 14-page manuscript, with OLC's penciled corrections, is in Berg–NYPL.

356. "Gush and vulgarity": SLC to S. E. Moffett, Apr. 25, 1899, Vienna (MTP). In this letter SLC told Moffett to write the biographical sketch for Bliss. On March 31, 1899, SLC sent his own draft of the sketch to Bliss with instructions for Moffett to put it in his own language. The sketch, signed by Moffett, was published in *McClure's Magazine*, October 1899.

356. Tall story: See DeLancey Ferguson, "Mark Twain's Comstock Duel: The Birth of a Legend." *AL*, XIV, No. 1 (March 1942), 66-70.

357. "The 20th Century is a stranger": *MTN*, 372.

Chapter Seventeen (pages 358-388)

358. "Younger and jollier": *LinL*, II, 138.
359. "It always puzzled me": *MF*, 217.
359. "I hate to have him": *MTH*, 735n.
360. Cash income: *MTN*, 380.
360n. Final accounting: N.Y. *Times*, Feb. 22, 1964.
361. "Be *very* guarded": OLC to S. E. Moffett, Jan. 23, 1902, Riverdale, N.Y. (MTP).
361. Celebrity: Daniel J. Boorstin, *The Image* (New York, 1962), 57.
361. "Mark's spectacular personality": Ferris Greenslet, *The Life of Thomas Bailey Aldrich* (Boston, 1908), 220.
361. "But they would not let it go": *MTH*, 735n.
362. "I must really complain": *MTH*, 763-64.

362. "Corn-Pone Opinions": *W*, XXIX, 399-406.
362. "I think that England sinned": Boston *Transcript*, Dec. 14, 1900.
362. "I bring you": N.Y. *Herald*, Dec. 30, 1900.
363. "I am not expecting anything": *L*, 704-5.
363. "Oldest and best models": *L*, 763.
363. "The Tom Sawyer of the political world": *Eruption*, 49-51.
363. "It is simple, direct": *MTN*, 394.
364. "In ten years": *L*, 715.
364. "O compassionate missionary": *W*, XXIX, 249.
364. "Nothing but such a book": SLC to Frank Bliss, Aug. 21, 1901, Saranac, N. Y. (MTP).
365. "Even half a friend": SLC to Frank Bliss, Aug. 29, 1901, Saranac (MTP).
365. Tom and Huck stories: Notebook No. 34, MTP.
365. "It all seems so small": Paine, 1168.
366. "Standard Oil": Paine, 1076.
366. "When we contemplate": SLC to "Mr. Day," Mar. 21, 1901 (?), New York (MTP).
366. "My instincts": SLC to Dr. Barbour, Jan. 8, 1906, New York (Berg–NYPL).
367. "The whole truth": Paine, 1234.
367. "If we can build": M. R. Werner, *It Happened in New York* (New York, 1957), 242. In addition to Werner's account and Paine's (1279-1286), I have drawn on the following sources for the Gorky affair: Louis J. Budd, "Twain, Howells, and the Boston Nihilists," *New England Quarterly*, XXXII (September 1959), 351-71; Alexander Kaun, *Maxim Gorky and His Russia* (New York, 1931; Kaun quotes Franklin Giddings' "social lynching" article); Ernest Poole, "Maxim Gorki in New York," *Slavonic and East European Review*, XXII, No. 58 (May 1944), 77-83.
368. "Custom is custom": SLC, "The Gorky Incident," *Letters from the Earth* (New York, 1962), 156.
369. "I more believe": *LL*, 344.
369. "Almost the only crime": SLC to Clara, May 20, 1905, Dublin, N. H. (MTP).
369. "Sozodont": Undated note (Berg–NYPL).

370. "Poor Livy": *L*, 728.
370. "The last name": *LL*, 339-40.
371. Breach of contract: SLC's deposition is in MTP.
371. "Passing off the stage": William Lyon Phelps, *Autobiography* (New York, 1939), 456-57.
371. "Pathetic something": *L*, 756.
371. "Full of remorse": *MTN*, 387.
371. "A calamity": *MTN*, 388.
371. "Bereaved circumstances": *MTN*, 387.
373. Later he claimed: SLC to Elizabeth Wallace, Aug. 27, 1909, Redding, Conn. (MTP).
373. "The dinner scheme": SLC to George Harvey, Sept. 21, 1905, Dublin, N. H. (MTP).
373. "Harvey the Magnificent": W. F. Johnson, *George Harvey* (Boston, 1929), 85.
374. Publicity stunt: Isabel Lyon's notes (Berg–NYPL).
374. "Hated Persons": List in MTP. In Notebook No. 36, MTP, SLC said, "I wish all publishers were in hell."
374. "Sit by the fire": *L*, 774.
376. "My biographer": SLC to "Any friend or acquaintance of mine," Mar. 1, 1906, New York (MTP).
376. "I don't want it done": SLC to Clara, June 19 or 20, 1905, Dublin, N. H. (MTP).
376. "Damned fool": SLC to S. E. Moffett, Feb. 7 or 8, 1907 (MTP).
376. "All private letters": SLC to S. E. Moffett, July 28, 1900, London (MTP).
377. "Lost confidence in Paine": Isabel Lyon's notes (Berg–NYPL).
377. "Those privacies exposed": *MTH*, 828.
378. "Dramatic and unconscious": *MTH*, 780.
378. "Remorseless truth": *MTH*, 782.
378. "When I was younger": Paine, 1269.
379. "Dewy and breezy": *MTH*, 778.
379. "Poor man": *Selected Letters of William James*, ed. Elizabeth Hardwick (New York, 1961), 228-29.
379. "When I think": Paine, 1323.

380. "Magnificent *coup*": *MMT*, 96.
380. "Microscopic dust": *AU*-1959, 368-70.
381. "As widely celebrated": *AU*-1959, 349.
381. "Butter wanted": *Mark Twain's Letters to Mary*, ed. Lewis Leary (New York, 1961), opp. 67.
381. Carlotta Welles: Carlotta Welles Briggs to Dixon Wecter, Nov. 4, 1947 (MTP).
382. "Greatest American writer": The interview with Shaw was published in *Harper's Weekly*, July 20, 1907.
382. "My dear Mark Twain": G. B. Shaw to SLC, July 3, 1907, London (MTP); except for the salutation, the letter is in Paine, 1398. Writing *Saint Joan*, Shaw told Lady Gregory in 1923 that he had not read SLC's *Joan of Arc* for fear "of being influenced by him"; in his preface to the play (1924) Shaw said SLC's Joan was "an unimpeachable American school teacher in armor."
384. "Principal intimate": *AU*-1924, I, 251.
384. Thank-you notes: Carnegie papers—Library of Congress.
384. "Money-lust": *L*, 770.
384. "Cannot be altogether bad": SLC's account of the Aldine Club lunch is in *Eruption*, 96-105.
385. "Mr. Rogers": *MF*, 278-79.
385. "Poor fellow": *MTH*, 838.
386. "My father died": SLC to Clara, Hamilton, Bermuda, Mar. 24, 1910 (MTP).
386. "Unaccountable freaks": *MF*, 279.
386. "The irony of it": SLC to Clara, Redding, Conn., July 18, 1909 (MTP).
386. "Caught Miss Lyon": SLC to Melville Stone, Sept. 14, 1909 (MTP).
386. "A liar": SLC to Clara, Mar. 6, 1910, Hamilton, Bermuda (MTP).
387. "For the fun of it": *MMT*, 99.
387. "I hear the newspapers": Paine, 1549.
388. "You never wrote anything greater": *MTH*, 851.

INDEX

Index

Index

Index

Index

Index

Index

Index

Index

Index

Index

Clemens' hatred for, 271, 291-292, 337, 344, 355
Webster, Daniel, 76
Welles, Carlotta, 381-382
What Is Man?, 340, 347
"Which Was the Dream," 345
Whitman, Walt, 20, 49, 58, 81, 152, 158, 281, 284, 300
Whitmore, Franklin G., 286, 288
Whittier, John Greenleaf, 296, 348, 354
Wilhelm, Kaiser, 312, 363
Williams, True, 199
Wilson, Pres. Woodrow, 373
Wilson, Theodore, 326
Winans, Thomas De Kay, 177-178

Woodhull and Claflin's Weekly, 157
Woodhull, Victoria, 157
World, The, 367
World's Work, 384
Writings of Mark Twain, The, 355

"Yankee in Czar Nicholas' Court," 367
Young, John Russell, 242, 304

Zola, Émile, 353